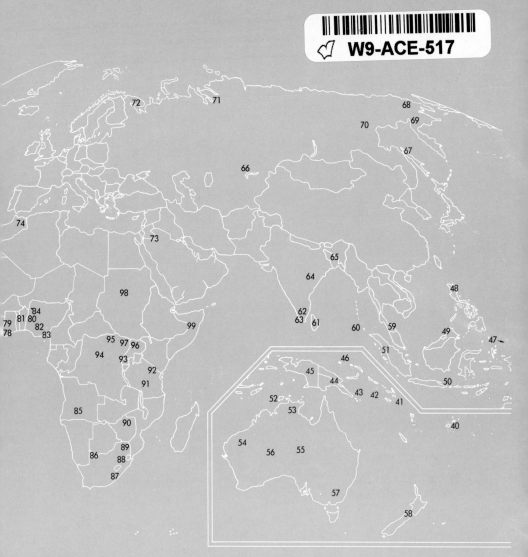

EURASIA

59. Sakai, Semang
60. Andamanese
61. Vedda
62. Kota, Toda
63. Nayar
64. Baiga, Munda, Gond
65. Naga
66. Kalmuk
67. Ainu
68. Chukchee
69. Koryak
70. Tungus
71. Samoyed
72. Lapps

AFRICA
(including Arabian Peninsula)

73. Ruwalla Bedouin
74. Berbers
75. Tuareg
76. Mende
77. Mano
78. Ashanti
79. Tallensi, Nupe
80. Yoruba
81. Dahomeans
82. Ibo (incl. Anang)
   (Ibibio)
83. Igbo, Tiv

84. Kanuri
85. Ovimbundu
86. Bushman
87. Zulu
88. Swazi
89. Thonga (BaThonga)
90. Tonga
91. Barabaig
92. Masai

93. Ankole (Banyankole)
94. Pygmy Tribes
   (Mbuti, etc.)
95. Azande
96. Ganda (Baganda),
   Nyoro (Banyoro)
97. Lugbara
98. Nuer
99. Somali, Galla

BARTON M. SCHWARTZ, Ph.D., University of California, Los Angeles, is Associate Professor and Chairman of the Department of Anthropology at the California State College at Los Angeles. He previously taught at Washington State University and Lehigh University. Dr. Schwartz has done anthropological research in Trinidad, Mauritius, and Fiji.

ROBERT H. EWALD, Ph.D., University of Michigan, is Professor of Anthropology at the California State College at Los Angeles. He has done anthropological research in Guatemala, Panama, and Peru.

Culture and Society

AN INTRODUCTION TO
CULTURAL ANTHROPOLOGY

BARTON M. SCHWARTZ

ROBERT H. EWALD

BOTH OF CALIFORNIA STATE
COLLEGE AT LOS ANGELES

THE RONALD PRESS COMPANY · NEW YORK

To

Lynn and Robyn Schwartz

To

Pat Ewald

Preface

This book is written for the beginning student in cultural anthropology. Our primary goal is to provide the student with an understanding of the central concept of anthropology—*culture*. Culture is presented as a unifying concept which provides a coherent frame of reference for more specialized studies such as religion, economics, political systems, and social organization. In this way, we enable the student to see the interrelation of sociocultural phenomena: the relationship of particular parts to the whole of culture. Comprehension of this relationship results in a more complete understanding and appreciation of human behavior.

As an example of this integrated approach, a separate chapter is devoted to religious phenomena as essential parts of cultural systems, but ritual, belief, and religious organization are made integral parts of the chapters focusing on social control, political systems, economic organization, and culture change. Still another example of this integration is found in the presentation of the history of anthropology. Historical materials are incorporated throughout the text and are discussed where relevant. In this way, the development of anthropological thought is presented in more meaningful terms. Also, this same unified presentation is extended to the major theoretical approaches within cultural anthropology—historicalism, evolutionism, structural-functionalism. They are shown to be mutually compatible with one another and logically consistent with a more general theory of culture. Finally, two chapters dealing with the biological dimension of man are included. Consistent with our major aims, this information is related to the remainder of the book and shows the intimate relationships among biological and cultural factors in human evolution.

The dynamic nature of sociocultural processes is an important focus of this book. Culture is approached from the inside, so to speak, allowing the reader to understand the dynamism of organizational and social processes. Sociocultural behavior and organization are seen as adaptive mechanisms used by man in a variety of situations and in a variety of ways. Societies adapt to continuously changing conditions with corresponding cultural and organizational modifications. Social systems are dynamic, not static.

Wherever possible or desirable, traditional ethnographic materials are utilized to illustrate concepts. It is important that students be familiar with groups traditionally cited by anthropologists: the Arunta, the Trobriand Islanders, the Eskimo; and the institutions frequently used to illustrate social and cultural concepts, such as the *kula* or the *potlatch*. But to achieve freshness in presentation and to make the reader more aware of contemporary anthropological research, more recently published works to illustrate social and cultural concepts are emphasized.

In writing a book of this kind, authors inevitably incur debts of gratitude to different people. Many of these are those intellectual debts that any writer incurs over the space of many years—to his own teachers, and colleagues, to his students, and to the countless other writers in anthropology who must remain anonymous because their ideas have merged inextricably with and become part of the general stock of knowledge and understanding. If we have drawn freely from this stock, we hope that this book will, in turn, contribute to it. We offer our thanks to those who have given unstintingly of their time and whose enthusiasm has been a frequent and much-needed source of encouragement. Marian Post and Jacqueline Yee have done a major part of the typing of our manuscript, including the many rough drafts. Special thanks to Greta Kwik for much of the preliminary art work, and for many pages of typing. Patsy Thompson did much of the painstaking work of compiling terms for the glossary. A debt of gratitude is owed our colleague Mary Woodward for her critical reading of our section in linguistics; these pages gained much from her comments and suggestions. We wish to express, also, our appreciation to Mrs. Jo Dorsey of the American Museum of Natural History and to the United Nations photographic Library for their assistance. Additional acknowledgments appear throughout the book.

BARTON M. SCHWARTZ
ROBERT H. EWALD

Los Angeles, California
January, 1968

Contents

I

ANTHROPOLOGY AND HUMAN BEHAVIOR

1

The Science of Anthropology

INTRODUCTION

Anthropology as a professional field has grown very rapidly in the past fifteen years. The word itself is becoming increasingly current in the vocabulary of the general public. Yet the public at large has a quite varied and often inaccurate notion of what anthropology is. Most commonly, anthropologists seem to be identified as "bone diggers," as people who dust off old Egyptian papyri, or excavate ancient pyramids, or rifle old Indian mounds of their contents. Still others identify them as scholars who record exotic sex customs of little-known peoples or observe the antics of apes and monkeys. Though not completely inaccurate, these notions are not strictly accurate, for they do not show the full range of things anthropologists do or why they do them.

SCOPE OF ANTHROPOLOGY

"What is anthropology, and what do anthropologists do?" The most efficient way of answering this question would be to define the term and then systematically outline the activities of anthropologists. But before we do this, to give the reader some of the color and flavor of our field, we present two examples of the human phenomena which are the bases of all anthropological writing and theorizing. An examination of these passages will show what we study, the kinds of questions raised by our studies, and the kinds of answers we strive for.

3

I

When Kenge woke me the sun was not yet up, and the birds were still silent in the trees. It was three days after Balekimito's funeral, and the previous night it had been decided in a general discussion [that we should build a new camp]. . . . Already the Pygmy village was alive with women bundling up their household possessions in the baskets they would carry on their backs. The men were busy checking their hunting nets, examining their arrow shafts and testing their bows. . . . The older girls carried an extra basket bulging with plantation foods, or else they carried a baby brother or sister on one hip. . . . Some of the older boys carried their fathers' hunting nets, proudly, leaving the more experienced hunters free to set off in pursuit of any game they might come across on the way. . . . I went over to where a group of men were drinking *liko*, a brew of forest berries and nuts and herbs. . . . Only Ekianga sat silent, outside his hut, watching his third and youngest wife, Kamaikan, cooking his breakfast. He ignored his two other wives. . . . As Kamaikan squatted over the fire, fanning it until it glowed red, I saw that she was pregnant, and I gathered from the look she cast after her two co-wives that her condition was the cause of some jealousy in the household. . . . I heard later that Kenge considered himself above acting as a porter; he apparently thought of that as a job fit only for people of the village, not people of the forest. Any self-respecting Pygmy carries his own load and no one else's. (Turnbull 1962:46 ff.)

II

A word should be added about leavings which are said to be used in sorcery. Anything which has been in direct contact with a person (fragments of a bark skirt or net bag, a woman's netted hair snood, an arm band, anklet, or belt) and anything which has been part of his person (hair, nail parings, bodily excretions) is in a sense an extension of himself. Through such material, an essential ingredient in most types of sorcery, he is vulnerable to anyone who wants to do him harm . . . [therefore] men as well as women quite often destroy discarded fragments of food—not just throwing them into the fire, but making sure that they are completely burned. (Berndt 1962:211 ff.)

The literature from which these selections are culled is enormous, and thousands of others could be cited. However, if we delve deeply enough into them, these two examples will reveal much of what anthropology is all about.

First, anthropology has been characterized by an orientation toward primitive, non-literate, non-western peoples; it has been concerned with groups of people not commonly studied by any other discipline. While the scientific investigation of such cultural groups remains diagnostic of contemporary anthropology, as exemplified by the above descriptions of African Pygmies and a New Guinea mountain tribe, anthropologists do not restrict their studies to such groups. Indeed, many anthropologists are engaged in intensive studies of contemporary emergent nations, modern western civilization, urbanization processes, industrialization, and similar topics.

Second, field research—collecting information through intimate, first-hand experience among the people being studied—is a necessary part of anthropological investigations. Accounts such as those given above can be based only upon this type of intimate and continuous involvement. A temporary visitor to a Pygmy camp, even if present the morning of a camp move, could not recognize or identify the simultaneous activities described, much less understand and interpret them intelligibly in cultural terms.

Third, specific information and generalizations derived from such information are essential to anthropology. Even the very brief examples of the Pygmy camp and of sorcery in New Guinea demonstrate the importance of detailed cultural facts for anthropological research. No detail of everyday life is so minute or so insignificant that it would justify an ethnographer's failure to take note of it. All possible cultural facts are important to any valid analysis of the broader aspects of culture—social organization, religion, political action, social control, language, or economics.

Finally, the subject matter of anthropology is more comprehensive than that claimed by any other science. The full range of things the anthropologist studies—daily camp routine, diet, attitude, tools, beliefs, customs, dress—covers all men in all places at all times; he is interested in and investigates all human behavior. Whether it is the behavior of the entire human species (*sapiens*) or the behavior of a small group, it is the concern of anthropology. *The subject matter of anthropology is man and his culture*—using the latter term in a much broader sense than it is sometimes used in daily speech.

Not every anthropologist studies all of man and all of man's culture. Like other scientists, anthropologists specialize, pursuing a wide range of interests which to the layman may seem quite unrelated. This is revealed by an examination of the contents of any professional anthropology journal (*American Anthropologist, Southwestern Journal of Anthropology, Ethnology, Current Anthropology, Man, Journal of the Royal Anthropological Institute of Great Britain and Ireland, Human Organization*). Articles included in one issue might report on such diverse topics as African secret societies, art, Eskimo kinship terminology, symbolism, values in American culture, the social functions of magic, toilet training of Japanese children, warfare practices, cannibalism, witchcraft, human genetics, primate locomotor behavior, and fossil man. While this list is heterogeneous, all topics included have one common denominator—man and his culture.

Human behavior is cultural behavior. With some consistent variation a human is a product of his culture—his behavior is based largely upon the cultural system into which he is born and in which he is raised and lives. The behavior of the human individual cannot be explained or completely understood apart from the culture in which he lives. Therefore, and perhaps paradoxically to the layman, to explain the behavior of human individuals the anthropologist studies not the individual as an individual but the culture in which he participates. The culture of a human group is treated as a system. The anthropologist analyzes this system by determining its properties—its constituent elements and their relationships. Individual actions are explained and understood by viewing them against this totality.

This does not mean that the individual is irrelevant to anthropological studies. Individual behavior is important to the anthropologist for two reasons. First, the individual is seldom, if ever, isolated from other individuals—he is a member of a group. Because of this relationship, the behavior of each individual constitutes part of the behavior of the group to which he belongs. Second, the individual is the carrier of culture. Individual acts are cultural acts. However, particular events (individual behavior) are of interest to the scientist only as members of or as related to a class of events—culture, in this case. Thus, individual behavior provides the anthropologist with basic information (particular events), whereas behavior of many individuals, viewed as a totality, is the class of events (culture). The class of events provides the context within which particular events are explained. This explanatory approach is not unique to anthropology; most scientific disciplines use it. The physicist, for example, is interested in the behavior of a falling body only as a member of the class "falling bodies." A particular body, due to its shape and the action of friction upon it, may not fall precisely like any other body. Therefore, a mathematical formula which describes the behavior of falling bodies *in general* may not accurately describe that of a particular body. Nevertheless, the general statement provides us with a context for understanding, and even predicting in a *general way*, the falling of particular bodies.

Our earlier selection on sorcery in New Guinea illustrates this principle when applied to the realm of culture. The anthropologist is discussing a general category of culture—sorcery. Sorcery is any act by which the practitioner attempts to harm an enemy by magical means. The anthropologist continues his explanation by attempting to demonstrate that sorcery, or the threat of its use, serves a positive social function. It is a means of maintaining social order, just as the ultimate threat of force serves to maintain order in our society. Further, because open warfare between hostile neighbors is no longer permitted in New Guinea (by colonial governments), sorcery serves as a medium for expressing hostility between them. Such statements about the function of sorcery in this New Guinea culture refer to a class of events. Individual acts of sorcery are considered only as members forming the class.

Sorcery is but one aspect or category of culture, but its use in explaining individual behavior illustrates an important principle in the analysis of cultural systems. The totality that is culture is classified by the anthropologist into such categories as social order, kinship systems, family life, religious rituals, art, diet, marriage customs, and sorcery. Each category summarizes innumerable individual instances of behavior. Therefore, classification serves the purpose of reducing an otherwise unmanageable maze of things and events to a relatively few manageable categories. Specific items of behavior then become understandable as examples of one of these more general classes. The relationships among these categories, as parts of a whole, can be explored meaningfully, enabling the anthropologist to explain specific behavior as it is related to all other human behavior. Such categories can be analyzed cross-culturally. Thus, a relationship was postulated between the categories *sorcery* and *social control* in the New Guinea tribe. These same two categories can be studied among a wide range of cultures to determine if the same relationship occurs cross-culturally.

In summary, anthropologists study whole cultures—*the total cultural patterns of particular human groups*. In this context they may emphasize major parts of a culture, such as economics, political organization, or religion, but each separate part is examined and explained in relation to the total culture. They also deal with *culture as a whole*, as species-wide behavior without reference to particular time or place, or to particular human groups. This latter concept—culture in general—is the most comprehensive in the social sciences.

But why, we may ask, is a separate and distinct science of anthropology necessary at all? Other sciences and humanistic disciplines are concerned with particular aspects of man's behavior—sociology, economics, psychology, political science, comparative religion, and history —and taken collectively these disciplines cover most of man's behavior. Why then do we need another discipline which grandiosely styles itself the science of man? It is the function of an introductory anthropology text to make explicit the place of anthropology among the sciences, but there are many ways of answering the question, "Why anthropology?"

First, anthropology is the only science which has fully explored the biological basis for human behavior and the biological limitations on man's behavior. Anthropology studies the relationships between man's biological evolution and the evolution of his culture—the totality of human evolution. Up to this point we have been talking only about culture or about cultural anthropology, but in fact it was modern anthropology that demonstrated that culture originated in the course of man's biological evolution.

Second, the cross-cultural methods used by anthropologists constitute an important contribution to science and have resulted in more meaningful and valid generalizations about man and his culture. It has become axiomatic in modern anthropology that valid generalizations about human behavior must be based upon comparative studies of human societies from every part of the world and at every technological level. Almost from the beginnings of written history, scholars writing about the nature of man—about human nature—have implied that their statements were universally valid or true of men everywhere. Whether describing man as a social animal, a political animal, or an economic animal, it is clear that they felt they were talking about man in general, not just about men in their own societies. But when one justifies his behavior with the plaintive cry, "I am only human," does he imply that his motives, his desires, his basic anxieties are exactly like those of an Eskimo, a Russian, or a Zulu? If they differ, are these peoples not human? Anthropologists have always attempted to base their generalizations about man upon sufficient evidence of man everywhere—upon extinct as well as contemporary cultures.

Third, anthropology seems to have acquired "squatter's rights" to an area left unoccupied by other sciences. Anthropologists study so-called primitive societies or other societies not ordinarily within the purview of western social science. This is a matter of preference as well as of default. Anthropologists have no doubt that such studies are completely and scientifically justified in their own right. We cannot claim universal knowledge of man or universal validity for our generalizations unless we include primitive societies in our study. Equally important, by focusing on relatively simple, small-scale societies, we can more readily isolate relationships, describe and understand cultural processes, and thus explain total cultures.

Fourth, anthropological procedures applied to small-scale societies not only provide microcosmic analyses of culture, but also result in contributions to a body of theory and method for the more difficult chore of studying and understanding our own and other more complex cultures.

Fifth, only cultural anthropology has dealt in a systematic way with the totality of human behavior—with culture as a unified whole. It is this "holistic" approach to social, economic, political, religious, linguistic behavior as interrelated parts of a single system that is the enduring and continuing contribution of anthropology to the studies of man. The significance of these factors will be emphasized and expanded throughout the book.

FIELDS OF ANTHROPOLOGY

Anthropology is an extremely broad field, for it is concerned with all of human behavior. This does not mean, however, that each anthropologist is fully competent in or even interested in every aspect of his discipline. The field as a whole has become so complex that no one individual can hope to master more than a small part of it. Anthropology, as we have mentioned, has become highly specialized. There are anthropologists who concentrate upon the study of the genetics of human blood groups; others formulate mathematical models for the study of kinship systems; some study social change in Latin American peasant societies, or concentrate on the cultural background of mental illness. Nevertheless, such specialized pursuits always relate in some meaningful way to the work of other anthropological specialists. The individual who is engaged in kinship studies makes use of numerous prior studies of social organizations; a study of blood-group genetics is related to work in the more comprehensive area of population genetics, and both subjects are directly relevant to the broader science of human biology. In these ways, the entire field of anthropology achieves a high degree of integration among its numerous specialized parts. Each of the parts relates to a single constant: man—man as an animal and man as a cultural being.

While specialized interests are many, the science of man has two main dimensions: *biological* and *cultural*. Most anthropologists, therefore, recognize the basic division of their field into physical anthropology and cultural anthropology. Each of these broad areas may be further subdivided in a number of ways, and our outline is but one of several classifications possible.

Physical Anthropology

Physical anthropology has become a vast and complicated field of study in its own right and has advanced far beyond the crude racial classifications and bone measuring (anthropometry) of less than a century ago. Contemporary physical anthropology is concerned with human origins, human evolution, and human variability. Each of these three major problem areas is based upon extensive specialized study, but the specialists (paleontologists, geneticists, serologists, constitutional anthropologists, primatologists, and others) all claim the broader designation of physical anthropologist as well. This is more than a terminological integration; it is a real one. For example, the human paleontologist studies the fossil evidence of man's evolution. The fossils he unearths in many parts of the world provide us with the only direct evidence bearing on this problem. Studies of living primates and their relation to the problem of man's evolution are the task of the primatologist. But living primates provide only *indirect* or parallel evidence of man's evolution. The human geneticist provides basic, causal information in most areas concerned with man as a biological organism—structural changes in the biology of man, biological capacity for adaptation to a given environment, genetic variability, rates and types of evolutionary change. All of these are equally important for understanding man the animal as well as man the cultural being: there is a biological foundation of culture. The many specialized fields within physical anthropology all contribute to a comprehensive understanding of man. The interdependence of these specialties, each of which is based upon and directly related to a single constant, man, necessarily results in the integration of the entire field of physical anthropology.

Cultural Anthropology

In spite of the basic division of anthropology into physical and cultural, the reader must remain aware of the essential interrelatedness of the two fields. Human evolution, seen in broadest perspective (macroevolution), is a single process. Though we separate it into biological and cultural evolution and talk about each *as if* it were a separate, independent process, understanding is severely limited unless it is recognized that cultural factors profoundly influence biological evolution and that biological factors influence cultural evolution. The physical anthropologist is distinguished from the human biologist precisely by this awareness—the importance of culture in shaping the course of man's biological development and the influence of biological factors upon culture.

Culture is the behavior of a particular kind of biological organism— man. Certain "universals" of culture—tool production and use, family organization, regulation of sexual activities, protection against the natural environment—reflect the biology of man. As man evolved biologically, his capacity for culture also evolved. The possession of culture, in turn, influenced man's continuing biological development. Eventually, culture developed to a point of such complexity that it became the overriding factor in human evolution. This development resulted in the evolution of culture according to its own laws of process, not those of biology. Biological factors continue to influence its development, but culture has reached proportions whereby it logically warrants separate analysis, and this is the province of cultural anthropology.

The following subdivisions reflect the more specialized approaches to the study of culture.

Archaeology. Archaeology consists of the accumulation and interpretation of data from cultures that have become extinct, usually cultures that have left no written records. However, some archaeologists are concerned primarily with the reconstruction and analysis of classical civilizations—Rome, Greece, and Egypt—which have left written records of their culture. Historical or classical archaeology (the study of extinct cultures with written records) is somewhat analogous to cultural studies of contemporary complex societies, while prehistoric archaeology (the study of cultures without written records) is most analogous to cultural studies of relatively simple contemporary societies. Archaeology legitimately claims the area of prehistory as well as the historical period.

The task of the archaeologist concerned with prehistoric cultures is a difficult one. He is obliged to reconstruct extinct cultures from scant artifacts randomly preserved by nature for hundreds or even thousands of years. Because the culture has become extinct, behavioral patterns, which are crucial to studies of contemporary cultures (ethnography), are not available to the archaeologist. Yet, from the material remains uncovered—stone axes, arrow points, bone tools, or fragments of pottery—archaeologists are able to infer logically the major social patterns that existed during the time the culture was viable. Such logical inference is based upon the assumption that culture is an integrated whole and implies that the material objects made by man reflect his behavior and other non-material aspects of his culture. In some cases, the archaeologist is fortunate enough to find large quantities of material remains. These might even include bones of fish and game animals, evidence of plants, or the artifacts used to procure these food products. More "spectacular" remains—pyramids, tombs, burial mounds, caches of gold or jade—are equally important for archaeological analysis.

Interpretation of these diverse remains provides some understanding of life as it was lived in the past. Establishing the age of remains, determining the climatic and general environmental conditions prevalent at that time, establishing relationships with other cultural remains from surrounding areas (possibly as evidence of cultural borrowing, migration, or trade), and making inferences about cultural patterns not directly revealed by the artifact materials uncovered are part of the interpretive process. In addition, the archaeologist relies heavily upon the specialized knowledge of the geologist, the geographer, the paleontologist, the ethnologist, and even the botanist and chemist to complete his interpretation of the cultural and natural materials uncovered.

Archaeology, then, is a major source of data for the cultural anthropologist. The magnitude of the archaeologist's contribution to the study of culture becomes apparent when it is remembered that man's total span on the earth has been at least 1 million years (and probably closer

The excavation and restoration of an archaeological site at Pacha-camac, Peru, revealed an extinct Indian civilization dating back thousands of years. The artifacts recovered from this site enabled archaeologists to infer much about the cultural patterns of the society. (Photo by Robert H. Ewald.)

to 2 million years). Written documents, on the other hand, have a maximum history of only 5,000 years. Therefore, our knowledge of more than 99 per cent of man's cultural history is based upon the findings of the archaeologist.

Ethnography. Ethnography is the description of the culture (lifeways) of a particular human group at a single point in time. Theorizing, extensive interpretation, or cross-cultural comparisons cannot be legitimately included within ethnography. The ethnographer describes as clearly and as objectively as possible the events he witnesses. An example is the following description of possession among voodoo adherents in Haiti.

People possessed start by giving an impression of having lost control of their motor system. Shaken by spasmodic convulsions, they pitch forward, as though projected by a spring, turn frantically around and around, stiffen and stay still with body bent forward, sway, stagger, save themselves, again lose balance, only to fall finally in a state of semiconsciousness. Sometimes such attacks are sudden, sometimes they are heralded by preliminary signs: a vacant or anguished expression, mild tremblings, panting breath, or drops of sweat on the brow; the face becomes tense or suffering.

In certain cases trance is preceded by a sleepy condition. The possessed cannot keep his eyes open and seems overcome with . . . languor. This does not last long: it suddenly gives place to a rough awakening accompanied by convulsive movements.

This preliminary phase can soon end. People who are used to possession pass quickly through the whole range of nervous symptoms. They quake, stagger, make a few mechanical movements, and then, suddenly—there they are: in full trance. . . .

Sometimes . . . the person possessed seems unable to come out of his stupor. I remember one woman, seized by the *loa* Agassu, who remained a long time on her back with eyes closed, her arms flung out like a cross. She might have been thought to have fainted, had she not thrown her head from side to side and had her body not been subject to mild spasms gradually reaching her shoulders, which she shook rhythmically. With great difficulty she managed to kneel. She then opened her eyes: they were fixed and estranged. She kissed the earth and got up with the heavy movements of a person weighed down by pain. Like a sleepwalker she went and kissed the *poteau-mitan*. Tears rolled down her cheeks. Losing balance, she fell to the ground, where she resumed her previous position. The *hungan*, rushing up to her, alternately cajoled and entreated her gently. She wiped her tears, got up, and went and sat on a seat where she remained motionless, her face fixed in a sad, farouche stare. (Metraux 1960:407–9.)

In this excerpt there is no theory, no interpretation, and no comparison save literary analogies that are inserted to allow the reader to feel greater empathy with the events the ethnographer has observed. However, this descriptive passage will be interpreted, will be used in comparison with other descriptive reports, and will provide data for cultural theory. The ethnographic descriptions obtained by anthropologists are prerequisites for analysis and, as such, constitute the raw materials which allow subsequent interpretation, analysis, and theorizing about culture. A parallel exists between the archaeologist, whose province is extinct societies, and the ethnographer, whose province is the culture of contemporary groups: both describe culture.

The ethnographer makes use of all available data in describing the way of life of any society. These include historical sources such as missionaries' accounts, travelers' renditions and impressions of the culture, census data, and other available materials. But most ethnographers rely primarily upon the method of direct observation, as shown in the above example. It is this aspect of ethnography, direct observation, which has most captured the imagination of the layman and which has come to be uniquely identified with the anthropological method. Direct observation, an integral and basic part of field work, is the ultimate source of data collected by cultural anthropologists. It provides the basis for anthropological analyses of human behavior.

To the student and layman, there is often glamour in the prospect of taking up residence among an exotic people in a far-off land—the "jungle," a remote Pacific island, the Andean highlands, the Amazon river basin—to record their way of life. The ethnographer's work is often visualized as a continuous round of witnessing fascinating rituals or marriage and burial customs, of eating strange foods (the reader enjoys shuddering vicariously at such accounts), and perhaps being a privileged witness to forbidden, esoteric acts. This, like many other notions about anthropology, contains some truth but much folly.

There exists an enormous literature of published ethnographies in many languages, dating back many years. The authors of the more sophisticated descriptions are usually trained social scientists, but many valuable accounts have been written by missionaries, traders, colonial officials, and others who have lived among "far-off" peoples, gaining an intimate knowledge of their life-ways. This literature embodies a large portion of all we know about man, past and present. It provides the basis for much scientific theory, and apparent gaps in this literature often stimulate additional ethnographic research.

Ethnology. Ethnology is the explanatory, interpretive, and theorizing branch of cultural anthropology. As a categorical term, ethnology has had several meanings in the brief history of anthropology. In Europe, "anthropology" traditionally was used to refer to the study of biological man, while "ethnology" was similar to the meaning we now bestow upon cultural anthropology. To a generation or more of early American anthropologists, ethnology was, essentially, the historical approach to culture. Focus was upon the spread of customs from their centers of origin and the geographical distribution of cultural items as a clue to their history.

Contemporary ethnologists use the comparative method to establish similarities and differences among diverse cultures, and derive valid generalizations from such studies. They attempt to: (1) formulate general laws to which cultural systems apparently conform; (2) state the conditions under which certain events can, cannot, or will occur; (3) relate selected cultural events to other significant cultural occurrences; and (4) classify cultural data into various categories as a preliminary step to exploring the relations between these logically derived categories. In short, anthropologists, like other scientists, formulate concepts and logical constructs *about* culture (culture, itself, is one such construct), and then logically refine their concepts to arrive at more precise analyses. The end results are explanation, understanding, and the ability to predict —possibly even control—human events.

Thus we see that cultural anthropology, as a science, has much in common with the procedures and methods of other sciences. Data accumulation—whether utilizing archaeological techniques, research into historical documents, or ethnographic research—is an important part of anthropology. Such data are often incorporated into systematic descriptions called ethnographies, and the interpretation and explanation of ethnographic data is called ethnology. Explanation is a goal of all sciences. Anthropologists are interested in understanding the phenomena they observe and in making predictions based on this understanding.

Linguistics. Linguistics is the scientific study of language as an aspect of culture. A language is a system—a set of rules—according to which significant, minimal units of sound called *phonemes* are combined into larger, meaningful units called *morphemes,* and morphemes are combined and arranged into meaningful utterances. The rules involving morphemes constitute the grammar or, more precisely, the grammatical structure of the language. The actual behavior of individuals in producing utterances according to the rules of their language is called *speech.* Speech is learned behavior and is part of culture.

The study of language has a number of aspects which are related to studies of culture. Traditionally, linguists have studied the structures of languages as if they bore no relationship to any other aspect of culture. This approach is called *structural linguistics* and subsumes two kinds of study—*phonology* and *grammar.*

Phonology refers to the characteristic sounds in a given language and the sequences they may form. A phoneme is a minimal unit of significant sound. The human vocal and auditory apparatus is capable of producing and distinguishing hundreds of distinct sounds, but a given language will utilize a finite number. English, for example, depending upon the dialect (a local variant of a language), has approximately 46 phonemes (Gleason 1961:50). All languages of the world, ignoring the extremes, range between 30 and 45 phonemes. Phonology also concerns itself with the sequences in which phonemes may occur. In English, for example, the sound combination /ts/ occurs at the end of some words but never at the beginning. Therefore, a foreign loan word like *tsetse fly* is difficult for English speakers to pronounce because they have not learned this particular sequence. Phonemes as such do not have meaning. They must be combined into larger units—morphemes and words—which do have meaning. Morphemes and their arrangements in a language are part of the grammatical structure of language.

Grammar is the study of the minimal units of sound sequences that have meaning (morphemes), the ways in which these units are combined to form larger utterances, and the rules governing their order. A morpheme may be coextensive with a word but capable of standing by itself, in which case the linguist calls it a "free morpheme." Or, a morpheme may not stand alone and may be used only in combination with other morphemes to form a word, in which case it is called a "bound morpheme." Examples of free morphemes in English are such words as *eat, sleep,* or *cat.* These are minimal units; they cannot be divided into shorter meaningful units. A word like *untied,* on the other hand, consists of three morphemes: *un-tie-d.* The second of these can stand alone as a free morpheme, the first and third cannot. The two bound morphemes—*un* and *d*—nevertheless do have meaning (*un* = not; *d* = past tense).

Grammar also involves the rules governing the arrangement of words in longer utterances. The phrase, "This is a book," clearly follows rules of English grammar. If the first two words were reversed, the meaning of the utterance would be altered, and any other order would result in nonsense or in "incorrect" English. The rules of English grammar will not apply strictly to another language, not even to a related language like Spanish or German. Each of the thousands of languages known to linguistics has its own phonological and grammatical patterns.

Another important aspect of linguistics has to do with the historical relationships among languages. Since such relationships are established by comparison, this branch of linguistics is sometimes called *comparative* or *historical linguistics.* A comparison of a selected vocabulary list from English, German, and Russian would establish that many similar words are shared by English and German but fewer are shared by these two languages and Russian. We would unhesitatingly postulate a more recent historical relationship between English and German than between German and Russian or English and Russian. The study of the geographical distribution of languages and the relationships among them often provides the ethnologist with a valuable technique for historical reconstruction. The anthropologist might postulate that two geographically separated but similar languages once represented a single speech community, or that an intervening language represents a recent invasion which divided speakers of the first language into two or more groups, driving them apart.

Structural and historical linguists sometimes treat language as if it were quite independent of other aspects of culture. In fact, the nature of the relationship has not always been entirely clear. Culture, we have seen, exhibits all the characteristics of a system; its various parts and subsystems are clearly interrelated. The kinds of ritual a people perform or the beliefs they hold will depend on the organization of their society, which in turn may be intimately related to their technology or economy. A major task of ethnology is the demonstration of such relationships. But, until relatively recently, there has been no apparent relationship demonstrated between the structure of a language and any other aspect of a culture. Thus, the culture of a group may change quite dramatically within a short time span, whereas their language (aside from vocabulary changes) would undergo no noticeable change. The implication of this would be that language and culture can vary quite independently of one another.

In recent years, however, there has been a growing exploration of this relationship. A number of scholars now believe that a relationship exists between the grammatical structure of a language and the thought processes or the general philosophy of the members of a society. The late Edward Sapir and his student Benjamin Whorf were outstanding pioneers in this field of language and culture, also referred to as *ethnolinguistics* or *psycholinguistics*. Their statement concerning the relationship between language and culture has come to be known as the "Sapir-Whorf hypothesis." According to Hoijer, "The central idea of the Sapir-Whorf hypothesis is that language functions, not simply as a device for reporting experience, but also, and more significantly, as a way of defining experience for its speakers . . ." (see Fried 1959:221). According to this point of view, the world about us is never observed or perceived objectively. Rather, our perceptions of that world are subtly and unconsciously structured by the grammatical forms that shape our very thoughts. Hence, the "world view" of one society will be presented differently from that of another because their languages differ.

While the conclusions of ethnolinguists are tentative and controversial, their line of inquiry does promise significant new dimensions of understanding in the study of man and culture.

Finally, the techniques of linguistic analysis have provided the ethnologist with an important tool for conducting research in the field. Anthropologists have found that a knowledge of structural analysis greatly facilitates the learning of languages, particularly languages that are not written. Lacking such techniques, the fieldworker is forced to work through the medium of interpreters, and inevitably his work will suffer in quality and in depth.

Social Anthropology. In addition to the more commonly recognized branches already described, other interest-areas and pursuits do exist and are important parts of anthropology. Culture and personality, applied anthropology, political anthropology, urban anthropology, medical anthropology, and others are examples of and can be properly subsumed under the major categories we have given. We will not discuss all of these specialized interest-areas separately, but there is an additional field within anthropology that deserves more extended consideration, if only because of the frequency with which its designation, *social anthropology,* is used.

Persons who regard themselves as social anthropologists are often quite explicit in distinguishing their field from cultural anthropology. Today, this distinction is more apparent than real. Social anthropology is considered by its practitioners to be the study of social man, of social relations, and of human society. Indeed, social anthropologists sometimes insist they are sociologists, distinguishing themselves from other sociologists only because they investigate primitive, preliterate, or nonwestern societies, and use anthropological techniques for gathering and analyzing data. For the social anthropologist, the various parts of culture—beliefs, customs, rituals—are conceived as aspects of a social system and as products of social interaction. The primary task of the social anthropologist is to lay bare the system of organization of the society he studies—including its structure, actions, and functions. As a "comparative sociologist," he attempts to derive universally valid generalizations by comparing analyses derived from a wide range of cultures.

APPROACH TO CULTURE AND SOCIETY

We do not believe, nor do most social anthropologists, that culture and society are mutually exclusive categories. As practiced by modern scholars, cultural anthropology and social anthropology differ more in emphasis than in kind. Culture is the more inclusive category. Culture as human behavior not only includes tools, architecture, art, beliefs, rituals, and customs, but encompasses the entire range of social interaction, the area which the social anthropologist has selected as his subject matter.

Our approach, and it should be emphasized that this is but one of many possible valid approaches, is to treat culture both generally—as species-wide behavior—and specifically—as particular group behavior. In the first or general approach, the unit of study is the totality of human behavior, including its growth and development through time without reference to specific human groups or geographical divisions. The usefulness of this type of analysis is demonstrated in the chapters which focus on culture as a process—culture history and cultural evolution. Based upon this general knowledge and understanding, a specific approach to culture is presented. Because culture is always the property of specific human groups—societies, tribes, communities, or nations—we shift our emphasis to an analysis of the ways in which human groups organize their culture. Part II of this book will explore the intimate relationships between social organization *as one aspect* of culture and all other parts of culture, individually and in conjunction with one another.

Throughout, it is crucial that the reader keep in mind that culture and society are both useful and necessary concepts for a scientific study of man. Culture should be seen as the broader, more inclusive category. Social interaction and organization are major parts systematically related to all other aspects of culture. It is this view that will be detailed in subsequent chapters.

2

Anthropological Field Research

INTRODUCTION

Field research, conducted through actual residence among the people being studied, is more characteristic of anthropology than it is of any other discipline. Anthropologists carry on their research wherever human society and culture are found. Field work is an expected part of the training of all anthropologists. It is a rare scholar in anthropology who has not collected information first-hand in this manner.

When an anthropologist considers doing field research, several complex problems must be defined and solved: what preparations must be made for entry into the field; how can sufficient rapport be established with the people being investigated; what theoretical assumptions and what problem orientations are to be used in approaching the research; what hypotheses can be formulated and/or demonstrated by this research; how are personal and cultural biases to be recognized and minimized; what specific techniques of data collection are to be used; how will the data collected be validated—how can observations be checked and rechecked; how does this research relate to and contribute to existing generalizations about man and his culture? These and other problems comprise six distinct but not mutually exclusive categories of the research operation: *preparation for field research, establishing contact, establishing rapport, data collection, analysis of data collected,* and *the research report.* Each of these is a necessary part of the overall research process. While they have a logical and sequential order, these activities do overlap. One does not necessarily end when another begins.

PREPARATION FOR FIELD RESEARCH

Often an anthropologist's first field trip is part of his requirements for the Ph.D. The majority of universities offering advanced degrees in cultural anthropology make ethnographic field research such a requirement. Today, the usual procedure in earning the Ph.D. is (1) completion of undergraduate training (B.A. in anthropology in most, though not all, cases); (2) formal graduate training—course work, extensive reading, graduate seminars; (3) successful completion of two language examinations; and (4) passing written and oral comprehensive examinations in the various fields of anthropology. During a candidate's graduate training he is expected to develop an interest in a specific geographic area—Africa, Oceania, Middle America, Australia, South Asia, the Middle East. Further, the student is expected to be able to formulate and present significant hypotheses which can be tested by means of field work in his area of interest. Most frequently, though there are exceptions, the student will have successfully completed all these requirements prior to undertaking field research. First-hand collection of data will give the degree candidate the information necessary to complete his final requirement—the doctoral dissertation and its oral defense.

In addition to or as part of his formal graduate training, the degree candidate will make certain other preparations for entry into the field. He prepares for field work by (1) reading the available literature pertinent to his investigatory interest, (2) consulting maps, (3) conferring with people who have knowledge of the area in which the field work is to be done, and (4) familiarizing himself with relevant archival material. Some of these preparations will necessarily be completed after arrival in the country where the research is to be done. Archival materials, for example, may be unavailable except in that country.

In each of his preparations the anthropologist must evaluate information critically and objectively, and he must become aware of existing bias which can distort the information being considered. A missionary or traveler might misrepresent the religious life of a tribal people. An earlier scholar might focus so exclusively on economic or political aspects of the culture in question that the result is an incomplete or even inaccurate impression of its other aspects. A reputable scholar can unconsciously select his data so as to support a preconceived theoretical position. Unskilled observers see things they expect or wish to see and may fail completely to record other crucial data. Unless the anthropologist is aware of these and many other potential biases, he will fail to gain an objective view of his area from such sources. Objectivity is a consistent goal of the professional anthropologist.

Another very important consideration in preparing for field work is the language in which the research is to be done. The ideal condition of all ethnographic research is to work in the language of the people under investigation. The anthropologist either learns that language (if there are tutors or materials available to help him), or acquires sufficient linguistic training to learn the language as rapidly as possible when he arrives in the field. When neither is possible, the anthropologist must find an interpreter.

ESTABLISHING CONTACT

If he has managed to gain financial support—from his graduate school or a research foundation (known in university jargon as "getting a grant")—the candidate is ready to leave for the field. Days or even hours later he may arrive in the country he has chosen. His manner of reaching his final destination will depend, of course, on what people he has chosen to study. The last part of his trip could be a comfortable taxi ride, a harrowing bus ride over winding mountain roads, a torturous week on horseback, or several days' squatting in a dugout canoe. Often, in professional circles, though it is scientifically unjustified, the prestige that accrues from field work varies according to the accessibility of the people to be studied. Studying a remnant Indian population inside metropolitan Los Angeles or San Francisco confers less prestige than busing to a village 20 miles from Mexico City. And the latter yields in prestige to a venture in which a three-week schooner voyage is climaxed by a two-week walk into the interior of New Guinea. This superficial academic "prestige" bears no relation to the real value of the work done or the data collected. *All field work adds to the body of anthropological knowledge.* The fledgling anthropologist may choose any of hundreds of areas in which to do his research, but he must undergo this *rite de passage* before he can achieve professional maturity.

An analogy between the anthropologist's first field experience and a primitive rite of passage is really not so far-fetched. Psychologically, and even physically, this first field experience frequently approaches in intensity the trial by ordeal experienced by the primitive youth who is obliged to demonstrate his manhood to the adult males of his society. First, though not necessarily most important, there is the sheer physical discomfort of field work, often aggravated by disease. The anthropologist Elman Service dedicated one of his books (1958): "To anthropological field workers, who have been defined as 'otherwise intelligent and literate persons who do not accept the germ theory of disease.'"

The fieldworker, alone among a people who do not speak his language, and hours (perhaps even centuries!) away from modern medical aid and suffering with malaria or dysentery, may find himself temporarily envying the primitive youth who is staked out on an anthill but surrounded by sympathetic relatives.

Still, the physical discomforts experienced by the anthropologist are often quite secondary to the psychological trauma of suddenly finding himself completely alone among a strange people whose speech, culture, and most basic assumptions are totally foreign to his own. Few other experiences can match this loneliness. No matter that the natives may be completely friendly; how long can strangers grin amiably at one another before both parties become uncomfortable? The situation is improved immeasurably, of course, if the fieldworker already has some knowledge of the language. Even for the best fieldworkers, this experience can be initially traumatic and often continues to be lonely, tedious, and frustrating. On more than one occasion the first shock of field work has been too much for the novice, who has gone home to seek a more congenial profession.

Culture Shock

Anthropologists employ a picturesque term for this unpleasant experience. They call it "culture shock." Most of us, whether we have traveled or not, have probably experienced culture shock in one form or another. It most commonly takes the form of a reaction—disgust, ridicule, contempt—to customs or beliefs belonging to another culture. Culture shock is ethnocentrism in a crisis situation. It demonstrates clearly that we are products of our culture.

If a motion picture showing Australian tribesmen stuffing roasted grub worms into their mouths threatens you with nausea; if a written account of Aztec human sacrifice fills you with horror; or if you are simply an American tourist appalled at the quality of European plumbing, you have experienced a certain amount of culture shock. The newly located fieldworker might experience shock in similar ways—finding local food unpalatable, reacting to what he regards as needless cruelty toward animals, having his modesty outraged at being unable to perform certain natural functions in private, finding displeasure with the ways of the host culture, or experiencing an inability to communicate.

One anthropologist expresses it as, among other things, ". . . a feeling of helplessness and a desire for the company of people of one's own nationality, and 'a terrible longing to be back home, to be able to have a good cup of coffee and a piece of apple pie, to walk into that corner drugstore, to visit one's relatives, and in general, to talk to people who really make sense.'" (Foster 1962:187–88.) According to another writer, "In nearly every prolonged contact that a person schooled in one culture has with that of another, some shock and forced readjustment occurs. It is compounded of frustration, exasperation, irritation, and the strain of heightened attention to strange cues and signs in a foreign situation." (Arensberg and Niehoff 1964:186.) A third anthropologist, Oberg, suggests:

> Culture shock is precipitated by the anxiety that results from losing all one's familiar cues. These cues include the thousand and one ways in which we orient ourselves to the situations of daily life: when to shake hands and what to say when we meet people, when and how much to tip, how to give orders to servants, how to make purchases, when to accept and when to refuse invitations, when to take statements seriously and when not. Those cues to behavior . . . words, gestures, facial expressions . . . are acquired in the course of growing up and are as much a part of our culture as the language we speak. All of us depend for our peace of mind and our efficiency on hundreds of cues, most of which we do not carry on a level of conscious awareness. (Foster 1962:188.)

Culture shock is based upon unfamiliarity, lack of understanding, inability to communicate and interact effectively, and the inability (though temporary in some cases) to adapt to alien situations. Since personal values are involved, all individuals react to culture shock in different ways. An anthropologist's reactions can seriously affect his field work. Situations may be encountered where the behavior of informants threatens or contradicts the basic values and moral principles of the fieldworker. An extreme example, which no anthropologist is likely to encounter today, is human sacrifice. Should the anthropologist stand by passively taking notes as though he were scrutinizing the activity of organisms under a microscope? Should he attempt to stop the proceedings—which are tantamount to murder in his culture? Certainly these are two alternatives available to the anthropologist.

Perhaps less improbable, suppose the anthropologist was invited to accompany a headhunting expedition and witnessed the ruthless killing of women, children, and men and the decapitation of adult victims. Or suppose, in a different situation, he observed his informants killing a female infant as an adjustment to an extreme food shortage. Certainly the fieldworker concerned would have to make some kind of decision: jeopardize his work by interfering; flee in helpless anger; or remain a dispassionate observer, trying to convince himself that morals and ethics are all relative and that he should not allow his own cultural standards to intrude into this situation. In any case, the anthropologist will experience some shock based upon the differences between his culture and the one he is studying.

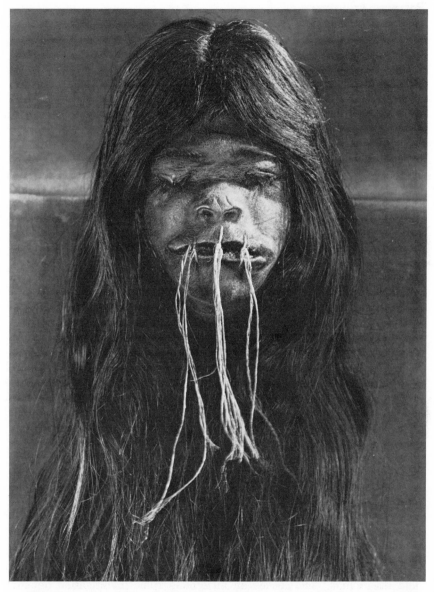

Situations are often encountered where the behavior of another culture threatens and contradicts the basic values of the fieldworker, as in the case of the head-shrinking of the Jivaro Indians of Ecuador. (Courtesy of the American Museum of Natural History.)

Personal Adjustment

Actual examples, not as dramatic as these hypothetical ones, could be related by most fieldworkers. Most such situations involve personal adjustment. How quickly the fieldworker adjusts, if he ever does, is largely a matter of his own previous experience, maturity, tolerance, and adaptability. He may adjust in a matter of weeks, thereafter thoroughly enjoying his experience, or he may never adjust. In the latter case, the anthropologist seriously handicaps effective research and may fail completely.

His personal adjustment may involve simply understanding and adapting to different conceptions of time. One of the authors made his first field trip to Guatemala. He was adequately warned of the Latin American attitude toward time, but to no avail. On one occasion he arranged to meet an informant three days later at 7:00 A.M. to walk with him to a distant cornfield where they would spend the day conversing and working. The anthropologist rejoined his family in a nearby town, but returned on the morning in question at the exact hour agreed upon. Expecting his informant to arrive promptly, he had even turned down the breakfast offered him by his landlady, though she had assured him that he had sufficient time. This was an understatement. Later in the day, after hours of waiting, he found that his informant had left for the coast on the previous afternoon and would not return for two weeks. Incidents of this kind can be very disturbing to the fieldworker. Should the author have confronted his informant with charges of unreliability and lack of courtesy? The informant might have responded: "You were very insistent in making this appointment, and since we are a courteous people, I told you what you wanted to hear. If you knew our ways you would not have kept the appointment either." Examples like this characterize most, if not all, anthropological field work.

ESTABLISHING RAPPORT

Establishing sufficient and proper contact with the research population—the people to be studied—is a basic and consistent problem of all field researchers. The success of all ethnographic investigation depends upon rapport. Most peoples of the world today, no matter how isolated, have had some contact with the outside world. Many times the contact has not been pleasant, and if not unpleasant it usually has been purposeful—missionaries attempting conversion or governmental representatives collecting taxes. If the anthropologist's initial contact with the people is through a government tax collector or a zealous missionary, he must be wary about taking on the coloration or values attributed to his introducer.

At the same time, the researcher wants to observe first-hand and even participate in the culture of the people being studied. The combination of these two techniques—*observation* and *participation*—is one of the major contributions of anthropology to field research. Effective use of this combination is not automatic, but depends upon rapport—free, sincere, harmonious understanding and interaction—being established and developed between the researcher and the research population.

The result is *participant observation,* which means involving oneself in the life of the community, becoming as inconspicuous as possible, and thereafter attempting to share the life of the people. The observer eats with his hosts, works with them in the fields, plays their games, and attends their funerals, weddings, and festivals. He learns their language as a key to understanding and empathizing with the local values, symbolism, and world view of his subjects. These activities, and many more, are the ideals of participant observation. If the anthropologist succeeds, he will acquire a depth of understanding for which there is no substitute—though we recognize that many other techniques can provide a valuable supplement.

Most fieldworkers probably fall far short of this ideal, and success is a highly relative matter. What are some barriers to success, assuming that the fieldworker himself is a capable, adaptable, tolerant, and sympathetic individual? First, of course, there is the question of rapport—a word much on the lips of field researchers. How does one gain the acceptance, trust, and respect of his subjects; how does he establish good relations of a sort that permits participation in the life of the community? Certainly they are not to be achieved by refusing the hosts' hospitality, violating their customs, being stingy where they are generous, and in general exhibiting bad manners. But a fieldworker can be aware of these basic rules of conduct and still fail to establish good rapport.

A powerful and frequent factor militating against good relations, regardless of how tactful and friendly the fieldworker may be, is a general hostility toward all outsiders on the part of his hosts, stemming from experiences in the past. Any stranger may potentially mean forced labor recruitment, appropriation of lands, increased taxes, and so on. Peasant peoples, whose insufficient land is their whole life, are especially prone to such suspicions. One of the writers, on his first trip to Guatemala, found what many fieldworkers have encountered—a difficulty in explaining his role, and a mistrust of him in the role in which the people cast him. His first guide and friend was, unfortunately in this case, a known Protestant missionary, and this association was not easy to offset in a

Anthropologist J. L. Clark poses with two Pygmy women of the Congo. Acceptance into a society may be the most difficult task the fieldworker faces. (Courtesy of the American Museum of Natural History.)

predominantly Catholic population. Still other peasants had their suspicions aroused by the anthropologist's questions concerning landholdings. Guatemala was in the midst of an agrarian reform program, and many people had had land appropriated by the national government. The anthropologist, for all they knew, was an agent of the government gathering information for further land seizures.

The anthropologist's role, or perceived role, may pose a threat to certain vested interests. If he is overly generous with his stock of medicines and gains some success as a curer, he may find himself threatening, in a very real way, a local curing specialist. Such persons can easily start whispering campaigns to discredit the anthropologist and his motives. One ethnologist, writing of his field research among the Quechua of Peru, described the reactions of his subjects to him in this way:

A popular rumor about me held that I was a PISHTAKU, an evil supernatural being who is said to steal the fat from people. . . . Many people believed that I was a rapist, and women were warned that sexual contact with me
would bring about venereal disease in the victim or, at the least, that such contact would be extremely painful because of the size and shape of the sexual
organ concerned. . . . Jokes focussing on my role as a castrator of men were
frequent. (Stein 1961:x.)

The examples of such difficulties are numerous; we cite just one more.
Maud Oakes, who studied a village in Guatemala, once was called in to
save a sick child, but was too late, and the child died. The angered
grandfather, a *shaman* (religious specialist), spread the word that she
was a sorceress, with evil powers. Later, an epidemic was blamed on
her photography, it being claimed that when she took pictures, she
carried away the spirits of her subjects. Soon nearly everything she did
was interpreted as evidence of supernatural powers. Indeed, when she
was observed eating Rye Crisp, the word went about that she could eat
wood. Only the shift to a new villain saved her from this role of scapegoat. (Paul 1953:439.)

To a people who attribute any kind of misfortune to magic or witchcraft, it is no great jump to the conclusion that the outsider is the evil
influence, and this may be no laughing matter to the unfortunate victim.
Anthropologists have been driven out of communities for less.

Needless to say, all such incidents detract greatly from the pleasures
of field work. To quote the late Oliver LaFarge (1947): "Given as they
are to dire suspicion and ready hostility, in these close-knit groups I
myself can testify that the general assumption of an unpleasant attitude
can take most of the joy out of life, even though it is accompanied by
no overt action of any kind, but only by whisperings as one goes by, an
unfriendly laugh when one has passed, and a constant turning of suspicious eyes in one's direction as one walks about." And, we might add,
this general discomfort can arise when the child of an informant whom
you had believed to be your good friend unknowingly refers to you by
some unpleasant term (e.g., *gringo*) that he obviously learned at home.

But, let us assume that some initial rapport is established. The anthropologist hands out free photographs, drinks regularly with the men,
demonstrates some skill in local games, adds to entertainment through
his musical ability, and generally makes himself popular enough to begin
to be accepted. This is only the beginning. A lingering suspicion of all
outsiders and the inability to communicate fully in the native language
will always be important barriers. The anthropologist is an outsider, and
nothing can alter this fact. His presence must always affect the behavior of those he is observing. He is, in short, a factor in his own data.
The astute anthropologist accepts this and tries to treat the reactions of

his subjects to him as part of his data. He can never assume that people are behaving in front of him as they would if he were not present. But the anthropologist can minimize scepticism and increase rapport with the research population, thereby increasing the amount and variety of information he collects.

DATA COLLECTION

A research sequence can be formulated for anthropologists engaged in field research. Based upon his rapport with the research population, the researcher achieves particular status levels that are directly related to the derivation of information. Conscious recognition of this sequence allows anthropological fieldworkers to be more effective by being more precisely aware of the behavioral limitations that coincide with the particular status they have achieved. This sequence is as follows:

Status	*Degree of Information*
1. Outsider	No information derived.
2. Partial Observer	Limited information derived through the process of observation only.
3. Full Observer	Increased information derived, but restricted to the process of observation.
4. Observer-as-Participant	Increased information derived through the combined processes of observation and participation, but the emphasis is still upon observation with only limited participation possible.
5. Participant-as-Observer	Increased information derived through the combined processes of participation and observation, but the emphasis is now upon participation.
6. Participant Observer	Most intensive derivation of information with extreme emphasis upon participation.
7. Full Participant	Increased derivation of information, but highly biased and non-objective.

Limitations to Data Collection

Participation and observation, no matter how effectively used, must have limitations. Even the most enterprising researcher can see only so much and be in only one place at a time. Many situations will occur outside his field of observation; others will not occur at all during his stay. Conceivably, there will be no burials, no marriages, no punishment of crime, and so on. If such is the case, the anthropologist must rely on other techniques to gain information about events he has not observed. There are many techniques available to the anthropologist in the field. In addition to observation and participation, surveys, questionnaires, directed and non-directed depth interviewing, attitude scaling, photographic techniques, and the like are used to record the activities, beliefs, values, and behavior of the people being studied. But these too have limitations which must be recognized.

While interviewing-type techniques are valuable supplements indispensable to a field researcher, they are not adequate substitutes for being there and seeing with one's own eyes. Anthropologists are only too well aware of the discrepancies between what informants say is done, or should be done, and what actually transpires when a situation arises. Let us explore this idea.

Anthropologists commonly distinguish between what is referred to as *ideal culture* and *manifest culture*. Manifest culture, simply enough, refers to what people actually do in a specific situation. An Australian hunter, returning to his camp with game, can be observed calling out his relatives and distributing the meat according to customary rules. A Hopi Indian can be seen turning aside with a show of embarrassment when he confronts his mother-in-law along the trail. A Guatemalan Indian tips his hat when meeting a *Ladino* (non-Indian). The whole range of readily observable behavior recorded by the anthropologist comes under the heading of manifest culture. People till the soil, make flint implements, fondle their children, tell tales around a fire, decorate pottery, dress themselves in a favored costume. But there is always a great deal more not readily observable by the anthropologist.

Under the heading *covert culture*, anthropologists include everything not directly observable: conscious or unconscious dispositions that form part of individuals' personalities, beliefs, attitudes, *ideals*, and *values*. The covert sector includes ideal culture—that which people of a certain society think ought to be or should be, whether it is ever done in practice or not. Values, which are favored, admired, prestigeful patterns of action, are often expressed as moral commandments, though not necessarily so. A given society values honesty, generosity, cooperativeness, tact, and so on. Individuals who behave in these valued ways (ideal culture) are admired and enjoy enhanced status. Those who depart from these valued ways meet with some public disapproval.

Frequently these two patterns—ideal and manifest—are in close agreement. The values of a primitive hunting band may enjoin generosity, and the majority of all successful hunters will, in fact, share with their neighbors. In our society we value outward show of patriotism, the assumption being that this outward display mirrors inner feelings. Few people will remain seated during the playing of our national anthem or will fail to at least move their lips when the group is pledging allegiance to the flag. There is always some correspondence between manifest and ideal patterns of culture.

In any culture, however, this correspondence between values (ideal culture) and behavior (manifest culture) is imperfect. We profess ideals, enunciate ethical principles, verbally uphold values, but simultaneously behave quite differently. Examples from our own culture are endless. Each of us could make up a list of the discrepancies that are part of our everyday life. While such variance between ideal and manifest culture may be more characteristic of a complex, rapidly changing, heterogeneous society like our own (if only because of the high number of cultural alternatives available to the society's members), some variance does exist in all cultures.

Recognition of the variance between ideal and manifest culture is essential to field research. The fieldworker who derives information from informants must be aware of the possibility of discrepancies between verbal accounts and actual behavior witnessed. Discrepancies between actual behavior and ideal statements about behavior are valuable data. Most professional anthropologists could cite examples of ethnographic writings in which behavioral patterns are described as though they were both real and ideal: every male marries his second cross-cousin; every young couple takes up residence with the groom's family; every individual greets the new moon with an appropriate ritual. Such accounts are static and unreal and overlook or ignore the dynamic aspects of all social systems. A writer who depicted Americans as living wholly without departure from the ideals they profess would not only be presenting a distorted picture, he would preclude automatically the possibility of understanding why discrepancies do exist, how they originate, and what they tell us of American character. Discrepancies noted between ideal and manifest behavior provide the researcher with important information about how the society functions.

The seemingly endless pitfalls that await the fieldworker—culture shock, inadequate preparation, failure to understand the language, failure to establish rapport, hostility of the subjects, inability to distinguish real and ideal culture, and many more—may make the uninitiated doubt the possibility of ever accomplishing a successful ethnological study. Occasionally these obstacles do spell disaster or at least seriously limit the effectiveness of the fieldworker. But there are good fieldworkers and poor ones, fortunate and unfortunate. All of the obstacles, depending on the individual and his particular circumstances, can be overcome to some degree.

ANALYSIS

If anthropology stopped with the collection of data or the description of a particular people and their culture traits, the discipline would not merit being called a science. One of the most important obligations of any science is *explanation* of the entire range of phenomena that constitute the subject matter of that science. Anthropology seeks to explain the phenomena we call culture.

In an ordinary sense, explanation frequently means relating a particular phenomenon or event to something else—another phenomenon, event, class of events, concept. Often such explanation assumes the form of antecedent relationships: that which is to be explained is related to prior phenomena or events. For example, we might "explain" the movements of a billiard ball by relating it to such antecedent conditions as the actions of the player, the prior movement of the cue ball, and the shape of the table.

An Eskimo explained in the following way why his cousin broke his leg:

> . . . they would say to one another, "What taboo could it have been that we broke?" Some wise old man's advice would be called upon, and he would be told of all the taboos which were observed, and then he would say, "How did you break your marrow-bone?" Some one would volunteer, "I broke mine with a stone." "Yes, and which hand did you hold the stone in when you broke it?" "My right hand." "Ah yes, that explains it; you should have held the stone in your left hand. That is why your cousin's leg got broken. You broke the marrow-bone the wrong way." (Stefansson 1962:408.)

Throughout our waking hours an endless series of events, if noticed at all, are "understood" by such relationships. In common speech, we frequently refer to antecedent conditions as "causing" the thing or event in question. At times, the causal antecedent may be observable, as in the case of the billiard ball causing a second one to move; it may be related to an observable event, as the Eskimo's breach of a taboo which caused his cousin to break a leg; or it may be related to a non-observable event such as a human desire. When individuals explain their motives for action—why they engage in a particular type of behavior—these motives become the explanation for the behavior.

Every society transmits to each incoming generation a vast store of knowledge, or understanding of things and events, arrived at in just this common-sense way. Indeed, for ordinary day-to-day behavior such explanations are accepted as adequate. It is sufficient for the billiard player to relate the outcome of a shot to his prior actions and subsequently modify or correct his actions to affect the quality of his game. The Eskimo may break his marrow-bone holding the rock in his left hand rather than risk another broken leg for his cousin. We can usually cope adequately with events in our natural and social environment on the basis of common-sense knowledge ascertained by isolating the antecedent conditions. Often such understanding is implicit rather than being explicitly formulated.

Scientific explanation, however, is more than common-sense explanation. First, any observable event is unique and an explanation based on observing exactly the preceding events can explain that phenomenon only. The uniqueness of any event, cultural or natural, can be demonstrated as long as the available methods and techniques are sufficiently refined to obtain the desired results.

The importance of events for science lies in their differences as well as in their logical similarities. Science is less interested in a unique event than it is in events which are members of classes of events. Scientific explanation attempts to isolate the characteristics of a class of phenomena. The occurrence of a particular event is then explainable as a member of a class of events. But the uniqueness of any event or phenomenon takes on added significance when it is related to a class of events. In this way, it can be shown that the particular event is not completely the same as all other events in the same class but deviates in a particular way from those characteristics diagnostic of the class of events. By utilizing classes of events, the scientist can demonstrate the significant and logical similarities and differences among the many unique events which comprise the class. A description of how billiard balls *in general* behave under specified conditions (categorical behavior) will explain *approximately* the behavior of a particular ball (a unique occurrence).

Second, scientific explanations relate particulars to generalities more precisely than do common-sense explanations. Common sense, based upon observation, may tell us about certain general conditions, but, whereas common sense is often content with rough approximations and "shrugs its shoulders" at apparent exceptions to a rule, science is not so easily satisfied. The scientist attempts to specify exactly the conditions which determine an event. If a generalization is not validated by observation, the scientist is obliged to explain why. It is characteristic of the scientific attitude that when theories or generalizations do not "square" with empirical observation, then these generalizations must be re-examined and possibly modified or rejected.

Common-sense knowledge is often stubbornly or passively retained in spite of contradictions, or simply because common-sense generalizations are not subjected to critical testing that reveals contradictions. The scientist is more critical, systematic, and specific in stating the conditions said to determine any event. When an event seems to contradict a generalization or law, the scientist rechecks his observations, his theory, or both.

The processes and characteristics of scientific explanation can be made clearer by a specific example of anthropological research as it occurred in a field situation. The general sequence of operations is observation

The woman in this Indian family of San Antonio Sacatepequez is wearing the woven blouse or *huipil* characteristic of her community. (Photo by Robert H. Ewald.)

of the event, speculation about the event observed, formulation of a tentative hypothesis based upon the initial observation, additional observation to test the hypothesis formulated, and initial conclusions—presentation of statements of increasing generality which relate the observed phenomena to a known law or generalization, and then relation of these general statements to other established pertinent generalizations.

An Example of Analysis: A Peasant Village in Guatemala

The research took place in a peasant village located in the mountainous region of western Guatemala. The village is characterized by a high percentage of persons of Indian ancestry.

During the first few days of research the anthropologist devoted many hours to walking about the village in an attempt to orient himself, make initial contacts, and establish friendly relations. Frequently, he observed males removing their hats, bowing slightly, and softly giving respectful greetings when they encountered other males. In those cases where meetings occurred on narrow sidewalks, the first man stepped aside, allowing the other to pass. These were the anthropologist's observations.

What was the significance of these events? The anthropologist thought at first that what he observed was customary behavior for that area. In some ways it was similar to behavior in his own culture, but it was also different. Why did the people of this Guatemalan village act in this way under these circumstances? Did their behavior reflect a particular rule of etiquette? In his own culture, the anthropologist knew, the old and the young, men and women, employer and employee, teacher and student, tend to behave toward one another in certain patterned ways which are regarded as good manners or as proper etiquette. The action which the anthropologist observed in the Guatemalan village seemed to fit into the same general category of customary behavior characteristic of his own culture.

A group of *Ladino* males of San Antonio Sacatepequez, seated in front of the Town Hall. (Photo by Robert H. Ewald.)

To this point, the anthropologist had observed the repetition of specific, similar events; mentally he had categorized these events into a behavioral *class* of events. He had then related this class of phenomena to a similar general category of behavior, called etiquette, found in his own culture. The anthropologist now had a partial explanation which might satisfy completely a less critical observer: males tip their hats or bow to one another because this conforms to social expectations and good manners. He observed perhaps a hundred such incidents, no two exactly alike, but he did not try to explain each one as a unique event. Rather, he abstracted the element or elements common to all such incidents, related this common denominator to a general statement about rules of etiquette, and then attempted to explain each particular incident as an example of this class of behavior. This explanation remained incomplete and did not satisfy the scientist.

Reviewing his observations, the anthropologist decided that individuals who offered respect could be distinguished from those who received it in several ways. The class of people who received the more formal and conscious greeting wore shoes and generally dressed better than the shoeless persons who extended this type of greeting. The recipients were generally more European in appearance, whereas the group giving homage were more Indian-appearing. Also, the recipients were observed to speak a more precise Spanish than that of the Indian-appearing group. With this additional related knowledge, the anthropologist was able to refine his preliminary explanation about etiquette.

Initially, the anthropologist might have hypothesized that two distinct social groups, different from one another culturally, linguistically, and to some extent physically, coexisted within a single village. Further observation and inquiry suggested to the anthropologist that one group was identified locally as Indian and members of the other group were called *Ladinos* (or, by outsiders, *mestizos*—persons of mixed ancestry). With this additional information, the anthropologist modified his first hypothesis and then proposed that the behavior observed was socially patterned and occurred only between members of two different social groups. This hypothesis was confirmed immediately by local persons. They explained that Indians owed this kind of behavior to *Ladinos* since the former were biologically inferior to the latter. This hypothesis, while it was a refinement of the initial one and a more complete explanation, went little beyond what was common knowledge to the people of the village.

However, the anthropologist had similar information from other societies, not shared with his local informants. He formulated still more general statements about the function of etiquette in human society, and generalized that in any case of social interaction between members of different groups—male and female, teacher and student, officer and enlisted man—each of a pair of individuals will commonly behave in a patterned way that we call etiquette. In presenting this generalization, the anthropologist related one general statement about rules of etiquette to another general statement about groups of individuals.

The anthropologist had other information which he used to suggest further general hypotheses directly related to the events he originally observed (White 1959:225 ff.):

1. Members of any social unit may have aims, ambitions, interests, and values quite at variance or even opposed to those of other groups.
2. In social divisions there is potential conflict and disharmony.
3. Effective adjustment and survival of the social group demands that relations between its divisions be regulated.
4. Positive group relations compatible with effective adaptation are accomplished partially through a set of rules called etiquette.
5. These rules of behavior come to be identified with a particular social unit; they are, in some cases, symbols of membership in that group.
6. As such, they function to preserve group identity, simultaneously reinforcing feelings of loyalty among group members.
7. In any system, certain effective sanctions (reward and punishment) must operate to enforce adherence to rules of etiquette.

Having formulated a set of very general rules about the place of etiquette in human society, the anthropologist returned to his own data. This Guatemalan village was marked by a very sharp caste-like division in which two groups, Indian and *Ladino*, lived side by side and in mutual dependence, with both groups benefiting from the relationship. However, this social situation was clearly more favorable to one group than to the other. If the unfavorable status of one group were allowed to express itself in resentment and hostility, the stability of the overall system would suffer markedly. Therefore, *to maintain the system as it was*, all social intercourse between members of the two caste-like groups must be regulated—made orderly and predictable. Specific acts of courtesy of Indian toward *Ladino* were now explainable as behavior which facilitated interaction between individuals within a society, thereby enhancing the smooth functioning of the total social unit.

The more general statements made in the paragraphs above could not have been deduced from the single case of etiquette in this Guatemalan village. If such a hypothesis had been advanced on the basis of the Guatemalan case, it would have required testing through observation in many societies. Once the statement about a general relation between rules of etiquette and social systems has been made, it renders intelligible a very wide range of human behavior. An African subject prostrating himself before his monarch, a Polynesian crawling past a seated chief, an American removing his hat in an elevator, or an Indonesian commoner addressing his chief in a special ceremonial language, are not diverse, unrelated phenomena as we might at first have thought. All are members of a single class of events.

THE RESEARCH REPORT

Examples of general statements which explain particular phenomena are abundant in the literature of anthropology. Each year hundreds of field trips are made in all nations of the world. New ethnographic findings are added to existing anthropological materials, and will be made available to all anthropologists through papers written by the researcher and published in one of several kinds of journals: a special-interest journal devoted to a particular area or people, such as *Africa, Oceania, Caribbean Studies,* or the *Journal of Asian Studies,* or a more general, theoretically oriented periodical such as the *American Anthropologist* or *Current Anthropology.* In addition, books reporting anthropological research are published each year. All of these research reports extend the growth of scientific anthropology. The anthropologist planning field work looks to these writings for information that will increase the efficiency and value of his research.

The research report is presented in several different forms, but each of these forms shares certain characteristics. All complete research reports, whether articles or books, include:

1. Statement of the research problem.
2. Discussion of basic environmental and demographic information diagnostic of the area in which the research was done.
3. Explanation of data collection—the methods and techniques used in the research project.
4. Statement of the findings—the information collected.
5. Analysis of the information collected.
6. Conclusions derived from the research.

This total sequence, the research report, is a unified explanation of the research project. The anthropologist reports to other scientists exactly what he has done, how he interprets the information collected, and how he relates it to other similar information. In this way scientific anthropology is simultaneously extended and refined.

SUMMARY

Knowledge begets knowledge. Careful preparation for field work necessarily includes the serious study of existing research reports. This is followed by the observation and collection of information by the anthropologist, who then analyzes, interprets, and reports his findings. His reports are added to the existing published information to provide a more effective basis for future research. Each researcher thus provides steppingstones for the next. In this way man's knowledge about man is accumulated, extended, and refined accurately and consistently, according to the methods of science.

3

Anthropology and the Study of Culture

INTRODUCTION

While the term "culture" has been used frequently in the preceding chapters, it has not been explicitly defined. Some of the things that the term includes have been mentioned—clothing, customs, beliefs, dietary patterns, ritual behavior—but an expansion of this list would yield only an "enumerative definition" without providing the criteria necessary to identify an act or object as being or not being culture. The reader would be left to determine the criteria for himself.

DEFINITIONS

Several years ago two anthropologists (Kroeber and Kluckhohn 1963) published a book titled simply *Culture*. They presented more than 150 definitions of the word "culture" culled from the writings of many anthropologists, sociologists, psychologists, and others. By examination they were able to classify these many definitions into several main types.

1. *Descriptive or enumerative definitions*—those which list content without always specifying the criteria by which the list is to be selected. The classic definition of this type comes from the distinguished pioneer anthropologist E. B. Tylor (1958:1): "Culture or Civilization, taken in its wide ethnographic sense, is that complex whole which includes knowledge, belief, art, morals, law, custom, and any other capabilities and habits acquired by man as a member of society." Actually, the final phrase modifies this definition somewhat, causing it to overlap the next type.
2. *Historical definitions*—those which emphasize social heritage or tradition. Frequently it is stressed that the culture of any human group has been

handed down from generation to generation, as in Malinowski's definition: "Culture comprises *inherited* artifacts, goods, technical processes, ideas, habits, and values." Similarly, Linton refers to culture as "the total *social heredity* of mankind . . ." (italics supplied) (Kroeber and Kluckhohn 1963:90).

3. *Normative definitions*—those which emphasize social rules or socially patterned behavior. As Firth states, "the acts of individuals not in isolation but as members of society . . . the sum total of these modes of behavior [is called] 'culture'" (*ibid.* 1963:95). The emphasis upon "modes of behavior" suggests that idiosyncratic behavior is not properly culture.

4. *Psychological definitions*—those which emphasize learning: "Culture . . . is a statement of the design of the human maze, of the type of reward involved, and of what responses are to be rewarded" (*ibid.* 1963:111).

These four types do not exhaust the possibilities for defining culture, nor are they the complete list from Kroeber and Kluckhohn. They do, however, suggest the range of variation.

These definitions are not necessarily mutually exclusive, nor do they necessarily contradict one another. Consider, for example, the second and fourth categories. To say that the culture of a human group is handed down from generation to generation does not preclude an examination of the psychological processes wherein individual members of society learn the behavior appropriate to their group. In fact, these two in combination reinforce one another and make the definition more complete. Two criteria are provided—heritage and learning. Given these two criteria for ascertaining culture, specific items of culture that are learned can be enumerated, the existence of norms or patterns can be demonstrated, and it can then be shown that these are passed on to future generations.

The multiplicity of available definitions of culture suggests two questions: Which of these many definitions is the "correct" one? What is the value or purpose of attempting such definition at all? Answers to such questions involve a more general problem—the purpose of definition in the sciences. First, there is no such thing as *the* "correct" definition. Definitions are man-made, and are therefore arbitrary. Second, definitions are scientific tools used by the scientist to identify, pinpoint, or otherwise delimit the phenomena being studied. Third, definitions increase understanding of the phenomena being investigated.

CONCEPTIONS OF CULTURE

Reality and Abstraction

The term "culture" refers to two different but related ideas, both of which must be kept in mind when this term is defined. On the one hand, it includes phenomena—real things and events. A stone axe, a skyscraper, a collection of thatch huts, and a crucifix are all real things and are part of culture. Specific human activities—chipping a stone axe, selling an object in the market, etching a design on a pot, or addressing a person with a kinship term—are also culture. Each of these things, events, or series of events can be located in time and space, and each has the "reality" of any other phenomenon in nature. On the other hand, culture is a concept about or an abstraction from real phenomena —a way of thinking about them. Thus, when we say that it is part of American culture to eat three times daily at specified intervals, we have "abstracted" a pattern from the real behavior of millions of individuals. The statement suggesting that American culture is characterized by three daily meals is culture as an abstraction. The actual eating of meals by persons who are members of "American society" is culture as real phenomena.

These two conceptions of culture—culture as real phenomena and culture as an abstraction—are not contradictory in the sense that if one is right the other is wrong. Culture can be defined in both ways. Words mean what we wish them to mean. White (1959:3), who defines culture as "things and events dependent upon symboling," finds it necessary to conceptualize culture as phenomenal reality. However, when he wishes to speak about the evolution of culture, he shifts his focus and treats culture as a concept, an abstraction for purposes of analysis. Both are valid approaches.

Though the term is most often used by anthropologists for the purpose of explaining or rendering intelligible the phenomenal reality of human behavior, it is legitimate and scientifically defensible to define culture as phenomena, as an abstraction from the phenomena, or as an intellectual construct.

A scientist deals with concepts about phenomena and explores the logical relations among these concepts. While such logical manipulations may not appear to deal with reality directly, ultimately all concepts are based upon and relate back to "reality," to real things and events. Scientific laws are statements about logical relationships among concepts but simultaneously provide general explanations for the behavior of phenomena. Similarly, anthropologists make use of "culture as a concept" to explain "culture as phenomena" and thus make more intelligible human behavior and the material products of that behavior.

However, human behavior involves a wide variety of action. Certain actions are characteristic of particular categories of persons—males or females, adults or children, wealthy people or poor, Navaho or Hopi. While these actions are performed by individuals, the similarity of their behavior is due to the fact that they are acting as members of a particular social group, category, or community. While the members of a given social unit engage in similar action, such behavior is diagnostic of a particular group and, therefore, differs among groups. Males engage in behavior which is different from that of females, the young differ from the old, the Navaho from the Hopi.

Culture: A Behavioral Referent

If, in using culture as a concept, our goal is explanation of behavior, how are the various kinds of action compatible with this concept? It is important to recognize that the concept provides a referent against which real things and events are interpreted.

Idiosyncratic behavior, for example, is unique individual action which is seldom repeated and which is frequently unpredictable. White (1959:227) tells of a newspaper item which reported the idiosyncratic behavior of a Scottish gentleman at a bus stop in Glasgow. In this particular incident the gentleman doffed his hat to two ladies and bowed, exposing two small mice scampering about on his bald head. He was arrested. This act was identified as idiosyncratic behavior in his society, and culture was used as a referent for identifying this act as an idiosyncrasy. That is, the individual's behavior was evaluated in relation to other known cultural behavior which occurs in the same society. In this particular case the man's behavior was unique and unpredictable— so much so that the ladies complained and brought about his arrest.

But not all human behavior is idiosyncratic. The man in the example given above may enjoy meat immensely, and yet he may avoid eating it each Friday or on certain other days. The members of his family and certain of his neighbors may do the same. Test results may reveal that many other people refrain from eating meat on Fridays. These test results might establish that those who share the pattern of avoidance of meat on Fridays do so because each has equally deep and similar religious convictions; that each believes in the theological rationale behind the taboo (avoidance); or that each experiences emotional discomfort if he violates the taboo. We have not explained the operation of this taboo simply by showing that numerous individuals practice avoidance of meat on Fridays. But this hypothetical investigation does suggest that a certain pattern of behavior characterizes the members of a named group—people identified according to their religious beliefs and practices as Roman Catholics—and that this behavior is shared and is not idiosyncratic.

A further comparative study may reveal that Protestants do not share this taboo on meat, and that Muslims or Jews have no taboo against eating meat on Friday, but do avoid eating pork under any circumstances. A high-caste Hindu, on the other hand, avoids eating meat or meat products completely. In each of these cases membership in a religious organization imposes certain behavioral patterns upon each individual member; he is expected to adhere to specific behavioral prescriptions and proscriptions.

This investigation might be carried a step further to show that individuals who are identified as Catholics, Protestants, Jews, or Muslims, and who are therefore behaviorally different, act in ways that are highly similar; they share certain other behavioral patterns irrespective of their religious group membership. Thus, it may be observed that all individuals in our society, whether they identify themselves as Catholic, Protestant, or Jew, will stand in unison at the playing of "The Star-Spangled Banner," or that each will recite the identical words in pledging allegiance to the same flag on certain public occasions. But here the referent is not a particular religious organization but a much different social group; the individuals behave similarly because they are members of a larger sociopolitical entity called a nation.

To summarize briefly, the behavior of an individual can be idiosyncratic, or it can be shared with a significant number of members of some social group or category. In the United States an individual might be identified as a citizen of this country, as a member of an ethnic minority within the larger national whole, as belonging to a certain religious organization, and as affiliated with a certain socioeconomic class. In each case he shares certain behavioral patterns with many other individuals who have similar affiliations. These patterns serve to distinguish him behaviorally from persons having different national, religious, ethnic, or social class affiliations. If an individual's behavior is truly idiosyncratic, and limited to that individual alone, then explanation must focus on the individual himself, and on the unique circumstances which give rise to his action.

In our earlier example we characterized the behavior of the man with the mice as idiosyncratic. If, on the other hand, a number of individuals engaged in this activity recurrently, and under identifiable circumstances, then we would assume that the causes were supraindividual. In cases involving shared behavior, the behavior of individuals is partially explained by identifying them as members of some group or class and by relating this individual action to behavior which is diagnostic of that group or class. An individual who regularly arises at an early hour to attend a religious service which he calls Mass, who often wears a medal about his neck, who affixes a statue of a saint to the dashboard of his automobile, and who on Fridays may select fish or egg dishes rather than meat would reflect behavior most closely associated with our behavioral expectations of a Roman Catholic. In this particular analysis, the sex, citizenship, and social status of the individual are irrelevant.

The determinants of his behavior are to be seen as the behavioral patterns characteristic of his religious organization, not of these other groups or classes. In summary, the cultures or subcultures in which the individual participates provide the referent or context against which any item of behavior may be evaluated and understood.

Culture: A Deterministic Phenomenon

The concept of cultural determinism—the idea that an individual's behavior is somehow determined by the culture within which he lives—is more frequently misunderstood, and perhaps for that reason rejected, than most other concepts with which anthropology deals. Objections to this notion are raised by both laymen and professional social scientists. The objections of the layman are often based on emotion rather than on reason, especially when raised on theological grounds. For some the idea of cultural determinism evokes the image of culture as a blind, impersonal force which causes every human action. This contradicts the popular conception of man as a creative, determining force unto himself, and acceptance of the age-old doctrine of free will makes it difficult for many laymen to accept the anthropological concept of cultural determinism.

Cultural determinism can be seen in the relation of the behavior of individuals and their membership in or affiliation with certain cultural organizations. Peoples' food preferences or avoidances, their dress or ornamentation, their motor habits, and so on, are described as being derived from the patterns of their cultures. But cultural anthropologists mean more than this when they speak of behavior as being culturally determined. Behavior is much more than clothing, hairdress, or readily observable motor behavior. The term "behavior" also includes such things as thoughts, feelings, emotions, ideas, beliefs. It includes all the things we mean when we refer to overt (readily and externally observable) behavior and to covert (non-observable) behavior. In asserting that thoughts, feelings, ideas, or motivations are in some way imposed upon us from without—from our cultural environment—we are saying that nothing man does is free of cultural influences. Anthropologists working in the area between psychology and culture (sometimes called culture and personality or psychological anthropology) have been able to show convincingly that every sector of human behavior, even dreams, fantasies, neuroses, and psychotic manifestations, reveal cultural patterning.

Certain Australian tribes are famous in the anthropological literature for their very specific marriage customs in which the only acceptable mate for a man is his second cross-cousin (his mother's mother's brother's daughter's daughter). Marriage with a first cousin or any other second cousin is regarded as incestuous and punishable by tribal custom. Ethnographers have reported that these Australian men sometimes dream that they attempt to have sexual relations with a girl of a prohibited relationship, only to have the girl's mother appear in the dream to drive them off with a broom. But when the dream involves a girl of a permitted degree of relationship, the dreamed-of sexual encounter sometimes comes to a climax. An individual in our culture could not have a dream exactly like this one. True enough, an American male might have frustrated dreams, but certainly not about relations with someone who is not a second cross-cousin.

Each individual is born into an on-going social system having its own characteristic culture patterns. This culture existed before the birth of any particular individual. The philosophy, the value system, the religion, the customary forms of etiquette—the total culture—of this group have been handed down from previous generations, and will be passed on to future generations. Enculturation of the individual insures that as he matures this culture will become his culture. He will be rewarded in many ways for responding positively to expected behavior, and he will be punished in many ways, both subtle and obvious, for his attempts to deviate from the accepted behavioral patterns of his society. Enculturation begins so early, and is carried on so subtly, that no individual is ever fully aware of all the values and sentiments that he has acquired as a member of his group.

The process of cultural determinism is vital to the perpetuation and survival of societies, and is therefore vital to the perpetuation and survival of the human species. At any point in time a society and its culture represent a working adjustment to many problems of human survival. The culture of a society serves to articulate that society's members with their natural environment, with neighboring groups, with the supernatural world, and with one another. Group survival and continuity are more certain and efficient because each generation inherits more or less intact a set of ready-made solutions to the major problems of life. If each child were permitted to deviate as freely as he wished from accepted patterns of behavior, the patterns would cease to exist, as would social life as such. Social life is based upon predictability, and predictability means customary behavior. Therefore, no human group can permit complete freedom to its individual members. However, social life can never achieve complete regimentation. A social system must allow for individual differences, though deviation from social norms must be limited. Freedom of individual choice is a relative freedom only. Cultural determinism is a powerful, pervasive, and unavoidable force in human society. Culture is the source of the individual's customs, beliefs, values, ideals. *Human activity is cultural activity.*

Culture: Man's Adaptive Mechanism

The most important fact about culture, in understanding its significance as an adaptive mechanism, is its superorganic or suprabiological
character. By this is meant, simply, that the tools, techniques, knowledge, and social forms which make up the culture of any society are not
specifically linked to any feature of man's biology. Within broad limits,
all items of culture can change almost endlessly without any immediate
corresponding change in man's anatomy or physiology. Lower animals,
however, must adapt to their environments and to the changes that occur
in these environments through extremely slow biological, evolutionary
processes—mutations, natural selection, and the like. Often when the
environment has changed more rapidly than the species, the result has
been extinction of the species. Any animal species would have an enormous advantage in its adaptation and struggle for existence if it could
change rapidly in response to environmental change. In biological
terms, this is largely impossible, but in behavioral terms, through culture, it is commonplace. Most animal species lack the neurological
equipment—the central nervous system and brain—which makes such
rapid behavioral adjustment possible. They lack the capacity for culture.

The culture of any society represents an adaptation or an adjustment
to the conditions of life as people live it, including their physical, social,
and supernatural environment. There is nothing in any culture that is
inherent in the biological makeup of its carriers, and any culture is potentially capable of almost unlimited change.

Let us consider first man's physical environment, to which he must
adapt if he is to meet his basic biological needs, such as subsistence,
shelter, or protection from natural enemies. This environment is a highly
variable one, as a rudimentary knowledge of geography will tell us. In
the thousands of years that man has existed as *Homo sapiens,* his migra-
tions have carried him into almost every conceivable geographic zone.
He occupies such environmental extremes as the Arctic north, tropical
rain forests, arid deserts, mountainous country and lowlands, coastal regions and inlands. In every instance his means of adapting to these
habitats have been cultural. Hunting and gathering, horticulture, agriculture, animal husbandry, and many levels of industry have served
man's basic biological needs. Man has yet to exploit all the environments potentially available to him. He now approaches habitation of
the ocean floor and of outer space. The exploration of these zones has
been made possible by cultural advances, and if man successfully in-
habits such zones, it will be because he has devised new cultural means

for doing so. Wherever he has gone, he has quickly developed the cultural means for surviving in each particular environment. History and ethnography have documented again and again man's capacity for modifying his culture to maintain or to improve his adaptation to external conditions.

The technological means by which man accomplishes these things are, of course, a major aspect of his culture, but not the only aspect. Technologies are used by human individuals, but always as members of groups. Human behavior is, in short, social behavior. Men have always formed groups to exploit their environment, to afford protection from nature and natural enemies, and to provide many kinds of satisfactions. Man's social systems also regulate the important function of perpetuating his species. A universal aspect of social systems is rules of behavior which specify who may marry, under what conditions, to reproduce their kind. Those permitted to form social units for the purpose of procreation are also charged with the obligation of training their offspring, so that they will perform the tasks necessary for group survival, and so that they too will perpetuate their kind, as their children will do after them.

Social life is so pervasive a part of human existence that it has become as real a part of man's environment as his natural surroundings. Because men everywhere must adjust to the social environment in which they live, an invariable part of all cultural systems is complex rules of social interaction. That is, each individual, because he is a member of society, is required to interact with other individuals to a greater or lesser degree. Such interactions, however, are seldom random or haphazard; rather, they are structured by a system of relationships which direct, prescribe, and proscribe with whom an individual can interact, how he will act, and in what context such interaction will take place. All such interactions are defined by the groups within each society and by the society at large. The kind of organization—kinship, social, economic, religious, political—varies among societies, and so the mode of interaction among individuals also varies. Some societies are kinship-oriented; kinship, therefore, defines a large part of the interaction that occurs. Others are non-kinship-oriented, and voluntary associations, with their attendant values, goals, and obligations, are important in defining the interaction that takes place. Whatever the interactional definition one finds in any society, it is a form of cultural behavior which man uses as an adaptive mechanism.

Man does not restrict his adaptation to the physical and the social environment, but extends his adjustment to include the supernatural. Religion is universal in human society, though it takes many different forms. It serves man in many different ways. The supernatural is used to rationalize, to cure, to make ill, to cause death, and to give life; it is a means for success and a way to explain failure; it provides confidence in times of stress and fear; and it explains all that is otherwise not known by a society. The supernatural is viewed in many different ways: it is benevolent and malevolent; all-powerful and all-knowing; strong and weak; a provider and a destroyer; anthropomorphic and anthropopsy-chic; a force and an entity; large and small; visible and invisible. It can be all things to some men and insignificant to others. Whatever form the supernatural takes and whatever behavior is directed toward it, it is entirely cultural.

Culture's Relation to the Individual

Since A. L. Kroeber's pioneering article entitled "The Superorganic" (1917), many cultural anthropologists have subscribed to the point of view that culture may be treated as a phenomenon entirely apart from its human carriers. That is, for purposes of analysis, we may proceed as if man did not even exist: culture behaves according to cultural laws and is to be explained in terms of itself. Saying that culture explains culture is sometimes branded as circular reasoning. Anthropologists who disagree with this position believe that culture is ultimately the behavior of individual human beings and cannot be understood apart from these individuals. It is *always the individual* who thinks, acts, dreams, and revolts. Consistent with this latter approach is the belief that the study of culture begins with the individual. Anthropology is then construed to be a mental science. Kroeber emphatically rejected this in advancing his own "superorganic" view of culture. In support of his contentions, he considered the phenomenon of simultaneous invention. In the history of invention we find frequent repetition; when an invention occurs, it often occurs two, three, and even more times within a period of one or two years. Inventors working independently of one another, and unaware of each other's investigations, simultaneously produced the telescope (three times in 1608), the telegraph (five times around 1837), the telephone (twice in 1876), and the steamboat (four times between 1783–88). This phenomenon cannot be explained by individual psychology. Rather than a psychological interpretation, Kroeber recognized that supraindividual forces prevail which transcend personality. For the purpose of understanding the phenomenon of simultaneous invention, culture may be treated as a system of constituent elements (ideas, tools, processes, social institutions) which interact among themselves, frequently recombining to form new elements. The steamboat, for example, involved the recombination of boat, steam engine, and water wheel, a recombination of established principles resulting in a new cultural item. White (1949:190–232) has stressed that the simultaneous presence of necessary elements and a process of interaction make the resultant invention nearly inevitable. Neither Kroeber nor White, both of whom professed this view, would deny that individuals with their own unique personalities are involved in each invention. However, they believed that the individual is not an explanation for why, how, where, or when the invention occurs. An Einstein living at the time of Newton could not have formulated the theory of relativity, because the necessary antecedent cultural elements were not present. Knowing all about the personality of Einstein would add little to our understanding of the theory of relativity *as part of a culture system.* Analyzing culture as a thing in itself is perfectly valid. This is not to say that the anthropologist ignores the individual or individual psychology. Some anthropological problems necessitate an awareness of the individual's position in culture, which is that of a carrier and transmitter of culture rather than a passive recipient.

The individual is a dynamic element in the culture process. He is not completely free of its influences because he is reared in a cultural system and is a product of it. Inevitably, culture is the source for many of his ideas and perceptions, but he is not limited to mere acceptance of culture. As a dynamic entity he *responds* to his culture, and in the process modifies it in certain ways. His rejection of a behavioral pattern can result in its modification, especially if his response is echoed by others. Culture shapes individual behavior but individual behavior also shapes culture.

Overt and Covert Culture

Culture includes not only the outward, visible acts of individuals, but also behavior that is not readily observable—feeling, thinking, believing. The first category is often referred to as *overt* behavior, and the second as *covert* behavior. In either case the behavior in question is cultural behavior.

Overt culture refers to patterned behavior that is directly observable or to the material products which result from behavior. An axe, an arrow point, a basket, or any other artifact is a clear example of overt culture. These things are tangible and visible, and have discernible physical properties. This is equally true of action. A man swinging an axe or discharging an arrow from his bow, a woman weaving a basket or using it to collect seeds are performing actions which are observed directly. Actions can be relatively simple behavior performed by one individual, or complex behavior in which hundreds of persons participate.

Covert culture refers to patterned behavior that is not directly observable. Ideas, attitudes, feelings, emotional states, and beliefs are categorical examples of covert culture. These cannot be observed directly; rather, we *infer* from observable behavior that they exist. A person prays, and we regard this as evidence that he believes in the deity to whom he is praying. A neighbor regularly displays his flag on certain holidays, and we assume that he has patriotic commitments. In short, we assume that overt action is an expression of covert behavior, and sometimes we infer a causal relationship between the two. A temper tantrum, whether in a child or an adult, is fairly strong presumptive evidence for a powerful inner emotion, whether we label it anger, hate, or fear. On the other hand, if we infer deep feelings of piety in an individual because of his regular church attendance, we may be far from accurate. If the individual voices an expression of piety, this would further support our inference, but would still not be conclusive.

Anthropologists assume that covert behavior is characterized by social conformity, just as is overt action. There is impressive evidence to show that one's dreams, hallucinations, beliefs, attitudes, and ideals are very much the products of one's culture. Two native New Yorkers are more likely to experience revulsion at the thought of eating a roasted grub worm than are two Aranda tribesmen. Recurrent dreams in which one sees an animal spirit are more frequent among a people who believe in such spirits than among an urban western population. Individuals from one sector of our society will be more likely to share an ideal of racial equality than those from another sector.

Another related common assumption of cultural anthropologists is that people in a given culture behave alike outwardly because they share common values and beliefs; further, that the process of enculturation insures not only that the members of a group will act as society says they should act, but also that they will *want* to act in these socially required ways. The implication here is that there is a close congruence between overt behavior and covert psychological states. The assumption of this necessary congruence has led some scholars to infer personality traits of a given group almost wholly from their overt behavior patterns (rather than establishing them independently). Certainly, there can be and often is a relationship between overt behavior and covert motivation, as evidenced by much incontrovertible fact. However, we regard any assumption of complete congruence with skepticism.

Students of society are well aware of the importance of social sanctions for inducing conformity of behavior despite psychological differences among the group's members. One hundred soldiers can march together with admirable precision, but it does not necessarily follow that each feels the same thing. Possibly one man of the hundred genuinely loves what he is doing, while a second man feels he is doing his patriotic duty, and a third marches because he fears military discipline. It is a measure of the strength of social sanctions that they can exact conformity from a group of individuals who harbor highly diverse covert reasons for the same overt behavior.

The utility of the concepts of overt and covert culture is that they permit us to recognize two distinct categories of cultural behavior and to show the correspondence, as well as the lack of correspondence, between these two dimensions of culture. The members of a society may express similar external behavior and, simultaneously, share similar feelings, attitudes, or beliefs. Alternatively, members of a society may express similar external behaviors which are based upon divergent feelings, attitudes, or beliefs. Or, divergent external behavior may be expressed by a society's members, based upon similar feelings, attitudes, and beliefs. In any case, it is of scientific interest and importance to know the variations of overt and covert culture that exist and the possible correspondence between these two categories.

Culture: A System

The anthropologist sees human activity as taking many forms, depending upon time, place, and other circumstances. Each different kind of activity, carried on for different purposes and involving different groups of people, merits a separate designation. In our society a family on a picnic behaves differently from a family attending church, and a man accompanying his family in these two activities behaves differently from when he is in a conference room with a group of business associates. We might designate these activities under such headings as recreation, religious ritual, and economics, or we might speak of the family as a special cultural component and then classify religion and recreation under the heading of family activities or functions. Depending upon the purpose of the investigator and upon how accurately he observes and wishes to classify, he may analyze his culture into few or many such categories. If his purpose is that of exhaustive description, he might use dozens of separate categories of culture such as: technology and material culture; economic organization; the family, kinship, and marriage; rites of passage; political organization; art and recreation; supernaturalism and world view; magic and witchcraft. Frequently these categories of culture are conceptualized as parts related to a more comprehensive totality.

Culture is frequently conceptualized as a system, an organized whole made up of these interrelated parts. The action within one part affects the action within all other parts (in varying degrees), and all are influenced by the particular organization of the entire system. Obviously, this is a "man-made concept," a way of thinking about human phenomena. But what are the components of a cultural system?

Subsystems of Culture. One frequently employed and meaningful way of defining its components is to regard the cultural system as being made up of a number of subsystems, each equated with a different kind of human activity. Thus, in observing the behavior of the people of San Antonio Sacatepequez over a long period of time, it would become apparent that much of their behavior is directed toward exploiting natural resources (tilling the soil, cutting firewood, collecting wild plants), distributing these among the members of the community, or otherwise disposing of them. The anthropologist might arbitrarily lump all of these activities together into the single category of "economic behavior," and suggest that one of the major components of the culture of San Antonio is an economic subsystem. Quite clearly, economics can be subdivided into such categories as production, distribution, and consumption. How large the anthropologist makes his subsystems of culture, or how precisely he subdivides human activities, depends upon his purposes. The table of contents in any introductory textbook in cultural anthropology, or the chapter headings of any ethnographic monograph, provides some indication of how that author conceptualizes culture for the purposes of his study.

Typically, culture is divided into subsidiary concepts like kinship and social organization, economics, religion, political organization, and language. It should be recognized that all of these subsidiary categories are concepts, not things and events. They are not phenomenal reality, they are ways of categorizing and thinking about human activities. In order to illustrate this point, one might think of a hypothetical stranger entering a community about which he is totally ignorant. Without any preconceived categories to structure or organize his perceptions, all he sees is behavior—people doing things. He has not yet perceived different kinds of activities. But, to make his perceptions more intelligible, he may begin to classify the behavior he is observing, deciding that some behavior is similar or relevant to other behavior, and that still other behavior is dissimilar and has no apparent relationship. He makes the arbitrary choice that swinging a hoe, dropping seed in the ground, cutting down grown plants, carrying produce into the village, storing it or giving it to other individuals, perhaps in exchange for other goods or metal tokens (money), are related activities and should be classified under a single heading. In an equally arbitrary manner he decides that the act of carrying part of this produce to church, where some sort of behavior is directed toward it by a richly dressed outsider who happens to be present in the village that day, is a different kind of activity and should be classified with other activities that occur in that large and imposing building. Is the stranger's ordering of things and events good and useful, or bad and a waste of time? If his concepts (his cultural subsystems) enhance his understanding of local behavior, and perhaps even enable him to predict future behavior, then his concepts are "useful" in relation to his purposes.

Culture as a System: A Historical Perspective. The notion that the culture of any human group constitutes a system, an organized whole consisting of interrelated parts, certainly did not originate in twentieth-century anthropology. At least as far back as the eighteenth century the so-called social philosophers were beginning to appreciate the interrelatedness of human phenomena—law, customs, political institutions, and so on. But it remained for twentieth-century scholars consciously to advance this idea as a scientific principle, and to make it a basis for the study of culture and society. Many contemporary anthropologists associate the origins of this notion with two men above all others, Bronislaw Malinowski and A. R. Radcliffe-Brown. Malinowski (Kroeber and Kluckhohn 1963:90) defined culture as comprising "inherited artifacts, goods, technical processes, ideas, habits, and values." He regarded these things as forming an interrelated whole, in which all the parts were related to one another in a systematic way. Anthropological facts were to be explained by their *function,* not by their supposed history. The term "function" actually had a double meaning for Malinowski. The function of any item of culture is the need it serves, biologically and culturally. An agricultural tool, an arrangement for the division of labor, or a technique for food preparation ultimately serves to meet man's hunger need. Other basic human needs such as bodily comforts, growth, safety, movement, health, and reproduction are satisfied by other cultural responses. But his concept of need embraced much more than the biological and psychological needs of human individuals. It included also cultural needs—certain conditions that had to be met if a community was to survive and its culture to continue. The function of any item of culture meant, therefore, not only the individual biological need it served, but the contribution it made in preserving or maintaining the system of which it was a part. Radcliffe-Brown's ideas of society as a system, and of function as the contribution of any item of culture in maintaining that system, were very similar to Malinowski's conception (Richards 1957:17).

Today, few anthropologists agree completely with the idea of treating the culture of any human group as a logically closed system which can be explained entirely in terms of itself. Even the most isolated tribe of hunters and gatherers has relations with neighboring groups which will influence their respective cultures. For example, the existence of a standing army in any society would be unintelligible if we studied that society as a closed, self-contained system, but it becomes immediately intelligible when we see that society as part of a larger system which embraces neighboring states. Then it becomes apparent that the army's main function is protection of territorial rights against other groups outside the society. It is doubtful whether any culture can be meaningfully or successfully described or explained as a totally integrated whole, as Malinowski often stated the aim of anthropology to be. Malinowski, however, did succeed, brilliantly and meaningfully, in demonstrating the extensive interrelationships of the parts of culture and the way in which a single aspect of culture influences other aspects of culture.

An excellent example of how Malinowski views the interrelatedness of all aspects of culture is seen in his treatment of family economics among the Trobriand Islanders (1961:53–72). Among these matrilineal (descent traced through female kin) people, a boy's closest ties are not with his father but with his mother's brother, who is of his clan. Thus, a man works hard at gardening, not to support his wife and children, but rather his sister and her children. Up to three quarters of his produce is distributed to these matrilineal kinsmen. In this brief example is seen an obvious and immediate relationship between the kinship system and the economics of distribution. Malinowski extends this same idea when he shows that the Trobriand chief will marry several women, preferably those having wealthy brothers, thereby acquiring a number of wealthy brothers-in-law. Since their kinship obligations are to their sisters (the chief's wives), the Trobriand chief will accumulate significant wealth in the form of produce from his brothers-in-laws' gardens. Thus, in certain contexts this kinship and economic behavior also has political implications. The chief, however, does not hoard this accumulated food but redistributes it at occasional communal ceremonies, such as feasts for the return of the dead ancestral spirits. In so doing, he not only satisfies his obligations as a chief, but insures the continued proper distribution of accumulated wealth throughout the society. Still another example of Malinowski's acute awareness and appreciation of the interrelatedness of cultural phenomena is seen in his illuminating description of a Trobriander canoe. The following discussion, taken from his classic account of this society, shows the reciprocal interrelatedness of technology, sentiment, religious belief, and social organization (1961:105–23). In this discussion of canoes and sailing, Malinowski emphasizes that a canoe, taken by itself, is a material object and nothing more. Contemplating even a perfect specimen in a museum could never reveal its ethnographic reality:

> The canoe is made for a certain use, and with a definite purpose; it is a means to an end, and we, who study native life, must not reverse this relation, and make a fetish of the object itself. In the study of the economic purposes for which a canoe is made, of the various uses to which it is submitted, we find the first approach to a deeper ethnographic treatment. Further sociological data, referring to its ownership, accounts of who sails in it, and how it is done; information regarding the ceremonies and customs of its construction, a sort of typical life history of a native craft—all that brings us nearer still to the understanding of what his canoe truly means to the native.

But to the native, the canoe is much more—a thing of beauty, surrounded by an atmosphere of romance, a living thing having an individuality of its own.

Following a technical discussion of the complexities of making a canoe, Malinowski goes on to show how a thorough understanding of a canoe must take into consideration Trobriand social organization:

> In studying the construction of a canoe, we see the natives engaged in an economic enterprise on a big scale. Technical difficulties face them, which require knowledge, and can only be overcome by a continuous, systematic effort, and at certain stages must be met by means of communal labour. All this obviously implies some social organisation.

This leads Malinowski into a discussion of the complexities of Trobriand economic organization and magical beliefs. Each step in the manufacture of a canoe has its appropriate magical rituals. A belief in the efficiency of magic is to be found associated with all vital activities, not only those of canoe making, but of propitious sailing, of shipwreck and salvage, of trade, fishing, and protection against attack in foreign travels. Thus, the study of the ethnographic meaning of a canoe takes us deeply into Trobriand religion.

Further, there is the relationship between the object itself and the community in which it is found, a topic referred to by Malinowski as its ownership. Conceptions of ownership vary greatly from society to society, and understanding the native's ideas concerning canoe ownership forces us to unravel his notions of ownership in general, which in turn takes us into yet other areas of economics and social relations.

Finally, the greatest and most highly valued of Trobriand canoes are those used for the long-distance trading involved in the so-called Kula. This is a most complex institution in which men from many islands travel widely to visit Kula partners on other islands. The heart of this trade is the ceremonious exchange of certain objects which have little intrinsic value, but enormous emotional value for their temporary owners. This single, complex institution is taken by Malinowski as his point of departure in his book *Argonauts of the Western Pacific*. All other aspects of native life, including the canoe and its sociology, are woven into a functional description of Trobriand culture by tracing their relationships to the Kula. In theory the same systematic description of this culture could be achieved by starting with any other institution of Trobriand culture, and tracing its relationships outward to embrace all other aspects of the culture.

Largely due to the efforts of Malinowski and Radcliffe-Brown, most anthropologists have come to accept the significance of the functional interrelatedness of a culture. It has been demonstrated empirically, hundreds of times over, that changes introduced into certain sectors of a culture (especially the economic and technological dimensions) will inevitably lead to concomitant changes in most, if not all, other parts of culture—in family life, religion, ethics, moral conduct, and so on. No one has ever demonstrated, however, that every culture trait in a given cultural system is in fact related to every other item, or that a change will eventually affect every other trait of this system. The reader should be aware that the idea of culture as an organized whole, as a system having the properties of other natural systems, is yet another significant concept. It is an intellectual construct that enables investigators to view cultural items in a meaningful way. As a concept it is not an end in itself, and its value lies in its heuristic utility, in how well it can be used to explain.

Culture as Patterned Behavior

While it is true that no one has ever described a culture as a complete system, showing the interrelatedness of every part to every other part, the concept of system is a useful one. The student of culture can bring understanding to many aspects of the cultural system while accepting something less than complete description. He can, for example, conceptualize culture as a system of interlocking *patterns* without pretending to place every item of culture in a pattern or without expecting to demonstrate the interrelatedness of every pattern. His patterns can be relatively simple ones embracing a limited number of behaviors, or they can be extremely broad, embracing large areas of cultural activity.

We can illustrate briefly what is meant by pattern by drawing on an example used in the preceding chapter. We showed that in the Guatemalan town of San Antonio, individuals identifiable as Indians may often be seen tipping their hats, bowing, or otherwise exhibiting respectful behavior toward the non-Indian *Ladinos*. The *Ladino* in turn accepts this show of respect with characteristic behavior of his own. This customary behavior between Indian and *Ladino* constitutes a pattern made up of certain elements: tipping his hat, bowing, respectful form of address, stepping aside or off the sidewalk by the Indian; use of more familiar terms of address, keeping his hat on, not stepping aside, and otherwise exhibiting an overbearing manner by the *Ladino*. These elements are linked together in a predictable manner. Many other items of behavior performed by Indian and *Ladino* are not linked to these items and are, therefore, not part of this particular pattern.

Linton's Approach to Patterning. A useful way of approaching the study of patterns was developed by Ralph Linton (1936:397–400), although his terminology differs somewhat from that used in this book. He takes as his starting point the analysis of culture into units called *traits*, which can in turn be analyzed into smaller units which he calls *items*. Not only items of behavior, but any material object used by a culture can be referred to as a trait—a canoe, a bow, a loin cloth, or an automobile. A canoe, however, can be analyzed into numerous items, if we wish to do so: the kind of wood used, its dimensions, the structure of its bow, stern, or gunwales, and so on. Whether we choose to call an element of culture a trait or an item is, of course, an arbitrary matter, and depends on the purpose of our analysis.

"Although the traits which compose the overt expression of a culture can be isolated artificially, they are actually integrated into a functional whole" (Linton 1936:397). Traits are always associated in some way with other traits to form larger functional units. Linton refers to these as *trait complexes*, which correspond to what we have referred to as patterns. Thus, the individual behaviors of Indian and *Ladino*, given above, would be called, in Linton's terminology, traits. They are associated in a complex, or pattern, to which we can assign a name—greeting behavior or intergroup etiquette. Linton's own example is that of the Comanche bow. This trait is made up of several items: wood used, length, cross-section of the bow shaft, high polish of the wood, the type of bowstring and the method of its attachment. These items are individually insignificant, but together they constitute a distinctive trait in Comanche culture. The bow, in turn, is combined with other traits— the arrow, the combined bow-case and quiver, and the method of shooting—to form a trait complex, which is a larger unit of Comanche culture.

Linton identifies a still broader classification when he combines trait complexes into *activities* (*ibid.*, 397–98). The bow-and-arrow complex, for example, may be combined with the horse complex, the tracking complex, and other complexes to form what he calls the hunting activity. In a similar way, the pattern (trait complex) identified in our Guatemalan village may be combined with yet other patterns of behavior between Indians and *Ladinos*. Members of these two groups meet under many circumstances—in municipal government, in economic dealings, in church-related activities—and each calls for characteristic behavioral traits. Together these narrower patterns combine to form the broad pattern of intergroup etiquette. In Linton's words (1936:398), "The whole structure might be likened to a pyramid with the items, which are the most numerous, at the bottom and the number of units diminishing with each succeeding tier."

Linton recognizes that this method of analysis raises some questions and may be difficult to apply in some cases. For certain purposes we might not wish to limit ourselves to the categories of item, trait, trait complex, and activity. For other purposes these few categories may be too many and may imply a precision of analysis greater than can be achieved. For our purposes in this section, we have preferred to limit our analysis to patterns, which are made up of identifiable elements or traits and which, in turn, may combine to form ever more complex patterns. The important point to be stressed is that culture is not just an assemblage of unrelated traits. No matter how finely the anthropologist subdivides a culture to arrive at its constituent units, these units exist only in some kind of functional association with other units. Such units have little or no scientific meaning except as parts of broader behavioral complexes or patterns. These patterns, in turn, have limited meaning unless seen in their interrelations with other patterns. The pattern of behavior identified as the Trobriand family took on additional meaning when it was related to the patterns of matrilineal descent, the economic patterns of distribution and consumption of goods, and the pattern of political leadership. The achievement of this level of understanding did not require that every trait in Trobriand culture be combined into a pattern, nor that every pattern be related to every other pattern. The perspective gained by utilizing a functional approach does not suffer because we have fallen short of a complete functionalist description.

Benedict's Configurations of Culture. This chapter is concluded with a brief discussion of a special application of the concept of cultural patterning which gained prominence through the writings of the late Ruth Benedict a generation ago. In her influential book *Patterns of Culture,* published in 1934, she addressed herself to the difficult problem of characterizing whole cultures in terms of their total configurations, their dominant *genius* or *ethos*. She recognized that a culture is made up of many patterns, in the sense described above, but she wished to go further and show that in any culture these patterns are bound together in some consistent way that gives that culture its particular style, its unique configuration.

A culture, like an individual, is a more or less consistent pattern of thought and action. Within each culture there come into being characteristic purposes not necessarily shared by other types of society. In obedience to these purposes, each people further and further consolidates its experience, and in proportion to the urgency of these drives the heterogeneous items of behaviour take more and more congruous shape. Taken up by a well-integrated culture, the most ill-assorted acts become characteristic of its peculiar goals, often by the most unlikely metamorphoses. The form that these acts take we can understand only by understanding first the emotional and intellectual mainsprings of that society. (1946:42.)

Benedict, in her analysis of cultural systems, searched for some dominant philosophy or world view, a "super pattern" that could be expressed in psychological terms, that seems to underlie all other patterns and which gives them consistency in terms of the whole configuration. Such a dominant world view would influence individual behavior in all areas of existence, and, therefore, would be reflected in the many patterns that make up the total configuration.

To demonstrate this approach, Benedict selected three cultures for which there were good existing ethnographic descriptions: the Pueblo cultures of New Mexico, the Kwakiutl of British Columbia, and the Dobu of Melanesia. To characterize the Pueblos, for example, and to compare them with other North American Indians, Benedict borrowed from the philosopher Nietzsche, who distinguished "two diametrically opposed ways of arriving at the values of existence" (1946:72). The *Dionysian* is one who seeks to escape the limits of existence imposed upon him by his five senses. "The desire of the Dionysian, in personal experience or in ritual, is to press through it toward a certain psychological state, to achieve excess . . . he values the illuminations of frenzy." To illustrate this, Benedict showed that many North American Indian groups deliberately induced hallucination by means of self-torture and fasting in order to experience a valued "vision." Exaltation was widely associated with religion and might be sought through drugs or alcoholic intoxication. A Kwakiutl Indian would attempt to exalt himself and humiliate his opponents through a potlatch, involving the destruction of property, and through uninhibited boasting.

The other of Nietzsche's types, *Apollonian*, mistrusted all of this. He avoided and even outlawed the kinds of experiences valued by the Dionysian. This was the way of the Pueblo Indians. The Apollonian world view was, according to Benedict's analysis, dominant in all aspects of Pueblo culture. The Apollonian stays to the middle of the road by strict adherence to tradition. He distrusts individualism, which is re-

The inscription above the doorway of a Kwakiutl Indian house in British Columbia commemorates one chief Clelamen who "gave away with the help of his sons . . . property in blankets, canoes, etc. valued at 4000 dollars, this being his eighth large potlatch and feast that he had held." (Courtesy of the American Museum of Natural History.)

flected in Pueblo culture by the absence of any strong pattern of leadership. A chance vision or hallucination, far from being valued, is feared as a sign of death.

Benedict went on to characterize each of the three sample cultures in terms of one or the other of these dominant configurations. She did not suggest, however, that all the world's cultures are either Apollonian or Dionysian. Nor did she suggest that all cultures can be characterized in terms of a single, consistent, underlying ethos. What she did attempt to show is that within each of these three cultures numerous institutions and many diverse patterns of behavior become intelligible to us when seen as the expression of a single, dominant configuration.

Writers since Benedict have questioned the validity of her interpretation of Pueblo, Kwakiutl, and Dobuan culture. They have questioned whether any culture can be characterized in terms of a single or even a few dominant psychological drives. The problems raised by Benedict are, nevertheless, still with us. Like many writers before her, various writers since Benedict have sought ways of expressing, in scientifically meaningful terms, the character, the genius, the ethos, or the style of whole cultures. The feeling underlying all such attempts is that something remains to be explained or understood, even after we have analyzed a culture into its component patterns and have shown the systematic relations between them.

4

Evolution, Genetics, and Culture

INTRODUCTION

More than any other student of man, the anthropologist recognizes the intimate relationship between biology and culture. It is this awareness of the significance of cultural factors in man's evolution that distinguishes the physical anthropologist from other students of human biology. Similarly, the recognition and understanding of the biological dimensions of culture is one of the ways in which the cultural anthropologist differs from other students of human behavior. In this chapter, biology and culture are treated as dimensions of a single entity—man. Since man and culture are dynamic phenomena, it is more meaningful to deal with them over time, rather than at a point in time. Therefore, the biological and the cultural evolution of man are focused upon as the two major parts of human evolution, and their interrelatedness is emphasized.

RELATIONSHIP BETWEEN BIOLOGY AND CULTURE

The reader will become more aware of the relationship between man's biology and man's culture when he considers the following specific points.

1. *General biological evolution is a process characteristic of all living things.* Man, as an animal, is subject to the processes of biological evolution, and therefore has certain affinities with other living things. The same mechanisms that operate in the evolution of a bat, a fish, or a

gorilla—mitosis, meiosis, fertilization, mutation, selection, hybridization, genetic drift, migration, isolation, specialization, and many more—are at work in man's evolution.

2. *The unit of evolution among all animals, and therefore among men, is not the individual but the population.* The individual, to be sure, contributes his genetic materials to the total gene pool of the population of which he is a member. This he does by passing on his genes to future generations through sexual reproduction, so that they continue to be part of that gene pool. If his genetic materials are not passed on in this way, they die with the individual, and are irrelevant to the process of evolution. Evolution is a process in which *populations, not individuals,* are modified through time. This change, to a large extent, is based upon the frequency with which genes occur in any given population.

3. *Adaptation is the orienting factor in evolution and is common to all living things.* The adaptive process cannot be viewed in isolation, however, because it always occurs in relation to the environment.

4. *Man adapts to his environment both culturally, a highly mutable form of adaptation, and biologically, a relatively immutable form of adaptation.* These occur simultaneously. Culture, however, can overcome the immutable aspects of man's biological adaptation.

5. *There are many specific features of man's biology that in some way limit, condition, or determine his behavior as a species.* Culture is the behavior of an animal species having erect posture, bipedal locomotion, a grasping hand, stereoscopic vision, warm blood, and so on. Culture, as man's behavior, reflects his unique biology, just as the behavior of any animal species is directly correlated with its biological features. Indeed, there is such an intimate relationship between man's behavior and his biology that culture as we know it would be impossible for a species with a significantly different biological makeup.

6. *Culture has not always existed. It emerged in the course of man's biological evolution, as a consequence of biological changes taking place in man.* During a certain period in man's evolution, transformations were taking place in his biology—structural and physiological changes—which made possible a qualitatively new kind of behavior. A proto-hominid species was being transformed into a human species. Consequently, cultural processes cannot be completely understood apart from a consideration of biological evolution. They are part of the same, more comprehensive process of human evolution.

7. *Culture affects human variability, adaptation, and viability.* War, slavery, colonization, and the like, all affect population size and composition. Cultural institutions permit the survival and reproduction of individuals and groups of individuals who would be unfit for survival

without culture. Nuclear physics, medicine, and more efficient technology are examples of cultural items which have had direct effects on human biology.

8. *Culture is, first and foremost, an adaptive mechanism.* It is a means of meeting subsistence needs, rearing the young to maturity, achieving protection against climate and competitive groups, providing effective organization, and more. Man achieves with tools and organization what other species achieve through biological structural modification.

9. *Culture is mutable, and can evolve independently of biological man.* Man's techniques for coping with his environment can change, develop, and become more effective with little or no corresponding change in his biology.

For many reasons, then, an understanding of human evolution would be impossible without taking into account the intricate interplay between biological and cultural factors.

GENETIC COMPOSITION OF MAN

The genetic composition of man is the basis for his entire biological evolution. While culture has been a primary factor in the evolution of the human genetic system, that system in turn is the primary reason for man's capacity for culture. Every physical characteristic of man— his erect posture, his opposable thumb, his stereoscopic vision, or the manner in which his offspring are born (all of which are expressed in his culture)—is based upon the presence of particular genes and particular gene combinations. Genes are the non-observable causes of observable physical characteristics.

The science of human genetics, though an infant science, has made significant contributions to understanding man and his biological evolution. Much of this and future understanding is based upon knowledge of what might be called the genetic processes of life—mitosis, meiosis, and fertilization. These three processes are responsible for man's existence and his perpetuation in much the same way they explain the existence and perpetuation of other animal groups. Since mitosis, meiosis, and fertilization are inextricably linked to form a closed cyclical pattern, a sound understanding of these three processes is the basis for understanding all genetics and all biological evolution. Before these genetic processes of life can be discussed with understanding, certain basic information is necessary.

Each cell in the human body has two general parts, cytoplasm and nucleus, and each part is circumscribed by a protective membrane. Their arrangement is shown in Fig. 4-1.

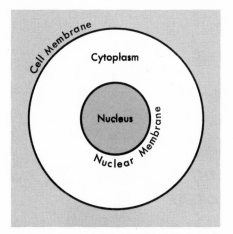

Fig. 4–1. Body cell.

Within the nucleus of each cell are found the hereditary material of man (genes), and the location of genes (chromosomes, or colored bodies). Genes and chromosomes both always occur in pairs and must be considered in this way. A gene has never been observed by man and remains a construct—a way in which man conceives of and refers to his hereditary materials. Chromosomes, however, are observable under a microscope. Observation of man's chromosomes reveals that these structures have various shapes: short rods, long rods, V-shapes, J-shapes. While the chromosomes are not readily observable at all times, they never lose their identity in the nucleus. In addition, there is a numerical constancy of chromosomes in any given organism. Each cell within the same organism has the same number of chromosomes. The constant number of chromosomes in man is 46, grouped into 23 pairs. The constant number of chromosomes in other primate species (chimpanzee, gibbon, gorilla, various types of monkeys, and others) ranges from 34 to 66. The number of chromosomes varies among species, but remains constant within a given species. The constant number of chromosomes for man (46, or 23 pairs) is called the diploid number of chromosomes. All cells in man are characterized by this diploid number.

The diploid chromosomes in man are of different sizes and shapes but, with one exception, they always occur in identical pairs. These pairs are called homologous (like) chromosomes. There are, therefore, 22 pairs of homologous chromosomes in man; they are sometimes referred to as autosomes to distinguish them from the 23rd pair of chromosomes that are not homologous in males—the sex chromosomes. In females, all 23 pairs of chromosomes are homologous. This singular, but very important, difference is responsible for the differentiation between the sexes.

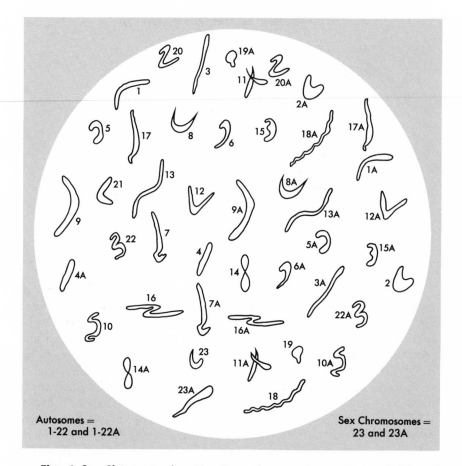

Fig. 4–2. Chromosomal composition of man. Autosomes = 1–22 and 1–22A. Sex chromosomes = 23 and 23A.

The diploid number of 46 chromosomes is made up of two chromosome sets, of 23 chromosomes each. Every normal individual receives one such set from his mother and one from his father. Each normal body cell, in every individual, will contain these two sets to make up the species-constant, diploid number of 46. Figure 4–2 illustrates the arrangement of human chromosomes. Autosomes 1–22 and sex chromosome 23 constitute the chromosome set inherited from the father; autosomes 1A–22A, and sex chromosome 23A constitute the chromosome set inherited from the mother. Figure 4–3 shows human chromosomes.

Each chromosome contains a series of *loci* (places) where the genes are situated. Therefore, in a homologous pair of chromosomes the adjacent loci would also be homologous. It follows from this that genes occur in pairs, each gene having a partner occupying the locus homologous to its own. In other words, the genes in a given pair occupy homologous loci (like places) in homologous chromosomes. Each of a pair

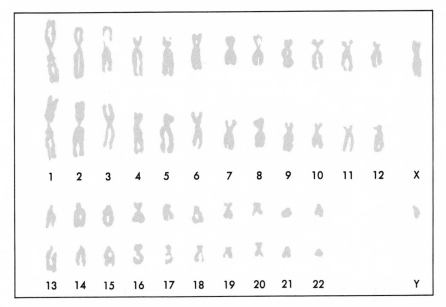

Fig. 4–3. The human chromosomes (autosomes 1–22, sex chromosomes X and Y). From a male cell in culture. The 46 chromosomes are from a photo-micrographic print, cut singly, arranged in pairs, and grouped according to sizes and relative lengths of arms. 3,200X. (From Stern's adaptation, 1960, of Tjio and Puck, "The Somatic Chromosomes of Man," from the *Proceedings of the National Academy of Sciences*, Vol. 44, pp. 1229–39, 1958.)

of genes is called an allele (meaning "the other one"), emphasizing its occurrence in a combination of two. Unlike the chromosomes in man, the number of genes is not known. Various estimates have been offered ranging from 2,000 to 50,000 pairs of genes in any one human individual.

The total particular combination of genes for any individual is his genotype (genetic composition), and no two individuals, except for certain rare exceptions, are ever exactly alike in their genetic composition. The particular combination of genes occurring at any given locus in an individual constitutes his genetic composition (genotype) for that locus. The genotype of any individual is fixed at the time of conception, when the male sperm fertilizes the female egg. The genotype of any individual may be treated as a constant, although we recognize that genetic changes, such as mutation, may take place.

Genes are non-observable, hereditary materials, but they are expressed externally. This external expression of the genetic composition of any individual is his phenotype, and the external expression of genes occurring at a given locus is the individual's phenotype for that locus. Phenotypes, therefore, are the external expression of genotypes. It is

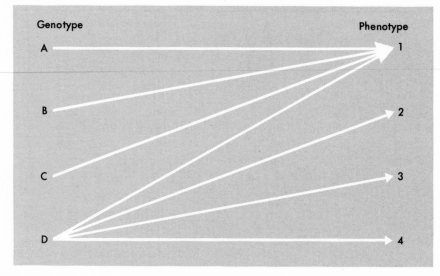

Fig. 4–4. Relationship between genotypes and phenotypes.

important to note that no simple correlation exists between phenotypes and genotypes. A given external expression (phenotype) may be the result of genes occurring at numerous loci. Conversely, a given gene, occurring at a single locus, may influence several different phenotypes.

Though hypothetical and oversimplified, Fig. 4–4 shows that genotypes A, B, C, and D are the basis for phenotype 1. Here four pairs of genes occurring at four different loci are responsible for a single external expression, phenotype 1. In addition, genotype D is partially responsible, or influences, four different external expressions, phenotypes 1, 2, 3, and 4. The diagram is left incomplete in order to insure easier understanding of the fact that no simple correlation exists between genetic composition and phenotypic expression. In reality the situation described probably would not exist in such simple terms.

The phenotype is a variable based upon the genotype and the interaction between the genotype and its non-genetic environment. Phenotypes can be readily changed—individuals who are light-skinned lie in the sun to darken their skin, bald persons attempt to grow hair or use wigs, fat people exercise to make themselves thinner. Genotypes, however, are not so readily modified.

GENETIC PROCESSES OF LIFE

With this basic information, the reader can comprehend the genetic processes of life—mitosis, meiosis, and fertilization—without difficulty.

Mitosis

Mitosis is a process of growth. It is the way in which the human individual develops from the point of conception until death. The mitotic process takes place in all viable human organisms, in all cells of their bodies, during their entire life span. The mitotic process is commonly referred to as cell division. While the designation is incomplete, cell division certainly is an important part of mitosis, for the cells (and all their materials) divide as a necessary part of their reproduction. The mitotic process includes two main parts: reduplication and division. Each cell undergoing mitosis will produce two cells that are exactly like the first cell. These two like cells are called daughter cells. Once these two cells are produced, each will, in turn, produce two daughter cells; the process continues in this way, so that four cells become eight exactly like the first four, and so forth. Since all body cells are derived from a single, original cell, all are exactly like this initial cell in genetic composition.

The initial cell for any individual is created at the time of conception, when the egg of the female is fertilized by the sperm of the male. Commencing with this single fertilized cell (called a zygote), mitosis takes place. The zygote develops (grows) into an embryo which, after nine months in the female body, is expelled to continue its development outside the environment of the mother's womb. Here, one cell produces two, two produce four, four produce eight, eight produce sixteen, and so forth. All cells are exactly like the original cell genetically, and are produced by the mitotic process. This process continues as long as the individual is alive.

A closer examination of the mitotic process reveals other important information. While the two processes of reduplication and division occur simultaneously during the initial phase of mitosis, a clearer understanding of the total sequence can be achieved if they are shown in a more distinct sequence.

In the first phase a tiny body called a centriole, located outside the nuclear membrane, divides into two, and the two new centrioles migrate to opposite sides of the nucleus. At the same time the 46 chromosomes have reduplicated themselves, forming 46 identical pairs. Their arrangement now becomes distinct and observable. [See Fig. 4–5(a) and 4–5(b).]

Following this stage of the mitotic process the reduplicated chromosomes arrange themselves along an equatorial plane in preparation for normal cell division. Each chromosome aligned along this plane is attached to a spindle thread which radiates out from one of the centrioles. Meanwhile the nuclear membrane has dissolved [Fig. 4–5(c)]. Now, each new set of 46 chromosomes is pulled toward its respective end of the cell by the spindle thread. A new membrane forms about each set of chromosomes, division takes place between the two nuclei, and the cell separates [Fig. 4–5(d) through (f)]. Each of the daughter cells, which have the same genetic materials as the original cell, resumes a premitotic arrangement before each enters into mitosis again [Fig. 4–5(f)]. The entire process is completed in less than one hour.

Summary of Mitosis.   Several important characteristics of mitosis should be reiterated:

1. Mitosis is a process of growth.
2. Mitosis occurs in all parts of the body.
3. Mitosis takes place during the entire life of a given individual from the time of conception until death.
4. Mitosis is characterized by a single cellular division.
5. Mitosis results in the production of cells which are exactly like the original one.
6. Mitosis occurs at different rates during the life of an individual—very rapidly from the time of conception until the major growth period has ceased, at a constant rate of replacement until old age, and at a decreasing rate of replacement during old age until death, when mitosis stops. This differential rate of mitosis is shown graphically in Fig. 4–6.

The entire process of mitosis for a given body cell, summarizing the various steps that have been explained, is shown in Fig. 4–5. When an aberration does occur (a deviation from the normal process, such as two chromosomes pulling apart unevenly, resulting in more than the normal genetic materials being pulled to one polar point and less than the normal genetic materials being pulled to the opposite polar point), those cells containing aberrated genetic materials will produce, according to the mitotic process, cells that are aberrated in exactly the same way as the original aberrated cell.

Meiosis

Meiosis is a process of the production of male sperm and female eggs, both of which are called gametes. Meiosis shows certain general similarities to mitosis, but is significantly different. First, the results of the two processes differ. Mitosis is a process of growth, whereas meiosis is a process of the production of gametes and has nothing to do with growth. Second, mitosis occurs in all parts of the body from the time of conception until the death of the individual. Meiosis occurs only in the sexual organs of the individual in the production of sex cells. It does not begin until biological puberty occurs and ends during the "change of life" in the individual, which takes place many years before

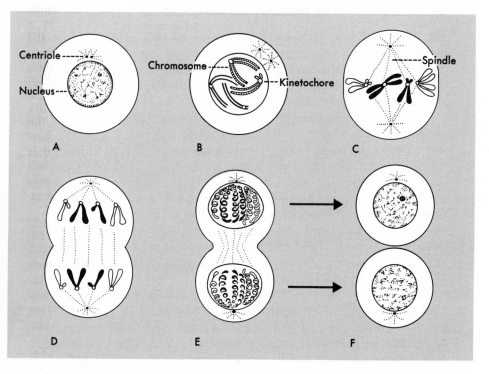

Fig. 4–5. Cell division and mitosis. C = centriole; N = nucleus; CH = chromosome; K = kinetochore; S = spindle. (From Curt Stern, *Principles of Human Genetics.* San Francisco, Calif.: W. H. Freeman and Co., 1960; p. 14, fig. 6.)

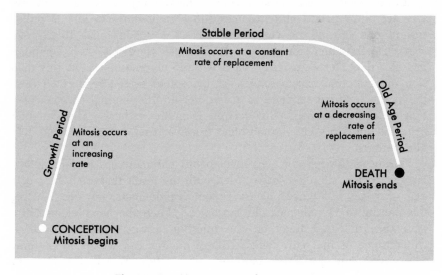

Fig. 4–6. Mitosis: rate of occurrence.

the individual dies. Therefore, meiosis occurs in a different place and during a much shorter period of time than does mitosis. Third, meiosis involves two cellular divisions whereas mitosis is characterized by a single cellular division. Other differences are best explained as the meiotic process is described.

Meiosis, occurring only in the sexual organs of the individual, is similar to mitosis in that it begins with a single cell (see Fig. 4–1). This cell contains the constant number of chromosomes that are contained in all other body cells—46 chromosomes grouped into 23 pairs. There are 22 pairs of autosomes and 1 pair of sex chromosomes included in the nucleus. The general processes of reduplication and division are characteristic of both the meiotic process and the mitotic process, except that division takes place twice in meiosis. Like the mitotic process, the cell undergoing meiosis shows the distinct appearance of the chromosomes contained within the nucleus and reduplication of these chromosomes. [See Fig. 4–7(a) through (c).]

At this point, however, the similarity between meiosis and mitosis ends. Following reduplication of the 46 chromosomes to produce 92, each of the reduplicated pairs comes together and intertwines in such a way that an exchange of genetic material occurs. This process, which is called crossing over, results in an exchange of genes between the intertwined chromosomes, so that none of the 92 chromosomes is any longer identical to those from the father or mother. The chromosomes now line up along the equatorial plane in homologous pairs (unlike the random alignment in mitosis). (See Fig. 4–7.)

As the nuclear membrane dissolves, the primary cell division begins. One set of 23 paired chromosomes (46 chromosomes in all) is pulled toward one side of the cell, the other set (an additional 46 chromosomes) to the other side of the cell. The cell constricts, then separates, and two daughter cells result, each with 46 chromosomes. In this division the maternal chromosomes (chromosomes originally derived from the mother) do not separate as a unit, nor do the paternal chromosomes (the chromosomes originally derived from the father). The daughter cells will contain some chromosomes from each set, but there is no definite pattern.

Pairing of the reduplicated homologous chromosomes is not haphazard but occurs in proper locus order, with the result that each gene of a pair of genes is aligned. There is some randomness, however, during this pairing of homologous chromosomes. When the homologous chromosomes are fused together, the question always remains for each chromosome of the pair: which will go on top and which on bottom? The positioning of the chromosomes at this time is called random or independent assortment and is extremely significant in terms of genetic

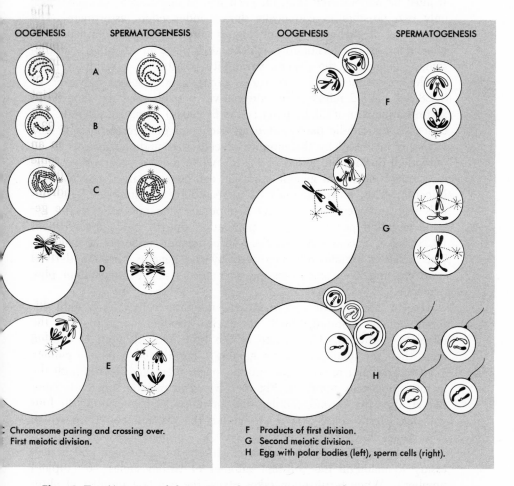

Fig. 4–7. Meiosis and formation of gametes. A–C. Chromosome pairing and crossing over. D–E. First meiotic division. F. Products of first division. G. Second meiotic division. H. Egg with polar bodies (*left*), sperm cells (*right*). (From Curt Stern, *Principles of Human Genetics.* San Francisco, Calif.: W. H. Freeman and Co., 1960; pp. 70–71, fig. 39.)

variation. *Genetic variation is the key to evolution.* Hence, independent assortment, though apparently a simple factor, is very important. It must be remembered that, for each pair of homologous chromosomes, only two possibilities can occur during independent assortment. The positioning of each pair of homologous chromosomes is completely independent of the positioning which takes place in all other chromosomes. Therefore, the genetic variability possible as a result of independent assortment alone is, for a single pair of genes only, 2^{23} or 8,388,608. The 2 refers to the alternatives possible, and the superscript 23 to the number of allelic pairs (pairs of genes) being considered. (In this case, one allelic pair located on each pair of chromosomes is 23.) If this is increased by the number of cells that undergo meiosis in an individual during the period of his life when meiosis occurs, then some measure of individual genetic variation can be ascertained (8,388,068 $\times$ N cells). This, however, must be increased by the number of individuals who are members of a given population, to approximate the genetic variation possible in that population due to random assortment (8,388,068 $\times$ N cells $\times$ N members of population undergoing meiosis). This result is significantly increased by the genetic variation derived from crossing over, since crossing over occurs as an independent phenomenon.

Due to independent assortment, the daughter cells may contain different genetic material, which affects the genetic composition of the offspring produced. The zygote at the time of conception is nothing more than the union of a male gamete (sperm) and a female gamete (egg). The final result of the production of these gametes through the meiotic process is shown in Fig. 4–7(h). The meiotic process is completed after the second cellular division takes place, resulting in four gametes (germ cells) which are unlike the original cell from which they came. Each gamete contains only 23 chromosomes and no pairs. This is the haploid (half) number of chromosomes for man and is necessary to maintain the constant number of chromosomes, 46 (diploid number). When fertilization takes place, the constant number of chromosomes will be restored.

Figure 4–7 summarizes the entire meiotic process. It is important, however, to point out the major differences between mitosis and meiosis to insure that no confusion exists. This is done in Table 4–1.

Fertilization

The genetic materials of any individual are restricted to that individual and die with him. There is no continuity beyond the life of the individual unless he can pass his genetic materials on to future genera-

Table 4–1

Variable	Mitosis	Meiosis
Process	Is a process of growth.	Is a process of production of gametes.
Time	Takes place during entire life of individual from conception till death.	Takes place between biological puberty and "change of life" in individual.
Place	Occurs throughout individual's body—in all cells.	Occurs only in the sexual organs of individual.
Rate	Occurs at a differential rate —increasing rate during growth period, constant rate during stable period, and decreasing rate during old age.	Occurs at a stable rate.
Cellular Divisions	Single cellular division.	Two cellular divisions.
Synapsis	Does not occur in mitosis.	Important part of meiosis.
Pairing of Homologous Chromosomes	Does not occur in mitosis.	Important part of meiosis.
Independent Assortment	Does not occur in mitosis.	Important part of meiosis.
Cellular Results of Process	Two daughter cells exactly like the original cell. Each cell contains 46 chromosomes (23 pairs).	Four gametes. Each gamete contains 23 chromosomes only—no pairs.
Evolutionary Significance	Not significant for evolution.	A source of genetic variability. Important for evolution.

tions through the process of fertilization—the production of offspring. Then, and only then, does the individual have active evolutionary significance; until then, he is of potential evolutionary significance only. Meiosis is responsible for producing the materials necessary for fertilization—gametes. Meiosis allows fertilization.

Fertilization is the union of the male and female gametes (sperm and egg) resulting in the production of a single cell called a zygote. Each gamete carries 23 chromosomes, and when joined through fertilization they produce a zygote containing 46 chromosomes, or 23 pairs. Each of the 23 chromosomes in each gamete is one of a pair of chromosomes. (See Fig. 4–8.) At this point, the union of the male and female gametes, the genetic composition of the individual is established. Barring mutation or aberration, the genetic composition of the individual will remain the same, and these genetic materials will be the only ones the individual can pass on to future generations. This is the individual's contribution to the gene pool of the population.

The three genetic processes of life—mitosis, meiosis, and fertilization

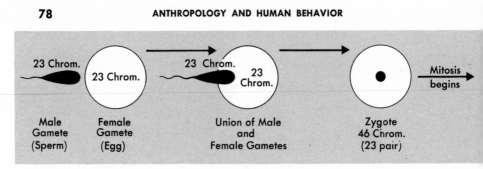

Fig. 4—8. Fertilization.

—constitute a unified cycle. Fertilization, which is allowed by the production of gametes, results in the formation of a single cell called a zygote. Once the zygote has been produced, it begins to grow according to the process of mitosis. After approximately nine months of such growth in the mother's womb, a newborn child is expelled from the mother's body. This offspring will continue its growth by the process of mitosis for its entire life. But as growth continues and biological puberty is achieved, the process of meiosis begins in the sexual organs of the individual. This enables the individual to produce gametes which, in turn, will be used to produce new zygotes through the process of fertilization. These new zygotes will undergo the processes of mitosis and meiosis and will then produce new zygotes by the process of fertilization. The total cycle continues in this way. (See Fig. 4—9.)

CULTURAL DIMENSIONS OF THE GENETIC PROCESSES OF LIFE

While mitosis, meiosis, and fertilization are biological processes, they are influenced significantly by cultural action. The most frequent and consistent cultural influence on these biological processes is selection of mates—determining who can mate with whom in any given society. The answer to this universal question is always a cultural one, and is phrased in terms of cultural rules for behavior: preferences, prescriptions, proscriptions, and the like. The genetic significance of these cultural decisions regarding mating is that certain gene combinations are excluded, or their possible frequency is reduced or increased. Genetic results of this kind are based upon cultural action which largely ignores genetic information.

Rules of exogamy (marriage outside a specified group or territory) and endogamy (marriage within a specified group or territory) are frequently occurring examples. Societies have various rules, written and

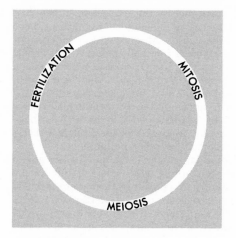

Fig. 4–9.   Cycle of genetic processes of life.

unwritten, that suggest, describe, prescribe, or prohibit an individual's marital partner or the person with whom he will mate. Caste endogamy is prescribed for much of India, ethnic group endogamy in the United States was very important during the nineteenth and early twentieth centuries, clan exogamy is a frequent behavioral rule among societies in much of the world, nuclear family exogamy is nearly universal. Each of these rules is a cultural rule, but each has genetic significance. In most instances, the genetic significance is not known simply because research of this kind has not been of sufficient depth or frequency. Nevertheless, enough genetic research has been completed, using specific cultural groups as the unit of investigation, to demonstrate that cultural decisions do have genetic results. Religious group isolation of the Jewish community in Rome is one such example.

Endogamy in the Jewish Ghetto in Rome

The ghetto community of Rome is probably the oldest still in existence on the European continent. . . . For more than 2,000 years its members have been more or less segregated from the rest of the city of Rome. . . . marriage records show that the members of the "small community" seldom marry outside their own group. . . . The present generation, their parents and their parents' parents, with remarkably few exceptions, were born in Rome—which means that they were natives of the city's Jewish community. . . . All the criteria . . . examined proved clearly that the remnant of the ancient Jewish community of Rome is in fact a distinct cultural sub-group within the city. . . . Inbreeding within this small population, continued over many centuries, would be expected to preserve or produce a distinct genetic pattern, and perhaps even peculiar genes which are not found at all in the surrounding population. . . . the remarkable blood studies of recent years, whereby biologists have discovered dozens of blood types and identified them with particular genes, have provided anthropologists and geneticists with a sharp tool for dissecting human heredity. . . . By this method significant differences in blood-gene frequencies have been found among the populations of the world. Most American Indians, for example, have group O blood; there are only a few with group A and almost none with group B. European populations have less O, more A, and increasing frequencies of B as one goes from west to east toward Asia. Asia has the highest frequency of group B in the world. In Africa populations south of the Sahara are distinguished by very high frequency of an Rh gene which is rare on other continents. In some parts of the world blood differences have been found between neighboring populations (e.g., segments of the Brahman caste) which are forbidden to intermarry by religious or other prohibitions.

We proceeded to type the blood of a large sample of the Roman ghetto population. . . . there emerged two peculiarities which marked the Roman Jews off sharply from other Italians. Nearly 27 percent of them were of blood group B, whereas among Catholic Italians not more than 11 or 12 percent have B blood. And the Jewish group was distinctly marked with an Rh gene which is rare among Italians, or for that matter among Europeans generally. This gene (known as ŕ or Cde) was present in about 5 percent of the ghetto members—a frequency five to ten times higher than in non-Jewish Italians. . . .

The ghetto population of Rome, then, does show definite biological differences from the rest of the Roman population. The blood tests confirm that this group has been genetically isolated in the midst of the metropolis in which it has been living for centuries. . . . We think we have established that the Jews of the Roman ghetto did maintain their cultural and biological identity as a distinct sub-community within a larger one, and that social forces can shape man's biology. (Dunn and Dunn 1957:119 ff.)

This description is a clear example of the influence of cultural behavior on the genetics of man, but there are hundreds of similar situations which have not yet been reported in such precise terms. Any cultural behavior which determines, influences, or in any way affects the selection of mates will of necessity influence the genetic composition of the offspring produced. Each individual is genetically unique and can only contribute the genes he has to his offspring. With this limitation of genes, the recombination of genes that can possibly occur in the offspring is limited.

Genetic Recombinations: The ABO Blood Group Locus

The ABO blood group locus provides an example of these genetic limitations. Only three different kinds of genes can occur at this locus: gene A, gene B, and gene O. An individual will have two genes (one pair) at this locus, which can occur in the following combinations only:

AA
AO
BB
BO
AB
OO

One gene at this locus was contained in the gamete produced by the individual's mother, and one gene at this locus was contained in the gamete produced by the individual's father. If the mother's gene was A and the father's gene was A, then the genetic composition of the individual would have to be AA at this locus—the recombination of A from the mother and A from the father. Given the genetic composition AA at this locus, the only gene that this individual can pass on to his off-spring is A, for this is the only kind of gene he has at this locus. Table 4-2 shows all the possible recombinations of genes at the ABO blood group locus.

Selection of Mates

Selection of mates is based on cultural factors and seldom involves genetics as a criterion. Nevertheless, genetics is involved. Individuals frequently use phenotypic expressions as a partial basis for selection of a mating partner. Mating based upon phenotypic expressions are of two general kinds: positive assortative mating and negative assortative mating.

Positive assortative mating is explained most simply as mating of like individuals. Such likeness is based on externally observable physical characteristics (phenotypes). A blond-haired, blue-eyed, tall male who mates with a blond-haired, blue-eyed, tall female is such an example. Negative assortative mating is just the opposite—mating of unlike individuals. In this case, a blond-haired, blue-eyed, tall male mates with a dark-haired, black-eyed, short female. In many societies throughout the world, and most typically in western societies, such phenotypes are an important part, and in some cases the only criteria, of mate selection. Since all phenotypic expressions are in some way related to genetic composition, genetic selection is being made whether the individuals are aware of it or not. Sometimes such selection may prove to be critical.

Brachydactyly, a condition which is expressed externally by short-fingeredness, is one example. Brachydactyly occurs in two forms: heter-ozygous and homozygous. A heterozygous (unlike) condition simply refers to the fact that the pair of genes at a given locus are different. A homozygous (like) condition is indicative of the fact that the genes occurring at a particular locus are the same. For the ABO blood group locus, individuals who have the genetic composition AA, BB, or OO are homozygous at this locus. Persons who have the genetic composition AO, BO, or AB are heterozygous at this locus. The heterozygous condition for brachydactyly can be expressed Bb (B = gene for brachydactyly and b = gene for the normal condition or non-brachydactyly). The homo-zygous condition for brachydactyly would be BB and the homozygous

Table 4–2

Genetic Composition of Mother	Genetic Composition of Father	Genes That Can Be Passed On by Mother	Genes That Can Be Passed On by Father	Possible Recombination of Mother's and Father's Genes	Possible Genetic Composition of Zygote	Phenotypic Expression of Zygote's Genes
AA	AA	A	A	AA	AA	A
AA	AO	A	A, O	AA, AO	AA, AO	A
AA	BB	A	B	AB	AB	AB
AA	BO	A	B, O	AB, AO	AB, AO	AB or A
AA	AB	A	A, B	AA, AB	AA, AB	A or AB
AA	OO	A	O	AO	AO	A
AO	AA	A, O	A	AA, AO	AA, AO	A
AO	AO	A, O	A, O	AA, AO, OO	AA, AO, OO	A or O
AO	BB	A, O	B	AB, BO	AB, BO	AB or B
AO	BO	A, O	B, O	AB, AO, BO, OO	AB, AO, BO, OO	AB, A, B, O
AO	AB	A, O	A, B	AA, AB, AO, BO	AA, AB, AO, BO	A, AB, B
AO	OO	A, O	O	AO, OO	AO, OO	A, O
BB	AA	B	A	AB	AB	AB
BB	AO	B	A, O	AB, BO	AB, BO	AB, B
BB	BB	B	B	BB	BB	B
BB	BO	B	B, O	BB, BO	BB, BO	B
BB	AB	B	A, B	AB, BB	AB, BB	AB, B
BB	OO	B	O	BO	BO	B
BO	AA	B, O	A	AB, AO	AB, AO	AB, A
BO	AO	B, O	A, O	AB, BO, AO, OO	AB, BO, AO, OO	AB, B, A, O
BO	BB	B, O	B	BB, BO	BB, BO	B
BO	BO	B, O	B, O	BB, BO, OO	BB, BO, OO	B, O
BO	AB	B, O	A, B	AB, BB, AO, BO	AB, BB, AO, BO	AB, B, A
BO	OO	B, O	O	BO, OO	BO, OO	B, O
AB	AA	A, B	A	AA, AB	AA, AB	A, AB
AB	AO	A, B	A, O	AA, AO, AB, BO	AA, AO, AB, BO	A, AB, B
AB	BB	A, B	B	AB, BB	AB, BB	AB, B
AB	BO	A, B	B, O	AB, AO, BB, BO	AB, AO, BB, BO	AB, A, B
AB	AB	A, B	A, B	AA, AB, BB	AA, AB, BB	A, AB, B
AB	OO	A, B	O	AO, BO	AO, BO	A, B
OO	AA	O	A	AO	AO	A
OO	AO	O	A, O	AO, OO	AO, OO	A, O
OO	BB	O	B	BO	BO	B
OO	BO	O	B, O	BO, OO	BO, OO	B, O
OO	AB	O	A, B	AO, BO	AO, BO	A, B
OO	OO	O	O	OO	OO	O

condition for normality (non-brachydactyly) would be bb. There are two genes at this locus, B and b, which may result in three possible combinations, BB, Bb, and bb. The phenotypic expressions of this combination are:

BB—severe skeletal disorder, semi-lethal, or lethal
Bb—short-fingeredness
bb—normal fingers

Persons who are heterozygous at this locus have the ability of producing all three types of offspring, whereas persons who are homozygous normal (bb) can only produce homozygous normal offspring. Persons who are homozygous for brachydactyly (BB) will not constitute part of the reproductive population since they frequently die prior to puberty. Table 4–3 shows the possible combinations at this locus.

Table 4–3

Genetic Composition of Mother	Genetic Composition of Father	Genes That Can Be Passed On by Mother	Genes That Can Be Passed On by Father	Possible Recombinations of Mother's and Father's Genes	Possible Genetic Composition of Off-spring	Phenotypic Expression in Offspring
Bb	Bb	B, b	B, b	BB, Bb, bb	BB, Bb, bb	BB—semi-lethal Bb—short fingers bb—normal
Bb	bb	B, b	b	Bb, bb	Bb, bb	Bb—short fingers bb—normal
bb	Bb	b	B, b	Bb, bb	Bb, bb	Bb—short fingers bb—normal
bb	bb	b	b	bb	bb	bb—normal

Phenotypic expressions are not the only criteria used to select mating partners. Many other cultural factors are involved, resulting in the exclusion of certain persons as mates, allowing others, and stipulating preferences for others. Rules of incest, a universal prohibition occurring in one form or another in all societies, preclude mating with particular persons in the society. In the United States, individuals identified as mother, father, brother, sister, cousin, aunt, uncle, daughter, son, and others, are non-mating partners. This is a cultural rule restricting mating, not a biological one. Nevertheless, recombinations of genetic materials of these individuals are excluded.

Phenotypic expressions and incest rules are only two of many cultural rules which function either to specify proper matings, indicate preferred matings, or prohibit improper matings. What is proper, improper, or preferred is, of course, defined by the culture. All of these will have a definite genetic result in spite of the fact that they are cultural rules of behavior. Cross-cousin marriage, parallel-cousin marriage, premarital or postmarital sexual activity, and other cultural stipulations that prescribe, prohibit, prefer, or in any way designate mating partners have definite genetic results. These genetic results are of two general kinds: an increase in genetic variation for the population or a decrease in genetic variation for the population. These two categories are of the greatest genetic significance for man in terms of his biological evolution.

MAJOR FORCES OF EVOLUTION

There are four major forces of evolution: *mutation, selection, hybridization,* and *genetic drift.* Each of these results in either an increase or a decrease in genetic variation for human genetic populations and for man as a species. Mutation and selection are operative in all human populations at all times, but hybridization and genetic drift occur only in certain contexts.

Mutation

Mutations are modifications, either physical or chemical, in the structure of a gene. They are known to derive from two general types of sources: internal sources and external sources. Internal modifications may be the result of biochemical action, or of physical aberration or rearrangement. External sources of mutations are probably more widely discussed. Such radiation agents as nuclear radiation, X-rays, alpha, beta, and gamma rays, and chemical agents such as mustard gas, formaldehyde, forms of nitrogen, and many others, are known to be mutagenic agents, that is, they can induce changes in gene structure. In all cases of mutation the general result is increased genetic variation—a new gene form is introduced into the population. When the mutation occurs in the somatic cells of an individual, it has no significant bearing upon evolutionary processes simply because it cannot be passed on to future generations, but is removed from the gene pool of the population when the person dies. However, when mutations occur in the germ cells of the individual, he will be able to reproduce the mutant gene and pass it on to future generations. One example of mutations occurring in the germ cells, frequently cited by physical anthropologists and human geneticists, is the case of Queen Victoria of England. These scientists believe the probability is high ". . . that the hemophilia occurring in the royal families of Europe during the nineteenth and twentieth centuries owed its origin to a mutation. . . . All affected individuals trace their ancestry to Queen Victoria of England, who, undoubtedly, was heterozygous Hh. Her father was normal, and nothing suggests that her mother was a carrier. Consequently, Queen Victoria seems to have received a new mutant allele *h* from one of her parents." (Stern 1960:449.)

Mutations are frequently harmful to the individual, but may be advantageous, in the long run, for the population. They are harmful to the individual because the phenotypic expression of the mutant gene can result in some deformity or malfunction, such as hemophilia. Further, the mutation does not affect one gene alone, but alters the complex relationships of that gene to other genetic materials. It was shown above (Fig. 4–4) that any given gene, at a single locus, can influence various phenotypic expressions. Indeed, because of the complex interrelationships among genes, any mutation has a high probability of being deleterious (harmful). Nevertheless, mutations are beneficial to populations in the long run, because they increase variability. The greater the genetic variety in a population, the greater its possibility for adapting to future changes in the environment. Evolution always occurs in relation to the environment, which is itself constantly undergoing change. Since the genetic composition of a population is the basis for its adaptation to the existing environment, any change in the latter will decrease the effectiveness of the adaptation—possibly resulting in extinction. Genetic variability therefore provides the population with insurance that it will be able to adapt to changing environmental circumstances. In effect, genetic variability, which is accomplished, in part, through random mutations, insures a higher probability that some segment of the population will have the genetic composition that is adaptive to future environments, whatever they may be. The occurrence of mutations in a population, by increasing genetic variability, "preadapts" a population to future change. That segment of the population having the genetic composition which is adaptive to the future environment will, on the average, produce more viable offspring. In this way, the new, successful mutations will become fixed in the population and will contribute to its perpetuation.

Selection

Anthropologists, geneticists, biologists, and other scientists agree that adaptation is the orienting factor in evolution; it is the process most responsible for the direction of evolution. Selection (or natural selection) is the process by which adaptation is achieved. Selection can never be considered meaningfully apart from the environment because it is the process whereby a population is adapted to its particular environment. The process works in two main ways: it selects for or it selects against particular genetic compositions in a given environment.

Selection against certain genotypes means the relative lack of viability of these individuals in their particular environment. This lack of viability is expressed in a number of ways: (1) The individual dies at or before birth and, therefore, is removed from the population. He cannot contribute his genetic materials to the population or to future generations since he does not reach the meiotic stage—he neither produces gametes, nor is involved in the fertilization process. In this case, the individual has a lethal condition and is selected out of the population. (2) The individual dies at an early age, either before he reaches the meiotic stage or shortly thereafter. He has a semi-lethal condition, is selected out of the population, and is also of no evolutionary significance for the population. (3) The individual reaches the meiotic stage, enters into the fertilization process, and produces offspring, but these offspring are not viable and die at birth or at an early age. In this situation, the individual has passed his genetic materials on to the next generation, but they are removed from the population at that time and have no long-range significance for the population. (4) The individual reaches the meiotic stage, enters into the fertilization process, produces offspring who live, but these offspring are not as viable as other members of the population; they are not as biologically productive, are subject to illness or disease, are less likely to be involved in the mating process, and so on; hence, their evolutionary significance wanes.

Differential Viability.   Selection for certain genotypes is the relative increased viability of individuals in a particular environment. Relative increased viability means that individuals have a particular genotype that is compatible with a particular environment and, therefore, are adaptive to the environment. They will survive longer, will produce, on the average, more offspring who are viable, and will pass their genetic materials on to future generations. They are extremely significant for the biological evolution of the population. Of course, viability of individuals in a single environment varies considerably. Not all individuals are as viable as all others; some persons have greater or lesser viability. For these reasons, selection is sometimes defined as "differential fertility."

The well-known example of sickle-cell anemia can be used to exemplify selection working against particular genotypes in a specific environment and, simultaneously, working in favor of other genotypes in the same environment. Sickle-cell anemia is an abnormal condition of the red blood cells, and results in sickle-shaped red blood cells as compared with the normal disk-shaped red blood cells. The individual with this condition is anemic.

Most sufferers from sickle cell anemia die in childhood. Those who survive have a chronic disease punctuated by painful crises when blood supply is cut off from various body organs. There is no effective treatment for the disease.

From the first, a great deal of interest focused on the genetic aspects of this peculiarity. It was soon found that some Negroes carried a sickling tendency without showing symptoms of the disease. This was eventually discovered to mean that the carrier inherits the sickle cell gene from only one parent. A child who receives sickle cell genes from both parents produces only hemoglobin S and therefore is prone to sickling and anemia. On the other hand, in a person who has a normal hemoglobin gene from one parent and a hemoglobin S from the other sickling is much less likely; such persons, known as carriers of the "sickle cell trait," become ill only under exceptional conditions—for example, at high altitudes, when their blood does not receive enough oxygen.

The sickle cell trait is, of course, much more common than the disease. Among Negroes in the U. S. some 9 percent carry the trait, but less than one fourth of 1 percent show sickle cell anemia. In some Negro tribes in Africa the trait is present in as much as 40 percent of the population, while 4 percent have sickle cell genes from both parents and are subject to the disease.

The high incidence of the sickle cell gene in these tribes raised a most interesting question. Why does the harmful gene persist? A child who inherits two sickle cell genes (i.e., is homozygous for this gene) has only about one fifth as much chance as other children of surviving to reproductive age. Because of this mortality, about 16 percent of the sickle cell genes must be removed from the population in every generation. And yet the general level remains high without any sign of declining. What can be the explanation? Carriers of the sickle cell trait do not produce more children than those who lack it, and natural mutation could not possibly replace the lost sickle cell genes at any such rate.

The laws of evolution suggested a possible answer. Carriers of the sickle cell trait (a sickle cell gene from one parent and a normal one from the other) might have some advantage in survival over those who lacked the trait. If people with the trait had a lower mortality rate, counter-balancing the high mortality of sufferers from sickle cell anemia, then the frequency of sickle cell genes in the population would remain at a constant level.

What advantage could the sickle cell trait confer? Perhaps it protected its carriers against some other fatal disease—say malaria. The writer looked into the situation in malarious areas of Africa and found that children with the sickle cell trait were indeed relatively resistant to malarial infection. In some places they had as much as a 25 percent better chance of survival than children without the trait. Children in most of Central Africa are exposed to malaria nearly all year around and have repeated infections during their early years. If they survive, they build up a considerable immunity to the disease. In some unknown way the sickle cell trait apparently protects children against the malaria parasite during the dangerous years until they acquire an immunity to malaria.

On the African continent the sickle cell gene has a high frequency among people along the central belt, near the Equator, where malaria is common and is transmitted by mosquitoes through most of the year. North and south of this belt, where malaria is less common and usually of the benign variety, the sickle cell gene is rare or absent. Moreover, even within the central belt, tribes in nonmalarious areas have few sickle cell genes.

Extension of the studies showed that similar situations exist in other areas of the world. In malarious parts of southern Italy and Sicily, Greece, Turkey, and India, the sickle cell trait occurs in up to 30 percent of the population. There is no reason to suppose that the peoples of all these areas have transmitted the gene to one another during recent times. The sickle cell gene may have originated independently in the several populations or may trace back to a few such genes passed along among them a thousand years ago. The high frequency of the gene in these populations today can be attributed mainly to the selective effect of malaria.

On the other hand, we should expect that when a population moves from a malarious region to one free of this disease, the frequency of the sickle cell gene will fall. The Negro population of the U. S. exemplifies such a development. When Negro slaves were first brought to North America from West Africa some 250 to 300 years ago, the frequency of the sickle cell trait among them was probably not less than 22 percent. By mixed mating with Indian and white people this figure was probably reduced to about 15 percent. In the absence of any appreciable mortality from malaria, the loss of sickle cell genes through deaths from anemia in 12 generations should have reduced the frequency of the sickle cell trait in the Negro population to about 9 percent. This is, in fact, precisely the frequency found today.

Thus the Negroes of the U. S. show a clear case of evolutionary change. Within the space of a few hundred years this population, because of its transfer from Africa to North America, has undergone a definite alteration in genetic structure. This indicates how rapidly human evolution can take place under favorable circumstances. . . .

For anyone interested in population genetics and human evolution, the sickle cell story presents a remarkably clear demonstration of some of the principles at play. It affords, for one thing, a simple illustration of the principle of hybrid vigor. . . . In a population exposed to malaria the heterozygote (hybrid) possessing one normal hemoglobin gene and sickle cell hemoglobin gene has an advantage over either homozygote (two normal genes or two sickle cell genes). And this selective advantage, as we can observe, maintains a high frequency of a gene which is deleterious in double dose but advantageous in single dose.

Secondly, we see a simple example of inherited resistance to disease. . . . Thirdly, the sickle cell situation shows that mutation is not an unmixed bane to the human species. Most mutations are certainly disadvantageous, for our genetic constitution is so carefully balanced that any change is likely to be for the worse. . . . Nonetheless, the sickle cell mutation, which at first sight looks altogether harmful, turns out to be a definite advantage in a malarious environment. Similarly other mutant genes that are bad in one situation may prove beneficial in another. Variability and mutation permit the human species, like other organisms, to adapt rapidly to new situations. (Allison 1956:88 ff.)

The Population as the Unit in Selection. Individuals may be adaptive to an environment at certain loci and non-adaptive or less adaptive at other loci. Adaptation to an environment is relative to the genotype of individuals at particular loci and to the total genotype. In all cases selection is operating. When a significant number of individuals in a given population are proved to be adaptive to the environment, a fact demonstrated by their viability, their ability to produce offspring, and their general success for survival, then the population is one that is adaptive to the environment. It is the members of the population who are the carriers of genes, who pass these genetic materials on to future generations, who produce offspring, who live, and who die. Evolutionary forces act upon individuals, but individuals are members of a large unit —the genetic population, in this case. As such, they make an individual contribution to the group, but it is the group which is of evolutionary importance, not the individual, and it is the group that is perpetuated; the individual is a member of the group for a limited period of time only.

The Role of Culture in Selection. The genetic contribution of individuals is not the only one that has evolutionary significance. Individuals, through their culture, have made non-genetic contributions which have had very important evolutionary consequences. The entire area of medicine is meaningful for human evolution, for increased medical knowledge has resulted in greater viability of the population's members and consequently in increased genetic variation. Hospitals, medicines, cures, and practitioners keep more people alive today than ever before. People who may otherwise die are provided with a greater possibility of reaching the meiotic stage, of mating, and of producing offspring of their own. Through culture (increased and more precise application of medical knowledge) these individuals are able to contribute their genetic materials to the gene pool of the population. They are of evolutionary significance.

Culture is extremely important in changing selective pressures of the environment. As man changes his environment through culture, so does he change the selective pressures. Eradication of malaria changes the selective pressure for the sickle cell gene. Once malaria is removed, the heterozygote person for this condition (Ss) is less adaptive to the new environment than a person who is homozygous normal (ss). Selective pressures for the new, non-malarial environment will be greater selection for homozygous normal persons and greater selection against heterozygotes.

The frequency of genes for some defective conditions has risen due to medical science. Stern (1960:633–34) suggests the relatively well-known conditions of diabetes mellitus, harelip, cleft palate, and pyloric stenosis as examples of this.

Other traits which used to reduce the likelihood of reproduction of affected individuals are harelip and cleft palate. These traits often appear together, since they may have a common embryological basis—the failure of lateral anatomic parts to grow together. Formerly, many infants severely affected by cleft palate died soon after birth on account of difficulties in feeding or as consequence of respiratory infections. Of those who survived and had less severe degrees of the defect, a number developed speech defects and minor malformations which reduced their chances of marriage or induced them to abstain from parenthood. Modern surgery has not only succeeded in keeping alive many affected newborns formerly doomed to death but frequently leads to aesthetically highly satisfactory repair of the congenital defects. In all probability, a rise in the frequency of the alleles controlling harelip and cleft palate has taken place in recent times.

Still another example of the fact that progress in medical procedures often results in the propagation of alleles which would otherwise be subject to selective elimination is the disease congenital pyloric stenosis. Occurring in from 2 to 4 of 1,000 live births, this condition is caused by constriction fibers at the opening of the stomach into the small intestine, owing to an extensive overdevelopment of the circular muscles. Before 1912, newborns who were affected with a severe form of the disease did not survive beyond infancy; but in that year an operation was devised which eliminates the condition, permitting the affected individual to attain adulthood and have children. Although the genetic details are not fully clear, there is no doubt of an important genetic component for the disease, probably a dominant gene with reduced penetrance.

Diabetes mellitus, harelip and cleft palate, and pyloric stenosis are relatively common defects. There are many others which are rarer when appraised singly, but which together add up to a considerable total for which medical knowledge and surgical skill have made possible not only survival but a normal life, including greatly increased chances of reproduction. This increased fitness of the bearers of abnormal genes, together with a presumably unchanged rate of mutation from normal to abnormal, is bound to lead to a higher accumulation of abnormal alleles responsible for the hereditary classes of such defects.

In addition to this general category, which results in greater viability of individuals and increased genetic variation for the population, man, through culture, can induce mutations in individuals which result in still further genetic variation, and, in some cases, possible increased viability for individuals. As man's knowledge of human genetics increases, an ever greater possibility of control exists. The entire eugenic movement has this very goal. Whether eugenic control will ever become fully instituted will depend not only on genetic knowledge, but upon cultural decisions, and whether instituted fully, in part, or not at all, there will be genetic and evolutionary ramifications due to culture.

Hybridization

This third major force in evolution also has the result of altering the genetic composition of populations. While logically a process distinct from mutation and selection, hybridization does not operate independently from these processes—rather, it complements them. Genetic changes introduced into one population through mutation, and fixed in that population by selection, can then be carried to new populations through interbreeding. Selection must again operate if these genes are to become fixed in the new population.

Hybridization, which is the production of new genetic combinations through interbreeding, occurs in most living species, including *Homo sapiens*. Hybridization increases genetic variation. In the case of man, however, culture again is a crucial factor. This becomes readily apparent when the factors that operate to bring populations into contact so that they can interbreed, or those that limit interbreeding between populations already in contact, are considered. The most significant non-cultural barrier to hybridization in man is geography—barriers like great distance, seas, rivers, mountains, or deserts. None of these barriers has remained completely insurmountable, however, as cultural advance has produced the techniques for overcoming them—horseback riding, the boat, the wheel, and so on. Migration has gone on continuously throughout human history, breaking down isolation and frequently resulting in the flow of genes from one population to another.

The decision to migrate, the reasons for migration (using this term for any movement of peoples), and the kind of contact situation that results are all cultural factors. The earliest European migrants came to North America variously seeking religious freedom, farm lands, commercial opportunities, or religious converts. The Spanish came to the New World seeking new wealth to support Spanish home institutions, but also seeking converts to Catholicism. Migration frequently is motivated by the desire for military subjugation, economic exploitation, and religious conversion. The impetus may be population pressure at home, necessitating new lands elsewhere. Migration is not necessarily always a deliberate or conscious process. Throughout the Paleolithic ages (Old Stone Age) of human history, man lived in small migrant bands which moved continuously in search of game. Increasing population density necessitated a gradual movement into new territories, but so slowly that people probably were not aware of any significant movement. North America was first populated in this way.

When new populations come into contact, interbreeding does not always begin immediately nor is it extensive. Again, cultural factors will be operative to restrict or even prohibit such miscegenation. Strong racial differences will, for example, limit intermarriage. If one group is dominant over the other, dominant-group males may have sex relations with subordinate-group females, the resulting offspring being relegated to the social group of the mother. Thus, gene flow will be in one direction only. A new immigrant group—for example, in a North American city—will often remain endogamous for at least one generation. Eventually, however, interbreeding does occur, producing hybrid populations and new genetic combinations.

The cases of hybridization in the modern world are almost innumerable. The population explosion and widespread migration of the past two or three centuries have left few populations untouched by interbreeding. Perhaps the most far-reaching effect has been raciation—the formation of new races. As the next section shows, race formation proceeds most rapidly under conditions where numerous small populations live in relative isolation from one another. Present-day conditions, where few populations are isolated, do not favor the formation of new races.

One important result of hybridization has been its effect on human evolution in the more distant past. Man's ability, through culture, ultimately to break down all isolation and maintain the flow of genes between breeding populations, has undoubtedly been a significant factor in his failure to develop into multiple species. Races develop into distinct species only through long-term breeding isolation. The number of hominid species extant at any point in man's evolution has long been a matter of controversy. Those who favor the view that there has never been more than a single species of man, or, at most, two or three at any time, have pointed to the crucial role of culture in promoting hybridization.

Genetic Drift

Genetic drift, also known as the Sewall Wright effect or the small population effect, is a process whereby gene frequencies change due to chance. The rapidity with which such changes occur is dependent largely on the size of the population. In general, the smaller the population, the greater the speed of change in such frequencies, and the more extreme the effects upon the genetic composition of the population. Genetic drift is suspected of being operative in all populations, but the results are more readily discernible in small populations and are difficult to distinguish in large populations. In small populations, an allele may "drift" out of the population completely (loss of allele), and, simultaneously, another allele at the same locus may increase significantly in the frequency with which it occurs in that population (fixation of an allele). In large populations, the results of genetic drift are expressed as slight changes in gene frequencies from one generation to the next. Figure 4–10 shows the differential results of genetic drift for the same allele in a small population and a large one.

The mathematics of this process as worked out by Sewall Wright are complex, but the basic idea can be expressed more simply. Genetic drift occurs in its most intensive form in a small, genetically isolated population where the frequency for at least one allele at a given locus is extremely low. Through statistical error and the factors of probability, this low-frequency allele may "drift" out of the population completely.

For example, if a small group of migrants leaves a larger parent population, they will carry with them a portion of that population's gene pool. Since genetics has nothing to do with who decides to migrate, the migrant group will contain a random sample of any given allele. Through chance alone, the small population will not carry that allele in

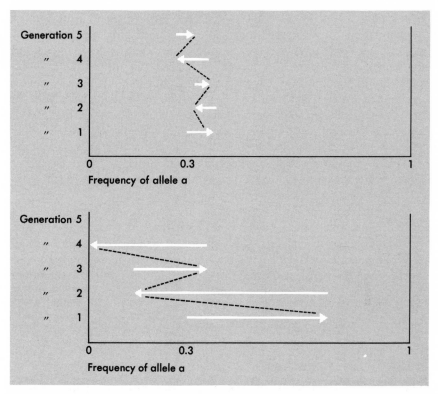

Fig. 4–10. Changing allele frequencies under the influence of drift. *Upper part:* Drift in a large population. Starting with the frequency of 0.3, the allele *a* increases slightly after one generation, and its frequency continues to fluctuate moderately in successive generations. *Lower part:* Drift in a small population. Again starting with a frequency of 0.3, the allele *a* drifts violently. After four generations, drift leads to the extinction of *a*. (From Curt Stern, *Principles of Human Genetics.* San Francisco, Calif.: W. H. Freeman and Co., 1960, p. 717, fig. 259.)

the same frequency as the parent population. Indeed, certain genes from the larger population may not be present at all among the migrants. This can be illustrated by using the ABO blood group locus, at which there are three alleles. If the hypothetical parent population is characterized by a low frequency for the O allele, then it is possible that by chance the migrant group will not include anyone carrying an O allele. At that particular locus the migrant group will be genetically and phenotypically unlike the parent group. However, the migrant population may contain a low frequency for this allele (O). If the frequency distribution at the ABO locus in the migrant population is 4 per cent O,

60 per cent A, and 36 per cent B, then the O allele may "drift" out of the population. If no new O genes are introduced into this small population, chance will operate in a way that will decrease the O allele and simultaneously increase the A and B alleles. All other things being equal, the higher the frequency of an allele in a population, the greater the chance for its continuance. Conversely, low-frequency alleles in small, genetically isolated populations have little chance of being continued. If this same situation applies, as it logically would, to many gene loci, there is a good chance that the migrants will, in a short time, produce a population that is genetically quite different from the parent group. Thus, through the operation of genetic drift, alleles can become lost to populations, or can become fairly rapidly fixed.

This process may well have been of considerable significance in earlier human evolution. For over 99 per cent of his span on earth, man was a food collector and lived in small groups which were parts of small breeding populations. Since small populations are most favorable for genetic drift, the result could have been a relatively rapid differentiation of local races. Their recombination through migration and hybridization would then have had the result of increasing the variability of the species as a whole. Unfortunately, because of the paucity of the fossil record for man's evolution, we cannot fully assess the importance of genetic drift in the overall pattern of human evolution. Gene frequencies refer to populations. Even if significant information of a genetic nature could be derived from fossilized bones and teeth, it would still require a much larger sample of fossils than will ever be available in order to make valid statements about the genetic structure of the whole population.

SUMMARY

The basic principles of genetics have been outlined, and brief discussions of each of the major processes at work in man's evolution have been presented. In this presentation a fact of paramount importance for understanding evolution was stressed: environment is of major importance for biological evolution, and culture is the single most crucial aspect of man's environment.

The concepts presented in this chapter were illustrated by research carried out on living populations—the Jewish ghetto in Rome, African Negroes, and so on. We must be much less specific in applying these concepts to early man, for detailed studies are not only lacking, but largely impossible. Nevertheless, genetic principles must have operated in the past as they do today. While the next chapter involves these same concepts, primary focus is upon the origins and evolution of man. The discussion of man's origins and evolution begins with the emergence of a hominid creature who had already achieved a bipedal posture and rudimentary tool use. Culture itself was just beginning to emerge and play a role in man's subsequent evolution. For culture to develop further, however, man's biological capacity for culture had to evolve. These things took place, in part, as a result of selection for more effective tool use. In short, once a rudimentary culture came into being, it became a crucial factor in man's biological evolution which, in turn, proceeded in the direction of a greater reliance upon culture. Culture is both cause and effect in this process, and its causal role cannot be understood without taking genetic principles into consideration.

5

The Biological
Evolution of Man

INTRODUCTION

In the preceding chapter we discussed the basic mechanisms of biological evolution. Long ago, Charles Darwin placed the study of man in the context of life in general. His knowledge of the mechanisms of evolution was not nearly as complete as that of today, but he established a principle which has not changed: the mechanisms of evolution apply to the whole of life including man. A study of man's evolution must, therefore, involve an understanding of the basic processes of life—mitosis, meiosis, reproduction, mutation, selection, hybridization, genetic drift.

Having placed man's evolution in the context of biological evolution in general, an important qualification must be added immediately: human evolution is not synonymous with biological evolution. In the first place, each living species has an evolutionary history which differs in its details from that of any other species. Thus, man's evolutionary history is unique in its details. More important, man's evolution differs qualitatively from that of any other species; there are factors operating in his evolution which are not to be found to a significant degree in the evolution of other animals. As we have seen, natural selection always operates with reference to a specific environmental situation; it works on the genetic materials of the species to fit it to its particular environment. Man's evolution differs in kind because his environment is unique. Sociocultural systems constitute for man an environment which is qualitatively different from that of any other known species. Articulate speech, tools, division of labor in economics, rules of exogamy, and religion, among other factors, are part of man's environment and have affected in some measure the course of his biological evolution. Culture did not come into being full-blown, but only gradually as part of the same process that produced *Homo sapiens*. It is this intricate, intimate, and mutual involvement of biological and cultural factors that makes human evolution at once so complex and so interesting, and it is primarily this concern with the cultural dimensions of man's evolution that distinguishes the physical anthropologist from the human biologist.

In this chapter we apply, insofar as is possible, the previously discussed principles of biological evolution to the evolution of man's family, the hominid. Our study will, of necessity, involve much speculation and inference, since the kinds of information necessary for detailed genetic descriptions of early populations are completely lacking. Practically all of our knowledge of human genetics is derived from comparative studies of the phenotypic characteristics of the living. Individuals can be blood typed, described in terms of other phenotypic characteristics (eye color, the secretion of blood antigens in the saliva, the presence of anomalies such as albinism or brachydactyly, or any other observable characteristic for which the genetic mechanism is at least partially understood), and pedigrees can be worked out (we can describe these same characteristics for the individual's family members). On these bases we can determine, by mathematical computations, the probable genes which are transmitted from generation to generation and which underlie phenotypic characteristics. We can describe entire populations or breeding isolates in terms of the mathematical frequencies for these postulated genes. The previous chapter presented in some detail the known genetic mechanisms for the ABO blood group and for brachydactyly. However, as soon as attention is shifted from the living to the dead—as represented by skeletal remains—the numbers of observable phenotypic characters with which we deal are significantly reduced, and our problems are increased many times over. For example, the genetics of the skeletal system are not well understood. Also, we can know nothing of the pedigrees of individuals represented by skeletal remains unless these have been recorded during the individuals' lives. We are, therefore, denied a powerful tool for genetic analysis. Finally, for older remains we rarely have more than fossilized skeletal fragments and teeth. With these formidable handicaps before us, can we say anything meaningful about early human evolution? We can confidently answer yes to this question.

It is a procedure of science to begin with what is known and then proceed to the unknown. An impressive body of knowledge concerning the biological mechanisms of evolution is available and is used as a basis for constructing a logically consistent theory of how evolution works. In addition, paleontology provides us with a nearly unbroken fossil record for many animal species that is highly consistent with our theory of evolution. If the processes of meiosis and mitosis as described in the last chapter accurately describe cell division as it occurs today; if genetic materials are subject to sudden changes (mutations); and if selection operates on genetic materials to adapt animal forms to their habitats today, then these processes must have been in operation 100,000 or 100,000,000 years ago as well. Like the pioneer geologist Lyell, we must assume a doctrine of "uniformitarianism." That is, those natural principles which can be observed at work in the world of today must be assumed to have been in operation in the past.

Our task, then, is to apply known evolutionary principles to the material we have available to us: the fossil record, however scant, and the natural environment in which those forms lived. The archaeological record, however, provides us with valuable supplementary information. The fact that early hominid forms used tools and that they relied increasingly on tools with the passage of time is significant. These are known facts to which we must apply known principles. If our speculations occasionally carry us a little beyond the known, this too is the way of science. These speculations are offered as hypotheses to be tested; they can always be refuted by the results of future research. In this way science validates its findings and its hypotheses.

The procedure followed in this chapter is to present the data available from paleontology, geology, and archaeology, and then to interpret these data in terms of a coherent evolutionary theory. This discussion includes the following major areas.

1. Man's so-called protohominid ancestor, and the environment in which he lived, is reconstructed. Information is derived from the fossil record, geology, paleoclimatology, and any other source of information or understanding available and directly pertinent to this reconstruction.

2. The evolution of the protohominids during the long ages preceding the emergence of modern man is traced. The accumulated fossil remains are arranged in a time sequence in an effort to determine the evolutionary trends that characterize this sequence. This procedure results in an outline of the main developmental stages through which man has passed in his evolution during the past million years or more.

3. Known evolutionary principles are applied to the known fossil record—a very general discussion, for reasons already given. The relationship between tool use and erect posture is the point of departure in this discussion. Next, the complexly interrelated processes wherein cultural factors first emerged and began to affect the course of hominid evolution are discussed. This discussion stresses how man's biological evolution resulted in an increased capacity for culture, and how this capacity in turn influenced the further modification of man's physical form in a mutually reinforcing way. By the time a fully human-appear-

ing creature emerged, articulate speech and all the other basic elements of cultural systems had made their appearance also. Rather than considering one factor—biology or culture—as simply the cause or the effect of the other, our stress throughout is on the "feedback" between these two processes. In fact, we show that they are two separate processes only from the standpoint of logical analysis. In nature they are a single process: *human evolution.* All these things are to be understood in terms of the operation of biological principles in a human environment.

TAXONOMY AND THE CLASSIFICATION OF THE PRIMATES

Most students will be familiar, at least in a general way, with the system of taxonomy whereby all living forms are classified or placed in categories on the basis of their similarities to other living forms. Such classifications are referred to as *phyletic,* because they are based on presumed phylogenetic relationships. That is, two or more species which are placed together in the same genus are assumed to be descended from a common ancestral form. We will concern ourselves only with those taxonomic categories most relevant to the study of man. One of a dozen or more very broad categories of animal life is that subphylum of the Chordata known as the Vertebrata or the vertebrates. There are five classes of vertebrates, including the fishes, amphibians, reptiles, birds, and mammals. Among the hundreds of thousands of living species which belong to the animal kingdom, man clearly falls into the latter class, the mammalian, because he shares with other animals so classified such characteristics as the manner of giving birth, the possession of external mammary glands, warm bloodedness, body hair, and others. The class of mammals includes many animal forms occupying a diversity of habitats and differing from one another very noticeably in size and outward appearance. A major subdivision of the taxonomic category class is referred to as an order. There are approximately 35 mammalian orders, among them the order of primates, which was given its name centuries ago by the great naturalist Linnaeus. This order is understood today to include all species, living or extinct, of men, apes, monkeys, and the rather tiny primitive creatures known as the prosimians. Figure 5–1 expresses, in greatly oversimplified form, the relationships commonly accepted to represent the living members of this order.

This classification, while it presents only living forms, is intended to reflect phylogeny, or evolutionary descent. For example, placing the families Hominidae and Pongidae under the single superfamily heading of Hominoidea, means that in the opinion of the taxonomist they are

SUBORDER	INFRA-ORDER	SUPERFAMILY	FAMILY	SPECIES POPULAR NAME
Prosimii	Lemuriformes	Tupaioidea		Tree Shrew
		Lemuroidea		
		Daubentonioidea		
	Lorisiformes	Lorisidae		Loris
	Tarsiiformes		Tarsiidae	Tarsier
Anthropoidea		Ceboidea	Cebidae	New World Monkeys
			Callithricidae	
		Cercopithecoidea	Cercopithecidae	Old World Monkeys
			Colobinae	
	None	Hominoidea	Pongidae	Gibbon
				Gorilla
				Chimpanzee
				Orangutan
			Hominidae	Homo sapiens (man)

Note: The reader will observe that no superfamilies for the infraorder Tarsiiformes, nor any infraorders for the suborder Anthropoidea are given. In taxonomic terms, the designations species, genus, family, order, class, and phylum are said to be "obligatory" ranks (Harrison, et al. 1964:17). That is, each higher rank must be subdivided into the ranks beneath it. Other ranks, such as suborder, infraorder, superfamily, or subfamily, are to be used only if the taxonomist finds that "not all the information he wishes to convey about a group can be expressed in the obligatory categories . . ." (*ibid.*). Thus, we do not have sufficient information about the Anthropoidea to divide this suborder into infraorders. A taxonomic system classifies things, and the accuracy of any classification will depend in part upon the quantity of things we have to classify. The fossil record for the Anthropoidea is very poor, and the living species are very few. Hence, we are unable to subdivide more accurately. A much more extensive classification than that given in the chart would be possible, however, especially for the Ceboidea and Cercopithecoidea, since there are hundreds of species and genera of monkeys alone.

Fig. 5–1. Classification of the order Primates.

more closely related to one another than to either the Ceboidea or Cercopithecoidea. The implication here is that living apes and man share a common ancestor more recent in time than their common ancestry with any monkey. The various superfamilies of prosimians, on the other hand, have a common ancestor which they do not share with the anthropoids.

Another way of conveying this same information would be by means of a "family tree." In such a diagram the living forms listed in Fig. 5–1 are the end products of evolution and are analogous to the top branches of a tree. If, therefore, we say that Pongidae and Hominidae are separate but related branches, we mean that, as we go back in time, they converge until they join as parts of a single ancestral branch. (See Fig. 5–2.)

But what do we call the ancestral branch, and how do we know its characteristics? According to Fig. 5–2, this is the hominoid branch, which gave rise to both pongid and hominid branches. We might reconstruct the features of this ancestral hominoid on the basis of a comparison of all living forms of apes and man, but such a reconstruction would be highly speculative in the absence of more direct evidence. The ideal situation would be to find a collection of fossilized skeletons representing this ancient ancestral form. But how would we

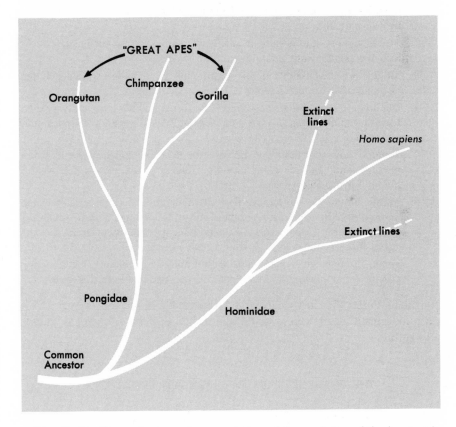

Fig. 5–2. General schematic presentation of the evolution of the hominoid line.

recognize this ancestor even if we should find it? We will take up below some of the problems involved in accumulating and interpreting a fossil record. We must add, however, that any simple family-tree type of representation of primate evolution should be used only to help clarify the relationships among different kinds of primates or primate fossils. It cannot portray accurately the enormously complex process of evolution. Further, we should stress that in the discussion which follows, we will concern ourselves only with the hominoid superfamily and, more specifically, with the hominid family and its divergence in the distant past from the family of pongids.

Recognizing that the student may become confused by the profusion of terms relating to different phases of hominid evolution, we offer the following clarification of terminology:

1. Hominoid(ea)—that superfamily of the suborder Anthropoidea which includes all varieties, living and extinct, of men and apes. It does not include monkeys.
2. Protohominoid—the earliest or ancestral hominoid form that gave rise to both the pongid and hominid families.
3. Pongid(ae)—that family of the superfamily Hominoidea which includes all living and extinct varieties of apes.
4. Protopongid—the earliest of the ape-like forms following their divergence from the hominid line. (See pages 106–07 for discussion of taxonomic relevance.)
5. Hominid(ae)—that family of the superfamily Hominoidea which includes modern man, and all ancestral forms following the divergence of the hominid and pongid lines.
6. Protohominid—the ancestral or early hominid form that gave rise to later hominid species. The protopongids and protohominids may be regarded as contemporary, each evolving in its own direction away from the ancestral form common to both—the protohominoid.
7. *Homo*—the only surviving genus of the family Hominidae. It is a matter of controversy how many fossil hominids are assignable to this genus.

It will be noted that in the text the formal suffixes -ea and -ae are often dropped, resulting in a more colloquial usage of terms—pongid, hominid, and so on.

THE FOSSIL RECORD FOR HOMINID EVOLUTION

Students of human evolution, or of primate evolution in general, commonly complain that the greatest handicap to their work is the sparsity of the fossil record. The only direct evidence of the early evolution of the hominids is their fossilized remains—usually of bone fragments or teeth, but sometimes of casts or impressions of these as well. Unfortunately for the primate paleontologist, primates do not often live in surroundings favorable to the preservation and subsequent fossilization of bones and teeth. Many live in the tropics, where decay of bones is far too rapid to permit the very slow process of fossilization. Consequently, the percentage of primate (or more specifically, hominid) individuals that become fossilized, in whole or in part, is very small when compared with many other creatures. The human paleontologist cannot help feeling a little wistful when he contemplates the vast bulk of fossilized remains with which the marine paleontologist, for example, can reconstruct the evolution of some of the marine species.

In addition to the scarcity of primate fossils in the earth's crust, there are practical considerations that militate against the scientist's finding more than a small percentage of them. A fossil does not become scientifically valuable until it is recovered, and its recovery is most valuable when it occurs under controlled circumstances. The context within which a fossilized bone or tooth is discovered can be as important as the object itself. Its location in the earth's crust may, for example, be the only indication of its age. An ancient tooth discovered in a Chinese apothecary (where they were once sold for medicinal purposes) cannot have the same value for the paleontologist as one uncovered under precisely known geological conditions. While salvage archaeological excavations, which precede construction crews, have increased significantly over the past 15 or 20 years, we can only guess (and most paleontologists would prefer not to think about it) the number of fossils destroyed each year by bulldozers and other construction equipment.

It must be stressed, then, that the fossil record of primate evolution in general and of hominid evolution in particular is not nearly as complete as we would like it. Many important questions remain unanswered and perhaps unasked. Only scant clues explaining the time or nature of the hominid divergence from the pongid line are available, and many of the fossils that have been recovered cannot be placed with any degree of certainty in man's own line of descent. Nevertheless, the fossil remains that are available constitute a very important body of data enabling the specialist to reconstruct the evolution of man much more completely than the non-specialist commonly appreciates. Understandably, due to the sparsity of the record, honest difference of opinion among specialists is frequent. They disagree on the age of a separate hominid line; on which fossils, if any, are ancestral to both hominid and pongid lines; on the relationships between specific fossil types, and so on. It is not our task in this book to resolve controversy among experts. Therefore, although we sometimes choose between alternative interpretations, we attempt no lengthy justification for our choices. At best, we caution the student when our choice of interpretations is controversial or doubtful.

The Dryopithecines

Our specific interest is in the Hominoid radiation, when the line or lines ancestral to the Pongidae and Hominidae separated from that of the Cercopithecoidea. However, the single most important group of fossil types for our consideration of hominoid evolution is that known as the Dryopithecinae. This term includes a number of finds from Miocene deposits in India, Europe, and East Africa. (See Fig. 5–3.) Some authorities would classify this group as a subfamily of the Pongidae, as shown in Fig. 5–4.

The Dryopithecinae are described as generalized anthropoids, that is, showing none of the later specializations of either the great apes or the hominids. "They were, no doubt, ancestral as a group to the present-day great apes, but what is more significant some of these dryopithecines and, in particular, the lower Miocene form *Proconsul*, could have been very close to the ancestors of the first hominids" (Harrison, et al. 1964:43). Carleton Coon (1962:199) states that all African varieties of the dryopithecines belong to a single genus, *Proconsul*. This genus occurs in three varieties, varying in size from a form comparable to a large gibbon to other forms the size of the modern gorilla, and dating from the Miocene in East Africa. They are generalized in that they resemble, morphologically, earlier and more primitive primates, but they also show some specializations to indicate that they were evolving in the pongid direction.

Many other dryopithecine specimens have been found in Europe and India, all indicating evolution in the same pongid direction. Some of these forms persisted into the Pliocene, the latest Cenozoic epoch, which began about 12 million years ago and lasted until about 2 million years ago. (See Fig. 5–3.) Whether these various specimens are to be referred to as protohominoids (ancestral to both pongids and hominids) or as protopongids (ancestral to the apes only) is not clear. They are not, however, regarded as protohominids (ancestral to man's line only) with one possible exception—*Ramapithecus*, a dryopithecine specimen found in India, and a more likely candidate for this status. According to Coon (1962:205), a detailed examination of the teeth, a fragment of the right maxilla, and the reconstructed palate reveals a more hominid-like specimen than the other dryopithecines. He suggests that India and China might well have been the breeding ground of the Hominidae.

It is apparent that while these Miocene dryopithecines were more

ERAS	In millions of years	PERIODS	EPOCHS	FOSSIL TYPE
CENOZOIC	(10,000 years)	Quaternary	Recent (Holocene)	Homo sapiens
			Pleistocene (Ice Age)	Neanderthal Australopithecus Homo habilis Zinjanthropus
	2			
	12	Tertiary	Pliocene	
			Miocene	Dryopithecus Proconsul
	25			
	35		Oligocene	Parapithecus Propliopithecus
	50		Eocene	
	70		Paleocene	Prosimians
MESOZOIC		Cretaceous Jurassic Triassic		Insectivores
	200			
PALEOZOIC		Permian Carboniferous Devonian Silurian Ordovician Cambrian		First reptiles First vertebrates
	500			

Note: The beginnings of mammalian evolution go back at least to the Triassic, and possibly earlier—200 million years or more into the geological era known as the Mesozoic. The separate primate radiation begins in the Paleocene Epoch of the Cenozoic Era, possibly 70 million years ago. Most of the fossil primate specimens dating from this very early period are identifiable, however, as belonging to the suborder Prosimii. Fossils representative of the beginnings of the suborder Anthropoidea are not clearly present before the Eocene, and possibly the Oligocene—about 40–50 million years ago. Numbers in the second column from the left indicate, in millions of years, when each epoch began.

Fig. 5–3. Geological time scale.

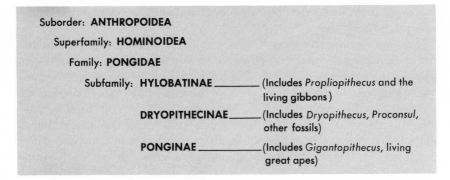

Suborder: **ANTHROPOIDEA**

Superfamily: **HOMINOIDEA**

Family: **PONGIDAE**

Subfamily: **HYLOBATINAE**———(Includes *Propliopithecus* and the living gibbons)

DRYOPITHECINAE———(Includes *Dryopithecus, Proconsul,* other fossils)

PONGINAE———(Includes *Gigantopithecus,* living great apes)

Fig. 5–4. Classification of the suborder Anthropoidea. (Adapted from Harrison, et al., 1964:25, by permission.)

ape-like than monkey-like in certain features of their dentition, they had not yet acquired what some authorities regard as the distinguishing features of the hominoid level of primate evolution—brachiation, or locomotion using the arms and hands. Whereas monkeys and prosimians go through the trees on all fours and jump from branch to branch, the apes are brachiators: they proceed hand-over-hand, suspended vertically from the branches, and if they walk on their hind legs, the arms and hands may be used for support.

Brachiation is commonly accepted as a necessary step in the evolution of erect posture, a step which ultimately freed the human hand from locomotor use (Brace and Montagu 1965:112). Brachiators have a chest, shoulder, and arm structure not found in quadruped primates (monkeys and prosimians), and the best explanation for the similarities between modern man and the living apes in these respects is evolution of the hominids from an ape level of brachiators. But there is no evidence whatsoever that *Dryopithecus* or *Proconsul* were brachiators. We are faced, in fact, with a long gap in the hominoid fossil record. "Somewhere within the ten million year blank of the Pliocene, brachiation must have developed among the Hominoidea" (Brace and Montagu 1965:120), but direct evidence in the form of fossils is lacking. Further, if man's ancestors shared in this development of a brachiating adaptation, then at a somewhat later time the Hominidae must have begun to diverge from the Pongidae to form what Brace and Montagu (1965:107 ff.) refer to as the "human grade" of evolution out of the earlier "ape grade." But what, precisely, distinguishes the hominid grade from the pongid?

Pongid and Hominid Divergence and the Principle of Taxonomic Relevance. We have already seen that the ancestral apes diverged from the monkey grade of evolution in their locomotor adaptation, that of brachiating. The living apes either brachiate in the trees (generally confining themselves to the lower, heavier branches), or move on all fours on the ground. They are, however, capable of progressing for short distances in a semi-erect posture. Brachiation is an adaptation to an arboreal life.

Man's ancestors shared in this development long enough to develop the shoulder, chest, and arm structure of the brachiators, but they then apparently shifted to a terrestrial habitat, and under new selective pressures gave up brachiating in favor of bipedal walking. Hominids are characterized by erect posture, in which the hands are not used in locomotion. We shall stress later that man's basic means of adaptation is culture, but to acquire culture he had to undergo many structural modifications. The basic structural adaptation making all of this possible was erect posture, which freed the hands for tool use; this in turn led to many other modifications in the structure of the skull and pelvis, in the size of the teeth and the shape of the face, in the conformation of the spinal column, and more. Therefore, in studying the fossil record and in assigning some fossils to the pongid line and others to the hominid, we must focus on those anatomical characteristics developed independently by the two lines.

A comparison of living man with living apes reveals many common features of anatomy and physiology which presumably have been inherited from a common, ancestral hominoid form. These features are what Le Gros Clark (1959:25) has called characters of common inheritance and would include the features of limb and shoulder structure adapted for brachiation. When these two forms of primate life began to diverge as a result of adaptation to different ecological niches, each began to acquire anatomical traits not shared with the other. These Le Gros Clark refers to as characters of independent acquisition. He goes on to show that as evolutionary divergence proceeds, characters of the first type (common inheritance) become progressively fewer, while those of independent acquisition become more numerous. It follows that in classifying fossil remains, and in assigning them to one line or the other, we should focus on the latter type of character. This is consistent with the "principle of taxonomic relevance" (Le Gros Clark 1959:11 ff.). To illustrate, let us suppose that we have found a new fossil hominoid and are uncertain as to whether it belongs to the ape grade or the human grade of evolution. The skull and jaw look very primitive, very "ape-like," but there is also evidence of erect posture. One taxonomist might be impressed most with the ape-like features and classify this form as a pongid. According to the principle of taxonomic relevance, the evidence for erect posture should place this fossil in the hominid line: the ape-like features of common inheritance would not be considered taxonomically relevant. Therefore, in studying the fossil record for hominid evolution, those specimens which have clearly diverged from the pongid line in the direction of modern man are considered most significant.

The principle is clear, but unfortunately the evidence is not always sufficient. Thus, due to the sparsity of the fossil record, it is impossible to set a precise date for the beginning of the hominid divergence from the pongids. We have seen that *Proconsul,* or the dryopithecines in general, is the likely candidate for the generalized ancestral hominoid before the development of the brachiating adaptation. But by the time the fossil record becomes at all clear we have arrived at the late Pliocene —about 2 million years ago—when a man-like creature was already in existence, perhaps having already evolved along his own separate lines for several millions of years.

The Australopithecines

Many of the specimens that constitute the fossil record were brought to light during the nineteenth century and in the early years of the twentieth century. None of this earlier material, however, represents the initial stages in hominid evolution. The history of the discovery of the fossil evidence for earliest man does not begin until 1924, when a young man named Raymond Dart discovered a small fossilized skull near Taung, Bechuanaland, in Africa. Although this skull, of an immature individual, was fairly certainly a hominoid specimen, it was not too clear whether it should be regarded as an ape-like man or as a hominid-appearing ape. Dart interpreted his find as an extinct form of ape intermediate between living anthropoids and man (Le Gros Clark 1967:16) and named it *Australopithecus africanus* (literally, southern ape of Africa). Dart's contention that this form had already evolved some distance in the direction of man met with severe criticism. The bulk of critical opinion seemed to favor the view that the specimen belonged in a taxonomic category with either the chimpanzee or gorilla, and that it was clearly an ape.

Ten years passed, following this initial discovery, before additional fossil finds of a similar nature were made in Africa. In 1936 another paleontologist, Robert Broom, made a fresh discovery at Sterkfontein, a site near Johannesburg in South Africa. This was a nearly complete skull (characterized by teeth of a human pattern and evidence that the spinal cord entered the skull at a point well forward) indicating or at least strongly suggesting erect posture. (Dart had made a similar claim for his Taungs skull, but on insufficient evidence.) Broom named his find *Plesianthropus transvaalensis*. Just two years later, Broom's researches were rewarded with another discovery, again near Sterkfontein. He named his new fossil *Paranthropus robustus,* feeling that a different genus and species designation was justified because this form had molar teeth much larger than those of *Plesianthropus*. The estimated brain size for the australopithecines, it should be noted, ranges from 450 cc. to 700 cc.; the *Paranthropus* types are in the higher range.

Once again, ten years passed before research on the australopithecines (as this material came to be collectively labeled) resumed. In the years following 1947 many new discoveries were made, again by Broom and Dart, the latter resuming his work in this field after many years. Broom's discovery, near Sterkfontein, of half of a pelvis (assigned by him to the *Plesianthropus* genus) was particularly important, because it confirmed earlier opinion that this creature had bipedal locomotion—it walked on its hind legs. In these same years a new site rich in australopithecine materials was uncovered at Makapansgat, about 200 miles northeast of

Sterkfontein. There, in 1947, Dart found material resembling his earlier *Australopithecus africanus,* but because of supposed evidence that this creature used fire, he christened it *Australopithecus prometheus.* In the following years, Makapansgat yielded great quantities of animal bones —mostly shattered fragments—of Lower Pleistocene age. Some of these bones, Dart believed, had been used as tools, and as a whole they were evidence of hunting activity, which to Dart meant that *Australopithecus prometheus* had culture. Again Dart's findings became the target of numerous skeptics, but the years since 1950 have produced increasing evidence of stone tools in the same time levels as the australopithecines. A claim is commonly made that the tools were produced by a more modern and as yet unfound hominid species, but this remains without substantiation today. It appears increasingly certain that Dart was right in his contention that *Australopithecus africanus* was a tool-using hominid.

There is now a very respectable body of fossil evidence assignable to Lower Pleistocene times (a half-million to one and a half million years old) which bears the label australopithecine. If we were to accept the taxonomic designations given each separate find by its discoverer, we would have to accept at least four genera, and six or more species of australopithecines. Taxonomists today, however, are more impressed with the similarities underlying all of this material than with what are regarded as relatively minor differences. The tendency has been, there-fore, to reduce the number of taxonomic categories. Thus J. T. Robinson (1963) speaks of only two genera—*Australopithecus* and *Paranthropus.* Brace and Montagu, expressing a view which we favor, recognize the differences between these two types but relegate both to the single genus *Homo.* This makes the australopithecines generically the same as modern man on the basis of their having had culture. These authors use the terms *Australopithecus* and *Paranthropus* to label substages in what they call the australopithecine stage of human evolution (1965: 224):

> Substage Australopithecus includes the finds made at Sterkfontein, the Maka-pansgat limeworks, and the original Taung discovery, to which we can probably add the Pre-Zinj child found by Leakey in Olduvai Gorge in 1960. Substage Paranthropus includes the Swartkrans and Kromdraai finds as well as Megan-thropus of Java and Zinjanthropus of Olduvai Gorge. All the indications point to the fact that Australopithecus occurred at an earlier time level than Par-anthropus, and we believe that Australopithecus is the logical ancestor.

The paragraph above refers to two finds not yet mentioned, the "Pre-Zinj" child and *Zinjanthropus.* These finds, made in eastern Africa in 1959 and 1960 by the Leakeys, are of great importance because of the age attributed to them. The first fossil discovery in this series was made by Mrs. Leakey in 1959 at a site known as Olduvai Gorge in northern

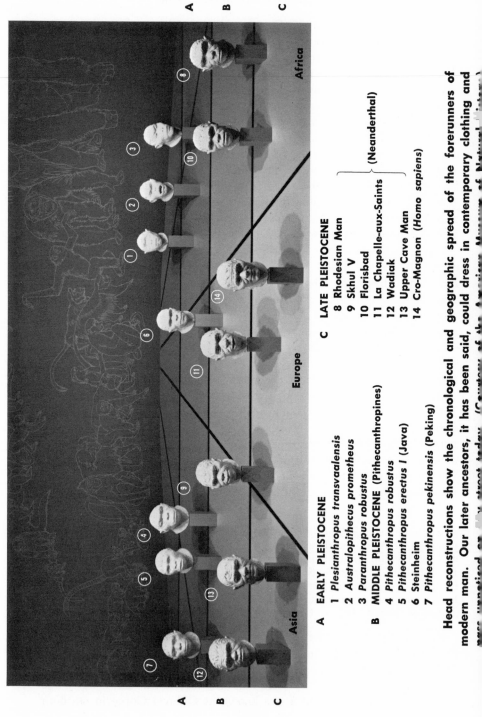

A EARLY PLEISTOCENE
1 *Plesianthropus transvaalensis*
2 *Australopithecus prometheus*
3 *Paranthropus robustus*

B MIDDLE PLEISTOCENE (Pithecanthropines)
4 *Pithecanthropus robustus*
5 *Pithecanthropus erectus I (Java)*
6 Steinheim
7 *Pithecanthropus pekinensis (Peking)*

C LATE PLEISTOCENE
8 Rhodesian Man
9 Skhul V
10 Florisbad
11 La Chapelle-aux-Saints } (Neanderthal)
12 Wadiak
13 Upper Cave Man
14 Cro-Magnon (*Homo sapiens*)

Head reconstructions show the chronological and geographic spread of the forerunners of modern man. Our later ancestors, it has been said, could dress in contemporary clothing and pass unnoticed on the street today. (Courtesy of the American Museum of Natural History.)

110

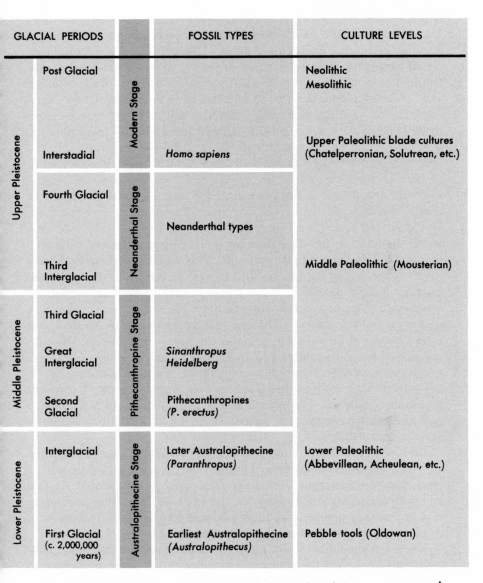

GLACIAL PERIODS			FOSSIL TYPES	CULTURE LEVELS
Upper Pleistocene	Post Glacial	Modern Stage		Neolithic Mesolithic
	Interstadial		Homo sapiens	Upper Paleolithic blade cultures (Chatelperronian, Solutrean, etc.)
	Fourth Glacial	Neanderthal Stage	Neanderthal types	
	Third Interglacial			Middle Paleolithic (Mousterian)
Middle Pleistocene	Third Glacial	Pithecanthropine Stage		
	Great Interglacial		Sinanthropus Heidelberg	
	Second Glacial		Pithecanthropines (P. erectus)	
Lower Pleistocene	Interglacial	Australopithecine Stage	Later Australopithecine (Paranthropus)	Lower Paleolithic (Abbevillean, Acheulean, etc.)
	First Glacial (c. 2,000,000 years)		Earliest Australopithecine (Australopithecus)	Pebble tools (Oldowan)

Fig. 5–5. Correlation of glacial periods, hominid evolutionary stages, and the sequence of cultures.

Tanganyika. It consisted of a number of fragments which, when reconstructed, constituted most of a skull. ". . . the discovery of the skull and the context within which it was found constitute one of the most important—if not *the* most important—single contributions to the understanding of human origins ever made" (*ibid.*, 205). The "context" referred to was the clear indication that the owner of the skull had manufactured tools of stone. Leakey had previously found a long sequence (i.e., covering a long time span) of stone tools in Olduvai Gorge, ranging from very ancient and crude "Oldowan pebble tools" to more finely made hand-axes. But, because no skeletal remains of australopithecines had been found in association with these tools, and since no tools had ever been found in the same deposits containing australopithecine bones, authorities were disinclined to grant these creatures hominid status. *Zinjanthropus boisei*, as Leakey named the new find, was clearly a tool maker. Geologically the deposits in which *Zinjanthropus* was found are of Pleistocene age. (See Fig. 5–5.) Since one million years was commonly accepted as the time span for the Pleistocene, Leakey estimated that this new find was 600,000 years old. This would seem to indicate that *Zinjanthropus* could not be ancestral to modern man, since the pithecanthropine finds of Java (see below), which were much more modern in appearance, were of approximately that age. However, the development of a new absolute dating technique, the potassium–argon method, has forced human paleontologists to revise sharply their thinking. The date established for the Leakeys' find by this new method is one and three-quarter millions of years, which would indicate that the Pleistocene age itself extends back much further than was heretofore believed. The reader should be cautioned, however, that the potassium–argon technique is new and subject to unknown inaccuracies. Not all authorities accept its age determinations.

In 1960 the Leakeys continued their activities and were rewarded with still further remains from Olduvai Gorge, from a slightly earlier level than *Zinjanthropus*. This "Pre-Zinj" child is represented by jaw and skull fragments and by bones of the left foot. The latter are important in that they provide additional evidence for the bipedal locomotion, or erect posture, of these very early hominids.

Leakey, it should be noted, no longer regards his first discovery, *Zinjanthropus*, as a direct forebear of man, but rather as an offshoot that became extinct. The Pre-Zinj material, on the other hand, he places in man's direct line of descent, and has named it *Homo habilis* (Le Gros Clark, *op. cit.*, 45). Not all authorities, however, are prepared to accept this conclusion on the basis of such limited information.

Taxonomy of the Australopithecines. There is a growing tendency among physical anthropologists to treat all of the above-mentioned fossil remains in the single major category of australopithecines. This is not a taxonomic category, however, and there is some difference of opinion regarding how this material should be classified. J. T. Robinson (1963: 385–416), on the basis of a detailed analysis of all the existing remains, postulates the existence of an ancestral australopithecine which gave rise to all later forms. This ancestral type had already made the anatomical shift from quadrupedal posture to fully erect bipedal locomotion, and was a vegetarian adapted to a wet climate. Robinson then goes on to classify existing australopithecine material into two genera: *Paranthropus* and *Australopithecus*. *Paranthropus*, according to Robinson's analysis of teeth and other evidence, was a vegetarian and represents a continuation of the ancestral line, little changed, in a wet environment. Therefore, he refers to the ancestral line as *Paranthropus*, and maintains that this line gave rise to the *Australopithecus* line. This came about with the inclusion of meat in the diet, and ". . . was a direct response to altered and altering environmental conditions. Increasing aridity over much of Africa, from which the vast majority of Australopithecine specimens are known, brought about the change in diet" (*ibid.*, 412). This change in diet, says Robinson, placed a premium on tool using and on increased intelligence. Thus, changed climatic conditions provided the stimulus for rapid evolutionary change, based on the potentiality inherent in erect posture and freed hands.

Brace and Montagu favor a somewhat simpler taxonomy of the australopithecines than does Robinson. They recognize the division into *Paranthropus* and *Australopithecus*, but do not treat them as separate genera. Their interpretation is as follows: the smaller *Australopithecus* is the earlier type and was not only using but making tools. He "must have possessed culture in order to have survived in the grassland environment which the fossil animal bones tell us was his habitat" (1965:226). *Paranthropus*, which is the larger of the two types, is then seen as developing from *Australopithecus*. These authors reject Robinson's interpretation (as does Le Gros Clark, *ibid.*, 63), that *Paranthropus* was a vegetarian. Thus, the two types are seen as substages of an australopithecine stage in human evolution. The various finds discussed above can be classified as follows:

Substage *Australopithecus* (earlier):
    Taung (*Australopithecus africanus*)
    Sterkfontein (*Plesianthropus transvaalensis*)
    Makapansgat (*Australopithecus prometheus*)
    Olduvai (Pre-Zinj child)
Substage *Paranthropus* (later):
    Swartkrans (*Paranthropus crassidens*)

Kromdraai (*Paranthropus robustus*)
Java (*Meganthropus*)
Olduvai (*Zinjanthropus boisei*)

Though based on admittedly sketchy evidence, if the interpretation of these authors is plausible, we can speak of an australopithecine stage —the earliest known stage—in man's evolution. It began at least in the early Pleistocene, or nearly 2 million years ago according to some potassium–argon determinations, and extended to about 600,000 years ago (into the Middle Pleistocene). We accept here the Brace and Montagu contention that these fossil types should all be classified as belonging to a single genus, *Homo*, on the basis of their most crucial adaptation, culture (not all authorities accept this interpretation). Whether *Australopithecus*, or *Paranthropus*, or any of the individual specimens should be classified as separate species does not concern us here. We do not believe that there is sufficient evidence to subdivide the australopithecine material into species, and, furthermore, such a classification is not important for our subsequent discussion of the biological foundations of culture.

The Pithecanthropines

One of the most famous fossil discoveries in the history of human paleontology, and one which predated Dart's first australopithecine discovery by more than 30 years, was made in 1891 almost halfway around the world from East Africa. The site was Trinl, a village on the Solo river in Java. The discoverer was a young Dutch physician named Eugene Dubois, who was stationed there as a health officer in the service of his nation's colonial army. In that year he found a "skull cap," having earlier found fragments of a jaw and a molar tooth. In the following year, in the same general area, he discovered a complete femur (thigh bone) and another molar. According to Dubois' interpretation these belonged to an extinct variety of chimpanzee, which he first named *Anthropopithecus erectus* (erect-walking man-ape). Later, on the basis of its skull capacity (about 900 cc.), he revised his interpretation to stress the nearness of this creature to man and renamed it *Pithecanthropus erectus* (erect-walking ape-man).

The skull of *Pithecanthropus* is low and "keeled," and is marked by a massive supraorbital torus, or brow ridge. The brain cavity of about 900 cc. is well below the average for modern man (about 1,400 cc.), but is much larger than that of any living ape. The jaw is massive, and lacks the protuberance which we call the chin. The teeth, though somewhat large compared with modern man's, are essentially modern. The rest of the skeleton, judging from fragmentary evidence, was not significantly different from that of modern man, and most anthropologists today would classify *Pithecanthropus* as belonging to the genus of modern man.

Another important find, or rather, a set of finds, was made at Choukoutien, near modern Peking in northern China. The bulk of this material was uncovered during a 10-year period beginning in about 1927 by Dr. Davidson Black, and later by his successors. The name given the fossil type represented by this material is *Sinanthropus pekinensis,* or China man of Peking (colloquially, Peking man). Actually, Dr. Black coined this term in 1927 on the basis of a single tooth, but subsequent excavations bore out his prediction that China would yield new evidence of fossil man. An abundance of fossilized skeletal fragments, representing several individuals, has been unearthed at Choukoutien. *Sinanthropus* looked very much like Java man (*Pithecanthropus*) in many respects, including the massive skull and jaw and the large teeth, but he lived much later, and his brain capacity exceeded that of the latter specimen. The capacities of various *Sinanthropus* specimens range from 1,000 cc. to 1,300 cc., the latter very close to the average for modern man.

Once more we face the problem of taxonomy and are confronted with the common tendency of human paleontologists to give each new fossil a different genus and species designation. Few anthropologists today would deny that the materials from Java and China are so similar as to merit at least a common generic designation, and many would even assign them to the same species, a view which we favor. Neither *Sinanthropus* nor *Pithecanthropus* is a good taxonomic term; we will retain these labels only for convenience when we wish to refer specifically to the China or Java fossils. Since we regard them as belonging to a later stage in man's evolution, one growing out of the australopithecine stage, we will follow the Brace and Montagu usage, and identify the stage with one label and the taxonomic category with another. These authors label this second stage in human evolution the pithecanthropine (1965: 233). Following an established usage, they name the fossil type *Homo erectus,* but this name admittedly has its shortcomings, since both the predecessors and the successors of the pithecanthropines had erect posture. To avoid confusing the student with a multiplicity of terms, we will omit discussing possible alternatives. Our principal concern, in any event, is with the general pithecanthropine level.

Homo erectus, or the pithecanthropine stage of human evolution, occurred largely within the Middle Pleistocene, perhaps one-quarter to one-half million years ago (see Fig. 5-5). This type evidently had a much wider world distribution than is indicated by the Java and Peking finds alone. During the past 60 years or more, a number of very ancient fossils have been uncovered in Europe and Africa; according to prevailing practice they were generally given separate genus and species status. Today many of these are seen as being essentially like *Pithecanthropus* and are, therefore, considered as belonging to that stage of man's evolution. One of the most famous is the "Heidelberg man," represented by a jaw discovered near Heidelberg, Germany, in 1907. It was found in a geological stratum of first interglacial or second glacial age (about 450,000 years old). Lasker (1961:112) finds that this jaw does not fit too well with either *Pithecanthropus* or *Sinanthropus,* and Brace and Montagu (1965:238) state that in the absence of a skull the assignment of this fossil to the pithecanthropines must be highly tentative.

In 1960 Leakey made yet another discovery at Olduvai Gorge, this in the so-called Bed II, which is geologically younger than the bed in which *Zinjanthropus* had been found. His 1960 find, a skull, was later supplemented by the discovery of jaws and teeth. Equally important, tools found in the same level were hand-axes which clearly evolved beyond the earlier pebble tools of Bed I. Brace and Montagu classify this later find as pithecanthropine, and regard it as clear evidence that australopithecines were ancestral to the pithecanthropines (*ibid.,* 207 ff.).

These two additional fossil types do not exhaust the list, but simply help indicate the wide geographic spread of pithecanthropines from early Middle Pleistocene onward. If the previous interpretation is correct—that the larger *Paranthropus* evolved out of the smaller *Australopithecus*—then the pithecanthropines show a continuation of earlier trends, especially in the enlargement of the brain. That is, man evolved an essentially modern skeleton with fully erect posture before attaining his modern size, while his brain was still only slightly larger than that of the gorilla. By the early Middle Pleistocene, man had attained a sufficient size, and his brain had evolved to such a capacity that it is no longer justifiable to classify him as an australopithecine. Due to the sparsity of the fossil record, this transition to a pithecanthropine stage seems sudden and dramatic. A much more complete fossil record (which we shall probably never have) would show the emergence of one stage out of the other as a gradual process with a complete series of intermediate forms.

The Neanderthals

Very probably, the mere mention of "Neanderthal man" will evoke in the minds of many of our readers a picture of an Alley Oop-like individual, perhaps walking along in a slouched posture, knuckles at knee level. Indeed, the very name of this much-maligned hominid has become synonymous with brutishness and low intelligence. The history of this misconception would take us too far afield, but a misconception it probably is. Neanderthal man did differ from men of today, especially in some of his varieties, but his brain had attained a fully modern size, and his tools show a progressive refinement of those of the pithecanthropine stage. In evolutionary perspective, Neanderthal man was a stage in man's evolution, intermediate between the pithecanthropine and the stage of fully modern man. Some writers are even inclined to grant him *Homo sapiens* status. While the fossil record is again scant, the cultural record becomes increasingly richer with time, and abundantly documents this picture of continuous, unbroken evolution.

The fossil record for the last 100,000 years or so of the Middle Pleistocene is unusually sparse, and so the record for Neanderthal man really begins about 100,000 years ago with the beginning of the fourth and final Pleistocene glaciation (see Fig. 5–5). Fossil remains attributable to this level of man's evolution are found over a vast area covering much of Africa and nearly the entire southern half of the Eurasian continent. There are, of course, noticeable differences between fossils in geographically separated areas. Modern man is an almost infinitely variable species, and there is no reason to expect that Neanderthals would not also exhibit great geographical diversity. Perhaps the most striking variant was first found in 1856 in a cave along the Neander Valley near Düsseldorf, Germany; it is from this type specimen that the whole series derives its name. Due to the completeness of the remains—a skull cap, thigh bones, pelvis, scapula, and fragments of ribs—it is believed that this was a deliberate burial. In later years highly similar materials were found elsewhere in western Europe, and less similar ones in southeastern Europe, North Africa, Palestine, Central Asia, and China. The western European type is best represented by a nearly complete skeleton found at La Chapelle-aux-Saints in France. Lasker (1961:101 ff.) describes this type as follows:

The skull has a capacity of over 1.6 liters [1,600 cc.], large even for modern man. The skull size has led to the assertion that Neanderthal man exceeds modern man in the volume of his brain; taking all specimens into account, however, Neanderthal skulls range down to about 1.3 liters, duplicating the range of the modern European populations. The Neanderthal skull is flattened down and has a large mound-shaped frontal torus over the orbits. . . . At the back of the head there is a backward extension of the occiput and an occipital torus. The foramen magnum, the hole in the skull through which the spinal cord connects with the brain, is well back on the skull base; this is associated with long single spines on the vertebrae of the neck—a sign of more powerful back muscles than are found in modern man. . . . The face is long and wide, with jutting jaws. . . . Neanderthal teeth are large and set in large jaws, but the teeth are completely human. . . . The chin is absent, and the jaws are robust with a wide area for attachment of the chewing muscles.

This type is sometimes referred to in the literature as "Classic Neanderthal," to distinguish it from other "neanderthaloid" types which lack the prominent brow ridge, vertebral spine, and other more primitive appearing features, and therefore look more modern. It is the generally "ape-like" appearance of Classic Neanderthals that has led many writers in the past to give them separate species status—*Homo neanderthalensis*. An artificial mystery of long standing has been, "What happened to Neanderthal man?" A general consensus has been that he became extinct, perhaps being wiped out by later migrants into western Europe. This is not the only possible interpretation.

As with other fossil types from earlier levels, Brace and Montagu have attempted to clarify and simplify the picture for Neanderthal man. Their discussion is based on a paper by Brace (1964:107–27) in which he defines Neanderthal as ". . . man of the Mousterian culture prior to the reduction in form and dimension of the Middle Pleistocene face." He presents the point of view that the massive facial skeleton, large teeth, and prominent brow ridges were early Neanderthal characteristics, and were much like those of earlier pithecanthropines. The teeth of these early forms were used for a variety of tasks later to be performed with improved and specialized tools. With the evolution of these superior tools, and with the adaptive significance of large teeth having been reduced, there followed a reduction in tooth size and in the form and dimensions of the "Middle Pleistocene face" (*ibid.*, 126).

Brace and Montagu (*op. cit.*, 244 ff.) go on to suggest that the only area in which the Neanderthals differed greatly from modern man was in the face, and "From the neck down, the Neanderthal skeleton is scarcely distinguishable from that of modern man. . . ." As to what happened to the Neanderthals, Brace (*op. cit.*, 126–27) suggests, ". . . it was the fate of the Neanderthal to give rise to modern man, and, as has frequently happened to members of the older generation in this changing world, to have been perceived in caricature, rejected, and disavowed by their own offspring, *Homo sapiens.*"

It should be stressed that this interpretation is not accepted by everyone. There are still those who see Classic Neanderthal as a relatively late offshoot of the main human line, doomed to eventual extinction. We favor the view of a Neanderthal stage of human evolution—again, because of its relative simplicity and because it takes into account the cultural factor. What archaeologists have called Mousterian culture has a wide distribution across southern Europe, North Africa, and the Middle East. A comparable level of culture (what Brace and Montagu call a "Mousterian-derived culture") is found elsewhere in Africa and eastward across southern Asia, covering the area of the so-called neanderthaloid fossil remains. We see no reason to accept the formation of separate and distinct hominid species within this area of relative cultural uniformity. In fact, we accept the point of view expressed long ago by the distinguished anthropologist Franz Weidenreich, that there has never been more than a single human species at any one time. Neanderthal in his early form was an evolutionary outgrowth of the pithecanthropines before him, and in his continuous evolution he eventually gave rise to modern man.

Modern Man

Neanderthal man and the Mousterian culture we attribute to him are both Middle Paleolithic phenomena. The dividing line between Middle and Upper Paleolithic times is, by definition, a cultural one: the end of Mousterian culture and the beginning of Chatelperronian and other "blade" cultures (see Fig. 5–5). For convenience, we use this same dividing line to mark the transition from Neanderthal to fully modern man, *Homo sapiens.* We say "convenience" because the transition was a gradual one. If Neanderthal became extinct at all, it was in the sense of evolving into a new species, and even this is not certain. In other words—and there are those who support this view—Neanderthal could possibly be classified as *Homo sapiens.*

Upper Paleolithic fossil materials greatly outnumber those for all previous ages, but evidence for the transition from Neanderthal to *Homo sapiens* is still scarce. The famous Cro-Magnon, first discovered in southwestern France in 1868, is generally regarded as belonging to the early part of the Upper Paleolithic, but the circumstances under which these materials (partial remains of five different individuals) were found preclude accurate dating. Nevertheless, the fossils were associated with remains of extinct animals and with Upper Paleolithic tools. Many other specimens from this period were also, unfortunately, discovered in earlier days under equally dubious circumstances. The reader should remember that the first clue to the age of any fossil is its geological context: if the fossil is contemporaneous with the earth layer in which it is found, then dating the earth layer may also date the fossil (barring significant modification of this layer). If the context is lost due to unscientific or accidental excavation, there is often no clue as to the age. To repeat, then, early transition to modern man is not well documented. For later times, from perhaps 25,000 or 30,000 years ago onward, the record becomes much more complete. Not only are fossils more abundant, but due to the practice of burial we more often encounter entire skeletons, and it is possible to present a fairly complete reconstruction of the appearance of Upper Paleolithic man.

It should be emphasized that man in the Upper Paleolithic was generally not identical in appearance to man of most recent times. Evolution has continued during the past 20,000 years or so. Existing fossil material shows that early *Homo sapiens*, like his successors today, was a highly variable species. In general, he was more robust than man today. His skull size, and therefore his brain size, had reached modern proportions. He had a vertical forehead and a developed chin, but his face was broader, on the average, than most recent man's. It seems likely that the part of the face associated with the teeth was more massive, and that a progressive reduction in dentition has occurred since that time (Brace and Montagu, *op. cit.*, 255). It is this reduction, as well as a somewhat less robust skeleton, that chiefly distinguishes most recent man from earlier *Homo sapiens*.

In conclusion, *Homo sapiens* may be seen to be the culmination of

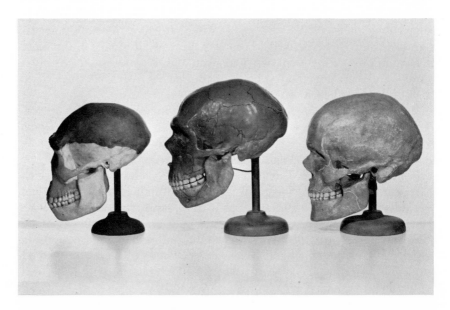

A comparison of the skulls of *Pithecanthropus* (left), Neanderthal (center), and Cro-Magnon (right). Note the evolution of human skull form—flattening of the face, reduction of the brow ridge (supraorbital torus) and sagittal crest, development of the nose and chin, forward placement of the skull–spinal cord junction (through the foramen magnum), and general reduction of the massiveness of the skull. (Courtesy of the American Museum of Natural History.)

a number of evolutionary trends which began over 2 million years ago. He can be described using the same anatomical terms with which we describe any other primate species. *Homo sapiens* is that hominid (or primate) species characterized by fully erect posture, bipedal locomotion, a vertical forehead, a high vaulted skull with a mean brain capacity of about 1,450 cc., a face which tends to be vertical with pronounced chin, a foramen magnum centrally located and oriented straight downward, cervical spines absent or rudimentary, and a grasping hand with fully opposable thumb. This is, of course, only a partial list.

THE MEANING OF HUMAN EVOLUTION

Man is a biological organism and a cultural being. Up to a certain point in his development, the evolution of man the organism was inseparable from the evolution of his culture. They were aspects of one and the same process—human evolution. Each aspect has been and still is a significant influence upon the other. Culture, however, has not always existed; it had to have a beginning. But with its first, rudimentary beginnings (themselves a function of the protohominid biological makeup), culture qualitatively transformed man's biological evolution. From that time on, culture became the crucial element in man's environment, and one to which he had to adapt. But the earliest men did not have the biological capacity for the complex cultures of later times; this capacity had to evolve first. Thus, the evolution of culture, and of man's capacity for culture, proceed hand-in-hand, as mutually reinforcing parts of the same process.

The Operation of Evolutionary Principles

In applying the principles of biological evolution to the known facts —the fossil record, the archaeological record, and the evidence from paleoclimatology—we make certain assumptions. Some of these have already been alluded to. The mitosis of somatic cells and the meiosis of sex cells characterized the growth and reproductive processes of primates in the remote past as in the present. Then, as now, the units of inheritance were genes, arranged in some kind of order along chromosomes, whose number was characteristic for each species. Random assortment of genes was an important source of variability in breeding populations. Genes were subject to occasional sudden changes, or mutations, which were the ultimate source of variability in any population. Selection, operating with reference to the total environment in which any population happened to find itself, favored certain genotypes over others. Isolation, gene drift, and hybridization are basic evolutionary processes which operated in the past as they have operated in recent times.

In the discussion which follows, selection in particular, but also isolation, drift, and hybridization are major referents. Mitosis, meiosis, and mutation are basic mechanisms (they go on all the time, in all species, and in any environment) and are treated as constants. Since frequent reference is made to selection, a word of caution is offered the reader at this point. It is all too easy to point to any characteristic of a fossil specimen, such as size or shape of teeth, bony ridges on the skull, or structure of the hand, and attribute it to "selective pressure." Natural selection does operate to fix and maintain any heritable character in a living population; it is not that "selective pressure" fails as an explanation. Rather, it is a constant factor, like mitosis or meiosis, and as such cannot by itself explain specific facts, e.g., why one species has small teeth and another species large teeth. Both are the result of selection, but to make the explanation more complete, other factors must be related to the character being explained. An evolutionary interpretation of the origins and development of man and culture increases in value as more facts and more kinds of facts are logically included as explanatory materials.

Man's Protohominoid and Protohominid Ancestors

Modern man is a hominid, according to the scheme of classification presented earlier in this chapter (see Fig. 5–1). He shares this classification with extinct ancestral forms going back at least to the earliest australopithecines, about 2 million years ago. The hominid line of evolutionary descent is distinct from the pongid line, which includes living and extinct forms of apes. As we work backward in time, tracing these two lines into the distant past, they converge—according to the commonly accepted theory—into a single ancestral form. This form, which we call the hominoid, or protohominoid, is best represented in the fossil record by the dryopithecines of Africa and Asia. This Miocene form (about 20 million years ago) had already diverged from the cercopithecoid line (Old World monkeys), but had not yet developed the distinctive specializations characteristic of the later pongid and hominid radiations.

What was this protohominoid ancestor like? He had already acquired important anatomical characteristics which, with further modifications, would become crucial to his future way of life. He was, in the terminology of Napier (1962:60), a tree-climber as opposed to a tree-runner. The early tree-running primates depended on sharp claws in moving about in the trees. The living tree-shrew is representative of this very primitive stage in primate evolution. A later development, dating possibly from mid-Eocene times (about 55 million years ago), was that of prehensility, or the ability to wrap elongated fingers around an object or a branch. This ability is to be seen, first and foremost, as an adaptation to arboreal life. Our protohominoid ancestors most probably had this characteristic: "In *Proconsul,* of the early to middle Miocene of 20 million years ago, the fossil record discloses a fully developed tree-climbing primate. His hand was clearly prehensile" (*ibid.*).

What else may be said of this ancestral type, as represented by *Proconsul* in the fossil record? Hockett and Ascher (1964:135–68) have attempted a detailed reconstruction of the protohominoids in which they stress the important point that these creatures stemmed from arboreal ancestors from whom they inherited such important preadaptations to ground dwelling as keen vision, freely movable arms with manipulative hands, and a larger brain. They are described as small, hairy, tailless animals. They probably showed little sexual dimorphism (little difference in body size between male and female), and they were diurnal (searched for food by daylight) and nested by night in the trees.

Their constant search for food often took them to the ground. Their bipedalism, like that of present-day gorillas, was infrequent, but standing erect permitted them to look above tall grasses, and their keen stereoscopic vision, which developed during their arboreal life, must have been an advantage. They were capable of some tool use and possibly even modified their tools as chimpanzees are observed to do today. Hockett and Ascher speculate that these protohominoids were largely vegetarians, but that they consumed some insects, hunted slow game, and perhaps scavenged. They also assume that some form of intragroup coordination was necessary for collective activities such as hunting. This coordination could have been affected by some form of communication, probably a call system. A call system, like that of present-day gibbons, consists of a limited number of vocal signals, each an appropriate response to a recurrent and biologically important situation (e.g., the approach of predators). A call system is not a language, but human speech must have eventually evolved out of such a system.

Livingston (1962:301–15) sees this protohominoid ancestor as a "generalized ape" living on the fringes of the tropical forest when the forest area was already shrinking due to widespread dessication. Like the modern gorilla, he was not a true brachiator (the gorilla lives largely on the ground, but uses his arms and hands to support himself when in the trees), and could rise to a bipedal posture for attack or for self-defense. This behavior, says Livingston, would preadapt this form to the carnivorous, bipedal, open grassland ecological niche which later hominids apparently occupied. His use of forelimbs while standing erect would also have preadapted him for tool use. Natural selection for a changing way of life would then explain changes in the lower limbs for erect posture and the use of forelimbs for holding tools in predation.

It seems likely that the terrestrial phase of human evolution followed on the heels of *Proconsul*. At that time, it is well known, the world's grasslands expanded enormously at the expense of the forests. By the end of the Miocene, 15 million years ago, most of the prototypes of the modern plains-living forms had appeared. During this period, apparently, the hominids also deserted their original forest habitats to take up life on the savanna, where the horizons were figuratively limitless. (Napier 1962:61.)

Livingston, and Hockett and Ascher, see this dessication of eastern Africa as giving rise to two basic radiations—the pongid and the hominid —from the ancestral protohominoids. The operation of mutation, selection, and other biological mechanisms on the genetic materials of the plains dwellers resulted in an evolutionary movement in the hominid direction. Adaptation to the new environment was the crucial process. The same mechanisms, acting on the same genetic materials in a different natural environment (the forest and forest fringes), resulted in the divergent, pongid line of development. In short, those large primates that remained in or near the trees evolved into the modern apes. Those that left the trees became protohominid bipeds, ancestral to later hominids. With prehensile hands freed from the requirements of locomotion, they began to follow a unique course of development.

Bipedalism and Tool Use. Just how and why the protohominid line left the trees for open grassland remains a major problem. There was probably, before the divergence of this line, more than a single protohominoid species occupying the transitional woodland–grassland environment, and these species were in competition for food. The smaller varieties probably were pushed to the edges of the groves and, occasionally, out into the grasslands. The problem of how and why this should have required the development of bipedalism remains a perplexing one. Hockett and Ascher invoke what they call Romer's Rule to explain this adaptive change (*ibid.*, 137):

> *The initial survival value of a favorable innovation is conservative, in that it renders possible the maintenance of a traditional way of life in the face of changed circumstances.*

The favorable innovation referred to is bipedalism, and the authors argue that this new adaptation was conservative in that it facilitated movement from one grove of trees to another. In other words, these protohominids were not "trying" to move into a grassland ecological niche; rather, they were trying to maintain a woodland way of life. But why would bipedalism facilitate movement from grove to grove?

Couldn't these animals have moved just as effectively and more rapidly in a quadrupedal posture? The answer would appear to be that bipedalism and erect posture freed the hands for the carrying and use of tools. The grasping function, we have seen, evolved during the proto-hominids' life in the trees, when the hands were used in locomotion. The hands had, in other words, been preadapted for tool use. Hockett and Ascher point out that the ability to carry and use tools would have been of great value to the early hominids.

DeVore and Washburn (1963:335–67), in their study of baboon social life, have shown what an enormous advantage would accrue to baboon

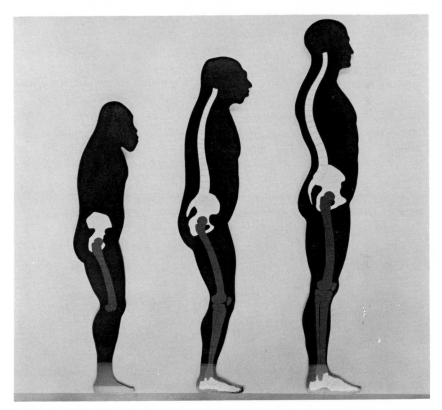

To walk habitually in an erect posture required profound modifications of the human skeleton, particularly in the pelvic region. The transition from *Australopithecus* (left) to Neanderthal (center) to modern man (right) is marked by a broadening of the iliac crest and a corresponding shortening of the ischium, giving the support and mobility needed in bipedalism. (Courtesy of the American Museum of Natural History.)

troops in their quest for food from the ability to use a simple digging stick. They suggest that the early hominids' environment was much like that of present-day baboons, and that they exploited much the same food resources. Thus, bipedalism and the ability to carry such simple tools as wooden sticks or sharp stones had survival value. The total environment in which these protohominids lived, their genetic materials and phenotypes, the survival value of improved tool use, and the continued occurrence of genetic mutations and selection automatically operated to bring about the evolution of a physical structure better adapted to bipedal locomotion.

But what of the hand, which was certainly crucial in the evolution of tool using? Is it sufficient to say that a prehensile hand developed during arboreal life and was later adapted to tool use? As Napier has shown (*op. cit.*, 56), human anatomists have traditionally favored the view that modern man has a "primitive, generalized" hand, which differs little from that of the monkeys or from that of the protohominoids of many millions of years ago. It is man's more highly evolved brain and nervous system, according to this view, that makes possible intricate tool use. Napier's researches, supported by new fossil material, especially that of *Zinjanthropus,* have shown a progressive evolution of the hand in the direction of complete opposability. An opposable thumb is one that can rotate across the palm, so that the ball of the thumb can touch, or oppose itself to, the fleshy tips of the other fingers.

Proconsul, says Napier, had an imperfectly opposable thumb. The Leakeys found, at Olduvai Gorge, some 15 hand bones of *Zinjanthropus.* These are evidence of a hand quite different from that of modern man in some respects, but different from that of the apes in other important respects. The thumb was opposable, and the hand was clearly capable of manufacturing the crude pebble tools found in the same deposits. Napier suggests, however, that this hand lacked the development for the precise movements required to make the more advanced tools found later in the archaeological record. Finally, the pongid hand shows an evolutionary specialization in quite another direction, that of brachiation. The bones of the hand would, in short, be most taxonomically relevant in consigning later fossil types to either the pongid or the hominid line. Unfortunately, these bones are rarely preserved.

Hockett and Ascher (*op. cit.*) have suggested that as a by-product of bipedalism and the freed hand, there was selection for memory and foresight. The ability of men to hunt cooperatively would have increased the quantity of meat in their diet. Game animals provide sufficient food to permit sharing (something which cannot occur when animals forage individually, with each small item of food going directly into the mouth), and the sharing of food would have been a step in the socialization of the hominids. It was probably during this time, also, that language evolved out of a primate call system, and our ancestors became men.

This is getting ahead of the story, however, and some of these developments could not have come about until much later—possibly not until pithecanthropine times. The entire process of evolution from protohominoid to protohominid to later hominid was a gradual and a complex one, and must have taken several millions of years from the time the pongid and hominid lines diverged. Washburn (1960:1–15), addressing himself to the problem of the specific evolutionary processes involved in this transition from early hominid to *Homo*, makes an important point: "It was the success of the simplest tools that started the whole trend of human evolution and led to the civilizations of today" (*ibid.*, 3). Until recently, many anthropologists were of the view that man had to evolve almost to his present form before he was capable of tool use. The discovery in eastern Africa of crude pebble tools in association with the bones and teeth of an ancient protohominid has forced us to revise this opinion.

Now it appears that man-apes—creatures able to run but not yet walk on two legs, and with brains no larger than those of apes now living—had already learned to make and to use tools. It follows that the structure of modern man must be the result of the change in the terms of natural selection that came with the tool-using way of life. (*Ibid.*, 3.)

The first well-documented phase of hominid evolution, as revealed by the Leakeys' finds at Olduvai Gorge, is that of a very small man-ape (Washburn's term for the australopithecines) who was small-brained, plains-living, tool-making, and a hunter of small animals. He was adapted more for bipedal running than for walking, in the opinion of Washburn (*ibid.*, 7 ff.), who maintains that bipedal walking is primarily an adaptation for covering long distances, and is essential for efficient hunting. The fossil record shows that this did not happen until about 500,000 years ago, by which time man was an effective hunter of large animals. Nevertheless, because of their limited bipedalism, the early man-apes had their hands free to carry and use tools. The advantages conferred upon them by tools led to more efficient bipedalism and more efficient tool use. Each of these factors—bipedalism and tool use—is both a cause and an effect of the other, because in natural selection cause and effect are interrelated. It has been suggested by various writers that bipedalism alone, without some compensating factor, would have been of no advantage to the australopithecines. They lacked the speed to escape danger, and their jaws and teeth were not powerful enough for defense against predators. These creatures would have been poorly adapted for survival without tools. "It may be, then, that the development of culture and erect posture were necessarily related occurrences, and that the earliest recognizable hominids are therefore the earliest possible men" (Brace, 1962:344).

A first trend, then, in human evolution, and one inseparable from cultural origins, was the assumption of fully erect posture. This development was probably well under way in the Pliocene, and was the first of the distinctively hominid characteristics to come into being. The primary skeletal evidence for erect posture is the pelvic structure of the australopithecines. "No part of the postcranial skeleton shows a more marked contrast between the modern anthropoid apes and modern man than the bony pelvis. In the former it is constructed on the same common pattern as that of quadrupedal mammals in general. In *Homo sapiens* it has become profoundly modified in adaptation to an erect

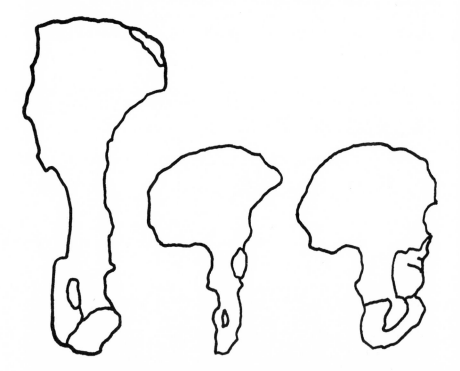

Fig. 5–6. Pelvic bones of ape (left), australopithecine (center) and man (right), showing differences between quadruped and biped. Upper part of human pelvis is wider and shorter than that of apes. Lower part of australopithecine pelvis resembles that of ape: upper part resembles that of man. (Copyright © 1960 by Scientific American, Inc. All rights reserved.)

posture and a bipedal gait" (Le Gros Clark, 1967:87). The available australopithecine pelvis bones show several significant differences from those of modern man, but they are clearly hominid in their general configuration (*ibid.*, 91). There can be no question then, on the basis of pelvic information alone, that the early australopithecines had erect posture. (See Fig. 5–6.)

Dentition and the Skull. Another trend in hominid evolution which was directly related to erect posture and tool use was a reduction in the size of the dentition and of the face. In the apes and monkeys in general, the males have large canine teeth and powerful jaw muscles. These have a defensive function that is of utmost importance to the survival of ground-dwelling apes and monkeys. Washburn (*op. cit.*, 9) reports having seen male baboons drive off cheetahs and dogs, and cites other reports of leopards having been put to flight. The australopithecines, who were plains dwellers, lacked these large canine teeth. The defensive functions of the teeth had already been taken over by tools. Since evolution is a very slow process, this would suggest that the hominids had been using tools for a very long time. (This fact would seem to lend support to the potassium–argon date of 1.75 million years for the "Pre-Zinj" fossil of Olduvai Gorge.) With increased reliance upon tools for defensive purposes, there was no further maintenance selection for large canines, and random variation resulted in a gradual reduction in their size.

Teeth are only one aspect of the total morphology of the skull, and any change in their size must be accompanied by corresponding changes elsewhere in the skull and face. Thus, the massive dentition of male apes and monkeys is related to such things as the length and robustness of the jaw, the size and configuration of facial bones, facial musculature, and the skull in general. Large, powerful jaws require heavy musculature, and this in turn must be attached to the face and skull at various points. In the gorilla, for example, the zygomatic arch (cheek bones) is extremely large; there is a massive supraorbital and occipital torus; and the attachment of muscles at the top of the skull results in a saggital crest. Further, according to Washburn, animals that fight with their jaws and teeth also develop powerful neck muscles. Therefore, reduction in size of the teeth had to be accompanied by changes in those parts of the skull and facial morphology related to the use of the teeth. The jaw became shortened, and the reduced musculature resulted in the reduction of various bony ridges on the skull. The result was a skull much more human in appearance. (See Fig. 5–7.) "The skull of the man-ape is that of an ape that has lost the structure for effective fighting with its teeth" (*ibid.*, 9). Washburn goes on to show that the hands took

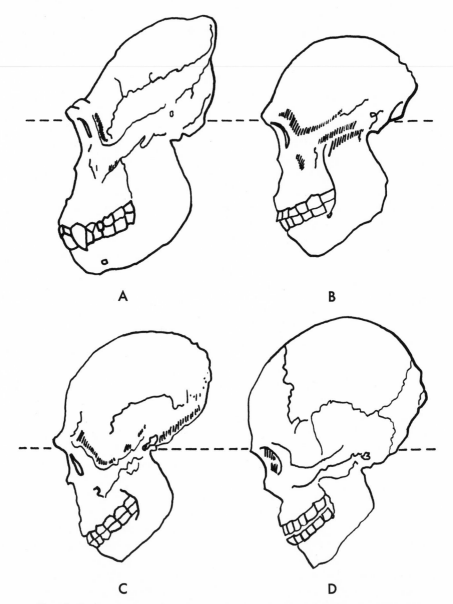

Fig. 5–7. Evolution of skull from ape (A) to australopithecine (B) to ancient man (C) to modern man (D) involves an increase in size of brain case (part of skull above broken lines) and a corresponding decrease in size of face (part of skull below broken lines). Note size of canines, zygomatic arch, supraorbital torus, and occipital torus in ape skull. (Copyright © 1960 by Scientific American, Inc. All rights reserved.)

over other functions of the teeth, such as seizing and pulling, thus resulting in reduced size of the incisor teeth.

The use of tools apparently did not replace any of the functions of the molar teeth, which are employed in grinding. The molar teeth of the australopithecines were large, and human molars continued to be large until very late in man's evolution. The reason for the eventual decrease in size appears to be the lack of positive selection for large size. That is, had large molars continued to be of value to the hominids in adapting to their environment, then continued selection would have maintained their size. It may well be that man's acquisition of fire, and the subsequent cooking of food, were factors in the decline of selective advantage in large molar size.

Brain Size. Another important biological change in the early hominids, also related to their changing way of life, was that of increased brain size. The rapid growth of the brain, which resulted in the achievement of fully modern size, was a very late development. The australopithecines, it was seen earlier in this chapter, had very small brains. Nevertheless, there is reason to believe that some growth did occur from protohominid times to the emergence of the pithecanthropines. The gradual evolution of tool using was achieved through the evolution of the hand and thumb, and perhaps of eye–hand coordination. But these could not be achieved without some corresponding evolution in the brain, especially in the size of the cortex. "The selection pressures that favored a large thumb also favored a large cortical area to receive sensations from the thumb and to control its motor activity" (*ibid.*, 13).

Similar reasoning could apply to other areas of the brain. An expanded cortex would have been required for the development of a variety of motor skills employed in tool making, tool use, and hunting. Large areas of the human cortex are also related to such intellectual activities as memory, foresight, planning, symbolization, and the language that is based on symbol using. These are, Washburn points out, the mental activities which make human social life possible. Much has been written, mostly in a highly speculative vein, about the social life of early man and the transition from primate to human social life. A full treatment of this complex subject lies beyond the scope of this chapter, and the following brief discussion necessarily does not take into account all that is known of primate sociology.

EVOLUTION OF HOMINID SOCIAL LIFE

Social life is important to the survival of all primates. There have been many studies in recent years of the social behavior of apes and monkeys in their "wild" condition. Social organization among primates differs widely from one species to another, varying with such factors as the size of the animal, reproductive physiology, degree of sexual dimorphism, whether the species lives in open grassland, on the forest floor, or high in the trees, the presence or absence of predators, or the nature of the food supply. Whether the group consists of a single mating pair and their offspring (gibbons), of a troop of a dozen or so individuals (gorilla or chimpanzee), or of a horde of upwards of 50 individuals (baboons and many other species of monkeys), it is clear that group organization serves a number of needs.

Primates enjoy the company of their fellows; an excellent illustration is to be seen in the social grooming that is found among many species. A gibbon, for example, will present his back to a member of his group, expecting him to explore his coat removing lice and dirt or flakes of dead skin. After a time the positions are reversed so that the other can, in turn, enjoy the process. Protection is another function of the primate band, and is especially crucial to those species subject to attack by predators. DeVore and Washburn (1963) show how a baboon troop on the move will group itself so as to afford maximum protection to infants and juveniles. If attacked by a predator, the dominant males will fall back to meet the threat. Survival of the individual members of the group depends on the continuous presence of adult males.

Human Social Life

Human social life differs from that of subhuman primates in a number of very important respects, perhaps the most important being that the human group is a cooperative organization. Cooperation, as we employ the term, refers to planned, concerted action toward a conscious shared goal. This definition would exclude the behavior of the social insects because their behavior is not planned and there is no consciousness of a goal even though action is concerted. By this same definition, subhuman primate social behavior is lacking in the cooperative principle. Lower primates are, of course, capable of concerted action, and this was undoubtedly an important precondition for the evolution of true cooperative behavior. Some significant parallels may be observed:

1. The primate ability to manipulate objects as tools provided the basis for the emergence of human tool using.
2. The capacity of primates to communicate through the use of a call system was probably a precondition for the development of language.
3. The primate capacity for engaging in concerted action provided the biological basis for the emergence of cooperation.

In the process of evolution nothing grows out of nothing. True cooperation, however, is a kind of social behavior that requires foresight, the ability to conceive of desired ends, and the ability to communicate one's thoughts to others and to plan a course of concerted action. Above all, this would require language—a communication system qualitatively different from the call system of lower primates.

Hockett and Ascher (*op. cit.*) state that as soon as the hominids achieved upright posture, bipedal locomotion, the use of the hands to manipulate, carry, and manufacture tools, and language, they had become men. All this, they believe, occurred by 1 million years ago, and only after this did the brain begin to increase greatly in size. A large brain, they maintain, achieved survival value only after the hominids had acquired language and culture. Language and culture, in other words, were man's means of adapting to his environment. In a rudimentary form, these things did not require a large brain. But once culture came into being, there was further selection for a larger brain, which in turn made possible more complex social life, greater technical skills, and therefore greater success in survival.

Mother–Child Relationship and Its Consequences. Washburn, writing in a similar vein, shows that the rapid development of man's brain would have created an "obstetrical dilemma" (*op. cit.*, 13 ff.), stemming from the following considerations. An infant ape or monkey clings to its mother, sometimes grasping her body hair and riding upside down as the mother moves along in her quadrupedal position. The mother's hands and arms are not free to carry her infant. To be able to do so, "the baby must be born with its central nervous system in an advanced state of development. But the brain of the fetus must be small enough so that birth may take place." What was early man's dilemma? He (or she) had achieved upright posture, but in the process the bony birth canal had become smaller. At the same time, natural selection was going on for a larger brain. This was resolved by the delivery of the fetus while the brain was still quite small and, therefore, not fully developed. This infant was far more helpless than the infant ape or monkey and could not possibly cling to its mother. But, with her bipedal posture, the human mother's hands and arms were free to carry her immature infant. As a consequence of this "premature" birth, a far greater proportion of human development had to take place in the postuterine phase of life, but such an infant eventually developed a much bigger brain than the ape or monkey fetus can possibly develop in its mother's uterus. On the other hand, there was a much longer period of dependency upon the mother and of maternal responsibility. The human mother was much more restricted in her movements than the female ape. Burdened for several years with a helpless infant, she could not be a hunter. However, by the time this development had taken place, man was already a full-fledged hunter, and in all probability was the protector of his group, against predators or other men.

Natural selection, we reason, favored a human group in which the male specialized in hunting and the female in child care—the first true economic division of labor. We have already commented on the possibility that a meat diet would permit the sharing of food. A successful hunter could kill more game than he could possibly consume on the spot. This fact alone did not "cause" him to carry it back to camp. Nor did the fact that a mother, handicapped by nursing one infant and caring for one or two other small children, might be unable to gather enough plant or insect food close to home to feed both herself and her children determine whether or not the male brought his game home to share. On the other hand, the new mother–child relationship could never have evolved in the first place unless some pattern of cooperation were evolving simultaneously. This long-term dependency of child on mother would have been highly unadaptive in a non-cooperative society. However, the development of symbolic thought and, with it, language would have made possible and would have greatly facilitated the development of cooperation. The very growth of the brain, which ultimately necessitated human cooperation, also made cooperation possible. Once more we see the intimate, intricate relationship between cause and effect. To quote Washburn (*ibid.*, 13): "The reason that the human brain makes the human way of life possible is that it is the result of that way of life. Great masses of the tissue in the human brain are devoted to memory, planning, language and skills, because these are the abilities favored by the human way of life."

We can visualize, therefore, an early human society in which males hunted, defended the group against natural enemies, and possibly participated in other more arduous tasks, such as building shelters. They probably also made their own tools. Females, on the other hand, were more restricted in their movements by periodic pregnancy and the need to nurse small infants or to care for other small children. To them fell the tasks which could best be performed, or had to be performed, near the campsite—cooking, preparing animal skins for clothing, and scouring the vicinity for plant food, insects and insect larvae, and possibly "slow" game. These two sets of activities were complementary and maximized the group's chances for survival. Language, tools, possibly the use of fire and cooking, a social system based on cooperation—in short, culture —was their mode of adaptation to the environment. Even in a rudimentary form, culture conferred an enormous advantage upon these early humans in their struggle for survival, and natural selection would automatically bring about the anatomical modifications that would permit the development of still more complex culture.

The Structure of the First Hominid Society

This discussion of the functions of the early human group has said nothing about its form, size, or structure. Did the entire group consist of a man, a woman, and their children, or what anthropologists call the nuclear family? Did it consist of several such families? Or did it consist of men, women, and children, with no regularized pairing of males and females? Admittedly, we are on uncertain ground in attempting to answer these questions. Many studies of the sociology of contemporary primates and of recent or contemporary hunting and gathering peoples are available, but neither group of materials provides direct evidence for man's social beginnings. We must continue to do as we have done throughout this chapter: reason from the known to the unknown to create a picture that is logically consistent and plausible. In so doing, we recognize that alternative explanations are possible and that our conclusions must remain open to modification and even rejection in the future.

It would seem that primates living on the ground or in open grassland must form large groups for protection. The baboons of eastern Africa illustrate this point well. Perhaps the protohominids of several million years ago formed similar troops, with the males falling back to confront predators when flight to the trees was not possible. Lacking tools and depending upon brute strength when fighting became inevitable, large numbers would have been a compensating advantage. Early men, however, had a rudimentary culture, which eliminated the necessity for very large groups. Several men, armed with weapons and possessing the mental capacity to formulate a plan for cooperative defense, would be a match for a single predator. Thus, the factor of defense and the value of cooperative endeavor in hunting game would militate against groups consisting of only a mating pair and their children. Eventually the use of fire would serve to ward off cats or other predators by night, and four or five men might be sufficient for defense and for hunting. But did the desire for human companionship, and the need for defense against human enemies, favor large troops? We suggest that large groups were inhibited by a positive and purely ecological factor: the food supply is limited in any area, and the larger the group the more it must move about in search of food. We suppose, therefore, that the optimum group for early man was large enough for cooperative activities, but small enough to live on the food available in an area, that is, small enough for convenience in hunting. Studies of living hunters and gatherers suggest a group varying around a modal number of about 30 members.

Sexual Patterns. The problem of the internal arrangement of such a group is a different one and involves a different set of assumptions. Anthropologists of the last century postulated an original human condition of "primordial promiscuity," in which every male of the group had sexual access to every female, and in which there was no regulation of sexual conduct. This assumption was based upon the supposed behavior of apes and monkeys in the wild. Modern studies of primate behavior make it doubtful that such a condition could ever have existed. There are, however, other logical possibilities. "Group marriage," an alliance in which a limited number of males form a mating unit with a number of females, is one possibility. As a second possibility, one or two dominant males in a group could claim all the females, establishing their dominance through occasional bloody fights with younger males. Finally, there could be more or less permanent matings of single males and females.

Much of the speculation on this subject in the past has rested on the assumption of a "high" sex drive among the primates in general, associated with a corresponding high degree of sexual jealousy. An early study of baboons in captivity showed a highly competitive situation where dominant males gathered "harems" of females about them and fought off all challenges by younger deprived males. The latter bided their time, and there were frequent fights to gain or maintain dominance. In the absence of other studies it seemed reasonable to extrapolate from baboons in captivity to the entire primate order. Thus, White (1959:65 ff.) sees sexual attraction as a major force in primate social organization and the primary factor in the formation of permanent bonds between male and female. Human society began when man, by cultural means, equalized the distribution of mates and formulated laws to regularize sexual behavior. The unequal distribution of mates in subhuman society (which White assumed) was maintained by physical dominance. Language and tools, however, permitted deprived males to arm themselves and formulate plans to overthrow the dominant males. Conversely, Sahlins (1960:3 ff.) sees the sex drive as posing a disruptive threat to early human societies:

> Sex is not an unmitigated social blessing for primates. Competition over partners, for example, can lead to vicious, even fatal, strife. It was this side of primate sexuality that forced early culture to curb and repress it. The emerging human primate, in a life-and-death economic struggle with nature, could not afford the luxury of a social struggle. Co-operation, not competition, was essential.

It was culture, therefore, that brought primate sexuality under control, subordinating this biological drive to the economic needs of the group.

In fact, we know virtually nothing about the nature of the sex drive in the protohominids, and we are just now beginning to accumulate reliable comparative knowledge of living primates. Living primates vary widely in group size and composition, as we have already indicated, and there is no clear-cut correlation between these factors and sexual activity. They also vary in the reproductive physiology of the female, showing at least three basic patterns (Harrison, et al. 1964:93–96), and there is a wide range in the intensity of sexual interest and activity. Washburn and Hamburg (1965:611) give the following comparisons: in more than a year of observation of the mountain gorilla, the observer witnessed only two cases of copulation; in over 400 hours of observation of the gibbon, mating behavior was rarely seen; in a two-month period, by contrast, a single observer saw 168 baboon matings. "There appear to be widely different patterns of sexual activity, all of which are compatible with keeping the females pregnant. Sexual activity is far from constant among different kinds of monkeys and apes. It certainly plays a much larger role in the social life of some groups than of others."

A factor that must certainly have a bearing on our discussion is the reproductive physiology of a particular species. Harrison, et al. show that the human female and the gibbon female share a pattern that does not occur among other primates. The gorilla, chimpanzee, baboon, and some other monkeys share a menstrual cycle in which, at ovulation, there is a swelling and discoloration of the sexual skin around the external genitals. The females of these species are ". . . maximally receptive about midway in the menstrual cycle and mating may take place within a restricted period of a few days at this time" (op. cit., 93). Male interest, on the other hand, does not fluctuate, and among these species it is found that the males will seek more than one female attachment. The result is competition among males for a number of consorts, or for "harems." Apparently, it is this tendency that was carried to an extreme by baboons in captivity, where there was no danger of predation and when the search for food was eliminated. There, sex did indeed become a primary concern.

This restricted period of receptivity is absent in the menstrual cycle of the human and gibbon female, in whom ". . . sexuality is more diffuse, [and] the male's interest in a particular female becomes continuous" (ibid., 95). It is significant that among gibbons in the wild, the family group typically consists of a single male, a single female, and their dependent offspring. The male and female are of approximately equal size, and there is not the degree of male dominance found among baboons or other anthropoids. "This lends support for the belief of a 'monogamous' system in *Australopithecus* which, like modern man, also displays a relatively small degree of sexual dimorphism" (*ibid.*). These authors are in agreement with a point made earlier by Sahlins (*op. cit.*), that in man sexual relations are largely free of hormonal regulation and come increasingly under cultural control.

Internal Arrangement of the Early Hominid Band. We cannot say for certain what the internal arrangement of the earliest hominid band was like. It does not seem likely, however, in the absence of marked sexual dimorphism, that individual males could maintain large "harems" by physical force. Further, the reproductive physiology of the female—if it was indeed the same as that of the human female today—would have provided the basis for permanent attachments between a single male and a single female because each would have been physiologically capable of providing for the sexual needs of the other. White's postulation, described above, of a human monogamous family being brought about, by cooperative force, out of a pre-existing "polygynous" society may therefore be unnecessary. Such units may already have been present. Cultural factors would then have operated not to create such units, but to formalize them, give them social sanction, forbid parent–child and sibling mating (see below), and punish deviance (i.e., alternative unions).

The nuclear family, as we show in a later chapter, is well adapted to the needs of primitive hunters and gatherers. Aside from providing an equitable distribution of mates, thereby maximizing the chances of equal sexual satisfaction for everyone, such a family has other practical consequences. One of these relates to the scarcity of food and the nomadic way of life. Even a small band, consisting of no more than 30 persons, would occasionally place a strain on the available food and water supply. Seasonally, water, game, and plant food would become so scarce that the band would have to break up into its constituent nuclear family units, each going its own way to eke out its subsistence. Since an economic division of labor along sex lines makes for complementarity of male and female roles, this mutual dependence would make it unlikely that the seasonal breakup of the band would follow any other than nuclear family lines.

It seems plausible, therefore, that the early human social group consisted of small bands of nuclear families. For reasons to be taken up in Chapter 15, such families were probably related, the husbands being brothers. How closely spaced the bands were was related to the food supply. Historically known band societies, including a few that still exist today, have generally been exogamous. That is, a man or woman is not permitted to marry within the band and must seek a mate from some other band. From the standpoint of the male, any girl of his band would be treated as a sister, and marriage between them would be regarded as incestuous. Every society known to anthropology has defined certain unions as incestuous, and therefore culturally deviant. Rules prohibiting such unions are universal. Leslie White has argued that human society began when early men evolved this concept of incest and formulated laws requiring that a man seek his mate outside his own group (White 1949:303–29). This came about, White maintains, because it was essential to human survival. Endogamous or in-breeding human groups would have been isolated from one another and would have lacked any means of establishing intergroup ties. Yet ties of cooperation or mutual aid between groups vastly increased the chances of human survival; their importance, in terms of survival, was too great to be left to chance.

How did early man achieve such intergroup cooperation? Through the definition and prohibition of incest, early man forced intermarriage between bands. Powerful bonds of kinship that united the members of bands into cooperative groupings were extended across band lines. Through systematic intermarriage, members of neighboring bands all became kinsmen to one another. For example, a man's married sisters would all reside with neighboring bands; his mother would have come from another band; and his wife's kinsmen would live in other bands as well. Subsequent chapters will enlarge upon the extent and effectiveness of mutual aid between kinsmen in primitive society. Our assumption is that once the protohominids bridged the gap that separated them from fully human status, their social organization had to be much like that of ethnographically known primitive hunters and gatherers. A hunting and gathering technology, powered by human muscular energy and applied to the semi-arid savanna environment of eastern Africa, would have imposed severe limitations on human social development with results similar to those still to be observed among primitive hunters and gatherers of today.

SOME OTHER EVOLUTIONARY PRINCIPLES

Most of the preceding discussion is phrased in terms of selection. This principle operated on the genetic materials of a certain hominid population which had already acquired certain preadaptive characteristics: prehensile hand, bipedalism, stereoscopic vision, the ability to manipulate tools, perhaps a true menstrual cycle, and others. It operated on these genetic materials, including continuing mutations, in reference to a total environment: arid or semi-arid savanna, the presence of dangerous predators, the presence of competing protohominids, and a slowly emerging cultural environment.

We have said nothing of such important biological processes as isolation, gene drift, or hybridization. These are operative in all species, but they take on a special significance in man's evolution because of the cultural factor. We will confine our discussion here to a single, very important fact about the human species: man is a single species. The only significant geographical varieties of man are subspecific. It is relatively rare in biological evolution to find a genus containing only a single species. Most typically, a species becomes separated, in time, into a number of breeding populations, each isolated from the others. Through the operation of mutation and selection, along with continued isolation, they eventually become separate and distinct species of the same genus. This process of change is referred to as cladogenesis, whereas a process in which a species changes through time, but without splitting into separate new species, is called anagenesis (Dobzhansky 1963:352–58). The fact that the genus *Homo* contains but a single species would seem to suggest the operation of anagenesis in man's evolution. Does this mean that there has never been more than a single species of *Homo?* An extreme anagenetic point of view would hold that this is so. On the other hand, the taxonomic practices of generations of physical anthropologists, wherein each new fossil specimen was assigned not only a new species, but even a new genus designation, would suggest an almost extreme cladogenetic point of view.

Few authorities today would support the extreme cladogenesis implicit in some of the older taxonomic schemes. If, on the other hand, the fossil and archaeological evidence seems to support the view that there has been no more than a single hominid species for at least a half-million years, then this position (anagenesis) is a reasonable one, even though logically extreme. Our interest, however, is in explaining why anagenesis has been the dominant, even if not the exclusive, process in hominid evolution. This explanation must lie in cultural factors.

Isolation has occurred in human evolution, as it has in the evolution of other species. This is a most important process, because it is through isolation that new, favorable mutations become rapidly fixed in human populations. The reasons for isolation in the human species are primarily cultural rather than geographical. Cultural, linguistic, ethnic, religious, social, and similar barriers to cross-breeding are usually only temporary, but while in force they do have the result of in-breeding. Breeding populations which are geographically adjacent to one another are often culturally isolated long enough for them to become genetically distinctive.

In the hominid line this divergence is never permitted to go far enough to result in the formation of separate species (cladogenesis). Sooner or later cultural barriers break down, and hybridization occurs. This is highly desirable from the standpoint of the evolutionary success of the species, because it means that new and favorable mutations, once fixed in a single breeding population, have a chance to spread throughout the species. The result is greater genetic variability which, we showed in the preceding chapter, is of great survival value to any species. Anagenesis has been a concomitant result of continued hybridization within the hominid species throughout its evolutionary history, and it is culture, again, that is the primary factor at work. Wherever human populations have come into contact they have been able, eventually, to overcome cultural barriers and have interbred. The process has not always been the same. Groups can meet as equals and engage in intermarriage or in clandestine mating. Or they can be brought together by conquest, so that dominant-group males mate with subordinate-group females. Slavery in the United States inevitably had this latter result. Perhaps the former situation was much more common early in man's history. Whatever the specific factors, wherever and whenever human groups have come into contact, their ability to communicate, even across linguistic boundaries, has ultimately led to hybridization. And no large segment of the genus *Homo* has ever remained in isolation sufficiently long to form a separate species.

SUMMARY

Julian Huxley has stated that sometime in the mid-Pliocene period, ". . . some five million years ago, all the purely physiological and material possibilities of life had been exhausted—size, power, speed, sensory and muscular efficiency, chemical coordination, temperature-regulation and the rest. After nearly two thousand million years, biological evolution on this planet had reached the limit of its advance" (1956:6). He goes on to show that evolution itself did not end with the attainment of these biological limits; rather, it shifted to a new phase, the "psycho-social," or cultural. It was late in the Pliocene or early in the Pleistocene that a protohominid primate form developed a qualitatively new means of adaptation to the environment in the form of a rudimentary culture—tools, cooperation, and speech. At this point, Huxley suggests that evolutionary advance began to take place in a new and scarcely exploited potentiality of life. "The still unrealized potentialities of life were its possibilities of fuller awareness, its mental or psychological attributes; and the hitherto unexploited capacity whose fuller utilization not only made possible the rise of man to evolutionary dominance but initiated a new phase of evolution, was the cumulative communication of experience" (*ibid.*, 6–7). Huxley also shows that with the advent of culture, the biological phase of human evolution became relatively insignificant, because what evolved thereafter was not man's genetic nature, but something superorganic called *culture*.

This should not be taken to mean that man ceased to evolve biologically as soon as he acquired culture. We have already seen that this was not the case. Early manifestations of culture were crude and limited because early man's biological and mental capacities for culture were limited. We have shown that during the long australopithecine stage of human evolution, man experienced continuous biological modification: more efficient bipedal locomotion and erect posture, better eye–hand coordination, greater body size, reduced size of teeth and jaw, and probably some increase in brain size. These in turn meant a greater reliance on an increasingly improved cultural adaptation. By the time man attained the pithecanthropine stage in his evolution, 500,000 to 750,000 years ago, he had approached his modern body size, had evolved a brain at least double the size of the australopithecine brain, and was making hand-axes which were superior to the pebble tools of the previous age. Even then, however, he had not ceased to evolve biologically. He did not attain a brain of fully modern size, and with it his full culture capacity, for another half-million years.

At precisely what point in his evolution man acquired his present-day capacity for culture building, no one can say. According to conservative estimates, man achieved the status of *Homo sapiens* at least 50,000 years ago, and it seems reasonable to assume that he had approached, if not fully attained, his modern mental capacity by that time. Indeed, as we have seen, there are those who would grant *sapiens* status to the Neanderthal phase of human evolution. But whether this development occurred 50,000, 100,000, or 250,000 years ago, it is at that point that biological evolution "transcended itself." At that point, biological change became relatively insignificant in man's adaptation to his environment. Henceforth, man's principal and immediate means of adapting and adjusting to his external world were cultural. Therefore, a new phase of evolution, the cultural phase, was initiated. In the past 10,000 years, cultural systems have grown and developed enormously, and the laws governing this evolutionary advance have been cultural, not biological laws. In a later chapter we treat cultural evolution as a process logically separate from biology.

6

Evolution: A Cultural Process

INTRODUCTION

Cultural evolution was a major approach to the study of man and culture during much of the nineteenth century. Most of the pioneers in anthropology pursued their studies in this framework. These men were interested in demonstrating the origins and subsequent development of such human institutions as marriage and the family, religion, and law—all of which are cultural phenomena. In spite of this historical fact, evolution is sometimes regarded as an exclusively biological process. It has frequently been claimed, by those who support this view, that an evolutionary interpretation of cultural phenomena is a misapplication of the concept based on mistaken analogies. It is true that some writers in the past have applied specifically biological concepts to cultural phenomena. However, these mistaken attempts do not invalidate the use of evolution, as a developmental process, to explain culture. *Culture can change and develop independently of biological changes in the human organism.* Evolution is the name given to that process which explains the change and development of culture. While the specific applications of evolution to biological and cultural phenomena will differ (these are qualitatively different phenomena), some of the same general principles of evolution are applicable to both. *Cultural evolution is not a misapplication of a biological concept, nor was the concept ever entirely original to biology.*

EVOLUTIONARY THOUGHT IN HISTORICAL PERSPECTIVE

Classical Evolution

Some nineteenth-century cultural evolutionists, such as Herbert Spencer, were undoubtedly impressed by the successes of Darwin and others in applying the concept of evolution to life in general. It must not be forgotten, however, that evolutionary interpretations of social and cultural phenomena were present long before the time of Darwin. As Evans-Pritchard (1951:21–42) has shown, social philosophers of the early eighteenth century were concerned with formulating general laws of progress which would explain in naturalistic terms the development of all societies through certain stages of growth. These scholars— Montesquieu, Condorcet, Turgot, and Saint-Simon in France; David Hume and Adam Smith in Great Britain—were interested in society as a whole and society as a natural system. Because they were looking for broad general trends underlying the unique events of history and were not interested in the unique events themselves, these social philosophers emphasized social institutions in their investigations.

They also stressed the need for empirical studies of society, but actually knew very little about the living primitive tribes who, they supposed, were representative of earlier stages of human social evolution. The few "facts" at their command (they were often less than reliable) were generally used to support theories which were the products of pure speculation (*ibid.*, 27). Nevertheless, their writings laid the foundations for the much sounder scholarship of the nineteenth century.

Classical evolutionists of the mid-nineteenth century—Lewis H. Morgan in the United States; E. B. Tylor, Sir Henry Maine, and J. F. McLennan in Great Britain; and J. Bachofen in Switzerland—were interested in establishing universal stages of culture growth through which societies everywhere had passed in the course of their development. Morgan traced the growth of culture through the general stages of savagery, barbarism, and civilization (see below). He also postulated an evolutionary sequence for marriage and the family, a development in which the group marriage of brothers and sisters grew out of an earlier stage of promiscuity (complete absence of regulated sex behavior), and gave way through intermediate stages to polygamy and finally to monogamy. Maine, who studied law, and Tylor and J. Lubbock, who studied religion, formulated evolutionary schemes to account for the origins and development of these aspects of culture.

Like their eighteenth-century predecessors, these scholars based their evolutionary schemes on speculation, and then proceeded to look for evidence to support them. But, unlike their predecessors, they had access to greater quantities of data from a variety of different societies, and were able to study social institutions—law, marriage, the family, religion —more systematically and precisely than the earlier writers.

The general approach of the nineteenth-century classical evolutionists involved certain basic assumptions:

1. Mankind everywhere exhibits similar mental characteristics. Consequently, men everywhere will respond in a like manner to similar situations. This concept—*the psychic unity of mankind*—explains the independent origins of similar culture traits and the constancy of developmental stages in widespread parts of the world.
2. Because of the psychic unity of mankind and therefore of independent origins of like cultural traits, the cultures of human groups everywhere evolve along similar lines. This theory of *parallel evolution*, in its extreme form, would hold, for example, that human groups everywhere have passed through each of Morgan's stages and substages of savagery, barbarism, and civilization (see Fig. 6–1).
3. While earlier stages of culture give way to later ones, the earlier stages do not completely die out. Thus, contemporary hunters and gatherers or primitive horticulturalists would be identified by the classical evolutionists as living examples of earlier stages and, therefore, "proof" of the existence of these stages.

In this way, classical evolutionists established by speculation a series of evolutionary stages in the development of law, the family, religion, and culture as a whole. The classical evolutionist searched the ethnographic literature for examples illustrative of each stage. When such examples were found, he felt that his scheme was validated. This "comparative method" was criticized severely by later anthropologists.

Morgan's Stages of Evolution. One of the earliest and best examples of a classical evolutionary scheme was provided by Lewis H. Morgan in *Ancient Society* (1877). According to this formulation, mankind has progressed through three great stages, the first two being divisible into three substages, as shown in Fig. 6–1.

Morgan recognized that within these major stages of development there occurred several parallel developments: subsistence, government, language, the family, religion, house life and architecture, and property. Each of these is treated separately and at length. Further, he equates progress through these various stages with increasing control over food sources, indicating that "It is . . . probable that the great epochs of human progress have been identified, more or less directly, with the enlargement of the sources of subsistence." (Morgan 1877:19.)

Major Stage	Substage	Distinguishing Criteria
III. Civilization	(no substages)	From invention of phonetic alphabet to the present time.
II. Barbarism	3. Upper status of barbarism	Begins with smelting of iron ore, use of iron tools.
	2. Middle status of barbarism	Domestication of animals; irrigation agriculture in New World.
	1. Lower status of barbarism	Begins with the invention of pottery.
I. Savagery	3. Upper status of savagery	Begins with the invention of the bow and arrow.
	2. Middle status of savagery	Begins with the acquisition of a fish subsistence and the use of fire.
	1. Lower status of savagery	From infancy of human race to commencement of next period.

Fig. 6–1. Morgan's stages in the development of civilization. (Read from bottom to top.)

Morgan stresses the importance of archaeological data for his scheme of evolution, but points out that archaeology does not provide enough complete information to illustrate all stages in the growth of civilization. A very important source of information concerning earlier stages in that growth are the living or historically known peoples of the world. The ethnographies of living peoples supplement knowledge derived from archaeology in completing descriptions of earlier cultural levels. Thus, the Australian aborigines of Morgan's day could be classified, in his judgment, as belonging to the middle status of savagery, whereas the Iroquois of New York State belonged, by virtue of their horticultural practices, to the lower status of barbarism. Morgan's stages are levels of cultural development, and living primitives are regarded as typifying lower, earlier levels. The point Morgan makes is crucial for evolutionary theory, that while each of the general stages of culture is succeeded by later and higher stages, representatives of each stage continue to live on into the present.

Many modern anthropologists agree with Morgan that productive technology—the tools and techniques whereby a people exploit their natural environment—is the basic aspect of every culture system and, therefore, of culture in general. A culture is an adaptation to a total environment, and the single most important factor in that adaptation is technology. Population density, group size, social complexity, the division of labor, and the complexity of religious life are determined within

Arunta tribesmen of Australia prepare for a dance and feast held at the grave to commemorate the deceased. The Arunta have been called our "contemporary ancestors," possessing a technology characteristic of Upper Paleolithic man 20,000 years ago. (Courtesy of the American Museum of Natural History.)

narrow limits by this factor. Therefore, if a living people like the Arunta of Australia have a technology much like that which archaeology demonstrates to have been characteristic of Upper Paleolithic man 20,000 years ago, we then have some justifiable basis for assuming a correspondence between other aspects of Upper Paleolithic culture and Arunta culture. As Service (1962:8) has asked, "But if the aboriginal culture of the Arunta . . . is not a form of adaptation to a particular kind of (total) environment made long, long ago and preserved into modern times because of its isolation, then what is it?" Living representatives of an ancestral *form* of culture are, then, as Service aptly describes them, our "contemporary ancestors." Morgan anticipated this argument when he related the general level of cultural development to subsistence technology.

To a limited extent, classical evolutionism persisted into the twentieth century, but, in general, these evolutionary theories had fallen into disrepute even before the turn of the century. Men like Morgan, Tylor, Maine, and McLennan are still looked upon with great respect by modern anthropologists, but this respect is for their other contributions. Morgan is credited with founding the modern comparative study of kinship systems, Tylor and McLennan are almost universally admired for their researches into primitive religion, and Maine is recognized for his research into law. But, we repeat, their attempts to discover origins and then trace subsequent developmental stages for the family, religion, or law were almost completely discredited by their successors. This rejection took different forms among different scholars.

Reactions to Classical Evolution

Three names commonly associated with the rejection of classical evolutionism are Franz Boas in the United States and Bronislaw Malinowski and A. R. Radcliffe-Brown in England. All three agreed that the classical evolutionists were attempting to write history, and pointed out that to write the history of any civilization, or of mankind at large, requires facts; history deals with what actually happened. They asserted that the classical evolutionists had no facts from the remote past and, therefore, had to rely on sheer speculation to reconstruct cultural origins and subsequent developmental stages. For this reason Boas, Malinowski, and Radcliffe-Brown, among others, branded classical evolutionism as conjectural history, pseudo-history, or just plain guesswork. They felt that such reconstruction was a meaningless exercise, since we can never know how religion originated, what man's first legal systems were like, or what form was taken by the first family.

These three men were not antihistorical. Boas, in fact, founded the American historical school of anthropology, which operated on the premise that to know anything significant about a culture you must know its history. Malinowski and Radcliffe-Brown believed that history was largely irrelevant to a functionalist interpretation of culture. Functionalism is essentially non-temporal. A cultural system is analyzed at a point in time to determine its structure and the interrelatedness of its parts. The function of a ritual, for example, is its contribution in maintaining the system of which it is a part. The mutual participation of the members of a lineage in a ritual of ancestor worship serves to strengthen the bonds that unite them and, thereby, enhances the solidarity of the lineage. This is its system-maintenance function. While the anthropological historian might well argue the importance of knowing the history of the particular ritual, the functionalist would claim that such a detailed history is irrelevant since it does not help to explain the contemporary function of the ritual in its present cultural context. Another example will clarify this distinction further.

It is appropriate behavior among some social classes in the United States for a man to walk on the street side when accompanying a woman. The historian would point out the origins of this custom, indicating that during an earlier period in our history this courtesy afforded protection for the lady against the splashing of mud from passing horses or carriages. The continued performance of this custom in contemporary society is a survival from a former time. The functionalist, on the other hand, might interpret this behavior within the context of etiquette, explaining that etiquette functions to preserve fundamental social distinctions—between the sexes in this case. The custom in question could be understood in this context even if nothing was known about its history or its origins. Knowing the history of etiquette adds nothing to a functionalist interpretation. Thus, functionalists such as Malinowski and Radcliffe-Brown were relatively disinterested in history, whether accurate and detailed or not. Since they regarded evolution as a kind of history, a pseudo-history, they dismissed it as being of little or no value for their investigations.

Boas and his followers were the most systematic and vigorous among their contemporaries in their rejection of nineteenth-century evolutionism. They shared with others the basic objection that classical evolution was conjectural history, but they had more specific criticisms of nineteenth-century scholarship.

Boas' Objections.   Boas' objections included the following:

1. The sequences postulated by the classical evolutionists were purely speculative. No one can ever demonstrate specific cultural origins. Even archaeology—the field of anthropology that deals with the past—is severely limited in deriving valid information about extinct cultures.

2. It is invalid to arrange cultures in a developmental sequence, placing the lowest cultures at one polar extreme and the highest cultures at the other. What is high and what is low will depend upon the ethnocentric bias of the person doing the arranging. Nineteenth-century anthropologists showed their ethnocentric bias by rating their own civilization most highly. This might have been justified on the basis of the advanced technology of western civilization at that time. However, if some criterion other than technological complexity were employed in the ranking, for example, complexity of kinship systems, then many so-called primitive cultures (such as that of the Australian aborigines) would rank high on

this evolutionary continuum, and technologically advanced civilizations (such as contemporary western society) would rank very low.

3. Living primitives are not representative of very early stages of cultural growth. All societies, including primitive ones, have unique and extensive histories—all societies change through time. The primitive cultures of today cannot be equated with the cultures of 50,000 or more years ago and, therefore, are not illustrative of earlier stages of culture.

4. The idea that mankind everywhere has passed through predetermined and identical stages of culture growth, and the related concept of parallel evolution (that all basic elements of culture originate independently many times over in various parts of the world because of the psychic unity of man) is not valid. Anthropological information is available which shows that independent invention of cultural elements occurs at most once or twice, and that once arrived at these elements are spread through a process of diffusion from one area to another.

It has been asserted by some contemporary anthropologists that Boas and his followers were not only non-evolutionist in their thinking—they were antievolutionist. It must be stressed, however, that their approach was not just a negative one. These anthropologists were concerned with historical problems, and they felt that the concept of evolution had nothing to contribute to their solution. It is true, nevertheless, that during the decades Franz Boas and his students were the dominant element in American anthropology, cultural evolutionism was absent from the writings of anthropologists in the United States.

The Resurgence of Cultural Evolution

Today, the concept of evolution is well established in cultural anthropology, as a result of a neoevolutionary movement in the United States led by Leslie White and, later, Julian Steward. In re-establishing evolutionism in culture theory, these men have found it necessary to take issue with some of the criticisms leveled against cultural evolutionism by Franz Boas and his contemporaries. First, these men believe that evolution is not conjectural history because it is not history at all. History deals with unique sequences of particular events: what has happened in particular places and on particular dates. When Hitler's armies overran Poland in 1939, it was a historical and a particular event. This identical event never occurred before and can never occur again. We cannot, therefore, generalize from it. Since history deals with particular things and events and their occurrence in time, and with unique sequences of events, it is not compatible with scientific generalization. Evolution, on the other hand, deals with things and events only as members of classes. Its goal is the explanation of general processes:

how culture as a whole or how specific cultural systems have developed through time. General statements can be made about the properties of cultural systems, and general laws governing the evolution of such systems can be derived. Evolution is a generalizing approach to cultural phenomena, history is a particularizing approach. Both are valid, and neither is a substitute for the other.

Second, the modern evolutionists suggest that the search for cultural origins is not vain conjecture. There is direct and valid indirect evidence bearing on such origins, from primatology, from archaeology, and from the ethnography of living peoples. According to White, it is valid to use living primitives as evidence of earlier stages of cultural growth. Since technology is the most important determining factor in any cultural system, and all early cultures were based on a technology of hunting and gathering, they cannot have been substantially different from recent, historically known hunters and gatherers. Therefore, the latter *are* evidence for earlier stages of culture and cultural growth.

Third, it is not necessarily invalid to rank cultures from low to high, nor must such activity reflect ethnocentric bias. The criteria used to rank cultures should, of course, be capable of objective application so that scholars working independently of one another can arrive at similar rankings. This factor alone would preclude the use of criteria involving personal judgments such as superior moral values, higher religion, better ethical principles, and the like. It is possible, however, to compare and evaluate cultures objectively, using criteria such as institutional complexity, economic productivity, or energy utilization. A statement indicating that contemporary American civilization harnesses greater quantities of energy than did the sixteenth-century Aztecs, and that the latter harnessed more energy than do contemporary Eskimo hunters, does not involve ethnocentric bias.

A valid theory of evolution does not require that every society pass through a fixed sequence of stages. While it is true that some nineteenth-century evolutionists suggested a theory of parallel evolution, in which cultures everywhere developed along identical lines, scholars such as Morgan and Tylor were not referring to the development of specific cultures. Clearly, they were referring to the evolution of culture in general, which is not the same thing as the culture history of specific societies. Culture in general *has* evolved through certain stages, and it is possible to explain this growth process in scientifically acceptable terms. In any event, even if the specific use of evolution by some nineteenth-century evolutionists is open to question, this should not invalidate the concept of evolution *per se*. It is still a useful concept, because it offers a kind of scientific understanding not provided by any other explanatory concept.

WHAT IS EVOLUTION?

Evolution is a developmental process which is not dependent upon specific time and specific place. As soon as attention is shifted from what has happened historically in specific world areas or in specific cultures to the common denominators underlying all such sequences, specific times and specific places become irrelevant. Incipient farming, for example, can be explained meaningfully as a stage within a sequence of technological development without referring to any particular time, place, or cultural group. Thus, incipient farming grew out of and was preceded by a previous technological stage of food collecting as part of a general process of development. This statement can be amplified by indicating that farming first appeared in the Middle East about 8000 B.C., but this is a historical fact that neither adds to nor subtracts from the validity of the more general formulation.

Evolution is one kind of process, history is quite another. History is sometimes defined as a temporal sequence of unique events. Evolution, however, is a temporal sequence of *forms.* Cultural forms are logically distinct from unique events. They can be subsystems of cultures (economics, religion, language), stages in a developmental sequence of culture (incipient farming, incipient statehood, food collecting), or total cultures (Pygmy culture, Bushman culture, Semang culture). As a cultural form, incipient statehood, for example, can be explained as a stage in the evolution of political organization which has emerged out of an earlier cultural form and which will, in turn, evolve into still another cultural form.

Evolution and evolutionary sequences are abstractions from reality. This idea of evolution as an abstraction which does not refer to unique events, times, or places should not be misunderstood. Any general proposition (such as evolution), if it is to be more than an entertaining intellectual exercise, must relate ultimately to empirical reality. A mathematical formula describing the behavior of falling bodies purports to describe in a general way the behavior of real, observable, measurable events. Similarly, a general law of cultural evolution must ultimately relate to the empirical reality of culture history. These historical particulars, classified and arranged into historical sequences, are the empirical reality from which evolutionary concepts of culture are abstracted.

Valid generalizations about the evolution of culture, as a whole, are derived by logical analysis from empirical reality. These general propositions—that during the course of acquiring an advanced agricultural technology, social systems always increase in size and complexity and develop a state level of political organization; that as states expand to the limits of their productivity, they tend to make war on their neighbors in order to appropriate economic resources and products—are abstractions from empirical reality, but are related directly to it. These propositions are part of the broader generalization that warfare emerges at a certain stage in cultural evolution under certain conditions. This is quite different from a factual, historical statement about a particular instance of warfare. The evolutionary generalization has explanatory value for understanding particular instances of warfare at different historical times and in different historical places; the historical statement does not.

Evolution is a process of change, over time, in a general direction. Most of the empirical evidence which demonstrates this developmental process is found in the archaeological record. Since writing emerged only about 5,000 years ago, archaeology is the only source for knowing about more than 99 per cent of man's culture history. In spite of the sparsity of cultural remains, due largely to the perishability of artifacts produced from organic materials, archaeologists have been able to gather important information about earlier human occupation in all major world areas except Antarctica. In some world areas—the Americas, Oceania, and Australia—archaeological remains are relatively recent, indicating the late arrival of man, while in other world areas—Europe, Africa, and Asia—datable cultural remains exceed 1 million years. Sometimes, these latter cultural remains are found in close association with fossilized skeletal fragments, and together they constitute our earliest evidence for human origins.

A summary of the culture history of a major world area, embracing much of Europe, North Africa, and the Middle East, is given in Fig. 6-2. The historical information contained in this chart is placed in the form of a sequence of horizontal levels; the oldest known levels appear at the bottom of the chart, and the most recent levels appear at the top. These named sequential levels—Paleolithic (Old Stone Age), Mesolithic (Middle Stone Age), Neolithic (New Stone Age), Bronze Age, and Iron Age—can be regarded as great historical time periods. But they are also representative of general stages in culture growth. An examination of the materials listed in the right-hand column in Fig. 6-2 reveals a progressive refinement—from earliest times until latest—in stone-working techniques, along with an increase in the variety of tools. Late in the sequence, man began to apply his stone tools to the practice of farming; soon after, he extended his technical mastery to the smelting of metals and the firing of pottery. From about 3000 B.C. on, his technical innovations appear with ever increasing rapidity. Further, it is assumed that definite developmental processes paralleled the developments illustrated (see the list on page 155). The left-hand column of the figure shows that all de-

GEOLOGICAL AGE	PERIOD NAME		ARCHAEOLOGICAL DESCRIPTION
1,200 b.c.	Iron Age		Iron metallurgy: coins, alphabetic writing
3,000 b.c.	Bronze Age		Bronze metallurgy: religious architecture; urban centers, writing invented
10,000 b.p.	Neolithic	Late	Polished stone adzes, axes, querns, mullers, pottery
		Early	
18,000 b.p.	Mesolithic		Rude pottery, microliths
50,000 b.p.	Paleolithic	Upper	Magdalenian, Solutrean, Aurignacian, Perigordian — specialized blade tools; cave art; bone tools
400,000 b.p.		Middle	Mousterian — composite tools, flakes (skin clothing?) (first use of fire?)
750,000 b.p.		Lower	Acheulean hand-axe — Levalloisian; Abbevillian biface hand-axe — Levalloisian flake tools
1-2,000,000 b.p.	Pre-Paleolithic (Eolithic)		Olduvai Gorge, eastern Africa Pebble tools

Geological ages (left, vertical): Recent (Post-Glacial) spans 1,200 b.c. through 18,000 b.p.; Pleistocene (Ice Age) spans 50,000 b.p. through 750,000 b.p.

Note: Estimate dates given as years b.p. = before present

Fig. 6–2. A generalized culture history chart for Europe, North Africa, and the Middle East.

velopments up until 10,000–20,000 years ago occurred within the Pleistocene (the Ice Age).

The archaeological materials summarized in the figure are very scanty for earliest times, but become increasingly frequent for later periods. Based on these materials, and certain inferences that can be drawn from them, a number of general statements can be made about the stages in cultural growth referred to above. These statements are strengthened by later historical materials and, indirectly, by ethnographic knowledge of contemporary peoples. First, there is definite evidence for cultural beginnings at least 1 million years ago in the general area represented in Fig. 6–2. Second, this culture has changed over time (1 million years) in a definite direction (from simple to complex) in the following general ways:

1. From one technological base to another; from a food-collecting to a food-producing to an industrial technology.
2. From sparse population and small social groups to dense population and larger groups.
3. From structurally simple to structurally complex groups; from those based on a simple division of labor and very little economic specialization to those based on a complex division of labor and much specialization.
4. From social groups regulated primarily by kinship to those regulated by a formal political system.
5. From nomadic bands to settled communities to incipient states to full-fledged states to empires.

Comparative historical materials from the archaeological record of other world areas—China, India, Japan, Middle America—show that every major world area has historical depth going back well before the advent of writing. Over the years, archaeologists have worked out local, highly specific cultural and time sequences (histories) for hundreds of sites, and somewhat more generalized time sequences for broader regions the world over. These sequences all differ from one another in detail, just as the histories of modern tribes and nations differ. Nevertheless, an examination of all sequences having sufficient time depth reveals certain common denominators. For each of several major world areas—the Middle East, Middle and South America, China, India—a highly similar sequence of developmental stages can be identified. Similar sequential development suggests the operation of similar processes underlying the more specific developments in these world areas. An understanding of these processes is essential for understanding the process of evolution.

True evolutionary schemes include more than directional change through time—they also include process. Evolution is change, over time, in a general (but definite) direction, according to a *constant process*. This process explains how change takes place over time, and why it proceeds in a certain direction. Any valid process that explains one part of the evolutionary record must be able to explain all parts, that is, the process which explains must be a constant. It is process that distinguishes evolutionary typologies from true evolutionary theories and laws. There are numerous theories of evolution which fail to explain how developmental change occurs. They simply list cultures in some sort of sequence from early to late or simple to complex. These are evolutionary typologies. One major theory of evolution that does include process is that given by Leslie White.

White's Energy Theory of Cultural Evolution

White (1959) regards energy as one of the most fundamental concepts in all the sciences, because all natural processes involve the capture and expenditure of energy. The simplest living organism, in order to maintain the life process and reproduce itself, must take in energy from outside itself. It is meaningful to phrase the entire process of biological evolution in terms of energy. *Evolution is a process in which ever greater magnitudes of energy are harnessed and incorporated into increasing numbers of living forms (both new individuals and new species), and into forms of increasing size and structural and organizational complexity.*

Man is an animal organism, and like any other organism he must harness energy to maintain his life processes and reproduce his own kind. The means by which he does this are cultural. A primitive hunter stalks, kills, and then disposes of his game using knowledge and tools which have been handed down to him by his ancestors as part of his cultural heritage. The social arrangements by which he cooperates with his fellows in the hunt, and then shares his game, are equally part of his culture. Since all human behavior is cultural behavior, and since culture may be validly treated as a system for purposes of analysis, *it is meaningful and valid to speak of cultural systems as harnessing energy.* The means by which cultures harness energy are technological, a point which will be explained below.

Cultural systems not only capture energy, but they capture a surplus which permits a multiplication of human individuals. Increased human population density, in turn, permits the expansion of human groups into new natural habitats, with the resultant appearance of new sociocultural systems—a process analogous to speciation in the biological world. Further, and this is the heart of White's cultural evolutionism, increasing quantities of energy harnessed and put to work by cultures result in the evolution of higher cultural forms out of lower—higher in terms of the size of human groups and the complexity of social, economic, political, and religious structures. White expresses these relationships as follows (1959:39–40):

> . . . culture is produced by man and therefore derives its generic nature from its source. Since the fundamental process of man as an organism is the capture and utilization of free energy, it follows that this must be the basic function of culture also; the harnessing of energy and putting it to work in the service of man. . . . Cultural systems expand qualitatively by developing

higher forms of organization and greater concentrations of energy. Degree of organization in any material system is proportional to the amount of energy incorporated in it. As the amount of energy harnessed by sociocultural systems increases per capita per year, the systems not only increase in size, but become more highly evolved; i.e., they become more differentiated structurally and more specialized functionally.

White thus states a very fundamental relationship: cultures harness energy and expand in the process. How may we make this relationship more explicit and therefore more useful? White answers this question in the following way:

> Culture, as a thermodynamic system, may be analyzed into the following factors: energy, tools, and product. As we have seen, culture is a mechanism for serving the needs of man. And to do this it must harness energy and put it to work. The use of energy requires technological apparatus, and we may extend the use of the term *tools* to cover all the material means with which energy is harnessed, transformed, and expended. We shall designate all goods and services capable of serving the needs of man that have been produced or formed by the cultural use of energy, the *product*. Thus, catching fish, shooting game, making pottery, cutting hair, piercing ears for pendants, filing teeth for beauty's sake, weaving cloth, and a thousand and one other cultural processes are examples of the control and expenditure of energy by instrumental means in order to serve some need of man. (*Ibid.*)

For purposes of showing how a cultural system captures and harnesses energy and how this energy is transformed into ever more complex systems, White suggests that the system be analyzed into three major sectors: technological, sociological, and ideological (for certain purposes he adds a fourth sector which we shall disregard). He visualizes the cultural system as a truncated pyramid of three layers. The lowest or broadest layer is *technology;* resting on this technological base is the level of *sociology,* the organizational sector of culture. The top layer, comprising all of man's beliefs, values, and philosophical systems, is labeled *ideology.*

If the basic function of culture is that of energy capture, then it is clear why White regards technology as the material basis of his system. It is through technology that man exploits the resources of his natural environment in order to meet his survival needs—subsistence, shelter, and protection. Until man's survival needs are met he cannot develop along other lines—art, science, religion, recreation, and so on. These things are all part of the cultural product made possible by energy utilization. White (*ibid.*, 40) expresses the relationship with the formula $E \times T \to P$, ". . . in which E represents the energy involved, T the technological means of utilizing it, and P, the product or result which serves a need of man." This is not a mathematical equation since we cannot attach precise numerical values to these three factors. Nevertheless, it is a convenient shorthand way of expressing a fundamental relationship.

Energy is basic to cultural systems, and it is with tools (or technology, embracing both tools and techniques for using them) that energy is harnessed to achieve cultural ends. During the enormously long period of food collecting, the only energy source harnessed by man was his own muscle power. Therefore, in White's formula, E is synonymous with human muscle power and was a constant factor (did not vary) throughout this time period. P, however, did not remain constant throughout the archaeological ages from the Lower Paleolithic through the Mesolithic. Archaeology has shown a steady progression in the number of tools made and used, in their quality, and in the creation of more specialized tools. It seems to be a fair assumption that culture was also becoming more complex in its non-material aspects—religion, social organization, art—and that population density was increasing as well. Now, if E was constant, but P (as revealed by archaeology) was increasing, then the value of the factor T must also have been increasing. According to White's interpretation, as tools improved in quality and became more specialized (adapted to more specific tasks), and as man acquired superior techniques for using them, he was able to utilize his muscle power more effectively. Thus, a sharp stone axe employs human muscle power more efficiently than does a crude one, and a bow and arrow employs that power more effectively than does a wooden throwing stick.

White recognizes that there was an inherent limitation to the development that could be achieved by cultures powered by human muscle energy alone. During the long stone ages the slow improvement in tools did serve to make human muscle power more efficient, but this power was still directed largely toward the collection of wild foods. Theoretically, unless man had developed some new technological device for harnessing significantly new sources of energy, his cultures could never have transcended the level achieved about 20,000 years ago.

Energy, therefore, is made the dynamic factor in the evolutionary process. Culture expands and develops only with the improvement of the technological means for harnessing ever greater quantities of energy. Technologically advanced cultures are those that capture and harness relatively great magnitudes of energy. Technologically simple cultures can harness only limited quantities of energy, and such cultures must remain meager in their material aspects and simple in their organization. This point of view is implicit in the description of the general evolutionary sequence presented below.

First, however, it must be shown more clearly how and why the technological aspect of culture shapes and influences the sociological and ideological aspects. Technology has an adaptive function: it articulates man with his natural environment and serves his basic survival needs.

Since survival is man's primary concern, the basic function of social organization is to organize man into effective groups for using his technology. In a primitive hunting band, the male will employ the spear or bow and arrow to hunt large game. The woman will use a digging stick and basket to collect roots or grub worms. This simple but effective division of labor is all that the simple technology requires. However, if the technology is one of irrigation agriculture, a larger number of persons is needed to construct the irrigation works, patrol and maintain them, and regulate the distribution of water. This implies a form of leadership absent and unnecessary in the primitive hunting band. *There is always an intimate relationship between the kind of technology wielded by a human group and the kind of group that is formed.* And, says White (*ibid.*), the primary determining role is that of technology. Through history, as man's technological means of exploiting his habitat have developed and grown in complexity, he has had to develop new social arrangements for employing that technology.

The so-called ideological sector of culture is also determined in its general features by the technological sector and by the organizational one. The ideas, beliefs, values, and general knowledge of a people are always delimited and conditioned by the level of technical achievement. The spirit beliefs and rituals appropriate to a hunting and gathering people do not serve equally well the needs of an early farming people, nor are the sun gods and mother-earth goddesses of a simple farming people appropriate to a people having an advanced industrial technology. A people possessing no tools or knowledge beyond that required for collecting wild plants cannot possibly measure the surface temperature of the sun or the physical composition of the stars. On the other hand, those who possess such knowledge are unlikely to deify and worship the sun and the stars. In short, throughout history, major changes in man's technological capacities have been followed by major social realignments, new principles of organization, and the abandonment of old doctrines for new. For these reasons, the stages in the simplified evolutionary scheme which are presented in the next section of this chapter are primarily stages in technological evolution.

Having discussed in a most general way man's historical past and having presented a statement of what is meant by cultural evolutionism, an evolutionist interpretation of the archaeological and historical record can be presented meaningfully. First, a vast and extremely complex array of historical facts is placed into the context of a general developmental process. It is shown that culture in general has evolved in an orderly way through three main stages, and that this growth has been governed by certain principles. In doing this, a context is provided for a later discussion (see Chapter 15) in which is traced the separate evo-

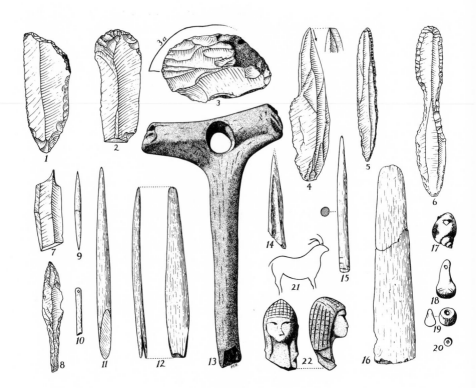

(One third natural size)

1. Knife of flake, straight edge, curved bluntly chipped back. Audi type. France.
2. Endscraper of flake, bit end rounded by chipping. France.
3. Endscraper of core (keelscraper) viewed from above; profile indicated. France.
4. Burin or engraving tool with transverse chisellike bit — the simplest of several allied forms. France.
5. Incising tool or pointed knife of flake, with straight bluntly chipped back. Gravette type. France.
6. Notched sidescraper or drawknife. France. After H. Breuil.
7. Perforator prepared from flake by chipping near point. France. After D. Peyrony.
8. Stemmed point prepared from flake by chipping. Font-Robert type. France.
9. Double-pointed bone implement, possibly used in place of fishhook. France. After D. Peyrony.
10. Needle of bone, fragmentary. France. After L. Didon.
11. Dart point of bone with slant base for hafting. France. After D. Peyrony.
12. Dart point of bone with slit base for hafting. France.
13. Lance shaft straightener of antler, sometimes called baton-de-commandement. France.
14. Awl or perforator made from bone splinter. France.
15. Hairpin(?) of bone, circular cross section. France.
16. Spatulate implement of antler, perhaps for working skins. France.
17. Pendant or bead of univalve shell, perforated. France.
18. Pendant or bead of reindeer(?) tooth, incised ornamentation. France.
19. Bead of bone, basket-shaped. France.
20. Bead of stone, disk-shaped. France.
21. Profile of ibex(?) engraved on cave wall — early style. France. After J. Dechelette.
22. Head of female figurine carved in ivory. France. After E. Piette.

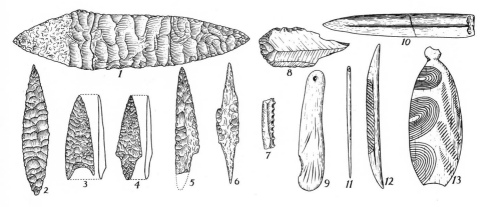

(One third natural size)

1. Knife or spear point (laurel leaf type), pressure chipped all over on both faces. France.
2. Spear point or knife (willow leaf type), chipped both faces, pointed base. France. After J. Dechelette.
3. Arrow point(?) chipped on upper face only, concave base. Spain. After H. Obermaier.
4. Arrow point(?) chipped on upper face only, stemmed. Spain. After H. Obermaier.
5. Lance point or knife, chipped on upper surface only, stemmed, with single barb or shoulder. France.
6. Perforator, double pointed, of flake chipped on upper face only. France.
7. Saw or denticulated flake. France. After H. Martin.
8. Combination endscraper and burin. France.
9. Pendant of perforated pebble. France. After D. Peyrony.
10. Awl or pointed implement of antler, longitudinal groove. France.
11. Needle of bone. France. After D. Peyrony.
12. Harpoon point(?) of antler, curved, double pointed, flattened for lashing. Spain. After O. Menghin.
13. Pendant of ivory, incised ornamentation. Moravia. After O. Menghin.

In White's energy theory, cultural systems harness energy into forms of increasing size and complexity. To utilize this energy, tools are manufactured, allowing man to meet his basic survival needs. The implements on the preceding page are from the Aurignacian period. Typical implements from the Solutrean period are shown above. Those from the Magdalenian period are shown on the following page. (Courtesy of the American Museum of Natural History.)

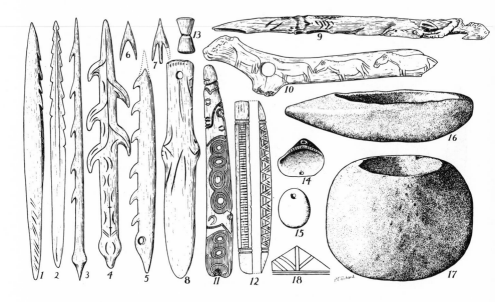

(One third natural size)

1. Dart point of bone, small barbs one side. France. After H. Breuil.
2. Dart point of bone, small barbs both sides. France. After H. Breuil.
3. Harpoon point of antler, lateral knobs on stem, barbed one side. France. After H. Breuil.
4. Harpoon point of antler, lateral knobs on stem, barbed both sides, incised ornamentation. France. After H. Breuil.
5. Harpoon point of antler, perforated stem, barbed one side. France. After H. Breuil.
6. Arrow point(?) of bone, forked base — called fishhook. France. After H. Breuil.
7. Arrow point(?) of bone with stem and barbs — called fishhook. France. After H. Breuil.
8. Dagger of bone, perforated and ornamented. France. After H. Breuil.
9. Spear-thrower of antler with carved image of mountain goat. France. After J. Dechelette.
10. Arrow shaft straightener or baton of antler with horse engravings. France. After Lartet and Christy.
11. Wand or baton of ivory with curved line ornamentation. France. After H. Breuil.
12. Spatulate implement of bone with straight line ornamentation. France. After G. Backman.
13. Bar-button or toggle of bone. France. After G. and A. de Mortillet.
14. Bead or pendant of bivalve shell, perforated. France. After G. and A. de Mortillet.
15. Pendant of small pebble, perforated. France.
16. Lamp of stone. France. (From cast.)
17. Mortar of stone. France.
18. Game trap or house frame(?) painted on cave wall. France. After G. and A. de Mortillet.

Typical implements of the Magdalenian period are shown above. (Courtesy of the American Museum of Natural History.)

lution of the various aspects or subsystems of culture in general—social organization, political systems, religion, and economic life. Finally, the analysis which follows allows increased understanding of the great range of culture types in the present world—primitive hunters, peasant societies, and modern nations—and how and why they coexist in time.

THE GENERAL EVOLUTION OF CULTURE

The Food Collectors

Modern anthropologists have characterized the food-collecting era of cultural evolution in a variety of ways, yet there is substantial agreement among these conceptions. White (*ibid.*, 42–45), we have seen, characterizes it as the stage of human muscular energy. The energy embodied in wild plant and animal food was put to work only after it had been transformed into muscle power. V. Gordon Childe (1960:99) speaks in a similar vein: human muscle power, he states, ". . . was the only force, apart from fire heat used in cooking and for hardening spears, available to earlier societies. . . ." Childe, like many other writers, does not focus upon the concept of energy *per se,* but rather on the fact that these early men were forced to rely exclusively on the food supply available in nature in the form of wild animals, fish, insects, and plant food. The possession of a food-collecting technology is an overriding factor in determining the general characteristics of any culture based on that technology. As Wolf (1962:50) expresses it, ". . . a hunter and gatherer of wild food is a slave to his food supply: if his game or wild food crop is abundant, he may live the life of a savage Riley; if it decreases or vanishes, he may face extinction with it."

The era of food gathering was an enormously long one, beginning with man himself, and ending in a few parts of the world just 10,000 years ago. In some isolated world areas this technology persists to the present day. As a stage in the evolution of culture, it corresponds to the pre-Paleolithic, Paleolithic, and Mesolithic eras described in the archaeological chart (see Fig. 6–2), or to Morgan's status of savagery. Cultures of this era, or present-day cultures existing on a similar technological base, necessarily share certain features. Since these will be discussed in greater detail in Chapter 15, only a few salient facts are presented at this point.

The population of food collectors cannot be any greater than the environment will support. Groups must be nomadic to follow the food supply, and, of practical necessity, must be small. A group of 50 persons must cover twice as much ground in search of food as one of 25, other things being equal. Material goods must be limited to what a migrant people can carry on their backs, and shelters will be rude and temporary. In most years, the environment will not provide sufficient food for a reliable or dependable surplus; ordinarily what surplus there is cannot be stored. Therefore, the food quest is an unending one. There is no economic specialization, and the only regular division of labor is that which occurs between the sexes. Typically the group will be what anthropologists call the *band*—several closely related families, perhaps a number of brothers, their wives, and their children. There are different kinds of bands, however, and we will return to this point in Chapter 15. Finally, in the absence of any kind of specialists to devote their time to such matters, there is generally no sophisticated development of art, philosophy, or religion.

The following general statements summarize food collectors:

1. The population density is rigidly set by the natural environment.
2. Group size ordinarily will be small.
3. The way of life is, of necessity, nomadic.
4. A nomadic people will not ordinarily accumulate much in the way of portable wealth.
5. In the absence of a reliable, predictable surplus, there can be no permanent, non-food-producing specialists.
6. Kinship will be a sufficient basis for regulating most social relationships. Therefore, political organization is rudimentary.

Such cultures, in comparison with those based on a more advanced technology, represent a low level of development.

The Agricultural Revolution

As long as man's technologies consisted of tools and techniques applicable solely to the collecting of wild foods, a rigid limit was set upon further cultural development. Those hunting and gathering tribes that persisted into historical times have not demonstrably exceeded the cultural level attained in the European Upper Paleolithic 20,000 years ago. Eventually, however, men in several parts of the world, stimulated perhaps by climatic change and a dwindling food supply, began to intervene in the natural processes of plant growth and of animal reproduction. The eventual result was man's control over his food supply. The consequences of this technological innovation, in terms of culture building, were truly revolutionary.

This development first occurred somewhere in the Middle East, and possibly in western China, as early as 8000 B.C., and perhaps as early as 6000 B.C. in the New World. Archaeologists have long named this new era, inaugurated by the beginnings of agriculture and animal domestication, the Neolithic or the New Stone Age. Compared with the excavated remains of earlier periods, the most notable characteristic of Neolithic artifacts is that they are made of ground and polished stone, rather than of chipped or flaked stones as in the previous ages. This new stone-working technique gave the era its name.

In terms of technological evolution, however, the crucial change was not from chipped to ground stone, but from food collection to food production. In White's terms this constituted an energy revolution. It was this development that released man from his "slavery" to his food supply and permitted his population density to rise beyond its previous environmentally determined limits. Within 5,000 years the process of cultural evolution, triggered by this technological revolution, had culminated in the urban civilizations of Egypt, Mesopotamia, and India. Indeed, the level of culture attained by these ancient civilizations was not greatly exceeded for the next 4,000 years, until the Industrial Revolution of the eighteenth century. This long period of time—from 10,000 years ago until 200 years ago—extends over a number of archaeological and historical time periods. It begins with the Neolithic, spans the Bronze and Iron Ages, and extends far into the period of recorded history.

Are we dealing here with one stage in cultural evolution, or several? White (op. cit.), whose focus is on energy as the prime mover of cultural evolution, points out that plant and animal domestication, as devices for harnessing energy, remained as man's highest technological achievement until the Industrial Revolution. Therefore, he treats this long period as a single stage of cultural evolution. The so-called Bronze and Iron Ages are but phases within the Agricultural Revolution. Childe (1936), on the other hand, is most impressed with the development of urban life around 3000 B.C. He speaks of this development, with its concomitant development of metallurgy, writing, astronomy, mathematics, massive architecture, the wheel, great irrigation works, and complex religious systems, as the Urban Revolution. This term is not entirely satisfactory, however, since comparable (though later) developments in the New World did not always culminate in urban life. The Maya civilization of southern Mexico and Guatemala, for example, achieved many of the things listed as concomitants of urban civilization in the Middle East without a developed urban life.

It is meaningful to recognize a number of substages in the agricultural stage of cultural evolution, with each higher substage having a more highly developed agricultural technology and correspondingly higher social, political, and religious developments. Steward and Faron (1959:70) refer to the earliest phase of the Agricultural Revolution in South America as that of "incipient farming." A similar phase can be identified for the Old World. The earliest farmers, judging from scanty archaeological evidence, did not immediately give up their hunting and gathering way of life, but combined the two pursuits. Only as the new way of life became increasingly productive were they able to give up their nomadism completely. This incipient farming phase reached its climax when man had achieved a nearly sedentary way of life, living in scattered, politically autonomous farm villages. This level was probably achieved as early as 4000 B.C. in the Middle East and by 1500 B.C. in southern Mexico and in the Central Andean region of South America. Archaeologists would classify these cultures as late Neolithic.

Before 3000 B.C. in the Old World, and by 1000 B.C. in the New World, irrigation agriculture was being practiced, permitting larger population densities and larger population aggregates. Politically, this development was accompanied by the formation of small, multicommunity states. American archaeologists refer to this period in Middle America and South America as the Formative or Pre-Classic period, because the foundations were being laid for the later "classic" developments in civilization. In the Old World this development immediately preceded the urban Bronze Age civilizations. In the older archaeological literature this late Neolithic phase is referred to as the Chalcolithic Age, when raw copper nuggets were hammered into usable shapes without smelting.

By the time the Classic era had arrived in the New World (early in the Christian era), and Old World civilizations were in the Bronze Age, agricultural and animal-breeding technology had very nearly reached the maximum development they would attain before the Industrial Revolution. Socially and politically this technological development was accompanied by the formation of large conquest states and empires. During the next 4,000 years countless new states and empires arose and fell, but the general level of social and political complexity attained by these early civilizations was not exceeded. Many new technical and other innovations appeared—iron smelting, the domestication of the horse, the invention of the alphabet and money, the water wheel and the windmill, and many more. But none of these things, in White's terms, constituted an energy revolution. Plant and animal husbandry, utilizing human and animal power, remained the technological basis for these civilizations. The "underdeveloped nations" of today's world are those that have yet to feel the full impact of the next development in cultural evolution and, therefore, still retain many characteristics of these preindustrial agricultural civilizations.

The Industrial Revolution

The latest stage in cultural evolution, the Industrial Revolution, began very recently and is abundantly documented by written history. It does not correspond, therefore, to any of the ages of archaeology. The classi-

Guatemalan Indian peasants till the soil with hoes. The so-called "underdeveloped nations" of today's world are those that have yet to feel the full impact of the next development in cultural evolution and, therefore, commonly retain many characteristics of pre-industrial agricultural societies. (Photo by Robert H. Ewald.)

cal evolutionists had little to say of this important stage. Morgan's status of civilization began with the alphabet, long before the birth of Christ. He discusses the industrial developments of his own day, but does not assign them to a separate substage in his evolutionist scheme.

Many modern scholars, particularly specialists in the history of technology, have addressed themselves to the social and political implications of the industrial age, but anthropologists in general have not made this a major concern. White was one of the first to incorporate a "fuel revolution" into his scheme of cultural evolution, as early as 1943, and more recently Rodnick (1966) has provided an extended treatment of the industrial age. Many anthropological fieldworkers have studied the impact of modern industrial civilization on native peoples throughout the world, but relatively few have studied western civilization by itself.

To the historian the Industrial Revolution had its roots in the fifteenth and sixteenth centuries and embraced many developments—social, economic, and technical—over a long span of time. Reference is made to the breakdown of the medieval guild system, and its replacement by the so-called domestic system; to expanding market systems, with the accompanying greater pressure for increased production and improved production methods; to the growing importance of the new middle classes in England, Holland, Germany, and France; and to the many new technical inventions which made their appearance in the earlier phases of the Industrial Revolution. The invention of the flying shuttle in 1753 represented the first great change in textile-weaving technology in many centuries. This was followed soon by Hargreaves' "spinning jenny," and by Cartwright's "power loom," which replaced human muscle power with that of the horse. These and many more inventions are products of the rapid social, economic, and political developments of the eighteenth century, but none provided any new sources of power.

The Industrial Revolution as a new stage in cultural evolution properly begins, therefore, with the appearance of an effective steam engine. As early as 1712 Newcomen's highly inefficient steam engine was being used more or less satisfactorily in English coal mines. It was not until 1769 that James Watt patented a workable steam engine, and even then many more years of steady improvements had to follow before this engine gained general acceptance. Thus, it was 1800 before this invention was widely adopted by the textile industry, and it was not until the decade 1840–50 that George Stephenson's earlier locomotive gained widespread use in England. This development of the steam engine was, of course, inseparable from other developments of the so-called coal and iron age. Nevertheless, we accept the steam engine as the single most important invention in harnessing the enormous energy stores locked up in the earth's huge coal reserves. Its appearance in 1769 heralds the beginning of the Industrial Revolution.

Consequences of the Industrial Revolution. Rodnick (*ibid.*, 182) refers to the consequences of the Industrial Revolution as constituting a Secondary civilization. The earlier Primary civilization was peasant-based and tradition-oriented, whereas the new Secondary civilization would be urbanized, factory-organized, and market-oriented. There can be no doubt that the changes following the invention of the steam engine were revolutionary in nature. There are masses of statistics from many sources to show the sudden and radical increases in industrial production in those nations immediately affected by the revolution— those favored with coal and iron reserves. It would require many pages just to summarize the changes suggested by Rodnick in the above reference. The social, political, and economic consequences of steam-powered transportation form a major part of this story. The phenomenal rise in world population, and the vast movements of people from the country to the cities where factories were located is another story. The emergence of modern nations and empires, the military and political struggles for the world's raw materials and for domination over world markets are important parts of the total story that we are still living today.

Still another important consequence of the Industrial Revolution amounted virtually to a second Agricultural Revolution. The reader may have wondered why the extremely rapid developments of the earlier Agricultural Revolution tapered off around 3000 B.C., when agricultural productivity had clearly not achieved its potential (indeed, it has yet to reach that potential). The answer is that *it had achieved the fullest development possible with a non-industrial technology.* To exploit more completely the potential inherent in plant domestication, man first had to develop a modern machine technology, systems of rapid transportation, advanced techniques for food storage and preservation, and a modern scientific knowledge of agronomy. These things were achieved during the Industrial Revolution, and agriculture became revolutionized in their wake. Today's agricultural technology is able, potentially, to produce an abundance for everyone—something not possible in a pre-industrial, peasant economy.

SUMMARY

In terms of the general formulation above, there is a close relationship between the technological aspect of any cultural system and its organizational and ideational aspects. When the perspective is culture in general (rather than specific sociocultural systems), the primary determinism in this relationship is exerted by technology. With this long-range perspective, we saw that each of two major technological revolutions was followed by sweeping changes in the other two major sectors of culture (the organizational and the ideational). There is nothing in this theory which demands, however, that changes in social organization and in cultural ideologies occur at an equal rate, or that either keeps pace with technological change. On the contrary, social patterns and belief systems are far more resistant to change than are technical devices and processes, and we should expect a lag in the adjustment of these sectors of culture to a changing technology. Thus, it is not inaccurate to say that the world is still adjusting to the consequences of the Industrial Revolution. There is widespread starvation in a world that has the technological resources to feed its many millions. Hundreds of millions of people die of diseases which modern medicine can conquer and has conquered in more favored nations. Countless millions more are landless and cannot find alternative employment in commerce and industry. We have not yet evolved the social, economic, and political institutions for allocating the world's resources (agricultural and industrial products) among the world's peoples and nations. Many other social ills such as crime, the breakdown of traditional institutions, and the prevalence of socially disapproved behavior patterns of many kinds are closely related to this great lag between technological advance and social organization.

II

ORGANIZATION
OF CULTURE

7

Organizational Basis of Society

INTRODUCTION

One of the main objectives of this book is to provide the reader with a precise understanding of the concept of organization as it relates to culture. This is a crucial concept because human behavior is always carried on in some kind of organizational framework. A major purpose of this chapter is to show how human groups organize themselves to carry on the activities that make up part of their culture.

At the outset, this objective may appear to be one which can be achieved rather easily. Each one of us has some idea of what is meant by organization, and, if necessary, could provide some kind of definition. We are confronted with the idea, if not the term, in the course of our daily existence. News media make constant reference to organized groups such as the Democratic or Republican party, the Catholic Church, the Organization of American States, a professional sports team, a labor union, the Congress of the United States, and innumerable "lettered" organizations such as CORE or NATO. Each of these suggests to us a particular and distinct group of individuals who are united in a specific way, who carry on particular activities, and who seek to achieve specific objectives and goals through their unity and their behavior. Similarly, though we may not consciously think of them in these terms, we belong to smaller groups which are an integral part of our daily lives, and which are characterized by organization. In fact, one of the significant features diagnostic of all effective groups is organization. The particular type of organization may vary with the complexity or the type of group being considered, but there are certain principles of organization which are found in all groups, large or small, formal or informal, simple or complex.

MAJOR COMPONENTS OF ORGANIZATION

All organization has three major components: *structure, action,* and *function.* Organization is further divisible into two major dimensions: the structural dimension and the behavioral dimension. The behavioral dimension of organization refers to the reality of human culture, whereas the structural dimension refers to the expectations of human culture—how the *people themselves* conceptualize their behavior. The general relationships among the components of organization are shown in Fig.

Structural Dimension	*Behavioral Dimension*
Expected structure	Real structure
Expected action	Real action
Expected function	Real function

Fig. 7–1. Organization.

7–1. These terms are defined briefly now, and a more extensive explanation of each is presented later in this chapter.

1. *Real action,* which is the most accurate starting point for all analyses of organization, is the actual behavior of human individuals—it consists of real events.
2. *Real structure* refers to the positions individuals fill and the ways in which these positions are actually related to one another. For example, several named individuals who occupy a dwelling, more or less permanently, to the exclusion of other individuals, who refer to one another by certain socially acceptable terms, who expect a particular and unique kind of behavior from each person called by a different term, and who have certain rights and obligations in relation to one another, constitute a real structure called a family or a household.
3. *Real function* refers to the *results* of the action performed by the individuals who occupy the positions that make up the structure. If the actions of the members of a hypothetical family result in the procreation of children, their care and feeding, the sexual satisfaction of the adult members, and so on, then these things are said to be real functions— actual results of behavior.
4. *Expected structure* is the positions (statuses) and their interrelationships that "should" occur in a given social group. Expected structure may be thought of as an ideal blueprint of a social group or of the total society. Frequently, the analyst finds that the expected structure is different from the structure that actually exists.

5. *Expected action* is behavior which "should" be performed. It is behavior expected of individuals who occupy or who "ought" to occupy those positions that make up the expected structure of a group or of a society. Clearly, this is not the same thing as real action, because the actual behavior of individuals may depart quite radically from that which is expected of them.

6. *Expected function* refers to the expected results of action which should be performed. There are numerous ideal structures in United States society (the nuclear family, police forces, labor unions, political bodies, and so on) which are expected, through the behavior of their members, to achieve certain results. Their actual functions (the results of real behavior) may be quite different, as subsequent discussions will show.

The Nuclear Family: An Example of Organization

At the beginning of this chapter it was stated that everyone has some idea of what is meant by organization. The reader could certainly illustrate what he means by organization by employing a social unit very familiar to him—the family. Because of the familiarity of the reader with the family type diagnostic of United States society (frequently referred to by anthropologists as the nuclear family), it will be used to illustrate the discussion presented in this chapter.

If asked, we would offer the terms father, mother, son, daughter, husband, wife, sister, and brother as labeling members of such a family unit. While each of us may have in mind particular individuals when we use these terms, they are also an efficient shorthand method for describing particular social positions characteristic of a specific social group—in this case, the nuclear family. The term brother, for example, labels not only particular individuals, but also a class which includes all male siblings. Similarly, the term son labels that class which includes all of one's male offspring. Furthermore, these terms label social positions (statuses) which are meaningful only in relation to some other position. One social position implies another. The status of husband, for example, is meaningful only in relation to another status, wife, and the term father implies the existence of other statuses, son and daughter. While each of these pairs of relationships is important in itself, their greatest significance, individually and in sum, is in relation to the group. Taken together, these statuses form an integrated and internally coherent structure, the nuclear family. The structural design of the family is given in Fig. 7–2.

Careful examination of Fig. 7–2 also shows the specific statuses that make up the nuclear family, as well as the particular types of relationships that occur among these statuses. Based upon the number of statuses that occur in any social group, the number of possible relationships

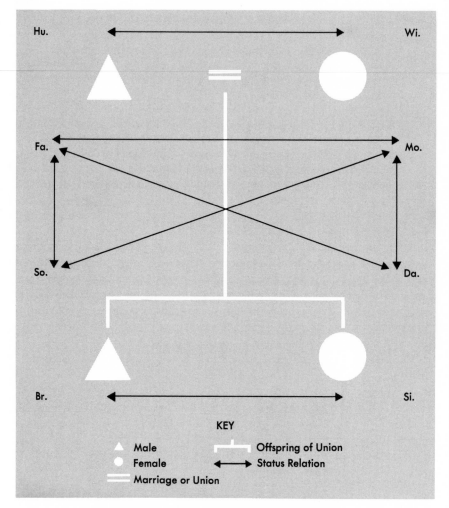

Fig. 7–2. Structure of the nuclear family.

that can conceivably occur may be determined. For the nuclear family, eight statuses and twelve logically possible relationships represent the maximum numbers. The twelve relationships that occur within the context of the nuclear family are of definite types. There are seven logically possible *dyadic* relationships that can occur, four *triadic* ones, and a single *quadratic* one. These relationships are listed systematically in Fig. 7–3.

Isolation of the statuses that occur within a nuclear family unit and of the specific interrelationships that are present does nothing more than define the *structure* of this particular group. It is essentially a blueprint

Dyadic Relationships	Triadic Relationships	Quadratic Relationship
1. Husband–Wife	1. Father–Son–Daughter	1. Father–Mother–Son–Daughter
2. Father–Mother	2. Mother–Son–Daughter	
3. Father–Son	3. Father–Mother–Son	
4. Father–Daughter	4. Father–Mother–Daughter	
5. Mother–Son		
6. Mother–Daughter		
7. Sister–Brother		

Fig. 7–3. Types of nuclear family relationships.

of the unit, or the way the parts are put together. This methodological technique for isolating structure is not restricted to social groups but is applicable to all things. The same procedure may be used by the geologist for determining the structure of a rock, by a chemist to arrive at the structure of a compound, or a biologist to ascertain the structure of an amoeba. This type of analysis emphasizes the more general fact that all things are characterized by a particular structure. A rock, a tree, a nation, and a football team all have a structure which can be isolated, identified, and described.

Structure as a Component of Organization

Structure essentially involves two things: the unique parts that make up the total unit, and the relationships among these parts. All things, animate and inanimate, have a structure made up of related parts. We are not concerned for the time being with either inanimate or biological structures, but with social structures, and, in particular, human social structures. What are the parts that make up a human social structure and how are they interrelated?

Real and Expected Structure. If any one of thousands of United States citizens were asked to describe the structure of the family in the United States, he would probably do so in terms of the unit just described—two adults, united by marriage, and their offspring. If it were pointed out to him that in his own neighborhood some homes were occupied by families lacking a male parent, by couples lacking children, or by a nuclear family and one or more grandparents, he would very likely regard these as departures from a *general rule*. This fact suggests a further distinction: between *real structures*, which are empirically derived, and *expected structures*, which people regard as ideal or upon which they model their own behavior. In other words, the people who live in a society will very often have a *conscious model* of how their society is structured—of what its parts are and how they are arranged.

Real structures, which are observable by an anthropologist, sociologist, or census taker, may, and often do, depart from this ideal.

It must be emphasized that an expected structure can also be something created by the social scientist, something arrived at analytically on the basis of his observations. The anthropologist's "blueprint" of United States society may be quite close to the expected structure of the "man in the street," at least with respect to a structure like that of the nuclear family. The chief difference may be that the anthropologist's description would show the range of variation that exists, whereas the layman would be only casually interested in such departures from the ideal. The social scientist's analysis, since it is more precise, may reveal structures of which the lay members of a society are unaware. Such structures are often highly significant for understanding the functioning of a social system. In the United States, for example, a formal analysis of our political structure, such as may be found in a high school or even a college textbook, may omit many informal but highly significant structural relations of which few persons are aware. In many Mexican villages, a researcher would find a formal political structure consisting of, among other things, a mayor, a town magistrate, an elected council, a number of salaried officials, and so on. Very often, however, there is a powerful individual, a *cacique* or boss, who operates behind the scenes, and who, locally, is not really thought of as part of formal political life. Nevertheless, the anthropologist's analytically derived structure, his blueprint of the community, should include this position, and the lines of power between it and other formally recognized positions should be specified.

The term *expected* is used here in both ways—the people's ideal model and the social scientist's analytically derived model. In either case, the expected structure will bear some relationship to real structure, but very often the two will not coincide exactly.

Animate and Inanimate Structure. We may generalize, then, that all organizations are characterized by structure. However, the converse statement, that all structures have organization, is not true according to our conception of organization. Animate and social structures are characterized by *behavior*. Behavior involves action, which makes such structures dynamic. Let us examine the significance of this distinction.

An inanimate thing, for example, a rock, is characterized by a structure consisting of certain parts and a particular relationship among these parts. It is, nevertheless, a static thing. It is only when forces external to the rock are applied in a particular way, as when it is thrown by a boy, that we can speak of action associated with it. Even then, we are not speaking of the same rock, but of a rock which has been momentarily modified by adding this externally derived animate element. Similarly, an artifact, such as an arrow point, is characterized by a structure, but lacks the active coefficient associated with animate or social things. Only when man unites the point with a shaft, picks up a bow, directs the point toward a target, and applies muscular power in a special way, is the point put into action. In each of these activities, which ultimately achieves action in relation to the point, external forces are applied. Consequently, the correct postulate must read: *all things have a structure, but only animate and social things are characterized by organization.* Those things which lack the capacity for action by themselves are completely static. This is a crucial concept, because static things also lack the capacity to adapt to changing conditions, if indeed there is any need for them to adapt at all. The only possible change that can occur is one which is imposed by external forces. Adaptation, however, is vital to animate or social structures. Action is the dynamic aspect of organization.

Action as a Component of Organization

A description of the structure of a society or a human group does nothing more than specify the structural positions that exist and the relationships among them. Such a description is incomplete until the individuals who occupy these positions, and their behavior as occupants, are considered. As we indicated above, it is action that distinguishes dynamic structures from static, inanimate ones, and permits us to consider social structures as aspects of organization. Action can be defined, therefore, as the behavioral coefficient of structure.

Much of individual human behavior is associated with the occupancy of certain social statuses, or structural positions within a group. In the United States the statuses husband and father (these are clearly not identical, though usually occupied by the same person) have a number of behavioral characteristics. A man occupying these statuses can often be observed to act as provider, disciplinarian, or protector of those occupying the reciprocal statuses of son or daughter, or as companion to the woman occupying the status of wife. In the United States there are certain behavioral characteristics associated with each of the positions in the nuclear family. These behaviors are expected of those who occupy such statuses. However, if the behavior of a number of individuals who occupy the same status was observed, it would soon become obvious that not all these persons behave in exactly the same way, and not all of them perform all the actions expected of their respective statuses. Therefore, the same distinction made for structure is equally true of action.

Real and Expected Action. Each structural position in a social group or system has a certain complex of behavior associated with it. Depending upon the particular status involved—priest, judge, father, fraternity brother, friend—the associated behavior may be highly explicit or very general. Thus, the behavior associated with a priest in United States society can be described in fairly explicit terms, whereas that between friends is only loosely specified. On the other hand, in some societies there is a custom of *institutionalized friendship:* a more formal relationship characterized by explicit behavioral expectations. In much of Latin America, for example, a special relationship is established between the father of a child and the godfather at baptism. These men become *compadres* (coparents) to one another, based upon their relationship to the child. Frequently, the behavior associated with this status (*compadre*) is more specific than that for the status of brother or cousin.

It is a matter of observation that different individuals occupying the same status will not behave exactly alike. Some fathers in United States society provide economic support for their wives and children, others do not. A mother may be slack in the performance of her domestic duties or in the care and training of her children. A medical doctor may refuse to call on a patient, or a clergyman may break a vow of celibacy. There is, in short, a difference between *real action* (what people actually do) and *expected action* (what society anticipates they will do as occupants of particular statuses).

Expected action is a complex of behavior, attached by custom or convention to a particular social status, and expected of anyone who fills that status. In cultural terms, expected action may be translated as *ideal* culture, as opposed to *manifest* culture (what people actually do). It is what people say they should do, or are expected to do, as opposed to what they actually do (real action) in any situation.

It is through the complex of expected behavior that statuses are linked to one another in a reciprocal manner. That is, certain behavior is expected of a wife toward her husband, and of a husband toward his wife; of a father toward his son or daughter, and of children toward their father. Any social system—any set of linked statuses—may be defined, therefore, as a system of mutual expectations. Subsequent chapters on social, economic, and religious life will make these points more explicit. There are few human activities that do not, in some measure, reflect the manifestation of status-linked behavior or the expectation of such behavior on the part of others.

Human behavior, which is real action carried on by individuals occupying certain statuses as a consequence of social expectations, is nearly always directed toward some culturally desired goal—social, religious, economic, political, and so on. These goals relate to needs, desires, and interests of individuals and of groups. If the expected behavior patterns are carried out, some of the socially desired results are achieved. This brings us to function, the third component of organization.

Function as a Component of Organization

Function refers, simply, to the results of action that occur in relation to a particular structure and/or structural position. Our use of the term function is in accord with popular usage. The function of the human heart is that of pumping blood; of an automobile carburetor, that of mixing air and gasoline; of a refrigerator, that of cooling and preserving food; of a canoe, that of transporting someone or something. In each case, the functioning of the object in question achieves certain results, which we define as being the function of that object. Function, therefore, includes the results of action of individuals occupying particular statuses.

Real and Expected Function. The same distinction applied to structure and action may be applied to function, and for the same reason: the discrepancy between what is observed to happen and what ideally should happen. The difference between expected function and real function can be brought out by using, once more, the example of the nuclear family in the United States.

One expected function of the family is to produce offspring, and perpetuation of the society depends on the fulfillment of this function. The production of offspring (an expected function) is related to the expected action of members of the family unit, in this case, prescribed sexual behavior between those occupying the statuses of husband and wife. However, in actual practice, the persons filling these statuses may not perform according to social expectations. Possibly one or the other is frigid or impotent. Possibly one or both are sterile. Therefore, the expected function of the family may not be realized. To be realized, this function clearly depends upon the real action of the individuals who fill the particular statuses of husband and wife.

If there are children, and if these children produce offspring of their own outside the marital union, then we could maintain that the family has fulfilled a real function, but not one that accords with social expectations. In this case, the real action is not coincident with expected action, that of husband and wife producing offspring, and that of premarital chastity. If, however, offspring are produced in accordance with the prescribed rules of behavior, then the real action will coincide with the expected action. In that case, real function and expected function will be one and the same; complete coincidence will be achieved. More frequently, however, there is significant variation between expected action and real action. Since function is the result of action, the same variation will be found between real and expected function.

The Function of Material Objects. The emphasis throughout this chapter is on culture as *socially organized* behavior. Our stress, therefore, is on action. An anthropological definition of culture, however, includes artifacts, or material culture. Is it meaningful to include material objects as part of human behavior? Anthropologists, who regard culture as human behavior, have resolved this logical difficulty by extending their definition to include the "material results of behavior." It is only by relating function to action, however, that it becomes meaningful to include material objects in a definition of culture. As we have already stressed, inanimate objects are incapable of action, and their function depends upon human intentions or motivations and human action. These intentions or motivations are, in turn, associated with certain statuses or structural positions—an axe is used by a man; a cooking pot or a digging stick is used by a woman. The object in question has no expected function independent of the intentions of its user, and it has no real function apart from the action of its user. As explained above, it is only when an animate, external force is applied that an inanimate thing acquires a real function. A wrist watch, although people speak of it as having a function, is incapable of either expected or real function unless man winds it or reads it. It is the *use* of material objects by man that makes it meaningful to speak of them as parts of culture, and therefore of human organization. The crucial factor, once more, is that of action; expected function and real function are dependent upon action.

THE RELATIONSHIPS AMONG STRUCTURE, ACTION, AND FUNCTION

Social organization, like any other concept in the sciences, is used as an explanatory concept. That which is to be explained, in this case, is the action of human individuals and of human groups. The starting point for these analyses must, therefore, always be human behavior or action. The complexity of our phenomena requires more than a common-sense approach. We have refined our analysis to include six logical constructs: real and expected structure, real and expected action, and real and expected function. Each is logically distinct from the others, but all are based upon human behavior, and all are related to one another as aspects of organization.

This relationship can be illustrated best by returning, again, to the nuclear family, and then by showing how the family is linked through behavior—real and expected—to still other structures.

Just as expected behavior is attached to a particular social status in a given social group, and is expected of the individual who fills the status, similarly, the *group itself* has a specific behavioral complex associated with it and expected of it. The behavioral complex associated with the nuclear family is at least the sum of the total expected behavior of all the statuses included in its structure, but it is usually more than this sum. The behavior expected of the nuclear family unit in the United States does more than satisfy individual or family objectives; it is directly linked to the necessary goals of the society. The family is expected to provide and train progeny who are able to contribute positive behavior to the society, which in turn contributes to the perpetuation of the total society. The failure of the nuclear family to accomplish this goal, or to accomplish it in an effective manner, threatens the existence of the society. That is, each nuclear family unit must produce offspring who, in turn, will form their own nuclear family units to produce further offspring. The primary way in which societies recruit new members is through birth, and this is a primary function of the family. A larger society is generally made up of groups other than the nuclear family, but their membership is derived from that of the family. Occupational groups, religious groups, social clubs, political organizations, labor unions, all are made up of structural positions which must be occupied by individuals. If the family failed in its essential function of producing offspring, it follows that there would be no individuals to occupy these statuses. The existence of the society would be threatened.

Each social group within a larger society has a structure—an interrelated set of structural positions or statuses—peculiar to itself, and a complex of behavior associated with this structure and expected of it. These social groups are, themselves, structural units which are linked together to form the total social structure of the society. They are linked to one another because the same individuals occupy statuses and perform the behavior expected of those statuses in a number of groups. To illustrate: in United States society, a single individual can be a member of his natal family (his family of orientation), his own family established through marriage (his family of procreation), an occupational group (factory, corporation), a church, a number of social clubs, a college fraternity, a home owners' association, and many more. All are linked by the fact of his membership and participation in each of them.

To summarize briefly, structure, action, and function are the necessary and sufficient major factors of organization, with action being the single most significant and diagnostic factor. Structure defines the parts and their interrelationships; action is the dynamic aspect of such relationships; and function is the result of such action associated with a particular structure. The structural dimension of human social organization (or for that matter any animate or social thing) taken by itself is a static construct. It may be seen, for purposes of analysis, as a model against which the dynamic aspects of organization are measured. Real action, in other words, is described and explained in the context of an expected structure. This relationship between action and structure is of

This man, pictured with his four wives and one child, fills the roles of husband, father, and chief of the Zongos in British Togoland. (United Nations.)

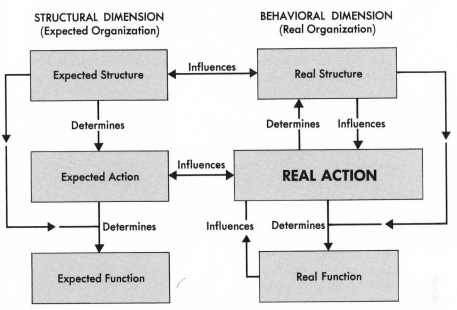

Fig. 7–4. Necessary and sufficient factors of organization.

even greater significance when it is recognized that it is real action that causes structural modification or change, an important consideration in the study of culture and society.

A Hypothetical Case

The three most important ideas involved here are (1) the distinction between organization and structure and its application to different classes of objects, (2) the significance of action for the concept of organization, and (3) the method for analyzing all forms of organization. These ideas and their interrelationships, as discussed to this point, are presented in Fig. 7–4. The figure becomes even more meaningful if the following hypothetical case materials are inserted in the relevant boxes, and the relationships among them are traced (the arrows of influence and determination in the figure):

1. *Real action:* A father in United States society "separates" from his wife, but continues to contribute to her support and to that of his children. He visits his children regularly, and shows much affection for them; occasionally, he gives them advice. They, in turn, reciprocate his affection, but do not recognize his authority. They show more fear and respect for their mother.

2. *Real structure:* In this case, a dwelling is occupied by a woman (mother) and her dependent children, but with no adult male (husband and father) present. The real actions of the individuals concerned—the payments made by the father, his visits to his children, sexual avoidance between him and his wife, etc.—are all *influenced* by the real structure. This real structure is *determined* by the real actions of these individuals.

3. *Real function:* The results of the actions of the family members, behaving within this real structure, are the financial support of mother and children by the absentee father, limited shows of affection between children and father, and sexual continence on the part of both parents. This continence is expected behavior in this case, but the other functions (results of action) are less than are expected for a "complete" nuclear family.

4. *Expected structure:* For this society, the expected structure is that of a father, mother, and children all present. Each status is occupied by an individual or individuals. All the dyadic, triadic, and quadratic relationships illustrated in Fig. 7–3 are present. This expected structure influences real structure. Thus, periodic visits of the father to see his children temporarily complete the structure. In the society at large, far more families (real structures) are "complete" than not. Through custom and tradition this type has come to be expected. Expected structure is, in other words, influenced by what actually occurs.

5. *Expected action:* Each of the structural positions in the expected family structure carries with it certain socially expected behavioral patterns, including financial support by the father, shows of affection between all individuals, shows of authority by the father, and so on. These social expectations influence the real action of the father—he visits his children and continues his support. It is expected that the mother will permit these visits, and in this case she does.

6. *Expected function:* The expected function of the family (as an ideal or expected structure) is to produce children, socialize them, provide sexual satisfaction for husband and wife, emotional satisfactions for all individuals, economic support for mother and children, and certain domestic services for all members. These results ideally come about through the expected actions of those occupying the statuses within the ideal structure.

NORMS AND NORMATIVE ACTION

All organized and effective activity in human society (effective in the sense that it contributes to socially desired or approved goals) is characterized by *normative behavior*. Similarly, all organizations and all structural positions within organizations are characterized by *norms*. Basically, norms are cultural rules for action which may be viewed as choices from among an almost unlimited range of possible alternatives in a given situation. An example might be the behavior of two male friends meeting after a separation of weeks or months. Such behavior probably takes hundreds of forms in the world at large, but in a given culture the alternatives are few. Latin American males commonly embrace. In the United States two males will most commonly shake hands. Two Barabaig males (eastern Africa) will clasp hands much as it is done in the United States, then shift the grip to the thumb, and then back to the handclasp, all in rapid succession (Klima 1967). Among a neighboring group, men were observed to spit into each other's right hand (*ibid.*). Each pattern of behavior constitutes a cultural rule, a cultural choice among conceivable alternatives. By our definition, each represents a cultural norm.

Ethnographic Examples of Normative Action

The following ethnographic examples will permit a more refined analysis of this concept.

"If a man sees a *sister* somewhere, he says to her: 'Sister, give me some areca nut; I don't have any with me.' But if a man meets up with any other woman not yet senile the latter runs and hides; she must not talk with him." (Oliver 1955:255.)

This statement by a Siuai (a Solomon Island society) male illustrates three normative patterns of behavior. First, behavioral interaction ". . . between opposite sex siblings of all gradations is friendly interaction and mutual generosity absolutely devoid of any suggestion of sexual intercourse" (*ibid.*). Second, this behavior implies that an incest taboo applies to all opposite sex siblings. Third, an avoidance taboo between non-siblings of opposite sex is expressed.

Another example from the literature:

[Martron, a resident of a French village] . . . had tried to arouse our suspicions against the Provins by saying, "I advise you to stay clear of the Provins family. I'm not saying why, you understand, and we'll pretend I have said nothing. It's a friendly warning. Take it as you will." His significant wink was intended to imply that he could give us plenty of proof if he weren't so discreet and kindly disposed. (Wylie 1964:197.)

The remarks here constitute an overt expression of the norm of *brouillé:*

If you are *brouillé* with someone, it means literally that you have been *mixed up* with him; your mutual relationship has become *confused.* You have quarreled and are now "on the outs." You have broken off relations. You avoid passing each other on the street, and when you cannot avoid passing you turn your head to avoid having to speak. You try not to be caught in a social situation in which you would normally be expected to shake hands. Through your behavior you try to create the impression that the person with whom you are *brouillé* has ceased to exist.

Even though you do not injure your opponent through physical or legal action, you may still harm him by attacking him orally. Oral aggression is socially acceptable, it rarely endangers the aggressor, and it may sometimes be even more effective than other types of aggression. The purpose of oral aggression is to arouse suspicion and resentment of your opponent so that he will be destroyed socially. (*Ibid.*, 196–97.)

The norms expressed in the following example refer to the sexual behavior characteristic of a social group of "withdrawees" (those who have dropped out of school) in Elmtown:

A withdrawee boy who had not "laid a girl" by the time he was old enough to leave school claimed that he had to protect himself from being called "a sissy," or "a pansy," by his clique mates. A boy who is known or believed to be a virgin is not respected by his peers. A boy is condemned severely, however, if he does not have enough knowledge of contraceptives and prophylactics to keep from getting "in trouble." "Trouble" involves two things, "knocking a girl up" (impregnation) or "getting a load" or a "dose" (venereal disease). (Hollingshead 1961:421.)

Each of these examples is an expression of *normative action* for a particular group, or a particular status within a given group; each is a manifestation, in actual behavior, of a cultural rule which defines action. It should be clear from this discussion that norms always refer to a social group or to some structural position (status) within a group.

Distinction Between Norms and Behavior

In the above examples a norm is a cultural rule which prescribes or proscribes certain action for Siuai siblings, for a boy in Elmtown toward his peers, for male Barabaig toward one another, and so on. Since norms characterize all social statuses and all social groups, all societies will be characterized by a wide variety of norms. However, not all the norms found in any one society will be compatible with one another. In fact, norms are often incompatible with one another. Using the Elmtown study as an example, it should be very apparent that membership in a peer group prescribes behavior that would be proscribed by membership in such other social units as the community, the family, or the church. In another situation, there may be incompatibility between the norms for an adult as prescribed by his church, and those prescribed by his suburban community. Being a social success in one's community may, for example, require a degree of drinking that is quite at variance with the norms of one's church. Actually, in any given society, we may find every degree of compatibility and incompatibility among its various norms.

The individual, whether as a member of a society or a social group within the society, or as the occupant of a certain status, will not always

Normative action is seen in the salutation of the Japanese Ainu. When a woman sees a man coming she gets down on her knees, bowing her head and at the same time moving her hand across her lips. The man sees her, folds his hands and bows, granting her permission to rise. (Courtesy of the American Museum of Natural History.)

behave exactly according to the norms for any given situation. In fact, individual behavior will always tend to vary about a norm. Therefore, it is necessary to distinguish between norms and normative action. Individual behavior or action is normative if it tends toward or approximates behavior called for by the existing norm. In order to distinguish more clearly between norms and normative action, it is necessary to explain the relationship between the concept of norms and the concept of expected behavior.

The reader may well ask whether the concepts of norms and expected behavior are not identical; are they not different ways of saying the same thing? A refined analysis of social organization requires that they be logically distinguished. The status of a religious specialist in our society, a minister or priest, will serve to illustrate this distinction. The expected behavior associated with this status includes the most exemplary conduct—either celibacy or strict monogamy, abstention from gambling and drinking, dignified demeanor, and so on. However, the minister who serves a sophisticated congregation may find it necessary to keep close to his people through such devices as moderate social drinking, laughing agreeably at off-color stories even if he doesn't tell them, becoming good at sports, and so on. Such behavior may actually become the norm for ministers in a given community without altering expectations of more exemplary conduct (expected behavior). In such a setting, the minister who insists on more "straight-laced" conduct will be departing from the norm, but will be adhering more closely to the expected behavior for his status. In this case, norms and expected behavior do not coincide. However, in other situations expected behavior and norms may coincide to a high degree or may be widely divergent.

What is the value of this distinction? Principally, it contributes to understanding social organization as a dynamic process. Social structure would be a static concept without the essential ingredient, action. Real action departs from expected action for any status or structural position in a society. Such departure, however, is never a disorganized or haphazard process. Even the departures occur within specified limits and may become normative in themselves. Thus, in the example above, ministers or priests may behave closely in accordance with community expectations. In this case, the norms and the expected behavior will be nearly congruent or coincidental. Where social factors favor a more relaxed attitude on the part of the clergy, expected action and normative action will diverge. But clergymen will, under these circumstances, tend to depart from expected behavior in similar directions, thereby establishing a new pattern or norm. This is one way in which new norms come into being: when actual behavior shows a general shift away from an established pattern. Such a process goes on continuously in any society. Isolating the causes for such shifts is an important part of the study of culture change.

The concepts of norms and normative action are to be seen, then, as additional dimensions in the analysis of social organization. They are clearly related to the concepts of expected action and real action, but they help us to emphasize that real action is socially patterned and varies only within culturally prescribed limits. These relationships between real and expected action, and norms and normative behavior, may be diagrammed as shown in Figs. 7–5 and 7–6.

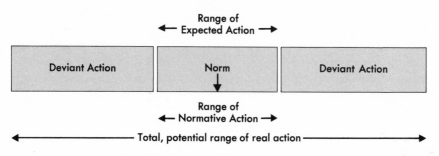

Fig. 7–5. Relationships among real action, expected action, norms, normative action, and deviant action.

A Guatemalan Example. Figure 7–5 may be illustrated with a special case. Many Guatemalan villages are characterized by a closed stratification system—an upper class of non-Indians or *Ladinos* and a lower class of Indians. Not only is there a lack of marriage between the classes, but no Indian male may ever have sexual relations with a *Ladino* woman. This is a community *norm*. So rigidly are such sex relations proscribed, even a slight departure from the norm would be regarded as punishable deviant behavior. The range of *normative behavior* is, therefore, very narrow. It is *expected*, by everyone in the community, that this proscribed relationship will not occur. Finally, although the potential range of real action is wide, the greatest majority of actual cases of behavior will occur at point X and will coincide with the norm. In such cases, there is almost complete coincidence (agreement) among these variables: norm, normative action, real action, and expected action.

Lack of agreement among these variables is probably far more common in human groups than is complete coincidence. Figure 7–6 may also be illustrated with data from a hypothetical Guatemalan village. A

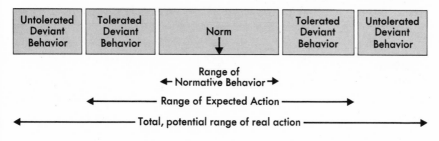

Fig. 7–6. Relationships among norms, real action, expected behavior, normative behavior, and deviant behavior.

Ladino male may not marry an Indian woman, but may, with relative impunity, have sexual relations with Indian women. Most *Ladino* men will boast of the number of such conquests and of the number of their children by such informal unions. This is a typical (normative) way of reasserting one's masculinity, an important value among *Ladino* men.

The *Ladino* cultural norm is that of males having sexual relations with Indian women, or at least boasting of such relations. The frequency of such relations will vary, however, and a man's behavior will fall within the range of normative behavior whether he seeks such relationships frequently or only occasionally. Thus, a relatively high frequency of behavior will depart from the norm, but will still be normative action. The deviant can be a man who either rejects extramarital relationships of this kind altogether (thereby losing esteem in the eyes of his fellows), or who seeks such relationships so indiscriminately and openly as to earn community disapproval. The range of expected action in this community may extend beyond the normative into the deviant. It is accepted locally that there are individual differences in behavior, and a mild degree of deviance in either direction is expected. Such limited deviance does not result in censure or punishment.

In this case, the community norm is not nearly as rigidly defined as in the first case, and the real action of all the adult *Ladino* males of the community can be distributed along nearly the entire range of potential real action. Thus, a specific hypothetical action (X in Fig. 7–6) will not coincide with the norm or the range of normative action, but will coincide with some point along the scale of expected action.

To summarize, in any given society there will be certain norms that are so rigidly prescribed (or proscribed) that the range of normative behavior will be very narrow (as in Fig. 7–5). The punishment for deviance will be so strict that real action will rarely depart from the norm. In all such cases, coincidence among norm, real action, expected action, and normative behavior will be high. A far greater proportion of norms, however, will permit a degree of latitude (as in Fig. 7–6), and the range of expected behavior will be correspondingly great. Figures 7–5 and 7–6 do not, of course, exhaust all of the logical possibilities. In United States society, for example, a father may overprovide (be deviant in one direction) without falling outside the range of expected behavior, whereas underprovision is not expected, and can lead to censure.

The figures also explain, in graphic form, the statement that manifest culture often fails to correspond to ideal culture. A statement of how priests or ministers should behave, or are expected to behave, is a statement of ideal culture. How they actually behave is manifest culture, whether this behavior corresponds exactly to the ideal or departs from it in some degree.

Behavioral Conformity and Deviance

Normative behavior is, of course, always a matter of degree. It would be fallacious to think of normative behavior as complete conformity on the part of all individuals within a society or social group. Complete conformity would be impossible, if for no other reason than that no two human individuals are ever exactly alike. A norm defines conduct within a given social situation, and in that situation no two individuals will behave exactly alike. Individually, their behavior is idiosyncratic and unique, but will tend toward a certain common pattern. That pattern we call a norm, but we also recognize that individual deviance from that norm will always be present in some degree. Deviation from norms occurs, then, because it must—it is rooted in the biological and psychological uniqueness of the individual.

It is important to understand, also, that complete conformity on the part of all individuals would be socially undesirable, even if it were possible. Every *effective* society or social group provides alternative patterns of behavior which receive some degree of acceptance within the group and which lead to ends similar to those achieved by normative behavior. Even among the members of a primitive hunting and gathering band, there will be alternative ways of weaving a basket, chipping a flint arrow point, tracking game, or constructing a house. A society in which alternative modes of behavior are completely lacking is a static society, one lacking in potential for change and therefore lacking the capacity for successful adaptation.

Social groups differ in the degree to which normative behavior corresponds to norms or to expected action. Some kinds of groups, by their very nature, will manifest a high degree of behavioral conformity, and there will be close congruence between norms and expected behavior. An extreme example of this would be a military unit, whose effectiveness in combat depends upon a high degree of conformity. A university faculty, on the other hand, will pride itself (unjustifiably perhaps) on its relatively broad toleration for individual differences. In theory, the degree of congruence between norms and normative behavior in any society will depend upon a variety of factors, including the composition, structure, and function of the group itself, the complexity of the larger society in which it exists, population density, the size of the society, and many more. The range of behavior that may occur in any social group or society in relation to a single norm is represented graphically in Fig. 7-7.

Figure 7-7 shows that normative behavior is the most frequent type of behavior which actually occurs. However, not all normative behavior is completely coincidental with the norm. Limited deviation from

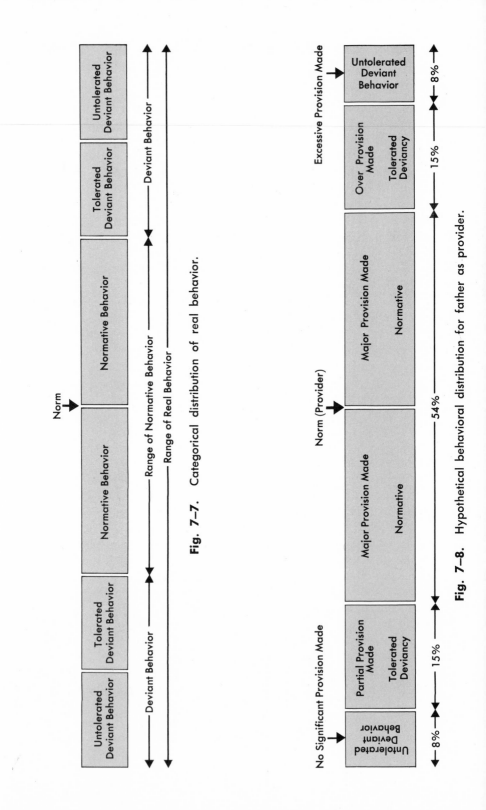

Fig. 7-7. Categorical distribution of real behavior.

Fig. 7-8. Hypothetical behavioral distribution for father as provider.

this cultural prescription or proscription does occur. In addition, some non-normative behavior, which is accepted or at least tolerated by the social unit, is present. This tolerated deviant behavior constitutes behavioral alternatives available to members of the social group, and it frequently acts as a stimulant to or a source of social change. Behavior that is tolerated deviant behavior at one time may be normative behavior at another time for the same social group. Also, some deviance occurs (non-acceptable behavior) that is not tolerated by the social group.

Consequently, in analyzing any social unit, it is crucial to determine (1) the range of normative behavior, (2) the tolerated deviation from the normative range, (3) the untolerated behavioral deviation present, (4) the degree of coincidence between the norm and normative behavior, and (5) the degree of coincidence among norms, normative behavior, and expected behavior.

A Hypothetical Example. An example may help to demonstrate this more specifically. If "provider" is accepted as one norm for the social status of father in contemporary United States society, the general range of behavior, given above, can be translated into more meaningful terms. By analyzing the behavior of 100 hypothetical individuals who fill the social status of father, a distribution similar to that given in Fig. 7–8 might be found.

In this example, the behavior of 54 per cent of those who fill the social status of father in contemporary United States society falls into the category of normative behavior. Within this category, only a small fraction of the behavior actually coincides completely with the norm. On the other hand, 30 per cent of the cases, while acceptable behavior, deviate significantly from the norm, and in 16 per cent of the cases the behavior of the individuals filling this social position is regarded as unacceptable by the society. In the category of untolerated deviant behavior, both under- and overprovision are defined as undesirable.

This example points out certain characteristics of normative behavior. First, normative behavior is shared behavior which is accepted by the members of the society, as opposed to other possible cultural alternatives which are less acceptable means of behaving in the same situation. For example, the father who spends his entire income on drink or gambling (underprovision) is not behaving normatively, nor is the father who radically overindulges his children. Second, normative behavior is not only acceptable behavior, it is also repetitive. That is, this type of behavior will be repeated sufficiently often by a significant number of individuals filling the particular social status involved, that such behavior becomes socially standardized. If provision were made for the family by only a few fathers, and this only sporadically, then it would not rep-

resent a socially standardized kind of behavior. It would not be sufficiently repetitive. Third, where such behavior is sufficiently repetitive
and does achieve significant standardization, it may be established as a
social expectation: the members of the society will expect this behavior
from those persons occupying the status involved. In United States
society there is a social expectation that fathers will provide financial
support for their wives and offspring. Fourth, normative behavior is
consistently dynamic and is always changing. Consequently, any high
degree of coincidence among expected action, real action, norms, and
normative behavior is always temporary and relatively short-lived. In
the earlier example, the model behavior held up as a norm for clergymen
gave way to new patterns of actual behavior as new social circumstances
dictated a more relaxed attitude. Fifth, normative behavior reflects social norms in varying degrees. It is an expression of the way in which
particular activities are repeatedly carried out and achieve standardization.

It should be apparent now that the concepts of norms and normative
behavior are essential to the concept of organization. The preliminary
discussion of organization, summarized in Fig. 7–4, is incomplete without the addition of these concepts, and for specific reasons. (1) Real
action, defined as the unique behaviors of individuals, is never completely haphazard or completely unique. Because of the existence of
cultural rules for behavior (norms) the several individuals occupying a
given status will tend to behave in a similar manner, that is, they will
behave normatively. Most real action, as Fig. 7–8 indicates, is normative action. (2) The statuses which make up a social structure are
linked together, therefore, by real action, much of which is normative
behavior. It is by studying normative behavior that we specify the real
relationships among the various social statuses in a group, and in so
doing define the real organization, objectives, and goals of that group.

The concept of normative behavior as part of organization can be
further illustrated by using other members of the nuclear family. The
person designated as mother is the bearer of children, is an individual
who may supplement the economic support of the group, is charged with
the responsibility of caring for the young children, and is one who performs the daily household tasks. Son and daughter in this context are
labels for persons engaged in activities which will prepare them for full
adult status and responsibilities in the near future. If we view the totality of these activities in relation to one another, it will become clear that
they all contribute to the achievement of a common group goal—generally, the maintenance and perpetuation of the family unit. The father
who provides the economic necessities and protection for the family insures the daily continued existence of the family. The mother, by pro-

viding new offspring, and raising and training small children for adult status, also contributes to the daily maintenance of the family, but in addition, makes a basic contribution to the continued perpetuation of the family unit in years to come. The son and daughter, by accepting the training necessary for successful participation as adults in the society, insure the perpetuation of the family unit for the future. Each of the members of the family has a vested interest in achieving these goals.

COMPLEMENTARY HETEROGENEOUS BEHAVIOR

A slightly closer examination of the activities of family members reveals the complementary nature of their normative behavior. That is, all members of the family do not do the same thing (although in some cases the activities of more than one member may overlap). Rather, they exhibit *complementary behavior:* they do different things which complement each other and which, together, achieve common goals. This example illustrates still another major aspect of organization, that all effective organizations must be characterized by different kinds of behavior organized in a complementary fashion. Complete homogeneity (the same action by all members of a group) will result in a less-than-effective organization in the long run. However, heterogeneous behavior which meets the new demands of the changing environment allows the organization to continue as an effective form. Effective organizations must continue over a period of time. To do this requires some degree of adaptability, because external conditions are continuously changing. It is heterogeneous behavior which provides a large part of such adaptive capacity.

Heterogeneous behavior functions in a manner similar to that of mutations in biological species. That is, variety in behavior provides a greater degree of insurance for success in new situations. There is a greater probability that an organization with heterogeneous behavior will adapt to new situations more readily and effectively than one characterized by homogeneous behavior. Of course, these are two extremes of a situation which can be treated as a continuum. In hunting and gathering societies, where there tends to be a general division of labor according to sex, complementary economic endeavors exist which reinforce and in fact permit one another. Often the gathering of vegetable products is the task and responsibility of females, while males assume the obligation of hunting animals. Although game animals will normally provide a greater supply of food for the group than the vegetable products gathered by the women, the male hunters are not always successful. During this period of temporary lack of success, the group must still eat, in order to be able to hunt in the future, and the supply of vegetable products contributed by the female will become the major source of food. If all members of the group engaged in the same type of activities (homogeneous economic behavior), they would probably have less chance of surviving. This shows how complementary behavior tends to achieve a common goal for the group. All cases, even among hunting and gathering societies, are not as dramatic as the hypothetical one given here, but the same concept applies.

An illustration of this idea is found in a description of the Tiwi of northern Australia, among whom heterogeneous complementary behavior can be seen clearly.

By shortly after dawn each day, the household was up, and after a light breakfast, usually of leftovers from the previous night, everybody left camp to go to work. The women and children (except perhaps the five-to-ten-year-old boys, who were rather useless at that age) scattered in every direction from the camp with baskets and/or babies on their backs, to spend the day gathering food, chiefly vegetable foods, grubs, worms, and anything else edible. Since they had spent their lives doing it, the old women knew all about gathering and preparing vegetable foods, and they supervised the younger women. . . . The meat, fish, and game provided for the large household . . . was obtained by the young men. . . . (Hart and Pilling 1960:33 ff.)

Not significantly different from the basic concepts illustrated by the Tiwi is the heterogeneous complementary behavior which occurs among "Class II" families in Elmtown.

The family's income is earned largely by the male head through active daily participation in the practice of a large independent profession (law, medicine, engineering, dentistry); in the operation of a family-owned business; as a salaried executive in an enterprise owned by Class I families . . . ; or as a salaried professional in a public office. . . .
Wives as homemakers, mothers, and social secretaries run their home with the help of one general servant, usually part-time, or the hourly services of a scrub woman. . . . Both college and non-college fathers and mothers emphasize the need for a college education to their children. The children expect their parents to assist them materially in reaching and consolidating a desirable future. The boys are headed for business or a profession. The girls are steered toward a desirable marriage after an education has been secured; for they must be trained for the kind of life that is expected of them. (Hollingshead 1961:91 ff.)

An examination of the available evidence from published ethnographic and sociological works suggests that a high degree of complementary heterogeneous behavior exists for each social group. Whether such behavior exists at an optimum cannot be easily determined in practice. Theoretically, however, the nearer the achievement of this optimal point, the greater the stability of the group, and the greater the probability for the perpetuation of the social unit involved. Significant deviation from this optimum heterogeneity will decrease the stability of the group and the probability for its perpetuation in its current form. Such deviation may occur toward either extreme. On the one hand, too great a degree of homogeneous behavior in an activity will not provide insurance against failure. On the other hand, a high degree of heterogeneous behavior which lacks the minimal complementary characteristics will result in a lack of coordination, or anarchy. However, all groups will tolerate, without significant destructive results, a relative degree of homogeneous behavior and non-complementary heterogeneous behavior by its members. The heterogeneity of complementary behavior will occur in different degrees and at different levels in different groups. Thus, in the nuclear family there tends to be relatively little homogeneous behavior, little non-complementary heterogeneous behavior, but a high degree of complementary heterogeneous behavior. However, a band in a hunting and gathering society is characterized by a higher degree of homogeneous behavior than occurs in each family within the band.

INTEGRATION

An effective social system is one which carries on certain activities successfully: it provides subsistence needs, shelter from the elements, protection against enemies, and minimal psychological satisfactions for its members; perpetuates itself through some form of membership recruitment; regulates the conduct of individual members or of subgroups; and, in general, maintains an adjustment to its total environment which permits it to carry on these necessary activities and realize definite goals. All these activities imply an allocation of tasks and responsibilities among the individuals who make up the membership of the group. These tasks are allocated not to individuals *per se* but to individuals as occupants of certain structural positions. It is this structure that gives continuity and predictability to social life. Individuals die, but statuses persist over many generations.

An effective social system is, therefore, one in which there is a structure for the performance of all essential activities; in which real action tends to be normative; in which there is sufficient complementary heterogeneous behavior to make possible continued adaptation to changing conditions. It functions effectively because there is a certain "fit" among its parts. *Integration* is a measure of this fit and is another characteristic of organization, one which aids in examining and explaining the major components of organization, structure, action, and function.

Real and Expected Integration

Integration, as with structure, action, and function, is characterized by a real and an expected dimension. If the reader were asked to create a table of organization for a new business enterprise, a social fraternity, or a local labor union, he would probably first experiment with various organizational charts. Such a chart should be based, however, on some conception of the purposes or goals of the organization, i.e., the expected functions of the new group. These functions should, in turn, be translated into specific activities (expected behavior) necessary to realize the goals of the organization. The essential task, then, would consist of devising enough structural positions to embody the required authority, responsibilities, tasks, and so on. Lines would be drawn to indicate how the various statuses relate to one another—president, treasurer, executive secretary, executive council, public relations, rank-and-file members, and so on. The anticipated smooth and effective functioning of this organization would be its *expected integration.*

Once this new organization began to operate, it might soon be found that some essential tasks had been overlooked; lines of authority might be ambiguous; friction might develop between certain structural positions (e.g., president and other members of the executive board). Unless the organization were revised, its necessary functions could not be achieved. There would, in other words, be deficiencies in *real integration,* and real integration would not be exactly the same as the integration expected.

Expected integration, therefore, is a result of the structural dimensions of an organization—the parts and their relationships, the expected action, and the expected function. The "fit" of this complex of structural components is precise "on paper," because *actual* behavior is omitted. Real integration, on the other hand, results from the real structure (the real parts and their relationships), real action, and real function. Real integration is usually a much less precise fit than that which is expected. It may be found, for example, that in a rapidly changing society the nuclear family no longer serves all of its expected functions. Educational functions of the family may possibly be abrogated, with a resultant failure to transmit traditional values to the children. Discipline and authority may pass from the hands of parents to school and police authorities. The reciprocal relationships between the nuclear family and other structures in the society are, therefore, no longer as balanced as they were in the past. To this extent, the integratedness of the organization has diminished.

The social sciences have yet to develop precise measurements of integration or the lack of integration in social systems. In United States society there are many things that are regarded, *a priori*, as symptomatic of a reduction in integration: crime, delinquency, increasing illegitimacy, increasing divorce rates, seeming changes in moral standards, and many more. It would, of course, be plausible to relate such things to changes in structural aspects of our organization: shifting norms, changing social expectations, and a resultant breakdown in the real functions of many parts of our society. A precise determination, we repeat, is lacking.

SUMMARY

In this chapter, the reader has been presented with a method which can be used to analyze any kind of organization, but especially human social organization, into its principal constituents. Starting with the crucial referent of real action, this analysis reveals both the real structure of the organization and its real function. Further analysis lays bare the structural dimension of these factors—expected or ideal structure, expected action, and expected function. The additional concepts of norms and normative behavior have been shown to be especially relevant to an understanding of social organization as a dynamic process. Finally, integration, both real and expected, has been shown to be yet another significant dimension of organization, though it cannot as yet be as precisely measured or specified as the others.

With the exception of continual reference to the nuclear family in United States society, this discussion has been presented in a very general way, with little reference to the particulars of organization for any society. Human societies exist at many levels of technological complexity. They occupy a wide range of natural and cultural environments, and each society is the product of its own unique history. As a consequence of all these factors (and more) acting in combination, every human society has its own unique organization. Each differs from all others in the details of its organization, in its principles of organization, and in its organizational complexity. The particular ways in which groups are organized, the differences and similarities between them, and the levels of complexity represented by these organizations are treated extensively in the remaining chapters of this book.

8

Organizational Membership and Relations

INTRODUCTION

A human society is more than a collection or aggregate of people. It is organized. One of the principal ways of organizing the members of a society is to distribute them among various groups. All human societies are differentiated in this general way, but human groups are formed in many different ways. Whatever the specific type of group formation, it is always consistent and compatible with the concept of organization. All human societies and all human groups can be analyzed in terms of structure, action, function, and integration; that is, a society is organized into groups which themselves have a unique organization. Obviously, behavior cannot occur without individuals. A crucial aspect, therefore, in the study of society is group membership. All social groups must have members, who fill particular structural positions, who act in relation to the behavioral expectations of these structural positions, and whose action achieves certain functions (results).

GROUP MEMBERSHIP

Not all the individuals in any given society are members of all the groups found in that society. This is especially true of complex societies because of the increased differentiation that characterizes them. In the United States, to use an example of extreme complexity, each of us may belong to a variety of social groups—nuclear family, church congregation, schools, political clubs, business groups, lodges, and potentially many more. No two of these groups have an identical membership, although the membership of one group may overlap to some extent that of another group. Definite criteria are used by each group for determining who should and who should not be a member. Not all members of an individual's church, for example, will share with him all of the characteristics that qualify the person for membership in other groups to which he belongs. If he is a male, the women of his congregation are automatically excluded from membership in his men's club or bowling team. The criteria referred to so far are general; they define membership at the group level. One must be a Catholic to join the Knights of Columbus, or a woman with a special genealogy to join the Daughters of the American Revolution. Groups themselves, however, are organized into a number of structural positions, and more specific criteria are employed to determine who may fill such positions within each group. The characteristics that qualify an individual for membership in the Rotary Club may not qualify him to be an officer in this same group. Some relationship always exists between these general and more specific criteria. The latter are usually further refinements of the criteria of group membership. Thus, an individual may need a doctor's degree to join a university faculty, and this degree must be in a certain subject area to qualify him for membership in a particular department. In addition, he must have tenure to serve on certain academic committees. The more specific criteria of membership presuppose the more general.

The relationships between specific and general criteria are highly variable and are dependent, in part, upon the group, the society, and the context in which the group and the society are involved.

REQUIREMENTS FOR MEMBERSHIP

There are two general categories of requirements for membership in human social groups: universal requirements and relative or non-universal requirements.

Universal Requirements

Two criteria used universally to define membership in social groups are age and sex. These criteria are applied, however, in various ways. They can be used to include or exclude members, to restrict them in certain ways, or to prescribe membership. Numerous groups, in many of the world's societies, are restricted to either male or female membership. Plains Indians' military societies, the Poro society found among the Mano of Liberia, the Elks and Masons in the United States, as well as many professional sports teams in this country are open only to males. The American Association of University Women and the Job's Daughters in the United States, a novena (prayer) group in many Latin American communities, or the elite body guard of a king of Dahomey (Africa) completely exclude males from membership. Certain other groups will emphasize one sex without excluding the other. Male membership is emphasized in such kin groupings as patrilineages or patrilineal clans, and female membership is emphasized in matrilineages or matrilineal clans, or the so-called matricentric family (see Chapter 10). Alternatively, society may prescribe both male and female membership in certain groups (nuclear family, caste groups, kindreds, the PTA, and so on).

Age is used as a criterion in a similar way. It may be used to include certain persons in a group and to exclude others. The age grades characteristic of much of Africa join together individuals in a particular age range and exclude all others. Each man belongs to his own age grade with men in his age range. Public office, military service, or holding a job may be restricted to individuals between certain ages—for example, 21 to 65. One must be 35 or older to occupy the presidency of the United States.

Very often age and sex are used in combination to define group membership. In some Middle American Indian communities, earlier in this century, public affairs were run by a council of *principales* (important old men). Advisory councils in many societies are made up of older male members. All societies use age, separately or in conjunction with other criteria, for assigning group membership.

The use of sex and age as general criteria for group membership is generally further specified by the structural positions within the group, to which they become intimately linked. The nuclear family serves as an example of this. The nuclear family in all societies employs sex and age as criteria for membership. The use of these criteria dichotomizes this group in two distinct ways. Sex divides the family horizontally, and age divides the family vertically, as shown in Fig. 8–1.

Sex distinguishes between the two general kinds of members, male and female. Age segregates the members into two general temporal classes. Taken by themselves these categories are not very significant, and do not tell us any more than is obvious. It is obvious, for example, that a female child cannot occupy the status of father, or that an adult female cannot be a son. (See, however, the discussion below of cultural definitions of age and sex.) But these structural positions are linked to expected behavior, for sex and age are the criteria for the allocation of tasks and responsibilities to status positions. Let us consider, for a moment, the statuses of son (young male) and father/husband (adult male). In a hunting society, like that of the Arunta of

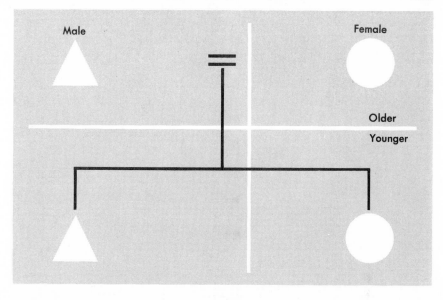

Fig. 8–1. Horizontal and vertical dimensions of the nuclear family using sex and age as criteria.

Australia, only an adult male has the strength and experience to qualify him to be a full-fledged hunter, which he must be in order to undertake the responsibility of a family. The subadult male, lacking the qualities of age and experience, is relegated to the society of women and children. In making the transition from one status to the other the boy must leave behind the company of women and children, and accept the demanding and arduous responsibilities of an adult male. So important is this transition that it is dramatized by ritual performances and a series of painful ordeals that extend over a period of several months. Puberty observances for boy or girl, involving isolation, painful ordeal, and dramatic rituals, are a recurrent feature of many of the world's societies. These serve to illustrate very clearly the definite ways in which societies conceptualize the statuses based on age and sex.

Relative Requirements

Age and sex, singly or in combination, are rarely the exclusive criteria for determining membership in a group or status position within that group. Most often they are used in combination with relative criteria (those not utilized by all societies or by all groups within a society). Relative criteria are of a more specialized nature and include such things as heredity, religious or ethnic affiliation, residence, special skills,

Sex may be a requirement for group membership, as shown here by the Men's House of the atoll of Woleai in the Western Caroline Islands group. The Men's House is a sort of social club for the male population of the island. (United Nations.)

monetary worth, personality, and many more. These criteria are relative in the sense that they are applied only to certain groups or certain kinds of groups within a society. Frequently, they are intimately linked to particular structural positions within the group and, in such cases, may define a specialized requirement for membership. A religious specialist, for example, may have to be the son of a religious specialist, may have to be able to go into a trance, or may have to acquire specialized knowledge—divining the future, curing disease, controlling the weather, and so on. Satisfaction of these relative criteria allows an individual to fill a particular structural position within a certain social group in a particular society. The combination of criteria is *relative* to a particular group or status position. The same combination would not qualify the individual for filling other status positions. However, membership in one group may be used as a requirement for membership in other groups.

Membership in a caste group in India requires that a person's mother and father be of the same caste; economically based social groups frequently require certain minimal skills for membership (trade unions, for example, often have explicit rules regarding apprenticeship through which an individual acquires the skills of his trade, and only upon meeting these and other requirements can he become a full-fledged "journeyman"); evidence of material wealth, education, knowledge of appropriate behavior, modes of dress, and patterns of recreation are among the criteria for distinguishing members of one social category from another in the social class system of the United States, England, and other complex societies; ethnic group membership, religious affiliation, and

The subadult Arunta male is relegated to the society of women and children. In making the transition to adulthood, he must undergo months of exclusion and painful ordeal before accepting the responsibilities of an adult male. (Courtesy of the American Museum of Natural History.)

hereditary characteristics (especially those popularly used as indices of race) are very familiar relative criteria of group or status membership in the United States. These and many other relative criteria are discussed in their relevant contexts or are implicit in other parts of the book, and need not be treated further at this point.

RELATIONSHIP AMONG MEMBERS

The relationship among the members of a social group is, to a greater or lesser extent, reciprocal and obligatory. The degree to which reciprocity and obligation occur in a social group depends on several factors, including size of the group, complexity of the group, specialization within the group, degree to which common goals and values are manifest in the group, and the critical needs which must be satisfied by group action. In all social groups, however, some definite relationship occurs among the members.

Group membership is never a singular phenomenon; it is always a relative one. An individual is a member of a social group and fills a structural position within that group in relation to other group members filling other structural positions. Members in a social group are meaningful only in relation to other members. Father and mother, for example, are meaningful only in relation to son or daughter; sister is meaningful only in relation to brother or another sister; and grandparents (grandmother and grandfather) are meaningful only in relation to grandchildren. Application of the concepts *procreation* and *orientation* to the nuclear family further explain and emphasize the relationship among members.

The *family of procreation* is the family formed by marriage and the production of offspring. The *family of orientation* is the family into which a person is born and/or raised. Both the family of procreation and the family of orientation are equivalent to the nuclear family. There is no structural difference; only the referent has changed. (See Fig. 8-2.) Each referent, however, is the reciprocal of the other. Father and mother are the major referents in the family of procreation—they are the ones who give rise to the family; son and daughter are the reciprocal. Son and daughter are the major referents in the family of orientation—they are the ones who are born into and raised in this family; mother and father are the reciprocal (they are the members who procreate and raise son and daughter). The family of procreation and the family of orientation combined equal the complete nuclear family. A

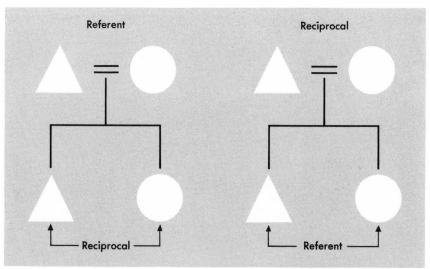

Fig. 8–2. Families of procreation and orientation.

male, for example, is the father in his own family of procreation, but he is a son in his family of orientation (the family in which he was oriented or socialized to his society and culture).

Bases of Relationship Among Members

The bases for the relationships among members of social groups fall into two generally recognized categories: *kinship* and *non-kinship*. Kinship-based groups are those formed by marriage and descent, or by some "fictive" process such as adoption. Non-kinship groups can be based on religious or economic interests, or they can be purely social in nature, to list but a few of the many cultural bases for groups. These distinctions of kin and non-kin refer to the basic ways in which group members are related. Siblings (a kinship bond) in a nuclear family are related through descent from common ancestors, their parents.

In a business establishment the relationships of co-workers and employer–employee are basically economic and non-kinship. The two categories are not, of course, mutually exclusive. Most if not all kinship-based groups are united by additional social, economic, or religious bonds. In fact, kinship statuses are generally defined in these terms. One's father is not only one's immediate ancestor, he is also one's economic support, disciplinarian, religious instructor, and so on. The nuclear family, especially in structurally simple societies, is frequently an all-purpose unit.

Visitors to a local aboriginal clan are painted with the particular clan designs. In this "fictive" form of kinship, members claim descent from a common ancestor, usually an animal, although family kinship may also be involved. (Courtesy of the American Museum of Natural History.)

Non-kinship groups may, on the other hand, be without any kinship basis. Not uncommonly, however, non-kinship groups are perceived in terms of kinship. Members of a labor union, a social fraternity, or a religious congregation address one another as brother or sister. A priest is addressed as father and in turn addresses his parishioners as sons or daughters.

Non-kinship groups and relationships are generally more numerous in human society than are those based on kinship. Kinship tends to be the primary basis of organization in socially and technologically simple societies, and non-kinship relations tend to multiply as the scale of social and technological complexity increases.

Kinship Bases of Relationship. Three general kinds of kinship relations occur in human society: *consanguineal* relations, *affinal* relations, and *fictive kinship* relations. Consanguineal kin are those persons who are recognized by society as related biologically, directly or indirectly (father, son, grandfather, mother, daughter). Affinal kin are those persons who are related, either directly or indirectly, by some socially recognized marital union (husband, wife, mother-in-law). Fictive kin are those persons who are related on a socially recognized but fictitious basis. A common feature of clans, for example (as shown in Chapter 10), is that members claim descent from a putative ancestor, which may be a totem animal such as a kangaroo, and all men of approximately the same age are brothers by virtue of this descent. Also, clans commonly practice adoption, and adopted members become brothers or sisters. In these cases, there is no traceable genealogical relationship among persons addressing one another by kin terms, and we refer to this basis as fictive.

All three types of kinship are socially real and define the relationships that occur among members of social groups. Consanguineal and affinal relationships, however, are more frequent than fictive relationships. These three categories of kinship relations are not mutually exclusive and may coexist in a single social group. The nuclear family, for example, includes both consanguineal and affinal relationships, and may include an adopted child. A totemic clan, the members of which claim descent from a common, animal ancestor, always includes consanguineal, affinal, and fictive relationships.

Levels of Kinship Relations. Kinship relations vary also in accordance with the degree of directness of the relationship. Direct relationships involve less genealogical distance, and indirect relations involve greater genealogical distance. Murdock (1949:94 ff.) describes four general orders of relationships associated with degrees of genealogical distance: primary relations, secondary relations, tertiary relations, and distant relations (those more distant than tertiary relations, such as quaternary or quinary relations). He suggests (*ibid.*, 96) that ". . . any individual in any society has potentially seven different kinds of primary relatives, 33 of secondary relatives, 151 of tertiary relatives, and geometrically increasing numbers of distant relatives to various degrees." While some overlap may occur, not all of a person's relatives are exactly the same as those of any other individual. Figure 8–3 gives examples of primary, secondary, and tertiary relatives, and also shows the similarity and differences that occur among the relatives of related individuals.

A person's primary relatives are his father, mother, sister, and brother (those relatives included in his family of orientation), as well as his

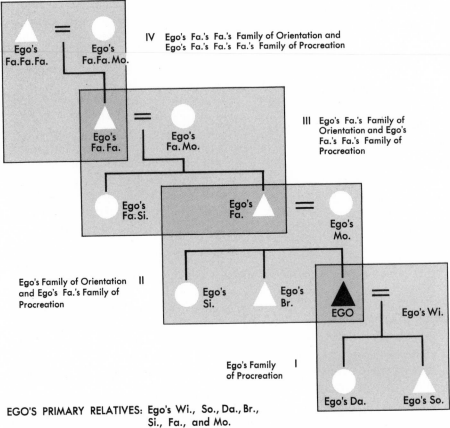

IV Ego's Fa.'s Fa.'s Family of Orientation and
     Ego's Fa.'s Fa.'s Fa.'s Family of Procreation

III Ego's Fa.'s Family of
     Orientation and Ego's
     Fa.'s Fa.'s Family of
     Procreation

Ego's Family of Orientation II
and Ego's Fa.'s Family of
Procreation

Ego's Family I
of Procreation

EGO'S PRIMARY RELATIVES: Ego's Wi., So., Da., Br.,
                                              Si., Fa., and Mo.
EGO'S SECONDARY RELATIVES: Ego's Fa. Si., Fa. Fa., and Fa. Mo.
EGO'S TERTIARY RELATIVES Ego's Fa. Fa. Fa., and Fa. Fa. Mo.

Fig. 8–3. Levels of kinship relations and families of orientation and procreation.

wife, son, and daughter (those persons included in his family of procreation). An individual's secondary relatives include his father's father, his father's mother, his father's brother, his father's sister, and so on. Each of a person's (ego's) primary relatives has his own primary relatives who are, also, secondary relatives to ego. Ego's tertiary relatives include such persons as his father's father's father, his father's father's mother, his father's brother's children, and many more. Ego's tertiary relatives are the same as the primary relatives of each of ego's secondary relatives. Figure 8–3 helps to clarify this complex set of relationships.

KINSHIP ORGANIZATION

The ways in which relationships among individuals in any society are defined are subject to very definite cultural rules. Every culture has its own rules for defining such relationships, and no two cultures are identical in this respect. On the other hand, no culture is entirely unique in its system of relationships. Cross-cultural comparison reveals certain systematic patterns which are characteristic of these relationships and which extend beyond the limits of any single culture.

Kinship systems, as these relationships are most commonly called, are not social groups in any sense of the word, because they always cut across group boundaries. But they do specify and define the relationships that occur within and between groups. Some kinship systems, for example, specify in a particular way the relationship of an individual to persons of his own generation, and are labeled by anthropologists as cousin systems. Others attract our attention by the way in which they define the relationship of a person to individuals of the first ascendant (parental) generation, and are labeled avuncular (uncle) systems. Regardless of the particular focus or the particular relations, all kinship systems accomplish the following: (1) they group particular kinds of persons, with reference to ego, into single named categories; and (2) they separate different kinds of persons, again from the standpoint of ego, into separate and distinct named categories. As a result (always using a hypothetical ego as the point of reference), all the persons related to ego through ties of consanguinity, affinity, or fictive kinship, are placed in one or another of a finite number of distinct named categories. These groupings are not achieved randomly, but result from the operation of definite principles. The distinctions that can be made among individuals of the same generation in United States society provide a clear illustration.

Cousin Systems

In the United States an individual's (ego's) father's brother's children, father's sister's children, mother's brother's children, and mother's sister's children are all grouped into a single named category, which is labeled with the kinship term cousin. All persons who belong in this category stand in the relationship of cousin to this individual (ego). Among these children are offspring of four different sets of parents. Some are male and some female, some are older and some younger than ego, but no significant terminological distinction is made among them. They are all referred to as cousins. This is not true of all societies, and many logical distinctions are possible.

If, for example, a society were to apply the criterion of sex, ego would have two kinds of relationships in this category—male and female cousins. If we were then to specify the set of parents from whom they are descended, two kinds of relationships would become eight:

1. Ego's mother's brother's male offspring.
2. Ego's mother's brother's female offspring.
3. Ego's mother's sister's male offspring.
4. Ego's mother's sister's female offspring.
5. Ego's father's brother's male offspring.
6. Ego's father's brother's female offspring.
7. Ego's father's sister's male offspring.
8. Ego's father's sister's female offspring.

Using yet another criterion, the sex of the connecting relative, many of the world's societies distinguish between *cross-cousins* and *parallel cousins*. Ego and his cross-cousins are offspring of siblings of the opposite sex, and would include his father's sister's children and his mother's brother's children. Ego's parallel cousins are children of siblings of the same sex as ego's own parents, and include his mother's sister's children and his father's brother's children. Figure 8–4 depicts these relationships. The two categories of cousins are distinguished in relation to ego, based upon the sex of ego's parents' siblings. It should be stressed that this is not a purely arbitrary distinction, but one which reflects other cultural rules in the society in which the distinction is made.

Murdock's Classification of Cousin Systems. Other kinship distinctions can be recognized among persons of the same generations (Murdock

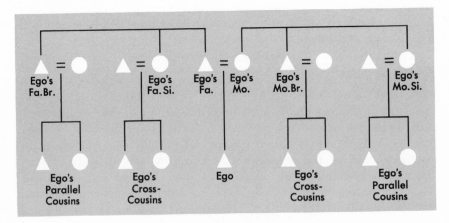

Fig. 8–4. Cross- and parallel cousins.

1949). These distinctions are based on similar principles. First, all offspring of an individual's (ego's) parents and all offspring of the same person's parents' siblings may be grouped together in a single named category. No significant terminological distinction is made among these individuals; they are all called by the same kinship term denoting the same kinship relation to ego. (See Fig. 8–5.) Of course, these persons are distinguished from one another by sex. A and A' are used to differentiate males from females only. Both A and A' are of the same kinship order to ego. Only one category of kinship relations results from this grouping (Murdock's Hawaiian Cousin System).

A second alternative is the exact opposite of the first: all offspring of ego's parents' siblings are distinguished from one another and from ego's siblings. Five categories of kinship relations to ego result from this kind of separation (Murdock's Sudanese Cousin System). (See Fig. 8–6.)

A third possibility involves grouping all offspring of ego's parents' siblings together in a single category and separating them from ego's siblings, who are placed in another kinship category. Once again, these persons are distinguished from one another on the basis of sex, but only two kinship categories of relations to ego result (Murdock's Eskimo Cousin System). (See Fig. 8–7.) The reader should recognize this system as characteristic of the United States, with the exception that sex is disregarded in United States cousin terminology.

The fourth system, like the third one, includes the principles of combination and separation but in a different way and with somewhat different results. Cross-cousins (ego's father's sister's children and ego's mother's brother's children) are combined into a single kinship category. Ego's parallel cousins (ego's father's brother's children and ego's mother's sister's children) and ego's siblings are grouped together and placed in another category different from that for ego's cross-cousins. Two categories of kinship relations result (Murdock's Iroquois Cousin System). (See Fig. 8–8.)

The combination of some relations and the separation of others to form kinship categories have been simple and straightforward to this point. Now, however, an additional variable is introduced. The next two kinship systems described use the same principles of combination and separation, but they simultaneously ignore the distinction that occurs between generations in relation to certain kinsmen. Segregation of relations by generation is meaningful in United States society and is taken for granted. This, however, is not the case in all other societies.

The fifth kinship system, and the first which ignores the generational variable, combines into a single named category ego's siblings and ego's parallel cousins. Ego's cross-cousins are differentiated from this group and from each other. Thus, ego's *patrilateral* cross-cousins (his father's

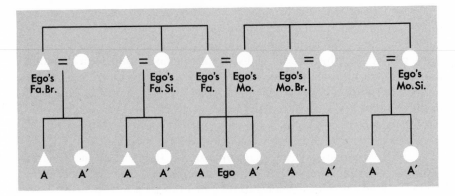

Fig. 8–5. Hawaiian Cousin System.

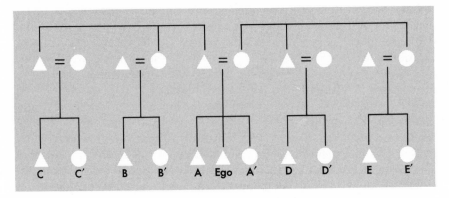

Fig. 8–6. Sudanese Cousin System.

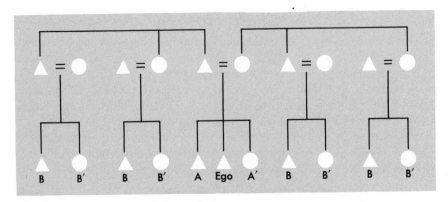

Fig. 8–7. Eskimo Cousin System.

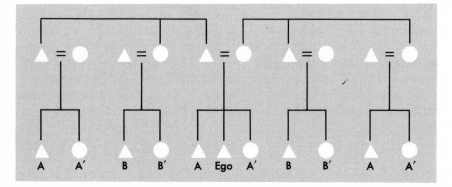

Fig. 8–8. Iroquois Cousin System.

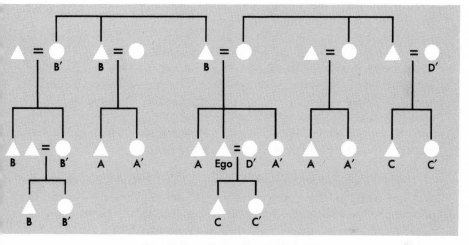

Fig. 8–9. Crow Cousin System.

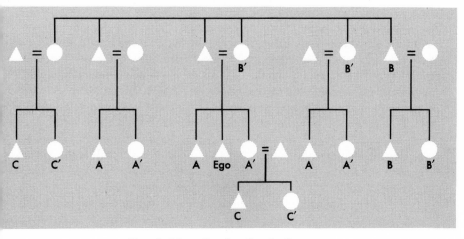

Fig. 8–10. Omaha Cousin System.

sister's children, labeled B and B' in Fig. 8–9) are placed in a different kinship category from that in which his *matrilateral* cross-cousins (ego's mother's brother's children, labeled C and C') are placed. The kinship term used to refer to ego's father's sister's children (B, B') translates as "male (or female) of my father's lineage." Ego employs this same term in referring to all other kinsmen labeled B, B' in Fig. 8–9: father, father's brother, father's sister's daughter's children, and all other persons who belong to his father's lineage. The significance of this terminological usage, so different from that in the reader's own kinship system, is that all these individuals stand in a similar kinship relation to ego. They are members of his father's lineage, an important category in societies having Murdock's Crow Cousin System. They are all grouped into a single kinship category, and ego calls them all by the same term—"male (or female) of my father's lineage."

In this same system, ego's mother's brother's children are equated with ego's own children and are called by kinship terms (C, C') which translate as "son" or "daughter." This occurs because ego's mother's brother's wife's relationship to ego is similar to his own wife's (both are D'). Three principal kinship categories result from the application of this system: (1) ego, his siblings, and his parallel cousins; (2) members of ego's father's lineage; and (3) ego's own children, and his mother's brother's children. Figure 8–9 explains this Crow Cousin System.

The final kinship system involves the same principles for combining and separating relations into categories. Like the previous system, this one ignores generational differences at certain points. Here, ego's parallel cousins are grouped along with ego's siblings into a single named category (A, A' in Fig. 8–10). His matrilateral cross-cousins (his mother's brother's offspring) are combined with his mother, his mother's sister, his mother's brother, and others into a different category (B, B') and called by a term which translates as "male (or female) of my mother's lineage." As is the case with the father's lineage in the Crow System, the mother's lineage constitutes a culturally significant category in this type of system. It should be stressed once more that such nomenclature is not meaningless or completely arbitrary, but rather reflects the social system in which it is found. Ego stands in a special relationship to all members of his mother's lineage, which makes them equivalent from his point of view, regardless of generational differences. The final category in this system groups together ego's patrilateral cross-cousins (his father's sister's children) with ego's sister's children (C, C'). They are referred to by a term which means "son (or daughter) of a female of my father's lineage." Thus, three principal categories of kin result from this system also. Figure 8–10 represents this system (Murdock's Omaha Cousin System) in graphic form.

Avuncular Systems

Principles of combining and separating kinship relations are not restricted to ego's own generation. They can, in fact, be applied to any generation. When applied to the first ascendant generation (ego's father's generation), and particularly to ego's mother's brother and ego's father's brother, the resultant systems are referred to as avuncular (uncle) systems.

The first avuncular system uses only the principle of combination: ego's father, ego's father's brother, and ego's mother's brother stand in the same kinship relation to ego and are grouped, therefore, into a single named kinship category. Since all of these relations are of the same generation, this system frequently is termed a *generational avuncular system*, emphasizing the grouping together of persons who belong to the same generation. [Figure 8–11(a) shows this avuncular system.] The principle of combination of persons in the same generation to form a single kinship category is exactly the same as that used in the first cousin kinship system (Hawaiian System), shown in Fig. 8–5.

The second avuncular system is completely different from the first one. Ego's father is placed in one category, ego's father's brother in a second category, and ego's mother's brother in a third. Complete separation is the only principle used, and it is exactly the same principle used in the second cousin system (Sudanese), shown in Fig. 8–6. This avuncular system, which is shown in Fig. 8–11(b), is referred to as a *bifurcate collateral avuncular system*, i.e., distinguishing among (bifurcating) relations who stand in a parallel position (are collateral) to one another. Father, father's brother, and mother's brother occupy a parallel (collateral) position to one another.

The third avuncular system employs both principles (combination and separation) in a manner that is similar to that used in the third cousin system described (Eskimo), in which ego's siblings were distinguished from ego's cousins and all of ego's cousins were grouped together in a single category. (See Fig. 8–7.) This avuncular system does the same thing, but in the first ascendant generation. Ego's father is placed in one category. Ego's father's brother and ego's mother's brother are grouped into another category distinct from that of ego's father. [See Fig. 8–11(c).] This avuncular system is called a *lineal avuncular system* because it separates the lineal relation (ego's father) from the lineal relative's collaterals (ego's father's brother and ego's mother's brother)

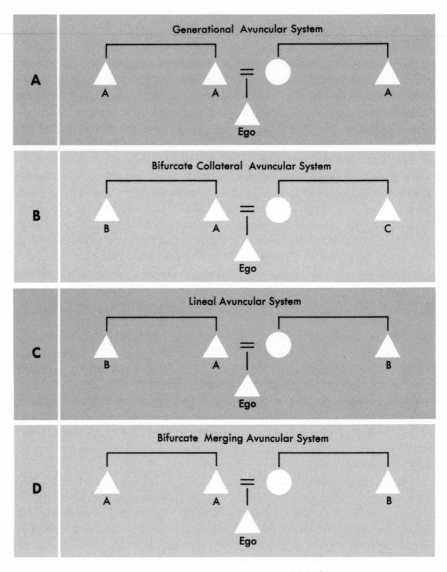

Fig. 8–11. Avuncular systems of kinship.

and groups these collaterals into a separate, single category. This system is characteristic of United States society, in which a person refers to his lineal relative as father and addresses the collaterals of this lineal relative as uncle. No distinction is made among uncles; both ego's father's brother and ego's mother's brother are called uncle.

The final avuncular system also uses the principles of combination and separation, but in a slightly different way. The emphasis of combination is upon ego's father's relatives, while the principle of separation is applied to ego's mother's relatives. Father and father's brother are combined into a single kinship category, and ego's mother's brother is placed in a second, distinct category [see Fig. 8–11(d)]. This system is referred to as a *bifurcate merging avuncular system*. It is called bifurcate because ego's father's side (father and father's brother in the first ascending generation) is split or separated from collateral kinsmen (mother's brother) on ego's mother's side; and merging because ego's lineal kinsman (father) is grouped together (merged) with collateral kin, the father's brothers in this case. The same principles of bifurcation and merging are found in the Iroquois (Fig. 8–8), the Crow (Fig. 8–9), and the Omaha (Fig. 8–10) Cousin Systems.

Kinship and the Structural Dimension of Organization

All of the kinship relations described, and in fact all kinship relations regardless of the system in which they occur, are named. The particular terms used to designate these relations are determined by the culture in which they occur. In all cases, however, the term used for a kinship relation designates it as a structural position (status) within the society and relates it to another structural position—its referent. Father, for example, is a named kinship status, but father is not significant unless the referent son or daughter is designated. A kinship term, however, does more than designate a particular status; it also indicates the behavior that is expected of any person who fills this status in relation to its referent. Ego is expected to behave in a definite way toward the person he calls mother, and ego's mother is expected to behave in a particular way in relation to ego and all persons she calls son or daughter. Son and daughter are the structural referents for the kinship statuses mother and father, and mother and father are the structural referents for the kinship terms son and daughter. The way in which ego is expected to behave toward someone he calls father is different from the way in which he is expected to behave toward someone he calls uncle, cousin, sister, or brother. Kinship terms name structural positions and, simultaneously, define the behavior expected of persons filling these structural positions in relation to persons filling other related kinship positions.

Any individual fills numerous kinship positions at the same time, because he stands in a different kinship relation to different people. For example, an individual in the United States fills the kinship position son in relation to his father, nephew in relation to his uncle, cousin in relation to his cousin, brother in relation to his sister or brother, father in relation to his son or daughter, grandson in relation to his father's father, and so on. Certain results are expected from the action performed by persons occupying these kinship statuses. In other words, *this network of relations has an expected function.*

The reader should recognize the application of the concepts discussed in the preceding chapter to the three items analyzed here: the kinship term, the behavior expected of a person filling the position which it labels, and the results expected of his action. Together they constitute the structural (expected) dimension of kinship organization. The actual or real dimensions of these factors may or may not coincide with the expected dimension. Our discussion of the nuclear family relationships in Chapter 7 illustrates the varying degrees to which these two dimensions can coincide.

The Validation of Relationships

Relationships among individuals are not effective (do not produce socially desired or expected results) unless they are validated. By this we mean that the persons reciprocally united in such relationships are aware of them, accept them, and behave in positive ways to bring about the expected results of these relationships. Validation can sometimes be highly formal and involve the use of meaningful symbols. A husband and wife relationship, for example, is validated in our society through the use of ritual, legal documents, public pronouncements, and various symbols such as rings, bridal bouquets, and special dress. The *couvade,* a custom widespread among South American Indians, in which the father takes to his own hammock while his wife is in childbirth, can be interpreted as a ritual validation of the father–son/daughter relationship. Public, ceremonial, symbolic acceptance of certain relationships is found in all societies. Our stress, however, is on the behavioral aspects of validation.

There are three principal ways in which individuals can respond to particular relationships. First, corresponding to our definition of validation above, a person may accept his relationship with another person and engage in positive behavior which will recognize this relationship and simultaneously validate it. A male who acknowledges his wife's child by giving it his name, who provides the child's economic support, and who acts as a father in all the ways expected of his status in his society has validated the father–child relationship. Second, a person may recognize the existence of a relationship but not engage in behavioral recognition or validation of it. The male in the preceding example may legally marry a woman and confer his name on her children, but engage in little of the behavior expected of his status. Finally, a person may reject a relationship to another person and engage in behavior which demonstrates his rejection of it and which indicates his failure to recognize it as a valid relationship. Within the context of the nuclear family this can be illustrated in various ways. The confirmed bachelor in our society, who not only does not marry but ostentatiously flaunts his freedom, has rejected marriage as a valid relationship. A married couple who place their child for adoption, or a child who leaves home with the intention of permanently breaking his parental ties, are further examples.

This third alternative, the complete rejection of a kinship relationship, would in most cases be regarded as deviant behavior. In many of the world's societies, for example, a man acquires full adult status only after he has married, i.e., has accepted a relationship and validated it through his behavior. In peasant societies the world over, a woman's primary obligation is to bear and rear children. Not only would she be guilty of the most deviant behavior by refusing to have children, thereby rejecting the mother–child relationship, but barrenness on her part would justify her husband's divorcing her to seek a more fruitful union.

The rejection of relationships is not always deviant behavior, because any society provides certain socially acceptable, legitimate alternatives to many of its relationships. In some cases the acceptance of a certain status will preclude the acceptance and validation of kinship relations. A Catholic priest, by his vow of celibacy, rejects the husband and father statuses which are expected of most men. In other cases, the assumption of a new kinship status either precludes or compromises the continuation of an existing one. In many societies the nuclear family adheres to the pattern of *neolocal marital residence,* that is, a newly married couple takes up residence apart from the families of both husband and wife. This separation can significantly weaken, or even completely break, the former parent–child relationship. If, for example, the bride's parents reject the groom (their new son-in-law), the girl's loyalty to her husband may preclude a continuation of her filial relationship with her parents. In societies in which the nuclear family and neolocal residence form the dominant pattern, an individual's primary obligations are to his family of procreation. He must validate this relationship (to his wife and children) even if it means withdrawing financial support from an aging parent. One final example can be cited. In societies that permit divorce, it is legitimate to break one marital relationship and establish a new one. Law or custom may require, however, that certain of the expected behaviors of the previous relationship be continued, such as alimony, child support, or gifts on special occasions.

Our emphasis in this discussion has been on the validation of kinship relations, but these concepts apply equally to all social relations. Organization, in its structural dimension, is made up of numerous linked status positions. Individuals occupying these linked statuses are related to one another in various ways—through kinship, economics, religion, and so on. Structure, we have said a number of times, is static without the crucial ingredient of action. If no one occupies the structural positions in a society, or if no one contributes positive, effective action to the relationships implied in linked statuses, these relationships cease to be culturally significant.

These concepts are important to a study of cultural change. In any society, over a period of time, new statuses become incorporated into the social system, old statuses become non-functional and disappear, or the behaviors characteristic of existing relationships change in some or in all of their aspects. A few examples from United States society will serve to illustrate these points. It is clear that in many sectors of our society the godparent relationship is no longer validated. This relationship is ritually established through the act of sponsorship of a child at baptism, but for many people this terminates the relationship. The status position of godparent, however, remains in the expected structure of our society. Many of the collateral kinship relations in United States society have also ceased to be valid. A high degree of geographical mobility tends to separate newly married couples from all of their kin and minimizes relations between them and all but their siblings and parents. Frequent visiting, exchange of gifts, dining, or exchanges of confidences between an individual in United States society and an uncle, aunt, cousin, niece, or nephew is no longer the pattern. Change often begins with an alteration in *some* of the behaviors that characterize a relationship. Changes already apparent in nuclear family relationships in our society would include increasing contribution of the mother to the economic support of the family; abrogation of responsibility for discipline to school or police; sharing of domestic duties by wife and husband. Old relationships are no longer validated, or they are being validated in new ways. In these ways social systems are changed.

Kinship: A Cultural Phenomenon

Kinship is a cultural phenomenon, although it is confused frequently with biology. Kinship terms, categories, behavior, systems, and organizations are arbitrary designations and rules for social relationships. By arbitrary, we mean that kinship usages are not rooted necessarily in biological fact. Our discussion of cousin and avuncular terminology shows clearly that societies can interpret relationships in many different ways. The particular usage adopted by any society is, therefore, a matter of cultural choice. We use the word choice, of course, in a metaphoric sense to describe a complex and largely unconscious historic process. But if biological facts do not determine kinship usages, neither are they completely irrelevant to the cultural choice among alternatives. In the United States, for example, the kinship term father is generally interpreted to mean one who has actually contributed his genetic material to the child he calls son or daughter.

Procreation and Kinship. To clarify the distinction between a biological relationship and a kinship one (which is cultural), the biological act of procreation must be distinguished from the occupation of structural positions in a social group. The English language does not make such a distinction easy precisely because we so commonly confuse the two concepts; and we confuse them because the two so often coincide in actual practice. For convenience, we will label *progenitor* a man whose genetic materials are borne by his offspring. Siblings are those who are biological offspring of the same parents. Father, son, daughter, brother, and sister are labels reserved for kinship statuses. Mother, similarly, will refer to one who stands in a socially defined relationship to a son or daughter. The biological mother, who may be and usually is the same person, is the woman who actually gave birth to the children in question. The socially defined relationships of father–son, husband–wife, brother–sister, and so on, are validated only when individuals accept these relationships and behave in socially expected ways. Cultural behavior, then, is crucial to this distinction. The following discussion will serve to illustrate these points.

In our own society, if a man visits a prostitute and, probably without the knowledge of either party, impregnates her, is he subsequently a father? In popular usage the answer would be yes, even if he never knows or acknowledges the child. Properly, according to our definition, he is a progenitor, for he has not accepted fatherhood as a valid relationship, and it does not socially exist. If this male is married and his wife becomes impregnated in a clandestine relationship with another man, does her husband become a father when she delivers her child? Yes, if he accepts this child as his own and validates the father–child relationship. No, if he learns of the child's origin and rejects the relationship. In neither case, however, is he a progenitor. We might add that, in general, if a man in United States society accepts the marital relationship as valid, he will also accept his wife's children as "his own," barring proof or suspicions to the contrary. In an unknown percentage of all cases, he is not actually the progenitor but he is socially the father.

The case of mother and biological mother is somewhat more difficult, partly due to the almost sacred aura with which motherhood has become invested in United States society. It is part of our folklore that an instinctive bond unites mother and child. (Indeed, the reader may recall novels in which a mother and child, separated at birth, are mysteriously drawn to one another in later life.) It is true that in United States society biological maternity and sociological motherhood merge almost completely. The major deviation from this general proposition comes through adoption, when the biological parents may not even be known. Nowhere is our folklore concerning the mystic identity of biological parent and child clearer than in adoption. Adoption laws often require that the "real parents" not know who has adopted their children, as a protection against their making future claims. Great pains are sometimes taken by adoptive parents never to let the child know that they are not "really" his parents. Novels, which reflect our folklore, will sometimes depict such a revelation as a most traumatic experience. Even the law has occasionally recognized the prior claims of biological parents, over sociological parents who may have accepted and validated this relationship for many years. There have been known cases in which legal technicalities have nullified adoption proceedings. In short, there is, in United States society, much confusion and conflict between biology and kinship.

SEX AND AGE: CULTURAL PHENOMENA

This confusion between biology and culture is further based, to a large extent, upon the way in which sex and age are construed. Sex and age are defined most frequently in western society as purely biological phenomena. This interpretation seems to be supported by common sense. A person is or is not a male or a female. Our custom of recording birth dates and our use of a calendrical system provide us with an absolute criterion for fixing age. A person 21 years of age is obviously biologically older than another person 15 years of age. In cross-cultural perspective, however, age and sex are both biological and cultural phenomena. In the United States, for example, we insist that sex is a biological phenomenon only. For this reason, it is difficult for many of us to understand sexual distinctions as cultural phenomena. Father, for us, should be a biological male. While this idea is widespread, there are societies in which a biological female fills the structural positions of father and husband. Among the Nuer of eastern

Africa, one socially acceptable form of marriage involves the union of an older woman with a younger female. The older woman, who is father and husband, hires a young male to perform the biological act that she as a woman is incapable of performing. However, this is an independent and temporary contractual relationship which in no way affects the older woman's status as father and husband. She is the father of all children that ensue, and these children are her legitimate heirs.

A similar situation is present in United States society, but we fail to recognize it as socially acceptable behavior and, therefore, discourage it. Homosexual individuals may assume a social position contrary to their phenotypical biological expressions. Biological females may assume the social position of husband and even father under certain conditions, and biological males, under other conditions, may assume the social positions of wife and mother. This situation is not restricted to the United States; in several European countries, entire communities of this type exist and are perpetuated. They are even tolerated and accepted in varying degrees by the more general society.

The common point of view in western society, that age is a purely biological thing, is also reflected in kinship usages. Parenthood, for example, is associated with biological maturity or adult age. A child cannot be a "father," or a "mother," as we define these terms biologically. An uncle must be someone old enough to have siblings of childbearing age. A grandfather must be of sufficient age to have children who can procreate. Age, therefore, is treated as a natural phenomenon and as an independent variable. Kinship (which is regarded as biological) is treated as a dependent variable. As one becomes biologically older he can also "become" a father, an uncle, or a grandfather. It therefore appears to us incongruous, and even amusing, when this relationship does not hold. If, for example, a woman has children over a period of 20 or more years, her latest born will be infants when their older siblings are already married. A newborn infant can be an uncle to a child several years his senior.

Such occurrences are regarded, in our society, as amusing oddities. Kinship usages followed in non-western societies are likely to be thought of as far more incongruous. This is best illustrated by societies in which generational differences between certain kinsmen are ignored. In the Crow System, for example, it was seen that ego refers to his father's sister, her daughter, and her daughter's daughter by a single kinship term. A very common kinship usage (especially in societies where three generations live in a single household) is a reciprocal terminology in which a grandchild and his grandfather address each other with an identical kinship term. If we translate these usages into our language, as earlier generations of scholars sometimes naïvely did, it would appear that an old man calls a small child "grandfather," or that an individual calls his female cousin "aunt." Because our system associates kinship positions with biological age, these kinship usages appear incongruous, as though the people concerned "do not know the facts" of biology.

SUMMARY

Kinship is, in summary, a cultural phenomenon *which may or may not coincide with biology.* Biological age and biological sex are independent of kinship factors as defined by culture, although there can be a great deal of correspondence between them. The correspondence is high in our society, where statistically the sociological parents very often are the progenitors of the children they acknowledge. Many interrelated factors explain this high correspondence. According to our traditional morality, childbearing is a function of a legally constituted marital union. There is a social stigma on illegitimacy (a cultural conception) and on "unwed mothers." Because of the complete independence of the nuclear family unit, we lack larger social units to take care of fatherless children. For these and perhaps other reasons, the law prescribes that a person is responsible for the results of his biological actions. As a consequence, our social norm is that of a nuclear family, consisting of a husband, a wife, and *their* dependent offspring. The reader will readily see from our previous discussion, however, that the congruence of norm, normative action, expected action, and real action is not complete. In many other societies, where the above conditions are absent or are interpreted in different ways, the perceived relationship between biology and kinship is also much different.

There are many other aspects of kinship with which we could further demonstrate its cultural nature. Since they also show the ways in which kinship is intimately involved in social groups, they are best taken up in our discussion of the ways in which social groups are organized.

9

Behavioral Conformity, Deviance, and Control

INTRODUCTION

No two individuals are exactly alike, and no two individuals behave in an identical manner at all times. Nevertheless, human society is predicated on a certain amount of uniform behavior among its individual members. There is nothing contradictory about these two statements. Complete homogeneity of behavior is biologically and psychologically impossible, and complete heterogeneity is socially impossible. An effective human society must achieve some balance between variation and similarity in behavior.

FORMS OF HUMAN BEHAVIOR

Viewed in this way, human behavior has three logical forms: widespread similarity of behavior among all individuals, some similarity, and no similarity. There are some actions shared by all men (universal conformity), some shared by only some men (social conformity), and some actions unique to the individual (idiosyncratic behavior). Universal conformity is related to man's biological or animal qualities, as modified and expressed through his culture, and is taken as a constant. The satisfaction of hunger and thirst through culture, the regulation of sexual behavior and procreation by kinship systems and rules of incest, the organization of individuals and resources are all essential to man's adaptation and are found wherever man exists. In each of these examples, the particular

ways in which different groups of men satisfy these universal requirements vary. The members of one society do not eat meat, but eat vegetable products; milk is not consumed in one society, but is preferred in
another; marriage to one's cousin constitutes incest in one society, but is
preferred in another. However, the fact that all men satisfy hunger and
thirst through culture, that all men have rules regulating sexual behavior
and procreation, and that all men organize themselves, makes these general forms of behavior universal, that is, they are found in all societies. At
the same time, we know that not all members of any society adhere
consistently or exactly to all behavioral expectations; idiosyncratic behavior occurs, and is responsible for significant behavioral variation
within any society. While the activities characterized by universal conformity are important, the more significant and revealing aspects of behavior, for our purposes, fall into the categories of social conformity
and idiosyncratic behavior. These two categories embrace culturally
relative behavior, and are, therefore, subject to significant cross-cultural
analysis.

Social conformity and idiosyncratic behavior, however, do not have
to be evaluated in relation to the total society. More often, they are
evaluated in relation to specific social groups within the society. All
societies contain smaller social groups that operate within the larger
framework of society, and it is these groups that are largely responsible
for the patterns of daily behavior which individuals follow. The behavior of an individual as a member of a subgroup may be entirely
appropriate to his membership in the larger society, but this is not
necessarily so. Whether an individual's behavior conforms to the requirements of his subgroup and to the requirements of the total society
depends upon the norms that characterize the subgroup and the society.
If the norms are similar for both, then the individual's behavior, insofar
as it is normative, will meet the requirements of both. However, all
societies are made up of a number of subgroups, and each is characterized by its own norms. It is possible, therefore, that an individual,
by following the norms of one subgroup, will be departing from the
norms of another subgroup or of the total society. Nineteenth-century
Mormons, for example, in following their own group norm of polygynous
marriages, were violating the norm of monogamy of the larger society.

Two important points emerge from this discussion: (1) social conformity and deviance exist in all societies and in all social groups within
each society, and (2) social conformity and deviance must always have
a referent (an individual conforms to or deviates from a particular
standard). The referent must be known specifically if valid statements
concerning conformity or deviance are to be made.

THE ADAPTIVE VALUE OF VARIABLE BEHAVIOR

The intimate balance in society among behavioral conformity, deviance, and control is crucial to the general successful adaptation of man. In fact, the balance achieved among these variables provides an index of the effectiveness of all other parts of culture in any society. A penetrating analysis of conformity, deviance, and control reveals such things as the capacity of a society for change without significant disruption; the static aspects of a society; the relative ability of a society to perpetuate the diagnostic parts of its culture; and the effective reciprocal integration among all parts of culture as manifest in a society.

The balance between deviance and conformity varies greatly in the known societies. Complete deviance, which implies completely idiosyncratic behavior, would mean the negation of social order, and exists nowhere. Complete conformity, which is equally impossible, would mean a static society: one unable to meet the constantly changing environment, both physical and sociocultural. Behavior in all societies falls somewhere between these two logically possible but socially impossible extremes. Thus, mechanisms fostering conformity and controlling deviance are found in all societies, but, by implication, all societies allow a certain degree of deviant behavior. Within this body of deviant behavior lies the ability of the society to meet new challenges, to continue successful adaptation, and to make necessary transitions in a relatively orderly, non-disruptive fashion. A meaningful analogy can be drawn between social deviance and the genetic variability found in any animal population. Both provide the "raw materials" for adaptive change.

Cultural Limits of Deviant Behavior

All groups do and must allow a certain degree of deviant behavior, but deviance has social limits. These limits are set by the particular culture; when they are exceeded, mechanisms of control will be set in motion. The control of deviance applies not only to individual members but to groups whose norms fall too far outside the accepted range of behavior as defined by the larger society. While such limitations appear to foster behavioral homogeneity, it remains true that no two individuals are exactly alike, and idiosyncratic behavior will and must occur. No individual can adhere completely to all norms characteristic of his society or to those of the subgroups within that society of which he is a member. Every society must, we repeat, permit a certain latitude in individual behavior—it must permit deviance.

In all societies, therefore, we find norms, deviance from those norms (both organized and individual), socially allowable limits to deviance (within the larger society and within its subunits as well), and mechanisms of control which seek to maintain these limits through social action. It remains now to determine the kinds of norms that exist in societies, the kinds of deviance that occur, the toleration limits that prevail in relation to deviance, the mechanisms of control that operate when these limits are transgressed, and other pertinent factors, all of which together will explain the range of social action found in the area of control.

SOCIAL NORMS AND CONFORMITY

In any society, most individuals adhere to certain customary behavioral patterns, and the result is a similarity in their actions. Their behavior may indicate shared attitudes, beliefs, and values, but whatever the underlying motives, the fact remains that a large part of the behavior found in any society will be shared to a greater or lesser extent by a significant proportion of its members. This sharing of overt actions is indicative of the existence of social norms.

Norms (any accepted modes of action or belief) may assume various forms: rules, codes, laws, or, more generically, customs. They are the accepted blueprints for social action. In order for a norm to exist, it must be accepted by a significant part of the membership of a society or a subsection of that society. Since all members of a given society do not necessarily accept or adhere to all of the same norms, and because norms are characteristic of parts of a society as well (classes, castes, occupational groups, religious orders and sects, etc.), norms assume a hierarchical relationship to one another within any society. That is, most members of a society will accept and share a general body of norms by virtue of their membership in the society, but these same individuals, as members of subgroups within that society, will also accept and adhere to norms peculiar to those subgroups and not shared by the society at large.

Norms are highly diversified and extremely numerous. It would be nearly impossible to list all the norms for all societies, or even to itemize all of the different kinds of norms that occur. Yet there is some similarity among norms in all societies, and this similarity allows us to categorize norms in terms of definite referents and then come to a clearer understanding of this concept.

Norms must have a definite *referent*. All norms are directly associated with something in society—the society itself, a group within society, a particular status position, or any other item diagnostic of human social organization. Second, a norm must be accepted by the members who constitute the referent in question, whether it is the society, a subunit, or another referent. Such acceptance may be expressed in laws, rules, maxims, and the like, and may be acted upon in any number of ways—with enthusiasm, with simple acceptance, with mere non-rejection, with approximate compliance. Whatever variations occur, norms must be accepted by the membership of the referent involved.

Norms which characterize an entire society may represent a generalized conscious cultural model for action. In our own society, for example, we have general norms of democracy and democratic processes that provide a model for our behavior, a model for action to be attempted regardless of whether it is actually achieved. Similar situations exist for the Soviet Union in terms of communism and for other societies professing a conscious model or organization which requires specific action. In spite of the fact that these norms may never be achieved fully in action, the model will still be retained as long as it has acceptance, and behavior will be based upon these norms.

Norms may, in addition, act as organizational blueprints for social groups within society. The family provides a clear-cut example of such a blueprint. The norms for the family in our society indicate that it should have a particular structure, itemized in terms of status positions (mother, father, husband, wife, son, daughter, sister, brother). Also, a particular type of behavior is associated with each position, and the person filling it is expected to *attempt* to achieve this normative behavior. Mothers are expected to behave in certain ways, whereas fathers are expected to engage in other types of behavior, as are sons and daughters, sisters and brothers, husbands and wives. In short, the norms associated with the family unit, and with each of the status positions within the family, tell the individuals who fill these statuses and who make up the family how to act. By this behavioral definition, a great deal of apparently random or haphazard action can be seen, upon closer inspection, as part of a homogeneity of action which all families in the society share to a greater or lesser degree. However, the norms associated with the family unit do not exist in isolation, but provide, in addition, a series of expectations upon which society and its members base other action. Norms in one social context may be directly related to and, at times, dependent upon norms that exist in a somewhat different social setting.

The norms associated with marriage not only provide us with another example of social norms, but demonstrate the relationships among norms that exist in two related but different social contexts. In our society, one of the norms directly associated with marriage is monogamy. Most marriages in the United States are of this variety, which demonstrates that the norm has been accepted.

The existence of a norm of monogamy tells individual members of the society several things. First, it provides a specific definition of the marital structure—one male and one female. Second, it indicates the type of action associated with this structure—one male and one female are given license by the society to live together in the same house, engage in sexual intercourse, have offspring and rear them, combine economic resources as though they were a single unit, and so on. These are some of the norms of action associated with marriage of the monogamous type in our society, and they specify some of the action expected of those who are involved in a monogamous marital union. Societies characterized by polygamy would define a somewhat different structure and behavior for members filling the status positions involved. The structure in polygynous marriage would involve the union of one male with two or more females, and, in polyandry, one female with two or more males. But in each of these cases, as with monogamy, there is a definite prescription (and at least an implied proscription) of the elements of organization (structure, action, and function) with their attendant norms.

The norms associated with a particular type of marriage are, therefore, directly related to the norms associated with a particular type of family. In our society, monogamous marriages are highly consistent with a nuclear family organization and are inconsistent with polygynous and polyandrous marriages. On the other hand, polygamous marriages are more consistent with composite family organizational types than with nuclear family organization. Not only are the structural norms different in the two cases, but so is the behavioral norm. If there are multiple wives involved in a family organization, the behavioral norms which guide their behavior will not be the same as those of a family organization in which one wife constitutes the norm. Frequently, in a polygynous society one wife is held responsible for all other wives of the family. This responsibility reflects particular behavioral and structural norms which cannot possibly exist in a family organization in which only one wife is involved.

A third way in which norms are manifest is in providing an expression of the custom diagnostic of the group, which is sometimes even deemed necessary for the perpetuation of the social unit. Etiquette, dress, cosmetics, and mannerisms—including speech, facial expressions, and bodily movements associated with language—are part of the norms of any society; they are some of the ways in which a group or society differentiates itself from other groups or societies. Such customs set one group culturally apart from other groups, while simultaneously promoting solidarity or unity within the group. Through similarity of action, customs express the shared norms of the group. Symbolic unity may be expressed by our flag and its associated behavior, by the golden stool of the Ashanti and its associated behavior, by the *molimo* trumpet of the Pygmy and its associated behavior. The fact that individuals will or will not belch at the table after a meal is indicative of norms in a particular society. If it is expected that a person will belch, failure to do so provides an instance of deviance from the norm; in societies where the norm is not to do so, an individual who belches is engaging in deviant behavior. Some examples of norms which occur in specific societies will contribute to a more precise understanding of this concept.

Ethnographic Examples of Norms

BaMbuti Pygmies. In the following example from a contemporary ethnography (Turnbull 1962:105–8), some of the norms found among the BaMbuti Pygmies are mentioned specifically, others are implied, and the mechanisms of social control are brought into play and directed toward a member who has transgressed the limits allowed for deviant behavior:

Cephu walked into the group, and still nobody spoke. He went up to where a youth was sitting in a chair. Usually he would have been offered a seat without his having to ask, and now he did not dare ask, and the youth continued to sit there in as nonchalant a manner as he could muster. . . . Manyalibo stood up and began a rather pompous statement of how everyone wanted this camp to be a good camp, and how everyone wanted the molimo to be a good molimo, with lots of singing, lots of eating, and lots of smoking. But Cephu never took part in the molimo, he pointed out. . . . And now, he added, Cephu had made the hunt a bad hunt.

Ekianga leaped to his feet and brandished his hairy fist across the fire. He said that he hoped Cephu would fall on his spear and kill himself like the animal he was. Who but an animal would steal meat from others? There were cries of rage from everyone, and Cephu burst into tears. Apparently, during the last cast of the nets Cephu, who had not trapped a single animal the whole day long, had slipped away from the others and set up his net in front of them. In this way he caught the first of the animals fleeing from the beaters, but he had not been able to retreat before he was discovered. . . .

Cephu tried very weakly to say that he had lost touch with the others and was still waiting when he heard the beating begin. It was only then that he had set up his net, where he was. Knowing that nobody believed him, he added that in any case he felt he deserved a better place in the line of nets. After all, was he not an important man, a chief, in fact, of his own band? Manyalibo tugged at Ekianga to sit down, and sitting down himself he said there was obviously no use prolonging the discussion. Cephu was a big chief, and a chief was a villager, for the BaMbuti never had chiefs. And Cephu had his own band, of which he was chief, so let him go with it and hunt elsewhere and be a chief elsewhere. . . .

Cephu knew he was defeated and humiliated. Alone, his band of four or five families was too small to make an efficient hunting unit. He apologized profusely, reiterated that he really did not know he had set up his net in front of the others, and said that in any case he would hand over all of the meat. . . . He clutched his stomach and said he would die; die because he was hungry and his brothers had taken away all his food; die because he was not respected.

This example points to the norms of the Pygmy society: cooperation, friendly and reciprocal interrelations, mutual leadership, and respect given on the basis of conforming behavior. The mechanisms of social control are shown to be public show of disrespect, public indictment for the deviant behavior, and ultimately, the threat of ostracism, which in this case could mean starvation. The display of competitive initiative by Cephu, which would be regarded in our society as at least partially praiseworthy, or normatively conforming, is directly deviant from Pygmy norms.

Adolescent Americans. A brief example from an ethnography (Hollingshead 1961:316) dealing with an American midwestern town further illustrates norms and control mechanisms:

SMOKING. The 77 per cent of the boys and 29 per cent of the girls who smoke know when and where to smoke. Boys approve of smoking for boys in the pool hall, the hangout, in a private car, on the street after dark, on dates, and out of town. Smoking is taboo around the high school, at high school athletic games, dances, church, and Boy Scout meetings. Girls may smoke in the clique and on dates, but not on the street. Freshman girls lose face with both boys and girls if they are known to smoke. This rule is violated by a few girls, both in their cliques and on dates, but if the violation becomes known, the offenders are gossiped about, snubbed, left out of parties, and generally treated with contempt.

The norms of this small town, in regard to adolescent smoking habits, are clearly understood among the youngsters. In this case, the adolescents are indulging in conforming behavior for their subgroup, but deviant behavior for the larger society. Besides their own methods of ostracism and ridicule, other control mechanisms are implied as coming from the larger society: only among themselves, in their "clique" or "hangout," or on dates, did either boys or girls feel free to smoke openly. This acknowledges their awareness that the larger society considers such behavior as "outside the limits," and their desire to avoid the penalties the society could impose.

DEVIANCE

The concept of deviance is intelligible only in relation to the idea of norms or normative behavior as manifest in a particular society. Behavior must deviate from something in particular (a definite referent) in order to determine the existence of deviance. There are two major types of deviance: tolerated deviance (that which is allowed by the society or the social group) and untolerated deviance (that which the society or the social group deems as unacceptable). Untolerated deviant behavior, against which the society acts and directs its efforts to control, is interpreted as threatening the existence of the present form of society; in many cases it does just that. To cite an extreme example, no society can tolerate unrestricted homicide. Consequently, any instance of murder threatens the society's existence. At the same time, it must be recognized that deviance provides increased heterogeneity of action, and, by contributing to the viability of a society, also increases its ability to adapt to future sociocultural environments. A static society is a nonviable society. Thus, some deviance in behavior is desirable in all societies.

Varieties of Deviance

Deviance can take many forms, and occurs in all sectors of culture. Individuals will almost always deviate to some extent from the behavior that is expected of them when they fill particular positions in society. The degree to which they fulfill the behavioral obligations attached to their statuses is in part a function of their own interpretation of what is expected of them. For example, a college professor who grades with unusual severity may interpret this as maintaining the standards expected of his status. A person's performance in a status position can also be affected by the way he has been trained to fill that position—a function of the enculturation process in his society.

All societies carry on processes whereby individuals are trained to assume certain social responsibilities and obligations within the society. Whether we label them enculturation, socialization, or education, it is by these processes that the culture of the group is transmitted to each incoming generation. As part of his training, each individual must be made aware of the values, attitudes, and norms of the society and of different groups within the society. He must learn the kinds of behavior that are regarded as unacceptable, and the consequences that will predictably result from such deviant behavior.

Societies and social groups, through the processes of enculturation, emphasize the knowledge they believe will lead to desirable and positive social action and, simultaneously, the ways in which society acts against those persons who choose to behave in an unacceptable manner. The family, the school, and the church, among other groups in United States society, emphasize and train individuals in behavior which is acceptable to each of these groups and to the total society—not to harm other persons physically, to respect other persons' property, to render aid to other individuals when possible, and so on.

Positive rewards are sometimes specified for those individuals who engage in positive, acceptable behavior. At the same time, individuals are warned about the consequences that will result if they do not engage in such positive behavior. If a person kills another, he will be apprehended, placed in confinement, and possibly lose his own life because of his deviant behavior. Warnings of the dire results that may occur from practicing deviant behavior are supported and reinforced by the social action that is directed against those individuals who have actually participated in this type of behavior. In complex societies, mass news media report such instances daily.

It appears to be common, the world over, to utilize threats of supernatural retribution in the socializing of children. Every culture has "bogeymen" who can be invoked by parents when children depart from acceptable behavior. Whether threats of sanctions actually deter other persons from engaging in the same or similar types of deviant behavior has not been answered satisfactorily. Examples of deviant behavior may, under certain circumstances, encourage deviant behavior of the same type. Nevertheless, it is important to recognize that groups who are responsible for enculturating individuals generally believe that one way in which they can encourage positive rather than deviant behavior is to show the negative and undesirable results of non-positive or deviant behavior.

Overplaying and Underplaying of Behavioral Obligations. Norms are sometimes thought of as *central tendencies,* the implication being that actual behavior might depart from the norm in either of two directions —too much or too little. The military officer who is overly lax in the enforcement of discipline is underplaying his role, as is the father in United States society who underprovides for his wife and children. The military officer who acts as a highly rigid disciplinarian is overplaying his role, as is the father in our society who extravagantly indulges his children's wants. A significant departure from the norm in either direction may constitute deviant behavior, and can result in action by the society, through its agencies of social control, against the deviant individual. The action may be to inform the individual that he is engaging in deviant behavior, or to warn him that he must substitute a more acceptable form of behavior for his deviance. Thus, during a "grace period," a traffic policeman may stop offenders to notify them that they are breaking a new traffic law, or he may stop a "speeder" but dismiss him with a warning to drive more slowly. Frequently, however, the society will punish the individual for his deviance. A traffic offender may be summoned into court and punished with a fine, loss of license, etc. These actions on the part of the social agency are considered to be deterrents to future deviance.

The overplaying or underplaying of roles can, of course, occur within acceptable limits. The father who slightly indulges his family may be held up as a model to more "normal" fathers, and an underprovider, within limits, will not always be reported to a corrective agency by his neighbors. A certain amount of deviant behavior, as we have suggested, provides a society with the variability desirable for continued adaptation to changing conditions. We have also shown, however, that some norms admit of very little deviance. Any departure from the norm or from the range of normative behavior, for example, murder in most societies, may be recognized very readily and immediately branded as unacceptable.

Etiquette. Etiquette refers to a broad and socially important area of customary behavior. In Chapter 3, we discussed etiquette as customary behavior between members of different classes in society. The classes may be male and female, young and old, those of subordinate or super-ordinate rank, and so on. The term can also refer to a wide range of customary behavior between status equals, where deviance may be defined as "bad manners." Proper observance of etiquette ("good manners") is an important mechanism for maintaining good social relations. Deviance in this respect in our society results in the employment of many sanctions: exclusion from intimate social ties or from membership in a desirable social group; criticism and ridicule; loss of employment. These and many other sanctions are leveled at the person guilty of improper dress, unacceptable grammar, obscenity, inappropriate mannerisms, and similar apparently minor acts. Appropriate behavior, it should be noted, is defined by group or class membership. Good manners, however defined, are a matter of group norms, and must be observed in interaction between status equals. Interaction with members of a different class may be regulated by quite different norms.

Norms of etiquette, like any other culture traits, differ greatly from culture to culture. Among aborigines in Australia, a traveler approaching a strange encampment would sit down or squat at a respectful distance, and remain there—for many hours if necessary—until approached by his hosts, because it is extremely bad manners to approach directly without an invitation. Etiquette for an Indian toward a *Ladino* in a Guatemalan village, we have seen, requires strictly deferential behavior. In all such cases, there is a range beyond which deviance is socially unacceptable and punishable.

Ethical and Moral Standards. Deviance from ethical and moral standards is of greater concern to members of a society than deviance from standards of etiquette. Behavior such as incest, adultery, physical injury, theft, or the taking of life is considered deviant behavior in most societies and social groups throughout the world. These types of deviance generally constitute more serious offenses which jeopardize the society's well-being, and therefore other agencies of social control may operate against the individual. It is not unusual to find that multiple sanctions, imposed by additional agencies of social control, may operate against the same individual for the same offense. Supernatural sanctions are frequently placed upon an individual when he commits murder, in spite of the fact that social sanctions have already been imposed by the agencies of social control of the society. In the United States, for example, since murder constitutes an act of deviance against the secular state and against the supernatural, both sanctions are invoked. In addition, society applies social pressures of various types even after an individual has "paid his debt to society" according to the legally constituted means and becomes subject to supernatural punishment in the future (at his death).

Probably, the more serious the offense (and this will be defined by each society), the greater the number of sanctions imposed upon the violator. Such a hypothesis is, however, subject to the related variable of cultural complexity. In order to have multiple sanctions placed upon a violator (beyond the general secular and supernatural agencies), multiple agencies of social control must exist in the society. In order for multiple agencies of social control to exist, the society must be relatively complex. Simpler societies frequently have a single agency that deals with a wide variety of deviant behavior; there is little if any specialization in coping with such behavior. In addition, the alternatives available to an individual in a simpler society are fewer than those in a more complex society. Therefore, the greater the complexity of the society, the greater the number of social groups that exist, and the greater the number of behavioral alternatives. These factors, in turn, permit a greater range of deviant behavior which requires more specialized agencies of social control to enforce and encourage acceptable behavior. The acceptance of this hypothesis should not, however, lead us to neglect the possibility that the greater the number of cultural alternatives in a society, the greater the acceptance of new cultural alternatives, and the broader, therefore, the latitude of acceptable, though deviant behavior.

In the social sciences, if not in society at large, we are becoming aware of the fact that deviant behavior is a major source of innovation. Many of the most important inventions and discoveries of modern times have been made by persons who, in their own time and in their own society, were regarded as deviants. This has been true, to some extent, of the inventors of the airplane, rockets, the automobile, and many other technological devices of present-day civilization. The anthropologist is not infrequently thought of, outside of academic circles at least, as being somewhat of a deviant.

Deviance is not restricted to the secular area of culture, but extends into the area of supernaturalism as well. Impiety has been regarded as serious deviant behavior in many societies. This was one of the crimes that theoretically merited the death penalty in ancient Aztec society. Impiety, or any suspected departure from rigid dogma, often led to severe punishment in seventeenth-century New England. The most serious charge was that of witchcraft, and the execution of persons as witches during the Salem trials is a well-known chapter in United States history. Even in more recent times in western society, the failure to practice a religion or to fully support one's church has been regarded as deviance. Being charged with atheism is no trivial matter in many sectors of our society today. However, much change has taken place in our society at large, and non-participation in a religion is no longer the serious matter it once was.

THE PROCESS OF SOCIAL CONTROL

When untolerated deviant behavior occurs, for whatever reasons, some system of social control is expected to be set into motion, and some agency of social control is expected to act. In very simple societies, such as the Pygmy, the agencies of social control may be equally simple, perhaps no more than a public gathering of the members of the hunting band to indict the errant member or, in the case of minor offenses, to show disrespect for him. In more complex societies, specialized agencies of social control exist and each acts to control specific types of deviance; the system of social control is more complex and specialized. There are groups that apprehend violators, different groups that judge alleged offenders, other groups that enforce the judgment.

A process of social control, to be defined as such, has six necessary and sufficient elements: norms, violation of norms, recognition of violation, report of violation, response to violation, and enforcement of this response. Together, these factors constitute a minimal process which is found not only in technologically advanced societies having complex, codified legal systems, but in very simple societies which have no written laws, and in which the entire social group is the agency of control. Each of these six elements will be discussed in turn.

Norms

Norms, as we have emphasized repeatedly, are any accepted cultural rules. They are also referents, or standards against which variation of behavior is recognized and measured. If deviant behavior is to be recognized, the behavior that is acceptable must be known. Thus, deviance must be determined within a definite social and cultural context. Behavior which is recognized as deviant in one context may be completely acceptable in a different context, depending upon the referents used to judge deviance.

Violation of Norms

Once norms are present and accepted, violations of these norms can occur. Not all members of any social group behave in exactly the same way, nor do all members of a social group necessarily accept all the norms of the group. Invariably, people behave in a way which can be judged deviant. Violations of norms are frequent in most social groups, but only when deviant behavior exceeds the limit tolerated by the group does the behavior constitute a serious violation.

Recognition of Violation

All serious violations must be recognized if an agency of social control is to act in relation to these violations. An agency of control cannot act if it has not been made aware that a violation has occurred. For example, monogamy is the norm for marital unions in the United States. Bigamy and polygyny are serious violations of this norm, and police authorities and the courts act in response to these violations when—and only when—they are aware of people involved in polygynous or bigamous relations. If they do not know of such instances they have no justifiable basis for action. There must be recognition of a violation of a norm if the process is to continue. Recognition, however, does not have to be by a member of the agency of social control. Frequently, it is not; anyone can recognize the violation. Deviance is recognized in some areas of behavior earlier than in others, and this also changes from time to time and from place to place. Some variation in the recognition of deviance is probably true of all human groups.

Report of Violation

Once a violation is recognized, however, a report must be made if the process is to be continued further. A person who recognizes the violation of a norm but does not report it disallows any possible action by agencies of social control. If, for example, an individual becomes aware of a person practicing bigamy, but decides it is "none of my business" and tells no one about it, the agency of social control does not become aware of the situation and cannot act. Reports of violations can come about in many ways. They may be made to the violator himself, to constituted authorities, to friends or kinsmen, and so on. The process may be quite informal. If a woman in a rural peasant village becomes aware of an adulterous situation, she may pass it on as gossip to other women at the well. They in turn may tell their husbands, and so on, until the affair reaches the attention of the village elders. However it takes place, a report must be made ultimately to the agency of social control if that agency is to respond to the violation. Otherwise the process stops, and the minimal process has not been carried out.

Response to Violation

When a report of a violation of a norm is made to the agency of social control, the agency must respond to the report in some way. There are many types of responses: investigations, formal charges, trials, penalties, reprimands, restorative action, and many more, or any combination of these. The effectiveness of the agency of social control will depend not only upon the fact that a response to the report of the violation has been made, but upon the type of response made.

Enforcement of the Response

When a response is accomplished, the agency of social control must be able to enforce it, for the ability to enforce the response also determines the effectiveness of the agency of control. An agency of control that imposes a fine upon a violator but cannot collect this fine is ineffective. In some situations where multiple agencies of control exist, they are in conflict with one another because they attempt to control the same types of violations; one detracts from the other's effectiveness of enforcement. Where western legal systems were imposed upon traditional agencies of control (as in British India and in Africa), an alternative was provided to violators. They no longer had to accept the judgment of the traditional agencies; instead, they could have their cases tried in the court of law introduced by the colonial government. This alternative detracted from the enforcement ability of the traditional agencies.

Types of Responses.   Three major kinds of responses can be made by agencies of social control: punitive, restorative, and punitive–restorative. Punishment of various types—fines, expulsion, confinement—may be imposed upon violators, and the enforcement of this response (payment of the fine imposed, leaving the society for a specified period of time, serving a period of time in confinement) is interpreted as satisfying or compensating for the violation. Theoretically, the violator resumes his previous life in society upon compliance with the punitive response imposed by the agency of control.

Social control in a Guatemalan village. Indians working in lieu of a fine. (Photo by Robert H. Ewald.)

Restorative action by the agency of social control does not seek to impose formal punishment upon an offender; rather, it attempts to "recondition" the individual in a manner that will enable him to assume his previously normal and acceptable place in society. Retraining is thought to be the most appropriate and effective response to violations, whether deviance is deliberate or due to ignorance of the norm.

Combined punitive and restorative responses are probably the most frequent ones issued by agencies of social control, especially in contemporary western societies. Violators are punished (fulfillment of this punishment is construed to mean that the offender has paid for his violation), and then they are retrained in an effort to prevent them from repeating the same or similar unacceptable behavior. Thus, in the United States, a person who is apprehended for a traffic violation frequently pays a fine to the state because he has behaved unacceptably, and is then required to attend instruction which attempts to explain and demonstrate to the offender why he should not behave in the unacceptable way. A similar sequence of events, though lengthier and more complex, is applied to more serious offenses. Psychiatric care, counseling, and rehabilitation of offenders are forms of retraining directed toward restoring the violator to his "proper" place in society. Some examples of the ways in which agencies of social control actually work will illustrate these concepts more concretely.

THE BAIGA OF INDIA: AN ETHNOGRAPHIC EXAMPLE OF SOCIAL CONTROL

The Baiga are a tribe of *bewar* (slash and burn) agriculturalists of the state of Orissa and of the Central Provinces in India. The endogamous Baiga tribe is divided into several endogamous *jats* (caste-like groups), each of which is territorially differentiated. Each *jat* is composed of numerous exogamous, non-totemic units—*garh*, which correspond to the usual village group.

Norms and Their Violation

Many of the Baiga norms, and their enforcement, are concerned with ". . . maintaining the integrity of the tribe on the one hand, and its prestige on the other" (Elwin 1939:196). The preservation of group solidarity through the maintenance of group integrity and prestige both explains and aids in maintaining Baiga endogamous relations, rules of commensality, and concepts of pollution. Thus, committing adultery with a non-Baiga presents the risk of introducing "alien blood" into the tribe; the acceptance of food from an alien defiles a Baiga and, in turn, makes him a threat to the entire society. Even the touching of earthenware cooking pots by a non-Baiga results in their defilement, and they must be destroyed. These are only a few examples of the tribe's attempt to maintain group solidarity.

Another aspect of the attempt to remain "pure" is found in the vanity of the Baiga. A Baiga considers himself as ". . . lord of the earth . . . master of wild animals, . . . the master of magic, the adept inventor of love-charms, the controller of wind and rain and fire" (*ibid.*, 197). Such vanity is especially true of the men. It is a grave offense, resulting in social exile, if a man allows his wife to beat him or allows her to take the lead in sexual intercourse; the Baiga set forth the maxim, "She must not ride upon her husband. Her place is below" (*ibid.*, 198). The hair, to which the Baiga pay a great deal of attention, cannot be barbered by alien hands. It is considered an extremely important secondary sexual characteristic, and, as such, defilement of it would betray the sexual integrity of the tribe. However, the regulations designed to achieve the Baiga goals are not to be explained simply in terms of Baiga and non-Baiga; there exist, in fact, gradations of the breach of solidarity. For example, if a Baiga receives a beating, he has committed a very serious offense; he has impaired the integrity of the tribe, because the Baiga believe that they are the *Bhumia-raja* (lord of the earth), that no person can equal their status and therefore no one should be able to beat them. Conversely, and consistent with this belief, the administering of a beating by a Baiga is proper, and no penalty is imposed. However, Baiga agents of control recognize the reality of the situation—Baiga *are* beaten from time to time by non-Baiga. Consequently, the seriousness of the offense of being beaten depends upon who administers the beating. A Baiga who is beaten by a Chamar or an Agaria (caste groups in India) may ". . . be excommunicate for ten years and then have to give a six days' feast with four goats before he would be forgiven." However, a similar beating at the hands of a Gond (a tribal group in India) is not as serious, and if a beating is administered by an Englishman there is no penalty. Realistically enough, the police and forest guards (governmental representatives in the Baiga territory) are excluded from the application of this rule ". . . for this happens so frequently that the Baiga would be financially ruined if they took it too seriously" (*ibid.*, 197).

These are only a few of the rules that characterize Baiga society. There are a great many more, as there are in all societies. Some of the behaviors considered deviant by the Baiga are tearing of the ear, vermin in a wound, killing a dog, cat, or cow, bestiality, breach of the menstruation rules, allowing oneself to be beaten, incest, marriage outside the tribe, piercing of the nose, impotency, or unmanliness. All of these and others are considered as untolerated deviant behavior and constitute an offense against society. These rules have been established through custom and precedent. Some have a traditional or mythical origin. The rule pertaining to allowing oneself to be beaten stems from the mythical belief that the Baiga is the lord of the earth, and may be traced to the myth of "The Blessing of the Baiga" (*ibid.*, 317). Others originated in the religious beliefs of the Baiga, or are the result of culture contact (e.g., exclusion of the English forest guards and police from application of certain Baiga rules for behavior, and those rules which have been adopted as a result of Hindu influence—killing of a cat, dog, or cow). Of major importance, though, is the fact that these are viable rules which are generally adhered to and which constitute and express the goals and values of the society.

Recognition and Report of Violation

One of the important agencies of social control among the Baiga is composed of the village women. This group is, among other things, an initiating body. Through the use of social pressures (mainly gossip and avoidance) and by influencing the male population, they are able to bring the process of social control into action. This unit is more of an agglomerate. Little, if any, rigidity of structure exists, and there is no leader, no specific number of members, no formal rules or requirements for membership other than sex, and no formal meetings. The way in which this informal social unit operates is expressed with clarity in the following statements by a Baiga:

'Suppose a girl has gone to a Panka [member of a lower caste]. Someone has seen her. She begins to talk. Then one evening, when that girl goes to the well to get water, the women draw away from her, they say, "Don't touch our water pots, don't come too near us." A few days afterwards, when the women have had time to talk to their husbands while they sleep together, perhaps the girl's father or her brother is sitting with the men. They say, "No, we won't take your pipe, we can't smoke with you." Then the family knows that the girl has committed some fault. When next the village gathers together for a festival or a dance, then the girl's father calls out, "What has my family done that you won't share our pipe or eat with us?" Then all the people tell him, and generally he gives a small feast to the elders of the village on behalf of the family, and after that they share his pipe again. But the girl's fate is decided by the *panch*.' (*Ibid.*, 200–1).

Village women are intimately involved in the process of social control among the Baiga. In the example given, members of the women's social unit were responsible for (1) recognition of the violation (pollution), and (2) report of the violation (to other women and to their husbands, who in turn reported the violation to the remainder of the village). The response to the report of the violation was made first by the male members, directed to the male members of the offender's family (failure to accept the pipe and smoke with these men), and second by the entire village, directed, once again, toward the offender's family. In this case, the family of the offender automatically assumes some of the guilt based on the action of the female offender. This in itself is a violation and is dealt with by the men's group and by the entire village. But the specific violation committed by the offender is dealt with by another agency of social control, the *"panch"* (or *panchayat*), a more formal council which, in this case, has received the report of the violation from the entire village based upon their previous action.

The *panchayat* is a more formal agency of social control, but it is also characterized by some latitude. First, as the name implies, the *panchayat* must be composed of at least five members (*panch* = five). Second, these members must claim some prestige within the village, but the source of this prestige—integrity, sagacity, economic wealth, many sons, tribal loyalty—matters little. Third, the group meets only when neces-sary: when requested to do so upon the report of a breach of acceptable behavior, when an individual is to be reinstated to his position in Baiga society after he has been excommunicated, or for other reasons of simi-lar importance. Fourth, there is no presiding officer, no maximum num-ber of members, and no full-time specialists. A *panchayat* may be composed of five members for deciding certain cases and five totally different members for deciding other cases.

Response to Violation

The actual procedure of the *panchayat* culminates in a decision re-garding the guilt or innocence of the accused. If a verdict of guilty is returned, the *panchayat* decides upon the punishment to be imposed. In arriving at such a decision, oaths may be taken, the genealogy of the family considered, the status of the individual weighed. The verdict and the penalty imposed, if any, constitute the response by the agency of social control. As in many societies and agencies of social control, nu-merous factors are considered when making a decision (not all of them objective in the western sense) and various things influence the mem-bers and the decision.

One of the most consistent factors that influences decisions by agen-cies of social control, and the society's ability and willingness to abide by such decisions, is the status of the offender. Persons with a great deal of economic and/or political power, prestige, or charismatic quali-ties may be able to compromise the response of agencies of social con-trol. It is a fairly recent phenomenon where such persons have felt the full force of decisions rendered by agencies of control. The effect of status can be seen in the case of a prominent and highly respected Baiga magician who entered into sexual intercourse with his daughter-in-law. Excommunication, a total of 8 rupees for liquor, 2 goats, and 6 *khandi* of rice was the penalty imposed for this violation. However, the offender did not accept the penalty imposed. In order to avoid being shamed in public, he paid 2 rupees for liquor but ". . . declared that he didn't care whether the people ate from him or no" (*ibid.*, 203). According to the Baiga rules, this individual should be an outcast for he is an excommunicate. Still the people drink liquor, smoke, and sit with him, and there is no definite evidence that his practice as a magi-cian has suffered. He is in demand everywhere, and his magic seems to be as powerful as ever. "He is regarded with great reverence, and his popularity is undiminished" (*ibid.*, 204).

Another example of influence upon agencies of social control occurs among the village women in Baiga society, who apply social pressure through gossip and avoidance in the course of their daily activities. Thus, they act as agents of social control and/or as mechanisms through which a decision made by an agency of social control is enforced. In either case, the application of social pressure by the village women is greatly intensified if the women have cause to resent the offender, though just the opposite may occur where an offender is well-liked by the women. Thus, a woman, of whom the village women have cause to be jealous, would be subject to very intensive social pressures if she committed an offense. This was not so in the case of a very young and pretty girl, who was well-liked by the women and who never gave them cause for jealousy. So well was this girl liked that, when she had relations with a Panka and subsequently with a Mussalman, no one said anything (no one put the process of social control into operation, because no one reported the violation though they recognized that it was a violation), and the girl was not penalized in any way (*ibid.*). The agency of social control must receive a report of a violation before it can respond.

Although the penalties imposed by the Baiga *panchayat* have been described as analogous to the fluctuating prices in a bazaar, they do follow some sort of order. As would be expected in any society, the more extreme violations call for more severe penalties, and lesser violations are associated with minor penalties. Thus, offenses such as allowing oneself to be beaten, or marriage outside the tribe, carry rather heavy fines in addition to excommunication of a serious nature, while the lesser offenses, such as bestiality or allowing vermin to get into a wound, call for lesser fines and a minor degree of excommunication, if any at all. Finally, there are numerous very minor violations (analogous to misdemeanors in the United States) that call for a minimum flat-rate penalty, usually a small fine.

Excommunication is imposed upon the offender for minor offenses and upon the entire family of the offender for more serious offenses. The extension of a penalty to the family of the offender is based upon the Baiga belief in contagion and contamination. Excommunication of the lesser degree may be expressed merely by the village members' refusing to share the man's pipe, and may be atoned for by a small dinner or feast provided for a few of the villagers. Restoration following the major form of excommunication involves the giving of three feasts, the third being the crucial one for complete restoration of the individual to

Baiga society. These are quite costly, and some Baiga, once excommunicated for a serious offense, are never able to raise funds sufficient to restore themselves to their former position, and remain outcastes for the rest of their lives.

Enforcement of the Response

Since there are no means for physical confinement in Baiga society, the means of enforcement revert to social pressure. Once excommunication has been specified, the members of the community will not interact with the guilty party or his family. While the offender is physically present in the group, he is no longer an effective member as long as he remains excommunicated. Social interaction, responsibility, obligation, expectation, and dependence are removed. The offender becomes a social isolate.

Severe excommunication, however, is an ultimate sanction. Since the major and most frequent objective of the entire Baiga system of control is the maintenance of group solidarity, restoration of the individual to his proper place in society is of foremost importance. Long-term or permanent severance of an individual from society not only disrupts the complex web of social interactions of which the individual was a part, but it decreases and even precludes the ability of the society to control the excommunicate. Accordingly, the Baiga realistically defend against resorting to the ultimate expulsion of an individual from the community by compromising the enforcement of penalties imposed. In the words of a member of Baiga society, " 'We demand a seven days' feast, with seven goats and twenty rupees' worth of liquor. We think ourselves lucky if we get a three days' feast with a pig, and ten rupees' worth of liquor' " (*ibid.*, 200).

The description of penalties readily shows that any regularity of penalization that occurs among the Baiga is a reflection of their hierarchically ranked values, as it is in any society.

AGENCIES OF SOCIAL CONTROL

Most societies are characterized by multiple agencies of social control, each of which achieves a different degree of success and effectiveness. The particular agency that operates is dependent upon the specific social unit to which it is related, and all agencies of social control are related to one or more social groups or total societies. The number of agencies of social control extant in any society depends upon (1) the number of distinct social groups in the society, (2) whether each group controls its members itself or has delegated this obligation to another agency, (3) the effectiveness of the agencies of social control in relation to one another, and (4) the complexity of the society.

Group Agencies

In less complex societies, and in some of the intermediate ones, it is not uncommon to find the agencies of social control bound up with political offices and groups. In fact, this is a logical unification, since social control may be viewed as one dimension of the political organization (the internal dimension dedicated to controlling the behavior within society as opposed to the external dimension of political organization which is concerned mainly with the defense of territory and property *vis-à-vis* other political groups). No matter how one conceives of the area of social control or of its agencies, it cannot be disputed that such

A native court of justice at Bama, British Cameroons, consists of the judge, an alkali, and his assessors, forming an Alkali's Court. (British Information Services.)

agencies are linked directly to particular social groups (including political, economic, and religious groups), and their main purposes are to encourage and maintain acceptable behavior and limit deviance.

Agencies of social control may include the total effective group, such as the Pygmy (a description of which was given earlier in this chapter) and the Eskimo hunting bands. The Eskimo song duel is frequently cited by anthropologists as constituting one example, whereby the total society (the effective social group) constitutes the agency of social control and decides the innocence or guilt of the accused. A decision in these cases, however, has nothing to do with the actual facts. Instead, the decision is based upon the way in which the accused and the accuser perform in the duel. If an individual who has committed an act of deviance (such as wife stealing) can perform in a manner which is more acceptable to the group than his accuser, he will not be convicted. A decision by the group is based upon their approval of the duel and is voiced extemporaneously at the time the duel is proceeding. The one who is deemed the loser of the duel by the group is shamed and frequently leaves to pursue his life alone—a hazardous task in the far northern environment. He may, at some later time, return to the group.

Representative Agencies

Representatives of groups are probably the most frequent agencies of social control. Many social groups have councils that act in this capacity. Indian society, for example, is characterized by at least two local agencies of social control, which cross-cut one another but are at the same time distinct from one another. These are the caste *panchayat* and the village *panchayat* (*panchayat* = council). The caste *panchayat* is composed, generally, of five or more members (this is not always actually the case) and is a council which represents the entire caste group. It is concerned with maintaining proper behavior by members of that particular caste. All castes have a caste *panchayat* which serves this function for their group. A person who pollutes himself, who infringes upon the rights of other caste members, or who in some way deviates from the behavior acceptable by the caste will be subject to action taken by the caste *panchayat*. When this group meets to respond to the report of the violation, many things are taken into consideration (genealogical relationships, past behavior, ritual piety, economic and political power and status, and others) as pertinent facts. Objective consideration of facts related only to the deviant act, as theoretically occurs in our society, is not universal. Certainly these are considered, but other items are equally important to the case. It appears that where members are reciprocally or intimately linked with one another, there is consideration of more comprehensive information and not only of those factors related to the isolated instance of deviance.

The second agency of social control in rural India is the village *panchayat*. Since many of the rural Indian villages are multicaste, it is necessary to have an agency of social control which can maintain acceptable behavior among castes; hence, the village *panchayat* is a multicaste group. This agency of social control is concerned with deviance that occurs among members of two or more different castes in a single village and which affects the entire village. A dispute that occurs between members of two castes regarding payment of goods or services would be a case for consideration by the village *panchayat*. The village *panchayat* deliberates in a way similar to that of the caste *panchayat*, considering all relevant information and not only that relating to the particular act of deviance. The examples given among the Baiga, though a tribe, explain in general terms the ways in which these councils operate.

Supernatural Agencies

Some agencies of social control do not rely upon individual or group decisions completely. African societies are frequently cited for their use of a trial by ordeal, in which other external (e.g., supernatural) agents decide the guilt or innocence of the accused or contribute to such a decision. The main idea in these cases is that an individual who is innocent will survive these trials (swallowing of poison, being thrown into a body of water with a heavy weight tied around him, and the like), and one who is guilty will be identified as such by supernatural powers and simultaneously punished. In many societies, such as our own, supernatural decisions and agencies may remain as separate entities that make decisions independently of the secular action or agency. These decisions of guilt or innocence may be a cumulative consideration of all acts of deviance in relation to all acts of positive behavior, or they may be a net consideration of the total behavior of any given individual during his life. In many of the world's religions, the supernatural acts in the capacity of an agency of social control and decides the guilt or innocence of the person. The Christian, Islamic, and Hebrew conceptions of the day of judgment illustrate this belief.

However, in some religions the supernatural may act through secular agencies to make more immediate decisions. Such is the case with Hinduism: a person is born at a lower status if he has not acted properly (has not fulfilled his *dharma*) and at a higher status if he has engaged in proper action. The social status a person occupies in any given life is considered to be a result of his proper or improper action in a past life.

Relationships Among Agencies of Control

The range and types of agencies of social control on a cross-cultural basis are as numerous as the types of social groups that exist. Some agencies of social control are kin-based, others are parts or representatives of voluntary associations, of political associations and groups, of ritual associations and groups, of territorial groups or administrative units, and so on. As with social groups in the more complex societies, agencies of social control stand in a hierarchical relationship to one another. While each agency of social control generally acts within a specified realm and is linked to a specific group or association in order to enforce that group's norms, certain agencies of social control overlap one another. This is especially true on a vertical plane. It is in such instances, or in cases where two agencies of symmetrical groups at the same hierarchical level overlap, that a distinct hierarchical relationship among agencies of social control and an order of priority are seen. The legal system in the United States is an example. The segmentary lineage system that occurs among African societies such as the Nuer is another. The *panchayats* in India, where there are levels of agencies of control within each social, political, or administrative unit (caste, village, or territory) are still another.

The Munda of India

The Munda, an agricultural tribe of Chota Nagpur in India, exemplify many of the ideas included in the above discussion. Many of the rules that characterize Munda society, like those of the Baiga, are concerned with maintaining group solidarity and restricting the entrance of alien elements. In addition, the Munda have numerous regulations regarding property. Many of the cases reported are concerned with this aspect of their control.

Judicial authority at the village level of Munda society is vested in the *Hatu panchayat* (village council). This is not a standing body, but meets only upon request. It is convened to decide private disputes and minor offenses. Once it has been formed, a definite structure is presented. When a dispute arises, each party to the dispute will gather a set of *Panches* (usually people of their own *kili*, an exogamous kinship group) who constitute a partisan faction. The two sets of *Panches* are brought together, and the *Munda* and *Pahan* (headmen of the village) then select three or more men from each faction. Those persons selected constitute the *Select Panch*, who, in turn, elect from their members a *Sir Panch* or President. This accomplished, the *Select Panch* will choose two or three individuals to serve in the capacity of *Kajuiidiagus* (messengers). All present are seated in a definite manner, according to the positions they fill.

Once this agency of social control has been duly formed, the case begins. The initial step is the reiteration of the charge (stated by the *Kajuiidiagus*), followed by an explanation of all depositions taken and a recapitulation of the evidence gathered by each side. Several men from each faction (the *Panches* initially gathered by each side who were not chosen as members of the *Select Panch*) are then questioned by the *Sir Panch*.

After this process of the investigation has been completed (during which oaths and ordeals may be administered in order to arrive at the truth), each member of the *Select Panch* then retires to consider privately all that has been presented in support of both sides. The *Sir Panch*, after sufficient time has elapsed, asks each member for his opinion and the reasons supporting it. Opinions with their attendant reasons are also elicited from members of both factions by the *Sir Panch*. After considering all opinions and reasons, the *Sir Panch* issues a *hukum* (decree) and explains his reasons.

It should be recognized that the *panchayat* in this instance is a body formed by very specific procedures, encompassing both selective and elective processes, and that the *Hatu panchayat* (village council), once formed, is rigidly structured. As regards the procedures of the *Hatu panchayat*, great precision is used in arriving at a verdict, thorough investigations of the facts and circumstances are made, and evidence as well as opinion is relied upon heavily. This concern with the opinion of all persons involved in the case is reflected in the decisions of the *panchayat*, which generally take the form of compromise and thus reveal their basic goals—restoration of group solidarity and the return of the individuals to their proper places in society.

When serious disputes or offenses arise, or when the decision of the *Hatu panchayat* is disputed, the case is brought before the *Parha panchayat*. This group constitutes the agency of social control and the judicial authority for the *Parha*, the larger territorial units of the Munda. Offices within the *Parha panchayat* are more numerous than those of the *Hatu panchayat* and are filled by the headmen (either the *Munda* or *Pahan* or both) of the constituent villages that make up this larger territorial unit. The principal officers of the *Parha panchayat* are the *Parha Raja* (president), the *Pande* (who makes the arrangements for the *panchayat* to convene and assembles the necessary participants), the *Pahan* (the religious member who officiates at the necessary sacrifices and feasts which are incorporated into the proceedings), and the *Dewan* (collector of fines), among others. These offices are hereditary according to particular villages, and the villages themselves take the name of the offices. For example, the village in which the *Parha Raja* resides is known as Raja, that of the *Dewan* as Dewan, and so on.

The proceedings of the *Parha panchayat* are initiated by the aggrieved individual. He notifies the *Munda* (headman) of his village, who, in turn, informs the *Parha Raja.* Having been informed of the complaint, the *Parha Raja,* through the *Pande,* assembles the members of the *Parha panchayat* and informs the villages concerned of the date when the proceedings will take place. Such meetings always take place in the village of the accused.

The manner of procedure is very similar to that described for the *Hatu panchayat,* and there is not enough significant variation to reiterate the details. By way of summary, the charge is made and explained by the *Parha Raja,* evidence and depositions are heard from both sides, and after due consideration the verdict is announced by the *Parha Raja.*

Penalties imposed by the Munda *panchayats* appear to be characterized by a significant degree of regularity and reflect all facts revealed by the judicial proceedings. In this way, it seems that the Munda have succeeded in accomplishing a formula to maintain group solidarity by satisfying both parties. This attitude is further stimulated by the Indian governmental courts. The Munda dislike interference with their system of dispensing justice, and pride themselves upon the fact that few cases are referred to the courts. This necessitates careful, sagacious, and satisfying decisions on the part of the *panchayats,* since the party who considers himself slighted in the dispensation of justice has the opportunity of reporting the offense to the governmental courts (an alternative agency of social control).

Penalties imposed by the Munda, as with the Baiga and with all other societies, reflect the degree of abhorrence with which they view specific violations. Major and significant deviations, such as sexual relations with those outside the tribe, call for a heavy fine as well as expulsion; violation of *kili* exogamy brings forth similar penalties; theft, however, is not met with as great a degree of abhorrence and usually calls for a fine equal to the value of the goods stolen and a promise not to commit the same offense again upon pain of a greater penalty.

Enforcement of the penalties imposed is accomplished in several ways. First, the decision handed down by the *panchayats* is regarded as an inspired decree, thus imposing a supernatural sanction. Second, the verdicts are usually accepted by the people, because those who sit in judgment are people who command respect and confidence (Sachchidananda 1957:131). If these subtle forms of enforcement fail, the ultimate measures are force and additional penalties. "Pitiful indeed is the condition of the convicted offender who refuses to bow to the decision of the Panchayat or pay the fine imposed. The recusant is often severely thrashed, and always outcasted. He cannot find wives for his sons or husbands for his daughters, and is turned out of his lands . . . if possible." (Roy 1912:420; much of the above factual information regarding the Munda system of social control is based upon this source.)

East Indians of Trinidad

Agencies of social control do not have to be formal bodies, as are the *panchayats* in India and the courts and police in the United States; they may be of a more informal nature. An example is that of the *pandit* (religious specialist) among East Indians in Trinidad.

For the most part, attempts by this religious specialist to maintain control within the village are limited to the settlement of disputes beween two or more individuals or families. These controversies seldom, if ever, involve serious crimes. Translated into the language of our legal code, conflict situations in which the pandit is involved would come under the category of civil action or minor torts.

There are several obstructions which prohibit the success of the pandit in such procedures. A pandit requested to act in an extra-legal capacity usually recognizes that: (1) his recommendations are not always accepted; (2) his decisions may not be treated as final; and (3) his suggestions are not always viewed as the best alternatives possible. In spite of these restrictions for success, the pandit's participation in matters of this type is continued and constitutes a significant contribution to the maintenance of social control among East Indians in rural Trinidad. Moreover, such extra-legal participation is intimately related to the pandit's other activities.

Several considerations explain continued extra-legal action by this religious specialist. First, he considers it his "duty" to act as an arbitrator. This concept of duty is derived from his stated obligation to help men to live in peace with one another. Second, success attained by the pandit allows him prestige in secular matters and tends to elevate his overall status in the community. In turn, this adds to the reputation of the pandit in sacred activities. Individuals rationalize that just and logical action by the pandit in secular matters are indicative of his devotion to God and man. They will, therefore, seek the services of a pandit successful in secular activities to conduct rituals, for curing, for divination, and the like. The religious specialist fosters this idea by publicly revealing that God has given him the power to arbitrate in order to help men live peacefully with one another, much the same as God has given him the power to cure and to conduct ritual activity properly. According to the pandit, these are merely diverse aspects of the same thing, e.g., his devotion to God. Third, availability of the pandit serves as a relatively effective alternative for resolving conflict situations. The necessity for having an alternative is explained, in part, by the mistrust that the villagers have of the police and the courts. Skepticism, mistrust, and sometimes fear of these governmental agencies is based upon: (1) the concept of racial bias and persecution by the Creole of the East Indian, a belief which occupies a formidable position in the latter's daily thoughts; (2) previous court decisions considered by the East Indian to be unjust, costly, and unduly long; (3) a concept of the police as a force which contrives against the East Indian and (which) treats the East Indian unfairly;

and (4) the belief that another East Indian, especially a religious specialist, will be better able to understand the entire situation and will consider the motives, complexities and hidden details of the matter more fully. In spite of these feelings, governmental agencies are used most frequently by the East Indian. There exists the overriding factor that the courts have the undisputed ability to enforce their decisions quickly and effectively. Moreover, they are an established organization to which the individual has recourse. Nevertheless, the contradictory skepticism held by the East Indian allows the existence of alternatives. Finally, the East Indian adheres to the attitude that problems pertaining to their ethnic group should be settled internally. Recourse to the pandit attempts to satisfy this need. However, even when the pandit is employed, the courts are constantly used as a threat during the entire proceeding; a fact which further exemplifies the importance of the courts.

The following case will illustrate the preceding discussion. This case was related to me by the pandit and is reported as told. Seventeen cases of this type were recorded during the course of the research.

Case Number 1

This Sanka, he has a piece of land. The land is not belonging to him, but the wife he is living with has a piece of land—a piece of swamp land. But he wants to, being as he is living with the woman, he protects the woman and he wants to take care. He has a nice piece of swamp land there where a lot of grass grow and animal eat. But some days the animal get away, bust rope and things and went and eat the grass. So once the fella by the name of Ram Nath, his bull went in there and eat some of the grass. And he hold the bull, this Sanka, and tie it. No! He carry it to the pound. The fella went and pay for it and get it out from the pound. He brought him up in court. I think for damages. This fella, he came to me when he got the summons, this Ram Nath. He say, "Well pandit, my animal gone and get away, and if you see what he eat, a very little piece of grass. I mean it only an animal and the man bring me up. I beg you that you come and settle the matter." I say, "All right." I went to them—to Sanka, Sanka's place, and I told them, I say, "Well, I understand that you bring this man up for animal damages." He say, "Yes, pandit, I always talk to this man, and he times me. And when he know I am not home, he let go the animal. And today, the day when this thing happened, he was out on the road and I was out on the road . . . too, and when I come I went down in the land and I see in the rice land this animal. So when I see the animal, he come to get it. So he have to pay me because many times he doing this thing." So I say, "Well, all right. If he eat your coconut, coconut have use, but this is grass. Animal will eat grass. How many grass did he eat, this animal? The animal hungry. If you hungry, you look for food, and if the animal get away, it is grass he eat. You didn't plant the grass, the grass grow in the swamp there. So don't make no fuss about that man, if you are the right person. Tell him again in front of me, warn him. Let him sign you a paper that he will not let go of the animal." I say I will make the paper. He say, "No! I want to put him in court. If he didn't pay, I will settle it." I say, "All right. How much do you want him to pay for the damages?" He say 80 dollars for damages for bringing up and everything. He say he give the lawyer 40 dollars already to proceed with the case and what not. I say, "Well you shouldn't hold a lawyer around all the time. The day of court you could have hold a lawyer. Get rid of the lawyer." He say, "No! I done pay him 40 dollars there." I know that the man is pulling a fast one. I know that! So I tell him, "Well look now, for pete's sake, I come in this matter now to beg you and I want you to settle this thing before we go in court. You will have plenty money you will lost. How many times the case will be postponed. Lawyers will take money. And this man is poor, he will have to pay too. So when you think you win, you lost in court. Nobody wins. For the amount of time you will have to run. I'm putting this to you. So if you go in front of the magistrate, one magistrate alone, what he tell you, you going to obey him. And I, who am living with you people here come to beg you. You must understand that we are human beings. You must have respect and regard for a person who tell you something, you must." He say, "Yes, but he have to pay." It is 80 dollars he want. So I say, "Let us try and come to a feeling, a human feeling, and you charge at something less." He say, "Less? What less I could charge?" I say, "Well let me tell you how much you must charge." He say, "All right. I leave it to you now, let me see." I say, "Well, the most thing I could give you is 40 dollars." He say, "NO! NO! NO! NO!, that can't pay me." I put it to him, I beg him, I talk to him in all different way. I call the wife and I say, "Look, so long the land was in abundant bush. You just cut grass in people land. This man is just pick up and this man is give him trouble. Leave this man and go away. You too have to live by the people and they will take advantage of you." The man get vexed and he say, "So what you mean? I is an ogre and I will run away?" I say, "If you get sick or dies and this thing, ain't you have to sleep by these people in the village yet. So let us bring peace and you take 40 dollars. I should say take nothing; Because he no produce that damage. But still if you want some money, and you have trouble and this is the way you want to take the money, well, take it. Take 40 dollars." He say, "All right, what you say, I leave it to you, pandit. What you say, I will do. I won't make trouble on it." I give him 40 dollars and I make him a paper, a receipt that on Tuesday, so and so date of court, he will not attend court. Why? Because we are settled here for damage. Damage settlement of 40 dollars. He stamp the receipt and I keep the receipt in my possession. I say to Ram Nath, "That after the case any time you will call for the receipt. And until the case went done, I will not give the receipt so that this man will not appear. And if he does appear, I have to go as a witness in front of the magistrate and tell where we settle the case already. You understand? Because if he could watch so near for 40 dollars, then he could watch again. You have to be frightened of this man. Your own people. And that's the case I settled."

Cases settled by the pandit, such as the one above, exhibit certain basic characteristics which are representative. First, the pandit is always solicited to participate as an arbitrator. He never intervenes in a conflict situation unless petitioned. Second, the major objective of the pandit is to keep the matter from being brought before the courts. Frequently, this is accomplished by using the courts as a threat. Third, the pandit is charged with the burden of proving that the settlement he has recommended is an equitable one. More, that it is one which will be adhered to without repercussions. Parties to a dispute must be assured that the case will not be referred to another agency of control. Fourth, moral precepts provide justification and precedent for the recommended settlement and are used consistently in arriving at a decision. In this way, the decision goes beyond the personal judgment of the pandit and is, therefore, more acceptable to the disputants.

The extra-legal activities of the pandit are not merely a cultural idiosyncracy, rather they are consistent with particular cultural patterns now extant. For example, marital patterns among East Indians in Boodram are ethnically endogamous. Ninety-nine percent of the marriages recorded during the research were among East Indians . . . a fact which is indicative of the tendency toward in-group behavior of East Indians. Related to this pattern of endogamy is the concept of internal resolution of problems by East Indians. The alternative of the pandit, performing as an arbitrator, provides an acceptable method which serves this function. In addition, the activities of the pandit in problem situations of this kind represent a minimal contribution toward unification of the East Indian community of Boodram. The case given above clearly demonstrates the stress placed upon shared cultural characteristics and the necessity for unified co-existence. Such emphasis is another dimension of in-group cohesion. Reinforcement for this type of behavior is derived from the broader range of political activities where analogous attempts at unification along ethnic lines are found. The Democratic Labor Party (DLP) is popularly construed as the East Indian political party, whereas the other major political organization, the People's National Movement (PNM), is associated with the Creole population of the island. In reality, both parties are multi-ethnic. Nevertheless, the majority of the villagers in Boodram make this ethnic group distinction. During the last election in 1961 considerable stress was placed upon ethnic and cultural identity during campaign activities of the DLP.

From still another point of view, the ability of the pandit to function successfully as an arbitrator is associated with related results. Increased intimate contact in secular matters is established with individuals. This allows the pandit to increase his range of services to the lay population, stimulate an interest in ritual activity, and ultimately foster the perpetuation of Hinduism in Boodram. At the individual level, this represents an attempt to strengthen the prestige and increase the clientele of the religious specialist. At the group level, it constitutes another means of achieving social and cultural unity.

Most important though, the extra-legal involvement of the pandit in Boodram is a conscious effort to perpetuate East Indian culture. By stressing shared cultural characteristics, stimulating participation in religious activity, and emphasizing ethnic group cohesion, the extra-legal activities of the pandit partially neutralize the impingement of alien cultural forces. Simultaneously, they foster the maintenance of transplanted patterns of East Indian culture.

In summary then, the extra-legal activities of the village pandit in Boodram constitute an alternative method of social control available to the village populace. This alternative, restricted in scope, represents a voluntary but conscious effort to maintain ethnic group cohesion among the East Indians in Boodram. As such it contributes to the perpetuation of transplanted East Indian culture in Trinidad. The specific procedures involved in settling matters of this kind are consistent with broader patterns of contemporary East Indian culture in Trinidad. At the individual level, the actions of the pandit as an arbitrator allow him added prestige and success in secular as well as sacred aspects of culture. It remains to expose how widespread such activities are among East Indian societies in other parts of Trinidad and in other areas where East Indian populations are found. (Schwartz 1965.)

Whatever the agency of social control, the society in which it exists, or the group it represents, the process itself must adhere to the necessary and sufficient factors defined for all effective systems of social control:

norms, violation of the norms, recognition of the violation, report of the violation, response to the report of the violation, and enforcement of the response. If these sequential variables are not met, the process stops, and the agency of social control is ineffective.

SUMMARY

The reader should, by now, have gained an understanding of what is meant by the organization of culture. All human actions or sequences of actions fall within our definition of culture. But such actions are never entirely haphazard; they occur within organized systems of behavior. One of the ways in which organization is achieved is through attaching expected behavioral sequences to specific statuses within social groups. While such behavior is highly variable, it tends to be distributed about certain modes which we call norms. Human society would be impossible unless there were a certain degree of orderliness and predictability to individual behavior, as it is expressed in normative behavior. Normative behavior is so crucial to the effective functioning and survival of societies that each social system has built into it a system which we have called social control. Our stress in this chapter has been on cultural behavior that departs from the norm sufficiently to be recognized as deviant. By implication, deviance is relatively less frequent than normative behavior. The range of normative behavior, then, in any society, covers by far the greater part of those human actions that we label culture. In subsequent chapters we will deal with more specific kinds of cultural behavior, especially economic and religious. In all cases, however, the student should be aware that such behavior is organized around norms characteristic of groups and status positions within groups.

10

Organization of
Social Groups

INTRODUCTION

Human social groups occur in an almost infinite variety of forms. The ways in which these groups are organized are not nearly as variable, and logical analysis reveals relatively few principles of organization underlying all human groups. The analysis of social organization in Chapter 7 has shown that all groups are characterized by structure, action, function, and, in varying degrees, integration. To these we have added the characteristic of membership. There are still other factors, however, that operate to produce regularities in group formation and that help to account for differences among social groups.

MARRIAGE AND GROUP FORMATION

Marriage is a major factor in group formation. There are several different types of marriage, each of which is based upon (1) the numbers of individuals united by the marriage bond and/or (2) the kinship relations between them. Each type of marriage contributes to the formation of one or more social groups in the societies in which it occurs, and each may influence, directly or indirectly, the ways in which other social groups are formed. Any type of marriage involves a number of kinship statuses within the group formed by the marital union, between it and other similar groups, or in the kinship system at large. Each type of marriage implies certain relationships among these kinship positions; the behavior expected of persons filling these positions; and the results expected of such behavior. The meaning of each of these factors is made clear in the discussions that follow.

This village in Togoland shows one of the many varieties of social organization. The village is made up of a series of family compounds, as many as one hundred families, which can have as many as twenty houses all connected with a mud wall. (United Nations.)

Types of Marital Unions

Monogamy. Monogamy, a union joining one man and one woman in marriage, is overwhelmingly the most frequent and widespread type of union in the world at large. The approximately equal, natural ratio of males to females in all societies is certainly a major reason that monogamy is so widespread. This is, of course, the type of marital union most familiar to members of western society. This relatively simple form of marriage creates a complex network of kinship relations. In addition to husband and wife, such kinship relations as mother-in-law, father-in-law, brother- and sister-in-law, and other more indirect relations are defined. Behavioral rules for interaction between the persons filling these positions are specified also. Examples of such rules have already been given in our discussion of the nuclear family in Chapter 7. Monogamy, however, does more: it specifies the type of family that can be formed—the monogamous nuclear family. The performance of behavior expected from the persons occupying the kinship positions of husband and wife will create, in fact, this type of family.

One of the social rights and obligations that exists between husband and wife is that of procreation—they are the socially acceptable mating partners. Behavior which exercises this right and which fulfills this obligation results in offspring, who occupy the kinship positions of son and daughter. This, in turn, makes *real* the previously *expected* structural positions of mother and father (the reciprocals of son and daughter), and also the expected positions of brother and sister. The monogamous nuclear family is the totality of these kinship positions. (See Fig. 10–1.)

Polygyny. Polygyny is one of several kinds of multiple marriage (referred to in general as *polygamy*—having more than one husband or wife at one time). Polygyny is the union of one man and two or more women. A polygynous marriage gives rise to three or more sets of in-law relations (the number of in-law sets will depend upon the number of wives), and, in addition, creates a new kinship status, co-wife. Each wife is linked to every other wife through the husband, who occupies the constant and pivotal kinship position in polygynous marriages.

Because of the multiple wives involved in polygynous unions, a somewhat different family type is created. Murdock (1949) classifies families resulting from polygynous marriages as composite families, but they can be viewed also as a variant form of the nuclear family. That is, each of a number of nuclear families has the structural positions of husband and wife, but the same individual occupies the position of husband in a number of such families, and the women in this cluster of families are

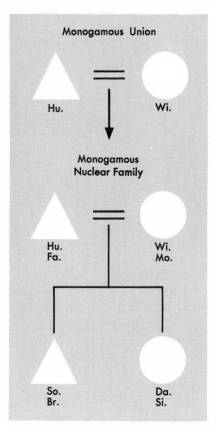

Monogamous Union

Hu.   Wi.

Monogamous
Nuclear Family

Hu.   Wi.
Fa.   Mo.

So.   Da.
Br.   Si.

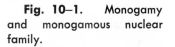

Fig. 10–1. Monogamy and monogamous nuclear family.

co-wives of one another. This is fairly common in Africa, and is described by Cohen (1967:43) for the Kanuri of Bornu Province, Nigeria:

> One out of every two Kanuri marriages is a polygynous one. Thus a woman is very likely sometime during her life to be in a situation in which she is one of two or more co-wives. Relations between co-wives is governed by strict codes of procedure. Each wife has her own hut in the back area of the compound farthest from the entrance hut or gate. Each wife cooks her own food and raises her own children who sleep in her hut while they are small. . . . Relations with the husband are strictly regulated. The general rule is that each wife performs her duties from sunset to sunset and the evening meal is taken after sunset. Every wife takes her own turn cooking the husband's food and that night she visits him in his hut. He may or may not have intercourse with her, but he must try to share sexual favors as equally as possible or else word about it will spread around in the family and cause tension between wives.

It would be an oversimplification, however, to regard such a family as merely a collection of nuclear families. The many activities carried on

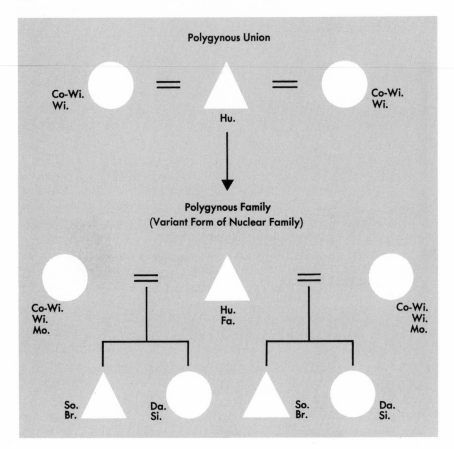

Fig. 10–2. Polygyny and polygynous family.

among co-wives, their subordination to a senior wife, and their joint residence in a single compound add dimensions to family life not found in single nuclear families (see Fig. 10–2).

Sororal Polygyny. Sororal polygyny is the union of one man and two or more women who stand in the relationship of sisters. This is a fairly common variant of polygyny in the world at large. Tension and hostility between co-wives is a universally recognized problem in polygynous societies, but it is often felt that sisters will make ideal co-wives; since they have already learned to get along with one another, their new status as co-wives will strengthen their already existing bond. It must be stressed, however, that relations among co-wives are often amicable. Indeed, a senior wife will frequently ask her husband to marry

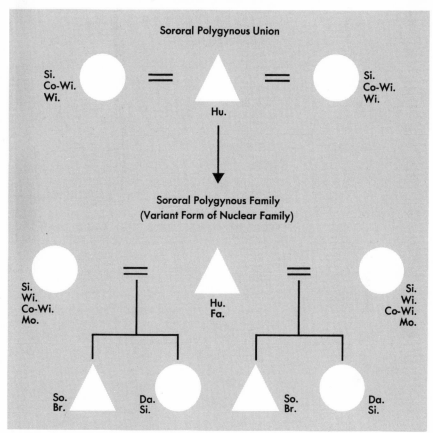

Fig. 10–3. Sororal polygyny and sororal polygynous family.

another girl to provide her with additional help or a desired companion, or to give her husband enhanced status, which the wife shares.

The family type formed by this marital union is the sororal polygynous family, a variant form of the general polygynous family. It shares all the features of the general type, with the additional factor that the women are all linked to one another not only as co-wives but as sisters. (See Fig. 10–3.)

Polyandry. Polyandry is another variant of polygamy and refers to the union of one woman with two or more men. The family type formed by this union is the polyandrous family, but this too can be viewed as a variant form of the nuclear family. In this case, however, one woman occupies the structural position of wife in two or more nuclear families,

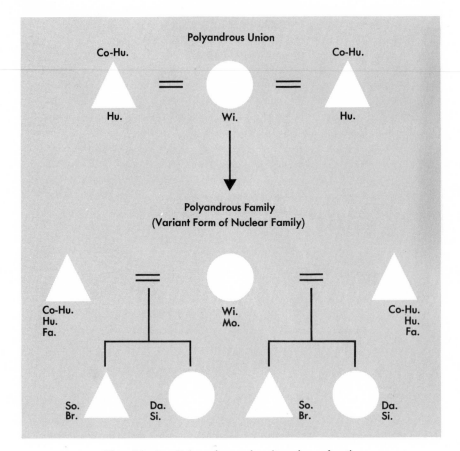

Fig. 10–4. Polyandry and polyandrous family.

whereas the structural positions of husband are occupied by two or more men. The constant and referential kinship position in polyandry is, therefore, that of wife. (See Fig. 10–4.) It becomes especially meaningful to think of the polyandrous family as a cluster of nuclear families when the husbands occupy separate households. This sometimes occurred among the Todas of southern India, who practiced polyandry as the preferential form of marriage. In such cases the wife would visit her husbands in turn, perhaps staying with each for a month at a time. Here too, however, the nuclear families so formed had characteristics not found in monogamous nuclear families. Thus, among the Todas it was customary for the first husband to perform the so-called "bow ceremony" upon the birth of his wife's first child. This ceremony made him the legal father of all her future children.

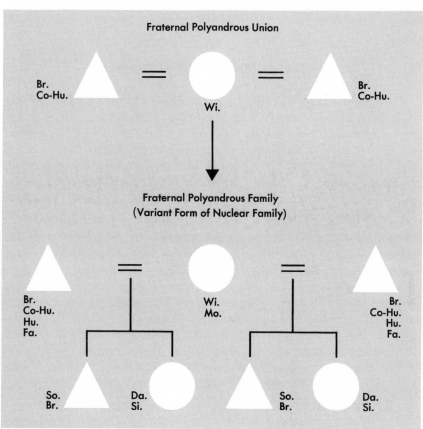

Fig. 10–5. Fraternal polyandry and fraternal polyandrous family.

Fraternal Polyandry. Fraternal polyandry, a special variant of polyandry in general, is the union of one woman with two or more males who stand in the relationship of brothers. These men become co-husbands through marriage, but also remain brothers. (See Fig. 10–5.) This kind of polyandry was formerly practiced by the Todas. When a woman married a man, his brothers became her husbands as a matter of course. Sometimes, however, co-husbands were not actual siblings, but clan brothers instead.

The Todas practiced polyandry consistently because of the unequal ratio of women to men, brought about by the frequent practice of female infanticide. The Eskimos were also known in the past to practice infanticide, resulting in a shortage of females, and occasionally an Eskimo would share his wife temporarily with a brother or even a friend. This kind of polyandry was not consistently practiced, however, as among the Todas.

RESIDENCE AND GROUP FORMATION

It should be clear from the foregoing discussion that the kind of marriage practiced in a society is an important factor in the kinds of groups that are formed. Polygyny as practiced by the Kanuri leads to a different kind of group than does the polyandry of the Todas or the monogamy of western society. Marriage is not, however, the only determinant of group formation. Another important factor is residence.

The Importance of Space

The place at which an individual resides is important for group formation in several ways. Among other things, residence emphasizes existing kinship, as well as other social relations. Certain groups, such as the household, are defined in terms of co-residence in a single domestic establishment. Continuous residence can contribute to the unification of social groups and, simultaneously, differentiate them from other groups. The following description by Middleton (1965:25) of the family among the Lugbara of Uganda, Africa, illustrates these points. This author employs the term "family cluster" to describe a larger residential unit made up of elementary and compound families:

> The family cluster is a small group, generally of about twenty-five people (about six adult men and their wives and children). It is not always a compact unit, though it may be. . . . Today it usually consists of a scattered group of homesteads, which may be up to half a mile across. The cluster has its own stretch of land, in which are its compounds, fields and grazing, and its own livestock; and its members have a strong sense of "belonging." When the cluster becomes too large to act as a single family group it may split in two. Thus at any particular time the unit under the authority of an elder may be a single compound family or a cluster of several families. But whatever its size, it has a single elder, and plays the same part within a wider system of similar groups.

A more complete description of residence in this society would show that a woman and her children reside together in a single hut. The married man and his wives (occupying as many huts) form a homestead or compound. This group is defined by co-residence. A number of contiguous homesteads, under a single leader, constitutes a family cluster. This unit is "home" to any man or woman. Spatial closeness contributes to the strong sense of "belonging" referred to by Middleton. Similar but separate units are spatially apart from one another. Residence, therefore, is a key factor in specifying all of these groups.

Postmarital Residence

Most of the anthropological research that relates to residence is based upon where a person lives following marriage. Concern with postmarital residence, as opposed to premarital residence, emphasizes the importance of marriage for group formation. In spite of this concern, disagreement exists regarding the categories for residential classification and the criteria used to determine these categories.

Murdock's Residential Types. Until recently, Murdock's (1949) fivefold classification of residential patterns was widely accepted among anthropologists. Using as his criterion the place where a newly married couple resides in relation to the kinsmen of one spouse or the other, he defines the major types of residence as shown in Fig. 10–6.

Type of Residence	Specification
1. Patrilocal	Couple takes up residence in or near the groom's father's house.
2. Matrilocal	Couple takes up residence in or near the bride's mother's house.
3. Bilocal	Couple may choose to reside in or near the house of the parents of either the bride or the groom.
4. Neolocal	Couple takes up residence in a house which is removed from the bride's parents' house and the groom's parents' house.
5. Avunculocal	Couple takes up residence in or near the house of the groom's mother's brother.

Fig. 10–6. Murdock's residential types.

The major types of residence recognized by Murdock do not exhaust the logical possibilities, some of which are found in actual practice. Thus, his first two types can be combined to form a new type—*matripatrilocal* residence, a form which Murdock treats as a variant of patrilocal residence. It occurs where a couple lives for a year or two, or until their first child is born, with or near the bride's parents, and then shifts permanently to patrilocal residence. A purely hypothetical situation, but logically possible, would be one in which an unmarried female takes up residence with a paternal aunt, and then brings her husband to live with her. This type Murdock calls *amitalocal residence* (*ibid.*, 71). Whatever the type of residence, all are based upon three factors: marriage, kinship relations, and place.

A number of writers have felt that Murdock's simple fivefold classification does not accommodate all the significant information available concerning residence, and that some of his terms lead to ambiguity. When we say residence is avunculocal, for example, do we mean the husband's uncle or the wife's? Do we mean the husband's mother's brother or his father's brother? The term patrilocal, it might be argued, tells us that the husband is living with his father, but does not describe accurately where the wife is living. For reasons such as these, a number of more specific classifications have been proposed.

Fischer's Residential Types. Fischer (1958) feels that a complete classification of residence rules should focus on individuals to indicate where each person, married or unmarried, lives. We should describe "the residence of husband and wife separately in terms of the relative who is the immediate sponsor of each in the residence group" (*ibid.*, 510). Thus, where a husband takes his wife to live with his mother's group (in a matrilineal society), we would say that he is living matrilocally, but his wife, because she is sponsored by her husband, is living virilocally. Figure 10–7 presents Fischer's classification in detail.

Fischer's chart omits mention of another important form of residence, that of a young, unmarried child living with his parents who, in turn, are residing neolocally. For this rule of residence he suggests the term

Type	*Kin Sponsor*
I. Neolocal	Self.
II. Consanguineolocal:	Any consanguine relative.
A. Patrilocal	Father or male patrilineal relative of ascending generation.
B. Matrilocal	Mother or female matrilineal relative of ascending generation.
C. Avunculocal	Mother's brother or male matrilineal relative of ascending generation.
D. Amitalocal	Father's sister or female patrilineal relative of ascending generation.
E. Fratrilocal	Brother or male parallel cousin of own generation.
F. Sororilocal	Sister or female parallel cousin of own generation.
G. Filiolocal	Son or son's son.
H. Filialocal	Daughter or daughter's daughter.
I. Nepotilocal	Sister's son or other male matrilineal relative of descending generation.
J. Heterolocal	Any other consanguine relative.
III. Affinolocal:	An affinal relative (almost invariably a spouse).
A. Virilocal (women only)	Husband.
B. Uxorilocal (men only)	Wife.

Fig. 10–7. Fischer's residential types.

parentilocal. This situation is especially common in contemporary United States society.

Carrasco's Residential Types. Carrasco (1963), in a further attempt to refine residential classification and increase its usefulness, suggests a threefold scheme which can be used in conjunction with existing classifications. Rather than focus on kinship sponsors, he refines the spatial dimensions of residence. Figure 10–8 presents an abbreviated form of his scheme, employing a limited number of examples.

Spatial Referent of Residence	Form Suggested	Example
Household	—domestic	Patridomestic—couple takes up residence in household of groom's patrilineal kinsmen.
Territorial division (e.g., wards or villages)	—vicinal	Patrivicinal—couple takes up residence in the ward or village of the groom's patrilineal kinsmen.
Distance relationships to households	—propinquous (close)	Patripropinquous—couple takes up residence close to the household of the groom's patrilineal kinsmen.
	—longinquous (distant)	Patrilonginquous—couple takes up residence distant from the groom's patrilineal kinsmen.

Fig. 10–8. Carrasco's residential types.

Carrasco's residential types can be used in combination to specify the total residential situation for a married couple. For example, he suggests ". . . that the Trobrianders' pattern of marital residence is neodomestic and avuncuvicinal, since a newly wed couple sets up a new household in the community of the groom's matrilineal kinsmen . . ." (*ibid.*, 133–34). A situation in which a couple takes up residence in the household of the groom's patrilineal kinsmen and, therefore, occupies a residence in the ward or village of these kinsmen would be called patridomestic patrivicinal residence. Where a couple takes up residence in a new household near the groom's patrilineal kinsmen and in the ward or village of these same kinsmen, the situation is referred to as neodomestic patripropinquous patrivicinal residence. Finally, where the couple takes up residence in a new household distant from but in the ward or village of the groom's patrilineal kinsmen, the situation is labeled neodomestic patrilonginquous patrivicinal residence.

This latter terminology is admittedly very cumbersome, but it has the advantage of telling the specialist almost precisely what the marital residential situation is. We have presented the Fischer and Carrasco classifications in some detail to indicate to the reader some of the complexities involved, because residence is an important variable in group formation. Patrilocal residence, for example, as defined by Murdock, tends to congregate kinsmen related through the male line, and matrilocal residence achieves the reverse. Marriage, then, is almost always accompanied by rules which specify just where a couple must live with reference to other kinsmen. In the following pages and chapters we will generally employ Murdock's simplified terminology, qualifying these terms where necessary to achieve greater precision of meaning.

DESCENT AND GROUP FORMATION

In the previous chapter we have seen that, depending on the system of classification employed in a society, an individual may have as many as 33 different kinds of secondary relatives and 151 different kinds of tertiary relatives. What is the individual's relationship to all of these kinsmen? Which of them have the strongest claims on the individual's loyalties, and to which of them may he turn for support of different kinds? Murdock (*op. cit.*, 14–15) has stated that all societies face the problem of defining for the individual that group of kinsmen with which he will have the closest ties. This is achieved through rules of descent. A third important variable in group formation, descent refers to the rules whereby an individual is assigned membership, and therefore can claim membership, in a particular group. These same rules define simultaneously all other members of this group. The rules of descent, by including certain members of the society in the individual's kin group, automatically exclude others. Anthropologists generally recognize four major patterns for claiming descent.

Unilineal Patterns of Descent

Individuals who claim descent along a single line (unilineally) do so in one of two ways: through the father's line (*patrilineal descent*) or through the mother's line (*matrilineal descent*). Both males and females are assigned to groups according to the prevailing rule of descent—matrilineal or patrilineal—so that brother and sister claim membership in the same group. Nevertheless, special importance is placed upon the males in patrilineal descent systems and upon the females in matrilineal descent systems. In groups formed by patrilineal descent, males form the core of the group and are responsible for its perpetuation. In groups formed by the matrilineal rule of descent, females form the core and are responsible for the group's perpetuation. Figures 10–9 and 10–10 illustrate the principles of patrilineal descent and matrilineal descent, respectively.

Patrilineal Descent. Figures 10–9 and 10–10 illustrate the principle of unilineal descent, but do not specify fully who will belong to ego's descent group in either system. In the patrilineal system, ego and his siblings belong to the descent group of the father, the father's siblings, the father's father, the father's brother's offspring (patrilateral parallel cousins), and so on. Females are of the same descent group as their father and brothers, but do not pass on their membership to their own

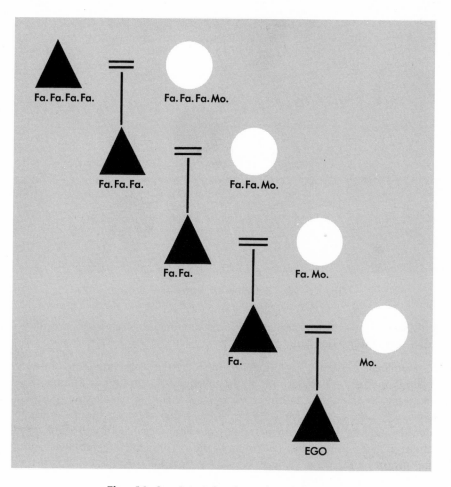

Fig. 10–9. Principle of patrilineal descent.

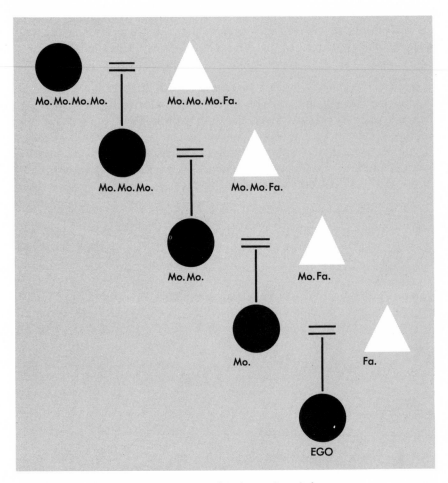

Fig. 10–10. Principle of matrilineal descent.

children. Under the patrilineal rule of descent their children are affiliated with the group of the husband.

Matrilineal Descent. In the matrilineal system, ego and her siblings belong to the descent group of the mother, the mother's siblings, the mother's mother, the mother's sister's offspring (matrilateral parallel cousins), and so on. Males are of the same descent group as their mother and sisters, but do not pass on their membership to their own children, who, under the matrilineal rule of descent, are affiliated with the group of the wife. The two descent systems are, then, like "mirror images" of one another.

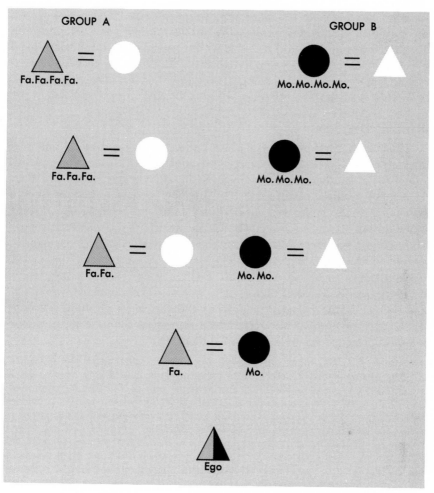

Fig. 10–11. Principle of double descent.

Double Descent. The unilineal principle of descent sometimes occurs in a double form in a single society and constitutes the third major type of descent. When an individual claims membership in a group along one line (either matrilineal or patrilineal), and simultaneously claims membership in a different group along the opposite line of descent, it is called *double descent* or duolineal descent. In such cases, it is important to keep in mind that the individual claims membership in two distinct groups, and does so according to two distinct unilineal principles. Thus, for certain purposes he would be aligned with the patrilineal kinsmen listed above; for other purposes, with the matrilineal kinsmen listed above. These are mutually exclusive groups, one containing the patrilineal kinsmen of the individual's father, the other the matrilineal kinsmen of his mother. The only persons with whom he shares membership in both groups are his siblings. Figure 10–11 illustrates the concept of double descent.

Bilateral Descent

The fourth type of descent most frequently recognized is one that characterizes United States society—*bilateral descent*. According to this principle, an individual claims membership in a single group but does so along two lines simultaneously. The kind of group so formed is a somewhat amorphous one, lacking the clear-cut boundaries of some other groups discussed below. It would include ego's near relatives on both his father's and his mother's side, but rarely going beyond his second cousins. In San Antonio Sacatepequez, Guatemala, this is the circle of kinsmen within which ego "feels" closely related, within which he visits frequently, feels obligated to attend wakes, funerals, weddings, and so on. Anthropologists sometimes call this loose grouping the *kindred*. Chance (1966:48 ff.) describes a somewhat different result of the bilateral principle for the Alaskan Eskimo:

> Aboriginally, the bilaterally extended family was the basic unit of north Alaskan Eskimo social structure. The recognition of kin through at least three generations on both the mother's and father's side of the family, combined with the extensive geographical mobility of the people of this region, provided an interwoven pattern of kinship linking together most villages. By means of a system of economic partnership, quasi-kinship groups were also formed, effectively extending cooperative ties to nonkin as well. Under this arrangement, all Eskimo who called each other by real or fictive kinship terms assumed a relation of sharing and cooperation (the extent of obligation depending on degree of distance from ego), and were seen by outsiders as being responsible for the actions of the entire kin group.

Bilateral kinship groupings are sometimes referred to as *ego-oriented* groupings, because they ramify (radiate) outward from ego. No one can share ego's kindred completely. Everyone is the center of his own bilateral kinship group.

There are two major distinctions between bilateral descent and double descent. While both use two lines, bilateral descent simultaneously combines these two lines of descent to achieve a claim of membership in a single group. The mother's and father's lines are not sharply differentiated, although ego is certainly aware of the difference between them. Double descent, in contrast, involves two lines of descent, each of which is independent of the other, and the opposite of the other, and results in the individual's claiming membership in two distinct social

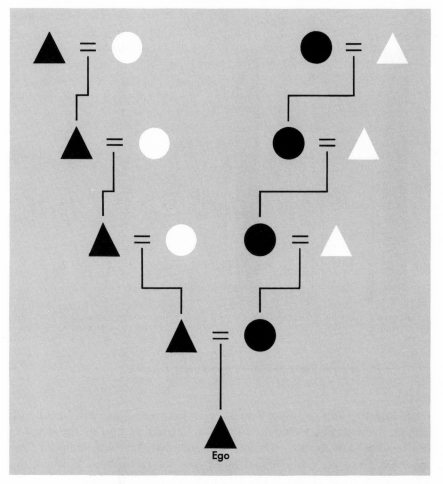

Fig. 10–12. Principle of bilateral descent.

groups. The individual associates himself exclusively with one or the other in different situations and for different purposes. These are significant differences and should be understood clearly. Figure 10–12 shows the principle of bilateral descent.

A slightly different representation of the major principles of descent is given in Fig. 10–13. Unilineal descent may be *either* matrilineal or patrilineal, and only membership in a single group is claimed on this basis. Double descent, however, combines both matrilineal and patrilineal principles, but independently of one another, and membership in two groups results. Bilateral descent does not segregate matrilineal and patrilineal kin, but combines them in a single group in which ego may

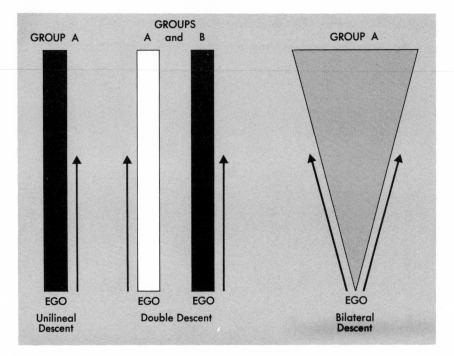

Fig. 10–13.   Principles of descent.

claim membership. Also, whereas ego's matrilineal or patrilineal kin groups theoretically include all kinsmen related to him in these lines, his bilateral kin group excludes some relatives on both sides. If he inherited all of his mother's and all of his father's bilateral kinsmen, he would have twice as many kin as either parent. A function of descent rules, we have stated, is to limit the number of potential kin.

COMBINATIONS OF MARRIAGE, RESIDENCE, AND DESCENT RULES

The three variable factors employed so far—marriage, residence, and descent—are related to one another both logically and empirically. Empirically, through ethnographic studies, we can identify societies which exhibit many different combinations of types of marriage, rules of residence, and rules of descent. In United States society, for example, we find monogamy combined with neolocal residence and bilateral descent. Not only do these variables define the dimensions of group formation, but they allow us to postulate combinations which are logically possible or empirically probable. Murdock, for example, has postulated a clan which would, theoretically, result from a combination of patrilineal descent and so-called amitalocal residence (*op. cit.*, 71). This combination is logically possible, but empirically improbable. An analysis of the three variables (marriage, residence, and descent) in this way can show us the restrictions on group formation as well as the possible variations that can occur among similar basic groups. These statements can be illustrated by using two basic forms of the family: the nuclear family and the minimal extended family. The nuclear family, as has been shown previously, involves eight basic structural positions, spanning two generations only, and related to one another in specified ways. The patrilineal minimal extended family includes two additional positions—father's father and father's mother (ego's paternal grandparents)—resulting in ten structural positions which span three generations. The structure of the nuclear family in relation to the minimal extended family is shown in Fig. 10–14, which includes a diagram of the expanded extended family for comparative purposes. It should be recognized from this figure that the nuclear family is a bilateral descent group (ego recognizes his descent from both his mother and his father, and a single group is formed), and the extended family is a unilineal descent group. This integration of a nuclear family within an extended family—one bilateral and the other unilineal—points out an important fact about social groups: the formation of one type of group does not necessarily

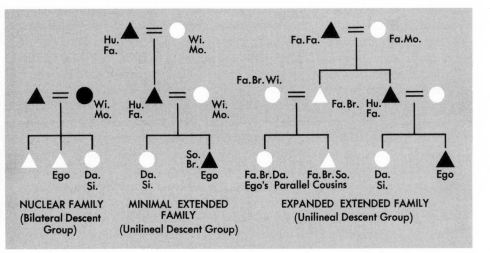

Fig. 10–14. Nuclear, minimal extended, and expanded extended families.

preclude, or conflict with, the formation and integration of other types of groups. It must be recognized, however, that when a nuclear family becomes bound up in the affairs of an extended family, its members engage in behavioral patterns not present in an isolated nuclear family. In an extended family, for example, a wife may be subordinate to her mother-in-law, and her husband to his father.

Taking as our point of departure the nuclear family and the minimal extended family, we are now in a position to combine them, systematically, with the variables of marriage, residence, and descent in all of their varieties. The results are shown in Tables 10–1 through 10–3. Table 10–1 combines these two family types with each of the five major marriage types to derive ten different social groups. In Table 10–2, each of these social groups is combined with each of five basic residential rules to derive yet another series of social groups. Finally, these latter social groups are combined, in turn, with each of three basic rules of descent—patrilineal, matrilineal, and bilateral—to produce a more finely specified series of social groups.

An inspection of these tables (Table 10–3 is only partially worked out for purposes of illustration) reveals several things. First, there are a limited number of logically and functionally possible social groups that can be derived from any combination of these variables. Second, each variable that is consecutively introduced into our calculations increases the number of possible combinations and, therefore, the number of possible groups that may be formed. Third, each variable introduced has the effect of further refining our definition of the social group. Thus, adding polygyny to the nuclear family creates the polygynous composite family; adding a rule of residence to the latter creates, for example, the patrilocal polygynous composite family; and this group is defined even more specifically (see Table 10–3) by the addition of patrilineality. Fourth, some combinations of variables are contradictory and incompatible, although to varying degrees. These appear as blanks in the right-hand columns of the tables.

By dividing the table into three separate parts, each of the three categorical variables can be introduced independently and in a cumulative manner. Since we use two family types, ten social groups are possible through the addition of five marriage types (Table 10–1). Combining these ten groups with five residential types would produce 50 combinations, but only 30 of these are logically possible (a matrilocal monogamous nuclear family would, for example, be a logical impossibility). Finally, applying three basic descent rules to these 30 types would produce 90 combinations, but only 56 of these are logically possible. We could not, for example, have a bilateral, matrilocal, sororal polygynous composite family. Tables 10–1 and 10–2 exhaust the numerically possible combinations; Table 10–3 gives a partial list of the 90 combinations possible. The reader can easily work out the remaining combinations for himself.

Table 10–1

Social Groups Based on Family Type and Marital Type

Family Type	+	Marital Type	=	Social Group Derived
Nuclear Family		Monogamy		Monogamous Nuclear Family
		Polygyny		Polygynous Composite Family
		Sororal Polygyny		Sororal Polygnous Composite Family
		Polyandry		Polyandrous Composite Family
		Fraternal Polyandry		Fraternal Polyandrous Composite Family
Minimal Extended Family		Monogamy		Monogamous Extended Family
		Polygyny		Polygynous Extended Family
		Sororal Polygyny		Sororal Polygynous Extended Family
		Polyandry		Polyandrous Extended Family
		Fraternal Polyandry		Fraternal Polyandrous Extended Family

Not all of the logically possible combinations are empirically probable (we have not found them and are unlikely to find them in society) because of degrees of incompatibility between our variables. Patrilocality, for example, is more compatible with patrilineality than with matrilineality, and the latter is more compatible with matrilocality or avunculocality. Patrilineality and patrilocality are more compatible with polygyny than are matrilineality and matrilocality, although matrilocality can occur with sororal polygyny. Matrilineality and matrilocality are more consistent with polyandry than are patrilocality and patrilineality, which in turn are consistent with fraternal polyandry. A sample survey of the world's societies would show the frequency of occurrence of our various derived social types. The probability of occurrence, however, is related to the degree of compatibility among the variables of group formation. The greater the compatibility among them, the higher the probability of their actual occurrence.

Marriage, Residence, and Descent as Expected Behavior

Each of the three variables discussed above is an expression of expected action when placed in specific cultural contexts. Avunculocal residence, for example, is the behavior expected of young Trobriand males upon marriage, and it is expected that the mother's brother will encourage and permit his sister's son to join him in this way. To the extent that Trobriand males actually reside in or near the household of their mothers' brothers, real action will coincide with the behavioral

Table 10–2

Social Groups Based on Residence, Family Type, and Marital Type

Social Group Derived (Table 10–1)	+ Residential = Type	Social Group Derived
Monogamous Nuclear Family	Patrilocal	—
	Matrilocal	—
	Bilocal	—
	Avunculocal	—
	Neolocal	Neolocal Monogamous Nuclear Family
Polygynous Composite Family	Patrilocal	Patrilocal Polygynous Composite Family
	Matrilocal	—
	Bilocal	—
	Avunculocal	—
	Neolocal	Neolocal Polygynous Composite Family
Sororal Polygynous Composite Family	Patrilocal	Patrilocal Sororal Polygynous Composite Family
	Matrilocal	Matrilocal Sororal Polygynous Composite Family
	Bilocal	Bilocal Sororal Polygynous Composite Family
	Avunculocal	Avunculocal Sororal Polygynous Composite Family
	Neolocal	Neolocal Sororal Polygynous Composite Family
Polyandrous Composite Family	Patrilocal	—
	Matrilocal	Matrilocal Polyandrous Composite Family
	Bilocal	—
	Avunculocal	Avunculocal Polyandrous Composite Family
	Neolocal	Neolocal Polyandrous Composite Family
Fraternal Polyandrous Composite Family	Patrilocal	Patrilocal Fraternal Polyandrous Composite Family
	Matrilocal	Matrilocal Fraternal Polyandrous Composite Family
	Bilocal	Bilocal Fraternal Polyandrous Composite Family
	Avunculocal	Avunculocal Fraternal Polyandrous Composite Family
	Neolocal	Neolocal Fraternal Polyandrous Composite Family
Monogamous Extended Family	Patrilocal	Patrilocal Monogamous Extended Family
	Matrilocal	Matrilocal Monogamous Extended Family
	Bilocal	Bilocal Monogamous Extended Family
	Avunculocal	Avunculocal Monogamous Extended Family
	Neolocal	—
Polygynous Extended Family	Patrilocal	Patrilocal Polygynous Extended Family
	Matrilocal	—
	Bilocal	—
	Avunculocal	—
	Neolocal	—
Sororal Polygynous Extended Family	Patrilocal	Patrilocal Sororal Polygynous Extended Family
	Matrilocal	Matrilocal Sororal Polygynous Extended Family
	Bilocal	Bilocal Sororal Polygynous Extended Family
	Avunculocal	Avunculocal Sororal Polygynous Extended Family
	Neolocal	—
Polyandrous Extended Family	Patrilocal	—
	Matrilocal	Matrilocal Polyandrous Extended Family
	Bilocal	—
	Avunculocal	—
	Neolocal	—
Fraternal Polyandrous Extended Family	Patrilocal	Patrilocal Fraternal Polyandrous Extended Family
	Matrilocal	Matrilocal Fraternal Polyandrous Extended Family
	Bilocal	Bilocal Fraternal Polyandrous Extended Family
	Avunculocal	Avunculocal Fraternal Polyandrous Extended Family
	Neolocal	—

Table 10–3

Social Groups Based on Descent, Family Type, Marital Type, and Residence

Social Group Derived (Table 10–2)	+ Descent Type	= Social Group Derived
Neolocal Monogamous Nuclear Family	Patrilineal	—
	Matrilineal	—
	Bilateral	Bilateral Neolocal Monogamous Nuclear Family
Patrilocal Polygynous Composite Family	Patrilineal	Patrilineal Patrilocal Polygynous Composite Family
	Matrilineal	Matrilineal Patrilocal Polygynous Composite Family
	Bilateral	—
Neolocal Polygynous Composite Family	Patrilineal	Patrilineal Neolocal Polygynous Composite Family
	Matrilineal	—
	Bilateral	—
Patrilocal Sororal Polygynous Composite Family	Patrilineal	Patrilineal Patrilocal Sororal Polygynous Composite Family
	Matrilineal	Matrilineal Patrilocal Sororal Polygynous Composite Family
	Bilateral	—
Matrilocal Sororal Polygynous Composite Family	Patrilineal	Patrilineal Matrilocal Sororal Polygynous Composite Family
	Matrilineal	Matrilineal Matrilocal Sororal Polygynous Composite Family
	Bilateral	—
Bilocal Sororal Polygynous Composite Family	Patrilineal	Patrilineal Bilocal Sororal Polygynous Composite Family
	Matrilineal	Matrilineal Bilocal Sororal Polygynous Composite Family
	Bilateral	—
Avunculocal Sororal Polygynous Composite Family	Patrilineal	Patrilineal Avunculocal Sororal Polygynous Composite Family
	Matrilineal	Matrilineal Avunculocal Sororal Polygynous Composite Family
	Bilateral	—
Neolocal Sororal Polygynous Composite Family	Patrilineal	Patrilineal Neolocal Sororal Polygynous Composite Family
	Matrilineal	Matrilineal Neolocal Sororal Polygynous Composite Family
	Bilateral	—
Matrilocal Polyandrous Composite Family	Patrilineal	Patrilineal Matrilocal Polyandrous Composite Family
	Matrilineal	Matrilineal Matrilocal Polyandrous Composite Family
	Bilateral	—
Avunculocal Polyandrous Composite Family	Patrilineal	Patrilineal Avunculocal Polyandrous Composite Family
	Matrilineal	Matrilineal Avunculocal Polyandrous Composite Family
	Bilateral	—

expectation. The frequency of avunculocal residence is probably sufficiently great in Trobriand society to constitute a norm which has a high
degree of congruence with expected behavior, and which provides a
referent against which patrilocal or neolocal residence can be judged
and declared to be deviant behavior.

Monogamous marriage is the norm in the United States and is expected behavior. In this case, as with the Trobriand residence pattern,
a high degree of congruence between the norm and expected action is
present. However, other forms of marriage do occur in the United
States—polygyny is the most frequent—which are defined as deviant
forms. Polygyny as practiced by the Mormons of Utah, on the other
hand, can be variously defined as tolerated deviant behavior or untolerated deviant behavior, depending upon the time period, the recognition by non-Mormons of such deviance, and the reaction of constituted
agencies to this type of behavior. Even if surrounding communities
tolerate Mormon polygyny, this form of marriage is illegal in United
States society at large and, therefore, is technically untolerated deviant
behavior. In nineteenth-century Mormon society, on the other hand,
polygyny was the norm, this type of marriage was expected of a Mormon
by his fellows, and a rigid adherence to monogamy would have been
deviant behavior. With the passage of time and the growth of opposition on the part of society at large, polygyny among Mormons has ceased
to be invariably expected, and, in an urban setting at least, monogamy
is no longer deviant behavior.

Generally, when anthropologists characterize a society or a social
group as patrilineal, matrilineal, patrilocal, matrilocal, and so on, they
are specifying the expected behavior of members and, frequently, are
defining the norms that exist. Let us examine a hypothetical statement:
"In society X monogamy is the most frequently occurring type of marriage; polygyny is highly desired, and is the preferred form of marriage,
but occurs only infrequently." This statement specifies monogamy as
the norm, polygyny as expected behavior, and other forms of marriage—
polyandry, for example—as deviant behavior. Other factors could be introduced into our hypothetical statement if we wished to belabor the
point, such as relating expected polygyny to high social status. That is,
in any society the norms and expectations regarding marriage, residence,
and descent can vary with relative social rank, or with membership in
social subgroups.

LINKAGE WITHIN SOCIAL GROUPS

It is meaningful to think of the relationships between the members of
social groups as constituting a series of *linkages,* among which we can

distinguish three major types—vertical, horizontal, and a combination
of the two, vertical–horizontal. Each of these general forms of linkage
has been described or referred to previously, but in different contexts,
and without specific reference. The particular type of linkage between
ego and another individual is defined according to such factors as directness of descent and the generation differences between them. Ego
is linked vertically to his father, for example, but is linked horizontally
to his own siblings, and vertically–horizontally to his father's brother.
All combined (vertical–horizontal) linkages are indirect ones. That is,
an individual is linked to another through an intermediate link or a
series of intermediate links. Indirect linkages are not, however, restricted
to the combined type. Vertical linkages which extend beyond a single
generation in either direction (ascending or descending) are also described as indirect. Thus, ego is linked vertically, but indirectly, to his
paternal grandfather through his father, or to his grandchildren through
his children. Generation, therefore, enters into a description of direct
and indirect linkage.

Horizontal linkage, however, is mainly direct linkage. It might appear, for example, that ego is linked horizontally and indirectly to his
parallel cousins because they are of the same generation. Actually, how-

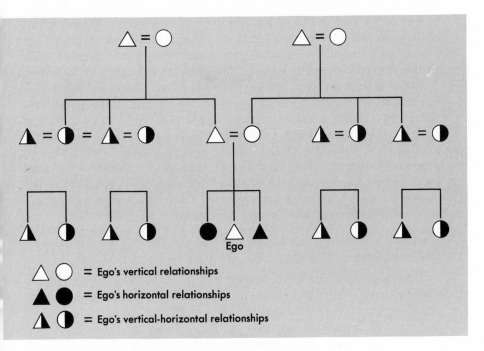

Fig. 10–15. Social linkage.

ever, the linkage is from ego to his father and mother, and through his father's brothers and his mother's sisters to ego's cousins. This link is a combined one, therefore, and is vertical–horizontal and indirect.

Figure 10–15 illustrates these forms of linkage. Ego is linked to his father and his mother in a direct and vertical way, but to his father's father, father's mother, mother's father, and mother's mother in an indirect and vertical way. He is linked to his brother and sister directly and horizontally, but to his parents' siblings, their spouses, and his cross- and parallel cousins according to the combined vertical–horizontal form. In Fig. 10–15 the relationships indicated by white are linked vertically to ego, those indicated by solid black are linked horizontally, and those indicated by black and white are ego's vertical–horizontal relations.

The concept of linkage is equally applicable to social groups, although here the principal criteria for defining the type of linkage are the types of descent, already described. The significance of this concept is made clear in the discussion of social groups which follows.

SOCIAL GROUPS BASED ON KINSHIP

In the earlier discussion of bilateral descent, it was shown that this principle can lead to the recognition by ego of a loosely defined group of kinsmen called the bilateral kindred. Many kinds of social groups are based upon specific kinship relations, and the membership of such groups can be defined in terms of the kinds of linkages just discussed.

Social groups such as families, lineages, clans, castes, and others are frequently categorized as *descent groups*, in contrast to territorial, economic, household, religious, ethnic, and other types of groups. The ways in which membership is defined, including the general and specific requirements, is highly variable among groups of these latter kinds. In descent groups, however, kinship and linkage are probably the most basic criteria for defining membership. Anthropologists generally recognize two basic kinds of descent groups: unilineal descent groups and bilateral descent groups.

Unilineal Descent Groups

Matrilineal and patrilineal descent groups, as unilineal types, emphasize the vertical form of linkage, as illustrated in Figs. 10–9 and 10–10. However, inspection of the structure of a unilineal descent group reveals that vertical linkage is not used to the exclusion of the other types. While the *core* of a patrilineage, for example (see below), will consist of vertically linked males, the total membership will include both horizontally and vertically–horizontally linked individuals.

The particular pattern of descent that characterizes a kinship group does more than define its members; it also reveals who the core members of the group are and which members are responsible for the perpetuation of the group, and indicates the social recognition of a common ancestor by the group members. Social recognition of a common ancestor, in conjunction with the fact that members trace descent to this ancestor, specifies the common ancestor as the major referent for unilineal descent groups. Newman's (1965:35) description of the Gururumba of New Guinea illustrates these points:

The term "sib" designates social groups whose membership is defined by descent, although the actual genealogical links between all the members cannot be traced. This is the case, for example, with the Gururumba sib named Wa'muJuhu. The Wa'muJuhu say they are descended from a pair of brothers, but the names of the brothers are not known, and no one knows who is descended from the elder brother and who from the younger. Common descent is implied rather than actual. The imputation of common descent means that all one's sib mates are, in a general way, regarded as consanguineal kinsmen.

Lineages. A lineage is a unilineal descent group composed of consanguineally related individuals who claim descent from a common ancestor, and who are able to trace this descent genealogically through a series of direct links. Figure 10–16 shows a patrilineage. The kinship positions represented in black are the consanguineal members of the

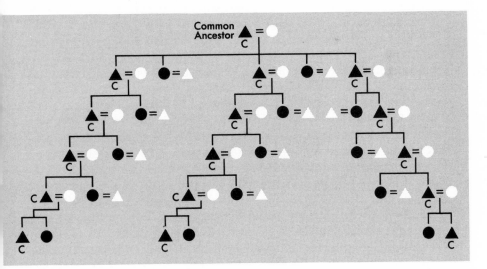

Fig. 10–16. Patrilineage showing consanguineal members and core members.

lineage. Those members who, in addition, are responsible for perpetuation of the lineage are labeled C. Inspection of the figure reveals that a female member of a patrilineage cannot perpetuate this group. The children she bears will claim membership in their father's lineage; they are not consanguineal members of their mother's lineage. In addition, Fig. 10–16 shows that all consanguineal members of the lineage can trace descent to the common ancestor according to this form of linkage and along a single line. Lineages based upon matrilineal descent (matrilineages) are just the reverse of this total diagram.

Clans. The term clan has been in the vocabulary of anthropology for a long time, and there is still much confusion in its use, partly because of the concurrent use of another term, sib (as in the quote from Newman above). Some anthropologists distinguish between them, using these terms to label significantly different kinds of descent groups. Murdock (*op. cit.*), for example, employs the term sib to label a non-residential unilineal descent group. He reserves the term clan for a descent group which also has residential features. Because of growing variance in this usage, however, we will consistently use the term clan in the former sense, and will give no specific recognition to the latter type of grouping.

A clan is a grouping whose membership claims descent from a common ancestor, without actually being able to trace genealogical links in all cases. Since descent is traced through either the male or the female line, clans are either patrilineal or matrilineal—patriclans or matriclans. A clan is exogamous, and bears a name whereby members identify themselves. Further, a clan is not ordinarily a localized group. In a patriclan, for example, the married female members will live apart from the males, and in most clan societies the male members of patriclans (or the female members of matriclans) will also be dispersed among several communities. Therefore, clans cross-cut local groups and are an important device for integrating tribal societies. (This point is discussed further in Chapter 15.)

The inability of members to trace all actual genealogical links to each other is an important feature of clans that requires further elaboration. Let us suppose that the clan ancestor in a patriclan was an actual individual who lived 30 generations ago, and that all of his descendants in the male line continued to trace their descent back to him. After 30 generations his descendants would number many thousands of individuals, and it would be difficult, if not impossible, for living individuals to know all the links, through 30 generations, that connect them to this ancestor. It would be equally impossible for the individual to trace his relationship to thousands of living clan members through actual genealogical ties. In practice this is not necessary, because the clan is named.

A newborn child is assigned to the clan of his father or mother, depending upon the type of clan, and throughout his life is associated with that clan name. If he is of the Eagle clan, e.g., wherever he goes his clan members are easily identifiable and are regarded as kinsmen. His clan kinsmen have certain claims upon him, and he upon them. This is an important function of clan organization—it extends the principle of kinship regulation of society to much larger groups in which actual relationships cannot be traced.

Middleton (*op. cit.*, 30) describes a Lugbara clan as follows:

> The members of a clan are dispersed and found in many parts of the country. Since the founding of Lugbara society the descendants of the clan founders, who were the sons of the hero-ancestors, have moved about the country, groups of kin segmenting and moving apart just as they do now. But there is almost always a main part of a clan that has not split up and that still inhabits a territory associated with the clan. It forms what might be called the localized core of that clan, and I call it a subclan. The founder of a subclan is thus the same man as the founder of the clan. A clan is a shadowy group that consists of a subclan living in the clan territory and a number of offshoots that have moved away at various times in the past and now live in other clan territories elsewhere.

This example is not an exact description of clan organization as it occurs everywhere, but it serves to illustrate the principles of clan organization in general.

It might be asked at this point how a clan differs from a lineage. Lineages, too, are unilineal descent groups and are exogamous. However, in a lineage an individual often can trace actual genealogical ties to other lineage members. The lineage ancestor is a known individual, even though he may have lived 8 or 10 generations ago. In the course of growing up as a member of a lineage, an individual may be expected to memorize the names of those ancestors through whom he is connected to the lineage founder. Further, it is not uncommon for all the male members of a patrilineage, or the female members of a matrilineage, to form a residential group, together with their affines (spouses) from other lineages. Very commonly, though not always, clans are segmented into lineages. Thus, Lugbara clans are segmented into a number of lineages within which descent is actually traced.

It should be pointed out that while a clan *per se* is not a residential grouping, core members and their affines do constitute residential units. If all the male members of a patrilineal clan, or the female members of a matrilineal clan, live in a single territory, we can speak of a *localized* clan. Most clan activities—clan rituals, for example—will then be carried on within that single locality, and very likely the affines (wives of patriclan members, or husbands of matriclan members) will participate to some extent. Affines who have married into a local group are never accorded full status in their spouse's clan, but they retain, in theory at least, clan rights in their own natal clans. Very frequently, however, members of two or more matriclans or patriclans will inhabit a single locality, and their affines from other clans will increase the number of clans represented locally. The net effect is to unite individuals in many communities with ties of clanship and with all the ritual and social obligations implied by such ties.

Phratries and Moieties. Phratry and moiety are terms which, like sib and clan, have been in the anthropological literature for a long time. There is no universal agreement, however, as to the significance of the groups so labeled. Some anthropologists regard them as unilineal descent groups, others do not. Most frequently they are found in clan societies and represent groupings of clans into larger units. A moiety system is a division of society into halves (by definition, a society may contain only two moieties). Where clans are distributed among three or more larger divisions, we refer to these divisions as phratries. Thus, the Crow Indians of the western plains were formerly divided into thirteen matriclans. These in turn were divided among six phratries, most of them having two clans only. Members of clans that are linked together to form a phratry will commonly think of themselves as being more closely related to each other than to other clans. A phratry or moiety may be exogamous. The feeling of kinship or of unilineal descent among phratry or moiety members is not as strong as that among lineage or clan members.

Extended Families as Unilineal Descent Groups. Technically, we can label as an extended family any domestic unit that includes relatives other than the parental couple and their offspring and extends over three lineal generations. However, the extended family can be and often is extended laterally, so that it may include a man and his wife, his sons and their wives, his brothers and their wives and children, and so on. In this section we are concerned with a group that stresses a single line of descent, the matriline or patriline, and has a corresponding rule of residence, matrilocality or patrilocality. The result is a matrilineal or a patrilineal extended family. Further, by definition, such a group should span at least three generations, though very rarely more than four. Figure 10–17 depicts a patrilineal extended family of three generations. The males born into the units constitute the core group, which alone can perpetuate the group. The affines are women who have married these core members. Daughters born into the family will leave the group upon marriage.

Descent in the family depicted in the figure is traced from the eldest living male. Conceivably this family could include this elder male's

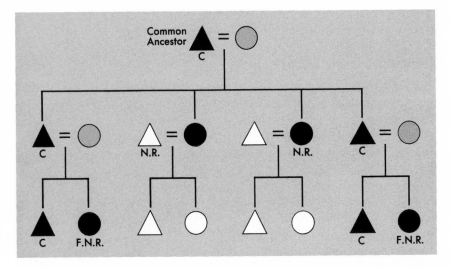

Fig. 10–17. Extended family showing consanguineal members (black), residential members (gray), consanguineal non-residential members (N.R.), consanguineal, future non-residential members (F.N.R.), and consanguineal, core members (C). (Assumes patrilineal and patrilocal situation.)

brother and his descendants; descent would then be traced back yet another generation to the deceased father of these two men.

The perpetuation of the extended family is a continuous process resulting essentially from the periodic removal, through death, of the highest ascending generation, and the addition, through birth, of new generations. Sometimes brothers will remain together following the death of the family's ancestor (their father), especially if they themselves have no grandchildren. Eventually, however, with the addition of grandchildren, the unit becomes too large for its purposes, and the brothers separate, each heading his own extended family. In some situations, however, land is plentiful and the division of labor—for farming, herding, food processing, spinning and weaving, and so on—requires a very large family. A number of brothers may then remain together under the headship of the eldest.

Where land is limited, where the extended family is not permitted to become too large, and where new extended families would be without resources, the eldest son may inherit the land, and if his brothers choose to remain with him, their children will be forced to leave as they reach maturity. This is often the practice in modern peasant societies in so-called underdeveloped nations. The alternatives for displaced family members include military service, wage labor on plantations or in the city, or the purchase of small plots of land elsewhere.

Bilateral Descent Groups

Bilateral descent groups are kinship groups based upon the simultaneous recognition of two lines of descent for the inclusion of members. Such groups may be ego-oriented, as was shown in our previous discussion of the bilateral kindred. No ego-oriented bilateral descent group can be the same for two individuals, although it will be approximately the same for siblings. Other bilateral descent groups are ancestor-oriented: a common ancestor is the major group referent. The members of a Hindu caste, for example, may regard themselves as descended from a common ancestor. Since the caste is endogamous, an individual's father's and mother's relatives will be of his caste. And because the caste has definable boundaries (which a kindred does not), the group is the same for every individual member.

SOCIAL GROUPS BASED ON NON-KINSHIP

Our discussion of the criteria of membership in the preceding chapter stressed the fact that many groups base their membership on factors other than kinship. Groups of this kind can appear in societies at any cultural level although, generally speaking, technologically simpler societies are predominantly oriented around kinship relations. In contrast, societies that are technologically advanced and socially more complex are characterized by increased cultural alternatives for group affiliation and tend to include fewer kinship-based groups. United States society, especially its urban sectors, has gone as far as any society in the world in de-emphasizing kin ties and kin-based groups. For many individuals in our society, a person's kin groups consist of his families of orientation and procreation and a loosely defined, functionally unimportant bilateral kindred. United States society embraces many subcultures, however, and the importance of kin ties varies among them.

If an individual in United States society, or in urbanized, industrialized western society in general, is affiliated with few kinship-based groups, his society provides him with many alternative group memberships: corporations, work groups, voluntary associations of many kinds, religious, political, and recreational groups, and many more. The members of such groups are not, in general, related consanguineally, affinally, or by fictive kinship ties, although this can and does occur. A family business would be a case in point. We have also discussed (see Chapter

8) the tendency for non-kin groups to cast themselves in a kinship mold, so that members address one another as brother or sister.

Rather than kinship, then, the criteria basic to membership in such groups include common goals, values, and interests; training; religious beliefs; political convictions; and the like. We have already discussed at length the criteria for group membership.

RELATIONSHIPS BETWEEN SOCIAL GROUPS

The social groups that make up a total society can be related in a variety of ways and for a variety of purposes. A brief example will introduce our meaning. The political structure of the United States includes not only a subdivision into 50 federal states, but a national governmental structure as well. This consists of the three branches learned by every school child, and innumerable departments and agencies, all constituting groups in the total structure. These are all related to one another directly or indirectly, so that the entire structure may function effectively. The ways in which many of these groups or structural units are related to one another are often the result of conscious, deliberate planning. Our constitution, and volumes of legislation, specify many of these relations.

There are innumerable social groupings in our society (and in all societies) that are related to one another in very definite ways, but whose relationships are not the result of design or conscious planning. Such relationships are a part of the structural dimension of the society and contribute importantly to its functioning.

Joint Membership

One of the ways in which two or more groups may be related to one another is through joint membership: the same individual or individuals can occupy structural positions (statuses) in each of the related groups. A most obvious example would be the position of an individual in both his family of orientation and his family of procreation. A male ego will illustrate this point. As a son in the family of orientation he provides the link in the important social relationships between his wife and his children, on the one hand, and his parents and siblings on the other. Marriage is often the means whereby family groups are united. This is especially important in non-western societies that stress kinship-based groupings. Among hunting and gathering bands, an individual will always occupy status positions in two or more bands because they consistently exchange wives (intermarry). Cooperative bonds between

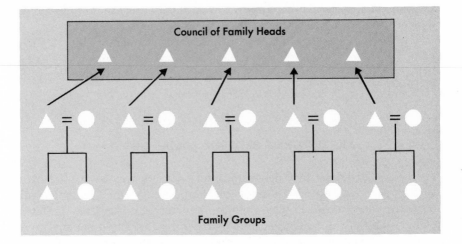

Fig. 10–18. Relationship of family to council based on common structural position.

groups are important to the survival of primitive hunters and gatherers, and it is the joint membership of individuals in two or more bands that establishes and maintains friendly, peaceful relations between them.

Another example can be derived from hunting and gathering bands. They are usually made up of nuclear families, each family containing the structural position of father. In addition, a band may contain a council of elders, whose membership is made up of all adult male family heads. Each individual adult male occupies two status positions: father in the nuclear family and elder in the council. Thus each family group is directly related to the council through the joint membership of adult males in both groups (see Fig. 10–18).

More complex linkages are to be found in more socially complex societies. Clans among the Bunyoro of East Africa are directly linked to the king and the administration through particular structural positions. In this society, only members of specified clans are authorized to fill certain structural positions in the administration. Beattie (1960: 31–32) provides a detailed description of this African monarchy. The king was traditionally surrounded by numerous court officials—custodians of the royal graves, men in charge of royal drums, custodians of court regalia, herdsmen, musicians, and many more. Some individuals served only on ceremonial occasions, attending the king. The way in which this system links the clans to the kingship is made very clear by Beattie:

This complex establishment is therefore not to be understood simply as an overcumbersome attempt to run a large household; neither in ancient times or now can it be regarded as an economical or even as a particularly efficient way of doing this. Sociologically, the point of it is that it provided a means of involving a great many different groups and kinds of people in a common interest in the royal establishment and so in the maintenance of the kingship itself. It did this both through the clan system (for different offices were often hereditarily vested in particular clans, all of whose members shared in the honor of representation at the palace) and through occupational specialization (since it meant that all of Bunyoro's crafts were represented at the capital). In these ways the huge royal establishment served to integrate the Nyoro people around their center, and so to sustain the political system itself.

Territory

Territory is often the basis for relating social groups to each other. For example, a moiety that is composed of several different lineages or clans may share a common territory, as opposed to the other moiety in the society, which occupies a different territory. Territorial relations of social groups are also related to administrative and political factors. Social groups sometimes occupy a definite administrative unit specified by territorial boundaries; all the groups within the unit are frequently related to one another in some way by reason of this common administrative identification. Caste groups in an Indian village, and their representatives, provide an example. Caste groups are part of an administrative unit—the village—which is unified by institutions such as the village *panchayat* and the *jajmani* system (an economic system involving interdependence of castes). At the same time, each caste segment in a village is related to other segments of the same caste in other villages, all segments forming a single caste group, which is, itself, territorially restricted.

SUMMARY

The ways in which social groups are related to one another are exemplified in greater detail as part of the discussions dealing with economics, ritual, and political dimensions of culture. However, certain general statements about the relations of groups to one another can be made here. The general ways in which groups are related to one another are similar to the ways in which members of social groups are linked to each other: vertically, horizontally, and vertically–horizontally.

Vertical relationships among groups are based upon such factors as the magnitude of groups in relation to one another; dominance of one group over another; the hierarchical arrangement of smaller, constituent groups to form larger, more inclusive groups; the factors of descent and residence, and many more. Any cultural situation which involves a hierarchy of groups will include, to some extent, vertical relations among

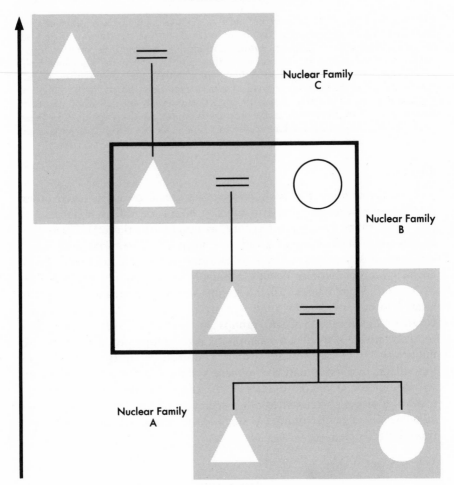

Fig. 10–19. Vertical relations of social groups.

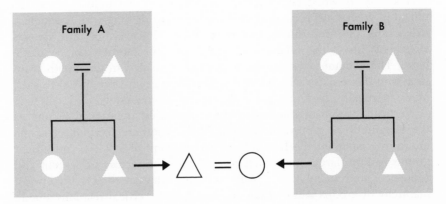

Fig. 10–20. Horizontal relations among groups.

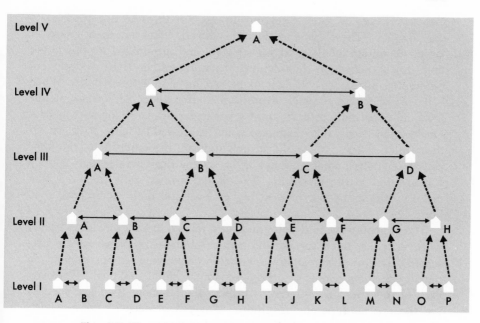

Fig. 10–21. Vertical–horizontal relations among groups.

groups (though the combined vertical–horizontal system of relations is also found in these situations).

The nuclear family, for example, as part of an extended family, is related vertically to other nuclear families on the bases of residence, descent, structural positions, membership, magnitude, and dependency (see Fig. 10–19). The extended family is dependent upon all nuclear families as structural components. In addition, a common residence and a definite pattern of descent join each nuclear family to every other one in a vertical manner. Finally, the extended family is of greater magnitude than its constituent nuclear families, and incorporates each of them within itself.

Horizontal relations among groups occur most frequently when the groups involved are in some way symmetrical to each other. For example, two nuclear families (symmetrical groups) are related to one another through the marriage of one member from each group. (See Fig. 10–20.) Common membership and common interests and goals are the factors that relate one family to the other.

Vertical–horizontal relations frequently occur in situations that are characterized by contraposition or reciprocal dependence, and by hierarchical differentiation. The segmentary lineage system that characterizes Nuer society (East Africa) is one example. Groups are segmented into levels, and at each level the groups are theoretically opposed to one another. These same groups are linked, however, to a group of larger magnitude at the next higher level and are unified by this larger unit. Such unification, hierarchically manifested, involves a system of differential allegiance which is expressed on a situational basis. When behavior which requires an expression of this allegiance occurs at one level, all units unify as a group at a particular level. When such behavior does not occur, this allegiance is not expressed. Figure 10–21 shows these relationships. The solid arrows indicate the opposition (the horizontal relations) among groups of a symmetrical nature that share a similar level in the hierarchy. The dotted arrows show the units that make up the groups at the next higher level and their hierarchical relations.

The general ways in which groups are related merely provide a framework in which more specific discussions of these relations can be presented. The specific relationships that occur among groups depend, in part, upon their realms of action—economic, ritual, political. However, each of these realms of action is responsible for more than just specifying the relationships among groups. Analysis of each of these aspects of culture reveals the existence of still other groups, specifies the organization that occurs, and sets forth the membership that is present. It shows the ways in which one part of culture is related to all other parts and the way in which one social group may cross-cut several aspects of culture. The succeeding chapters enlarge upon the organization of society and culture.

11

Economic Production

INTRODUCTION

The totality of the social behavior of the individuals that make up any society can be treated in a very general way, as has been done in Chapter 7, in the discussion of the basic principles of organization. The members of a society themselves, however, recognize that their behavior takes a variety of forms because it is directed toward a variety of goals. Depending upon these goals, social behavior can be described as political, religious, economic, and so on. Because behavior in each of these areas is social behavior, it is, within limits, orderly and predictable: it conforms to certain principles. Understanding of this order is based, in part, upon recognition of the more general principles of organization. Each category of behavior, however, has certain unique characteristics which are not wholly explainable in terms of these general principles. Economic behavior, for example, conforms to principles that are unique to the category of economics. It is for this reason that cultural categories such as economics, politics, or religion are isolated for purposes of analysis. Organization is the constant; the type of action is the variable.

While it is valid, for purposes of analysis, to isolate categories of behavior in order to achieve analytical refinement and greater depth of explanation, the material so isolated must be returned to its proper context before meaningful and valid generalizations can be derived. The analysis of behavior in a variety of logically derived cultural categories, while never losing sight of the necessary interrelatedness of these activities, has been a basic concept underlying the treatment of all material in this book. There is a necessary and intimate relationship among all parts of culture, and among the ways in which these parts are unified into an integrated whole according to common principles.

Some of the more basic ways in which economic behavior is organized could be illustrated equally well by drawing on any one of hundreds of ethnographically known societies. The Bushman of the South African Kalahari in hunting the giraffe, the Pitjandjara hunter of the Great Victorian Desert in Australia seeking the kangaroo, the Indian rice farmer in Trinidad or Guyana, the Masai cattle herder of East Africa, the American businessman or laborer—all engage in activity that is part of and illustrates the organization of economics. This behavior, like all other social action, is neither random nor a matter of individual choice; rather, it conforms to the principles of organization characteristic of each particular society. If a society is regulated exclusively by principles of kinship, for example, then economic behavior will be regulated by kinship rules. There are many kinds of organized economic activity in any society, each related to the others and to other aspects of culture. Regardless of the particular culture, however, economic activity is part of social organization in general and shares the necessary and sufficient factors of organization—structure, action, and function.

In addition to these general factors of organization, economic activity involves three major necessary and sufficient components that are unique to itself—*production, distribution,* and *consumption.* Obviously these three factors are expressed very differently in a hunting and gathering society, a preindustrial state, and a modern industrialized nation.

Production is the organization by the society of raw materials, technology (tools and techniques), and human effort in order to produce goods and/or services that are culturally desired. All societies known to us satisfy the requirements specified in this definition of production; *all societies are producers.* As a general statement, our definition also applies with equal validity to any regularized economic activity found in any society. Distribution and consumption are taken up in detail in Chapter 12. The remainder of this chapter is given to an analysis of production.

RAW MATERIALS, TECHNOLOGY, AND HUMAN EFFORT

While the products differ and the societies that produce them vary, the general factors involved in production remain constant. Raw materials, technology, and human effort, organized to produce a culturally desired item, are the universals of production. They are as necessary to production among the Pygmy of the Ituri Forest as they are to the General Motors plant in Detroit.

Cheyenne Women

The following description of the productive activities of Cheyenne women shows clearly how the basic factors of production are combined to produce a variety of culturally desirable items:

The basic household item of the woman is her stone maul—an oval river stone with pecked-out grooves on the short sides around which is fixed a supple willow withe firmly fastened with green rawhide. When dried out, the rawhide shrinks and holds the maul within the handle with the grip of a vise. With the maul she breaks up fuel, drives tipi pegs, and crushes large bones to be cooked in soup. With smaller handstones the housewife crushes her chokecherries and pulverizes her dried meat. The Cheyennes are essentially a Stone Age people.

Every household has its complement of horn spoons. These are made by steaming or boiling the horns of buffalo or mountain sheep until pliable. Tortoise shell and wood are also sometimes used. . . .

Each woman has a tanning kit of four tools: a scraper, flesher, drawblade, and softening rope or buffalo scapula (shoulder blade). The scraper is a prepared flat, oval stone held in both hands and used to remove extraneous meat and fat from the inner surface of the hide. Metal scrapers supplied by traders are also used.

The flesher is a more delicate instrument. Shaped like an adze, it is made of an elkhorn handle bent at right angle, with a sharp chipped flint lashed across the short end. It is used to hack down the inner surface of the skin . . . and a good fleshing tool is a cherished family heirloom. . . .

The drawblade is a slightly curved willow stick, into the concave side of which is glued a sharpened bone splinter. With the hide draped over an inclined pole, the woman worker shaves off the hair from the outer side of the skin.

Tanning calls for chemical applications; otherwise, the result is rawhide. Brains, liver, and soapweed provide the essentials of the working compound, which is mixed with grease to provide body. The stuff is well rubbed into both sides of the hide, which is then put to soak overnight. After drying in the sun, it is laboriously softened by being worked back and forth over a rawhide rope or by being pulled through a hole in a buffalo shoulder blade fastened to a tree.

A small lodge requires eleven buffalo cowhides, thinned and tanned. A big lodge takes as many as twenty-one. A woman does all the work on her lodge skins up to the point of the rope- or blade-softening process. For this last step she invites in her friends and relatives—one for each hide—and gives them a big feast. Each one is then given a hide to take home and finish, with a rawhide rope to use for the work. Meanwhile, she has to split and make quantities of thread from the buffalo sinews she has been hoarding. Her next chore is the preparation of another great feast, for the process of cutting and sewing the lodge is an all-day sewing-bee to which all her friends will bring the hides she has parceled out to them. At daybreak she must first seek out a woman known as an expert lodge maker, to whom she supplies paint and a cutting knife. Before the guests arrive, the lodge maker fits the pieces and marks them for cutting. The sewers subsequently arrive for breakfast and work all day long, with a meal in the afternoon and a supper at night—this last after the lodge has been raised and stretched on its foundation. For her pains, the expert lodge maker receives a small present.

A new home is a great thing for all the tribe, and it is so recognized in a ritual of dedication. Except for the women working on it, no one may enter a new lodge until the bravest man available has counted coup on it and has entered, followed by other outstanding warriors. The women have completed a hard and great piece of work, and in this way the men give recognition to their achievement. (Hoebel 1960:61–63.)

Each of the items produced by Cheyenne women represents the application of technology, by human effort, to raw materials to produce goods that are desired by the society. In each instance, the Cheyenne society has made the decision to produce one item rather than other possible alternatives; stone maul, handstone, horn spoon, tanning kit (scraper, flesher, drawblade, and softening rope), and lodge skin are deemed desirable cultural products.

Such decisions are not haphazard in any society. Among hunting and gathering societies, the decisions made to produce certain culturally desirable products may mean a significant difference in the degree of adaptive success, especially if the society resides in a very harsh environment. In deserts or icebound lands, misapplication of the strictly limited resources may mean a lack of adaptive success, and death to members of the society. The efficient exploitation of the environment, which maximizes the group's chances for survival, depends on the making of many optimal decisions concerning the use of limited resources.

Raw materials, technology, and human effort are, in summary, the necessary and sufficient factors of production. The members of a society organize these factors in particular ways to achieve culturally desired products. The producer begins the process with a desired product in mind, perhaps a pottery vessel, a canoe, a musical instrument, an item of clothing. Discounting at this time the element of human creativity, or inventiveness, the item visualized by the producer will always fall within the range of alternatives provided by his culture. A Cheyenne warrior might set out to make a tobacco pipe or an arrow point; within the limitations of his culture he will not even conceive of producing a blowgun or a walrus harpoon. The producer then selects the raw materials suitable for the product he has in mind. This choice will depend on availability and on cultural factors. Few peoples ever utilize all the potential resources of their environment. Finally, the producer applies his own effort and the technology at his command (tools and techniques) to the material in order to complete the production process.

Australian Aborigines: The Ngadadjara

Stone implement-making among the Ngadadjara, an Australian aboriginal group in South Australia, provides a detailed example of produc-

A tribesman from Northern Kimberley in Australia prepares a spear-point by pressure flaking. (Courtesy of the American Museum of Natural History.)

tion. Not only are the factors of production demonstrated explicitly, but the ingenuity of primitive technology is shown also in this description of a hafted axe:

. . . made and used by Tjupurula (his male class name), a man of about 60 years of age of the country west of Lake Christopher on the western border of Ngadadjara territory. He picked up the stone for this ['tjuna 'kandi] as a random flake of opaline silica at ['Patupiri], Kathleen Range, while engaged in a kangaroo hunt on the 7th November 1963. The following day he made the ['tjuna] handle from . . . a kind of ironwood (*Acacia*). He had sent his wife the same morning to the southern slopes of Gill Pinnacle to gather *Triodia* grass resin for the haft. The ['tjuna] had on it lines incised by running the edge of a stone flake ['kandi] around the ends of the shaft. These lines are called ['ŋamiri] and on tools, and particularly on spears, they serve as identification marks.

When found as a natural flake, to be hafted on this implement, it was discoidal in shape. I saw it before it was hafted. . . . There was no delicate trimming on its cutting margin when first inserted in the resin, but shortly afterwards during use in the making of the handle for a further chisel, it was sharpened. In doing this the cutting edge was tapped, using the rounded surface of one end of the second handle which Tjupurula was shaping with its aid. This single act of resharpening resulted in the appearance on the chisel edge of a regular series of tiny semi-circular stepped flake scars. . . .

During the sharpening process Tjupurula did not remove the stone from its setting in the resin. Among the Walpiri, at Yuendumu, skilled old men often remove the stone from the resin and reset it at right angles to the cutting position, before they tap off their sharpening flakes. This is considered particularly necessary when drastic resharpening is desirable; less so when only minor retouch is required. Among the Walpiri the sharpening is often done with taps from the flat face of a hunting boomerang. Such weapons are unknown in the Ngadadjara territory. The removal of trimming flakes in this manner tends to give the profile of the well sharpened stone, in section normal to the cutting edge, an outline which is concave; a similar silhouette to that of a hollow-ground razor. (Tindale 1965:135–36.)

ROLE OF THE ENVIRONMENT IN PRODUCTION

Environment, of course, is an important dimension of production, insofar as it limits and influences the kinds of items that are produced by a society. Particular raw materials must be available in the environment if the society is to make use of them for producing culturally desired goods. Though different types of raw materials may be used sometimes to achieve similar finished products, if none of these alternative materials is available, then the production of objects which require the use of these raw materials is precluded until the technology of the culture can provide adequate substitute material. For example, artifacts which require the use of metals such as iron, copper, or gold cannot be produced unless these metals are present in the environment and the society has the techniques available for extracting and making use of them. The Eskimo hunter of the far northern areas of Canada has little wood available to him due to the sparse vegetation and, therefore, will be restricted in the production of artifacts requiring the use of wood. Instead, such materials as bone, antler, skins, and ivory, which are more readily available, are utilized in the production of desired goods. The obvious alternative to extracting raw materials from the environment is trade. If a society can receive raw materials through trade, then the environmental limitations can be overcome, at least to the extent that the materials are offered as trade items and the society is able to produce other items that can be used in exchange. (Trade is part of the more general category of economic distribution and is discussed in this context.)

ECONOMIC PRODUCTION AND CULTURAL DESIRABILITY

When we speak of the cultural desirability of items of production, we are actually speaking of cultural choices from among possible or conceivable alternatives. The total inventory of items produced by human economic activity is an enormous one, and no society has ever selected more than a small fraction of these possible items to constitute its own cultural inventory. But why does a particular society desire (i.e., select for production) certain items and not others? Clearly, the choices made by men from among economic alternatives are limited by many factors. Time, availability of materials, and effort are certainly involved. Given the material available, the time necessary to produce an item, and the human effort that must be invested, man must make a choice of the items he wants produced. Shall he direct these factors to produce item A, B, or C? The answer to such a question is based on many other influencing factors. The general level of technological and sociocultural complexity attained by a society is one important limiting factor. It is obvious, for example, that the technological level attained by Bushman society would not permit production of automobiles or radios. Given the Bushman isolation and cultural level, these products are not even conceivable possibilities. A less extreme illustration would be the nomadic life of the Bushman, which limits the material items he can produce. His culturally desired items must be either immediately consumable or highly portable. In addition, the item produced must have some meaning in the context of his existing culture pattern. His environment and his way of life preclude his choice of such items as canoes, fishnets, or neckties. Finally, though this does not exhaust the list of limitations upon choice, economic choice, like all social behavior, is normative. Any people could, according to their way of life and available resources, select items for production which would meet their needs as satisfactorily as those they already have. Many items of production are highly desired because they are customary and are supported by the full force of tradition. No society is ever completely static, however, and preferences change. The archaeological record abundantly documents changing styles in pottery decoration, the shape of arrow points, house types, and so on, where the new product is not superior—in any absolute sense—to what it has replaced.

The items produced by the economic activity of any people are, then, to be defined as culturally desirable. However, the specific items and the range of items which any people can or will select for production are limited by many factors. Economic choice is not and cannot be a completely rational process. Man exists as he must in a complex natural and sociocultural environment, and none of his behavior is free from the influence of that environment.

A question might be raised at this point as to whether societies produce goods that are not culturally desirable, items which are evidently desired by some people but are objectionable to other people in the same society. It might be asked, for example, whether products such as LSD, morphine, firearms, switch-blade knives, or even automobiles are not objectionable in our society. To answer this question we must distinguish between the production of an item, and its consumption (the use to which it is put). Our society has decided to produce the items mentioned, and a portion of our resources (very sizable in some cases) is devoted to their production. LSD and morphine are produced for doctors and researchers to use in activities supported by society—medicine and research. Firearms of many kinds are openly produced for the use of our armed forces and police. The automobile is basic to our way of life, and the number of automobiles in use would suggest that this is a highly desired product. Yet these and many other items are found objectionable when used in ways not deemed acceptable to society. Not infrequently such usage is subject to strong social controls. Even the automobile is viewed as a threat to life, and its use is restricted in many ways. Society acts, in short, to prevent what is defined as the misuse of such items, but the items themselves remain culturally desirable and continue to be produced. It is a pattern of consumption or use that is not desired and is therefore subject to control or modification.

ORGANIZATION OF HUMAN EFFORT

One of the necessary factors of production is human effort, or labor. All societies, whatever the raw materials available to them and whatever their technology, organize the available human effort in order to achieve the ends (goods and services) they recognize as desirable. The ways in which a society organizes human effort for economic production are frequently referred to by anthropologists as the *division of labor.* Labor can be divided (tasks can be allocated) in various ways, some of which are found in all societies known to us and are, therefore, universal criteria for the division of labor.

Universal Criteria for Organizing Human Effort

There are at least two ways in which societies everywhere divide the human labor available to them in the course of economic production—

age and sex. In hunting and gathering societies, anthropologists consistently find that large game is hunted by the adult male while vegetable products are gathered by the adult female. In addition, non-adult males are consistently found to be associated with hunting small game animals, and non-adult females will perform tasks supplementary to the major gathering tasks of the adult females. Obviously the tasks of the younger members of society are directly related to training that will enable them to perform their tasks as full adult members in the society when the proper time comes. The supplementary contribution these younger members make may be economically negligible, but the training is necessary to insure the society's continuance. Examples of the universal aspects of the division of labor in various contemporary societies will provide an expansion of these ideas.

The Bushman. First, the Bushman, hunters and gatherers who live in the Kalahari Desert of South Africa.

Gathering veld food is the work of the Bushman women. . . . Dasina, Twikwe, and Tsetchwe walked in front, each with a digging-stick thrust in her belt like an enormous knife, each wearing a heavy cape, and Tsetchwe carrying her baby, who rode, carefree and swinging his feet, on her shoulder. . . .

We walked until we came to a patch of tsama melons, perhaps twenty of them lying together, shiny, smooth, and green in the grass. The vine that once had nourished them had dried away and already some of the melons were turning yellow, overripe, ready to open and release their seeds.

The women stopped and began to gather up the green melons, Twikwe picking them with a mechanical, stereotyped gesture. She first slipped her hand under a melon; then, twisting her elbow, she lifted the melon and held it pinched between the heel of her hand and her forearm, and with a scoop slipped it into the pocket of her kaross on the side. In a moment the side of her kaross was full, and she stood erect for an instant, looked at the sky, shifted her weight, and suddenly the melons rolled to the back of her kaross, leaving the side free for more. She was very efficient. In a moment she had a load. I was a little surprised at her, however, for now she would have to carry the melons with her all day whereas she might have gathered them on the way home. But Bushman women do not seem to mind this.

The women left behind the yellow melons which would have been bitter and rotten, touching them disappointedly with their toes instead. The false spring was hastening the time when all the melons would be gone, forcing the Bushmen to eat roots as a staple diet, not as desirable because of the uses that tsama melons have. Melons are eaten as both food and water, their pulp is added to meat which needs liquid for boiling, their seeds are roasted and eaten or ground into powder and used as flour, their rinds serve as mixing-bowls, as containers for small, loose objects, as cooking-pots with or without the pulp inside, as urine-containers for curing hides, as targets for the children's shooting practice, as children's drums, as resonators for musical instruments, and all this amounts to a serious loss for Bushmen when the melons rot or dry. (Thomas 1965:103–4.)

The Cheyenne. The Cheyenne Indians of the Great Plains region of North America provide another example of a rather strict division of labor based upon sex—one which is traditionally supported by ritual.

Women are the vegetable gatherers. The dibble, or digging stick, is their basic tool. It was given by the Great Medicine Spirit and it figures in the ritual paraphernalia of the Sun Dance, for it has its sacred aspects. Cheyenne dibbles are of two types. The short kind has a knob at one end and is pushed under the desired root by pressure against the stomach when the digger is down on both knees. The other kind is long, and is used as a crowbar. The sharp ends are fire hardened.

In many societies women are the principal gatherers of vegetable food products, like this Kamloop Indian digging roots. (Courtesy of the American Museum of Natural History.)

Some eight or ten different wild roots are gathered, including the bulbs of several varieties of lilies. . . .

Although root digging is a tiresome chore, the girls and women do not treat it as such. They leave the camp in the morning in small work parties without a male guard against enemy marauders. Their spirits are usually gay, for they look on the day's activity as an outing. Far out on the prairie they scatter to their individual tasks, for the actual gathering requires no cooperative effort. When they come together in the late afternoon, they often react to the monotony of their work by gambling their roots against each other in a game of seeing who can throw her digging stick the farthest, or by throwing "dice" of buffalo metacarpals. . . .

Women also go out in foraging groups to gather wood for their fires. Except for collecting expeditions, however, most of a woman's work when the camp is not moving is in and about the lodge preparing food, dressing hides, sewing and decorating clothing, robes, and lodges. A good woman is cheerful, busy, and skillful. The raising and lowering of tipis is solely the job of women, and they do it with skill and speed. In the more permanent camps they excavate the floor of the tipi four or five inches, leaving a sod bench around the outer part to serve as a foundation for the beds. The bare floor is wetted and packed down. A lodge lining is tied part way up the poles and folded inward over the bench so that no draft blows under the tipi cover on the sleepers. With the help of her children, the lodge mistress gathers bundles of grass to lay on the bench as padding. Mats made of horizontal willow withes which are attached to tripods are raised between the ends of each sleeping place and covered with buffalo robes to form backrests. In well-provided lodges each person therefore has a comfortable chaise longue as well as a private bed. A couple of buffalo robes are enough to keep the sleepers warm and comfortable within the tipi no matter how cold it may be outside. The areas under the backrest tripods form cupboards for the storage of gear and the parfleches of dried food. . . .

All clothing is made by the women. Unfamiliar with the art of weaving, they tan the necessary skins and loosely tailor the garments for themselves, their men and children. Awls are made of ground-down bones (animal or fish), or thorns. These, with thread and decorative materials, are kept by each woman in a hair-covered leather bag worn at her belt. Dresses are tubular sacks sewn together down the sides and reaching well below the knees. Short sleeves hang down from the shoulders. (Hoebel 1960:59–63.)

As opposed to gathering and clothes-making by the women, the Cheyenne men were essentially big-game hunters seeking mainly the bison, antelope, deer, elk, and wild sheep. Sometimes smaller game was taken for the furs only.

The Swazi. The Swazi of South Africa provide a contrasting example of a sexual division of labor. Production is also divided along the lines of sex, but the type of activity performed by each sex differs from that performed by the Cheyenne.

Every man, irrespective of his rank, knows how to build, plow, milk cattle, sew skins, and cut shields; every woman is able to hoe, thatch, plait ropes, and weave mats, baskets, and beer strainers. Swazi attach value judgments to activities over which one or other sex claims a monopoly by reason of assumed psychophysical attributes. Specific "masculine" tasks that carry high status include warfare, . . . animal husbandry, and hunting. Men are also the important public figures, the orators and councilors, and the family priests. A woman's life is restricted by domestic activities, and rearing of children, and the regular chores of grinding grain, carrying water, cooking foods, smearing the floors with cow dung. Men and women cooperate in agriculture and building, but the man's share is more spasmodic and energetic, the woman's more monotonous and continuous. (Kuper 1963:45.)

Age and sex are not always used by societies to separate labor completely, so that women always gather and men always hunt. Frequently, men and women will perform specific tasks on a cooperative basis with each contributing a particular task to produce a single product.

The Pygmies. The Pygmies of the Ituri Forest provide an excellent example of such cooperative production, especially in terms of their net hunting.

Ekianga and a few others made a brief reconnaissance, and when they came back they gave instructions as to the best direction for setting up the nets. The womenfolk, who had been foraging around for mushrooms and nuts, picked up their baskets and went ahead with the small children. They trod lightly and made no noise beyond an occasional crunch of a rotten branch, buried deep beneath the carpet of leaves. We all spread out in a long semicircle, each man knowing exactly who should be to his right and who to his left. I went with Maipe, who had been sent by Njobo with his net. We soon lost sight and sound of the others, but Maipe knew just where he would be expected to set up his net, and he took a short cut. I lost all sense of direction and could not even tell on which side of us the women were waiting for the signal to beat in toward our nets. We followed a little stream and paused by an enormous outcrop of huge stone boulders, almost perfectly square in shape, some of them eight feet across each face. Maipe looked around, then sat down to wait. After a few minutes Moke's nephew appeared to our left, stringing his net out through the undergrowth as he came.
  The end of the net stopped a few feet short of the boulders, and Maipe deftly joined it to his net; then, slipping each coil off his shoulder in turn, he hung his own net, fastening it to low branches and saplings. It stretched for about three hundred feet, so that one end was completely out of sight from the other. It stood about four feet high, and Maipe walked the length of it, silently adjusting it so that it touched the ground all the way along and was securely fastened above. If he found the net drooping where there was no support, he cut a sapling, stuck it in the ground and hung the net on it, bending the top sharply back, twisting it around and through the mesh so that the net could not slip. When this was done he took up his spear and casually sharpened it with a stone picked off the ground.
  It was about another five minutes before he suddenly stood up and beckoned me to do the same. He stood absolutely motionless, his head slightly on one side, listening; his spear was raised just a few inches from the ground. I listened too, but could hear nothing. The forest had become silent; even the crickets had stopped their almost incessant chirping. Maipe raised his spear higher, and then at some signal that I did not even notice there was a burst of

shouting, yelling, hooting and clapping, as the women and children started the beat. They must have been about a half mile away, and as they came closer the noise was deafening. We saw one antelope, a large red sondu, ears back, leaping toward the boulders as though it were heading straight for our net, but at the last moment it saw us and veered away to the left. Maipe could probably have killed it with his spear, but he said, "That is not for us. It will probably fall into Ekianga's net." Just then there was a lot of yelling from Moke's nephew. Maipe vaulted over the net and ran swiftly, leaping and bounding like the sondu to avoid obstacles. . . . The sondu had gone into Ekianga's net, just as Maipe had said, but while all the attention was in that direction a water chevron, the *sindula*, had tried to fight its way through Moke's net.

The sindula is one of the most prized animals; it is not much larger than a small dog but is dangerous and vicious. Moke's nephew had been left all by himself to deal with it, as the others in that area were helping Ekianga with the sondu. The youngster, probably not much more than thirteen years old, had speared it with his first thrust, pinning the animal to the ground through the fleshy part of the stomach. But the animal was still very much alive, fighting for freedom. It had already bitten its way through the net, and now it was doubled up, gashing the spear shaft with its sharp teeth. Maipe put another spear into its neck, but it still writhed and fought. Not until a third spear pierced its heart did it give up the struggle. (Turnbull 1962:97–99.)

In this example, women and young children (especially female ones) have the duty of driving the game sought by the Pygmy hunting group toward the nets set up by the adult male hunters. The males tend the nets and, when the game comes, are responsible for killing animals. Both jobs are of equal importance in this type of hunting activity; the failure or absence of either one would mean failure in producing food for consumption by the group. This activity is a cooperative effort which incorporates the division of labor by sex and age, the criterion of age being less distinct than that of sex.

Relative Criteria for Organizing Human Effort

In addition to the universally used criteria of age and sex for the organization of human effort, there are non-universal or variable criteria such as group membership, skill in performing a particular activity, inheritance, prestige, status, education, or physical ability and dexterity which a society may use to organize its human effort in production activities. The importance of each of these will vary from society to society, and, of course, not all criteria will be used by all societies.

Group membership is explicitly illustrated in the economic dimension of Indian caste (e.g., the *jajmani* or other similar systems found in various parts of India). Individuals who belong to the caste called *dhobi* traditionally engage in the activity of washing clothes. There are protective mechanisms (social sanctions arrived at by caste and village councils) that are intended to prevent others from engaging in the economic activities of the *dhobi* (washerman). The *chamar*, traditionally a leather worker, engages in leather work activities because he is a member of the *chamar* caste. So it is for each individual who is a member of a particular group—the Brahman, the Tailor, the Blacksmith, the Goldsmith, and all other caste groups actively participating in the caste system of traditional India. Their economic activities are largely defined for them by their membership in a particular group. But such a definition of economic action is not restricted to caste systems. An Aztec or an Inca engaged in particular activities, based upon the group to which he belonged. If a man was a member of the Aztec merchant class, the *pochteca*, he was expected to travel around the area distributing his wares, and simultaneously acquiring news from one place or another as a "secret service agent." He was the individual who reported information of unrest and possible revolt to the central authorities of the Aztec state. A member of the priestly class, however, would not engage in such activity but would devote his time and effort to carrying out the various rituals deemed necessary and desirable for the Inca or Aztec state. Commoners, or the Inca ruler himself, were subject to still other expectations. These are examples of hereditary economic activity.

The Trobriand Islanders. Another classic example—the case of the garden magician—occurs among the Trobriand Islanders. Malinowski's very clear description of inheritance of social status and, presumably, the ability to perform a particular type of economic action, demonstrates this point very well. The crop discussed is yams.

Among the forces and beliefs which bear upon and regulate garden work, perhaps magic is the most important. It is a department of its own, and the garden magician, next to the chief and sorcerer, is the most important personage of the village. The position is hereditary, and, in each village, a special system of magic is handed on in the female line from one generation to another. I have called it a *system*, because the magician has to perform a series of rites and spells over the garden, which run parallel with the labour, and which, in fact, initiate each stage of work and each new development of plant life. Even before any gardening is begun at all, the magician has to consecrate the site with a big ceremonial performance in which all men of the village take part. This ceremony officially opens the season's gardening, and only after it is performed do the villagers begin to cut the scrub on their plots. Then, in a series of rites, the magician inaugurates successively all the various stages which follow one another—the burning of the scrub, the clearing, the planting, the weeding and the harvesting. Also, in another series of rites and spells, he magically assists the plant in sprouting, in budding, in bursting into leaf, in climbing, in forming the rich garlands of foliage, and in producing the edible tubers.

The garden magician, according to native ideas, thus controls both the work of man and the forces of Nature. He also acts directly as supervisor of gardening, sees to it that people do not skimp their work, or lag behind with it. Thus magic is a systematising, regulating, and controlling influence in garden work.

The magician, in carrying out the rites, sets the pace, compels people to apply themselves to certain tasks, and to accomplish them properly and in time. Incidentally, magic also imposes on the tribe a good deal of extra work, of apparently unnecessary, hampering taboos and regulations. In the long run, however, there is no doubt that by its influence in ordering, systematising and regulating work, magic is economically invaluable for the natives. (Malinowski 1961:59–60.)

Not all Trobriand Islanders can engage in the types of economic activities described for the magician; they are restricted to those individuals who, by the fact of their inheritance, are qualified. This illustrates the use of a relative variable for organizing human effort: not all societies utilize inheritance for organizing activity, but some, such as the Trobriand Islanders, do.

The Central Eskimo. Among the Central Eskimo, religious specialists engage in certain activities deemed to be desirable services by the society, activities which cannot be performed by individuals who are not *ang'akut* (magicians). For example, in addition to other activities:

The hardest task, that of driving away Sedna [mistress of the underworld], is reserved for the most powerful angakoq [magician]. A rope is coiled on the floor of a large hut in such a manner as to leave a small opening at the top, which represents the breathing hole of a seal. Two angakut stand by the side of it, one of them holding the seal spear in his left hand, as if he were watching at the seal hole in the winter, the other holding the harpoon line. Another angakoq, whose office it is to lure Sedna up with a magic song, sits at the back of the hut. At last she comes up through the hard rocks and the wizard hears her heavy breathing; now she emerges from the ground and meets the angakoq waiting at the hole. She is harpooned and sinks away in angry haste, drawing after her the harpoon, to which the two men hold with all their strength. Only by a desperate effort does she tear herself away from it and return to her dwelling in Adlivun. Nothing is left with the two men but the blood sprinkled harpoon, which they proudly show to the Inuit.

Sedna and the other evil spirits are at last driven away, and on the following day a great festival for young and old is celebrated in honor of the event. (Boas 1964:196.)

This description of action by the magicians of the Central Eskimo provides an example of still another relative variable for the organization of human effort, in this case physical ability. Not all individuals have the physical requisites to be acceptable magicians, and among those who are acceptable, some are more successful than others. There is differentiation among individuals performing the same general type of activities, in that only some of the group's members may perform certain activities, such as driving away Sedna. A similar differentiation among individuals is applied when hunting and gathering groups make a distinction among good hunters and poor hunters. In doing this, they are not only providing cultural recognition, they are also applying another variable for organizing human economic effort in their particular society.

Cooperative Effort in Production

To describe productive processes solely in terms of who does them—young or old, male or female—fails to take into account another socially important factor of production: cooperation among individuals. The above passage describing the building of a Cheyenne lodge showed, for example, that while this was women's work, several women worked together to achieve the desired result. Cooperation is a social arrangement that can take many forms. By using ethnographic examples from a wide range of societies, three major categories of cooperative productive production can be isolated.

Homogeneous Productive Activity. In many kinds of activity, all the persons involved will do the same thing to produce the same item. For example, Bushman women work in groups to collect the vegetable products from their desert environment. It is true that this activity itself is not significantly cooperative—each collects food for her own family. The actual distribution of these products, however, extends throughout the band. Thus, all the women of the group are engaging in the same activity, performing the same tasks to obtain the same products—wild roots, melons, and so on—to feed the entire band.

Complementary Heterogeneous Productive Activity. Individuals performing different tasks to achieve a single product may be differentiated according to some of the relative variables already discussed—not only age and sex, but leadership status, kin-group membership, and others. This second category of cooperative human effort has already been illustrated by the description given of the communal hunt among the Pygmies.

The Kaoka. Another clear example is provided by the horticultural Kaoka of Guadalcanal in the Solomon Islands.

Cultivation is by the slash-and-burn method. The ground is cleared, the timber is destroyed, and two or sometimes three crops planted one after the other. The area is then abandoned for a period of ten years or more.

Yams, taro, and sweet potatoes are grown month by month, and at any given moment each householder has from four to six gardens at different stages. Yams, however, do a little better when sown during the height of the trade-wind season. Most persons plan therefore to have a few more plots prepared then. The tubers are ready at the tail end of the monsoon, a period known as *Walisi*.

Probably everyone makes an occasional small garden by himself, but in general the subclan members from the hamlet collaborate. They discuss the matter in the clubhouse during the evening and decide on which area and when they will begin. One or more of their number may at this particular time not wish to join in, perhaps on account of other commitments, perhaps because of a temporary shortage of seed yams, taro suckers, or sweet-potato runners, but the rest make appropriate arrangements. The older men take some of their young uterine nephews as helpers and also expect any married son living nearby to accompany them. Sometimes they also invite other relatives, including affines. Adult guests have to lend a hand in the clearing and fencing and are then allocated a section, which, of course, reverts back to the clan as soon as the last crop has been gathered in.

The oldest active man in the subclan is in charge; should leadership in any of the tasks be necessary, he directs the operations. He selects the patch to be used with reference to such factors as the presence of certain shrubs and the girth of trees. The first are regarded as indicators of the quality of the soil, the second as fixing the length of time that the ground has lain fallow. He orders the party to cut the brushwood, and later they fell the bigger timber. The rubbish dries out and is burned within a few weeks.

So far the males alone have been engaged in cultivation. The women now go along also to scatter the ashes over the soil and remove any further growth. In the meantime the men construct a stout fence around the block.

In the next stage the leader divides the clearing into plots, one for every household. The men mark the borders with flimsy palisades, then cut the plots into strips, one for every dependent. This final subdivision, although of little practical significance, serves to demonstrate the size of the garden, information that cannot otherwise be obtained in a community that lacks a means of measuring length or area.

Yams always form the first main crop. The men make a series of holes with a digging stick; later they and the women cut the seed tubers into pieces, each with an eye, which all go together and plant. After a lapse of some weeks the women make up a gang of weeders to clear the patch. Each may stick to her own household plot, but more frequently they combine and go from end to end in one long line. A few more weeks and the men have another turn. They cut stakes and fix them for the yam vines to climb on. Often, too, they build a shed or two to serve as shelter for any family that may wish to stay for a couple of days. Subsequently they fix shelves just below the roof so that the ripened yams can be stored, especially those that are picked out for seed. The women remove the weeds on one further occasion, and later on they dig up the tubers. The small ones are easily extracted, but harvesting the larger varieties, even though they weigh only a few pounds, is a tedious job demanding half an hour or more scooping the earth around each one. . . .

In addition to yams, each householder has patches of green vegetables and tobacco and also a few banana trees. The women plant and care for the green vegetables and tobacco; women and men plant bananas, and the men cut down the bunches of ripe fruit and carry them home. The tobacco leaves are first spread out in the sun, usually by the men, and then transferred to a shelf over the cooking fire. When fully matured they are rolled into bundles, each weighing about 4 pounds. A smoker cuts off a small wedge and rubs it in his palms before filling his pipe. . . .

Depending upon the type of soil, the second crop is either taro or sweet potatoes. If taro has been chosen, the women bring along the suckers from an old garden, and the members of both sexes combine to plant them. As before, the women do the weeding and harvesting. By this time the fences are probably falling into disrepair, and the subclan leader has to arrange with the men for their renovation.

The third crop, if the people decide to have one, is almost always sweet potatoes. Men and women cut shoots off the plants in another garden and dig one end of each shoot into the earth. The ripening tubers attract the pigs even more than do yams and taro, and the fence must now be regularly inspected and, if need be, strengthened.

The men carry all the very heavy loads, as, for example, when extra supplies have to be brought in for a feast; but it is women's work to take the daily food home from the cultivations. They put the yams, taro, or sweet potatoes into a flat basket, which they lift onto a woven ring of cane placed on top of the head. A weight of 80 pounds is not regarded as too heavy a load; and I have never seen anything fall. (Hogbin 1964:41–43.)

Specialization in Productive Activity

All individuals engage in different tasks to produce many different items. This third category of cooperative production is based upon the principle that all productive units, whether they be individuals or groups, contribute different tasks to an overall economic complex deemed necessary to achieve and maintain the desired "style of life" of the social complex or society. The organization of human effort for this sort of economy, while also complementary in its results, is significantly more complex than the two alternatives previously described, and of necessity involves more producing units.

The *Jajmani* System of North India. An excellent example is the *jajmani* system traditional in North India and similar systems such as the *malnad* system found in the southern part of India. One of the first descriptions of this system of economic organization is the now classic account provided by the Wisers:

At each of the two major harvests, Prakash calls to one of his fields the family washerman, the potter, carpenter, barber, and *kahars* who serve him. He gives one head-load of wheat and one of barley, or one head-load of corn and one of millet—about thirty pounds—to each one. They may also get rice, and eight pounds of the particular pulse just harvested. Others, who consider that they have a claim to some of his crop because of services rendered, must come without being called. The sewing man brings a garment for one of the smaller children. The *jadav* (leather worker) brings a leather thong. The grain parcher brings half a pound of a special sweet made from puffed rice. The bangle seller brings as many colored bangles as the daughter next to be married wants. The *mali* (flower grower) brings one or two marigolds. The cotton carder brings bits of twisted cotton, ready to be used as wicks for the small open lamps. The sweeper has nothing tangible to offer, but he comes. Those who appear—and they always do, if possible—receive from twelve to sixteen pounds of grain in a head load, and also rice, and perhaps five pounds of pulse. If they do not come, they get nothing. These same men visit other *jajmans* as well, to accumulate all they can for the lean months ahead. (Wiser and Wiser 1963: 150–51.)

The specific interrelationship among representatives of castes in the multicaste village is seen not only by the description of payments, given above, but also by the Wisers' description of the decline of the traditional *jajmani* system in the same village, a change brought about by newly established relationships between villagers and a town six miles away.

When I went to see a sick child in the house of one of the three oilsmiths, I expected to find the small ox going his steady round. Often I had watched him turning the heavy wooden pestle pressing oil from mustard seed, in the mortar made from a large tree trunk. But the mortar and pestle lay idle. The oilsmith showed me with pride what good wood there was in each part and talked of all the oil he could press. But he can no longer compete with the oil mills of Mainpuri. People find it cheaper to carry their mustard seed in to town and have the pressing done there. There is nothing else that he or his two brothers, whose presses also are idle, are trained to do. So they wait for jobs as day laborers on the land. When I asked them why they did not get work in one of the oil mills in the city, they said they could not manage the six-mile walk before and after a day's work in a mill. And bus fare, though little, would use up most of their earnings. If they had cycles they could manage it.

The cotton carder had a similar story to tell. Villagers say that he keeps more than his share of the cotton which they take to him to card and put into quilts for them. He says that he has to take this much if he and his family are to live. He realizes that the mills do it more cheaply than he can afford to, yet he has found no way of competing with them. Farmers going to town by cycle or with a load of grain or peanuts find it easy to bring back a finished quilt, and they no longer feel the responsibility which their forefathers always accepted for those who have served them. The sewing men likewise complain. Families on whom they could depend for the job of sewing their shirts and shorts, women's blouses, and clothes for the children, now prefer to buy some of their garments ready-made in town. They still have their ordinary clothes, those to be worn in the fields or courtyards, made by the sewing man attached to their family, but the earlier sense of security has been replaced by fear of growing competition. The *jajmans* say that there are too few sewing men left to do the work that needs to be done. Five have died in the past six years, but those who remain insist that they could do all the work required, if given a chance. (*Ibid.*, 188–89.)

South India. In the South Indian village of Gopalpur, this complex cooperative aspect of economics is exemplified by the actions of representatives of different *jati* (castes) who perform different tasks and serve different functions, each of which complements the other and all of which together produce the total desired style of life in this village. As Beals points out:

. . . the economic significance of jati membership lies not so much in the restrictions that jati membership places upon an individual's capacity to improve his economic position, as in guaranteeing economic cooperation outside the family circle. For the farmer, it is good business to be on good terms with someone who owns a large flock of sheep, for this provides access to a source of manure. Basketweavers, Carpenters, and Blacksmiths are sources of farm equipment. Delay in repairing a cart or plow, or inability to obtain a basket to carry manure to the fields, can make the difference between the success or failure of agricultural operations. Typically, the farmer is rich at harvest time, poor at sowing time. He must depend upon good will and credit in order to survive.

For essential services, the farmer tends to enter into a contractual relationship with the specialist. The Carpenter, Blacksmith, Barber, and Potter receive fixed quantities of grain at harvest time. In return, they provide services. Most individuals in Gopalpur wash their own clothing; a few have a permanent arrangement with the Washerman. The priests of the various deities do not ordinarily receive a fixed amount. They tend to be given grain in accordance with the quality of the harvest. The priests and their gods are expected to provide a good crop; if they do not do so, they cannot expect much grain in compensation. As a good businessman should, the farmer tries to maintain a friendly relationship with all relevant deities. Even a minor deity can spoil a crop or cause illness in the family. The Singer serving Hanumantha, the Mavla serving Muslim deities, the Brahmin serving Hindu deities, the Jangama serving the Lingayat deities, and anyone else who has any kind of priestly function in connection with any kind of godhouse, can expect to receive some sort of gift at harvest time. The tax collector, the landlord, any poor person, anyone who appears at the threshing ground receives his due.

The magnificent generosity of the harvest season enables the farmer to purchase the goodwill, credit, and protection that will enable him to carry on long after his grain storage bins are empty and long after the generosity of the harvest season has been replaced by the bleak stinginess of the man who lives on credit. Most people in Gopalpur are farmers who occasionally supplement their incomes by taking advantage of traditional specializations and privileges. . . .

To fill the gap between reality and the ideal pattern of economically cooperating jatis, there are social and religious obligations. To arrange a marriage, to set up the doorway of a new house, to stage a drama, or to hold an entertainment, the householder must call upon a wide range of jatis. The entertainment of even a modest number of guests requires the presence of the Singer. The Potter must provide new pots in which to cook the food; the Boin from the Farmer jati must carry the pot; the Shepherd must sacrifice the goat; the Crier, a Saltmaker, must invite the guests. To survive, one requires the cooperation of only a few jatis; to enjoy life and do things in the proper manner requires the cooperation of many.

Even in the economic field, cooperation extends far beyond any kind of formal arrangement. Fences, constructed of dried thorny branches, soon deteriorate. When the farmer is away, there is nothing to stop the herdsman from turning his cattle into the farmer's field. When the herdsman is away, there is nothing to stop the farmer from casting stones at the sheep that strays into his field. The belief that jatis are related to each other, like brothers, and that all jatis provide essential services for each other creates a unity within the diversity of jatis. (Beals 1962:39–41.)

SUMMARY

To summarize briefly, production is the organization of raw materials, technology, and human effort in order to produce goods that are culturally desired. Each of the ethnographic examples given demonstrates some particular part of economic production. The totality of these examples shows that there is a wide variety of ways in which raw materials can be taken from the environment with the use of many different kinds of tools. Equally varied are the knowledge and techniques used to extract raw materials from the environment and to fashion them into the products desired by the society. Finally, societies organize the human effort available to them in numerous ways. Universal criteria for the division of labor, such as sex and age, as well as relative criteria, such as inheritance, leadership, physical abilities, and many more, are used to bring about the production of things that are culturally desired by the society. Cooperative labor of three major kinds is recognized as an additional, but more general, way in which societies organize the human effort available: individuals are organized to do the same thing to produce a single item; individuals are organized to do different things to produce a single product; and individuals are organized to engage in different tasks to produce many different items. The particular ways in which such organization for economic production is manifest take on the flavor and the color of the culture in which they occur, as the ethnographic examples clearly show. However, the more general statements made about the organization of economic production are not restricted to a single culture, but are valid, cross-cultural generalizations that can be tested further in a wide variety of cultures and societies.

12

Economic Distribution
and Consumption

INTRODUCTION

Every society acquires—through its own processes of production, through trade, or by some other means—products which must be distributed among its members. Distribution, the second of the major components of economics, is the *flow of culturally desired goods and services*. The channels along which this flow takes place, together with the principles which regulate this flow, constitute one of the most significant aspects of any social system.

Cultural goods and services are never distributed randomly or arbitrarily. They may seem to be, at times, to the untrained observer, but upon investigation specific patterns can always be observed. The necessity for the regulation of distribution is explainable in part as a consequence of scarcity. Limitations upon production and trade result in limits on the goods and services available to any social group, so that individuals cannot claim and utilize such items with complete freedom and without social purpose. Claims upon economic products, as well as their use, are based upon particular rights and obligations held by specific individuals who fill specific structural positions within the society. A description of the channels along which goods and services flow, and the various structural positions involved, is, therefore, a description of the social reality underlying the economic system. A knowledge of the system of distribution helps clarify the social relations and interactions that occur.

While all societies can be described in terms of the distribution of economic goods and services, our emphasis in this chapter, as in the preceding chapter, will be upon the kinds of societies most commonly studied by anthropology. Kinship relations will therefore loom large in our discussion. The rights and obligations involved in distribution are part of the complex of expected behavior associated with structural positions in the kinship systems of the kinds of societies we are describing. The principal flow of products is along kinship lines. This is not to say that kinship does not influence the economics of distribution in societies like our own. As we show below, kinship is an important consideration in United States society in the reciprocal exchange of gifts. However, kinship is of relatively little importance in our total system of exchange, whereas it is the major factor in societies that rely on kinship as the principal means of regulating all social relations.

DISTRIBUTION AND KINSHIP

All hunting and gathering groups rely mainly upon kinship as a determinant of organization, and their organization of distribution is no exception. However, other factors are included as simultaneous indicators of how products should be distributed among members. Bushmen hunters who have returned from the hunt with a gemsbok provide the reader with an excellent example of how kinship relations will largely determine the distribution of this product. Individual members of the hunting band have a definite relationship with the hunters (the producers in this case) which entitles them to certain economic products.

. . . any animal is divided at once by a rigid system of rules, some meat given to each person rather than kept as a communal supply or portioned to families. . . . The gemsbok had vanished. All that remained from the butchering was the pile of squeezed, dry grass from the rumen and a few lumps of feces that the redheaded flies buzzed over. The meat, bones, head, hide, and brushlike tail all now belonged to people, and all the people had carried their portions away. Gai owned two hind legs and a front leg, Tsetchwe had meat from the back, Ukwane had the other front leg, his wife had one of the feet and the stomach, the young boys had lengths of intestine. Twikwe had received the head and Dasina the udder.

It seems very unequal when you watch Bushmen divide a kill, yet it is their system, and in the end no person eats more than any other. That day Ukwane gave Gai still another piece because Gai was his relation, Gai gave meat to Dasina because she was his wife's mother. After the meat had been divided again in this way and cooked, the cooked food was shared. No one, of course, contested Gai's large share, because he had been the hunter and by their law that much belonged to him. No one doubted that he would share his large amount with others, and they were not wrong, of course; he did. It is not the amount eaten by any person but the formal ownership of every part that matters to the Bushmen. (Thomas 1965:49–50.)

Two variables have operated as criteria for the distribution of economic products within this small Bushmen band: kinship relations and success in production. The successful hunter received the largest share of the meat, but the particular relationship of each person with the other was also a factor—perhaps the cardinal one—determining the amount and the portion of the game they received. Distribution of the type described (1) validates and reinforces particular relationships among members of a particular band and (2) simultaneously recognizes individual effort. Had an individual not been given his proper and expected share of the meat, this would have been a breach of expected behavior and would have resulted in serious disruption of the relationship and of the band. Maintenance and perpetuation of the entire band depend upon this type of distribution, for no single hunter will always be successful, and on the days he does not find game he is dependent upon his relationship to other successful individuals. The individual who fails to meet his expected distributional obligation may very well find himself hunting alone, which means, inevitably, many days without food essential for his survival.

Distribution along kinship lines does not have to be as extensive as that outlined for the Bushmen band; it is often restricted to a particular group, such as the family. Distribution along extended kinship lines is probably less common, in fact, than the type found in our own society, where distribution of products occurs, for the most part, within the residential unit (usually the nuclear family) with minor special or ceremonial exceptions such as marriages or birthday parties. We find a similar situation among the Tiwi of Australia, a society much different from our own.

The Tiwi themselves had no doubt about the close relationship between plural marriage and good eating. "If I had only one or two wives I would starve," the head of a large household once told a missionary who was preaching against plural marriage, "but with my present ten or twelve wives I can send them out in all directions in the morning and at least two or three of them are likely to bring something back with them at the end of the day, and then we can all eat." This was a realistic appraisal of the economic situation and it is to be noted that he put the emphasis on the food obtained by the women gatherers rather than that supplied by the male hunters. . . . the Tiwi ate pretty well, especially in the larger households. . . .

Even the smallest households nearly always contained at least one old female veteran of the food quest who knew the bush like the palm of her hand and could wrestle some food out of the most inhospitable district. The only households that ever went hungry . . . were the small households of only one or two wives, especially if both wives were young and inexperienced or young and flighty or both. Such households were uneconomic and were rare. On the other hand, the apparently absurd households such as those in which two young men shared their respective elderly mothers as wives, made good economic sense. Any attempt by two such young men to substitute two young wives or even four young wives for the two old ladies would have drastically reduced the standard of living of the household. When young wives arrived in Tiwi households they were not regarded as replacements for the old crones but joined as reinforcements and apprentices to the skilled workers—the veterans. The sexual aspects of marriage were necessarily subordinated to the housekeeping or food-production aspects, which is why in the previous section we spoke of every young man laying the foundation of his household by marrying an elderly widow usually long before there was any young wife in sight.

Since the bigger the household the more the food it produced for its own consumption, there was a tendency for the smaller and therefore hungrier households to hang around the fringes of the bigger ones. Though every household was autonomous and could camp and collect food anywhere in the band territory in which it roamed, it was rare to find all the households in a band distributed evenly over the available territory. . . .

. . . When the food gatherers returned in twos and threes in the late afternoon, each household would cook and eat at its own fires as a unit, but if they wished, members of the smaller households, in which food returns for the day were probably smaller per capita than those of the bigger households, would "drop in during supper" upon the latter and supplement their own slender meal. Such hospitality was always extended on an individual basis; some member of the bigger household, usually a senior wife, would offer to one of the visitors a piece of meat or a dish of *kwoka* and if rebuked by her husband she would justify her act by mentioning her own kin relationship to the visitor, as if to stress that the kindness was her own individual gesture and did not commit the whole household to friendliness. (Hart and Pilling 1960:34–36.)

Among the Trobriand Islanders, the distribution of economic products along kinship lines is important for the successful maintenance of total family groups. A married woman's brother is responsible for half, or even more, of the economic products she receives. Her husband, in turn, is economically responsible to his sister, and so on. This provides a somewhat different direction of exchange, but is based upon the same concept: distribution of economic products along kinship lines. The fact that a person provides half of the economic support of his sister and her family publicly demonstrates that (1) the brother recognizes the obligation he has and validates the kinship relation he has to his sister and (2) conversely, the female has made upon her brother the claim of kinship as it is manifest concerning economic products. In this situation a man's wife must make the same claim upon her brother and he must fulfill this obligation. Failure to do so would not only be individual deviant behavior, but would upset the entire system of economic exchange among kinsmen who are representatives of family units and whose families depend upon their kinsmen for economic assistance.

The preceding examples reveal an important fact about the economics of many non-western societies: the activities involved in the distribution of goods are not separate and distinct from all other social activities. The reciprocal behavior of giving and receiving is an integral part of the relationships among kinsmen, and serves to validate and reinforce these relationships. To give to or receive from a kinsman is to engage in expected behavior which recognizes and therefore validates the particular relationship. Economics is part of the total complex of behavior associated with kinship relations.

RELATIVE VALUE OF CULTURAL PRODUCTS

The claims made by individuals and groups in regard to cultural products (and, therefore, the distribution of such products) provide some clarification of the value attached to these items. In any society, there is a definite hierarchical arrangement of products according to their value, though this hierarchy of value may be more extreme in one society than in another. Claims will be made most strongly and will be enforced very rigidly when they are for products of high value, whereas claims for products of lesser value will usually be subjected to less rigid enforcement. Cattle in many herding societies of East Africa are of great value and are extremely important for achieving success in many areas of culture. Generally, in these herding societies, cattle are of primary importance in acquiring wives. Wives, in turn, provide additional status and produce children who, if female, will be instruments for the acquisition of additional cattle as a bride-price at the time they are ready for marriage. A fairly rigid repetitive cycle of distribution of economic products prevails in such cases. Cattle and wives are viewed as economic products that have great value, and claims are rigidly pursued and enforced in relation to these products. In fact, kinsmen of a female in such societies who do not set an adequate bride-price expressed in terms of cattle at the time of the woman's marriage negotiations will cast some suspicion upon her economic value and, therefore, upon her desirability. On the other hand, once a payment of cattle has been made to the bride's family, and they are distributed by her father among his kinsmen, her family will maintain pressure on her to make a success of her marriage. In the event of divorce, these valued cattle would have to be returned to the groom's kinsmen. The value placed upon them serves, therefore, to stabilize marital unions.

NON-KIN CHANNELS OF DISTRIBUTION

Economic products are not always distributed according to kinship relations, even in societies where kinship is of great importance. Cooperative fishing among East Indians in Trinidad is an example. A temporary economic group is formed for the purpose of obtaining large quantities of fish which are then dried and stored for future use. The group will include an individual who owns or who has the use of a boat, a person who will row the boat and sometimes fish, and perhaps two more expert fishermen. This group of four individuals is formed for the sole purpose of catching large quantities of fish. Each member has a special task to perform—actual catching of the fish, rowing of the boat to the fishing area and back, or maintenance of the boat during the fishing expedition. The economic production lasts only three or four days. At the end of each day, the fish caught are distributed equally among the four persons involved in production. Each then dries and stores the fish for his future use. Kinship is not a factor in the formation of the group or in the distribution of the products. However, each individual who is a member of the group may, and sometimes does, redistribute his share of the fish according to kinship relations. His father may claim a certain unspecified portion of the fish, and his brothers may do the same. Claims of this type may not always be made overtly, but the individual may feel an obligation based upon his kinship relation to these individuals, and the result is a distribution along kinship lines.

CEREMONIAL OCCASIONS FOR DISTRIBUTION

Economic products are distributed in all societies during ceremonial occasions. Rituals of various types, bringing together kinsmen who are not in daily contact with one another, may provide a person with his only opportunities for demonstrating his kinship relations and for fulfilling his obligations. Particular displays of etiquette may accompany the distribution of economic products. Such occasions as birth, puberty, marriage, and death—i.e., all the major rites of passage in a society— usually require that the sponsor (individual or group) provide at least shelter and food as well as some small token gift for the kinsmen who visit only at these times.

Gift-Giving

Birthday parties, weddings, births, engagement or baby showers, and similar ceremonial occasions in most western societies, and especially in the United States, involve the practice of gift-giving. While many explanations, reasons, and rationalizations are provided by individuals for giving gifts to other persons at these times, the fact remains that the giving of gifts on such occasions is .part of the economic distributive pattern. By giving gifts, kinship, friendship, and other types of relationships are emphasized, reinforced, or validated. The giving of gifts

Gift-giving is almost always one of the ingredients of a wedding. These bedouins usually inhabit the deserts of Asia and Africa. (Courtesy of the American Museum of Natural History.)

constitutes the behavioral fulfillment of an expectation which is a part of an existing relationship. Few persons forego the opportunity to provide their mother or father with some type of gift on Mother's Day or on Father's Day, no matter what their relations with their parents are at other times of the year. On these days, public proof is given that children recognize certain other persons as their kinsmen.

Christmas is of great importance to the economy of the United States, because of the frequency and the intensity of gift-giving that takes place at that time of year. In recent years, many billions of dollars have been spent annually in this country during the Christmas season. One cannot dispute the fact that gift-giving is an important part of the distribution of economic products. Many gifts are given to kinsmen, to friends, or to employees and employers. In each case an existing relationship is specified when a gift is given.

The relationships in gift-giving need not be between specific individuals. At Christmas time, many persons make donations in the form of gifts to agencies who serve the less fortunate or the needy. Each person has a particular reason for providing such economic products to these agencies, but, once again, the fact remains that this too is the behavioral and economic dimension of a kind of existing relationship. In these instances, a person is distributing economic products through gifts to a loosely defined class of persons—other men. In contemporary western society, the concepts involving man's relation to man are of daily importance. Certainly contemporary mass communications media make us aware of this relationship in many different ways, but the relationship is not completely the result of the mass media. The relationship is actually a revival of other concepts that have been present in western culture for many years. The same ideas are found in all humanitarian movements, in many religious codes of ethics, and in many nations' legal, moral, and ethical codes. Man feels a relationship with the generalized category of "mankind," and he frequently validates this relationship through the distribution of economic products. Our growing awareness, in the modern world, of human problems on a world-wide scale, has served to intensify these feelings. Values change and so do the behavioral expressions of these values.

Gift exchange is a significant part of economic activity, though there are individuals who would disagree with such a contention; persons indoctrinated in the values of western culture would assert that gift-giving is not motivated by economic concerns at all. They may believe that gift exchange is a free presentation of goods involving no obligations, and that it is a voluntary and disinterested presentation of products. Yet, ethnographic data overwhelmingly justify an equally valid, though opposite, explanation of gift-giving. This latter explanation is not a new one; it has been recognized for some time and has been expressed at various times in many different ways. One of the most direct examples is cited by Marcel Mauss in the following passage from the Eddas (quoted from Havamal with "Selections from Other Poems in the Eddas"):

> I have never found a man so generous and hospitable that he would not receive a present, nor one so liberal with his money that he would dislike a reward if he could get one.
> Friends should rejoice each others' hearts with gifts . . . , that is clear from one's own experience. That friendship lasts longest . . . in which friends both give and receive gifts.
> A man ought to be a friend to his friend and repay gift with gift. . . . Gifts ought to be paid in like coin. . . . a gift always looks for recompense. (Mauss 1954:xiv.)

This selection from early Germanic literature depicts gift-giving from both a social and an economic point of view. First, it emphasizes the idea that the exchange of gifts is the behavioral recognition, validation, and means for perpetuating existing social relations. Second, it points out that gift-giving or exchange is not a disinterested, voluntary, free presentation of goods, but a part of a very complex network of distribution which is deliberate, interested, and compulsory. Three obligations are involved in gift exchange as part of this total network and are partially responsible for its perpetuation: the obligation to give, the obligation to receive, and the obligation to repay. These obligations are a result of existing relationships and their perpetuation.

Gift-Giving as a Means of Establishing Relative Status

The distribution of economic goods can serve a variety of social purposes other than those of promoting solidarity or good feelings among kinsmen. Sometimes giving a gift can establish the status inequality between the giver and the recipient. Or, it may establish a new relationship in which the giver is clearly superior to the recipient. A very common situation the world over is that of a patron–client relationship which binds a status inferior and a status superior in a complex way. A Guatemalan Indian, for example, may look up to a wealthy *Ladino* as his patron. The patron gives him protection, rents land to him, and occasionally hires him for wages. In turn, the Indian pays for the rental of land and is available to his patron when he needs cheap labor. Rules of etiquette, of course, emphasize who is superior and who inferior. In addition, however, the *Ladino* on occasion will present his client with small gifts which are not to be reciprocated except through increased respect and gratitude. This *noblesse oblige* on the part of the patron establishes his status superiority. Housewives in United States society may have a similar relationship with a long-time family servant.

The recognized phenomenon in United States society wherein friends or relatives try to outdo one another in gift-giving expresses this struggle for superior status in a somewhat less structured way.

The Potlatch. One of the most famous examples of this kind of distribution in the anthropological literature comes from the Indians of the northwest coast of North America, and is called the potlatch. The distribution of economic goods is carried out for the express purpose of shaming one's rivals and correspondingly increasing one's social status. An individual, aided by members of his kinship group, gathers together large quantities of very valuable, socially desired products—fish oil, blankets, symbolic seals, and similar items. When sufficient wealth in the form of these products has been accumulated, he announces his intention of holding a potlatch, and invites other persons who occupy prominent places in the society. He seats them according to their rank at the time of the potlatch and demonstrates to them that he has no

These Kwakiutl Indians of British Columbia are holding a women's potlatch at Fort Rupert. (Courtesy of the American Museum of Natural History.)

regard or concern for these economic products by destroying them through burning, by throwing them away, or by giving them to the invited persons. Each time the individual makes a presentation, he makes a vainglorious speech extolling his own greatness and thereby shames the recipient and threatens his prestige and position in the society. In so doing, he validates or increases his own prestige and position. The only way the recipient of these products can revalidate his position and regain his prestige is by holding another potlatch, giving away more than he has received, and showing the same lack of concern for these very desirable cultural products. Each of these items is of great value in the society, and the more valuable the product one gives away the greater chance he has for increasing his own prestige and decreasing that of the person to whom he gives it.

TRADE

Trade is an important means of economic distribution. Most if not all societies are and have been involved in trade of various types. No society ever exists in complete isolation, and even the most primitive societies were involved in some kind of trade for some product which was valued or culturally desired. Vast trade networks have existed among Australian aboriginal tribes for many years; tobacco, red ochre, and certain woods are among the principal and most sought-after items. The northwest coast of North America was characterized by a large-scale trade network and trading centers prior to the advent of European contact. The Dalles regions along the Columbia River provided a trade center where groups from hundreds of miles distant congregated periodically for the exchange of goods. The Chinook (an aboriginal group occupying the territory on either side of the Columbia River in both Oregon and Washington) were recognized traders of the area and made long trips as far south as the northern coast of California for the express purpose of trade. In fact, a *lingua franca,* also called Chinook, developed which allowed the various trading groups of the area to negotiate for the products they desired.

Trade, of course, means that certain items are produced for the specific purpose of acquiring other culturally desired items. This is not to suggest that vast surpluses of goods are a prerequisite to trade. It means only that persons or groups have made a choice among products which are culturally desirable and which they cannot produce themselves.

Trade, under certain conditions, may actually increase production by providing groups with necessary raw materials that are not available in their own territories. The choice is to stop producing these items or to trade for the raw materials that are necessary for the production of these items.

Trading Networks

The area off eastern New Guinea is noted for its trading "rings"; among these, the network most frequently cited by anthropologists is the Kula of the Trobriand Islanders, made famous in the writings of Malinowski. This network links numerous island communities over an area 200 miles in diameter in the Bismarck Archipelago and involves the exchange of two primary items, shell necklaces and shell armbands. These Kula "valuables" move along a roughly circular route, one item passing from trading partner to trading partner in a clockwise direction, the other item in a counterclockwise direction. The exchange is accomplished in a highly formal, ritualized manner, and the partners who engage in this exchange stand in a special social relationship to one another. Great prestige accrues to a man who secures temporary ownership of especially famous necklaces or bracelets and keen interest follows their movements. However, along with this ritualized exchange a vast amount of exchange in economic products—food and craft articles, in particular —is carried on.

The Melanesian islands of the western Pacific have long been noted for the complex trading activities of tribal peoples. Harding has described an extensive trading system which links together hundreds of communities along a passageway that separates New Guinea from the Bismarck Archipelago:

> Unlike the trading "rings" of Papua, the trade system of the Vitiaz Strait is organized around a few centers. From these centers a small number of traders, in great two-masted canoes, range over an extensive land and sea area. Their voyages connect the islands forming the northern side of the Strait with the mainland to the south. . . . Exchange takes place in markets—traditional meeting places for trade purposes—on the platforms of sailing canoes, in conjunction with festivals, and during the inter-village visiting of trade-friends. The types of articles exchanged number only about three dozen; the social links or trade-

Helmsmen of the Kerema tribe in New Guinea navigate their rafts hundreds of miles among the surrounding islands to trade. (United Nations.)

friendships through which they are exchanged number in the thousands. (1967:4.)

Harding goes on to show that about 150,000 people live within this trade area. There is much regional specialization, some communities producing pots, others wooden bowls, bows and arrows, drums, food, or raw materials.

This example, and that of the Kula, illustrates an important fact about trade at the tribal level of society: the social relations established by trade are as highly valued as the products acquired through the exchange.

ECONOMIC SYSTEMS

Economic distribution is subject to some degree of regularity in society, so that certain types of economic systems and the regularity of economic activities can be isolated by analysis. Not only will this categorization serve to place distribution in a broader context, but it will help to demonstrate the ways in which economic action validates and maintains social relations and social organization. In addition, it will show some of the ways in which economics is linked to other parts of culture (religion, political organization, and the like).

Polanyi (1957:250 ff.) has suggested that there are two major types of economic systems that are meaningful in society: *status economies* and *market economies*. All economic systems can be explained in meaningful terms using these economic types as referents. The bases for the existence of each of these economic types are conceptually different. In both cases, however, explanation of the economic system necessarily involves some knowledge of other cultural systems in the same society. This isolation of economic types requires that the analyst be acutely aware of the culture as a whole. Economic behavior, we have stated, is not separate and distinct from other social activities. A complete analysis must inevitably link economics to other parts of culture.

Status Economies

Status economies are intimately integrated with the total social structure of a given culture. In fact, the activities that occur in a status economy are based largely upon the structural positions that an individual fills: a person's social position will largely determine the economic activities he performs in society. Such economic behavior is part of the complex of expected behavior associated with various structural positions in that society. An individual born into a particular caste, for example, occupies a particular status in Indian Hindu society. Because of his status designation, the probability is high that the individual will perform the major part of his economic activities in accordance with his social status. If he is a member of the *dhobi* caste, his major economic activity will be washing clothes—not officiating at particular ceremonies, or teaching school, or working with leather. Similarly, a *chamar*, because of his caste membership, will be a leather worker rather than a washerman or a goldsmith.

In another society a king may perform certain economic activities based on his social status as a king. He does not engage in the activities of a commoner, just as a commoner does not engage in the economic activities reserved for the status of king. The Swazi, a South African kingdom, demonstrate this very well.

Rank by birth cuts across distinctions of age and sex so that every Swazi does not participate to the same extent in manual labor. Aristocrats and leading councilors are responsible for providing suitable conditions for the success of the efforts of others rather than their own labor. They arrange for specialists to treat the land and seed; they summon men and women for work parties in district and national enterprises; they supervise the feeding and entertainment of workers when a task is complete. They are not, however, exempt from work with their subjects, and most of them perform a certain amount of service for the rulers. On occasion some chiefs have displayed long fingernails with obvious pride, but even the most noble women, including the queen mother, are expected to take part in cultivation. (Kuper 1963:45–46.)

Among the Bunyoro of East Africa, similar distinctions of economic activity occur, based upon the status of the individual as defined by the social structure.

What kind of work do chiefs do? There is a marked difference between the work of the two upper and the two lower grades. County and subcounty chiefs have to spend a lot of time on paper work; returns relating to tax collections, court cases, beer-brewing permits, food crops, vermin destruction, and many other matters have to be prepared and submitted monthly, and an extensive correspondence with superiors and subordinates has to be carried on. The formal hearing of criminal and civil cases in court may take one full day or more every week. All the chiefs are responsible for keeping order in their territories, for apprehending tax defaulters and other offenders, and for seeing that adequate food reserves are maintained. The collection of the annual tax is an urgent preoccupation, and it is common to see a subcounty or parish chief, with table, clerk, and policeman, established wherever money is being paid out—for example at cotton markets or tobacco-buying posts. All chiefs, but especially parish chiefs, spend a good deal of time in the informal settlement of village disputes "out of court."

The two lower grades of chiefs have much closer contact with the people than do the higher grades. Parish chiefs and village headmen have no office or clerical work to keep them at home, so they are constantly moving around among their people. They inspect growing crops, issue permits to brew the popular banana beer, supervise work on the roads and paths, organize and take part in communal hunts of such pests as wild pig and baboon, which do great damage to crops, tell cultivators where and what they should plant, summon people to court, and carry out innumerable other small day-to-day tasks. (Beattie 1960:44.)

Most of the societies we discuss and, in fact, most of the world's societies fall within the category of status economies. Status economies have significant differences, but they all share in common the fact that the social structure will define the economic activities of its participants. *Activities in the status economy are carried out on the basis of the status of an individual as defined by the social structure of the society of which he is a member—his social position will largely determine the economic activities that he performs.*

In addition, status economies are characterized by production for use: the reason for entering into the organization of production is basically to use the items produced. Use, of course, takes different forms— direct consumption, delayed consumption, and trade, among others. This does not necessarily mean that gains, surpluses, and profits are not found in status economies; they can be, depending upon how one defines these terms. However, the reason for production, for deciding to produce one item as opposed to other possible alternatives, is use.

In general terms, two distinct types of status economies have been isolated (Polanyi, et al. 1957), and two additional derivatives based on these major types can be recognized.

Reciprocal Status Economies. One major and distinct type of status economy is the reciprocal status economy. The crucial diagnostic factor is the reciprocal exchange of goods and/or services among *symmetrical* kinship units. General structural symmetry is probably the most frequent type for the successful distribution of goods along reciprocal lines. By symmetry we mean that the units engaged in exchange correspond to, are culturally analogous to, or balance one another. Exchange that occurs between two nuclear families, lineages, or castes within a society exemplifies the distribution of goods among symmetrical kinship units. These units are also structurally equivalent; one nuclear family, one lineage, or one caste is much like another.

Symmetry should not, however, be confused with equivalence. An example is provided by the traditional exchange between African Pygmies and their Bantu Negro neighbors. The Pygmy provides the Bantu villager with meat from the forest in return for vegetable products grown by the Bantu. The symmetrical units in this case are the Pygmy band and the Bantu village. This is cultural symmetry, since the band in Pygmy culture corresponds to (is symmetrical with) the village in Bantu culture. In addition, village families are linked to Pygmy families in a kind of patron–client relationship. These families are symmetrical kinship units, and the distribution of goods actually takes place between these kinship units.

The patron–client relationship that exists among families representative of castes in India provides another example of reciprocal status economic action. Here too, goods and services are exchanged reciprocally among structurally symmetrical units. First, each partner in the relationship is representative of a caste; the flow of goods therefore can be said to be among castes. Second, the specific exchange of goods and services is among family units, who are at the same time the caste representatives in that village. Thus, a member of a barber caste will serve a wealthy land-owning family, cutting their hair and nails, announcing certain ceremonies, and so on. Reciprocally, he receives payments and gifts. The same land-owning family will be the patron in a similar set of relationships with families of other "service castes"—washermen, goldsmiths, leather workers, and so on.

Redistributive Status Economies. A redistributive status economy, the second major type of status economy, is based largely upon the single diagnostic factor of *centricity* (control of a political nature). In redistributive economies, centralized control, usually of a political nature, is essential. Goods and services flow into a centralized point and are redistributed out of this central agency to the society. This may be the physical flow of goods into this central point, but it does not have to be. It may simply be a paper transaction or the recognition of ownership of goods and services in the society. In any case, if goods are to be received and then redistributed, it is crucial that there be a central point with sufficient control to achieve successful economic distribution of goods. There is no necessary equivalence between the payment of goods to the political center (either in amount, frequency of payment, or the population element involved) and the redistributive process *per se.* One individual may produce ten bags of grain on a certain plot of land, all of which will be received at the central point, but then he may receive only one bag of grain for his own needs; another individual in the same society who has not entered into grain production at all may receive three bags of grain. The Inca of Peru provide an excellent example of the redistributive process. In this society, the Sapa Inca (emperor), who was considered as a living deity and the ruler of the Inca people, theoretically owned everything, including the land. He distributed the land to the people in order that they might till it, but then received the produce of the land. The actual farmer received only one tenth of the redistribution of grain from the emperor. The nobility in this society also received their share of the grain even though they were not actually engaged in its production.

This factor of redistribution is one of the primary characteristics of the type of sociopolitical system known as a chiefdom (see Chapter 15). Obligatory payments, very often by peasant farmers, must be made to a chief, a priest, or a king who occupies the center of political control; they may be in the form of tribute to a temple, and may involve both goods and services. Peasant farmers in the early chiefdoms of Mexico (about 900 B.C.) not only contributed their agricultural surplus to the temple priests, but seasonally contributed their labor to the building and maintenance of religious structures. The state (a church-state or theocracy in this case), in turn, provided certain services such as keeping peace within the state's boundaries, and protecting its citizens from attack by other states, building irrigation works, or bringing new land under cultivation.

These same concepts of redistribution occurred in Trobriand society. A Trobriand chief accumulated surplus production in part by marrying the sisters of wealthier men or lesser chiefs. These latter, by Trobriand rules of distribution, were obligated to give a large portion of their own production to their chieftain brother-in-law. This wealth was used to underwrite Kula trading and to support great tribal feasts.

Reciprocal and Redistributive Combinations.   Few societies can be sharply categorized as reciprocal or redistributive. More frequently, societies display both types of status economic action in significant degrees. The two major factors of redistribution and reciprocity can be combined, showing in each combination the major emphasis: the reciprocal–redistributive economy, and the redistributive–reciprocal economic type. This recognizes that both elements are important in defining and organizing the economic activities, but in reciprocal–redistributive economies the ethnographic evidence would indicate that reciprocal economic action was the most significant, whereas in redistributive–reciprocal economies, the greatest significance is placed upon redistributive economic activities.

Such economic categories can be meaningfully combined or associated with other classifications to show the relationship of the various dimensions of culture in particular societies from still another point of view. For example, if these economic types were associated with particular community types, as given by Beardsley, et al. (1955), the general correlation would be as follows:

Community Type (Beardsley)	Economic Type	Ethnographic Example
Free wanderers	Reciprocity	Paleolithic hunters
Restricted wanderers	Reciprocity	Bushman, Yahgan, Semang
Central-based wanderers	Reciprocal–redistributive	Eskimo, Karok
Semi-permanent sedentary	Reciprocal–redistributive	Witoto, Chinook
Simple nuclear centered	Redistributive–reciprocal	Hopi, Creek, Natchez
Advanced nuclear centered	Redistributive	Dahomey
Supra-nuclear centered	Redistributive	Aztec, Inca

This very general correlation of economic type and community type is based essentially upon the *probability of occurrence*, which is derived from the presence or absence of centricity in the case of the redistributive systems and the presence or absence of symmetrical reciprocity in the reciprocal types. Where both occur, the combination is used. Within this group context, it must be remembered that persons who stand in a particular relation to others should behave in a certain way: a complex of expected behavior, frequently reciprocal, forms part of this relationship. Each and every time individuals in such a relationship fulfill this expectation, the relationship itself is validated and simultaneously strengthened. If such action proves to be completely deviant from the expectation that accompanies the status position, then the relationship, by virtue of the real action performed by the individuals involved, fails to validate, weakens, negates, or rejects the relationship.

Market Economies

The other major type of economic system that Polanyi (1957) has recognized is that of market economies. The organization of market economies is significantly different from that which characterizes status economies, for they are not based upon personal relations or status nor upon the social structure. Market economies are highly impersonal organizations and have no significant link with social status as determinants of economic organization. The existence of a price-making market is the crucial determining factor that defines the distribution of goods, as well as the other types of economic activities that occur. An individual participant in a market economy will not be involved in economic activities by virtue of his social status in that society.

While our own society is not characterized as a true market economy, it incorporates many of the significant elements found in such economic systems. One such element is that the individual can and does enter into any type of economic activity he desires, limited, of course, by his personal qualifications. Dependence upon social status for definition of economic activities does not operate in any significant manner and certainly it cannot be said that the entire economy is ordered upon the social structure. An individual born into the socioeconomic category labeled "lower lower class" is sometimes but not necessarily an unskilled worker. In our society, a person's position is partially determined by his economic activity, but the reverse is not true. An individual who is successful in economic activities which yield a high gain or profit is placed in the social category called "upper middle" or "lower upper." No one need remain an unskilled laborer because this was once his social position.

Market economies are further distinguished from status economies by the type of production that occurs. Status economies, it has been shown, are characterized by production for use, whereas market economies are characterized by production for gain. In market economies, *production for gain or profit is the diagnostic motive for entering into production— for allocating resources in a particular way as opposed to other possible alternatives.* Of course, not all producers will in fact make a profit or gain, but this does not negate these as reasons for entering into production. As in a status economy, production is primarily for use, but individuals may realize a profit. In this sense status economies are the reverse of market economies.

The kinds of production that are expected to result in a profit obviously change with time and with the goods that are culturally desired by the members of the society, with the availability of resources, and with the costs of production, among other things. The existence of a price-making market is instrumental in determining which types of production can be expected to result in a profit for the producer.

Market economies are not to be confused with markets or market centers. Markets and market centers exist in market economies, but they also exist in status economies. Peasant communities throughout the world are linked to market centers and market activities of various types. However, market centers and market activities which occur in status economies are not subject to the fluctuations of a price-making market, and the people who participate in such markets are not entering into production for the sole purpose of achieving a profit. Markets in Latin America, for example, are characterized by heavy participation. Vendors come many miles to sell their goods in the market, but many of them come to socialize, not only to make a profit. In fact, it is not uncommon for such vendors actually to suffer an economic loss by their participation in these markets. Traveling from one market to another in Middle America, from week to week, is as much a form of social activity as it is a form of economic activity, if not more so. In these markets, haggling over prices of commodities is another form of social entertainment and the individual who does not engage in haggling with the vendor is thought to be a deviant; he is expected while he fills the

The marketplace in a Guatemalan village reveals an economy where production is linked with *profit* rather than with *status* and personal relations. (Photo by Robert H. Ewald.)

status of buyer to haggle over the price just as the seller is expected to haggle in the opposite way. Buyer and seller in such markets are filling definite social structural positions where more than purely economic motives of profit and loss are involved.

Just as markets and market activities can occur in status economies, so status economic activities can occur in market or quasi-market economies. In fact, such programs as social security, retirement funds of various types (but not all), taxation, and similar heavily centralized activities are largely redistributive activities. Individuals pay money into a fund called social security in the United States; they receive no immediate redistribution of these funds nor do they receive other items in lieu of these payments. But other persons (those who have reached age 65 usually) are the recipients of these monies due to the redistributive system imposed and carried out by the government. However, deferred redistribution of monies is expected by the individuals who send their money to a central point (the government) when they reach the age required to receive similar funds. At that time, other persons, who will not be the recipients, will contribute money to the central point in order for this money to be redistributed. Many of the ideas and programs commonly thought to be associated with socialistic, communistic, or social democratic types of organization, each of which is characterized by a high degree of centricity, are redistributive programs, but they frequently exist (in actual practice) in market or quasi-market economies.

In addition to these redistributive aspects, reciprocal economic activities can also occur in a market-type economy. Gift-giving frequently occurs among symmetrical kinship units (families, kinsmen, brotherhoods) in United States society, as was explained in the section discussing gifts.

As with categorization of all kinds, no one category is ever able to account for all activities that occur within any society or any social group. The purpose of categorization is to show the most frequent, the diagnostic, the characteristic, the most meaningful, or any other kind of behavior considered important for explanatory purposes. Categorization contributes to explanation. Distribution has been placed in a variety of categories employing different criteria to show the reader the various facets of distributional activities in different societies, and the ways in which economic distribution cross-cuts and influences other dimensions of culture in all societies.

CONSUMPTION

Consumption, the third major variable included in our definition of economics, is to a large extent defined and explained by the discussion of distribution. It is the individuals who receive the goods and services who use them, but they use them in various ways. *Consumption is the organization of those individuals or groups in a society who utilize the goods and services produced and distributed.* Consumption is also a social process. In this sense, the organization of consumption is closely linked to and overlaps the organization of distribution. Because of the closeness of consumption and distribution in terms of their organizational aspects, much of the material provided in the discussion of distribution is pertinent and will not be repeated here; the reader should refer to the previous section where necessary.

Immediate and Deferred Consumption

A distinction may be made, however, between direct or *immediate consumption* and indirect or *deferred consumption*. The difference between these two types of consumption is based in part upon the type of goods involved. Goods and services that are consumed directly and immediately are *consumer's goods*. A major portion of production in tribal society is consumed in this way. Goods that are distributed and then placed into production in order to arrive at some other goods are *producer's goods.* There is an intermediate cycle of production and distribution that intervenes between production of producer's goods and direct or immediate consumption. However, the process can be viewed in another way: the producers are the consumers. The goods they receive initially are consumed by them as raw material, in a further productive process; consumption must then be distinguished on the basis of final consumption. If an item is produced, distributed, and consumed in such a way that it cannot or will not be placed back into the productive process, this is final consumption. On the other hand, if an item is received for the sole purpose of being placed into the productive process, it is as yet a factor in production and its final consumption has been deferred. Trade items are an important example of deferred consumption. In trading activities, goods are received by a person from a producer as part of the distributional system. The recipient may, then, place these goods into another distributional system (market exchange or sale). The goods will be received by still another person who will in turn use them. The intermediate consumer, who is actually deferring final consumption, is the vendor, and the final consumer is the person who received the goods and used them in a manner that will not allow them to be placed into production or distribution again. Vendors in peasant societies frequently engage in this type of activity. Individuals who buy or trade with growers or producers for economic products (fruits, vegetables, meats, baskets, and other items) do not use the goods themselves, but take them to the market place to redistribute them to other people who will act as final consumers. A tool or a household good may last many years, but this process of use is its final consumption.

Some goods are never finally consumed. These are usually products that are extremely scarce in a society, that have definite ritual value, or that for some other reason are perpetually distributed and only temporarily consumed. The shell bracelets and necklaces distributed by the Trobriand Islanders during Kula voyages, the copper plates distributed by some of the northwest coast Indian tribes at potlatches, trophies and plaques awarded for various accomplishments in our own society (where the recipients may only retain the award for one year and then must return it so that it can be awarded again to another person), and many other valued, sacred, or otherwise scarce items are examples of goods that are never finally consumed and never will be finally consumed unless the values of the society change radically.

Whatever the type of consumption, the acceptance and use of products constitute real behavior which may be compared with the expectations of the person filling the particular structural position involved. In such instances, acceptance of products is a behavioral fulfillment of social expectations, rights, obligations, and claims. For example, we have mentioned repeatedly that the father is the provider in the nuclear family. Of necessity, this means that mother and children must be consumers. They have a right, an obligation, and an expectation to accept the products which the father provides for their consumption. Failure to accept the father's provisions is deviance from the expectations for mother and children. Similar expectations based upon the fact that an individual is defined as a social consumer are found among members of an extended family, a lineage, or any other group based upon kinship relations. Kinship, however, is not the only determinant of consumption behavior. Any social status defined as consumer or involving the behavior of a consumer carries with it certain behavioral expectations. A buyer is defined by the seller as a consumer, and the former is expected to buy if certain behavioral expectations are met by the seller—if the price is reasonable, the products are considered to be of the proper quality, and so on.

SUMMARY

Consumption, especially in western societies, is frequently thought to be the efficient, non-wasteful use of products, but this conception is not universal. Moreover, what is considered wasteful in one society is not wasteful in another society. The storage of yams in front of a Trobriand house where they are allowed to rot, the destruction of property at a potlatch, or, even in our own society, the total range of conspicuous consumption are examples of what some societies would define as inefficient and wasteful use of products. At the same time, however, such consumption may achieve social recognition and prestige for the consumer. Consumption has multiple functions; numerous results may be achieved when consumers utilize the same product. Yams may be eaten and the result will be satisfaction of hunger. Yams, however, when stored in a pile in front of a house, may result in additional social prestige. Yams may be given to a chief to demonstrate allegiance and fulfillment of certain obligations, thus achieving conformity and fulfilling expectations. Finally, yams may be given to an individual's sister to provide for her family, resulting in the fulfillment of kinship obligations which are a crucial part of the distributional system and the integration of social groups in Trobriand society.

Consumption is obviously linked to the products and services available in the society, as are distribution and production. In turn, these are definitely restricted by the environmental potential (including trade).

In the United States, there are a great number of alternatives available both in what can be produced and in what can be consumed, and by whom. However, many other societies have fewer alternatives available to them, resulting in the organization of the major portion of their economic activities around the minimum consumption necessary for survival. The Bushmen of the Kalahari Desert provide an excellent example of consumption at this level.

In all societies, certain restrictions are applied to consumption. These restrictions are not only based on the limited resources, the limitations of the organization of production or distribution; they are also a result of the values and attitudes found in the society. Certain societies will not consume particular products or services because they are not deemed as desirable, whereas other societies, because they consider the same products as highly desirable, attempt to consume as much as possible. Cultural choices and decisions are important factors in determining what is to be consumed, just as they are important in determining what is to be produced and distributed.

13

Man's Organization of the Supernatural

INTRODUCTION

Man's adaptation to his physical and his social environment has been discussed and explained in earlier chapters. It has been shown that man exploits his environment through the totality of his economic organization. He organizes his human resources according to the principles of kinship, residence, and descent. He formulates particular rules governing the behavior expected of the members of society, creates agencies for the enforcement of these rules, and engages in numerous other activities, all of which are part of man's adjustment to his environment. Religion expresses still another dimension of man's environment—the supernatural.

Man has always been involved with the supernatural, and all societies are characterized by religion of one type or another. Man everywhere relates to supernatural entities, forces, and ideas (or their representations). He performs rituals directed toward them, derives support and confidence from and simultaneously fears these same supernatural entities, and invariably, though in many different ways, he includes the supernatural as an intimate part of society.

The supernatural is intimately integrated into man's daily life and aids him in his secular as well as his sacred pursuits. There is nothing supernatural, however, about man's behavior in the area of religion, in spite of the fact that such behavior includes and focuses upon interaction with phenomena defined by him as "supernatural." Religious behavior remains human behavior and, like all other forms of culture, is based upon man's symbolic capacity. It is subject to description and analysis in a way similar to that of all other types of human behavior. Religious behavior is organized; it is characterized by the necessary and sufficient factors of organization—structure, action, and function—as well as by variation, deviance, and conformity in the area of belief and in the realm of practice.

The particular ways in which man relates to and deals with the supernatural are varied. Men may band together to make offerings to, to appease, to propitiate, or even to oppose supernatural elements. They may use specialists to communicate with or manipulate the supernatural, and they may use the supernatural to rationalize, support, or justify human behavior and organizations. Men may use the supernatural to perform evil directed toward other men, as a protection against such attacks directed toward themselves, or as an explanation for success, failure, and the unknown. Religion and the supernatural (the referent of religion) are an important part of man's culture because they influence man's interaction with man and man's interaction with his environment. In fact, religion influences, to a greater or lesser extent, all other parts of culture in all societies.

WHAT IS RELIGION?

Scholars have been concerned with a definition of religion and its origins for many centuries but, oddly enough, in spite of man's interest, research, and general preoccupation with religion, a widely acceptable definition of religion apparently has not resulted from these endeavors. Some definitions are too limited for the purposes of cross-cultural comparison, others are too biased and reflect the values of a particular religious sect, others are so broad that religion cannot be distinguished from other parts of human culture (except by intuition or as based on the knowledge one has about his own society and culture), and still others combine these shortcomings. So diverse are the definitions of religion, one sometimes feels that religion is all things to all men. The following selected definitions illustrate the range of variation in man's conceptions of religion:

When I mention religion, I mean the Christian religion; and not only the Christian religion but the Protestant religion; and not only the Protestant religion, but the Church of England. (Fielding's *Tom Jones,* Parson Thwackum's dialogue, quoted in Lowie 1948:x.)

———

Religion, [is] the belief in Spiritual Beings. (Tylor 1958b:8.)

———

A religion is a unified system of beliefs and practices relative to sacred things, that is to say, things set apart and forbidden—beliefs and practices which unite into one single moral community called a Church, all those who adhere to them. (Durkheim 1961:62.)

[Religion is] . . . the normal psychological adjustment by which human societies build a barrier of fantasy against fear. And since, like any psychological adjustment, it is born in stress, it is therefore a source of emotion. (Howells 1948:22.)

Religion may be described as a system of beliefs and practices directed toward the "ultimate concern" of a society. "Ultimate concern" . . . has two aspects—meaning and power. It has meaning in the sense of ultimate meaning of the central values of a society, and it has power in the sense of ultimate, sacred, or supernatural power which stands behind those values. Viewed in this way, religion is concerned with the explanation and expression of the ultimate values of a society. . . . (Lessa and Vogt 1958:1.)

Regardless of the diversity of these definitions, they all have two things in common: the supernatural is the major referent (either explicitly or implicitly), and they all involve some concept of extrahuman power which is manifest in different ways. It may well be that these are the only two major diagnostic features of religion in all society, except for the fact that it is man who recognizes the supernatural and extrahuman power, and who expresses his interpretations of it. Without man, the supernatural would not be known to exist, and it is in this sense that religion is dependent upon man for its recognition and its expression. Other scientists express this idea in a slightly more extreme way, indicating that man creates religion *and* the supernatural, and without man the supernatural does not and cannot exist. This more extreme point of view, however, is opposed by the equally extreme idea that the supernatural exists independently of man. It is an ultimate constant, and it is the supernatural that allows man to recognize its existence: man has nothing to do with its creation or its perpetuation. In any case, one cannot dispute the fact that the supernatural exists as a cultural fact and that man relates to it through his religion and is intimately integrated with it.

Religion: An Adaptive Mechanism

Religion is one of several cultural mechanisms by which man adapts to his environment, both natural and cultural. While religion has the supernatural as its major referent, religious concepts and behavior are adaptive to the natural as well as the supernatural world and thus provide some degree of integration between these two "worlds." In fact, it is not unusual to find that societies conceive of the supernatural world as part of the natural world, a view which is different from that found in

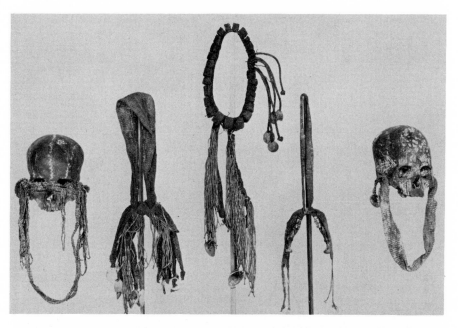

Man's belief in the supernatural is sometimes expressed through the wearing of charms. Shown here are human skull and human bone necklaces worn by natives of the Andaman Islands in the Bay of Bengal. (Courtesy of the American Museum of Natural History.)

many contemporary western nations, where the supernatural is most frequently seen as distinct from the natural environment, though links are recognized between the two. Those societies which are closer to the idea that the natural and the supernatural are a single unified environment, or are two integral parts of a single environment, express this idea by projecting their social structure, and, in fact, much of their culture, into the supernatural world. In this way, they create dependency relationships between the members of the natural and supernatural worlds.

Social Structure and the Hereafter

The Plateau Tonga of Africa are one example of (1) projection of the social structure into the hereafter, (2) the integration and reciprocal dependency that exists between the hereafter and the natural world, and (3) a less intensive distinction between the two worlds. As Colson (1958:397) indicates, the relationships that exist between the living and the *mizimu* (ancestral spirits) ". . . are a projection of those which exist between living persons organized in the kinship system. Mizimu and living members of a kinship group are parts of a single whole, and the ties between them transcend the bounds of time and space." The *mizimu* are extremely important in traditional Tonga culture, and the particular linkage of an individual with *mizimu* is a reflection of his membership in certain kinship groups and of the statuses he occupies in the society. For example, shortly after birth each person receives a guardian *mizimu*, from whom he derives his personality, and who is a symbolic identification of himself with his kinship groups. However, only those persons who have achieved householder status have a house *mizimu*, an additional ancestral spirit.

The integration, dependency, and, in fact, contractual relationship that exist between the living Tonga and the *mizimu* are expressed in very specific terms and can be summarized in four integrated steps that form a cyclical pattern essential to the perpetuation of this system:

1. Living persons propitiate *mizimu*.
2. *Mizimu*, in turn, assure the living of the good things in life (children, good harvests, herds of cattle, and an orderly existence).
3. This, in turn, allows the living to propitiate the *mizimu*.
4. The *mizimu* then continue to exist (the *mizimu* are dependent upon the devotion of the living, through offerings of beer and other items, for their very existence).

Obviously, it is to the mutual advantage of the living and the *mizimu* to maintain this contractual and dependency relationship.

However, deviant behavior occurs for many reasons in all areas of culture, and religious behavior is not an exception. Therefore, the *mizimu* may engage in evil deeds directed toward the living (though one of their main purposes is to protect the living from other evil beings —ghosts), lest the living Tonga forget their obligation to propitiate the *mizimu*. Propitiation by the living is the difference between cultural existence and cultural extinction for the *mizimu*. Also, it should not be forgotten that the *mizimu* are kinsmen of the living.

These reciprocal obligations are not categorically different from the complex of obligations that exist among members of the basic kinship unit in Tonga society, the matrilineal group (which fits the description of clans given in Chapter 10). The members of this group claim descent from a common ancestress (since it is matrilineal), but cannot trace this descent genealogically in numerous instances. The members of this unit have the ". . . obligation of visiting each other when ill, of mourning the deaths of members of each other's families, of helping to provide bride-wealth for the males of the group, of assisting each other to pay fines and damages, of purifying the spouses of those who die, and of finding the people to inherit the positions and mizimu of their dead. In case of need, they should assist each other with food and other gifts" (*ibid.*, 400). The behavioral, reciprocal dependency that exists among the members of this matrilineal kinship unit (because they are kinsmen and stand in a particular relationship to one another and, therefore, expect certain behavior of each other) in regard to the essentials of their life and their adaptation is of the same order as those that exist between the living and the *mizimu;* the *mizimu* are, in fact, members of this kinship group.

Similarly, Newman's description (1965:63) of nature spirits among the Gururumba of New Guinea illustrates the reciprocal dependency, interaction, and contractual agreements between man and the supernatural. Nature spirits, he states:

. . . have lusty sexual appetites, but since there are no female nature spirits they satisfy themselves with human females. The birth of twins . . . is attributed to such a relationship . . . ritual contact with a nature spirit can bring about good health and can increase a person's strength and productivity. Finally, nature spirits are motivated by ideals of reciprocity. One can enter into a relationship with a nature spirit that resembles a contractual agreement. . . . The man provides the spirit with a house, food from each of the gift exchanges he initiates, and information about his gardening activities and the disposition of his pig herd. In return the spirit takes a proprietary interest in the man's gardens and pigs. It protects the gardens against theft and rides herd on the pigs when they are not under human supervision. It may even "doctor" the pigs if they are ill or receive an injury.

Uchendu (1965:102) reports that among the Igbo of southeast Nigeria, reciprocity is the key factor in regulating the interaction that takes place with the ancestors.

Ancestors are scolded as if they were still living. . . . They are reprimanded for failing in their duty to their children, by closing their eyes to the depredations of evil spirits which cause death in the family, cause crop failure, and make trade unprofitable. No elaborate sacrifices are made to ancestors. They are given the ordinary foods eaten in the home: water, raphia wine, and a piece of kola may be all.

The spirits that occur among the Anang of Nigeria are even more specialized in their contractual obligations to members of the society.

In the economic sphere, particular ones promote the safe clearing of the bush, the successful growth of various crops and palm trees, the ability of craftsmen to produce articles that will command good prices in the market, and the prosperity of traders. In the political realm, certain others protect the members of each of the *iman* [a political unit], aid the villages' waging of war, and insure successful reigns for chiefs and community and patrilineage leaders. Some fulfil social functions by fostering reproduction, health, and longevity, by protecting the members of families and each of the secret societies, and by helping people to earn honorary titles. The greater number, however, are assigned religious tasks: to serve each of the types of religious practitioners by maintaining contact between them and the deity, to install souls and fates upon conception, and to observe the behavior of each human being and report it to Abassi for subsequent reward or punishment. (Messenger 1959:280–81.)

Social linkage between the living and supernatural entities is highly frequent throughout the world's societies, though there is great variation in the way in which it is manifest and the intensity with which it occurs. Traditional Chinese society is an example of this. Death of a member of a traditional Chinese family does not in the least remove him as a member. He remains a kinsman, and other kinsmen (the eldest son, in the case of the death of the father) have certain behavioral obligations to ensure his proper and continued existence through propitiation and maintenance of the family shrine (the abode of the family's ancestors). In turn, the ancestors are expected to protect the living and to aid them.

Kinship is a common form of expressing the linkage that exists between the world of the living and that of the supernatural. Among the so-called positive, major religions of the world, kinship terminology and behavior expected of such kin are practiced. Hence, in certain Christian sects, the major supernatural being (God) is frequently referred to as Father, and individuals behave in a way that demonstrates the reciprocal structural position of children. Even more specific use of kinship can be seen in the practice of Catholic nuns, who are symbolically married to Christ (though literally this would constitute an incestuous relationship if it were confined completely to the natural world). Nuns are the wives (an instance of polygyny, though the secular societies characterized by Catholicism largely forbid polygynous relationships) of Christ and therefore cannot marry other beings living in the natural world. Kinship terms and statuses of this type are frequent—Father, Son, Virgin Mother, priests referred to as father, nuns referred to as sister, and many more—but all are examples of man projecting his social structure into the supernatural and creating definite and intimate links between the natural and supernatural worlds. As has been pointed out, in some cases this causes the two worlds to be conceived of as a single environment or as two dimensions of a single environment.

TYPES OF SUPERNATURAL POWER

The particular types of supernatural power that characterize any given religion, and which therefore are found in a society, will be partially responsible for some of the ways in which the supernatural is manifest in the natural world. In general terms, there are two major categories of supernatural power: personal power and impersonal power. The basic distinction between the two is whether the extrahuman power is manifest in and used by a supernatural being, or whether it is a supernatural force independent of such beings. However, the distinctions between personal and impersonal extrahuman power are not always clear-cut, nor are they mutually exclusive, and both can be manifest in a single society. In all cases, while the supernatural is the obvious and explicit referent, man is the implied referent because, first, the power described as supernatural, whether it is personal or non-personal, is measured against the power of man—it is extrahuman power; and second, the very fact that man dichotomizes extrahuman power as personal and non-personal relates it back to himself. Man is the implied referent for the supernatural, however it is conceived and however it is thought to be manifest. This will be shown frequently throughout this chapter and is related to the idea previously expressed: the supernatural world would not be known to exist without man's recognition and expression of it.

Personal Power and Supernatural Beings

The idea of the personal power of supernatural beings is common knowledge in contemporary society. Any person who has read the Bible or who has been subject to religious teachings in the family, Sunday school, or church certainly is familiar with the idea of God. God is frequently described as all-powerful, all-knowing, and the Creator of all things—in other words, He is the possessor of extrahuman, supernatural power. This concept of God is not unique to Christianity, Judaism, or Islam; it is found in numerous religions, though it is not always found alone. However, at least one other society—the Pygmies of the Ituri Forest—expresses very similar interpretations of a god who has such supernatural power. For the Pygmy, the Forest is creator, provider, and protector, and has most of the other characteristics of the major supernatural deities in some of the world's major religions. As in many of the world's religions (though this concept is not expressed as candidly as it is among the Pygmies), the main supernatural entity is dependent upon the members of society.

"The forest is a father and mother to us, . . . and like a father or mother it gives us everything we need—food, clothing, shelter, warmth . . . and affection. Normally everything goes well, because the forest is good to its children, but when things go wrong there must be a reason. . . . when something big goes wrong, like illness or bad hunting or death, it must be because the forest is sleeping and not looking after its children. So what do we do? We wake it up. We wake it up by singing to it, and we do this because we want it to awaken happy. Then everything will be well and good again." (Turnbull 1962: 92.)

Few religions are characterized by a single supernatural entity, and even fewer religions have only one supernatural entity in whom all extrahuman power is manifest. Most if not all religions, including the so-called monotheistic ones, have multiple supernatural entities and, therefore, a distribution of extrahuman power. Frequently, this differential distribution of supernatural power is associated with a ranked hierarchy that adheres to or is similar to the general social structure of the society. The Nuer of East Africa represent such a situation. Among the Nuer, a major supernatural deity, Kwoth, is recognized, but there are multiple refractions (forms) of this major entity, and it is the social structure that determines the existence, function, and power of these multiple refractions.

The Nuer are characterized by segmentation of kinship and political units into a hierarchy of social groups. These groups are most prominently expressed and unified during conflict situations. The groups that unify, or display their differential allegiance *vis-à-vis* other social groups within the same society, depend upon the type of behavior (offense in this case) that has occurred. Where two groups are in direct conflict with each other, different manifestations of Kwoth are invoked by each social group that recognizes a particular refraction as being the property of the group. However, in other instances, where, for example, two groups are involved in a situation in which conflict is imminent but may still be prevented, both groups have a common interest, and so will invoke a single refraction of Kwoth, one to which they may both appeal in order to prevent the impending possible conflict between them.

In other situations, such as storms, drought, famine, and other major catastrophes which affect the total society, an even greater refraction of Kwoth will be invoked, all social groups calling upon a single supernatural entity. The concept of Spirit (Kwoth) can become associated with any social group, structural position, individual, or other unit in Nuer society. The particular social group with which a refraction of Kwoth is associated will provide this refraction with its particular limitations and scope of action; other refractions of Kwoth will be associated with groups higher up in the social hierarchy which will be invoked under other circumstances. The religious hierarchy of the refractions of Kwoth is a mirror image of the social structure of the Nuer. The most general and comprehensive events that occur in Nuer society and which affect all segments of the population are thought to be caused by the most comprehensive and powerful form of Kwoth (similar to our conception of God). However, the more specific the behavioral situation, the more specific, the less stable, and the less universal the refraction of Kwoth.

The multiple supernatural entities found in many religious systems are frequently ordered according to rank and are characterized by varying degrees of power and a specialization of behavior and function. Spirits of various types are found throughout the world: nature, ancestral, guardian, and household spirits; ghosts; minor deities and major ones; devils; gods of war, goddesses of wealth and happiness; creators and destroyers; and many others. Where a multiplicity of supernatural entities occurs, a specialization of behavior and function is described for these supernatural beings in relation to one another and to man and society. There is no society in the world that we know of that does not recognize the basic dichotomy of good and evil and that, therefore, does not have supernatural entities whose main function is to practice good, and others whose main function is to practice evil. *Mizimu* among the Plateau Tonga provide the good things of life for the Tonga as well as protect them from evil supernatural entities (ghosts). In Christianity and Judaism, the devil, along with other more minor supernatural specialists, is engaged in evil, whereas God, angels, and other specialists basically engage in good behavior and are man's protectors against evil. Few supernatural entities whose major behavioral characteristic is good adhere completely to this, for they are able to engage in evil if man does not fulfill his behavioral obligations to them. Thus, the Christian and Jewish God has destroyed men and spread disease; the Tonga *mizimu* can cause man evil in the form of disease and failure to provide the good things of life.

However, it is those supernatural entities whose main purpose is evil that are interpreted as being responsible for "bad" happenings. Frequently, evil caused by supernatural agents takes the form of disease and even death. Ghosts are sometimes cited as being the agents responsible for such results, as occurs among the Nyoro of East Africa (Beattie 1960:76):

"Yosefu's small daughter became ill, and shortly afterwards the son of Yosefu's full brother Yowana became sick too. The diviners were consulted, and it was found that the cause of these illnesses was Yowana's ill treatment of his father, who had died some months previously. Just before his death, Yowana had forcibly dissuaded his (Yowana's) wife from preparing food for him, on the ground that he had his own wife to take care of him. This had angered the old man; he had died without being reconciled to his son, and it was his ghost which was causing the children's illness."

Not all ghosts, however, are considered evil by the society in which they occur. Among the Gururumba, for example, ghosts attack the living because they want something (their bones cleaned), because the living did not pay them the proper respects at a ritual, or for other affronts. Newman (1965:84–85) describes one case where a ghost attacked an individual because he (the ghost) did not like to have his name called. This incident occurred during a hunting expedition, and one man, BoNgire, did not return to the camp when expected.

The men were beginning to wonder what had happened to him when suddenly he burst into camp. He was bleeding at the nose and his body was badly scratched. He rushed to the edge of the campfire where he stood for a moment without saying anything, then quite unexpectedly began shouting wildly and attacking anyone within reach. He was quite agitated and it took several men to restrain him. He was finally subdued and tied to a tree at the edge of the clearing. Judging from this behavior it was decided that he had been attacked by a ghost. . . . BoNgire continued to shout and speak incoherently and no one could communicate with him. Accordingly, the fire was built up a bit, and then smothered with wet leaves to create smoke. BoNgire was then suspended from a pole, in much the same way as when a pig is carried from one place to another, and was held in the smoke until he began to choke and vomit. Finally, after about five minutes of this treatment, he cried out in normal speech to be taken out of the smoke. This signalized that the dangerous contact with the ghost had been exorcised from him and that he was once more normal. A short time later, BoNgire was able to give his own account of what happened. He said, "I was in the forest looking for a tree-climbing kangaroo. I looked up into a tree and saw a nest. I knew there would be a tree kangaroo in it. I climbed the tree next to the tree with the nest. I went up. I kept on going up. When I got to the top I could see there was a tree kangaroo in the nest. I did not have my bow. I called to Usi . . . I said his name, but he did not come. Then I saw Usi's namesake in the tree with me [the ghost of a departed village mate with the same name], and he was red. Usi's namesake said, 'Why do you keep calling my name? I do not like to have my name called.' Then he bit me. I fell out of the tree. He kept on biting me. I could not see, I could not hear."

Man's Conception of Supernatural Beings

Frequently, man conceives of the supernatural beings with whom he interacts as having man's own characteristics. It is not uncommon to find that societies depict supernatural beings in *anthropomorphic* (in the form of man) and *anthropopsychic* (having human mental characteristics) terms. Hence, supernatural beings are thought to have the appearance of man, though in many instances this form is exaggerated since the supernatural being is extrahuman and is characterized by all the mental characteristics of man in extreme form. Supernatural beings, if they are anthropopsychic, can become angry, happy, moody, and in general enter into all the psychological states that are known for man. In addition, because supernatural beings are anthropopsychic, they are able to be cajoled, appealed to, manipulated, threatened, even tricked in some cases. Man views the supernatural in terms of his own characteristics, because the supernatural is based upon man's knowledge of his natural world. This is the only way in which man can depict his ideas of the supernatural. He has no other model. It is these ideas that become incorporated into his culture, to be passed on to future generations as part of the total range of knowledge necessary for members of the society to adapt successfully to the total environment.

The Dusun of Borneo, for example, recognize a male and a female creator pair.

The creator pair are said to reside beyond the limits of the universe—in a duplicate of the human world that is infinitely better where food is more abundant; where there are no diseases, accidents, loss of property; and where there are no arguments, fights, or wars. . . . In a general sense Dusun view their relationships with the creators as one of stability and fairness. . . . To Dusun the creators are all powerful, all pervasive, and the focal point of all known being. Creator beings are felt not to directly intercede in human affairs unless specifically requested by a male ritual specialist; such requests usually are made only with reference to community crises of famine, flood, drought or disease. (Williams 1965:11–12.)

However, man does not always view supernatural beings in anthropomorphic terms. The alternative seems to be to depict supernatural beings in no form at all, though frequently these intangible, invisible supernatural entities are viewed in anthropopsychic terms. Ghosts, spirits, souls, and the like are frequently described as invisible beings who can transform themselves into various forms, including that of man, and who are characterized by man's mental capacities. Therefore, they are treated accordingly—they are fed, appeased, favored, ignored, recognized, forgotten, ranked, and accorded all the behavior accorded to men.

The all-powerful deity of the Anang of Nigeria, Abassi, is conceptualized as being of ". . . gigantic proportions, invisible to human eyes, and . . . lives alone in a compound deep in the sky from which he occasionally emerges to roam about the earth" (Messenger 1959:280). However, the spirits who aid this all-powerful deity in controlling the universe and who act as intermediaries between him and the members of Anang society, are conceived in anthropomorphic terms. "All have normal, human, male and female figures and are visible only to religious specialists in a state of possession."

The Lugbara of Uganda (Middleton 1964:63) ". . . regard Spirit as an all-pervasive power that stands outside men. . . . It is omnipotent and timeless, and can create and destroy men and send them various sicknesses, disasters, and punishments as well as good and prosperity. Spirit is both good and evil. . . . Spirit is invisible and 'in the wind,' and is not personalized, because Spirit created persons and it can hardly therefore be a person itself." However, there is another form of Spirit which is ". . . thought to have the form of a tall man, white in color, cut in half down the middle, and hopping about on its one leg. It lives in streams, bushland, and on mountains, and if seen will kill and eat the ho glimpses it. It is often known as . . . evil Spirit . . . and feared. This aspect of Spirit comes into direct contact with can harm them in many ways."

Animism. Closely related to concepts of personalized power and to supernatural beings is the concept of a vital force or a soul substance which becomes manifest in animate things. It is described most frequently as the substance that gives life to the object; it makes the object animate, and when it leaves the object life is lost. However, it is recognized in some societies as being manifest in inanimate objects also. Sometimes this vital essence pervades all things—it is universal for the society, and in this sense is also closely related to the idea of impersonal supernatural power. Fraser (1966:56 ff.) reports this conception among the Malay fishermen of a southern Thailand village; the vital essence is *semangat*, and is universally present.

Its quantity, and perhaps quality, vary from object to object and from one part of an object to another. However, whether resident in inanimate objects, plants, animals, or men it is the same. . . . Villagers feel that it may leave the body of a person during dreams, and that therefore it is most dangerous to awaken suddenly a soundly sleeping man, for he might wake without his *semangat* which would then have no way of returning. In this same vein, the villagers believe that *semangat* ceases to exist with the death of its possessor, whether animate or inanimate. However, . . . a man may recharge his supply of *semangat* by contact with or, better, incorporation of some highly charged object.

The idea of an animating force separate from the body in which it is manifest has been one of the most stimulating concepts for investigation in anthropology, especially in the early days of scientific anthropology. Tylor, in fact, attempted to explain the origin and the total development of religion, including its universal variation in society, based upon this very idea. Man, according to Tylor, in answering certain basic physiological questions pertaining to death, waking, trance, sleep, and other natural behaviors, isolated the concept of a separable soul which animates the body. This belief constituted for Tylor the minimal basis of all religion—*animism*, the belief in spiritual beings. Animism was thought to be found in all religions regardless of their complexity or simplicity, though it occurs in somewhat different forms in various religions.

Whatever form it takes, the idea of a life-giving substance, a vital essence that is separate from the body, does occur in numerous religious systems throughout the world, including such contemporary religions as Christianity, Judaism, and Islam. The idea of a separable soul or life-giving substance leads to a complex of beliefs about the properties of this substance and its ability to be used and manipulated by man.

Hence, beliefs of soul loss and soul capture are frequently found in such societies, and are the explanation for various illnesses and diseases, and even for death in some instances. The idea underlying this theory of illness, disease, and death is a simple one. The vital essence is that which animates objects such as human bodies. When this substance leaves the body temporarily, the body goes into a sleep or a trance, and when it returns, the body returns to its normal animate situation. However, when the substance leaves the body permanently, the body dies or becomes lifeless. Therefore, a person's enemies will seek to cause an individual to fall ill or die by capturing or leading his soul astray. If the soul is captured or lost for a short period of time, only illness will result for the person, but if the soul is not returned to the body within a specified time period, the body will become permanently inanimate—it will die. Where there is belief in soul loss and soul capture, there must be counteractive beliefs using similar supernatural means for finding the soul and returning it to its proper locus. These ideas are discussed in a later section of this chapter.

Impersonal Power

Not all societies focus completely upon personal supernatural power and personalized supernatural beings. Beliefs in impersonal supernatural power also occur among most human societies: man frequently conceives of a supernatural power that pervades the entire universe but becomes manifest in beings and in things. Such is the case with mana.

Mana. Mana is most frequently associated with Melanesian and Polynesian religious systems, but the concept, called by different names, is found in many parts of the world. *Wakan* and *manitou*, for example, are terms used by the Plains tribes and the Algonquin-speaking tribes of North America to refer to a concept very similar to that of mana. Mana is construed as a supernatural power that pervades the universe. Therefore, it has an existence independent of the members of society, of the supernatural beings which may be involved with the society, and of any objects which are found in the society's environment. Mana, however, can become manifest in persons (natural and supernatural) as well as in things (objects). In this way, the force of mana is localized and becomes a part of man's environment to which he can relate and with which he can interact. An individual member of society may be imbued with mana, just as a rock, a tree, or an animal may contain mana. The presence of mana in these persons or things is cited as the cause for their unusual characteristics. An individual with unusual skill, extra strength, or keen sight; a person of high social status; a rock of an odd shape—all have mana.

Mana is not always constant in its manifestation. It may become manifest in a person or an object, but it does not necessarily remain there, and in this sense mana is characterized by instability and transferability. Ethnographic evidence shows that mana can leave one person and become manifest in another; leave one person and become manifest in an object; leave an object and become manifest in a person; or leave one object and become manifest in another object. Because mana is manifest in an object it does not have to be transferred to other objects only. There is no distinction of mana in terms of "object mana" and "personal mana," just as no distinction is made between good mana and bad mana—it is all mana of the same categorical type. The distinctions that occur are based on the way in which it is used by the person or thing in which it is manifest. Mana can be used for good or bad, but the mana itself is neutral; it is neither good nor bad.

Even though mana is transferable and is not completely constant, once it has become manifest in a person or an object, mana does tend, in certain societies, to remain with certain persons and certain groups of persons to a greater extent than it does with others. This is explained by the structural positions such persons fill. The terms chief, royalty, and religious specialists, for example, are categorical expressions of other-than-ordinary structural positions; they are indicative of special training, power, prestige, or authority. The persons who fill such structural positions, and who are imbued, therefore, with these special qualities, whatever they may be, are interpreted as having mana. In this sense, the differential distribution of mana adheres to the social structure of the society and provides a rationale for the social order. A chief has more mana than a commoner, a warrior more than a non-warrior, a king more than a noble, a noble more than a commoner, a religious specialist more than a layman, and so on. Because of this association of the degree of mana with social structure, all persons who fill these structural positions are thought to have the mana appropriate to their structural positions.

Mana, therefore, explains inequality, success, and failure in society. A Melanesian gardener, for example, who has consistently had a low yield of mediocre yams from his garden, finds an oddly shaped rock and places it in his garden. He believes that this object may have mana. His suspicions are proven correct when, at the next harvest, his yield is much greater and the yams are of better quality. The gardener can explain his success in terms of mana that has manifested itself in the rock which he has placed in his garden.

A person who is normally a mediocre swimmer, canoe maker, or warrior suddenly performs in a superior manner. His outstanding success may very well be explained in terms of mana that has become manifest in him. Mana can also explain social inequalities: it may attach itself in a hereditary fashion to a particular social group, and members of this group are thought to be born with more mana than other members of the society at large. This explanation not only justifies social group distinction, but it also helps to maintain the status quo where one group continues in its unequal position *vis-à-vis* other social groups in the same society. In this way mana tends to be perpetuated in particular social groups—royal lineages and families, warrior groups, religious orders—all of whom pass this on to their descendants through several generations.

Mana is potentially a dangerous force, and the person in whom it is manifested must be able to cope with the amount of supernatural power in him. Otherwise it can cause harm to his person—illness or even death. Further, it can bring harm to those who come into contact with him. Certain persons or things, therefore, must be avoided because of the mana in them. Thus, mana always implies a related concept, *taboo*.

Taboo.   Taboo (Polynesian *tabu, tapu, kapu*) is a word that has been in our English vocabulary since the voyages of Captain Cook to Polynesia in the eighteenth century. The word has taken on popular meanings that do not correspond closely with the Polynesian, although the common connotation of "forbidden" does not depart too far from the original. What is lacking is the sense of sacredness that taboo expresses in Polynesian usage. Anything that possessed mana was sacred and, therefore, was taboo to the uninitiated. For the ordinary person, to touch such things was dangerous. "No Tongan durst appropriate the remains of a superior's meal on pain of a sore throat; the cloak discarded by a Maori chief could not with safety be donned by an attendant. A Mangaia pontiff's body could not be tattooed; his equivalent in Tonga could not be either tattooed or circumcised like other men, since no one was competent to touch him with immunity, and when he was buried by his inferiors, as he inevitably had to be, these were reckoned infected for ten months" (Lowie 1948:79).

The preceding paragraph suggests that royalty in Polynesia were especially imbued with mana and were, therefore, highly taboo. ". . . no one was allowed to touch a superior's head or pass close behind him or eat in his presence. A Hawaiian whose shadow fell upon the king's house or back or who climbed over the royal stockade was doomed: to defy these taboos was tantamount to asserting oneself an equal or superior" (*ibid.*). A king or chief could make a canoe, a garden, or any private property his own by touching it or placing his mark upon it, thereby rendering it taboo. Thus, an entire complex of beliefs in the danger and power of mana served to set certain groups of people apart from others and to maintain and rationalize the idea of inequality.

It might be expected that notions such as these would render all normal intercourse between a king and his subjects difficult or even impossible. This was the case, and special rules had to be devised to protect those who had broken taboos. In Tonga the chief could absolve a person of a breach of taboo. If he were not present, the offender could purify himself by touching a special bowl consecrated by the chief (*ibid.*). In Hawaii, however, the whole system of taboos became so cumbersome and operation of the society so inefficient that by common agreement the Hawaiians rid themselves of their taboos. This was done on a prearranged day in 1819, on a ceremonial occasion when royalty led the way and deliberately broke all the old taboos. When no harm resulted, the Hawaiians took the pragmatic view that there was no longer any need to observe these old customs.

The concept of taboo, however, has been extended in its application, so that taboo means anything that is prohibited for whatever reason, but more particularly it refers to things or persons within the realm of the sacred that have supernatural or religious prohibition. In some cases, prohibitions are applied to items recognized as being potentially dangerous or unclean—menstrual blood and dead bodies. In other instances, however, they are prohibited (they are taboo) because the individual is not able to cope with the force or the presence of the person or thing.

Taboo, in fact, has been interpreted to mean many things. *Notes and Queries on Anthropology* (RAIG 1951:185 ff.), a guide for fieldworkers, points to various aspects of taboo: (1) taboo as negative sympathetic magic (originally Frazer's suggestion); (2) a negative sanction (based on Margaret Mead's interpretation of taboo); (3) a taboo not embodied in a legal code; (4) secular or sacred prohibitions; (5) the way in which man classifies and identifies transgressions; (6) the institutional localization of danger (based on Steiner's interpretation).

All interpretations of taboo have in common the idea that taboo is a prohibition which is recognized and identified by man, and which can be used for a variety of purposes. It may be used to maintain the status quo in society; to explain illness and even death; as a reason for magical acts; as a reason for perpetuating the basic social units in society, such as the family; as a means of identifying danger which allows individuals and groups to deal with such danger effectively; as a mechanism of social control; as a way of integrating supernatural power into the social structure of society; and in many other ways. The particular way in which the concept of taboo is manifest in a society depends upon the culture that characterizes that society. Each society has its own particular identification of prohibited items from which certain individuals must refrain. In all cases, taboos set persons and things apart from other persons and from other things.

One type of religious specialist is the lama, a priest of Buddhism in Tibet and Mongolia. He is shown here with a hand prayer wheel. (Courtesy of the American Museum of Natural History.)

THE RELIGIOUS SPECIALIST AND MAN'S RELATION TO THE SUPERNATURAL

In whatever form supernatural power occurs or whichever supernatural beings occur in a society, man will relate to these things and make use of them. Man uses supernatural beings and power in a variety of ways, but he also invariably makes use of specialists in order to do this most effectively, for all societies regard religious specialists as being closer to the supernatural power or supernatural beings man seeks to use. Therefore, man seeks out the religious specialist to provide his link to the supernatural. Individuals do, of course, relate directly to the supernatural in various ways without the complete aid or presence of a religious specialist, but during most ritual occasions a specialist is called upon to serve in some way.

There are many different types of religious specialists—priests, shamans, diviners, magicians, sorcerers, curers, and numerous others. It would be of little value, however, to list all the kinds of religious specialists that occur in society; it is the specialization of behavior in which these individuals engage that is most important for our discussion.

While such specialists are frequently distinguished from one another, the reader should not be led into the false notion that if a person is one type of specialist he is precluded from engaging in another type of specialized behavior in the realm of the sacred. In less complex hunting and gathering societies, such as the Bushmen, one individual may be diviner, curer, and performer of all rituals necessary for the existence of the group. In a more complex society, however, such as the Aztec or Nyoro, a person may be only a curer, another a diviner, another a priest, another a witch doctor, and so forth.

In general, the specialization of function in religion will be equal in degree to the specialization that occurs in economic or political organization. It must be recognized, of course, that disparate emphasis may be placed upon religion when it is compared with other parts of culture. There have been many societies in which religion has received more emphasis than any other cultural activity, and this degree of emphasis also has varied with time. Often, in more complex societies, which are characterized by a high degree of specialization, religion will not parallel the development in other areas. Some cultural lag can exist, as it does in our own society, where extreme economic and political specialization has occurred along with very rapid technological development. Religion has not kept pace with such developments and has therefore lost some of the emphasis that it has enjoyed at other times in history.

Religious Specialists and Ritual Behavior

The specialist rarely approaches the supernatural world in the same informal way in which individuals may approach one another. His behavior toward the supernatural is almost always highly formalized or ritualized. The term ritual, though often loosely defined, is generally taken to mean behavior of a definite, established, and repetitive type which occurs in relation to the supernatural. It is generally the religious specialist who performs or directs the performance of rituals in his society. On the basis of who participates in the ritual, we may recognize two general types of ritual behavior: *individually oriented* and *group-oriented*. In the past, however, this has led to a false distinction: individually oriented ritual behavior has been labeled magic, whereas group-oriented rituals have been referred to as religion. This basic distinction between magic and religion, which has pervaded the anthropological literature for decades, is a false dichotomy. In point of fact, magical rituals and non-magical rituals can both be individually or group-oriented and both are part of religion as we define it. We treat magic as part of the more general category of religion and subsidiary to it. We can logically distinguish between magical and non-magical aspects of religion, but not between magic and religion.

Magical Activities

Two general types of magical activities are most frequently recognized: *imitative magic* and *contagious magic,* both of which are based upon the idea of sympathetic relationships. These basic and general categories of magical activities were first set forth by Frazer in his classic *The Golden Bough.* Imitative magic is based on the idea that like produces like, and illustrates well the general concept of sympathetic relationships. The general public is probably familiar with the conception of making dolls or images and, by subjecting them to fire or "pin sticking," inflicting pain on the person whom the image depicts. The person himself may be many miles away from the place where "pain" is being inflicted upon the image. Among the Ainu of Northern Japan, for example, "If a man fashions an image of his enemy out of mugwort and buries it upside down with a curse, his victim will pine away as the image disintegrates. Similarly, one may fix an image of an enemy to a tree with nails through the heart and head, or set it adrift on a river in a miniature canoe of rotten wood" (Murdock 1934:182). Imitative magic of this type (image magic) is widespread and has been reported to occur in such geographically diverse areas as West Africa, Haiti, Trinidad, India, England, and the United States.

Contagious magic, the second major category of magical activities, is based upon the idea that something which has once been in contact with a person remains in contact even though it is physically removed. Since a connection between object and person remains, there is some idea of sympathetic relationship: magic can be performed upon the object and the effects will be experienced by the person. A person comes into contact with many things during his daily activities and, where belief in contagious magic prevails, the individual must be careful to make sure these objects are not used to harm him. Probably the most effective items that can be used for magical purposes are organic things (exuviae) that were once in contact with an individual—hair, nails, excreta, an umbilical cord, or any other physical object (hence the term exuvial magic). Other items, however, such as food, paper, rocks, or wood can also be used to perform contagious magic. These items, if once in contact with a person, are burned, stabbed, torn, or in some way harmed in order to cause physical harm to the person, who may be some distance away.

Some magical acts are directed toward an individual's soul, which is part of his physical person, and, in many societies, the most vital and susceptible part. Among the Siuai, for example, Oliver (1955:88) describes "dirt magic," a category of contagious magic, directed toward the individual's soul:

'cian captures part of his victim's soul and destroys it by any one of a
ways. Any part of the victim or anything touched by the victim will
.. this purpose: a hair, a fingernail, a piece of his clothing or ornament,
remains of food partly eaten by him, dirt from his footprint, etc. The most
common methods of destroying the captured soul are to feed the victim's
exuviae to an eel-demon, or to imprison it under the bark of a growing tree, or
to place it in a demon-ridden spot. Another variant is to plant a wild taro in
the victim's footprint; then when the taro plant matures, the magician makes
cuts in stalk and leaves, thereby causing sores to form on his victim.

Not all magical activities reveal the aspect of sympathetic relationships
in such a clear manner, nor do all forms of magic take place as immediately and as directly as those that have been described so far. Some
magical acts are conditional. Among the Manus of the Admiralty Islands, for example, Fortune (1934:65 ff.) describes a conditional form
of black magic (harmful magic) as a way of protecting property. In
such cases, the magic does not inflict harm upon anyone except an in-
truder or thief. The results of such conditional magical spells, used to
protect property, are specialized. "The forms that were known in Manus
were *souru*, which makes a woman barren, *rutchurutch*, which produces
lameness, *tchetche*, which produces a fever, *nam*, which produces stunted
physique, *bwokil*, which produces elephantiasis, and *palit a romot*, which
produces vomiting." An individual can protect his trees, for example,
by placing this conditional magical spell upon them. However, if someone else knows this particular spell, then he will know how to exorcise
(drive out) the spell from the tree and thus will not be subjected to the
results of the conditional spell placed upon it. Anyone who owns a
spell and who uses it must know also how to exorcise it from the tree
upon which it is placed, as a protective measure; if he does not relieve
the spell from the tree, he will not be able to pick the produce from it
without falling prey to the spell that he himself placed there.

Disease, Divination, and Curing

Magic, in its many manifestations, is recognized in nearly all societies
as the cause of evil in the form of illness, catastrophe, and even death.
Extrahuman power is invariably manipulated by a magician to bring
about these results. In this sense, religion provides a readily available
explanation for all kinds of misfortune. Because such misfortune is
caused by a supernatural force, religion must be brought into play to
counteract this harmful force through curing, weather magic, countersorcery, and so on. Before it is possible to ward off harm caused by
supernatural means, it is necessary to determine who is employing the
sorcery. In other words, a good curing specialist must know what kind
of magic is being used against his patient, who is using it, and how to

produce a cure through countermagic. In general, procedures for determining the unknown are referred to as rituals of *divination*.

Disease and other misfortunes are not always the results of intentional magic or of magic at all. The spirit world is often seen as having malevolent intentions. A spirit or deity who has been offended can take his revenge in many ways, including stealing the soul of his victim or causing his illness by some other means. Many societies believe in the existence of witches, certain persons who are born with the power to do evil. This is not magical power. In medieval Europe witches were thought to get this power from Satan, and witches were believed to bring disease to man and animals and to cause storms.

In all cases, the religious specialist is called upon to divine the causes of misfortune and to use magical or other techniques to counteract the evil. Magic can be used for other than evil purposes: to explain illness, for divination, and for curing. Each of these is taken up in greater detail below.

Disease and Illness.   All societies recognize a fairly wide range of illness and disease, and a general or a specific cause is usually associated with each particular type. Very often, the explanation for illness and disease takes the form of supernaturalism. This remains true even when contemporary medical knowledge is known or is available to the members of a society. In India, for example, Lewis (1965:273) notes that although the natural causes of typhoid are known and inoculation programs have been introduced and are somewhat successful, "A goddess, . . . Kanti Mata, is held responsible, and offerings are made to her to release the patient from sickness. Another explanation may be that evil spirits cause the disease, and Kanti Mata drives them out." Explanations of this type, specifying the supernatural as the cause or the explanation for the disease or illness, are extremely common.

Among the Lugbara of Uganda, it is believed that the dead are responsible for sending sickness, and they do so because the living have committed sinful acts; ghosts among the Plateau Tonga, and in some cases *mizimu*, are responsible for illness and disease; ghosts among the Gururumba may cause illness; and pollution of various types is a common cause of illness in many societies. Breach of taboos, contact with too much mana, and many other causes, all of which are in some way related to the supernatural, are used as explanations for the crisis situations of disease, illness, and death in most societies.

At the same time, it is not uncommon to find that illness or other harmful events are explained as being caused by members of society who are using supernatural means, rather than by a supernatural entity. Magicians of various types may be designated as the cause of such situations, and people frequently speak of black magicians (those who engage in evil behavior), though in many instances one does not have to be a specialist in order to perform such acts. Various types of imitative and contagious magic are cited as means by which magicians cause a person to fall ill or die. Sorcery and witchcraft are also identified as common causes of illness.

In many societies witchcraft and sorcery may be practiced unintentionally by a person. Whether intentional or unintentional, the result is the same—harm is inflicted upon an individual. Since witches and sorcerers are recognized as causers of illness, they are also used as scapegoats by societies in assigning causes of evil, whether they are in fact guilty or not. It is very common in many societies for completely harmless individuals to be identified as witches or sorcerers, despite their denials.

It is not to be expected, however, that those who work evil will readily admit it. Therefore, many societies that believe in witchcraft and sorcery will also have techniques for identifying the guilty. Trials by ordeal are very common in Africa to determine whether a person is in fact a witch or a sorcerer. If illness is attributed to witches or sorcerers, then society can effect a cure more readily than in some other cases—essentially, find the witch and release the spell that has caused the illness. Beliefs in witches and witchcraft are widespread, and probably have approached universal proportions at some time in history, if not at the present time.

The "Evil Eye." One does not have to be a witch or a sorcerer to cause illness. Illness, discomfort, or harm may be inflicted upon a person unintentionally by someone who is very close to the individual and who attempts to help the person rather than inflict harm. It is this very concern for the individual that results in illness. The "evil eye," for example, may cause illness and is frequently the result of glances of pride or even of love directed toward an individual. Among the East Indians of Trinidad, it is believed that if a woman nurses a baby in public, exposing her breast, and someone "watches" her breast (after all, they explain, it is an attractive thing) with love, the breast catches *maljo* (evil eye; Spanish: *mal ojo*) and then the child that is being nursed will not take the breast any more but will only cry. The mother's breast will burn and become hard like a rock. The only way to remedy this situation is to have a religious specialist treat it while the child is holding the nipple of the breast in his mouth.

Maljo is not restricted in its effects to humans, but may cause similar difficulties to animals and to plants, and is, in addition, used as an explanation for the cause of certain illnesses. In another case among East

Indians in Trinidad, it was reported that a family had several cattle which started to die suddenly. The family believed that someone had placed a "bad eye" on the cattle, and the only way to stop the cattle from dying was to have the religious specialist cleanse the cattle, and the area in which the cattle stayed, through prayer. Another instance, among the same group, tells of an Indian family who owned a pepper tree which produced the best peppers in the entire area. A stranger came to the family one day, and asked for some peppers from the tree. The family gave permission to the individual to pick some peppers from the tree. Several days later the pepper tree began to die. The family blamed this result upon the stranger who had picked the peppers, saying that he had a "bad eye," and from that day forward the family would not allow this individual near their household. Finally, among these same people, chicken pox is believed to be caused by a "bad eye." In spite of the fact that western medical knowledge is known and available, chicken pox caused by a "bad eye" can only be cured by a traditional religious specialist, according to the people.

In San Antonio Sacatepequez a child became ill with symptoms of chills and vomiting. When she failed to respond to a doctor's care her mother suspected *mal ojo*. It was thought that a stranger, or someone with "strong blood," must have looked at the child. A *curandera* (curing specialist) was called in. Her cure consisted of placing several ingredients in her mouth and masticating them thoroughly—peppers, seeds of the rue plant, cane alcohol, and a large, highly noxious beetle called *ixpin*. A white cloth was then placed over the child's face. The *curandera* placed her finger in her mouth to moisten it with this mixture, and used it to trace the sign of the cross on the child's forehead, arms, trunk, and legs. Finally, she expectorated the remaining potion onto the child's covered face, completing the cure. In this case, as in the preceding one, "evil eye" was regarded as a sickness about which doctors know nothing (see Chapter 17).

Divination. Wherever illness is thought to be caused by supernatural means, divination is frequently employed to ascertain the cause of the illness. Only after the cause has been identified and located can steps be taken to counteract or cure the illness that afflicts a victim. Diviners, although they may be full-time specialists, are most frequently engaged in other activities. Divining may take several different forms, but it frequently involves the use of trance, as among the Malay fishermen of southern Thailand.

Diagnosis is ordinarily accomplished by the *bomo* [a divining and curing specialist] putting himself into a trance, and inquiring of the spirits the exact cause. . . . It is . . . usual that contact cannot be made directly with the offending spirit at this time, but only with a knowledgeable spirit who is in the habit of supplying the particular *bomo* with information. . . . Occasionally, the *bomo's* spiritual informer will indicate the matter that is causing the displeasure on the part of the offending spirit and a cure can be accomplished without establishing direct contact with the spirit causing the disease. (Fraser 1966:58.)

Hand-trembling, according to Kluckhohn and Leighton (1962:210–11), is the most frequently used form of divination among the Navaho. The hand-trembler is usually arranged for by someone other than the ill person, and the ritual of divining occurs in the following general way:

When the hand-trembler arrives he sits down beside the patient. Water is brought, and he washes his hands and arms. He then takes pollen and, working from right to left, puts it on the soles of the patient's feet, his knees, palms of the hands, breast, between his shoulders, on top of his head, and in his mouth. [Additional pollen is placed upon the patient in various places.] As he puts the pollen from elbow to thumb he prays: "Black Gila Monster, I want you to tell me what is wrong with this patient. Do not hide anything from me. I am giving you a jet bead to tell me what the illness of this patient is." This prayer is then repeated for each finger. . . . The whole performance is repeated three more times. While this takes place, no one may leave or enter the hogan or walk around outside. . . . Then a song invoking Gila Monster . . . is sung in four verses. . . . As soon as the hand-trembler begins to sing . . . his hand and arm begin to shake violently. The way in which the hand moves as it shakes provides the information sought.

Wherever divination is used to detect illness, abnormality, unhappiness, or other disruptive states among members of society, it provides man with a specific way in which he can contact the supernatural and deal with it. In this sense, divination is man's way of transferring events from an extrahuman context to a human context in order that he may deal effectively with them. Divination, then, is one more way in which man links together the supernatural and the natural worlds.

Divination, however, is not restricted in its use to locating the causes of disease and illness (whether such maladies are brought about by ghosts, spirits, magicians, object-intrusion, spirit-intrusion, soul capture, or soul loss). It can be used to locate objects that are lost, to determine auspicious days for the performance of certain rituals or to enter into other types of behavior (lawsuits, economic contracts, production, and many more), to ascertain an appropriate name for a child, or to foretell future events for an individual. A Hindu religious specialist in Trinidad, where one of the authors carried out field research, was constantly requested to locate lost bicycles for individuals and frequently proved to be right in his ability to detect the location of such objects. In addition, he was used to determine the proper names for newborn Hindu children, to determine auspicious days for marriages, and to ascertain the proper days for people to make a court claim or to enter into a business venture. Those persons who used this specialist (whose activities certainly were not restricted to divination) were usually very satisfied with his prognostications.

Miner (1965:94) reports the use of marabouts (Islamic religious specialists) by families in the city of Timbuctoo, and likens the selection of a marabout by a family to the selection of a family doctor. One of the activities expected of marabouts is divination, and a marabout ". . . is consulted before arranging a marriage, buying a house or a horse, entering upon a large commercial venture, or any other serious undertaking."

Curing. Frequently, diviners are also curers, as in the case of shamans (religious specialists usually associated with Siberian, Eskimoan, and other far northern societies, but found also in Africa and India and in fact throughout the world), who are known to divine and cure almost simultaneously. Curing, by shamans and other specialists, sometimes involves the use of trances and the exorcism of souls or spirits as well as the expulsion of foreign objects that have entered into the body causing the person to fall ill. The idea involved, obviously, is to locate and rid the body of this foreign matter and the illness simultaneously, thus returning the body to its normal state. Shamanistic cures often involve sucking from the body foreign objects which may have been placed there by other supernatural specialists who have the power to cause harm. Shamans have been reported to extract (through sucking) a wide variety of materials from the bodies of patients—stones, crystals of quartz, worms, even frogs.

One of the authors was told by an informant of an instance where he sought the aid of a specialist who used sucking methods to cure. The informant was plagued with pains in his feet and hands. He explained his ailments to the curer, and after the necessary preparations and one or two visits, the curer extracted, through sucking, several needles from the informant's hands; at the next visit, he extracted needles from the informant's feet and knees. This resulted in the patient's being relieved of his pain and of course increased his belief in the powers of this specialist. The sleight of hand necessary for this kind of cure is a very common part of the shaman's stock in trade.

A different individual reported the cure of a widespread infection of his feet (one similar to what may be popularly called jungle rot) by a similar kind of religious specialist using the same type of method, sucking. The informant had attempted to have other religious specialists cure him and even resorted to the use of modern medicines for treatment, all of which he claimed did not help. In desperation, though he had doubts, he visited a curer who used sucking methods to cure. The curer, after the appropriate preparations, sucked the individual's infected feet, according to the informant's story, several different times. Strangely enough, the disease apparently did not spread to the curer, and the informant was reportedly cured of the infection.

The *bomo* of the Malay fishermen (Fraser 1966) uses exorcism to cure, much of which is directed toward spirits who have been molesting the individual and thus have caused him to fall ill. The *bomo* frequently uses trance to contact the offending spirit and has the alternatives of bargaining, debating, and negotiating with the spirit to stop harming the affected person and to arrive at some favor that the spirit will accept for the cessation of this harmful activity. However, the *bomo* has the alternative available to him, if he is not successful in his negotiations and if he feels confident, of attempting to exorcise the spirit completely by himself without the spirit's consent. Obviously, this procedure entails somewhat greater risk for the patient and for the reputation of the *bomo*. As with other curers, however, the Malay belief in the ability of the *bomo* further illustrates the widespread belief that man does have the ability to control and to manipulate supernatural elements and power to some extent.

Curing does not have to be a matter of directly expelling objects or exorcising spirits, but it may very well involve the use of supernatural agents to help the patient recover. Such aid from supernatural agents is requested by religious specialists or by the patient himself. Thus, in Christianity, God is frequently invoked to help cure persons who have fallen ill or who are involved in a crisis situation which threatens their life. Among the East Indians of Trinidad, ceremonies are sponsored by persons and families, and carried out by Brahmin priests (*pandits*) to achieve these very goals. The Hanuman *puja* (ritual), for example, is performed to acquire from Hanuman (the so-called monkey god) aid in restoring an individual to proper health, or in maintaining good health for the person's entire family; frequently, an individual vows to sponsor one or more Hanuman *pujas* if an ill member of his family becomes well. Very widely in Latin American peasant society, candles and prayers are offered to favorite saints to bring about a cure. In Guatemala, crosses placed at certain spots around a village will be approached in the same way.

No matter what the procedure used for the purposes of curing, a cure may also involve the use of various types of medicines. In contemporary western society, medicine is thought to mean exclusively drugs and prescriptions which are subject to definite regulations for dispensing and production. Elsewhere medicine frequently involves the use of substances or objects imbued with supernatural powers. Potions of various types are employed widely throughout the world, as are charms and fetishes, all of which may be used in curing or in the prevention of illness. The use of magical materials for the prevention or cure of illness is certainly not restricted to the less complex societies; many such uses pervade contemporary western society, even though its members have been educated to accept the idea of more objective medicine and cures. Many if not most of the societies that have been influenced by western culture, either through missionary activity, governmental health programs, or other types of contacts, have been introduced to western concepts of medicine. Very often, modern medical facilities and remedies have been made available to them, but the members of these societies employ both modern and traditional medicine as alternatives in effecting cures. They may, however, reserve certain illnesses for the traditional specialist and his medicines, while others are subjected to treatment according to western means. In some cases, traditional practices have recognized medical value, and not infrequently western medicines and knowledge of disease have been enhanced by contact with these less complex societies. Many drugs and their uses have been learned from these societies (see Chapter 17).

SUPERNATURAL SANCTIONS AND SOCIAL CONTROL

A very large part of all human behavior is religious behavior and is predicated upon the reality of the supernatural world. Because this world is real to man and is believed to affect him in countless ways, for good or for evil, it is essential that he be able to adjust to it or control it. Curing rituals, weather magic, fertility magic, rituals for supplicating or appeasing the spirit owners of game animals, and countless more, give man the comforting illusion of control where scientific and technological control are lacking.

There is a wide range of religious behavior whose immediate intent is to influence the supernatural in some way, but whose ultimate effect is to regulate or control the behavior of individual members of the human group. *Supernatural sanctions* are a major aspect of social control in many of the world's societies. There are many different ways, however, in which supernaturalism enters into the regulation and control of human behavior.

Sorcery and Witchcraft

Sorcery and witchcraft are very important aspects of social control in many societies. Persons may be induced to behave normatively in at least two ways: either through fear of becoming the victim of these practices or through fear of being accused of these practices themselves. Accusations of non-conformity, with the accompanying possibility of dire punishment, have been a powerful force for inducing conformity throughout history, and accusations of sorcery or witchcraft have been unusually common. In Puritan New England, the church fathers had no greater weapon against impiety or any other kind of deviance than the witchcraft accusation and public trial. Their logic seemed flawless. Who has a greater desire to destroy the church than Satan? It is a well known fact that witches are in league with Satan, and that they can assume human form. Therefore, what is more reasonable than to brand as a witch anyone found guilty of impiety? The victim could, of course, confess. In so doing he not only saved his life, but reconfirmed the popular belief in witchcraft.

Many scholars have postulated a relationship between a high prevalence of beliefs in sorcery or witchcraft and a lack of other legitimate social controls. As Swanson (1960:146) has stated: "The widespread use of black magic suggests a serious lack of legitimate means of social control and moral bonds. It implies that people need to control one another in a situation where such control is not provided by means which have public approval." He goes on to show a significant correlation between high prevalence of witchcraft beliefs and a breakdown in political structure and legal processes. This was especially true of the witchcraft hysteria in Europe from about 1500 to 1750. "Small local and regional units were giving way to national states. For at least two centuries the very allegiance of populations and the legitimacy of their governments were in flux." A similar situation, according to Swanson's researches (*ibid.*, 150), was present during the witchcraft trials in Salem, Massachusetts, in 1692.

Rewards and Punishments

Two general types of rewards are most frequently recognized as accruing from the performance of religious behavior: immediate rewards and deferred rewards. Although some anthropologists have tried to correlate immediate rewards with magical activities and deferred rewards with religious activities, the correlation does not apply to all societies and is certainly not exact in many of the world's societies. Deferred rewards may occur as a result of magical behavior and immediate rewards may occur as a result of non-magical behavior. Obviously, combinations of the two result, where a person receives some immediate rewards and some deferred rewards based on a single behavioral involvement. Conditional rewards resulting from magical practices are in fact deferred rewards as occur, e.g., when magical charms and amulets are used.

The relationships among members of many societies and the ancestral spirits which are intimately integrated with them emphasize the idea of reciprocal immediate rewards. Contractual and dependency relationships between ghosts, spirits, and other supernatural beings and the living members of society all involve immediate rewards; these occur among the *mizimu* and the living in Tonga society, and ghosts and the living among the Gururumba, to mention two of the societies discussed in this chapter.

Deferred rewards are most frequently those received at the time of death, or shortly thereafter, and are often based upon the individual's total action during his life. In Christianity, Islam, Judaism, and Hinduism, evaluations or judgments are made to determine whether a person will enjoy the more desirable association with supernatural beings by going to Heaven, by being reborn at a higher level in the social structure of the society, or any number of other rewards; or whether he will be punished in some way for his wrong behavior during his life. Deferred rewards do not contradict the possibility of more immediate rewards during the life of an individual, and in fact it is probable that most societies recognize both deferred and immediate rewards.

Supernatural rewards and punishments, whether deferred or immediate, function in many societies as effective stimuli for maintaining social control. Supernatural sanctions are frequently held out to individuals as reasons not to engage in deviant behavior. The idea is that of a double sanction: if secular means for controlling the deviance of a person are ineffective, then supernatural means will achieve this end.

Many of the complex religions associated with technologically advanced or socially complex cultures have elaborate codes of ethics which are in some way sanctioned by the religious system. In such societies, antisocial behavior of any kind is interpreted as an offense against the supernatural, and the punishment that is held out as a sanction against such behavior may be deferred until the afterlife. However, the rewards that are promised for proper behavior are also deferred. Christianity and Islam are prominent among world religions that hold out the promise of a blissful afterlife, and Hinduism promises rebirth at a higher level of existence.

On the other hand, many religions that offer deferred rewards will also promise immediate rewards and punishments for proper or improper religious behavior. Prayers and offerings for immediate benefits —recovery from illness, protection against danger, success in love or business, victory in battle or an athletic contest—characterize most world religions.

SUMMARY

In all considerations of the supernatural, man must always be seen as intimately involved in and as the object of supernatural action. Supernaturalism has no meaning apart from human societies. It is man, as a member of society, who recognizes and expresses the existence and organization of the supernatural. He alone can describe the characteristics of the supernatural world, how it relates to himself and the natural world in which he lives, and how he, in turn, must relate to it. Concerns such as these motivate and order large areas of human behavior in nearly all societies. Man and the supernatural are the two referents of religion.

14

Unification and Reciprocity of Social Groups

INTRODUCTION

The factors of integration and reciprocity within and among social groups have been treated in various cultural contexts. Integration, for example, has been described in Chapter 7 as the "fit" among structural positions within social groups or among social groups within the larger society. If, for example, the main tasks, activities, or functions deemed necessary for the operation of a society are allocated among the various structural positions and social groups in such a way that the goals of the society are effectively achieved, then there is a high degree of integration among these structural parts. Wasteful duplication of efforts or the lack of structural parts to carry on necessary activities indicates a low degree of integration. Another example, reciprocity, was discussed mainly in the context of economics (where it was described as the exchange of goods and services among social units—families, lineages, bands, villages, and the like) and in the context of kinship, indicating the reciprocal rights and obligations that prevail among kinsmen. It has also been shown that effective integration of a society's parts may be achieved by reciprocal exchange. In this chapter, these concepts are extended to show that many forms of cultural behavior which occur persistently throughout the world's societies are more meaningful when seen as substantive factors contributing to the *unification, integration, dependency,* or *reciprocity* of social groups.

Many cultural examples have already been given to show how unification, integration, dependency, and reciprocity are achieved in social groups. Kinship systems and the complex rules that regulate kinship

377

behavior are important examples of the integration of social groups and of the dependency relations among kinsmen. The distribution of economic products between the member groups of different societies (for example, the "silent barter" between Pygmies and Bantu Negroes or the Kula exchange of Melanesian islanders) illustrates reciprocal and dependency relations.

These and many other examples reveal a fact of major importance about human groups: no social group, whether a subgroup within a larger society or a total society itself, is ever completely independent. In much the same way that individuals within a group are dependent upon one another, social groups always depend on other groups. A lone Pygmy family, for example, could not engage in the mass communal hunts that are an important part of their economy. Economic exchange, division of labor, mutual defense, the exchange of wives, and many other activities imply the dependence of human groups on other groups. Dependency relations may extend beyond the boundaries of single societies, as in the Kula trade, and can unite groups otherwise separated by cultural and linguistic barriers. The particular types of relationships that occur, the ways in which they are established, and the means by which they are maintained and reinforced will largely determine the degree of unification, integration, dependency, and/or reciprocity that occurs within and among groups.

Similarly, no individual in human society is completely independent of other human individuals. On the contrary, each individual is dependent upon numerous other individuals who occupy the various structural positions in his group: father, son, wife, headman, chief, shaman, exchange partner, and so on. Each relationship can be looked upon as a set of mutual rights and obligations in which claims are made and certain behavior expected. The relationships within the nuclear family illustrate this well (see Chapter 7). The dependency relations between individuals are an important aspect of the total organization and the effective operation of all societies.

The various cultural principles of integration, unification, reciprocity, and dependency already discussed do not by any means exhaust the possible list, and in this chapter some universally important cultural complexes that achieve these ends are discussed.

CULTURAL MEANS FOR ACHIEVING UNIFICATION

All societies have certain goals, explicit or implicit, that by common agreement are worthy of achievement. These may be highly abstract—world peace, universal brotherhood, social equality, and so on; or they can be fairly specific—a home and children, education, good relations with a neighboring band, enough to eat, a large herd of cattle, prestige, or the admiration of one's fellows. A complex set of goals constitutes part of the culture of every human society, but these goals are much more than an abstract philosophy—they are socially significant. Because they motivate behavior, and because they are valued (their achievement or maintenance gives the individual something he needs or wants, such as comfort, well-being, prestige, pride), the individual members of the society strive for them in their everyday behavior. The acceptance of common goals and values by the members of a social group makes possible a high degree of homogeneity of social behavior.

Acceptance of Common Goals and Values

The acceptance of common goals and values is basic, then, to membership in any group. The individual who does not accept them, at least minimally, and who does not pattern his behavior after them, is regarded as a deviant. He may even be expelled from his group. The common goals and values of any group are important for that group's unification because they specify the group's behavioral objectives, define the range of social action, and indicate the social limitations of action. The goals a society strives for, and the means for their achievement, are part of the cultural norms and expectations for that society. Striving for them is normative behavior which contributes to the unification of the society, whereas rejecting them is deviant behavior and threatens the solidarity and the unity of the group.

Very often, the requirements for membership in a group are phrased in terms of the acceptance of that group's goals and values. Membership in some groups—family, lineage, clan, caste, or the total society—is acquired by birth, but the individual still must accept the goals that characterize them; this is usually accomplished through the process of enculturation. An individual may join other groups, voluntarily or otherwise, later in life, but membership in these groups also involves a conscious acceptance of their goals and values. A new convert to a religious group, for example, may have to declare publicly his acceptance of a creed that embodies that group's values. A military recruit must accept at least outwardly the goals of military discipline and efficiency.

No human group, whether a kinship unit, a school, a factory, a secret society, or a religious sect, can function effectively and maintain its unity unless there is a minimal acceptance of goals and values. This is a major principle of organization in all human groups and societies. A collection of human individuals without a common set of goals and values is not, properly speaking, a group at all; it is a temporary aggregate of people. It should be noted, however, that even large social aggregates, such as social classes in the United States or England, may be characterized by a distinctive set of values. The American upper middle class, for example, is often described by sociologists in terms of values—education, residence, style of dress, and general standard of living—which definitely govern behavior and restrict social interaction. Families classified as upper middle class tend to socialize and intermarry with families of similar social ranking. Practices such as these serve to isolate and insulate this aggregate from other social aggregates in the total society.

Endogamy and Unification of Social Groups

Some groups in society are characterized by endogamous marriage. Endogamy means marriage within a specified group, territory, or other defined unit. Some restriction of marriage is universal in human society. In all cases a specific unit is the referent for the practice of endogamous behavior, and failure to specify the group in which endogamy occurs makes a statement about endogamy unmeaningful.

Caste Endogamy. One of the most widely known examples of endogamy occurs in the Indian caste system. Persons who are members of a caste group (*jāti*) are required to select their marital partners from the same caste group. Failure to do so may result in action taken by the *panchayat* (caste council) against the individual, and may even result in his being outcasted. The severity of this sanction is obvious, because it removes the individual from membership in the group upon which his life depends. Endogamous caste marriages are supported, reinforced, and rationalized by ritual explanations, which are, in turn, manifest in everyday behavioral patterns. Concepts of physical pollution, for example, are related to the concept of caste endogamy. A person of a higher caste who comes into physical contact with a person of a lower caste (all castes are hierarchically ranked) becomes polluted, the severity of the pollution being dependent upon the relative rank of the two castes. Pollution means that a person is defiled and at that time exists in an other-than-normal condition. In order to restore the person to his proper social position, he must go through a rite of purification and may be subject to the sanctions imposed by the *panchayat,* because he has come into contact with someone lower than himself. Obviously, individuals of unequal rank cannot marry, since continuous physical contact is involved. Similar concepts of pollution apply to the handling of food, and a person of a high caste may take food of certain types only from members of certain caste groups; in all other cases he becomes polluted. One of the duties of the wife according to the division of labor is the preparation of food, and if the wife pollutes the food because she is of a lower caste, the marital situation would obviously be ineffective in terms of the reciprocal dependency among members filling the necessary structural positions in the nuclear family.

Endogamy, with all its attendant reinforcing concepts, such as pollution, helps to set one group apart from all others. It aids in creating a situation of contraposition among groups, and, like any cultural principle that results in segregation among groups, it simultaneously unifies the membership of any single group. It might be argued that there could be no such thing as an in-group or a "we-group" feeling without the existence of "they-groups" to act as foils which stimulate the sense of in-group unity. Taboo, a concept that is closely related to that of pollution (in fact, things that are polluting are taboo, though the sanctions imposed may be of a different sort in some cases), similarly achieves group unity if the taboos are linked to particular social groups and simultaneously set one group apart from all others. This is one of the ways in which royalty or upper-class groups are set apart from commoners or lower-class groups.

Ethnic and Religious Group Endogamy. While it is most rigidly expressed in the caste system of India, endogamy occurs in relation to other social groups throughout the world. Groups that are subjected to slavery, indenture, or some type of conquest situation are known to practice endogamy with a higher frequency than exogamy. Ethnic groups within larger societies also adhere to a pattern of endogamous relationships, a practice which has been an integral part of the history of the United States. Immigrant groups arriving in the United States—Jews, Irish, Japanese, Chinese, and others—have maintained endogamous patterns within their respective groups at least in the first generation and often through several succeeding generations. The actual length of continuing endogamous practices is dependent upon the ethnic group involved and the social circumstances in which it lives. In plural societies (societies with two or more distinct culture patterns) such as Trinidad, Indonesia, Guyana, Surinam, and Fiji, endogamous patterns among ethnic groups—East Indians, "Creoles," Armenians, Chinese, Fijians, and Javanese, among others—are the general rule. Similarly, endogamous marriage is common for religious groups, especially where two or more religious groups are in opposition, or are in any way antagonistic to one another. Wherever Hindus and Muslims, Catholics and Jews, Protestants and Catholics, or Protestants and Jews are found living adjacent to one another, to mention but a few of the possibilities, they maintain some degree of endogamy. It may be very powerful in some cases and less rigidly adhered to in others. Some deviation from this rule always occurs, even where the most severe sanctions are employed. This is an invariable fact of human behavior and occurs even in the caste system of India. It might be noted, as a further illustration of the previous discussion, that where endogamous groups do intermarry, one group may insist that the in-marrying member accept its goals and values or at least enculturate the children in its ways. Despite occasional breaches, endogamy is the most frequent behavior between the religious groups mentioned and is expected behavior.

Concepts of incest, which are culturally defined and expressed through kinship systems—a person cannot, for example, marry or mate with an individual he calls mother, sister, or daughter—also achieve group unification. They set apart certain members of a kinship unit from other members, and in some cases they segment a group and simultaneously unify its parts. Segmentary lineage systems, for example, such as occur among the Nuer of East Africa, are illustrations of segmentation, contraposition of groups, and simultaneous unification among groups and within groups.

Property and Unification of Social Groups

Property is still another cultural means for unifying groups or creating reciprocal and dependency relationships among and within groups. The passage of property to individuals within a particular group according to certain principles of descent—patrilineal, matrilineal, bilineal, ambilineal, or some other means—specifies the unification of the group around certain members who are representatives of different generations within the group. It establishes, through the differential distribution of property, the relative importance of members within social groups. For example, a group that transmits its property along patrilineal lines, such as a patrilineal extended family, will specify either the eldest son, the youngest son, the eldest brother, or another member to receive the major share of the property. This is done in order to minimize the fragmentation of property upon which the total unit depends if it is to keep its present structural form, and if it is to achieve the goals expected of it. Fragmentation of property among several sons at the time of the death of the father will not only spell the end of that extended family, it will make it impossible to form new ones. One of the major problems for the continuance of the extended family in peasant societies has been the shortage and fragmentation of land.

Property may be held in common by a large group such as a clan or a lineage. Greater unity among the members of the group is usually achieved through such common ownership because it provides a tangible item to which members of the group may relate, which they may claim, and to which they have exclusive rights. No single individual in the group owns the total property. It is group property, owned by all members in common.

Where property is used for exchange purposes among groups, a certain degree of integration, unification, reciprocity, and dependency is achieved. The exchange of meat products by the Pygmy for vegetable products from their Bantu neighbors is one such example, and the exchange is reinforced by ritual behavior that occurs between the two groups. The Kula of the Trobriand Islanders is another example of the reciprocal exchange of goods that leads to unification, integration, dependency, and reciprocity among the partners to the Kula exchange. Since the ritual items exchanged are limited and are highly valued, the factors of dependency and reciprocity are intensified to an even greater degree. In fact, all of the cases discussed in Chapter 12 dealing with economic distribution of products demonstrate these same principles. The *jajmani* system in India, the Kula ring among the Trobriand Islanders, the "silent barter" that occurs among the Bantu and the Pygmy, the redistributive patterns that are characteristic of societies or groups that have a high degree of centricity, such as the Inca, Aztec, and in some instances United States society, are all examples of cultural means for achieving group unification.

Members of Society as Property.   Property, of course, includes many different items and is not restricted to material products such as yams, taro, wheat, chairs, or beads. Wives, children, and mothers may constitute valuable property in certain societies. African cattle-herding societies—for example, the Barabaig of East Africa, the Tonga of Rhodesia, the Somali of East Africa, and the Swazi of South Africa—view their unmarried females as property which is at least as valuable as their cattle —the basis of the economy. Females are exchanged for cattle at the time of marriage, and cattle and wives measure a man's wealth in such societies. As one would expect, polygynous forms of marriage are frequent and are directly related to a man's wealth. An individual who can afford the cattle for many wives is considered a wealthy person. Of course, all female offspring that his wives produce will eventually bring him additional cattle, which will further increase and maintain his wealth. His wealth, however, will be decreased by the amount of cattle that he must use to buy wives for his male offspring.

Conceptions of property applied to members of a society are not restricted to females of marriageable age; in some societies mothers who have become widowed are defined as significant property and are indicative of the social and economic wealth of an individual. Among the Tiwi, for example, widows are used as bargaining power in marital arrangements among males (Hart and Pilling 1960:14–30). The Tiwi practice a cross-generational system of marriage whereby older males marry younger females. Since the younger males do not have mates of the same age (the older men have married the younger women), they must resort to marriage with older women. (Polygyny occurs also and is a factor in determining the lack of available marriageable females of a young age for young males.) This is, from the Tiwi point of view, a beneficial situation for the younger males, since it is the older women who are most knowledgeable about exploitation of the environment (the women are the major food producers among the Tiwi, as they are in many hunting and gathering groups). Therefore, a knowledgeable older wife will provide the necessary training of the younger wives whom a man marries as he gets older, and will therefore insure him of a prosperous household. For this economic reason, older women are viewed as valuable property, and they are one of the keystones of group formation at the family and household levels. A young male who marries a young, inexperienced female will not be as successful in creating a prosperous household. The older women are considered a source of additional wealth and power—economic, social, and political.

In India, China, and some other societies, child and infant betrothal occurs as a means of creating bonds between certain social groups. For this reason children (or even unborn children) are also viewed as significantly valuable property. Simultaneously this practice creates rights and obligations among members of social groups that must be satisfied in the future.

Exchange of Marital Partners

Exchange of marital partners creates a dependency relationship among groups in certain societies, based upon the various rights and obligations that attend these contractual agreements. One of the forms of exchange of marital partners reported for Australia occurs when two males contract or agree to exchange sisters for marital purposes. If this situation is adhered to by a significant number of people in the group over a sufficient period of time, then it may become institutionalized and form a definite cultural mechanism for unification and reciprocity among groups.

A more common form of exchange probably occurs among territorial units. Individuals from one community or village may tend to marry persons from one or more other villages, possibly resulting in a complex web of relationships based on reciprocity in marriage. Where social groups or aggregates follow exogamous patterns of marriage on a reciprocal basis, as occurs in the cases of moiety exogamy, certain rights and obligations are created by this exchange of marital partners. In

North India, a complex web of interrelationships is based upon the exchange of marital partners among numerous villages. Clan barrios of Middle America and Africa that practice exogamy with other clan barrios are involved in a similar complex of dependency and reciprocity based upon exchange of marital partners.

Economic Aspects of Marital Exchange. Marital arrangements frequently include the presentation and distribution of property by one social group to another. Where such distribution of economic products occurs, it tends to create direct or indirect relations among certain social groups and also provides some degree of reinforcement and support for the new group being formed by the act of marriage. The customs of bride-price, bride-service, and dowries are three related cultural means for the distribution of property and wealth among members of different groups and for integration among the two or more groups involved. In certain societies, and frequently in societies that practice a polygynous form of marriage, bride-price is an institutionalized phenomenon. Cattle and other products must be paid for the bride-to-be. Arrangements for the payment and negotiations to determine exactly the amount to be paid are usually undertaken by the kinship unit involved and by its representatives (go-betweens). The social unit to which the female belongs will attempt in most cases to arrive at a very lucrative price for allowing her to marry. The greater the price paid for the girl, the greater the prestige of the group and the greater the prestige and wealth of the male and of his kinship group, which pays the bride-price. A high bride-price bestows prestige and wealth upon both groups and both parties involved in the negotiations. In these societies, wives are a form of wealth, as has been explained previously.

In instances where persons and groups cannot afford to pay the price demanded for the girl, or where the economic wealth demanded is not forthcoming for some other reasons, the marriage may still be allowed to take place. Under such circumstances, an alternative to paying the bride-price or part of the bride-price is for the male who is entering into the marriage to perform bride-service for the kinsmen of the bride. Most frequently, the male will perform in this capacity for one year, during which time he will live with the kinsmen of the bride, and then will return to live with his own kinsmen (a system of matri-patrilocal residence). The frequency of bride-service is probably not as great as that of bride-price, but it is an important means for the distribution of economic wealth—in this case, in the form of economic services.

For both bride-price and bride-service, the underlying explanation is that the girl is an economic asset. When she marries, the social group to which she has belonged loses her services, which are economically valuable. The group that receives the girl through the institution of marriage will be gaining economic wealth (services) as manifest in the person of the girl, and therefore the receiving group must pay for her in marriage. There may not be a definite correlation between the actual economic value of any particular female and the bride-price that is paid. Nevertheless, her potential economic value, as expressed by her social group, is the basis for the amount of the bride-price they seek.

The distribution of property received through the bride-price is also indicative of this interest. It is not the bride herself who receives this payment, but her kinsmen. Since the kinsmen of the bride receive the bride-price, they also have a vested interest in maintaining the stability of the marital union. Divorce or some other dissolution of the union could result in the kinsmen of the bride having to return the bride-price to the kinsmen of the groom. Bride-price, therefore, is a stimulus to group stability as well as a cultural means for unifying social groups.

Dowries are composed of economic goods that the girl collects and takes with her at the time of marriage. In very few cases does she actually present this dowry to the groom or his kinsmen; rather, dowries are an economic supplement to the group that is being formed by the marital union. A female who has a large and valuable dowry is recognized as a greater social and economic asset by the members of the interested social groups and is therefore considered a more desirable mate. A dowry, since it is usually collected with the help and contributions of the bride's kinsmen, is a reflection of the social and economic position of the social group of which the girl is a member prior to marriage.

In all such cases—the exchange of property through trade, the exchange of wives, and the flow of property that accompanies these marital exchanges—it must be stressed that valued bonds are being established between different social groups. Families are united with other families, lineages or clans with other lineages and clans, and communities with communities. The net effect is to broaden the social and economic resources, and perhaps the defensive capacities, of each of the groups involved. The exchange of wives, for example, is the principal means whereby hunting and gathering bands unite to enlarge their circle of cooperative ties. Any custom that serves to strengthen and perpetuate these ties will also contribute to the unification and dependency of the larger social units so formed.

RITES OF PASSAGE

Certain periods in the life cycle of each individual are recognized by all societies as critical events. At these times, society gathers together its resources to give recognition to the occasion, usually in the form of a dramatic ritual performance which will assist the individual in his passage through the crisis situation. The four major life-cycle crises which are universally recognized are birth, puberty, marriage, and death. These are very critical times during which the individual is making a transition from one status to another. In many societies, he is thought to be especially vulnerable to supernatural influences during the period of transition and, at these times, may even pose a danger to other members of society. In many tribes, for example, girls are isolated for several days at their first menstruation, for the protection of both themselves and the community. The rites of passage which accompany these events are believed, therefore, to be very necessary for ensuring proper transition.

Phases Within Rites of Passage

Arnold Van Gennep (1960), one of the first scholars to study rites of passage systematically, identified three phases that occur in all rites of passage in all societies: *separation, transition,* and *incorporation.* Since the individual as a member of society moves successively from one significant stage in his life to another—childhood to young adulthood, young adulthood to married status, and so on—he must be ritually separated from each stage, go through a transitional period (though this may be symbolic and require no more than a moment), and then be incorporated into his new social status. These three phases taken together comprise a complete rite of passage and are incorporated into the life-cycle observances of most of the world's societies. Not all societies give equal recognition to all four of these major crisis events nor is each dramatized with equal intensity. Nevertheless, each marks the passage of the individual into a new status position in society, and the proper assumption of his new status is of deep concern to the entire group.

The passage from childhood to young adulthood, for example, is almost universally marked by some kind of ritual observance, usually called a *puberty ceremony.* The individual making this transition is felt to be leaving his childhood behind and is on the verge of full adult participation in his society. At first, full adult status may be marked only by greater economic participation. A boy begins to join the men in hunting or farming; a girl is expected to collect firewood, cultivate a garden plot, and in general carry on a full range of domestic activities. When the time for marriage arrives, these individuals will accept even more crucial responsibilities, those of setting up a household and rearing offspring. Unless the individual accepts the responsibilities (the expected behavior) of his new statuses, the survival and well-being of the group are threatened. Puberty and marriage may both be celebrated by

In the Nicobar Islands in the Bay of Bengal, the puberty ceremony involves the girl burning a chicken alive. (Courtesy of the American Museum of Natural History.)

extensive ritual performances, although in primitive societies the former tends to be more elaborate. The transition from childhood to adulthood is so critical that only the most dramatic of rituals can properly impress on the pubescent boy or girl the seriousness of his or her new responsibilities. Each of these things will be discussed in more detail below.

Society can be seen, therefore, to have a vested interest in both transformations—childhood to adulthood and unmarried to married. The supernatural world is often believed to have a vested interest in these events as well, a fact which is consistent with the incorporation of the supernatural into the social structure of human groups. Departed relatives, for example, may still be treated as kinsmen if death is considered a transition from one status to another. The spirit world is as interested in human affairs as the living are in supernatural affairs. Hence, the supernatural is often invoked to participate in rites of passage and to render additional aid. Sometimes the spirits of the dead are impersonated by the adult males as a high point in the rite of passage, in order to make the spirits' presence all the more dramatic and impressive.

The three dimensions of a rite of passage—separation, transition, and incorporation—need not be given equal weight in all passage rites, as Van Gennep noted. Mortuary rites, for example, often stress the separational dimension of the crisis. Even here, however, the other phases can also be involved. A concept such as purgatory, for example, could be interpreted as a transitional period followed by full incorporation into the supernatural (the afterlife); post-mortem rituals often have the function of easing or speeding the passage of the soul to its ultimate destination; and rites of ancestor worship may aid the incorporation of the ancestral spirit into its new status in the social structure of the supernatural. (This realm is very real to those who believe in it, and rites of ancestor worship are an important aspect of man's adjustment to the supernatural world.)

Marriage, according to Van Gennep, stresses the aspect of incorporation, but certainly the separation of an individual from a non-married status is an important part of such rites. Not uncommonly, in some parts of the world, marriage is preceded by a mock battle in which the bride is forcefully separated from her family, thereby dramatizing her entry into a new status. This separation may be stressed in a homily delivered to the young couple by a respected elder. A period of engagement or betrothal, on the other hand, can be interpreted as a transitional period between unmarried and married status.

Rites performed during or soon after the birth of a child also emphasize the aspect of incorporation. The child is given a name to signalize his acceptance by his social unit. However, in many societies birth is regarded as a transition into life from a previous existence. Concepts of reincarnation, or transmigration of the soul, are widespread and are found among primitive as well as among technologically more advanced societies. One expression of these concepts is the belief that it is spirits who impregnate women and, therefore, enter into the production of offspring. Among Australian aborigines, it was believed that if women walked near certain stones, spirits would enter their bodies, causing impregnation. In the context of such beliefs, spirits who leave the realm of the living by death can be incorporated into the natural world once again through reincarnation.

Rites and the Unification of Social Groups

Whatever forms they take, rites of passage are a major force for the unification and integration of society. These are times when groups unite in a body and, supported by the accumulated resources of all their members, express their unity in the performance of ceremonies. In part, these ceremonies are a symbolic reaffirmation of the unity of the group; memberships and alliances are renewed, reinforced, or formed. Often, for example, such occasions provide the only opportunity for courtship or for widely separated friends and kinsmen to see one another.

On the eve of his circumcision ceremony a boy rides a horse accompanied by dancers and musicians in the Legog village in Indonesia. (United Nations.)

In a very important sense, rites of passage are group undertakings. Marriages among Hindus, for example, are extremely costly ceremonies to perform, and it is not uncommon for kinsmen to contribute economic resources to make possible the proper performance of the ceremony. Entire families may incur, from the marriage of a single daughter, heavy debts which will take many years to pay off. Not only do such rites represent the unity of the group and afford proper passage of the person from one social status to the next, but it is at these times that the prestige and integrity of the social group responsible for the performance of such ceremonies are open for display, tested, and validated. Failure to perform ceremonies that are consistent with these social claims would probably result in the loss of much prestige.

In some societies, rites of passage are huge undertakings that require a special form of organization; puberty ceremonies, for example, are held only when the economic resources are sufficient for their proper performance. Many individuals must stop their normal patterns of activity and must assume new social positions for the purpose of the performance of this rite. For these reasons, puberty rites may be undertaken only every few years, and any individual who has reached biological puberty during this period will enter into these rites at that time. However, not until they have taken part in the complete performance of these rites do individuals actually achieve full adult status in the society and become recognized as adults.

An Example: The Poro. The Poro, sometimes called the "bush school," is a widespread phenomenon in western Africa, though it has been especially well described for the Mano of Liberia. At the time the Poro is held, a total reorganization of the society takes place. Individuals step out of their normal structural positions for the period that the Poro is in session, and new offices, filled by other persons, are responsible for the total operation of the society. The new organization is responsible for enforcing the behavioral rules that apply during the Poro, for constituting courts and agencies of control, for carrying on intertribal relations, political affairs, and even war. The Poro is essentially a school for the initiation of young males into full adult status. Its activities include the necessary instruction in tribal lore, and circumcision. (Among the Mano a similar institutionalized rite of passage called the Sande takes place simultaneously for pubescent females.) Although the main overt purpose of the Poro is the initiation of young males, this is one of the few times that members of various social groups, and even of different tribes, can congregate in a single place at a single time. At these ceremonies, persons display the markings that distinguish them from other social groups and in this way demonstrate the unity of each social group as opposed to all others. At the same time, the unification among groups is displayed by the very fact that they participate in a common Poro. In fact, one of the results of the Poro, since it involves the initiation of members of different social groups, is to create special kinship relations among individuals who have gone through the same Poro together. They are for all practical purposes brothers and have certain rights and obligations in relation to one another. These claims and obligations, based upon common initiation, are maintained throughout their entire lives.

In addition, the Poro is a time when man can interact more specifically and more intimately with the supernatural world. In Harley's terms (1948:349), "The Poro may be thought of as an attempt to reduce the all-pervading spirit world to an organization in which man may participate. It was the mechanism by which man might contact the spirit world and interpret it to people, where men became spirits, and took on godhood."

Initiation schools, where elaborate ceremonies are held on a large scale, where boys go through circumcision, where girls are sometimes subjected to the operation of clitoridectomy (as in the Sande), where men are in closer contact with the spirit world, and where members of society display their differentiation and simultaneously their unification in relation to the social groups present, are certainly not limited to Africa. They were (and still are, to a certain extent among some desert tribes) an important part of Australian aboriginal life.

TOTEMISM

In many societies in the world a special relationship exists between certain social units and some part of nature—an animal, a plant, meteorological phenomena, or even the stars and planets. This relationship can be of many kinds, but very often it takes the form of a belief in the descent of the members of a social unit from a natural phenomenon—the totem object. Totemism is frequently associated with social groups such as clans, lineages, or patrilocal bands, in which the totem plant or animal may be regarded as the ancestor of the group. Totemism need not, however, be associated with kinship groupings; it can be linked with most of the social units, classes, or aggregates in any society. As Radcliffe-Brown (1965) has pointed out, there may be many different kinds of totemism: sex totemism, moiety totemism, and clan totemism, among others. Indeed, even in contemporary society, the naming of athletic teams or military units after animals (e.g., "Eagle Squadron") has sometimes been referred to as a form of totemism. In its fully developed form, totemism is still another institutionalized aspect of culture which contributes to the unification and integration of social groups.

Totemic Groups: The Australian Aborigines

Australian aboriginal tribes are often cited as the best illustration of the practice of totemism. Among tribes such as the Arunta, each local group traced its descent from some mythological natural object—the emu, kangaroo, rock wallaby, witchetty grub, and so on. Further, each local group or band possessed a complex body of mythology which told of the founding of the group by the totem ancestor in the remote past. The most sacred objects owned by any band were its *tjurungas*, flat objects of wood or stone on which were etched a symbolic "map" representing the early wanderings of their ancestor in the remote "dreaming time." All the familiar objects in the landscape were said to be symbolically represented, and recognizable by the band elders. The manipulation of *tjurungas* was a most important part of certain ceremonies.

The possession of a totemic name, a body of sacred lore, sacred objects, and a distinctive set of totemic rituals all serve to give each band its unique identity. Since totemism sets each band off from all other bands, it is a powerful unifying force. In addition, totemism is intimately linked to the rites of passage at puberty among Australian tribes. The initiation of boys into the tribe takes place only at such widely spaced intervals as the available food supply allows. These initiations are the occasion for large tribal gatherings, when member bands assemble from far and wide. It is during the initiation, and not before, that the sacred totemic lore of each band is passed on to the male initiates of that band. So sacred is this lore that if a female or an uninitiated young male is exposed to this knowledge, even by accident, severe punishment (even death) is imposed.

On these same occasions, the members of each totemic group perform the traditional "increase ceremonies" that are part of their ceremonial lore. Very widely in Australia, the members of a plant or animal totemic group have the responsibility for maintaining the numbers and therefore perpetuating the species of their totem. Only if these complex increase ceremonies are performed properly will the plant or animal species reproduce itself. This practice among Australian tribes results in a strong element of group interdependence. A local group cannot ordinarily eat its own totem plant or animal; kangaroo meat is taboo to kangaroo people, emu meat to emu people, and so on. Therefore, the performance of the increase ceremony does not affect the food supply of the totemic group concerned. Rather, it works to the benefit of other local groups. The kangaroo people benefit from the performances of the emu people and of all other totemic groups, who in turn benefit from kangaroo increase rites. The net effect is to create a "ceremonial division of labor," which stresses the dependency relations between local groups. This is a further instance of social behavior, rationalized in supernaturalistic terms, which contributes to integration among social groups through mutual dependence. The meanings employed in totemism may be highly symbolic, but it is through real social action that the symbols are expressed.

It should be stressed, before concluding this discussion, that not all totemism is of the form just described. Indeed, so-called totemic practices take such a wide variety of forms in the world at large that some anthropologists have seriously questioned the propriety of labeling them all with this single term.

SYMBOLIC UNIFICATION OF SOCIAL GROUPS

We stated above that the common possession of a totem and a totemic name provides each band with an important means of unification. Each individual is readily identifiable as a member of his local group through his sharing of the totemic name, and is therefore set apart from other social groups. Very often, totemic meanings are given tangible symbolic expression through the use of pictures, carvings, tattoos, or some other visible representations. These are part of the total complex which serves to set apart one group from another and to promote the sense of identity and solidarity within the group. The members of any group are, of course, related to one another in various ways, but all societies multiply such ties in as many other ways as possible. In theory, the greater the number and the closer the ties that unite the members of a group (in other words, the greater the integration, unification, reciprocity, and dependency relations), the more effectively the group will be able to achieve its common goals and values.

Names and Symbols

Names (including totemic ones) are an important symbolic means of social unification in most if not all societies. They are, in fact, a primary means of identifying, and preserving the identity of, a wide variety of social groups. In a lineage system, for example, certain core members are responsible for perpetuating the lineage, which in turn may serve important functions in society—landholding, the administration of law, the performance of ritual, and so on. In a patrilineage, the identity of the core members is maintained by passing down the lineage name through the male line. In many societies the "family name" is a matter of great concern, and to receive the family name entails serious responsibilities, including the maintenance of certain standards of conduct and the production of male (or female, in a matrilineal system) offspring. The symbolic unification and perpetuation of the group are the responsibility of those individuals who receive the names of the group.

The idea of symbolic unification should not be an unfamiliar one, for symbols of one kind or another are constantly employed in more complex western societies to identify national or subnational groups. The symbols an individual recognizes or manipulates are an important source of information about him, and his sharing of these symbols with other members of his group is an added unifying bond among them. National flags are an example. All of the world's national entities have flags, and each specific flag stands for one particular country. The United States flag, when displayed or exhibited by any group anywhere in the world, immediately establishes the national identity of those who comprise the group. This flag symbolizes a major constellation of values and ideals to which a citizen of this nation is expected to subscribe. The sight of this flag often has the effect of evoking appropriate sentiments—pride, patriotism, national loyalty—in the beholder. Such feelings are consciously stimulated in groups of individuals through rituals such as the Pledge of Allegiance or the singing of the national anthem (another such symbol). United States society, like the society of any other nation, comprises many diverse social classes, ethnic groups, political subdivisions, and other regional, religious, and special interest groups. Powerful symbols of unity are necessary for expressing the national interests that all of these have in common.

Subgroups or subcultures within United States society may have their separate symbols of unification. Each of the 50 states has its own flag, its state flower, and even a state animal. All of these symbolic representations, including the state name, function to achieve the general unification of the group's members and to set them apart from all other equivalent groups. Units within the United States military system, or for that matter in any military system, follow a similar pattern of symbolic representation and unification. Companies, regiments, and battalions use names, sometimes flags, various badges, or even animal mascots, all of which are sources of pride and marks of group identity. Slogans, songs, dress, and behavior are related cultural means for the symbolic representation and unification of one group vis-à-vis other groups.

SUMMARY

Integration, unification, dependency, and reciprocity are related concepts used to describe the characteristics of human groups and social systems. They can be present within groups or among groups to varying degrees. The concepts labeled by these terms are not identical. Integration refers to the degree of "fit" among the various structural components in a social system. Unification is related to real action, for example, the results that flow from the joint participation of a group's members in a religious ritual. The same behavior may, however, contribute to the integration of structural units within the group. Both reciprocity and dependency relations among individuals or structural positions may contribute to integration and unification. The various means employed by a society to achieve these things are always cultural. Most if not all of the regularized, positive cultural behavior (customs, norms) of a society's members will contribute to such achievement. Obviously, as was shown in the discussion of deviance, not all behavior is positive in this sense. Individuals will refuse to engage in reciprocal patterns, to accept common goals and values, to respect symbols of unity, and so on, and such behavior may significantly detract from unification, integration, dependency, or reciprocity. The total organization of social groups, however, along with the behavior that is expected of individuals who occupy the various structural positions, is designed to achieve these qualities to varying degrees.

15

Evolution and the
Organization of Culture

INTRODUCTION

In Chapter 6, a general formulation was presented which showed culture as having evolved through three principal stages or levels. At that point, we were concerned only with the evolution of "culture as a whole," or what Steward (1955) has termed *universal evolution*.

Among modern anthropologists, Leslie White and V. Gordon Childe have been particularly identified with this general or universal approach to cultural evolution. Both are interested in general levels of cultural development, and neither concerns himself greatly with the specific differences between cultures *within* each level. For example, a direct relationship between technology and social organization may be postulated, all factors specific to particular cultures being omitted because the interest here is not in explaining the differences between cultures. Thus it can be stated that societies having a food-collecting technology will ordinarily live in small groups of the type anthropologists call the band, that at most they will achieve a tribal level of sociopolitical organization, and that, generally, such cultures will be meager in their material culture as well. Contemporary or recent examples of this level of culture are the Australian aborigines such as the Arunta or Tiwi, the Polar Eskimo, the Kalahari Bushman of Africa, the Yahgan of Tierra del Fuego, and the Paiute of the western North American plateau region. No two of these cultures are identical in their social organization or in the details of their technology and material culture. What they do have in common is a food-collecting technology and a band level of social organization.

The differences that could be considered, if an alternative method of analysis were followed, would relate not to the technological level, which is the same for these groups, but to specific features in their environments, their histories, or their contacts with neighboring groups. Both White and Childe eliminate such factors as irrelevant to their more general formulation. This is not to say that these men are unaware of the influence of environment on culture. White, for example (1959:49), shows how his simple formula may be modified to read:

$$E \text{ (energy)} \times T \text{ (technology)} \times V \text{ (environment)} \rightarrow P \text{ (productivity)}$$

Thus, in a comparison of the Tiwi and the Paiute, E and T can be held constant, and we can study the effect of their different environments on their respective cultures. But in most of their discussions, both White and Childe take the point of view that for culture in general the environment "averages out" and may, therefore, be treated as a constant.

Julian Steward (*op. cit.*) is among those who have taken the other approach, that the developments in specific cultures through time should be studied. Instead of a single line of evolution, Steward studies the evolution of culture along many lines; his is a *multilineal* approach. He accepts the general validity of the White and Childe universal approach, but finds it too general to answer many of the questions in which he is interested. Steward wants to know why the Paiute, Yahgan, and Bushman differed in details of their band organization. He accepts the fact that civilization developed along parallel lines through highly similar stages in such widely separated world areas as Peru, the Valley of Mexico, the Nile Valley, and the Indus Valley of India, but he is equally interested in the differences between these areas. According to Steward, these differences can be explained only by taking into account other factors, especially the environment; the form taken by any culture in its development is a matter of *cultural–ecological adaptation*.

Sahlins (Sahlins and Service 1960) has noted that the so-called universal approach (that of White and Childe) deals with the emergence of higher forms out of lower, whereas Steward's approach is concerned with the emergence of many particular forms of culture as a result of cultural–ecological adaptation. The first process he calls *general* evolution. The second process, which is analogous to speciation in biological evolution, Sahlins calls *specific* evolution. These are complementary approaches, and both are valid.

Both the universal and the multilineal approaches are used here. We show that, in general, higher forms of social and political organization have emerged or evolved out of lower, but at any level of development there can be significant variations. At the tribal level, for example, are found tribes that lack a clan organization, tribes that have patrilineal clans, and other tribes that have matrilineal clans. These differences cannot be explained by the technological level of cultural development, which is similar for all these tribes, but must be explained by features of the natural and cultural environment.

Any human group must adapt to the environment in which it lives. An important part of this adaptation is, of course, the group's technology (see Chapter 6), which will play a powerful, determining role in the level of social, political, economic, and religious organization that is achieved. However, other factors, such as climate, the nature and distribution of natural resources, and the nature of contacts with other human groups will influence the ways in which specific adaptation is made.

THE BAND LEVEL OF CULTURAL ORGANIZATION

We suggested in an earlier chapter that man, in the course of becoming human, evolved a kind of social organization that uniquely met his various needs. In the course of this evolution, a subhuman mating group became transformed into a human family. This grouping achieved an optimal distribution of mates, and thereby met, if not completely satisfied, man's sexual needs. The unit thus formed provided for the rearing of the helpless infant and for the transmission of knowledge from generation to generation. This same all-purpose grouping became the basis for economic life, with the division of labor by sex being primary. The biological facts of man's greater size and strength, and of woman's periodic disability through menstruation, pregnancy, and lactation cannot be discounted in explaining this economic arrangement. We know of no exception to the rule that the man is the hunter and the woman the gatherer, and we assume this was true in the distant past as well. A family serving these functions has been basic to the society of every historically known group of hunters and gatherers. Seasonally, in some parts of the world, this has been the maximal group. Thus, among the modern Bushman of the Kalahari, when food and water become extremely scarce, individual families go off on their own to maximize their chances of finding subsistence. The same has been observed in some Australian groups, the Paiute, the Central Eskimo, the Yahgan of Tierra del Fuego, and others.

There are compelling reasons, however, why the single family is rarely the maximal group, except in cases of dire necessity. Mere survival is a constant concern of the primitive food collector, and social life itself is a form of adaptation (one shared with many animal species). The basis of human social life, and the reason it is many times more effective than the social life of lower primates, is cooperation. In fact, the whole of cultural evolution may be interpreted as a gradual extension of this important principle.

One of the most significant forms of cooperation among food collectors is sharing. It seems to be a universal principle that when any family has food, no one goes hungry. Most known groups have precise rules governing the division of game animals when any man in the group returns successful from the hunt.

Group Life: An Adaptive Mechanism

Group life is survival insurance against a variety of dangers. An Eskimo family living alone on the Arctic ice sheet would be helpless if the male hunter became seriously ill, and all members of the family probably would die of starvation. Group life also affords protection against human enemies. Primitive hunters do not practice warfare as it is known among civilized people for conquest or dominion over land, but feuding is known. Years of bloody feuding between neighboring bands might be triggered by a murder, by trespassing on one band's hunting land, by the theft of women, or even by suspected sorcery. The Arunta of Australia, like many other societies, never accepted "natural causes" as an explanation for illness or death. A different reason had to be sought, and often the explanation was black magic worked by a member of another band. The suspected sorcerer might be made the victim of "countersorcery," or even be killed in a raid. The advantage of always being surrounded by kinsmen should be readily apparent. Finally, group life provides companionship. As we have seen, only sheer necessity will cause the member families of a group to separate, and they remain apart only as long as necessity dictates. Conversely, when food is unusually abundant, many groups will gather together until the food supply is depleted. Among the Yahgan of Tierra del Fuego the stranding of a whale on the beach might provide such a windfall. Frequently, this becomes an occasion for initiating the young into the tribe, amidst feasting, dancing, music, and general sociability. Many of man's cultural values can be realized only in group life.

It might seem that if group living is desirable, a large group will be better than a small one. There are limitations, however, on group size among hunters and gatherers, and the environment sets these limits in absolute terms. As we have already indicated, population density is controlled by the available food supply, and group size is related to this same factor. If a square mile of territory can feed one person on a given day, then two people together must cover two square miles. The actual size of a hunting band, then, is likely to be a compromise between these factors: the desire for sociability, the need for cooperation and protection, and the scarcity of food resources. Typically, hunting and gathering bands vary about a modal number of 20 to 30.

Residence and Band Composition

To state that a band consists of 30 members does not indicate who these members are or how they are related to one another. Are they kinsmen, or just a fortuitous grouping of families who have agreed to live together? In historical times many known hunting bands have been *patrilocal* or *virilocal*. That is, when a young couple marries, they will take up residence with the social group of the groom. Residence rules are always an important aspect of the social life of any human group and are rarely, if ever, completely arbitrary. What are the reasons for patrilocality among hunting and gathering peoples? First, the young man in question will not marry a girl of his own group, because all girls of his own age will be regarded as sisters. He must, therefore, find his wife among the girls of another band. But what determines where they will set up their residence? One logical possibility, among several, is that they will establish a separate residence (neolocal residence) apart from any relatives. However, for reasons already discussed, their survival will depend upon their alliance with a larger group. What are the reasons for living with the groom's family? From childhood on, the boy will have been trained as a hunter by his father and other older men of his group. He will have learned intimately the topography of the band territory, including game trails and water holes. This knowledge, as well as his familiarity with the land and its resources, and with supernatural dangers, will enhance his effectiveness as a hunter. Typically, it is the pursuit of game that determines a band's movements, and women will collect vegetable foods, insects, and slow game in the vicinity of whatever camp site is selected for hunting. Therefore, in economic terms, the woman gives up less in moving to the group of her husband than the male would sacrifice if *matrilocal* (or *uxorilocal*) residence were the rule. Systematic adherence to this rule of residence results in the composition anthropologists have observed for so many patrilocal hunting bands.

A young man's band will typically include his father and mother, his father's brothers and their wives, their sons and unmarried daughters, his own brothers and their wives, their children, and his unmarried sisters (see Fig. 15–1). As the girls of his age group marry, they join their husbands in other band territories. Therefore, the wives of the male members of his own group come from other bands. This exchange of women by adjacent bands has the effect of extending kinship ties over wide

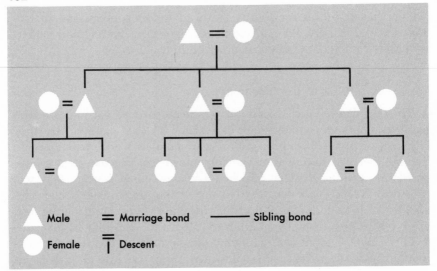

Fig. 15–1. Typical composition of a virilocal hunting band. Three generations are represented in this conventional kinship diagram. The top level is the grandparental. Each of the three sons, at the second level, is depicted as having a wife, who would have married in from another band. Their children, at the lowest level, include unmarried daughters, unmarried sons, and married sons with their wives from the outside.

geographical areas and has intrinsic survival value in times of extreme need.

Types of Band Organization

A number of types of bands can be identified with respect to their freedom of movement or territoriality, which in turn relates to the nature of the food supply. Beardsley et al. (1955) recognize three types of communities [wandering bands] using this criterion.

The Free Wandering Community. This type of band moves about frequently and without restriction; the nature of its wandering is dependent only upon the availability of food resources. This kind of "open territoriality" becomes necessary when the food supply in any area fluctuates so much from year to year that a band confined to that territory would frequently face starvation. According to Beardsley, there is archaeological evidence for this pattern in the Old World Paleolithic and also in the so-called Clovis culture of western North America (c. 10,000 B.C.). He gives no ethnographic examples for this type, but Sahlins (1959:190) describes a condition of non-existent territoriality and gives as modern examples the Shoshoni of the Great Basin region of the western United States and the Eskimo.

The Restricted Wandering Community. In this type of community the people wander about within a restricted area defined as their own. They have exclusive rights to its products and defend it against trespassers. This is restricted territoriality. Archaeologically, this community type is represented at certain Mesolithic sites in Europe and also at the earliest sites of human occupation in North America. Modern ethnographic examples include the Yahgan, the Bushmen, and the Semang of Malaysia. Sahlins adds to this list most of the Australians and the Ona, northern neighbors of the Yahgan. Relative dependability of food supply from year to year is the important factor permitting this kind of territorial occupation.

The Central-Based Wandering Community. In this community the people spend part of each year wandering and the balance of the year at a central base to which they may or may not return the next year. A seasonal abundance or scarcity of food contributes to this pattern. According to Sahlins (*ibid.*), "Local groups of Central Kalahari Bushmen . . . remain fixed in territories focused around water holes during the dry season; whereas, in the rainy season, such groups mingle and hunt together." Beardsley does not include the Bushmen in this category, but does list the Eskimo and the Maritime Chukchee of northeast Asia. Thus, while there is much correspondence between Beardsley's three community types and Sahlins' three types of territoriality, there is not complete agreement in the assignment of ethnographic types to these categories.

THE TRIBAL LEVEL OF CULTURAL ORGANIZATION

The tribal level [*] of society evolved out of the band level as a response to increased population density, made possible by either a very rich natural environment (in a relatively few instances, hunters and gatherers have achieved this level) or a technological revolution (farming, animal domestication, or some combination of these two with continued food collecting). Whereas at the band level groups are small, scattered, and loosely tied together through marriage and kinship, the tribal form of organization serves to integrate a denser population, and

---

[*] Service's (1962:110–42) description of this level of organization provides the basis for much of our discussion.

larger and more numerous groups. Characteristically such groups are more highly organized, internally structured, and unified by ties that are more numerous and to some extent different from those that unite bands.

What specifically do we mean by a tribe? The word tribe is one of the more ambiguous terms in the anthropological glossary and is frequently used to mean a political entity having some form of centralized government. Not uncommonly, westerners, in their dealings with native peoples of Africa, the Pacific, or elsewhere, have assumed the existence of such a level of political organization and have insisted upon dealing with "chiefs" where none exists. What Service (*op. cit.*), Steward and Faron (1959), and others call a *chiefdom* is yet another level in evolutionary development, and will be discussed later. There are ties of a political nature within the tribe, but characteristically this does not take the form of a central leadership.

Segmentation and Sodality

Tribal society is *segmented* * into a number of local groups that maintain geographic separateness but share a common language and culture. Superficially these segmented local groups may look like large bands, but the principles of organization are quite different. A second essential feature of tribal organization is that the segments are united by various bonds, but they fall short of a centralized political structure such as chieftainship. The means by which localized segments are united are called *pan-tribal sodalities* by Service, who defines a sodality (1962:21) as a non-residential association that has some corporate functions or purposes. In contrast with the patrilocal band or the local segment of the tribe, which are residential groups, the sodality is not a group at all. Its members are to be found in a number of groups and, therefore, the sodality cross-cuts residential groups. By way of familiar illustration, the United States is segmented into 50 localized divisions called states. Members of the Republican party, an association which is non-residential and which has certain functions or purposes, are found in all 50 states. The Republican party, therefore, has the nature of a sodality, and because its members are to be found throughout the 50 states, this sodality clearly cross-cuts these other units (the 50 states). This cross-cutting is crucial, for by definition it has an *integrating* effect.

---

* By *segmentation* we mean a division of society into a number of units which are structurally similar or identical and functionally equivalent. Thus, a university may be segmented into colleges or schools, an army into divisions, or a patrilocal band into nuclear families.

The Integrating Function of Sodalities. What is meant by the integrating effect of sodalities? If members of neighboring residential groups are also members of a non-residential association (sodality), this association serves to establish a link between the two residential groups. Among the Cheyenne of the western Plains, for example, the basic residential unit of the tribe was a band or camp (Hoebel 1960:31). In addition to these residential groupings, the Cheyenne in the nineteenth century had seven warrior or military societies, bearing such names as the Fox, Elk, Shield, Dog, and Bow-string. When a Cheyenne boy came of age and was ready to go to war, he could join one of these societies (sodalities). Aside from functioning in war, each society served a police function during the great communal buffalo hunts, when several bands were camped together to form the camp circle. In addition to a name, each society had various insignia, songs, and ritual paraphernalia. Thus, a strong bond united the members of the society. From the individual's standpoint, the fact that another band contained members of his own military society served to establish a relationship, reinforced by feelings of loyalty and friendship, between that band and his. As Hoebel phrases it (*ibid.*, 33): "Cutting across the . . . bands are the sodalities, or clubs, of the warriors. . . . While hunting is a male activity woven into the interests of the family, fighting was an activity institutionalized in the organization of the military societies. The interests of these societies were tribal rather than kin based."

This final statement serves to illustrate what is meant by *pan-tribal* sodalities. When membership extends beyond a single local group to include all or most of the local groups of the tribe, the integrating effect is pan-tribal. By definition, sodalities have a political, or at least quasi-political, function in that they serve to regulate interrelations among the various bands or residential groups.

Variation in Tribal Organization

This definition of tribal society categorizes as tribal many of the world's societies of today and the recent past. Indeed, tribal societies are far more numerous than those of the band level of organization and have been found in all world areas, usually in association with the practice of horticulture, irrigation agriculture, pastoralism, or some combination of these along with hunting and collecting. Tribes are, in short, representative of the technological level attained as a result of the Agricultural Revolution, which made possible a denser population and larger groups, which in turn required (or at least made possible) more complex forms of social organization. Examples of tribes from the recent or modern world, according to Service, include the Hopi and Navaho of the United States southwest, the Bororo and Guarani of South America, the Nuer and Boloki of Africa, the Reindeer Tungus and Samoyed of Siberia, the Comanche and Cheyenne of the Great Plains, the Ifugao of the Philippines, and others. Only occasionally has food collecting (in an unusually favorable environment) permitted a tribal level of organization.

While the Agricultural Revolution (or food collecting in a rich environment) "made possible" more complex social forms, higher productivity does not determine the specific form tribal society will take. A brief comparison of the tribes listed in the preceding paragraph would reveal that they differ both in the structure of the local residential group and in the kinds of sodalities which provide tribal integration. As White (1959) has stated, technology and energy levels determine only the general level of sociocultural organization, not its specific form.

To account for the differences between different tribes, other variable factors have to be introduced. Here, as we have already suggested, the environment becomes relevant. The presence of other societies as potential enemies, allies, or trading partners is as much a part of the environment as the climate, fauna, flora, and general topography. To illustrate, the head-hunting Jivaro Indians of eastern Ecuador are segmented into what are known as lineage villages, each occupying a single large dwelling. Warfare, for trophy heads, was once endemic among these communities, and frequently adjacent communities would form temporary defense alliances under a single chieftain. In times of peace, such alliances would disintegrate. This feature of Jivaro social organization would be unintelligible if the cultural environment of hostile, warlike neighbors were not considered. However, in most cases a simple relationship between a specific feature of band organization or kind of sodality and a specific feature of the environment cannot be demonstrated. At best, a certain kind of social arrangement, as a common form of adjustment to given environmental circumstances, can be shown without claiming a causal relationship. Thus, the patrilocal band commonly appears among hunters because of the *convenience* of having the man remain with his natal group. This factor does not, however, absolutely determine patrilocality.

The Lineage Village. One of the most common forms of the residential unit in tribal society is the lineage village, a local group. In Beardsley's (*op. cit.*) evolutionary scheme, it would appear as a *semi-permanent sedentary community*. A lineage village is made up of individuals who trace descent through a single line (either the male or female, from a common ancestor), their spouses, and their children. The consciousness among lineage members of lineal descent and of being a group apart from other similar groups is crucial to this definition. A patrilocal band, as defined above, resembles a lineage grouping in that the males grouped together by the rule of patrilocal residence are often descended from a common male ancestor, but there is no actual reckoning of descent and no consciousness of being a descent group. It may well be, of course, that lineage communities evolved out of an earlier band organization, with the addition of lineal descent reckoning being the crucial difference. The patrilocality of the hunting band provides a logically prior stage in the development of a band based on patrilineal descent.

In many of the world's tribal societies marital residence is matrilocal or uxorilocal (a newly married couple lives with the wife's natal family), and reckoning of descent is matrilineal (through the female line). Under this arrangement, a boy, at marriage, leaves his own natal group and goes to live in that of his wife. The core members of the group are females related through common descent, their mothers, their husbands, and their children. This type of marital residence is found so commonly among horticultural peoples of the world (the Hopi of Arizona and the Iroquois of eastern United States are examples) that anthropologists have been led to postulate a causal relationship between it and horticulture. Service writes as follows (*ibid.*, 121):

> The suggestion in this situation is that in matrilineal tribes the significant factor must be the collaborative activities of the women: tending gardens, having common harvest or food-processing labor and commonly-shared food storage, and in many cases . . . even common cooking for the whole longhouse. It may be that the cooperation of women makes their continued existence as a group a sufficient reason for uxorilocal residence, even though hunting and warfare may remain important collaborative activities of males.

He goes on to suggest that the relative importance of warfare on the one hand, and the collaborative raising, processing, storage, and distribution of food on the other, may be the factor determining whether a horticultural tribe will be virilocal or uxorilocal. Elsewhere, Service shows that, everywhere in tribal society, competition between tribes has resulted in an unremitting state of hostility. "The external polity of tribes is usually military only." This fact alone is sufficient to explain the necessity for internal unity of the tribe. This brings us back to the question of pan-tribal sodalities.

Clans and Age Societies. The lineal group of tribal society is based on kinship ties, reckoned in either the male or female line. Everyone in the group is a kinsman of everyone else, either through descent or marriage. One of the commonest kinds of sodality is an association based on the extension of kin reckoning and is called the *clan*. A clan may be described as an association of kinsmen who trace descent through either the paternal or the maternal line from a common ancestor, and which has the following characteristics:

1. A name, and other identifying insignia and dress; special ceremonies, songs, paraphernalia, clan mythologies, etc.
2. Exogamy; a man must find his wife in another clan, and, therefore, husbands and wives are always of different clans.
3. Non-residential; it cross-cuts residential groups. Its members may be found in all the bands or local groups comprising the tribe.
4. Clan ancestor, which may, in fact, be a mythological creature or an animal, and clan members often cannot trace actual descent. In other words, the ties between members are not always genealogical.
5. Corporate functions, that is, it acts as a unit in performing certain functions.

Since the clan is not a residential group, and its members are widely scattered (indeed they may never meet as a group), the possession of a name and other insignia is necessary for strengthening bonds among clansmen. If the clan were a residential unit, it would not, by definition, be a sodality. In accepting the principle of common descent, without being able actually to trace genealogical ties, a clan differs from the lineage. In fact, a characteristic feature of the clan system is the ready way in which clans adopt members. This form of organization can incorporate within it many more individuals than are usually found in a lineage. Therefore, it seems accurate to say that the clan system represents an extension of the kinship principle and can incorporate a much larger number of individuals than can actually keep track of blood ties. It serves the integrating needs of an expanding society which has not yet developed a political structure. The manifest function of the clan may be to perform certain ceremonies, such as burying deceased members or engaging in games with other clans, but its covert or latent function is that of strengthening tribal solidarity.

There are other kinds of sodalities not based on kin or putative kin ties. We have already mentioned one such association in the military societies of the Cheyenne. Another kind, found among many tribes of East Africa, are the *age societies*. Here, young men of many communities are initiated into manhood in a great common ceremony, and for the remainder of their lives the men initiated together comprise an age group or class, united to other classmates from other local groups by powerful bonds. Thus, the age group cuts across residential groups to achieve integration.

In summary, tribal organization is a higher level of organization than that which characterizes the band. Although it may have had its roots in the food-collecting era of technological development, tribal organization is an evolutionary stage which follows the band level. Apparently, it developed as a response to the needs of larger social groups living in closer proximity to, and therefore competing with, their neighbors. Tribal society marked an initial but very important step in the evolution toward progressively complex structures with increasingly differentiated functions. It was possibly the dominant organizational form among incipient agriculturalists everywhere and has remained typical of primitive horticulturalists in contemporary times.

THE RISE OF INCIPIENT STATES OR CHIEFDOMS

At both band and tribal levels of cultural evolution, the local group, whatever its ties with other segments or groups, remains politically autonomous. Interpersonal relations within the group are regulated by mutual bonds of kinship, and those between bands by kinship or kin-like sodalities. The members of a military society or age class, for example, think of one another as brothers, and political authority is minimal. At most, an elder kinsman within a band may acquire moral authority over the members of his group. Such an individual is not properly called a chief, but a *headman,* and his authority depends more on personal, charismatic qualities than on wealth or inheritance and usually is not transmitted to his sons or nephews. The headman's power may be greater if supplemented with supernatural appeals—if, for example, he is also a shaman. In any case, his authority never extends beyond his community to embrace neighboring groups.

Political authority of this kind appears only at a later stage of cultural evolution, as a concomitant of many other things—greater technical control of the environment, greater food surplus, economic specialization, the rise of non-food-producing specialists, denser population and larger population aggregates, the growth of regional specialization and trade, and the emergence (in some areas) of irrigation agriculture.

The next stage, therefore, in the evolution of the organizational aspects of culture occurs when a number of local groups give up or lose some of their autonomy to an outside leader. Local leadership develops in all communities, well beyond the headmanship discussed above, to a level described as chieftainship. Evolution is a gradual process, and there is no sharp dividing line between adjacent categories. When, for example, the chief of a community becomes sufficiently strong to impose his leadership over a number of neighboring communities, a new level of sociopolitical integration has emerged. This level of organization is an *incipient state* or a *chiefdom.* In overall evolutionary perspective, the chiefdom is a product of the Agricultural Revolution, and in the Middle East it emerged before the full Bronze Age. In Middle America and South America, the incipient state is associated with the Formative or Pre-Classic periods of archaeology (about 1000 B.C.); the early Monte Alban civilization of the Valley of Oaxaca and the early stages of the great civilization of Teotihuacan in the Valley of Mexico are illustrative of this development in the New World.

Factors in the Formation of Chiefdoms

Incipient states or chiefdoms differ in many important ways from tribal or band-level societies. The basic factors in their emergence appear to be economic and are related to increased productivity as well as to local and regional specialization in production. However, no simple or precise correlation can be made between the technology of farming or pastoralism and the emergence of chiefdoms. Environment is a primary factor preventing such a correlation. Under highly favorable environmental conditions, the most primitive hoe culture (or in some cases a food-collecting culture) can be productive enough to achieve and sustain this level of organization. As we pointed out previously, the earliest phases of agriculture were not very productive and did not lead to the formation of multivillage chiefdoms. In fact, many tribal-level peoples have been horticulturalists or pastoralists. On the other hand, food collectors, such as the salmon-fishing Kwakiutl of British Columbia, have achieved the chiefdom level of organization.

Regional Specialization and Trade. Farming *per se*, then, does not automatically mean high productivity, and high productive potential does not necessarily result in the formation of chiefdoms. We are still on uncertain grounds when we attempt to define the causes of any kind of organization. At best, we can isolate what seem to be relevant factors. Thus, among the known chiefdoms of the world, not only the richness of the land's natural resources but the geographical *distribution* of these resources seem to be factors. As Service has shown (1962:145), chiefdoms tend to exist in habitats which are topographically complex, offering a variety of environmental conditions within a relatively small area. A fairly small mountainous region can provide mountain forests, high grasslands, fertile valley floors, semi-tropical slopes, and a variety of other resources—faunal, floral, and mineral. This situation can serve to stimulate trade. Locally, communities living in such a habitat may specialize in lumber or wood products, fish, temperate-zone agriculture or tropical-zone agriculture, pottery, stone wares, and many other things. At the tribal level, significant exchange of products (trade) occurs between groups that differ in their economic specialization. In New

Guinea, for example, it is common for coastal peoples to exchange fish for horticultural products from inland people. The Congo Pygmies exchange meat and other forest products with their Bantu neighbors for plantains and other vegetable foods.

A surplus for trade may be produced, however, only through organized effort, and the growth of leadership at the tribal level may well have been a response to the needs for such organization. This same leadership could then regulate the ensuing intergroup trade and intragroup distribution of products received in trade. There must be some degree of organization and leadership since, as Service observes, such exchange is a matter of group interest. Thus, the potential for greater productivity stimulates the growth of organization and leadership, which in turn make possible greater surplus production. Cause and effect, as we have observed in other contexts, are intimately interwoven.

Chiefdoms as Redistributive Agencies

If managed cooperation *within* a group can result in increased productivity, it is equally true that similar cooperation *between* groups can lead to more effective production and distribution. Apparently, many chiefdoms have arisen under conditions where one of many neighboring economically specialized communities has assumed control of the surplus production of other groups. The means whereby this is accomplished vary greatly from one chiefdom to another, but the results are the same. In the Trobriand Islands, a matrilineal society, a district chief acquired control of surplus production through the exercise of marital rights, because in this culture a husband acquired rights to the surplus production of his wives' brothers. A chief, who was entitled to several wives, could marry the sisters of the locally important and wealthy men, thereby acquiring rich brothers-in-law. He, in turn, acquired a number of obligations to the people over whom he held sway. Among other things, he had the obligation of underwriting great feasts which all could attend, thereby redistributing the surplus acquired previously.

This points to an essential feature of chiefdoms—they are *redistributive* systems. By one means or another, a chief gains control over the productive activities of the people under him. This includes not only the surplus production, which can be highly varied from one community to another, but also the labor pool. He can redirect surplus goods from one part of his chiefdom to another, or even outside the chiefdom, and he can redirect the labor supply as well.

A chief who gains control over the activities of the member communities of his chiefdom can also exercise his authority in other ways. He can use his power to allocate land among his followers, demand their support in warfare with neighboring states, combine his political functions with his religious ones and serve as a priest of his community. In fact, it may have been as a religious specialist that he gained the prestige which led to his leadership in the first place. Since most early states were theocratic (led by politico-religious leaders), we may be justified in assuming that this tendency was present at the incipient state level under discussion.

Stratification in Incipient States

A division of society into ranked levels is referred to as social stratification. This phenomenon, based as it often is on accumulated wealth and political power, is the outcome of the same general factors that produced the chiefdom. Like the chiefdom, social stratification emerges gradually and tends to become increasingly more complex. Out of what prior condition, then, did stratification evolve? This question can be best answered by treating the evolution of stratification systems along with the evolution of the chiefdom itself.

It is possible that early in the development of chieftainship a man ruled largely through his personal, charismatic characteristics. The existence of a chieftainship depended on the presence of someone with the personal characteristics to wield such power. This does not imply that such a person occupied the *position* of chief, but rather that he *was* the chief. In contrast, and by way of illustration of this important point, the presidency is a position within the governmental structure of the United States, and a man occupies the position. His behavior in that position is dictated by what the Constitution and other legislative enactments say a president must do.

Ultimately something analogous happened in the evolution of chiefdoms. In time, a formal structure evolved with a position of chief as an integral part. This probably came about as chiefs became powerful and wealthy and passed their power and wealth on to their families. If, by tradition, a chief passed his position on to his son (his position became hereditary), then the chieftainship became a permanent position (an office) to be filled in each generation. A chief, his father before him, and his sons after him, would under these circumstances form a ruling lineage. Since a father could have more than one son but there was only one chieftainship to confer, other sons could be given other statuses within the chiefdom—religious leadership, military captaincies, and the like. As these became permanent, a structure of government emerged.

Differences in wealth and power and the presence of a hereditary ruling family show that there are rank differences in the incipient state, whereas, by contrast, band-level society is more equalitarian. Aside from the respect accorded the aged, a skilled hunter, or a religious practitioner, there is little rank differentiation in band society. In tribal society, however, membership in a military or secret society may confer prestige, and military exploits may be an important avenue to higher rank. Indians of the western Plains, during the days of mounted buffalo hunting, recognized a finely graded hierarchy of exploits, called counting *coup*. A warrior earned *coups* for various feats of bravery, including taking a scalp, being the first to touch an enemy, raiding an enemy camp unarmed to steal horses, and many others. But these were individual achievements. A son could not inherit the prestige of his father; it had to be personally earned.

At the level of chiefdoms the situation changes. A chief, by virtue of his redistributive function, is in a position to retain much of his society's wealth for himself. Permanent wealth, in the form of land, herds of cattle, or luxury items (perhaps produced by artisans under the chief's patronage) can be passed on to sons, daughters, or to younger brothers. The chieftainship itself becomes hereditary, and therefore remains within a single family. In short, individuals enjoy wealth, power, and prestige by virtue of being born into a family. In a developed chiefdom, there are a number of high-ranking families, all of whom claim descent from an original chieftain ancestor. Together, they constitute a social class that is superior to others by virtue of descent, wealth, and power. They keep themselves distinct and separate from lower classes in a number of ways: they claim greater purity or nobility of blood, practice endogamy (intraclass marriage, in this case), insist upon receiving courtesy and elaborate respect from lower-class members, and devise sumptuary laws which limit the consumption of certain luxury items to themselves alone (certain foods or gold and silver ornaments) and these items become symbols of higher class status.

THE DEVELOPED STATE

Our reference above to the chiefdom as being an incipient state implied a low level of state organization just emerging out of a lower stage of cultural evolution. What, then, is a developed or full-fledged state, and how does it come about? First, if a chiefdom is viewed as a system of diverse parts—minimally, separate communities—then the chieftainship itself can be seen as a sociopolitical mechanism of integration and control. It performs the functions commonly attributed to a state form of organization, which it exhibits in a rudimentary fashion. What are these functions that a state performs? A state exists to solve political problems, and politics, as Bohannan tells us (1963:266), is the utilization and control of force within a territorial framework. This force has two aspects—the internal use of force in law enforcement, and its external use in warfare. But, as Bohannan also points out (*ibid.*, 272), a society can perform these functions without having a state form of organization. Tribal society, for example, has mechanisms for protecting tribal territory against outsiders and for maintaining internal order.

A state is a *formal structure* in which political control (legal and military) is vested. It utilizes its authority and the force invested in it to maintain peace and conformity among its members through law and custom, and it utilizes physical force to "maintain territorial and cultural integrity against external threats . . ." (*ibid.*, 274). It is a formal structure composed of various statuses (structural positions) which have the attributes of power and authority. As with any structural position, regardless of its cultural context, a person occupying any of these political positions (offices) is expected to behave in certain ways. In each case, the power and authority necessary to satisfy the expectations of the office come to the individual by virtue of the position.*

In this sense, then, a full-fledged state differs from a chiefdom only in degree. A state functions on a larger scale than a chiefdom because it must regulate and control larger population aggregates or larger territorial units. The difference is not entirely one of degree, however, since with size and complexity a state develops new parts (structural positions) and new functions not present in the chiefdom. Further, as we shall see, early states were often *theocratic states:* they combined the exercise of physical force with the imposition of supernatural sanctions in a unique way so as to create a whole new organism of control, the *state-church.* This form of organization is only foreshadowed in the chiefdom. First, however, let us ask the question, how did states come into being? Were there new factors at work to produce this kind of organization or was there only a continuation of the same forces that brought the chiefdom level of organization into being?

The Origins of States

States have come into being in a number of ways, sometimes but not always as a continuation and extension of the evolutionary trends already discussed.

---

* This is not to say that a person will conform entirely to expectations. There is always some discrepancy between *real* and *expected* action, and a person may well bring charismatic qualities to a position. Indeed, the authority vested in a structural position may be increased or decreased depending upon the personal qualities of its occupants. This has been true of the presidency in the United States, as well as numerous other political offices.

Conquest States: The Kingdom of Ankole.   Very commonly, in the world at large, states have arisen through conquest.   A typical situation arose several times in East Africa when an invading group of pastoralists moved in among horticulturalists and imposed their rule upon them. Oberg (1940:121–62) has shown how the kingdom of Ankole in Uganda was formed in this way.   The general region forms a corridor connecting the grasslands to the north with the plateau region to the south.   The latter region was once inhabited by Bantu-speaking agricultural Negroes. Then, for reasons not fully known, waves of cattle-raising peoples, known as Hamitic peoples or Hamiticized Negroes, began to move down this corridor into Bantu territory.   Wherever they settled among the farmers, these pastoralists ". . . made a uniform adjustment, they conquered the agriculturalists, and established themselves as a ruling class" (*ibid.*, 121).   When the British came to Uganda around 1900, they found many such states in which the ruling pastoralists referred to themselves as the Bahima and the subordinate farmers called themselves the Bairu.

These Bahima had entered the land, carrying with them a tribal level of organization.   Now, to impose their rule upon the Bairu and exploit their production, they also had to reorganize themselves.

No longer were the Bahima cattle men free agents, united in extended families and loosely knit lineages and clans; they were now also members of a political group.   If the Bahima were going to further their interests as Bahima, they had to organize and act together as Bahima. [A special political bond] had to be created, had to be consciously entered into.   It involved leadership, co-operation, submission to authority.   It gave rise to kingship and the dynastic principle, the organization of military forces and chieftainship.   In short, it welded the Bahima into a State, the nucleus of the Banyankole kingdom. (*Ibid.*, 128.)

It was necessary for the rulers to create political institutions that would contain these two populations within the same territory, to regulate the relations between them, and to subject the horticulturalists to this rule. Not all states, however, have arisen in this way, and conversely, conquest does not always lead to the formation of a state.

Hydraulic States: Coastal Peru.   The formation of theocratic states along coastal Peru in the first millennium B.C. is illustrative of another process which has evidently occurred many times in arid regions of the world. Agriculture can support very dense populations in these arid river valleys provided that river water is more or less equitably distributed.   The use of river water in farming means, of course, some system of irrigation. The existence of farming communities along the entire extent of a river, from the coast to the western slopes of the Andes, presupposes that all communities will share in the distribution of water.   The water flowing along a river course is not inexhaustible, and many of the coastal rivers of Peru are reduced to a trickle at certain times of the year, but even at other times the communities downstream would suffer if those upstream made unlimited use of the water. Therefore, the construction of irrigation works, their maintenance, and their policing to ensure an equitable distribution to all communities implies some supravillage control backed by force. There is abundant archaeological evidence to show that systems of control did develop in many coastal valleys, as well as in highland areas where water control was also essential to support large populations. The resultant political institutions, because they achieved this particular function, have been called irrigation states or *hydraulic states* (see Wittfogel 1959:94–113).

The head of such a state is a priest-chief or a priest-king. His ability to control a large labor force is used not only to construct and maintain irrigation works, but to bring new land under cultivation through vast engineering projects (such as terracing mountain sides); to construct imposing ceremonial structures (such as Chavin de Huantar in Peru, or Ur in Mesopotamia); and to build fortifications, roads, and bridges. These things begin at the chiefdom level, and the state may be seen as a culmination of these earlier phenomena, a higher level achieved in this process of evolution.

Warfare: The Northern Andes. Finally, although this does not exhaust the possibilities, states can arise as a response to warfare. That is, scattered autonomous communities have this alternative when faced with the threat of a war-like neighboring state: if they are not to be swallowed up, they must somehow band together in common defense. Steward and Faron (1959:174–201) show that chiefdoms may have arisen in the northern Andes as a response to patterns of warfare in the south. And Service (*op. cit.,* 151) states: "It is possible that intense competition and frequent warfare among tribes was an important condition for the rise of chiefdoms in the first place, inasmuch as planning and coordination have obvious advantages in war." The process, once begun, can result in the formation of large and powerful states. States, while they can be seen as a fuller development of chiefdoms, have features of organization not to be found at the simpler level.

Characteristics of State Organization

A major diagnostic feature of most early states is that they combined political and religious leadership in a single state structure, and were in fact state-churches or theocratic states. (Both terms have gained common acceptance, but for consistency we will utilize the former.) Leslie White defines and describes the state-church as follows (1959:303 ff.):

Civil societies are characterized by a number of diverse parts and specialized functions, on the one hand, and a special mechanism for coordination, integration, and control, on the other. This special mechanism should have a name, and we have decided to call it the *state-church*. We do this because this mechanism always has both a secular and civil aspect and an ecclesiastical aspect; *state* and *church* properly designate *aspects* of this coordinative, integrative mechanism rather than separate entities.

He goes on to show that while state and church may be structurally distinct, as in the United States today, they were originally one. Since sacred and secular functions and authority rest in one and the same person (or at least a group of rulers), the head of such a state is commonly referred to by some name denoting this duality—priest-king, theocratic ruler, chief priest, and the like. White shows that the caliph in early Islam was such a ruler: "The only valid law of Islam is the sacred law given out by Mohammed; jurisprudence is, in reality, a branch of theology. And the chief duty of the caliph is the enforcement of holy law" (*ibid.*, 305). Further examples could be given to illustrate this same point. Early rulers of Egypt, Mesopotamia, or Iron Age Greece, as well as those of pre-Columbian America were all of this type, and in modern times the Emperor of Japan was regarded as a living descendant of a god.

What does a state-church do, and why should these two functions be so universally combined in early states? White states that the function is that of "coordination and control of parts and regulation of the system as a whole" (*ibid.*, 313). What are the parts that need coordination? States are marked by a complexity of structure and differentiation of function which are only foreshadowed in chiefdoms. A state is characterized, for example, by a division into several classes, whereas in early societies the basic division was into ruling and subordinate classes. The bulk of the subordinate class was made up of rural peasantry; thus, early states were divided along rural and urban lines as well. The rulers were often served by large numbers of artisans who lived in the cities and produced luxury goods for their patrons, supported ultimately by tribute from the peasantry. Within the dominant class, there can be a division of functions into commercial, military, and political, and the state itself might be subdivided into a number of territorial units. Tenochtitlán, the capital city of the Aztec state, was subdivided into 20 units called *calpulli*. Thus, a state can be divided in many ways, with the divisions differing greatly in power and having quite diverse interests. The lines separating them are lines of potential conflict and dissension, and conflict between classes or within classes over the division of wealth and power can occur. This situation is not unique among early states, but characterizes all advanced societies to some degree. "If the social system is to be kept intact, if it is not to explode in violence and subside in anarchy, the relationship of subordination and superordination between the classes must be maintained; in other words, the subordinate class must be kept in a condition of subjection and exploitation. It is the business of the state-church to see that this is done" (*ibid.*, 313 ff.).

Steward and Faron (1959: 94 ff.) provide a clear description of a state-church in their discussion of Mochica civilization of northern coastal Peru (about 200 B.C. to 400 A.D.):

> The state superstructure must have consisted of a large pyramid of nobles topped by the supreme ruler, the representative or incarnation of the god. This structure rested upon a vast number of specialists of lesser status. The servants of the lords included messengers, attendants, healers, and litter bearers. There were many minor state functionaries, such as architects, war captains, and lesser priests. There were also artisans, who specialized in ceramics, weaving, metallurgy, or carving. And there were doctors, musicians, and dancers.
> The basic population were the principal producers. They not only tilled the soil; they furnished manpower for the construction of state irrigation works, temples, and forts. They probably also served as soldiers, in which capacity they are portrayed with the shield, mace, and spear. Possibly as successful warriors they could acquire special status.

With modifications, this description could fit many early theocratic states. The same authors make the following statement of the functions of the state-church (*ibid.*, 100 ff.):

> A state functions in two capacities: first, it is an integrating and coordinating agency that serves the needs of its people; second, it is a consuming institution that demands goods and services from the people. In the first capacity, it arranges that a certain portion of the effort of its component communities and classes be channeled into projects that are beneficial to everyone. An irrigation state plans, creates, and manages waterworks that increase the yield of farm land, and it brings new land under cultivation. In order to do this, however, it must devise a political organization and a power structure. In a prescientific era, it may back its power with supernaturalism, that is, with a state church or cult; and it may have to employ military force if the groups that it seeks to bring into cooperation resist rational or supernatural appeals.

Religion, Politics, and the State. The final sentence in the above paragraph throws light on one of the questions we asked above: why should the religious and political functions be so universally combined in early states? At this early stage in the evolution of state organization, political institutions backed by force were not sufficiently developed to contain the diverse classes and segments that made up these relatively large population aggregates. Control over men's minds through the threat of supernatural sanctions provided a powerful additional aspect of this mechanism of control. Indeed, we might well argue that religious control emerged prior to political institutions, and, being insufficient to regulate and control subordinate populations, had to be supplemented by military force embodied in political institutions.

There is much archaeological evidence to show that one of the earliest power figures to emerge following the Agricultural Revolution was a religious specialist, the priest. Hunters and gatherers often employ supernaturalism to extend their meager technological controls over their habitat. This may take the form of hunting magic or of rituals to appease the spirits of game animals. Here, culture serves a very important adjustive function. As early man made the transition from food collection to production, the emphasis of his ritualism changed. Gods of rain and fertility replaced those of game animals. Farming can be as precarious a way of making a living as hunting or food gathering, and the specialist who wielded the "pseudotechnology" of ritualism was an important man in the community.

A recurrent feature in the archaeology of developed agricultural societies is the ceremonial precinct, a religious structure or series of structures set aside from ordinary affairs. Here, the priest, in elaborate dress, performed the impressive ceremonies that maintained the desired relationship between man and the supernatural. The timely fall of rain, the seasonal flooding of the Nile or the Tigris–Euphrates rivers, the fertility of the soil and the abundance of the harvest, or even the normal progression of the seasons, all depended upon the good will of the gods. The priest alone could guarantee that good will.

Religion, Economy, and the State. In the classical archaic states of the Middle East, India, China, and later the New World, the most impressive architecture was religious architecture. Even before the growth of large cities and great states, relatively small peasant populations were able to build impressive structures such as that of Chavin de Huantar in northern Peru. A pattern was established very early: in any given geographical region a ceremonial center would emerge. Its location would often be determined by preexisting trade relations; that is, it would be strategically located where people from diverse production areas would come to market, and market day would also be the occasion for worshiping at the temple or ceremonial precinct.

In time, either through supernatural appeals or through threat of supernatural sanctions, the priest induced the peasantry to devote time to building new structures or enlarging the old ones. They would also be asked to contribute a share of their agricultural surplus to the support of artisans whose task it was to add the refinements of sculpture or murals to the temples. Later, the priest could supply a theological rationale for this pattern by stating that all land belongs to the gods, and that man works it on suffrance. Therefore, in bringing goods and services to the temples, man is only returning to the gods what is their due. It would be a short additional step for the priest to proclaim himself the gods' representative on earth. In ancient Egypt and Mesopotamia the temples became great repositories for surplus grain, cloth, and luxury goods, and some of the earliest known specimens of writing are temple records, or accounts of tribute received and paid out and of land allocated to the peasantry.

From the beginning, therefore, the power or authority vested in the newly emergent priest class was much more than just religious power, because it extended into the realm of economics. It was shown above that one of the ways in which a state organization can come into being is through the control of local specialization areas within a larger region. The actual mechanism whereby such control was achieved could well have been that which we just described. What began as a periodic trip to market soon became a pilgrimage to a ceremonial center, not only to trade but to worship; what had begun as control by the priests over religious activities soon became control over economic production. The surplus brought to the temples by the peasantry not only supported the new class, but sustained a class of artisans who could produce luxury goods for the ruling priesthood. This was the start of the social class distinctions based on wealth and power which we have already discussed.

Later, the managerial activities of the ruling priesthood were extended into still other areas. In arid regions, agriculture could support a large population only if vast irrigation works were built and maintained, and the water equitably distributed. The cooperation necessary to achieve this does not come about automatically. It requires management backed by some sanction, supernatural or political. Eventually, in many world areas, states became so large and complex, and the potential antagonism and dissension so great, that supernatural appeals or threats could not provide sufficient control. The priesthood came to supplement sacred controls with secular police power. Warfare between neighboring states was also a very early development, and it may be that police and military power were exercised by one and the same organization.

Territorial Organization and the State. The fundamental organizing principle of the state is *territory*. By this we mean that the relationships of individuals and groups to the state are determined by where one resides. In our society each of us "belongs" to a series of territorial subdivisions of the national state, arranged in an ascending hierarchy from local, county, state, to national. All of our legal rights and obligations are held with reference to one or more of these. We pay taxes within each of these units, are subject to its laws, and exercise the right of voting as a member of each unit. At the opposite extreme, primitive societies are organized on the basis of kinship. Each individual member of a kin group enjoys certain rights and privileges, and owes certain obligations to other members, because all are bound together by ties of kinship. A man has certain rights and obligations with respect to his brother, and others with respect to his father, son, sister, mother's brother, etc. Custom may be quite specific as to what these mutual rights and obligations are. Such societies occupy a territory, to be sure, but this is significant only in the relations between groups.

In the course of cultural evolution, as band and tribal forms of organization gave way to the chiefdom and state, kinship lost its effectiveness as an organizing principle. The people within a state became organized into territorial subdivisions. As a transitional phase in this development, some former kinship groupings may have served as the basis for territorial subdivision. A tribal society, for example, may have been divided into a number of clans. Then, as this society made the transition to state organization, these clans may have served as nuclei for local subdivisions of the state. At that point they ceased to be clans, but the kinship ties within such units remained important for many purposes, especially landholding and inheritance. But the individual's relations to the state are dictated by his place of residence, not by his kinship ties *per se*.

Other Characteristics of State Organization. A state arrogates to itself the right to settle disputes and punish transgressions. The administration of law, therefore, is another function of the state. One of the commonest features of band and tribal society is that the balance between segments is maintained through blood feuding or private revenge. An injury to an individual is an injury to his kinsmen, and they in turn hold the right to exact vengeance upon the culprit or his kin group. Since there is no central authority in tribal society, revenge must remain a matter for individuals or groups of kinsmen. Where a state exists to regulate and coordinate its member communities, private revenge would pose a threat to the internal peace and stability of the state structure. The administration of law can no longer be left to individuals or private groups. A state can, of course, allocate powers in purely local matters to its local subdivisions. Characteristically, as states evolve, laws become codified, and may even be set forth as written documents. The law code of Hammurabi (Babylon, c. 1800 B.C.) is among the earliest known to historians.

A state maintains some sort of military force as one aspect of its relations with other states. It lies beyond the scope of this discussion to analyze the causes of warfare. We will only note that while feuding seems to be universal among tribal societies, and common to bands, warfare for economic gain or territorial conquest is a civilized institution. It came into existence with the emergence of chiefdoms and states. Early in the development of states, warfare serves a number of purposes. By raiding its neighbors, a state can bring back plunder to enrich the ruling class, or captives to serve as sacrificial victims, as household drudges or slaves, or as concubines for the conquerors. Ordinarily, in such warfare, no attempt is made to incorporate the conquered land and people into the state structure of the conquerors. This is apparently a later development in warfare. In the long run, conquest can be more profitable than raiding, because the productivity of the subject state can be regulated so as to provide a continuous flow of tribute into the coffers of the ruling state.

States regulate economic relations within their boundaries. In the ancient Aztec state all commercial transactions had to take place within the market, where state officials supervised weights and measures, levied taxes, and punished those who broke their laws. The state had a monopoly on long-distance trade with other states through a special guild of traders known as the *pochteca*. Wherever money comes into use, its coinage and issuance are always monopolized by the state.

White (*op. cit.*, 322 ff.) has summarized the functions of a state as follows:

> We have now seen how the state, by means of such governmental machinery as kings, lords, viziers, and ministers, assemblies or parliaments, courts, police, and penal institutions, integrates, regulates, and controls much of the life of civil societies. They defend them against aggression from abroad and from insurrection within. And they carry on or regulate many intrasocietal processes— of communication, transportation, irrigation, public health and welfare, finance and commerce, punishment of crime, education, etc.—which are essential or desirable to the effective functioning of the society. The goal or objective of these endeavors is security, continuity, and the effective functioning of the sociocultural system.

The classical states of antiquity reached their full flowering in the urban societies of Egypt and Mesopotamia by 2500 B.C., in the Bronze Age civilization of China around 1800 B.C., and in the classical civilizations of Middle America and the Central Andes in the first millennium after Christ. All the great achievements in technology, the arts, architecture, and religion were products of this state development. The ruling classes were the intellectual elite who created systems of writing, mathematics, and law, and from their astronomical researches complex calendrical systems were developed. Under their patronage, large classes of artisans built imposing architectural works and produced innumerable luxury items and works of art. Bronze, and later iron metallurgy, the wheel, and sailing vessels were among the many technological achievements of that era.

In general, the level of civilization achieved during what archaeologists have called the Bronze and Iron Ages was not exceeded until the next great technological revolution in the eighteenth century. In the many centuries that intervened, states and empires rose and fell; new civilizations came into being, flourished, and then decayed. The beginnings of Christianity, Islam, and Buddhism are all parts of this story. But despite the many changes that took place between 2500 B.C. and 1800 A.D., the general sociopolitical level of civilization remained the same: a monarchial or feudal state organization resting on a peasant economy.

Primary Civilization

Recent or present-day nations that are relatively untouched by the Industrial Revolution are sometimes referred to as *preindustrial societies*. They are characterized by a ruling elite, a large peasant population, and a small middle class of shopkeepers, white-collar workers, teachers, and other professionals. The wealth of such nations comes mainly from the land and is produced by peasants, employing what Wolf (1966:19) has called a *paleotechnic* technology.

In energy terms, the principal feature of such a technology is human muscle power applied to simple tools, supplemented by some animal power (e.g., oxen-drawn plows) and some limited use of water or wind to power simple machines. In their general features, such societies are not fundamentally different from small European or Asian nations of the sixteenth century. Another term to describe this level of cultural evolution, one growing in usage, is that of primary civilization (Rodnick 1966). In a primary civilization, the ratio of human muscle power to non-human power is relatively high. Social systems which rely on a preponderance of human muscle power are absolutely limited in their potential for development. Stated in simplest terms, the return in goods and services per unit of manpower expended is low. The peasant must work long hours throughout the year to feed his family and maintain his home, while still producing a surplus of goods and services to support the non-cultivators of his society. If a nation lacks industry, and if the greatest proportion of all arable lands is worked by peasants employing a primitive technology, then the gross national product must be low. A few can live lives of luxury, but many must remain impoverished.

THE INDUSTRIAL REVOLUTION: SECONDARY CIVILIZATION

We have already discussed the great technological revolution brought about when man learned to harness fossil fuels in the form of coal and oil. The perfection of a steam engine and its application to numerous industrial machines soon had the effect of replacing human muscle power and animal power for many purposes. This reduction of the human factor in the technology–culture equation is the major criterion for the definition of this new cultural level as secondary civilization (*ibid.*). Men are still an essential element, of course, but the mechanization of the many processes of production and distribution has had the effect of vastly increasing the return in goods and services per unit of manpower expended. Another consequence of the Industrial Revolution, one not always fully appreciated, is that it made possible a second Agricultural Revolution. The original revolution had certain inherent limitations; in particular, the science of the preindustrial era was extremely limited. The intellectual successes achieved by the theocratic ruling classes were directed mainly toward supernatural ends. In the preindustrial western world, free scientific inquiry was actually discouraged (violently at times) during the first fifteen or more centuries of the Christian era. One of the most important consequences of the Industrial Revolution, therefore, was the revolution in thought that brought about the birth of modern science. Thus, the application of machine-age technology, of modern transportation, and of knowledge of modern science to agriculture has had profound consequences for contemporary civilization. With the enormous increase in the ratio of agricultural productivity to each unit of manpower, a small proportion of each nation's population can now feed the entire nation, and release upward of 90 per cent of the population for other tasks. Less than 10 per cent of modern-day Americans are farmers, yet they are capable of producing a great surplus of foodstuffs over and above our national needs. This is not belied by the fact that many Americans have insufficient food. The problem today is often one of distribution, not production. The phenomena of government subsidies to inhibit further production, and of the wholesale destruction of food that cannot be sold at a profit are curious consequences of this second Agricultural Revolution.

We will not attempt a systematic analysis of this latest phase in cultural evolution, for two reasons. First, the details are part of modern history and are familiar to most students. Second, the story is so vastly complex that it lies far beyond the modest scope of this chapter, or even of this book. We conclude this chapter, therefore, with a discussion of a few salient features of this latest revolution.

In sociopolitical terms, this latest age has been marked by the separation of church and state and the emergence of giant nation-states. The size of modern states, such as the United States or the Soviet Union, is in part a function of population increase made possible by the second Agricultural Revolution. It is estimated that world population has increased sevenfold since the sixteenth century. This increase in population density is not a sufficient explanation for the size of modern political units, however, and we must also take into account such factors as the development of transportation and communications in the past century. The effectiveness of a state structure as a mechanism of integration and control can be no greater than these factors will permit.

In the absence of some means of rapid communication or transportation, the degree of control which a state has over its component parts decreases proportionately to their distance from the control center. This has been a problem with most great states and empires of the past: the weakening and breakdown of central control has always begun at the peripheries. The ancient Inca of the South American Andes were able partially to counteract the effects of distance by means of an extensive system of magnificent roads along which messages could be sent using a rapid relay service. This empire was just reaching the peak of its power when the Spanish arrived in the sixteenth century, and we may seriously question how long centralized control could have been maintained in the face of continuous rebellions along the frontiers.

The great political states of today, on the other hand, have come into being coincidentally with the development of modern high-speed transportation and telecommunications. The reader will recall that much of present-day United States was lawless frontier before the westward extension of the railroad and telegraph. Prior to these developments, news of an event in New York could not reach California for as long as three months. In today's age of electronic technology, newsworthy events can be transmitted in a fraction of a second to the most remote parts of the globe. Within a matter of minutes, or at most hours, civil disturbances can be put down in almost any part of a modern nation with the aid of rail or air transportation. These and innumerable other technological developments have made possible the almost fantastic complexity of modern political systems.

THE ACCELERATION IN CULTURAL EVOLUTION

The extremely rapid cultural development that has occurred since the Industrial Revolution illustrates well a further point about cultural evolution in general: culture evolves at an accelerating rate. That is, not only does culture evolve in the direction of greater complexity, but the rate of change increases. The rate of change can be related to what we call *cultural mass*. The culture of a small, unspecialized, undifferentiated primitive society is low in mass: it contains relatively few culture traits or elements. Change, in turn, can be viewed as an interaction between the elements making up the mass of a culture. Ideas act on ideas and on objects; objects act on social institutions, which in turn act on ideas. Anything new in a cultural system, an innovation, can be seen as a recombination of already existing elements. A simple culture, being low in mass, has relatively few elements to interact and recombine, and therefore has little potential for change. Thus, for untold ages, beginning with the dawn of mankind and extending until late in the Upper Paleolithic, cultural systems changed so slowly that archaeologists must measure change in terms of tens of thousands of years.

A technological revolution, like that of plant and animal domestication, makes possible increased population density and population size, occupational specialization, and regional specialization and trade. These result in increased culture mass, through internal innovation as well as through borrowing due to increased contacts between cultures. This increased mass also means increased potential for change; there are more elements present to interact and recombine. The changes recorded by archaeologists and historians for the centuries following the Agricultural Revolution were compressed into a moment in time, when compared to the vast preceding ages when change was all but undiscernible. Between 8000 and 2500 B.C., the great civilizations of antiquity attained their full flowering.

The cultural development that has been a direct consequence of the Industrial Revolution has occurred in less than two hundred years and has resulted in cultures enormously greater in mass than those of ancient Egypt or Mesopotamia. In relative terms, these latter developments have required less than 4 per cent of the time required by the Agricultural Revolution to attain its peak in 2500 B.C. And the Agricultural Revolution occupied but 0.005 per cent of the time elapsed since the beginning of what we have called the Human Revolution of 1 million years before. So rapidly is culture evolving that we appear to be in the midst of another revolution before we have even begun to realize the full significance of the Industrial Revolution.

Tertiary Civilization

Rodnick (*ibid.*, 182), as we stated above, refers to the civilization which began with the Industrial Revolution as secondary civilization. He describes it as follows:

The new Secondary civilization would be urbanized, factory-organized, market-oriented, literate (using schools rather than family life to spread the new culture), and opposed to provincialism and regionalism. Its spheres of influence would be wider, and the peasant would have little or no place in this civilization. In 1800, 95 percent of America's 5 million people were still living on farms. . . . In 1965, less than 7 percent of America's population was involved in farming.

We have discussed only briefly, and in very general terms, the features of this secondary civilization. But, according to Rodnick, we have already entered into the newer tertiary civilization. This newest civilization illustrates, once more, the acceleration of cultural evolution:

Secondary civilization spread further in less time than the old Primary civilization of the ancient city-states; it had transformed the old cultures more quickly than the Primary civilization had changed the Neolithic cultures that preceded it. But this new civilization would itself become transformed into Tertiary civilization within a matter of a century, with even newer drives and professions. In the Tertiary civilization, the factory worker would go the way of the peasant; and the aristocrat-warrior, who had become the merchant-manufacturer, would be transformed into a new professional manager. By the beginning of the twenty-first century, the latter may well change into an even newer group of professional problem-solvers.

What does this new phase in cultural evolution mean in terms of our earlier discussion of the role of energy and technology in that growth process? Are we, for example, in the midst of yet another energy revolution? It may well be that the harnessing of the atom, or eventually the direct harnessing of solar energy, will trigger off still another energy revolution. But coal, oil, natural gas, and hydroelectric power still provide all but an insignificant part of the motive power for our civilization. The nature of our present revolution, if indeed we wish to define it as such, seems to be not in the harnessing of new magnitudes of energy, but in the role of the human factor. The harnessing of coal by machines less than two centuries ago greatly reduced the relative role of human muscle power, and innumerable technological developments in the present century have had the effect of further reducing this human factor. As suggested in the two selections above, the factory worker appears to be on the road to becoming as obsolete as the peasant before him; and as numerous processes in production, processing, transportation, and communications come to be carried on by computer-controlled machinery, the role of the managerial class will become one of professional problem-solvers. To quote Rodnick (*ibid.,* 375–76):

The Tertiary civilization of the twenty-first century will be an automatic one, in which man for the first time in his existence will be able to tame the countless electrons of the universe to be his personal slaves. Primary civilization used the labor of human beings and domesticated animals; Secondary civilization employed the far greater energy derived from steam, electricity, and petroleum; but Tertiary civilization will exploit the tiny unseen electron in its many various forms.

SUMMARY

The Human Revolution was not, properly speaking, an energy revolution. The lower primates, including man's prehuman forebears, are capable of transforming solar energy, embodied in wild food, into muscle power. At first, man could do little more. The Human Revolution came as a result of a new mental faculty, expressed in articulate speech, which resulted in a qualitatively new way of harnessing that energy and putting it to work. This we call *culture*. For nearly a million years the energy factor in our equation remained constant, but the technological phase of culture did not. The magnitude of energy channeled into human thought processes may be insignificant compared with that channeled into pursuing game or hurling a spear, but the qualitatively different use of that energy made possible the progressive and cumulative improvement of tools. During this long age of muscle-powered technology, culture could evolve and develop within limits because these improvements in technology made possible the more effective use of human muscle power.

Then, with the Agricultural Revolution, man acquired the ability to harness solar energy more directly through plant and animal domestication, and by harnessing animal power to vehicles and plows, he found a substitute for his own muscle power. But the ratio of human to nonhuman power utilized in culture-building remained high. The Industrial Revolution brought about a drastic change in this ratio, with a potential for still greater change. Machines took over many of the tasks once performed by man and animal, and the always important role of technology in culture-building had increased to the point where machines could run other machines to produce new machines. This development, which we call *automation*, has been a rapidly accelerating one in the present century, due in particular to developments in the field of electronics.

The new revolution may well be a technological and a social one rather than an energy revolution. Machines are progressively reducing and often eliminating the role of human muscular energy in our equation. Even more important, however, is the fact that computer technology is replacing the human mind at many points, at least in the gross mechanics of mathematical computations. A properly programmed computer can perform in minutes fantastically complex calculations that would once have required the efforts of many individuals working continuously for many years. But machines do not create. Nothing comes out of a computer that the human mind has not put into it. The creative role of the human mind has yet to be replaced by machines, however complex and sophisticated. Thus, cultural evolution appears to have come full circle. The human revolution began with the emergence of man's symbolic mentality. For long ages the creations of his mind could be implemented only by his own muscle power applied to tools and later complex machines. Now his technologies have become largely divorced from his muscle power, and, increasingly, all that remains of man in the equation of culture-building is his creative mind, which is heir to a million years of accumulated knowledge.

III

CULTURE:
A DYNAMIC
PHENOMENON

16

Processes of Culture Change

INTRODUCTION

The reader must be aware that he lives in a civilization that is changing constantly. Some aspects of his culture change so slowly that they are little different today from the way they were in his grandparents' day. Other things change so rapidly that the process is visible almost from day to day. However slow the change that takes place, nothing in culture is permanent. In cultures less technologically advanced than those of North America or Europe, change seems to come about so slowly as to be non-existent, but no culture, however simple or isolated, is ever completely static. Expressions such as "the timeless East," or "the land that time forgot" do not describe anything in the present-day world. Some changes are highly momentous and bring about profound cultural transformations—the automobile, jet-propelled aircraft, developments in space technology, or the "wonder drugs." Other changes are relatively trivial—a "better mousetrap," a slight innovation in popular music, a new way of hafting a stone arrow point—but, given sufficient time, many small changes may add up to major shifts in cultural systems.

The concept of change has not been discussed explicitly up to this point, but it has been implicit in the preceding chapters. Social organization, for example, was portrayed as a dynamic process because it is based on real action. Where real action departs sufficiently from the norm, it is defined as deviant behavior, and deviance is an important source of change in sociocultural systems. All of the preceding chapters dealing with the organization of culture have shown that there is latitude in the expected behavior for any structural position in society. Such variations introduce an element of behavior into social systems which can result in a gradual drift away from established norms.

Change was also treated in Chapters 6 and 15, which deal with this phenomenon under the general heading of evolution. Evolution is change, but conceptually it is of a different kind from that just discussed. It is directional in nature, and it is sometimes referred to as *advance*. Preceding discussions in this book have suggested that two major types of evolutionary change may be distinguished: (1) general or macroevolutionary changes that take place in culture as a whole; and (2) specific or microevolutionary changes that take place in particular sociocultural systems. In dealing with the evolution of culture as a whole (macroevolution) we do not consider the environment—it "averages out" in the long run and, therefore, is held constant. Specific sociocultural systems, on the other hand, do occupy particular environments. Adaptation, then, is all-important because change is, more than anything else, a process wherein cultures adjust to new or changing environmental conditions.

In this chapter the focus is entirely upon specific changes that occur in particular sociocultural systems. The discussion is in two major parts. First, the various sources of cultural change—both internal and external— are discussed. Second, the concept of change as an adaptive process is considered.

Change comes about in sociocultural systems in many ways, and it affects the systems to varying degrees. Change may be a simple addition to the inventory of traits in a culture—a new tool, a new song, a slightly modified way of decorating a cooking pot, or a new word in the vocabulary—or it may be a process so sweeping that it changes the nature of the entire system. Any change, however, must originate and must take place somewhere. From the standpoint of particular sociocultural systems, two general categories of change can be recognized: (1) internal change, whose source is within the culture, and (2) external change, which originates and enters from outside the culture.

INTERNAL SOURCES OF CULTURE CHANGE

Changes that originate within a sociocultural system can be classified into a relatively few categories, each of which can be identified and described in fairly simple terms. The cultural processes involved in these changes are, on the other hand, quite complex. Therefore, each will be given separate attention.

Invention and Discovery as Innovative Processes

The reader may recall from his early school days that his education in American and European history included the memorization of significant inventions and scientific discoveries of modern times—the steamboat, the cotton gin, the steam locomotive, the discovery of bacteria, X-rays, or the principle of combustion. During his lifetime, he may remember the announcement of a successful polio vaccine, color television, or a supersonic passenger airplane. Each of these items represented a more-or-less significant addition to the existing cultural inventory in the form of new objects, new technical processes, or new knowledge. The terms invention and discovery need not be limited, however, to the products of science and technology; they can occur in all parts of culture —technology, art, music, religion, or even social organization. For example, a person who breaks away from an established religion, combines elements of his former religion with new elements of his own, and attracts a following, has invented a new religion.

Invention may be defined as a process wherein existing culture traits are recombined into new forms. White (1949:203) states that "An invention is a new synthesis of cultural elements." Childe (1936:17), writing in a similar vein, but stressing the independence of this process from biology, suggests that "An invention is not an accidental mutation of the germ-plasm, but a new synthesis of the accumulated experience to which the inventor is heir by tradition only." The inventor has available to him a stock of cultural elements: ideas, tools, technical processes, scientific knowledge, social institutions, customs, and so on. Invention may be a form of "cultural play," in which the inventor is experimenting with new combinations with no particular practical ends in mind and in response to no cultural need. Or, he may be seeking a cure for a deadly disease, an improvement in an old technical process, a solution to a problem in space flight, a better way to haft a stone axe, a new way to cook a yam, or a commercial product that will give his company a competitive advantage. A religious or social reformer is often motivated by dissatisfaction with existing forms and seeks to invent new ones. Whatever the stimulus to invention and whatever the resulting product, the inventor must work within the framework of his own culture or of other cultures to which he is exposed. He must start with an existing basis and work with existing materials. Invention is, therefore, a process involving resynthesis of existing elements. The invention of the automobile was preceded by numerous earlier inventions: the wheel, metallurgical processes, the internal combustion engine, and many more. In a very real sense, therefore, an invention cannot occur before its time. Unless tradition has provided the necessary accumulation of cultural elements, the inventor will have little or no basis for resynthesis.

What is the difference between an invention and a discovery? The distinction is not always a necessary or a useful one, but many writers have found it worthwhile to distinguish between these terms for certain purposes. Invention is sometimes said to be the creation of something new, a thing that did not previously exist. A discovery, in contrast, is the finding of something that was always there. Honigmann (1959:194) finds it more useful to define discovery as an addition to knowledge, and invention as the utilization or application of that knowledge to produce a new form. Where no clear distinction may be drawn, it may be more pragmatic to use the terms interchangeably or to use the more inclusive term *innovation*.

Innovation is an important source of change in all cultures. Innovations have occurred in the technologically most primitive societies. Hafting a stone axe to a stick was an important innovation that gave the wielder increased leverage and therefore more efficient use of his muscle power. The spear thrower mechanically extended the reach of man's arm, permitting him to hurl a spear farther and with greater force. The addition of some foreign material to clay before forming it into a pottery vessel prevented its cracking during firing, and was an important early innovation. Innumerable cultural innovations were the products of as many anonymous innovators living in the remote and recent past.

An examination of the history of innovation reveals a significant fact: the rate at which innovations occur has increased through time. Further, in more recent times they have occurred with greater frequency in more complex sociocultural systems than in simpler ones. An inquiry into the reasons for this will throw much light onto the process of innovation.

Cultural Complexity and the Rate of Innovation

Our definition of invention as a process of resynthesis provides the key to understanding differential rates of innovation. Primitive cultures are demonstrably less complex than technically advanced cultures. The technological inventory of primitive cultures contains fewer tools, fewer technical processes, smaller energy resources, and less scientific and naturalistic knowledge. At the level of social organization, primitive society has smaller social units, which are characterized by fewer structural positions within them and less specialization of function. The division of society into families and extended families results in the multiplication of functionally equivalent units—each is an all-purpose unit that performs essentially the same tasks. Finally, it is generally true of such societies that local groups live in relative isolation from culturally different groups. Members of such societies, as potential inventors, are not exposed to new ideas or knowledge significantly different from that already available. They lack intensive cross-cultural stimulation—an extremely significant factor in the growth of cultures.

Since primitive (less complex) cultures have fewer culture traits, it follows that there are fewer potential recombinations. If the total material inventory of a tribe of hunters and gatherers consists of the fire-hardened wooden spear of the man, and the wooden digging stick and bark tray of the woman, few new combinations of these things are possible. Obviously, no culture is as meager as this description. Nevertheless, when the cultural inventory is small, and isolation prevents its enrichment through contacts with different cultures, then change cannot and does not occur rapidly. Change, however, is a cumulative process. Each addition to a culture, however small, increases the potential for further change. The sociocultural systems brought into being by the Agricultural Revolution had a far greater potential for change than did the Stone Age cultures before them, and the civilizations made possible by the Industrial Revolution have been characterized by far more rapid change than the preindustrial civilizations. Culture change and culture growth are accelerating processes. A graph of man's cultural growth from earliest times, measured in terms of both material and social complexity, would show an upward curve rather than a straight line—the progression would be a geometric one rather than a straight-line arithmetic one.

Social Factors Favoring Innovation

The social environment in which the inventor operates is a very important factor for innovation. One of the major consequences of the Agricultural Revolution was its creation of a surplus of food capable of supporting classes of non-food producers. The eventual result was an economic, religious, and political division of labor in society, in which a wide range of new tasks became distributed among many new structural positions and specialized groups. The early agricultural civilizations of Egypt, Mesopotamia, India, China, Mexico, and Peru were characterized by such specialist classes and groups as priest-rulers, architects, stoneworkers, pottery makers, metallurgists, textile workers, traders, soldiers, musicians, and peasant farmers, to name some of the more important ones. Trade and other kinds of contact with other cultures resulted in an influx of new ideas and new materials. These factors provided a new environment which allowed specialist groups the training, leisure, and interest to experiment with new forms. Innumerable significant innovations in science, technology, and religion resulted. The potter's wheel, systems of mathematics, writing, agricultural terracing and irrigation systems, bronze metallurgy, wheeled vehicles—all were part of the new inventory stemming from such innovation.

The Industrial Revolution triggered an even more dramatic increase in cultural activity. Modern industrial civilizations are characterized by an almost inconceivably complex division of labor and specialization in every part of their cultures. An outstanding feature of these new societies is conscious, deliberate research. Highly trained and highly organized teams of specialists, supported by university, governmental, and business funds, are engaged in the investigation of nearly every aspect of modern culture: technology, health and medicine, outer space, social problems of every kind, the home, recreation, and many more. Basically, the motivation underlying all of this research is innovation—new additions to the existing cultural inventory, new processes, new and improved ways of doing things. This is an era of the scientific and technical specialist. The number and kinds of specialists on a modern university faculty would mirror fairly accurately the organization of research and innovation. Simultaneously, innovation is equally characteristic of the arts, philosophy, and religion.

Social Factors Limiting Innovation

Not only are inventions relatively infrequent in primitive and technologically less advanced cultures, but there are fewer conscious attempts at innovation. This is, in part, a function of the factors already discussed. Where there is little possibility for change to begin with, there will be less of a search for it. However, in tribal and peasant societies there are positive inhibitions to change. Such societies often exist along the border that separates survival from extinction. Their technical adaptation to a meager environment is often an ingenious one, but it is an adaptation that permits little margin for error. Complex social rules are worked out to achieve an optimal distribution of limited economic resources, and the entire adaptation to the total environment represents a complex integration of technological, social, and supernatural factors. The close adherence to customary ways of doing things takes on an importance that would appear exaggerated in our own society. A high value is placed upon traditional ways; change is feared and avoided. The innovator, far from being the culture hero he sometimes is in western society, may be regarded as a serious deviant. There are many examples from the ethnographic literature that illustrate the suspicion that greets the man who departs from established ways, and the social sanctions placed upon him.

Such cultural limitations to change provide a striking contrast with contemporary complex cultures. Any comprehensive summary of contemporary American values, many of which are shared with other industrial nations, shows the high value placed upon change. A constant expectation of change is found in many areas of culture. This is not to suggest that conservatism is completely absent or that all change is equally welcomed. Values, beliefs, and attitudes in religion and politics frequently are guarded carefully, and any questioning of them or any attempt to change them is branded variously as heresy, sacrilege, or political radicalism. A major political schism exists in United States society, separating those who desire rapid change in our economic or political life from those who favor the status quo or who cling nostalgically to a past they never knew. Regardless of such views, most members of contemporary complex societies favor change in such areas as science, technology, music, recreation, home furnishings, clothing, and material possessions. Change is sought, it is eagerly anticipated, and it is even considered to be necessary and inevitable.

Fashion

Nowhere is this desire for change illustrated more clearly than in the phenomenon called fashion. By fashion we mean periodic, short-term, cyclical changes in a wide range of cultural products. Seasonal changes in clothing, annual model changes in automobiles, or periodic changes in hair styling and cosmetics are obvious examples of fashion change in many western societies. Fashion can refer equally well, however, to many other areas of life. Popular music, dances, literature, even medicine—each has its cycles of change, and each reflects our keen interest in continuous change. Fashion changes often have little to do with technical or functional improvement. A new model automobile may embody many technical improvements, yet the advertisers will stress its greater beauty. In fact, a fashion change may even be harmful, as when new and untested hair dyes affect the texture of the hair and even result in baldness.

A. L. Kroeber (1948:391) has referred to fashion as a kind of "cultural play" activity. In the United States, for example, this kind of play is clearly related to such factors as great national wealth and abundant free time. Few societies in the world can afford to discard unworn clothing because it is "outmoded," buy a new automobile each year because a later model is available, or submit to expensive psychotherapy because it is the fashionable thing to do. The reader will recognize, of course, that important social class differences are involved in these behaviors. High prestige and social rank are rewards for those who move in the world of "high fashion." It seems reasonable to predict that if the gross national product of this country continues to increase, and if automation or general technological advance provides increased leisure time to enjoy this abundance, this cultural play activity will become increasingly important.

EXTERNAL SOURCES OF CULTURE CHANGE

Anthropologists have long recognized that no culture has ever developed in complete independence of other cultures. Internal processes such as invention and discovery can account for only part of the total inventory of any sociocultural system. Each is a complex blending—a "hybrid" product—of elements stemming from many sources. The process whereby culture items spread from culture to culture, or from one geographical region to another, is known as *diffusion*. However, when two or more sociocultural systems are in continuous, first-hand contact with one another, with each adapting to the presence of the other and borrowing cultural elements from the other, anthropologists label the process *acculturation*. These important external sources of change are taken up separately.

Diffusion and Cultural Growth

The process of diffusion has been explained in various ways by anthropologists. In the early part of this century a number of anthropological schools of thought formed in North America, England, and Germany which have been collectively categorized as diffusionist or historical schools in anthropology. According to the members of the *Kulturkreislehre*, or "culture circle school," which developed in Austria–Germany, there were several major world areas where culture originated and from which it spread outward in circles to other world areas. Any specific world area, therefore, received its culture in successive waves, the total culture being analogous to a series of superimposed layers. The culture circle school believed it was the task of ethnology to sort out these superimposed layers and trace them to their source.

A more extreme point of view, originating in England and found in the work of Grafton Elliot Smith and W. J. Perry, is sometimes called the "heliocentric" theory. This position holds that all major cultural development originated in Egypt and then spread through secondary centers to the rest of the world. The *Kulturkreislehre* position was generally based on much sounder scholarship than that found in the heliocentric theory, but both are regarded today as extreme diffusionist positions.

A sounder diffusionist school of thought developed in the United States under the leadership of Franz Boas. This school believed that man is essentially uninventive and that any invention is a somewhat improbable event, unlikely to occur more than once or, at most, a few times. Therefore, the presence of an invention in many locales can only be explained by diffusion. Much of the activity of Boas and his students consisted of studies showing how, when, and where culture traits spread once they had originated. The studies were generally valid and contributed to the general knowledge of culture history, but above all, these men demonstrated conclusively that all cultures owe much—indeed most —of their heritage to borrowing from other and earlier cultures. Kroeber (*op. cit.*) has provided detailed histories of the spread of several important inventions—paper, printing, systems of measurement, and even art styles—from their points of origin to their many ultimate destinations. The late Ralph Linton published a short tongue-in-cheek article entitled "One Hundred Per Cent American," which shows the great debt the United States owes to earlier civilizations. Linton traced a day in the life of an "unsuspecting patriot," from the moment he awakens until he settles back in his commuter train on his way to work. Nearly everything he uses, wears, or eats had its origins in some other part of the world. His last act before boarding his train is to buy a newspaper:

Once on board he settles back to inhale the fumes of a cigarette invented in Mexico, or a cigar invented in Brazil. Meanwhile, he reads the news of the day, imprinted in characters invented by the ancient Semites by a process invented in Germany upon a material invented in China. As he scans the latest editorial pointing out the dire results to our institutions of accepting foreign ideas, he will not fail to thank a Hebrew God in an Indo-European language that he is a one hundred per cent (decimal system invented by the Greeks) American (from Americus Vespucci, Italian geographer). (Linton 1966:254– 55.)

What is it that diffuses in the spread of culture? Is it the actual item itself? For example, following its invention by the Chinese, was paper physically transported from one country to another, or was it knowledge of the technical process for producing paper, or both? Anthropologists have analyzed the process of diffusion to show that it takes a number of forms.

In many cases an idea originates in a culture and is expressed by an invention. Then a neighboring culture becomes aware of this idea, accepts it, and expresses the idea in the same or a highly similar form. Kroeber (*op. cit.*, 367), for example, cites the case of the Australian ballot, which could be secretly marked and deposited in such a way as to eliminate fraud. This idea spread to the United States and led to an almost identical voting procedure. Therefore, we may say that the Australian ballot diffused to the United States.

A somewhat similar result is achieved through the import or export of cultural items through trade. A number of nations first received the automobile through trade, when manufactured vehicles were transported abroad and sold. Ultimately some of these nations (e.g., Japan) utilized the idea to manufacture their own automobiles. We can again say that the item diffused from the west to Japan and other nations.

Finally, there occurs what many anthropologists have called *stimulus diffusion:* a culture borrows an idea from another culture, but for some reason cannot or will not reproduce it in the same form. Kroeber provides an example (*ibid.*, 369), the invention of porcelain by the Chinese. This product was imported by Europeans, who made every attempt to reproduce it locally but without success. It was not until centuries later that Europeans finally succeeded in reinventing "china," stimulated by the earlier import of the idea from the Chinese.

Acceptance and Rejection of Cultural Items. The present-day generation of anthropologists is no longer interested in diffusion for its own sake. Few published studies in recent years have traced the spread of items of culture over the face of the earth. Far more significant for modern anthropological investigation are the processes whereby borrowed items are accepted and incorporated into the borrowing culture. A diffused item is not significant unless it actually penetrates a culture and is accepted into it. In most cases, the new item must be reinterpreted so that it is compatible with the existing inventory of the recipient culture; it must be given meaning in terms of the borrowing culture. This points up the significance of the process of stimulus diffusion—a people will often accept an idea, but will then give it their own outward expression. "Rock and roll" music in Peru, for example, is adapted to familiar Peruvian themes; "Chinese food" served in North American restaurants has been adapted to the American palate, and bean curds or certain marine worms common to Chinese cooking do not find their way into North American restaurant cooking. These are trivial examples, but more significant illustrations of this principle are readily available; some are presented in a later discussion of religious syncretism.

The main point is that members of society have three general alternatives when faced with diffusion of an item of culture: (1) reject the item; (2) accept and modify the item; or (3) accept the item as it is. Ready acceptance of the item is related to such factors as the "felt need" for the item, its familiarity to the borrowing people, or the ease with which it can be borrowed without serious disruption of existing cultural patterns. Certain items, for example, have always diffused readily to other cultures. Steel tools produced by western civilization—knives, axes, hoes—have found ready acceptance among primitives and non-western peasants because there is an existing counterpart in the borrowing culture, there is a need for them, and they are generally far superior to the stone items already in use. Also, aspirin seems to be generally acceptable to the same kinds of cultures. Headaches are a universal complaint, aspirin provides a ready relief, and apparently does not conflict with any existing belief.

Cultural innovations other than technical devices of obvious utility often appear in response to some internal cultural need and are invented by persons who share the goals, values, and beliefs of the majority of the members of their own society. When these same items spread to a foreign culture, they are likely to encounter quite a different social system characterized by significantly different values and behavioral norms. In order to accept the diffusing item, the potential borrowing culture must either reinterpret it to fit the existing patterns, or accommodate the diffusing patterns, or both. Sometimes the accommodation cannot be made.

The cyclical reappearance of short skirts in United States fashions fails to penetrate the culture of certain religious groups because existing norms of modesty in these groups preclude such acceptance. For centuries Islamic nations have resisted the penetration of such ideas as life insurance, photography, playing cards, and alcoholic beverages because these things are explicitly or implicitly forbidden by Islamic beliefs. The greater the conflict between a diffusing item and the value system of a borrowing culture, the greater the accommodation that has to be made, and the greater the probability that the item will be rejected, resisted, or profoundly modified in the borrowing. For example, Islamic nations have readily borrowed many items of western technology, but items of Christian belief being diffused to Islamic cultures have to compete with an established religious system that provides the basis for much of the culture. Christian missionary work rarely makes significant headway in such cultures.

Acculturation and Acculturative Situations

It is probable that throughout human history groups of people have had at least sporadic contact with other, culturally different groups. Certainly this can be observed in the few surviving hunting and gathering societies in the world today; wherever such groups have had more than passing contact with outsiders, their cultures have changed as a consequence. This process, wherein the culture of one human group or society becomes modified through more or less enduring contact with another group, is called *acculturation*. The nature of the contact can be highly variable. Change may occur through borrowing from one another, or it may be a result of the adjustments that each culture makes to the presence of the other. Conceivably no borrowing will occur at all, and yet one or both cultures involved will become drastically changed. One social group, for example, may pose a serious military threat to another, which will be met by the development of a defensive organization heretofore unneeded.

The term acculturation refers only to the fact of culture contact and to the changes that take place; it does not specify the nature of that contact or the different kinds of change that result. Acculturative situations may vary according to the relative dominance of the groups concerned, depending upon whether this dominance is primarily political, economic, religious, or a combination of these. Acculturative situations also vary according to whether contact is immediate and direct, or deferred and sporadic; according to the relative size or "mass" of the cultures in contact; and according to the duration and intensity of contact.

Military Conquest. One of the more common situations throughout history has been that in which groups—bands, villages, entire tribes—of a similar technological level have shared a common boundary. There may be occasional warfare or feuding among them, followed by periods of peace, and potential and actual hostilities will play an important part in their social organization. In Chapter 15, for example, we have seen that tribal-level organization is a response to intermittent warfare. In addition to this kind of social readjustment, however, many specific items of culture are diffused from one group to another with the result that each group becomes increasingly like the other. This type of acculturative situation is characterized by a lack of significant dominance.

Dominance of one culture over another can come about in many ways, but military conquest is probably the most frequent source of this kind of acculturation. The Spanish conquest of the New World is an outstanding example. In several areas—notably Mexico, Guatemala, and Peru—the Spanish found dense Indian populations organized into complex states or even empires. The Spanish came in relatively small numbers, but succeeded in deposing Indian administrative institutions and replacing them with their own political, economic, and religious institutions. Enforced acculturation resulted. Indians were forced to give up pre-conquest religious patterns and took on the outward forms of Catholicism; they were forced to raise new crops and herd cattle for the Spanish; and finally, despite the persistence of some parts of Indian culture, nearly every aspect of Indian life was profoundly affected. Acculturation, however, is rarely a unilateral process. Over the centuries, descendants of the Spanish took on many elements of Indian culture, especially foods and agricultural practices, and mixed descendants of Spanish and Indians (mestizos) bear a culture that is a complex blending of both parent cultures.

Conquest does not always result in the enforced acculturation of the subordinate group. China provides a notable exception. Over a span of many centuries, China was invaded and conquered repeatedly by militaristic tribes from beyond her frontiers, such as the Mongols or Manchus. Each invader set up its own ruling dynasty over the Chinese, and then within several generations lost its original culture. Each became absorbed or assimilated into Chinese civilization. This is not unique in human history; it has occurred in other times and places where militaristic, nomadic peoples lived on the peripheries of more opulent civilizations. The Aztecs were relative newcomers to the Valley of Mexico, where advanced civilization had been achieved centuries earlier. These militaristic upstarts were looked down upon as *Chichimecs*—barbarians—by the more established civilizations already occupying the Valley. By 1500 the Aztecs were the supreme power, and they had taken on much of the civilization of their predecessors.

Economic Dominance. Another kind of acculturation is that which involves economic dominance. Several nations in modern times—most notably the United States and England—have built up far-flung international trading relations. In some cases these nations have become the chief importers of the surpluses of less developed nations, especially those practicing monoculture (raising a single crop such as coffee, sugar, or rubber). These monocultural nations in turn imported the economic surplus of the more advanced nations. Consumer patterns and even individual aspirations of the peoples of the less developed nations are influenced by such trade. In rural Latin America, for example, it is a very remote village indeed where the visitor does not see signs advertising Coca-Cola or Alka-Seltzer, or where someone does not own a Singer sewing machine. Not uncommonly, where a dominant nation has developed extensive trade agreements with an "underdeveloped nation," these interests are fostered and protected through loans, aid missions, and occasional political interference. With the growth of nationalist sentiments, the peoples of such nations have come to resent the influence of the larger nation, which they brand as economic imperialism.

Importation of a Subordinate Group. The importation of African slaves into the New World provides an example of an acculturative situation in which the subordinate group entered the territory of the dominant group. Brazil illustrates this very well. At one time Negroes were the single largest element in the total population of Brazil; they are still dominant in some regions. The Negro of Brazil today is first and foremost a Brazilian. While he lives within the framework of a social, political, and religious organization that is predominantly Portuguese in origin, the Negro has also contributed to this culture—especially to its folklore and music, but also to its religion. Along Brazil's Atlantic coast, and in many of her cities, Negro populations are members of complex syncretic cults characterized by blends of Catholic and African cultural elements.

Religious Proselytizing. Acculturation often occurs over long distances and involves relatively few representatives of one of the cultures in contact. Religious proselytizing is a good illustration. Individual missionaries, missionary families, or small groups of missionaries, whose principal goal is spreading their own religious beliefs, often travel great distances to take up residence among peoples of foreign cultures. These missionaries are representative of their own culture, though certainly a specialized aspect of it, and bring this culture into contact with the native culture through their missionary work. If the native people accept new gods, clothe their nakedness, and give up polygyny, they have become acculturated to that extent. Many contemporary missionary groups stress culture change far beyond religious conversion. They often characterize themselves as medical or educational missionaries, and their goals are better health practices, improved farming practices, literacy, and so on. Many contemporary churches have become important private agencies of "planned culture change."

Acculturation of Subgroups. Acculturation need not occur between separate and distinct societies. The cultures in contact are frequently subcultures within the same larger society. A very common situation in highland Guatemala is one in which peoples identified as Indians live side-by-side with peoples called *Ladinos*. The Indian often speaks a Mayan dialect, wears a distinctive costume, practices a Catholicism strongly blended with pre-conquest Indian elements, and is generally culturally distinct from the *Ladino*. The latter is oriented toward national culture—speaks Spanish, is literate, votes, identifies with formal, orthodox Catholicism, and so on. He is the Indian's chief contact with national culture. Guatemala, like many Latin American nations, looks upon these modern Indians as a serious social problem. They participate little in political life, place no value on education, produce relatively little for the market, buy from the market in penny quantities, and are generally seen as obstacles to social and economic development. One of the authors (Ewald 1957) has shown how national legislation, designed to ameliorate some of these problems, has affected (acculturated) the Indian population of San Antonio Sacatepequez in western Guatemala.

Empirical studies of the past thirty years have yielded a large and significant body of literature dealing with acculturation, and it is far beyond the scope of this chapter even to summarize the findings in this field. However, there are two kinds of reaction to acculturation which

are highly significant: *revitalization movements* and *religious syncretism.*
Both are important for an understanding of the process of culture change.

Revitalization Movements. Wallace (1956:265) has proposed the term
revitalization movement to describe ". . . a deliberate, organized, conscious effort by members of a society to construct a more satisfying culture." Although other writers have described similar movements as nativistic, revivalistic, messianic, and vitalistic, Wallace finds that the above
definition describes what is basic to all of them. The members of a
culture engaged in this type of activity perceive their culture as unsatis-
factory and attempt to change it. Such movements *per se* are not acculturative, but they are sometimes stimulated by contact situations.

Under certain culture contact situations—notably those originating in
conquest—a subordinate population finds much of its former way of life
destroyed. Traditional ways of solving problems and of coping with
the environment, norms of social interaction sanctioned by traditional
social controls, patterns of religious behavior, meaningful values—all can
be destroyed under the highly disruptive effects of enforced acculturation. In the short run it is difficult for a society to achieve a reintegration of its parts, and under continued pressure a society might find
reintegration impossible. This situation provides fertile soil for a revitalization movement—a mass attempt to create a more satisfactory culture.
Often the movement has a strong element of fantasy or unrealism—the
members of the dominant culture will be driven into the sea, buffalo will
again roam the Plains, things will be as they were before. The movement may be purely secular, or it may be strongly religious, as in the
so-called messianic movements which are organized around a religious
leader.

The famed "Cargo Cults" of Melanesia are an example of revitalization movements. Cargo Cult movements have appeared in many scattered
locales in the western Pacific, and have been given many local names.
Among a Kaoka-speaking group of northeastern Guadalcanal there occurred a movement known as Masinga Rule (Hogbin 1964:95–98). These
tribesmen had not been subject to the bloody fighting that took place in
parts of Guadalcanal early in World War II, but nevertheless, under colonial dominance, much of their former culture was lost by 1945. Traditional headmen had disappeared, the great feasts that gave men prestige
were no longer practiced, missionaries put an end to native forms of worship and stamped out polygyny, and great trading expeditions and
traditional warfare were ended by the British colonial government. Simultaneously, the availability of wage labor—first on British plantations, and
later with the American military—gave the young Kaoka men economic
independence which contributed to the decline of traditional economic,

social, and political systems. Much of the culture that had given meaning to their traditional way of life was gone.

Masinga Rule was a response to this situation and was based upon elements of the contact situation. "The believers hold that, if they behave themselves in the manner divinely revealed to the leaders, the wartime American transports will return bringing all the goods of Western manufacture that are so ardently desired" (*ibid.*, 97). At first the movement was largely political, but soon other aspects were stressed.

> The generous American soldiers were distinguished from the niggardly British plantation owners of the pre- and postwar years, and the dogma was propounded that, if only the people had sufficient faith and carried out the ritual outlined by the Masinga-Rule chiefs, the former would come back to the Solomons with their landing craft and liberty ships. These would anchor in the harbors and unload cases full of cigarettes, tobacco, canned foods, axes, knives, machines, fishhooks, lines, clothing, and all the other things that had been there for the asking from 1943 to 1945. Fired with enthusiasm, the natives erected huge sheds for storing the cargo. Sceptics, they said, would be deprived of their land and punished. (*Ibid.*)

Wallace (*op. cit.*) has formulated a series of stages that occur when a revitalization process runs its full course. The following summary paraphrases his main points, adapting them to the context of this discussion.

1. *Steady state.* This situation reflects a condition of cultural stability and might describe Solomon Island society in the years before World War II. "For the vast majority of the population, culturally recognized techniques for satisfying needs operate with such efficiency that chronic stress within the system varies within tolerable limits" (*ibid.*, 268). Even with some interference from the colonial government, the peoples of Guadalcanal were able to devise new techniques for satisfying their needs without seriously disrupting other need-serving mechanisms.

2. *The period of increased individual stress.* Here, a progressive decrease in the cultural means for reducing individual stress is present. The reduced efficiency of the cultural system can result from many factors, including acculturative ones or political subordination. The individual reaches a point of increased stress and must find new ways of doing things. Though the data on Masinga Rule were not presented in this particular context, this stage appears to fit what was happening in the years immediately following World War II in Guadalcanal.

3. *The period of cultural distortion.* Prolonged stress and anxiety, based upon the prospect of changing one's ways of behaving, can result in a variety of individual reactions. Wallace speaks of certain regressive action systems: alcoholism, passivity and indolence, disregard for group mores, and so on. The culture becomes distorted: ". . . the ele-

ments are not harmoniously related but are mutually inconsistent and interfering" (*ibid.*, 269). Stress therefore continues to rise. The cultural distortion of traditional patterns in Guadalcanal was described above. The replacement of traditional forms of leadership with new leaders recognized by the district administration is an example of the "piecemeal cultural substitution" discussed by Wallace. The traditional sanctions behind leadership were lacking, the economic supports were gone, and the new patterns were not geared to traditional ways.

4. *The period of revitalization.* A society can disintegrate to the point of extinction unless some revitalization process takes place. A religious revitalization movement often begins with a single individual who, under stress, experiences something akin to a vision or a moment of insight. A supernatural being may appear to him and set forth a set of rules for revitalization. He communicates his vision to others, promising the protection of the supernatural being, as well as material benefits for him and his society if they adopt the new cultural system (cargo cult, nativistic cult, etc.). A group of converts may form, and an action program begins. These followers may also have visions or revelatory experiences. Often such movements meet severe resistance from the dominant power and must be gradually modified to make them acceptable. Eventually, however, significant reintegration may occur. "As the whole or a controlling portion of the population comes to accept the new religion with its various injunctions, a noticeable social revitalization occurs, signalized by the reduction of the personal deterioration symptoms of individuals, by extensive cultural changes, and by an enthusiastic embarkation on some organized program of group action" (*ibid.*, 275).

5. *The new steady state.* With the establishment of viable new culture patterns, the course of revitalization will have been run. The culture of the new state will differ in many ways from that of the earlier steady state, but a form of cultural stability is achieved once again.

Religious Syncretism in Acculturation. It is possible for a borrowing culture to accept a new idea and incorporate it, more or less intact, into its own patterns. Where this occurs, there is relatively little modification of these existing patterns. There is little evidence to suggest that Latin American Indian peasants, for example, have changed radically to accommodate to the presence of the European- or American-made steel hoe. This is not to suggest that technological imports are always so neutral. The importation of the gasoline-powered mill into Middle American communities has had the effect of releasing peasant women from the time-consuming drudgery of milling corn by hand. Their newfound leisure some day may have profound social consequences to which the peasant community will have to adjust.

Elements of two cultures are sometimes found in syncretism, as in the religious rites of the South American Indians. Priests from nearby Canelos have influenced the Indians to observe the Christian matrimony at Pacy Yacu in Ecuador. (Courtesy of the American Museum of Natural History.)

By far the most frequent process in acculturation is one in which both the borrowed item(s) and the existing culture undergo modification as they accommodate one another. The result is a process of blending to which anthropologists give the name *syncretism*. Syncretism can occur in any part of culture where there is borrowing, but nowhere is it clearer or more dramatic than in religious borrowing. The religious systems which arise as the result of this process are known, accordingly, as *syncretic cults*. These are world-wide in their occurrence. Very typically, where a major world religion (Islam or Catholicism, in particular) has been imposed upon a people already practicing a viable religion, the result is a blending: some elements of the new religion are rejected outright, some elements of the old religion are completely lost, and the resultant new system represents a compromise. The Vodun (Voodoo) religion of Haiti represents a blending of African elements with Catholicism, as do similar cults in Brazil. Worship of gods of pure African origin, while retaining much of Catholicism, is common. In such contexts, the gods may be known by both their African names and by the names of Catholic saints. "Xango, a god of lightning and thunder, is equated with St. Jerome (young Xango) and sometimes with St. Peter (old Xango). Ogun, a god of the hunt in the Yoruban pantheon, is St. Anthony in Bahia and St. George in other parts of Brazil" (Wagley 1963:243). The leader of such a cult may be known as the "mother . . ." or "father in sainthood."

Some of the outstanding examples of the religious syncretism that has occurred under conditions of acculturation are to be found where the Spanish imposed Catholicism upon Indians who had a highly developed church-state form of religion in pre-conquest times. This is notably true of southern Mexico, Guatemala, and highland Peru and Bolivia —areas occupied aboriginally by the Aztec, Maya, and Inca civilizations.

Madsen (1960:1–35) provides an excellent illustration of this process among contemporary Maya Indians of southern Mexico, Guatemala, and British Honduras. He shows how the forms of pre-conquest Maya religion were crucial to their ultimate acceptance of Christianity. The following brief examples are drawn from Madsen's more extended discussion. The ancient Maya conceived of their world as having four cardinal directions, corresponding to north, east, south, and west. At each of these corners stood a Bacab or skybearer. Each direction had its color, and the Bacab was a god of the world direction and color. Also at each corner stood a wild cotton tree (the ceiba), which symbolized abundance and which in Maya art was represented as a stylized cross. "To see the natives worshipping a cross no doubt interested the Spaniards a great deal" (*ibid.*, 8). These four world directions were prayed to in Maya rituals for rain, and were therefore associated in Maya thought with the Chacs (rain gods). Finally, a Maya village had four exits— perhaps symbolizing the world directions—each marked by a pile of stones. These stone piles entered into certain ceremonies and were of great importance.

The Spanish friars, following the conquest, set about systematically to destroy native religious institutions and practices—the native priesthood, all forms of public worship, idolatry, religious architecture, and so on. These were to be replaced in all cases with Christian supernatural beliefs, doctrines, and rituals. Often, the way in which this was done resulted in the peculiar blending that took place. The friars often converted older Indian shrines to Christian use, and one of their actions was to order crosses to be placed on the piles of stones at the village exits. A cross-like symbol (the ceiba tree) was already identified in the Indian mind with the four directions, and this new practice may have facilitated the Indian acceptance of the Christian cross. The result: a partial confusing and mixing of the two religions.

Another coincidence which undoubtedly added to the confusion and mixture of the two religions was the fact that the day of the Holy Cross fell on May 3rd which just about coincides with the coming of the rains at the end of the dry season, immediately after sowing. The Cross, as I have already pointed out, was associated prior to the Conquest with the four directions, and hence with agriculture and the rains. (*Ibid.*, 13.)

Thus, because of the fortuitous timing of Holy Cross, Catholic observances on that day could well have struck the Indians as a ceremony for rain, a conception strikingly similar to their own practices. Further, Spanish church architecture of the time often placed statues of the saints or archangels at the four corners of a square area, which may have contributed to a later identification of the archangels with the four Chacs. The Bible itself, Madsen shows, makes references to directions, the number four, and colors. He quotes *Revelation* vii:1 as follows:

"And after these things I saw four angels standing on the four corners of the earth, holding the four winds of the earth, that the wind should not blow on the earth, nor on the sea, nor on any tree." (*Ibid.*, 13.)

The writer goes on to show other circumstances that contributed to the blending in the minds of the Indians—such notions as the directions, the cross, rain, archangels, and many more. In *Revelation* vi:1–8 there appear the four riders of the Apocalypse, mounted on horses of different colors which correspond roughly with the Maya directional colors. This may have contributed to the final coalescing of the Chacs and the archangels, for ultimately the Chacs are seen as riding about on their colored horses, bringing rain as they ride.

Modern Maya Indians, like the descendants of the Aztecs in Mexico and those of the Inca in Peru, are nominally Catholic. They accept the major Christian supernaturals, have their children baptized, attend Mass when a priest visits town, and generally think of themselves as "very good Catholics." Nevertheless, their religion is most often a syncretic product, the complex blending of many elements to produce something neither Catholic nor "pagan," but a new product of both of them. Thus, Madsen finds, the cross is central to present-day Maya worship, but it is their own conception of the cross—a being that sees, hears, thinks, and can answer prayers.

SOCIOCULTURAL CHANGES AS AN ADAPTIVE PROCESS

Much of the stress to this point has been upon the appearance of new items of culture in sociocultural systems, whether from internal innovation or from external sources. These new items include technical devices and processes, ideas, religious beliefs, and potentially anything else that can be classified as an item of culture. These are not just "things," added to or subtracted from collections of other things. Rather, they are aspects of human behavior, and human behavior is organized. Man lives as a member of a group whose organization determines and shapes, to some extent, his behavior. This organization is based upon real action, which in turn relates to real structure and real function to form the behavioral dimension of organization. When culture changes, it is real action that changes. Thus, when a Latin American peasant woman abandons her primitive grindstone in favor of a commercially operated power grinder, it is her behavior as an occupant of the status of wife or housekeeper that changes. Because of this change in real action, in time the norms for that structural position may also change. Insofar as this change may alter the relationship between husband and wife, the change in real action also modifies the real structure of that society.

This aspect of change is of particular interest to many anthropologists today. To establish that a new culture trait has arisen through invention, that it has diffused to a culture over a great distance, or that it has been imposed through conquest, explains nothing about the crucial social processes that are involved. Little can be learned about the dynamics of sociocultural systems if investigation stops here. The significance of these statements becomes clear when the reader recalls a statement made many times in this book: culture is man's adaptive mechanism. Man uses culture to adapt to his total environment—natural and cultural—and it is through social organization that this adaptation is achieved. Men hunt, attack their enemies, till the soil, manufacture tools, dance, sing, pray to their gods, reproduce their kind, use kinship terms, and engage in all the other activities that collectively comprise their adaptation. These things are always done within an organizational context.

However, a social system is rarely if ever precisely adapted to the total environment. Integration or fit is never perfect, and numerous variables prevent such perfection. Dependency relations among groups are in permanent flux, the unification of groups is imperfect, individuals seldom accept all of the values and goals of their society, persons deviate from expected behavior in many ways, and a society's environment changes constantly. The appearance of an immigrant group may require new kinds of action—defense, trade, mutual aid, intermarriage, and so on. The sudden disappearance of a valued natural resource may require drastic economic changes; conversely, the acquisition of a new technological process may permit the exploitation of new resources. Many times in the course of human history the advent of a major innovation, coming from within or from outside a society, has had profound consequences for the existing social system. A social system is never a static thing. Change is a never ending process of readjustment and readaptation, as man responds behaviorally to ever changing circumstances.

Organizational Change

If we adopt the analysis of organization presented in Chapter 7, then logically change can be of three main kinds: behavioral, structural, and functional. The order of this list represents a logical sequence, since change—because it is a dynamic process—must begin with real action. Someone may take the contrary position that a legislative body can create a new structure to which real action must then conform. The Congress of the United States, for example, may begin by conceiving of a new function to be fulfilled—perhaps combating poverty. A new agency (an ideal structure) may then be created to serve this function; simultaneously the expected behavior of that agency is specified. Further, it may be expected that as individuals are appointed to the agency their real behavior will result in the structure itself becoming real and its expected functions being made manifest. This sequence can and often does occur, but the reader should recognize that the creation of the new agency itself began with real action. In this hypothetical case, the social scientist will not have to look far for the causes of this real action. He will have before him many of the diverse social, economic, and political conditions that result in poverty, that necessitate action to combat it, and that culminate in the action of the legislators.

Far more frequently the anthropologist finds himself studying and analyzing change in other cultures, where the factors involved are not so readily apparent. He begins, as field research must, with real action. From this he derives the manifest structure and function of real action. A more refined and sophisticated analysis may be required to specify the ideal dimensions of the organization. Upon completion of his analysis, however, change may not be apparent to him at all. Life in a peasant village, for example, changes slowly, and during a twelve-month or an eighteen-month visit changes are difficult to detect. As an anthropologist, however, he knows that even peasant societies change continuously, and he may be able to establish this fact if he has access to reliable historical information. Older people can be interviewed, local records can be consulted, and access to archival materials may be possible.

An Example: San Antonio Sacatepequez. One of the authors, using methods such as these, was able to reconstruct political changes in a Guatemalan village over a twenty-year period. Full and detailed historical information is always the most reliable source for establishing the facts of change and determining the structural and functional readaptations that have taken place. The action analysis of social institutions, however, provides us with a method for at least suggesting the direction that change is taking or is likely to take. As shown in Chapter 7, this may be achieved by focusing on discrepancies or incongruencies among real, normative, and expected action, and their possible influence on real structure. This can be illustrated briefly by the data from San Antonio Sacatepequez. These data were not collected with this mode of analysis in mind, and therefore do not permit us to do more than suggest the applicability of this method.

This community is characterized by a rigid system of stratification which some writers have referred to as a caste or caste-like system. The conscious model (expected structure) in the minds of the people bears out this definition of caste. The non-Indian *Ladinos* are the superordinate group in this hierarchy and regard themselves as superior in every way to the subordinate Indians. They often rationalize their superiority on biological grounds, though Indian and *Ladino* alike are often mestizos (of mixed ancestry). Ideally, there is no intermarriage and no upward mobility, and social interaction between members of the two groups is marked by extreme courtesy, almost servility, of Indian toward *Ladino*. A *Ladino* never performs wage labor for an Indian, whereas the latter is heavily dependent upon *Ladinos* for cash wages. This system began developing several generations ago and became quite stable early in the twentieth century, not only in San Antonio but in many other Guatemalan communities. Despite the differential privileges built into this system, it does provide for most of the basic needs and satisfactions of both *Ladino* and Indian. Many Guatemalan communities approximate the "steady state" postulated by Wallace (see page 448). Even when the community appears to be very stable, and when historical evidence for change is lacking, the observer can detect many indications of change in this system.

Various interactions between the two groups are regulated by norms —for example, rules of etiquette (discussed more fully in Chapter 2), rules of endogamy, and the occurrence of intergroup sex relations (discussed in Chapter 7). In each of these areas of behavior there is a high, though varying, agreement among the norm, normative behavior, and expected behavior. Nevertheless, real action is occasionally observed to diverge sufficiently far from the norm to approach or even reach deviance. Many of the younger Indian men are less formal in their etiquette toward *Ladinos* than the older ones, and today a wave of the hand may take the place of the tipping of a hat. Further, a young Indian male may approach a mixed group before the town hall and offer to shake hands with everyone, including *Ladinos*. On occasions where there is a good deal of drinking, young Indians are often openly disrespectful and even hostile toward certain *Ladino* males. In general, *Ladino* males, especially the older ones, are disturbed by such behavior.

Several *Ladino* males in this village live in common law with Indian women. In these cases the man refers to the woman as "my woman," or "my concubine," but not "my wife." In this way caste lines are kept distinct, because there is no actual marriage. Such common-law unions are the norm and are expected of lower-class *Ladinos*. It is not the norm for *Ladino* women to live with Indian men, yet one household in the village did consist of such a pair. In this case, there is some doubt about the Indian status of the man. In spite of the fact that ideally everyone is either an Indian or a *Ladino*, and the latter claim to be white or Spanish, there is occasional awareness of the logical inconsistency of this position where a *Ladino* is known to have an Indian grandparent or great-grandparent. The ambiguous reaction of the community to this behavior (the common-law union) indicates a discrepancy between real and expected structure.

Rules of intergroup etiquette require that *Ladino* males do not shake hands with or fraternize with Indian men. Yet two notable exceptions did occur. One of the most prosperous stores in the village was owned by an Indian, who also owned much land in another part of the country and had the only truck in the village. He employed a poor *Ladino* from a nearby large town. Whenever he returned from a business trip he was greeted respectfully by some *Ladino* men, who openly shook his hand. When questioned, they appeared embarrassed and insisted that this was no indication of their equality. Another Indian who lived in an outlying hamlet within the municipality of San Antonio owned much land near "the coast," dressed well, and rode a fine white horse. He occasionally drank with young *Ladino* men, and when he died very suddenly, many *Ladinos* attended his funeral. He was described to the author as "one of our better Indians." Again, there was a denial of equality.

It is significant, however, that in both of these cases the Indian male was well-to-do and independent of the patronage of any *Ladino*. It is precisely this patronage—the renting of land, provision of wage labor, giving of gifts, and the offering of protection by *Ladino* to Indian—that constitutes one of the strongest sanctions in this system of unequal privilege. Traditionally, most of the Indians of the community are bound by such a relationship with one or more *Ladino* families. The *Ladinos* also constitute the local political power, however, which gives them an additional and forceful sanction that can be used against Indians who deviate from customary behavior.

The data derived, though incomplete, suggest fairly frequent departures from the norm on the part of some Indians. Such behavior—for example, the frequent shows of disrespect by younger Indians—certainly is not normative but it seems to be expected. This expectation, however, seems to apply mainly to the younger generation of Indians, whereas their elders still follow the traditional forms of courtesy and occasionally can be seen teaching proper behavior to their children and grandchildren. What appears to be taking place is a shift in expected behavior which could someday result in the creation of new norms. This is what happens in culture change: new customary patterns replace old ones.

Apparently a number of factors are at work in San Antonio and other similar communities to bring about this shift. The young Indian men have generally had one or more experiences (such as military service) that have taken them outside the framework of the traditional system, thereby exposing them to new values, new goals, and new conceptions of their own identity. Each year a number of young men from the village are recruited into the army and, for the first time, are exposed to life outside their municipality. They enjoy spending money they have never had before, and they acquire many new wants. Other men have found increased opportunities, especially since the Revolution in 1944, for wage labor outside the municipality. When they return home, these men cannot accept the system as their fathers do. Finally, Protestant missionary work has created a number of converts, again among the younger people, who are often the same young men who are dissatisfied with the status quo.

As Guatemala itself experiences economic growth, as new industries create new jobs, and as expanded communications systems make geographic mobility relatively easy, the old economic base for a caste-like system is seriously weakened and gives way to an economic base that is more compatible with other social forms. If the cases of the two well-to-do Indians are any indication, new criteria of high status are emerging. It may be that a gradual shift from a closed status system to a somewhat more open system, where ranking is based on achievement, is taking place.

In summary, the caste-like system emerged from a particular set of economic, social, and political circumstances. It occurs in relatively isolated rural areas where Indians practice subsistence agriculture and are tied to the *Ladino* in various dependency relationships. The system is maintained through political and economic sanctions wielded by the superior group and through rules of customary behavior which regulate all intercaste relations. With relatively little influence from the outside world, this system was a very stable one. However, as a result of the factors listed above and of increased attempts on the part of the national government to draw the Indian into national economic and political life (Ewald 1957), the conditions within which the system remained stable have changed. The most apparent changes, as we should expect, are in real action. But there are already indications of changes in the real structure because of this new behavior. If and when intermarriage and upward mobility become possible, the ideal structure too will change.

SUMMARY

This brief example illustrates what happens in social change. In response to various factors, which collectively represent changes in the total environment, the social organization begins a process of readaptation. The existing latitude within structural positions permits only a certain amount of deviance in real action, which may come about as a response to these changing circumstances. Eventually, as new patterns of action become more frequent and acceptable, new norms will have come into existence. In some cases new requirements will result in the creation of new structural positions. The Hopi Indians, for example, under pressure from the United States government, found themselves with "chiefs" where they had none before. Eventually, the real structure of social organization will change to meet the new requirements. The reintegration or reunification of society may be more effective or less effective than in the previous "steady state" (to borrow Wallace's term), but the important point is that change occurs as a response to changing circumstances.

An earlier generation of anthropologists often took the position that rapidly changing tribal peoples could not be profitably studied in their present condition. They believed that western contacts had disrupted these societies to such a great extent that they no longer possessed a viable social organization. Therefore, field work by these anthropologists consisted of reconstructing these rapidly changing societies as they had been before contact. Various aspects of the social organization found at the time of investigation were interpreted as survivals or distorted forms of a formerly viable organization and were not deemed worthy of study. The present generation of anthropologists, however, increasingly appreciates the fact that whatever form of organization is found in any society—however ineffective it appears—represents some kind of adjustment, even if the society or the environment is changing rapidly. It is the study of these processes of change—how human groups cope with a rapidly changing world—that constitutes one of the most important contributions of contemporary anthropology.

17

The Applications of Anthropology

INTRODUCTION

In the preceding chapters, we have introduced the reader to both the depth and the breadth of anthropological knowledge. We have discussed what anthropologists do, and how they do it; analyzed at length the fundamental concept of our science—culture; explored the meaning of culture as a conceptual tool; related the origins of cultural behavior to man's biological origins; and studied the history of culture in the conceptual framework of evolution. Then, focusing on culture more specifically in the context of organization, we have examined the more significant areas of human behavior—economic, ritual, and political.

Implicit throughout this discussion has been the authors' belief, which is shared by most anthropologists, that such knowledge is a worthwhile end in itself. The pursuit of knowledge without visible practical ends requires no justification. Human nature, if this term has any meaning, must certainly include man's capacity for wondering and for speculating, and his desire to seek understanding. Undeniably, an important part of man's adjustment to his world is his efforts to make that world and everything in it meaningful and intelligible. Writing with this implicit conviction, we have not addressed ourselves to the possible uses and applications of our knowledge of man.

Nevertheless, the question inevitably arises, "Knowledge for what?" A distinction is commonly made in the physical sciences between so-called pure science and applied science. The former is often justified in terms of the latter. Quite possibly, the need for such justification reflects a dominant utilitarian value in our own culture. The scientist who quite happily pursues researches that have no foreseeable application to industry, medicine, or commerce may, because of this dominant value, feel compelled to point out that much "pure research" in the past has led ultimately to practical uses undreamed of by the researcher.

It would seem fair to ask, then, whether there is or can be an applied science of man; whether anthropological knowledge can be put to work to serve human needs or solve human problems. Our immediate answer would be a qualified "yes"—qualified because there are certain obvious cases of proven application, and other more controversial areas where application is claimed but not so clearly achieved.

Examples of the demonstrated uses of anthropological knowledge are many. An obvious illustration would be in the area of medicine. Many medicinal plants used by primitive or non-literate peoples have found their way into the modern pharmacopeias and the anthropologist has often been the medium whereby this knowledge was transmitted. This, however, is a by-product of anthropological knowledge, and is not entirely what we mean by application. A better example would be the uses to which physical anthropology has been put in recent years. As Lasker has stated (1961:3–4):

> The fourth phase of the postwar advances [in physical anthropology] was the application of proven anthropological techniques and their modification to meet practical requirements. World War II itself provided many opportunities for such new applications. It was necessary to clothe millions of men and women, using a limited number of uniform sizes; planes, tanks, and trucks had to be designed to accommodate live human beings; remains of war dead needed identification; geographic medicine was a concern of our far-flung armies; and the question of paternity was an aftermath of war.

Physical anthropologists now commonly hold positions in medical and dental schools. Because of their specialized knowledge of the structure and function of the human body, they have made recognized contributions to these fields. Our concern in this chapter, however, is with the possible applications of anthropology to sociocultural problems.

Two quite different questions are involved here: can anthropological theory and knowledge be applied to the solution of sociocultural problems; and can there be a science of *applied anthropology?* Sol Tax, commenting on this distinction (1966:418), points out that professional anthropologists encourage the use of anthropological knowledge by government and private organizations:

> Anthropological knowledge is used by administrators and managers with the wit to use it. If they wish professional assistance, they must turn to anthropologists. Anthropologists indeed become involved in management and administration, just as in social work, education, and public health.

Tax goes on to show that there is no profession of applied anthropology in the same sense that there are professions of engineering and medicine, despite the fact that a Society for Applied Anthropology has existed in the United States for many years. We will return to the question of whether there is or can be a science of applied anthropology. But first, can anthropological theory and knowledge be applied to the solution of sociocultural problems?

ANTHROPOLOGY AND CULTURAL PLANNING

The use of anthropological knowledge for social purposes can be placed in a much broader category—*planned* or *directed culture change.* This category has been defined as knowledgeable intervention into the culture of any group in order to bring about change in a desired direction. Looked at in this very general way, planned change is not new at all. When, for the first time in history, a militant state conquered and imposed its rule on a defeated people, it probably enforced some kind of economic reorganization to facilitate its exploitation. The Inca of Peru, in expanding their empire over many subject states in the fifteenth century, extensively reorganized local political, religious, and economic systems. This was certainly planned change in a direction desired by the conquerors for their own ends. The Spanish, during their conquests, imposed numerous institutions upon the Indians of the New World. Indians living on widely scattered homesteads were brought together to live in compact settlements called *reducciones,* and the *encomienda* system was instituted to mobilize Indian labor. Under this system, individual conquerors were given certain rights over the Indians occupying specified towns. A standardized political system was imposed at the local level throughout Spanish America, and the Spanish planned the replacement of all native forms of worship with the Catholic Church. These are but two illustrations of a process that has gone on in many parts of the world for hundreds, perhaps thousands of years— planned change through conquest.

Change through conquest was not brought about, however, through the conscious application of anthropological principles. This is not to deny that planners in the past sometimes employed a strategy that modern anthropologists would recognize as theoretically sound. In fact, the early Spanish clergy in the New World made much intelligent use of the pre-existent patterns of Indian culture to introduce new forms of worship. The ideas of baptism and confession to a priest, for example, were easily accepted by Indians whose native religions embraced very similar notions. This approach is consistent with the fact, learned by anthropologists involved in introducing change into different cultures, that items (objects, ideas, suggestions) entering a culture from the outside have a better chance of acceptance if presented to a people in a form that is familiar or intelligible to them.

Anthropological theory, and therefore its conscious application to sociocultural problems, is largely a product of the present century. In fact, it has only been during the past two or three decades that appreciable numbers of anthropologists have recognized that they are applied anthropologists. During World War II anthropologists were called upon by the government to use their knowledge of culture in predicting the behavior of the enemy following their defeat. In the postwar years, the United Nations and many agencies of the United States government

Costumed villagers in a remote section of Peru perform a ritual dance in greeting the arrival of a DDT dusting team. The intelligent use of pre-existent patterns of their culture by the UNICEF team is facilitating the success of this program. (United Nations.)

consciously inaugurated programs of planned change throughout the world, particularly in the so-called underdeveloped nations. It was recognized that technologically backward nations faced enormous problems in developing their economic potential and in overcoming the many concomitants of poverty—illiteracy, high infant mortality, substandard diet and housing, inadequate public health facilities, and many more. These programs of planned change approached the problems of underdeveloped nations (now more commonly referred to as recently developed or emergent nations) in various ways. The United Nations Economic, Social, and Cultural Organization (UNESCO) is particularly concerned with "fundamental education"; the United Nations International Children's Emergency Fund (UNICEF) has focused on the problems of children in emergent nations; Point Four (a program of the United States) was created to promote agricultural development; the United States Agency for International Development (AID) has contributed to the development of industry, agriculture, education, and more; and the Peace Corps, with its "person to person" approach, works at the local level in many nations to stimulate self-help. Meanwhile, the emergent nations themselves have attempted to cope with their own problems, though often with outside financial aid.

The Anthropologist and Programs of Planned Change

An important question intrudes at this point: What does anthropology have to do with technical assistance, economic development, or public health programs? If an emergent nation needs financial assistance, it might be argued, the appropriate international agency can arrange a loan. If it wishes to develop its economic potential, technical experts of other countries (economists, agronomists, conservationists) can be used on a temporary basis. The more prosperous nations can readily loan large numbers of educators, public health officials, and other personnel to any emergent nation requiring help. Unfortunately, offers of such aid, or its actual proffer, frequently lead to rejection on the part of those to be reached. Countless programs of aid (planned change) have failed, or have failed to live up to their potential. People whose culture we wish to change react negatively to offers of aid; they reject innovations outright, or accept them for a time and then allow them to fall into disuse. Why do people fail to modify their ways in "needed" directions or tend to reject innovation? Anthropology can determine the reasons for the failure or ineffectiveness of programs of planned change.

One clue to the problem of why people reject aid is found in the point of view expressed in this book: human behavior is cultural behavior. It is behavior which an individual knows and upon which he depends. Therefore, he is skeptical about changing it and is tenacious when external agents threaten to modify his customary way of life, especially when he does not know or understand the precise changes that will result. He is asked to give up the known for a "better" unknown.

The culture of the society or social group into which an individual is born or lives provides him with a limited number of responses (ways of thinking, acting, or feeling) in any given situation. The ways of accomplishing a given end—tilling the soil, cooking a yam, propelling a canoe, killing an enemy, or decorating one's body—may be potentially unlimited, but in any one society the alternatives are few. A farmer tills the soil in a stooped position using a short-handled steel hoe; his wife and the other women of his community share two or three yam recipes; body decoration is limited to the use of paint, employing a limited number of customary designs; and so on. Many factors—physiological, psychological, social, cultural—are at work, restricting individual behavior to this relatively narrow range of alternatives. On the physiological and psychological levels, a farmer may reject outright the suggestion that he lengthen the handle of his hoe, because this would force him to work in an unfamiliar and, therefore, uncomfortable position. The very thought of eating foods not already included in his diet may fill him with revulsion, to the extent that they would be literally indigestible to him. His culture may place a ban (taboo) on certain foods, such as pork. Geometric designs painted on the chest in white and red may appear highly aesthetic to him, whereas tattooing, pierced ears, or scarification may seem barbarous and hideous.

Directed culture change involves the presentation of new alternatives to a society in a way that they will be accepted. However, these alternatives are frequently ignored or even violently rejected. New alternatives may violate existing norms or even deep-seated taboos; they may fail to meet any felt or perceived need, may involve changing set habit patterns without offering any socially valued rewards, may prescribe unfamiliar action patterns, and so on. Cultural barriers or obstacles to planned change exist in all societies and must be overcome or circumvented if the proposed changes are to be successfully introduced. Only persons who know the culture of the society to be changed can even hope to succeed, and even they will have difficulty.

The place of the anthropologist in this entire process should be readily apparent. As the theoretician of culture change, or of culture in general, he is best equipped to do some or all of the following to increase the success and effectiveness of programs of planned change.

1. Using specialized techniques of data gathering and analysis, the anthropologist can explain to planners the social organization of the people in

question. Because he takes as his point of departure *real action,* he can define the existing social norms, the range of normative and expected behavior, and the limits beyond which behavior may not go without bringing about corrective, restorative, or punitive action.

2. He can advise planners of the perceived or felt needs of the people, and in this way direct the program more specifically.

3. He can foresee, or at least attempt to predict, cultural obstacles to planned innovations, and from his knowledge of action patterns, ideals, and values, can suggest ways of avoiding these obstacles or of changing the emphasis of planned change so as to negate them.

4. Because the anthropologist knows the totality of cultures and the interrelations of their parts, he can anticipate some of the consequences, both desirable and harmful, of specific changes introduced into the culture.

5. Finally, the anthropologist can provide valuable counsel at all stages of planning, implementation, and follow-up in programs of directed culture change.

There has, in fact, been an increasing awareness on the part of international, national, and private administrators of the crucial understanding that anthropology can contribute not only in planned change but in any area where intercultural understanding is required.

In answer to our original questions, we can say that while there is no well-established profession of applied anthropology, and the science of applied anthropology is in its infancy, we now have a reasonably firm foundation for further developments. The value of anthropological knowledge is widely appreciated, and more often than not the professional anthropologist is called upon to give advice in the application of such knowledge. For many years the British government employed anthropologists in colonial administration; American anthropologists were enlisted in the task of administering the Pacific Trust Territories following World War II; the National Indian Institute of Mexico is not only advised but is administered by anthropologists; anthropologists serve the United States Agency for International Development, the Peace Corps, and UNESCO; and anthropologists are cooperating fruitfully with other professionals in education, public health, urban affairs, and industry in the United States. In short, wherever there are human problems or areas that require intercultural understanding, the anthropologist can make an important contribution.

ANTHROPOLOGY IN TECHNICAL ASSISTANCE PROGRAMS

A major area of application in which United States anthropologists have been involved is technical aid. This term is used to refer to aid offered by trained specialists, in a variety of situations, to those lacking such specialized knowledge. The technical specialist may be an engineer, advising the government of an emergent nation about building roads, bridges, irrigation works, or dams; a public health specialist in epidemiology, advising an African or Central American nation about malaria or typhus control; an economist; an educator; or an agronomist. In each case, the technical specialist is expected to study the local situation, make recommendations for action, train host-country personnel, or in some other way contribute to the solution of problems in the host country. Since all of these take into account the culture with which the technical specialist is involved, technical assistance is obviously much more than a technical problem.

As we have already explained, a variety of cultural factors can decrease the success of the technical specialist. This is where the cultural anthropologist can help most effectively. He may be called upon as a consultant or an adviser, for a number of reasons:

1. The recipients of technical assistance are the societies in which anthropologists have been traditionally interested and have studied.
2. The anthropologist is qualified, by training and inclination, to do the painstaking work of analyzing the recipient culture.
3. He is aware of the gap that can exist between the culture of the recipient people and that of the team of technical specialists.
4. He can anticipate some of the obstacles to success.
5. He can serve as a "resident trouble shooter," making on-going judgments as to why a program seems to be failing, why some parts of a program and not others appear to be meeting with success, and can suggest techniques for greater success.
6. As the results of action begin to occur, the anthropologist can provide constant "feedback" into the program, permitting the technical specialist or the administrator to modify the course of action where this seems indicated.

It must be stressed that cases where the anthropologist advises the technical specialist are not examples of the operation of a precise science of applied anthropology. They are, rather, instances of the *application of anthropological knowledge* to human problems. These attempts gain in scientific precision if a cultural anthropologist is actually participating as an adviser, planning consultant, "trouble shooter," or simply as a source of information about the recipient culture. Few anthropologists engaged in such work would claim the distinction of being applied scientists, especially if this term implies rigorously controlled experimental conditions, great accuracy in selecting courses of action, or a high degree of precision in predicting the outcome of action.

We will return to this point at the conclusion of this chapter; we present now a number of case studies in directed culture change, to provide a basis for further generalizations about the process itself.

Case Studies

A number of heterogeneous illustrative cases in which aid has been offered to impoverished, technologically backward communities exemplify many of the ideas discussed above. These cases are selected because they illustrate the need for sociocultural understanding in carrying out any program of induced change, and the obstacles to be encountered when such understanding is lacking. Also, they provide the basis for a number of general principles and practical guides which are applicable to programs of change in general.

An Urban Squatters' Settlement in Peru. One of the authors conducted research in a *barriada* outside a large Peruvian city. This was one of many similar communities that ringed the city. They were formed when migrants, either from the center of the city or from outlying rural areas, invaded public or private lands and took up residence under conditions of extreme poverty, with its accompanying submarginal diet, housing, and sanitation. Typically, several hundred squatter families, living adjacent to one another, would organize themselves about a natural leader (a *presidente*), adopt a name, and in general take on the characteristics of a separate community. During the time of the research, the Peruvian government was in the process of taking title to *barriada* lands, in order to create planned communities in which each family would have legal rights to its plot of land. A separate program was inaugurated to provide low-cost housing to the squatters at very low interest rates. The *barriada* selected for this case had not yet undergone this transformation.

The anthropologist in the course of his research found that his *barriada* had not one, but two local *presidentes*, each presiding over his own "town council." This split occurred when the original *presidente* was accused of mismanaging funds which he had collected for community betterment. Thereafter, some of the families in the *barriada* aligned themselves with one of the councils, and the remaining families with the other council. The bitter hostility that existed between the two *presidentes* spread to their followers. As much as possible, each side occupied its own sector of the *barriada* and avoided members of the rival faction. Each Sunday a priest from the city came to the *barriada* to celebrate Mass in a temporary tent-like structure. Only families from one side of the *barriada* attended. The *presidente* of the other faction explained to the anthropologist that his people were not welcome "over there," and that it would be dangerous to send their children to the catechism class which was conducted as part of the services.

A medical doctor who taught at the local medical school began a weekly visit to the *barriada*, bringing along a number of students to conduct a free clinic. One of the two *presidentes* provided him with quarters in the council meeting hall. Members of the opposing faction, therefore, refused to attend the clinic, and insisted that it was not open to them. This bitter division was expressed in many other ways.

It was this situation that confronted a small group of Peace Corps Volunteers, who arrived to begin a program of urban community development for which they had been trained. One of their first goals was to establish a nursery school for preschool children. In spite of the great antagonisms existing between the two factions, the Volunteers managed to get approval in principle for two small schools—one for the younger age group, another for the older group. Classes were held in the meeting halls of the two factions, with the result that approximately half of the children were made by their parents to boycott the school belonging to the rival faction.

Meanwhile, one of the faction *presidentes* became aware of the availability of the Food for Peace program. The program, financed by the United States, had a headquarters in the city and was administered locally by a Peruvian. This *presidente* enlisted the aid of the Volunteers in bringing the food program to his *barriada*. The director of Food for Peace agreed to come to the *barriada* on a Sunday morning to outline the program to the assembled people of the community. The Peace Corps Volunteers exercised all of their diplomacy to prevail on leaders of both factions to stand together on a platform with the visitor. This they did, but not without a show of great reluctance. The Food for Peace director then explained what was available, and what the *barriada* would have to do to get this help. Food would be made available to provide a substantial breakfast for the smaller children of the *barriada*. All the people had to do was provide a space where the breakfasts would be prepared, and the labor to cook and serve the food to the children. He suggested they build a school for this purpose. Immediately the question was raised: On which side of the *barriada* would this building be located? Slowly, but with mounting intensity, charges and countercharges were hurled by members of the rival factions: who had founded the *barriada;* who had done the most to further its aims; who had its best interests at heart? This went on while mothers of hungry children begged the director for aid. He left the *barriada* when the proceedings erupted into a series of fist fights.

It should be noted that one of the authors was present in the *barriada* as an observer, and participated in none of the situations described above. Much more transpired in the months following this first visit of the Food for Peace representative, and after the departure of the author. But throughout their stay in the *barriada* the Peace Corps Volunteers were accused by each faction of showing favoritism to the other. A municipal agency came to the conclusion that the only solution to the problem would be to relocate the smaller of the two groups. This was an extreme solution to a vexing problem but, as is shown below, factionalism is one of the most difficult of all obstacles to planned culture change. This situation was not unique, since factionalism reportedly occurred in other *barriadas* about the city.

A Rural Cooperative in Mexico. For many years the Mexican government has financed a program of Rural Cultural Missions whose task is to visit rural communities and aid them in improving the conditions of their lives. These are essentially teaching missions, and a representative staff typically includes teachers of agriculture, construction, mechanics, entertainment and recreation, trades and industries, in addition to a social worker, a nurse, and a midwife. A mission staff of this kind operates out of a small town and serves a number of communities in the area for a period of up to three years. Its tasks are to improve agricultural and animal-raising techniques, teach new arts and crafts, promote sounder economic practices, teach concepts of sanitation and preventive medicine, develop an interest in recreational activities, and in general raise the social, economic, and cultural standards of the community.

We will not concern ourselves in this brief case study with the details of organization, philosophy, and methods of this extensive program. Rather, the activities of a specific mission in the small village of San Pablo, about six miles from the large city of Puebla (Whetten 1948: 440–47), are discussed. San Pablo, the administrative center for a larger municipality, had a total population of about 8,500 at the time the Mission did its work there. A large percentage of these people were Indians and speakers of Nahuatl (the language of the ancient Aztecs). Schoolteachers found that they had to devote most of their time to teaching children to speak Spanish. The illiteracy rate was very high—more than 80 per cent of the population over ten years of age.

The principal crop in this village, as in hundreds of Middle American communities, was maize (corn). The maize tortilla was not only the staple item in the local diet, but the principal industry of San Pablo. Over 1,500 local women were engaged in making tortillas for sale in nearby Puebla. Whetten describes the routine as follows: Each day the women carry their corn to a local mill to be ground into the fine dough known as *masa*. This dough is then taken back to the house, where the rest of the morning is spent in patting the dough into round cakes and cooking them on a large shallow dish over a burner. The following morning the women place their loads (about 25 to 50 pounds) on their backs, and set out for Puebla. There, they sell their tortillas, use part of their profits to buy corn for the next day's supply, and return home. Whetten estimates that about half of them walk both ways, while the others take the buses that shuttle every hour between San Pablo and Puebla. These buses are heavily loaded during the early and late hours, with the overflow passengers hanging from the sides or riding on top.

At the time of the Cultural Mission's work, San Pablo was dominated, politically and economically, by a local *cacique* ("boss"), a man who guided and controlled the activities of the municipal authorities and the entire municipality. This man was also prominent in state government. In spite of the practice of electing municipal officers, the *cacique* virtually appointed all officials, including an illiterate *presidente municipal* (*ibid.*, 443).

When the Mission team arrived, they experienced a cool reception and were the victims of much gossip. "Many expressed great surprise that the federal Department of Public Education should be so generous as to want to help them improve their homes and living conditions without obligating them in some way. 'Surely,' they argued, 'it is a trick of some sort designed as an excuse for increasing our taxes or of placing us under obligations to pay for the services at some later date'" (*ibid.*, 445). Eventually, after many delays, the missioners began to make friends, and within a few months they were able to begin work. A major proposal was to organize all tortilla makers into a large cooperative. They would buy their own electric-powered mills, invest in tortilla-making machines, and even buy one or two station wagons to transport the tortillas to Puebla. In addition, stands would be set up permanently in Puebla with permanent salesmen. No longer would 1,500 women have to make the daily trip individually. The director of the Mission took this plan to the state government, where he was told to consult with the local *cacique*. "Vested interests prevented the formation of the co-operative. The cacique threatened to fight the proposal to the bitter end. It is said that he has a monopoly on transportation and owns the buses which run between San Pablo and Puebla and which now carry full loads. He charges a fee for each person and each basket each way. Obviously, any proposal to substitute other forms of transportation or even to curtail the number of passengers would seriously interfere with his business" (*ibid.*, 446). Owners of the local corn grinders protested; the city of Puebla, faced with losing 1,500 market fees each day, was against the proposal; and consumers feared that machine-made tortillas would not taste as good as the hand-made ones. Because of the power of the *cacique* in state and local government, the director of the Mission decided to abandon the project.

A number of other cooperatives were established, however, and be-

A brickyard in an outlying area of Mexico City. (Courtesy of the American Museum of Natural History.)

came successful. Several brick-making cooperatives, each with about ten members, found a ready market for their product. Locally, people had made little use of bricks, because they had to be imported at high cost from Puebla. Now that they were available locally, and more cheaply, people began to make greater use of them. A market for these bricks also developed in the city. In addition to the brick-making cooperative, many people accepted the Mission's plan to raise better breeds of chickens. This proved successful and resulted in a vast increase in egg production for the area.

A Nutritional Program in Guatemala. Several years ago, an organization known as the Nutritional Institute of Central America and Panama (INCAP) undertook a program of nutritional experimentation in Guatemala (Adams 1955:435–58). One project in particular, begun in the Indian village of Magdalena, "was part of a program to determine what supplemental food elements, if any, were needed to improve the local diet, which appeared to be deficient in animal proteins" (*ibid.*, 436).

An Indian housewife prepares corn for tortillas, a traditional pan-cake dish among low income groups, while the children make mats of rushes. (United Nations.)

Each day the school children of Magdalena were brought together and given a food supplement under the direction of a member of the INCAP field staff. Each child was given a periodic physical examination in order to determine the results of nutritional supplements administered. These routine examinations included the collection of data on weight and height and the sampling of blood for laboratory analysis.

In order to secure the cooperation of the villagers, INCAP also established a medical clinic, which was staffed to provide daily services for routine medical cases. More difficult cases, such as those involving surgery, were referred to a hospital in a nearby city.

The initial INCAP staff included a doctor, who visited the village periodically; a nurse, who visited the clinic daily; and a project social worker, who spent most of her time in Magdalena. An anthropologist was added to this staff when difficulties were reported. These difficulties were of several kinds: villagers became antagonistic to staff members; staff members were rumored locally to be politically subversive; parents feared that the staff meant harm to their children. Little by little, cooperation for the program was being withdrawn, and some villagers threatened to have the entire project expelled. The anthropologist, on his arrival, found dissension within the INCAP staff itself.

He proceeded to carry out a program of research to determine the basis of the antagonism present. This involved, first and foremost, an analysis of local social and cultural patterns. On a general level, he found that the chief interests of the Magdalenos was in the "individualistic economy, their family life, and their religious activities" (*ibid.*, 439). Because of their particular view of life within this framework, they looked upon the efforts of INCAP as an attempt by an outside agency to interfere in their lives. It was necessary for the anthropologist to view the project through their eyes, from the inside out, in order to see how they perceived project activities, and how this perception could lead to an antagonistic response. It was equally essential that he analyze the culture (or subculture) of the INCAP personnel, to determine areas of misunderstanding between the two cultures. "Investigation disclosed that each instance of difficulty arose out of the interplay between the cultural practices and beliefs of the villagers and those of the project personnel" (*ibid.*, 440). Four aspects of village culture proved to be crucial to the difficulties experienced by INCAP.

1. There were two opposing factions in the village. One was anti-government, conservative, strongly Catholic; the other was pro-government, progressive, and included several Protestant and non-religious families. The rivalry between them was intense. The INCAP social worker happened to make her early friendships among the first group, and in so doing reduced her chances of gaining acceptance among members of the second group. The objectives of the program required the cooperation of both factions, but the latter faction tended to identify program activities with their rivals, and this led them to withhold their own cooperation.

2. In the Guatemalan political climate of the day, there was an alignment between pro-government and pro-communist forces, and the more conservative elements in the society identified with the strongly anti-communists. In Magdalena both factions were somewhat anti-communist, but the conservative faction much more strongly than the progressive. In the eyes of these conservative villagers their government was pro-communist; INCAP, though an international organization, was working with the government, and must therefore be communist; Americans

working with communists must be communist too. This attitude was an important factor in the increasing hostility and coldness of villagers toward project personnel. "With the villagers ready to see the threat of Communism everywhere, it was not surprising that the INCAP program was made a scapegoat" (*ibid.*, 444). The anthropologist made recommendations for direct action which dealt with this problem very effectively. The measures taken consisted essentially of visits by the social worker to all her friends, telling them that the rumor was not true; that Americans were anti-communistic (they were actually fighting them in a place called Korea); and that INCAP personnel were definitely not communists.

3. The villagers subscribed to a belief concerning the nature of blood that was contrary to western medical knowledge: blood, they thought, is non-regenerative, and loss of blood weakens the body permanently because once lost it is never replaced. To these Indians, a cut is a very serious matter. As the project progressed, parents became increasingly reluctant to send their children for medical examinations, and many refused outright. They could not understand why doctors, who claimed to be interested in the health of their children, could want to weaken them by taking their blood. The anthropologist's recommendations, which again proved effective, included a program of re-education, utilizing Indian beliefs. Since they already believed in a relationship between blood and health, it was possible to convince them that tests were necessary in order to determine whether their blood was "sick" or "well."

4. The anthropologist determined the existence of a fantasy, evidently very widespread in Guatemala, concerning the eating of children. Various investigators have reported a practice wherein mothers threaten children with a story that they will be eaten if they do not behave properly. Adams reports that in many places where UNICEF has provided milk for Guatemalan children, the rumor has arisen that these children were being fattened to be sent to the United States or Russia for eating. The INCAP social worker encountered this same problem in Magdalena. The nutrition program was supposedly designed to fatten the children The purpose of the blood test, it was rumored, was to determine if children were fat enough for shipment to the United States.

This matter, too, was approached directly. An INCAP worker invited a village leader to accompany him to the laboratory in the city where the processing of blood samples was explained to him. Later this man was instrumental in explaining to the villagers that blood testing had nothing to do with fattening of children. After a time the INCAP people heard nothing more of this "cannibalistic fantasy."

Finally, the anthropologist found that there was general dissatisfaction with the clinic (a program related to the nutritional one) and it operation. The reasons for this need not be discussed here. The significant thing is that this was one of a number of special programs (none of which succeeded) designed to attract attention and to promote the cooperation of the villagers. The anthropologist felt that the villagers had no reason to relate the clinic or any other program to the nutritional program. He concluded that any program should concentrate on its main goal, nutritional experimentation in this case, and that it should avoid auxiliary projects that complicate the issue. The clinic, for example, had at least one effect opposite of that intended. Since serious cases were not treated, villagers tended to lose their respect for the staff, rather than being positively impressed with what was done for them.

A Health Program in Rural India. When a serious outbreak of smallpox occurred in an Indian village, the frightened people went to the village priest for his help. He promptly sat down, crossed his legs, closed his eyes, and became "possessed" by the goddess Thalerani. He then declared that the epidemic had been visited upon them by the goddess in her anger. She could be pacified only by a sacrifice, followed by a great feast. At once the people set about to offer their worship so that the goddess would spare their children.

Meanwhile, local authorities heard of the outbreak and dispatched a vaccinator with medical supplies. This man immediately went about the village ordering women to send their children to him for vaccination. They knew nothing of vaccination and were quite suspicious of a man who would come unannounced and demand their children. As the alarm spread, he came quickly to be known as "the one who makes the babies cry." His efforts were totally fruitless, and he left the village.

Back at his headquarters, he met with the social education officer, who was also a stranger to the afflicted village. Together they returned and approached the village priest for his help. He denied them his assistance, saying that his villagers had faith which made their medicine unnecessary. However, before they left the village, the priest came to them, this time deeply disturbed. His nephew had fallen ill, and he insisted that they treat the child. He admitted that faith was enough for the simple villagers, but that his nephew would need medicine. The two men took advantage of his request to renew their demands for his help. This time he called the villagers to him and explained that they must allow their children to be vaccinated with a "magical herb." His own nephew received the treatment with no more than a whimper, and this changed the entire atmosphere. One by one the villagers went home and returned with their children. The priest even assisted the medical officer in instructing the people on the care of the vaccination sore. "Later on he showed a willingness to incorporate some general ideas about better health practices in his nightly sessions of religious discourses and . . . singing. Unwittingly, a new goddess was speaking through him" (Link and Mehta 1966:222–23). Thus the village priest became an effective ally to the medical workers. He showed himself to be unusually ready to introduce new ideas, and the confidence the people had in him contributed greatly to his effectiveness.

Recurrent Factors in Technical Assistance Programs

These four case studies differ greatly in their details, but in each case an outside agency has entered a community—peasant villages in three instances and an urban slum in the fourth—to offer some kind of assistance. The circumstances are highly variable. In Peru the Peace Corps was present by invitation of the national government to aid in the long-range development of a newly formed, impoverished suburban slum. San Pablo was one of many Mexican rural communities which were targets of a vast program of rural development. Magdalena was one of several communities selected for an experiment which, if successful, would lead to an internationally sponsored program to improve the general level of health in peasant communities. In India there was the immediate need to deal with an epidemic. In none of these cases had the community itself requested the presence of the outsiders.

The programs, in each case, were intended to deal with problems which may or may not have been perceived as problems by the recipients of this aid. Each of the groups offering technical assistance experienced difficulties in dealing with the people they wanted to help. In some of the cases their efforts were successful, whereas in others they were unqualified failures. Regardless of the great differences in the details of these four case studies, certain recurrent factors are found in each of them which are commonly found in technical assistance programs, and which are of interest to the applied anthropologist.

These factors—factionalism, indifference or hostility on the part of the recipients, the power of local leaders, the obstacles posed by vested interests, the importance of religious beliefs, the difficulty of communication between innovator and recipient, and many more—can be logically grouped into a limited number of categories. [Several anthropologists have published essays in which they analyze the factors operative in technical assistance programs: Erasmus (1954), Foster (1962), Niehoff (1966), Paul (1955), and Spicer (1952) have made notable contributions, and their writings have added much to the following presentation.]

In studying culture change anthropologists have always been aware of such phenomena as selective borrowing, resistance to change, or even outright rejection of new ideas. Whether an innovation originates within a cultural system or is being introduced from the outside, how readily it is accepted will depend upon a number of factors. Anthropologists have been especially aware of resistance to change when it is consciously and deliberately imposed from without, as in the four case studies described. Theoretical writings have tended to overstress resistance to change, an idea that is most commonly formulated by those engaged in trying to bring about change. Thus, says Spicer (1952:17), "It has become something of a commonplace to say, 'People resist change,' but a generalization that has many more facts to support it is the opposite: 'People accept change.'" Niehoff (1966:23–24) also notes that peasant peoples are often quite ready to accept new and better ways of doing things, and when they react against a program of planned change, it is as a direct result of the innovative techniques being employed. But whatever the cause, resistance does occur. Innovators (technical experts) do consistently encounter obstacles of many kinds in their attempts to induce change among peoples in need of technical assistance.

It is quite clear from most published cases that resistance stems, in part, from the nature of the recipient culture itself, which is compounded by the presence of the innovators' culture. Obviously, these are not mutually exclusive categories, and resistance results from interaction between the two cultures.

Attitudinal Factors. Attitudinal cultural factors of many kinds are known to present obstacles to planned change. Suspiciousness of peasant peoples toward all outsiders is reported again and again by technical assistance personnel. The reception accorded the Cultural Mission staff in San Pablo is one such instance. Why should their government want to give the people of San Pablo something for nothing? Past experience had made them wary of such offers. The Guatemalan Indians, for somewhat different reasons, were suspicious of the intentions of the INCAP staff, and the Indian villagers became seriously alarmed at the presence of the vaccinator, due in part to his heavy-handed approach. Suspicion on the part of the world's peasantry should not be viewed as something stemming from perverse ignorance, nor as something innate. Rather, it is an attitude growing out of the conditions of peasant life and, in particular, the peasants' relations with the outside world. This attitude has a number of sources, as illustrated in our case studies and other similar studies.

First, suspicion can stem from a misconception of the purpose of the technical assistance program. The Peace Corps Volunteers in the Peruvian *barriada* came as community developers. They were trained to help develop local initiative and to stimulate self-help, but they had no material resources. Their initial attempts at setting up a nursery school were not highly regarded by the council *presidente,* who saw the most pressing need of his people to be food, not education for small children. Hence he redirected their efforts toward securing the Food for Peace program for his community.

People who have traditionally lived in isolation are always likely to be suspicious of the presence of outsiders, especially agents of the national government. All too often in the past, as we suggested in Chapter 2, the presence of government officials has meant increased taxation, loss of land, military conscription, or some other unwelcome interference in their lives. Nothing in their experience enables them to comprehend the rationale behind a complex technical development program. Nor can they understand why strangers would want to help them. They are likely, therefore, to interpret the presence of the outsiders in ways that make sense to them. A deep-seated "cannibalistic fantasy" provided the people of Magdalena with an intelligible reason for the INCAP program of blood testing and nutritional supplementation.

Second, peasants have become cynical about well-intentioned efforts to better their lives. Especially since 1945, rural and urban communities in emergent nations throughout the world have been the targets of repeated attempts by a host of agencies—private, national, and international—proclaiming such intentions. It seems that such programs invariably begin and often end with a survey or census of the community. Latecomers to such communities, for example, Peace Corps Volunteers, often find a people weary of responding to lengthy questionnaires. A standard bit of humor in the folklore of anthropology illustrates this very point: an Eskimo family consists of a husband, wife, three children, and an anthropologist. If a census taker is substituted for the anthropologist in this formulation, it could well apply to households in many urban slums or peasant communities.

Finally, fatalism—an attitude of weary resignation, or the feeling that no matter what one does, he cannot alter an implacable future—is widespread among peasant peoples of the world. "Some people are so poor, have so little land and resources, and have previously failed to better their own conditions so often that they simply do not believe they can improve their own circumstances. Usually such fatalism is based on a fairly realistic assessment of true conditions . . ." (Niehoff, *op. cit.,* 38). Fatalism is frequently given a religious rationale. An anthropologist investigating high infant mortality in rural Colombia found a lethargic acceptance of this situation. If a child dies in infancy it is because God willed it so; if he recovers from illness, it is because God did not intend his death. Such an attitude toward life and death is widespread in Latin America. Needless to say, it can provide a serious obstacle to programs of medical assistance (Foster 1962:66–67). Foster attributes a high infant mortality rate among Egyptian peasantry to a similar attitude. Death is the will of Allah.

It must be stressed that these and other attitudes, while they pose serious obstacles to planned change, are not immutable. A most important part of the innovative strategy in a technical assistance program must be to overcome suspicion, hostility, fatalism, or the feeling that nothing can be done to help.

The Belief System. The belief system can also impose serious barriers which the innovator must surmount if he is to be successful. The Guatemalan Indians' beliefs concerning blood are illustrative. Adams observed in his study of Magdalena that religion was an area of primary concern to the Indian. While the beliefs concerning blood were not, in themselves, of supernatural origin, Guatemalan beliefs about health, medicine, and the body are based in supernaturalism. This is frequently true of peasant peoples the world over. These are important factors which the public health worker or medical technician must take into account if he is to succeed. It is widely observed that peasants, even when exposed to modern medicine, will maintain certain areas of belief that are immune to western science. A common belief in Guatemala concerns a disease called *susto* (literally, fright), sometimes caused by seeing a ghost, and often resulting in loss of the soul. Another belief, widespread in Latin America, is *mal ojo* ("evil eye"), usually an affliction of children, caused by the inadvertent gaze of a person of "strong blood." The point is that in neither case will the Indian go to a doctor or clinic for treatment, because it is believed that modern doctors know nothing of such illnesses and, therefore, cannot deal with them effectively. The traditional treatment may involve either magical or herbal remedies, applied by a local curing specialist or shaman. Again, while such beliefs pose problems to the innovator, these are not always insurmountable. In Magdalena, the anthropologist quieted the rumor concerning cannibalism in a way already described. He did not attempt to eliminate the beliefs concerning blood, but rather made recommendations that the INCAP staff utilize these beliefs in gaining acceptance for the program.

Communication. Another factor illustrated by our case material is communication among the recipient peoples themselves. Niehoff (*op. cit.*, 24) defines this category as "spontaneous communication among the recipients in regard to the change project," and he recognizes two kinds of communication: gossip and rumor-mongering. We have shown above that when the recipients do not comprehend the purpose of a project, they will interpret it in accordance with existing beliefs. Such an interpretation will often arise out of gossip and rumor.

Lewis (1955:403–34) has shown the negative effectiveness of rumor and gossip in the Mexican village of Tepoztlan. A team of researchers entered Tepoztlan to carry out a project of psychological research, but in response to requests by both the villagers and the national government, they also set up a medical clinic to provide treatment for the people. The psychological project involved the testing of school children, including a physical examination for possible defects. The testing program went well for some weeks, when suddenly the school principal put an end to it. He wished, he said, to investigate rumors that the children were being asked immoral questions. Apparently a local religious practitioner was the primary source behind the rumors. In part, he perceived the clinic as a threat to his own status in the community, and by discrediting the testing program, he was also discrediting the clinic.

Rumor and gossip probably accompany and contribute to many other difficulties that beset innovators. Gossip reinforced the belief that the Peace Corps Volunteers in the Peruvian *barriada* favored one or the other faction. The supposed communistic leanings of the INCAP staff were also "established" by rumors, some of which the anthropologist was able to expose. Apparently in this case the most direct response was the most effective one. The originators of the rumors were confronted, on the one hand, while the social worker countered the rumors among her friends on the other.

Social Structure. Another important source of resistance lies in the social structure of the recipient community. Two closely related factors within this category are those of *leadership* and *vested interests*. "There is little doubt that the single most important characteristic of the local society is its leadership. There is probably no way to ruin the chances of an innovation project more easily than to ignore the traditional leaders or to choose the wrong ones" (Niehoff, *op. cit.*, 31). Leaders can be of various kinds: officially elected, informal, sacred, or secular. In any case, the leader in question derives certain kinds of benefit from his position—prestige, power, wealth, personal satisfaction—and will react in some predictable way if he is threatened, ignored, or slighted. The leader has a vested interest in his community and seeks to keep it the. way it is, unless the change will benefit him. To enter a community without his approval can be interpreted as consciously ignoring his position, and his resultant loss of face can earn his hostility. The *cacique* in the village of San Pablo, though an informal leader, was a wealthy and influential man. The proposed tortilla cooperative threatened his lucrative transportation business and he opposed it. He was supported in his opposition by other vested interests, and the project was doomed to failure.

However, enlisting the aid of leaders can have positive results. The village priest in India contributed to a successful program of health education, and an influential man in Magdalena helped put an end to the rumors of cannibalism when he was taken to the blood-testing laboratory.

Factionalism. A further structural source of resistance is *factionalism*, which recurs in numerous case studies. Since factions often organize about different leaders, the problem of dealing with them must of necessity involve the problem of dealing with leadership as well. The Peruvian and Guatemalan cases above are fairly typical. Factions tend to occupy different sections or *barrios* in the community, and they sometimes represent different political philosophies. In the Peruvian case, one faction accused the other of strong communist leanings, which were as vehemently denied. The element of rivalry is, by definition, always present in factions and may result in strong hatreds.

The innovator in every case faces a serious dilemma. His program is usually intended to benefit an entire community, and he must therefore secure the cooperation of all its members. But he has to begin somewhere, and very possibly will be ignorant of the existence of factionalism until he has made his beginning. If he begins his work among the members and with the leadership of one faction, he is immediately identified with them and earns the hostility of the other group. The social worker in Magdalena became aware of this very thing when the members of the "progressive" faction identified her as a friend of their rival group. This is perhaps one of the most serious and difficult obstacles to planned change. Where the factionalism is well-established and feelings are deep, the innovator can take little direct action to change things. The people of the Peruvian *barriada* wanted food very badly, but the uneasy truce arrived at proved to be only a temporary solution. Official agencies executed the extreme measure of physically relocating one group.

Identification of Needs

Besides anticipating sources of resistance, the innovator of planned change must know the recipient culture for other reasons. The nature of that culture is highly relevant to the planning of change. The implicit assumption of the technical expert is that his program is going to change the recipient culture in some desirable direction by adding something new to it or by changing or eliminating something that is already there. The crucial question to be asked here is, "Desirable to whom?" It has been the experience of programmers the world over that innovations, seen as desirable or necessary by the technical expert, are not perceived as desirable by the intended recipients.

The importance of identification of needs becomes apparent when the overall, long-range goals of technical assistance in general are considered. A program should result in more or less permanent benefit to a community, whether in the area of health and medicine, economics, education, public administration, or housing. The technical assistance staff cannot remain permanently in the community, and at some point they must be able to say that their innovations have been accepted—a successful brick-making cooperative is functioning, people regularly seek medical aid or regularly boil drinking water, or an organization that did not exist prior to the program now exists for solving community problems. The technical expert should "work himself out of a job"; the process he institutes should become self-sustaining and self-sufficient.

In order to achieve this degree of acceptance, the innovation must fulfill a need already perceived by the people themselves; it must be a *felt need*. Most peasant farmers, for example, feel the need for greater crop yields. In an arid land, where irrigation water is scarce, a farmer is likely to welcome a program that promises an increased water supply. It is not a foregone conclusion, however, that any measure which will improve living conditions will be welcomed by the recipient culture. The felt needs of the planner (those derived from his own culture) are not always those of the recipients. One of the authors observed, in the Peruvian *barriada* discussed above, that excretion was performed in a broad ditch at the edge of the settlement. In a neighboring *barriada* an "action group" of educated middle-class Peruvians was working hard to convince the families of the "need" to build latrines, but they evinced little interest. Whose need was it? In this extremely dry climate, human waste dried out rapidly, and there was no problem with flies or odors.

Foster (*op. cit.*, 180) tells of a similar case in Iran, where despite evidence that the dry atmosphere quickly dried out human fecal matter, public health technicians insisted that there was a health problem with flies. "The program approach to this health problem, which logically had to exist, was the latrine which, when installed in numbers, became a fly breeder and villages previously free became infested."

Differential Perception of Needs. It might seem to be a reasonable assumption on the part of western medical specialists that people everywhere desire good health and long life and, therefore, will feel the need for any measure proposed to bring about these desired goals. Again, this is not necessarily the case. There are actually several points involved here.

First, technically backward peoples may not perceive health in the same way as the medical technician. As Paul has stated, "While sound health is everywhere sought, the quest for health may or may not rate high in the hierarchy of a society's value system, depending on the particular culture . . ." (1961:2). In the United States, health is generally defined as a positive value, a state of the body to be sought and maintained. An entire complex of behavior, involving exercise, proper diet, sufficient rest and fresh air, and, above all, cleanliness, is assiduously observed because it contributes to "good health." "Today, in the United States, prosperity, democracy, and frequency of bathing have become linked values. Americans say that cleanliness is next to godliness, an indication that bathing and cleanliness are affect-laden values in contemporary middle-class culture as well as a means to better health" (Paul 1958:1506). The people of a peasant community may suffer from frequent illness and from high infant mortality, and yet fail to view health as a positive state, that is, as one to be actively sought. Consequently, a technical assistance program which promotes such cleanliness measures as frequent bathing, covering of garbage, or the boiling of drinking water will bring no response.

Second, a very sound health measure, from a technical point of view, can often conflict with existing practices. Paul (*ibid.*, 1504) tells of a health problem in rural India, where people defecate in open fields, resulting in contamination of food and water through the agency of rodents and flies. A public health team attempted to alleviate this problem by installing numerous latrines. These were designed taking into account such cultural factors as local squatting postures and other factors such as available water and soil conditions. Nevertheless, the latrines were not used, especially by the women. "Every morning and afternoon women go in groups to the field, not only to relieve themselves but also to take time off from busy domestic routines, to gossip and exchange advice about husbands and mothers-in-law, and to bathe with water from tanks located in the field. The linked habits of going to the fields for social gatherings and for toilet and bathing activities meet a strongly felt need for community living and relaxation from daily toil."

This single case illustrates an important lesson for the technical specialist: customs rarely if ever exist in a vacuum. Almost any item of behavior is likely to be linked in some complex way to other items. When the planner of change is developing his program of action, he should view "undesirable" behaviors not in isolation but as items in a complex. An innovation has the best prospects for acceptance if it can fit into this complex rather than conflicting with it.

Finally, people often fail to perceive a need, even where serious problems exist, because there is no apparent connection between the proposed innovation and the goal to be achieved by it. A peasant is not likely to commit his limited time or resources to a project which gives him no readily apparent benefit. This is nowhere clearer than in the case of preventive medicine. A peasant is likely to welcome any measure that brings quick, recognizable relief from pain or discomfort—aspirin, an injection of penicillin, or any other therapeutic measure—but will be disinterested in a measure designed to forestall something that may never happen.

In the case study dealing with the smallpox epidemic in India, vaccination could not possibly have helped those who had already contracted the disease. To a people who interpreted this disease in terms of divine wrath rather than in terms of bacteria, there was no incentive to submit to vaccination. It was only when the priest explained the practice as a form of magic, and lent prestige to it by having his own nephew vaccinated, that the people began to bring in their children. Peasant women are equally ignorant of germs and may be very reluctant to waste time and scarce cooking fuel to boil water, especially when no immediate benefits result. Therefore, where an innovation fails to produce immediate results, it is usually not perceived as desirable by the recipient society, even if its eventual result is to alleviate hunger, sickness, or discomfort. To make such measures felt needs may require an extensive program of education or promotion in the recipient society.

Much more could be added to our brief analysis of these few case studies. Even the limited details given would suggest, for example, the importance of personality factors in the presentation of new ideas. The personal characteristics of the technical assistant, which are crucial to any program, include not only his technical knowledge and theoretical understandings, but the kind of person he is.

ANTHROPOLOGY, URBAN EDUCATION, AND THE CULTURALLY DISADVANTAGED

The application of anthropological knowledge to the solution of human problems is not limited to cultures that are foreign to the anthropologist. Anthropologists in the United States have become increasingly interested in problems of their own culture, especially in complex multi-cultured urban settings. They find themselves particularly involved in the areas of common interest between anthropology and education. As an indication of this, a number of scholars now hold joint appointments in university departments of anthropology and schools of education. A recent book of readings (Spindler 1963) is one of a growing number of books that explore these areas.

Very recently, anthropologists have become involved, tangentially at least, in increasing the effectiveness of educational programs directed toward those minority groups in the United States defined as "culturally disadvantaged." This involvement has been largely at the request of educators, who are invariably the directors of the programs, and who are realizing more and more that they cannot deal effectively with members of these cultural groups unless they know something about their culture. It is not uncommon to find that educational programs in the United States are attempting, at least nominally, to provide particular children with the opportunity to overcome or equalize what has been defined as their cultural disadvantage.

In order to achieve this general goal, educators seek to learn the characteristics of the disadvantaged child, the influences of poverty on family relationships, the results of *acculturation,* and the development of the child's self-image—all of which are largely areas of cultural information. Sometimes these categories of knowledge are stated as program objectives. In each instance, the educators view their programs from the point of view of the individual, but they find that they must rely upon the anthropologist to describe and explain the total cultural context in which the individual lives.

The following discussion is not presented as a series of case studies in education, as was the preceding discussion of technical assistance. Rather, we analyze the education of the culturally disadvantaged as a problem area into which anthropology has only begun to move. We emphasize the need for increased cooperation between anthropology and education, and we offer some suggestions for future action in this field. Our tone is, therefore, much more speculative than in the first part of this chapter.

Anthropologists should be pleased to find the use of the concept of acculturation among the objectives sought by these programs, for this is an anthropological concept. At the same time, most anthropologists would insist upon clarification of this concept if full value is to be derived from its potential. Acculturation is sometimes used as though it were synonymous with socialization or enculturation (a common error in our contemporary society, but a very serious one) partly because of the public's inadequate understanding of anthropology and its potential contributions. Acculturation, traditionally, has been defined as the continuous, intimate, first-hand contact between two or more cultures over a significant period of time. It is not teaching the child how to become a member of his society (socialization); it is not the parents' instruction about a cultural tradition (enculturation); rather, it is the transfer of cultural elements, directly and first-hand, from one culture to another. Such direct contact may and frequently does take the form of a superordinate–subordinate relationship, where one culture gives a significantly greater amount of its culture to another in a cultural exchange. However, it should always be remembered that cultural exchange within the context of acculturation always involves the receipt and transmission of cultural elements in both directions; it is never a unilateral process.

Acculturation and Urban Education

While the concept of acculturation was derived from research and observation of numerous and varied contact situations involving two or more distinct cultures, it has meaningful application to subcultures and groups in heterogeneous settings such as urban areas. For, when their context is examined, the contacts present among the so-called subcultures of the urban area are not categorically different from those where two or more distinct cultures are involved in an acculturative situation. Among the population units of an urban area, each is represented by different cultural forms and behavior (although expressed in terms of some similarity), each receives cultural elements from the other, and each is in continuous first-hand contact with the other. Also, the particular type of acculturative situation in the urban area is superordinate–subordinate, with so-called "middle-class American culture" occupying the superordinate position and subcultures or social categories such as "Mexican-American," "Negro-American," "Puerto Rican-American," "Spanish-American" occupying the subordinate positions. This condition is explained by various reasons and rationalizations, but is, more objectively and realistically, based upon the fact that these subgroups receive more cultural elements from the dominant "American" culture than they transmit to it. The contact among various social groups in the urban area is more than an analogy; while it varies significantly in its expression and form, it is a real acculturative situation.

The very fact that we (society) have made significant distinctions among the social groups that frequent the urban areas and have then used these "derived" differences as a basis for specialized educational programs is probably the best possible support for the claim that the urban situation is one of acculturation. Therefore, anthropology's methods of observing and understanding such situations are applicable, in modified form, in dealing with some of these urban problems.

Recognition of an acculturative situation has value, but there is more to the contemporary urban situation in the United States. Closer examination of specific contemporary educational programs reveals at least one factor shared by all such programs: the stated and conscious efforts to intensify the transmission of "American" culture and to minimize the receipt of cultural elements into it from the urban subcultures. This is exactly the process that is taking place, and because of such efforts it must be realized that this situation is not solely one of acculturation but is, more specifically, a derivative of the concept of directed culture change, i.e., conscious attempts to induce, maintain, and intensify the transference and acceptance of cultural items.

Today, wide-range programs such as Head Start, Teachers' Institutes for the Culturally Disadvantaged, Poverty Corps, and many other "equal opportunity" projects are numerous. Each of these is a program of directed culture change, and each is intent upon increasing the flow of items from the "American culture" to subcultures or groups existing in its midst, while simultaneously minimizing the intake or acceptance of cultural items in the reverse direction from these subgroups. All members of these projects are agents of directed culture change and are charged with the obligation of doing these things in accordance with stated educational processes and through specified educational channels.

Cultural Awareness of the Educator

However, if educators are to do this effectively (we shall not consider the merits of such goals but will accept the stated objectives of the programs), they must know a great deal about the groups with which they are working; they must know the subcultures to which they are to transmit these "American" cultural elements. If teachers randomly discharge the items they want these groups to internalize, the groups will continue to reject many of them, as they have done in the past, on the bases of lack of understanding, cultural incompatibility, or lack of value for them, or simply as being unimportant for maintaining or changing their style of life. In order to introduce "American" culture elements so that they will be accepted and internalized, the most vulnerable areas of the recipients' culture must be determined objectively and realistically. The areas of compatibility and similarity as well as the areas of difference between American culture and the culture characterizing these other groups must be specifically determined, not just as categorical similarities and differences, but in terms of their graded significance. To know the culture is to know these things.

If individuals involved in such programs are to be effective agents of culture change, and if they are to know the cultures that characterize the groups with which they are working, they must know how to learn about these cultures, how to evaluate and assess them, and how to seek ideas and analogies that can be used. In order to achieve this knowledge, the methods and techniques involved in such processes must be determined and known. When agents of contemporary educational programs have accomplished these things, they will be researchers, appliers, and educators simultaneously—they will no longer restrict their activities to education as it has been defined in the past. Education, if it is to be increasingly effective, means the derivation of information as well as its dissemination. The effective educator requires more varied and more effective skills than most other specialists in our contemporary society.

Robert Redfield has offered an analogy that is applicable to contemporary educators involved in these various programs, and is worth repeating here:

A fable, which Aesop somehow neglected to record, tells of a hen who was striving to instruct her chicks about their future sources of food supply while she and they were balanced precariously on a chicken coop which was being carried down a river by a flood. It was a long time since the hen had studied the forests on the bank and the account she was giving her chicks of forest resources was none too good. So she called to a wise owl on the bank for help. "You know the woods, oh owl, for you stay in this forest and study it," said the hen, "will you not tell me what to teach my chicks about life in the forest?" But the owl had overheard what the hen had been telling the chicks about the forest as she came along, and he thought it was scientifically inaccurate and superficial. Besides, he was just then very busy completing a monograph on the incidence of beetle larvae in acorns. So he pretended he had not heard the hen. The hen, turned back upon herself, proceeded as well as she could to prepare and put into effect an instruction unit on the food resources of oak forests, meanwhile struggling to keep the chicks from falling off the chicken coop. The chicks took the instruction very well, and later the chicken coop stopped at a point far downstream and the chicks all went ashore—to begin their adult lives in a treeless meadow. (Redfield, unpublished ms., "Research in the Social Sciences: Its Significance for General Education.")

While there is increasing participation by the owls—the social scientists—in educational programs that seek to incorporate and apply scientific research, educators cannot depend totally upon the owls in order to train the chicks. Teachers are not only the hens, but must also be the owls. They are, simultaneously, researchers, appliers, and educators. While the task is a comprehensive one, these three activities are intimately integrated, and their successful combination will yield more effective attainment of the programs' objectives. Teachers should always be searching for new data about the groups with whom they are working in order that they may become more effective on a consistent basis. Enduring success will not be achieved if they simply restrict themselves to the role of educator, or if they attempt to apply only what they learn in the university and college classroom or from texts. Information about each specific situation in which teachers are involved must be derived first-hand, combined with knowledge derived from other sources, and then applied through the educational channels that are available or through newly created ones.

Potential Contributions of Anthropology

Anthropology can help educators in all of these endeavors. Specifically, anthropology can and is providing knowledge about particular urban areas and about the contact and directed change of the "culturally disadvantaged" groups within these contexts. But in the final analysis, each individual teacher must derive information from his or her students, who are the representatives of particular social groups characterized by diverse social and cultural characteristics. Therefore, anthropology can provide more immediate and more significant aid in giving teachers general methods and techniques for deriving specific information about their specific groups in their particular situation. Anthropology can help make them aware of the necessity of knowing explicitly the values and goals of the subcultures with which they are dealing, and also the necessity of defining explicitly their own values, so that they may learn to look for and understand the relationships among these variables in a clear and precise manner. Once this is achieved, it will be a relatively easy task for the educator, with a little imagination, to make the specific adaptation to his or her particular group—an adaptation that should prove to be much more effective than the application of facts derived from one urban situation and applied in a significantly different urban context. While similarities obviously exist among urban subcultures, the variables usually are not specified sufficiently well, nor are they subject to the control necessary for transference.

The Research Sequence in Education. An excellent example of how anthropology can provide generalized practical methodology and techniques which can be adapted to specific situations by teachers is the research sequence which is used by anthropologists engaged in field research (this has been detailed in Chapter 2). The researcher achieves particular status levels which are correlated with the derivation of information, and which can be correlated with the application of such information and, in the case of educators, with the subsequent transmission of cultural elements. Conscious recognition of this sequence will ultimately allow educators to be more effective by being more aware of the behavioral limitations that coincide with the particular statuses they may achieve. This sequence is shown in Table 17–1.

As one of the authors has indicated elsewhere, "Although each of the seven techniques is not normally involved in every research program, each is a definite aspect of a composite field investigation. While the positions of complete outsider and full participant [see Table 17–1] are not usually accepted as techniques for the actual collection of field data, they do reflect the practical and logical extremes of the continuum. They are real situations which the investigator may encounter during the course of his research program, and are included, therefore, for proper perspective" (Schwartz n.d., 6). It should be recognized that this sequence is based upon a number of criteria, which also are relevant

Table 17–1

Status	Degree of Information	Application and Transmission of Information
1. Outsider	No information derived.	No application of data and no transmission of cultural elements.
2. Partial Observer	Limited information derived through the process of observation only.	No application of data and no transmission of cultural elements.
3. Full Observer	Increased information derived, but restricted to the process of observation.	No application of data and no transmission of cultural elements.
4. Observer-as-Participant	Increased information derived through the combined processes of observation and participation, but emphasis still upon observation with only limited participation possible.	Limited transmission of cultural elements and limited application of research data.
5. Participant-as-Observer	Increased information derived through the combined processes of participation and observation, but emphasis now upon participation.	Increased transmission of cultural elements and application of research data.
6. Participant Observer	Most intensive derivation of information with extreme emphasis upon participation.	Most significant transmission of cultural items and application of research data.
7. Full Participant	Increased derivation of information, but highly biased and non-objective.	Inability to transmit cultural elements or apply data effectively, objectively, and realistically in relation to the stated goals.

to the teachers' situations. They are: ". . . degree of rapport; objectives of the . . . program; composition, ecology, and history of the research population; time allocated for completion of the research; personal characteristics and training of the investigator; practical restrictions . . . ; and linguistic barriers" (*ibid.*). Probably the single most important criterion is that of rapport, for there is a direct correlation among each of the statuses indicated, the degree of rapport necessary to achieve the status, and the type and degree of data possible from each status level.

This sequence for researchers is not significantly different from one that many teachers follow during the course of their teacher training. Initially, they are complete outsiders in relation to a particular classroom or school; then they proceed to a period of observation during which classrooms are visited to watch teachers and students in action. This is followed by a stage of combined observation and participation, with an opportunity to teach on a limited basis under the guidance of a master teacher. In this stage the combined processes of observation and participation are employed on a restricted basis. Finally, the trainee achieves the position of teacher, where the emphasis is upon participation but observation is still retained as a supplementary technique. Since teachers are familiar with this sequence, it should not be difficult for them to apply it consciously when they operate as agents of directed culture change.

If this methodological sequence of status achievement is consciously maintained, the educator can increase the success achieved within the context of the stated objectives of his program. He will know when to introduce certain items of change and when not to; when he has established enough rapport to utilize the talents present in the classroom as an aid in introducing change; and when he will encounter conflict and resistance based upon a lack of rapport or failure to maintain it. He will be able to recognize when he has begun to achieve the non-objective and undesirable status of full participant and thus when to follow a pattern of action that will counteract this and return him to the more desirable and more effective status of participant observer. These are only some of the possibilities offered by the simple recognition of the teacher's position in relation to the group with which he is working, the group that he is trying to change.

Conflicting Subcultural Values

It is equally important that teachers recognize explicitly and remain consciously aware of the values of their own culture and those of the subculture with which they are working. Each should be viewed in relation to the other and in terms of the specific context. Reading, for example, is an objective that is stated to be a highly desirable, even a necessary, goal for all members of our society. If children are to have an "equal opportunity," we say, they must be able to read. The inability to read reduces one's ability to compete in our complex modern society. Those who cannot read are placed at a disadvantage; failures in our society are constant reminders of this, according to the generally accepted interpretations. We use such evidence to intensify our efforts to teach reading in the schools. By placing our values in the spotlight and remaining consciously aware of them, we are simultaneously losing sight of the variations of values that are characteristic of the subgroups to whom we are trying to teach reading. In too many instances, the "nonreading" child who is a representative of a subculture does not share the wider view of society that reading is a necessary skill for successful competition, nor do his parents or relatives. When educators lack specific knowledge of the culture and behavioral patterns of a subgroup, they cannot be explicitly aware of its differential values.

As illustrated by the perhaps familiar example of the misunderstood projective test, a child whose home has more cracked windows than non-cracked ones will not be able to explain what is "wrong" with a picture of a house whose windows are cracked. In an environment where most windows are cracked, it is a culturally meaningless statement to say, "Cracked windows are wrong." Similarly, where most adults are non-readers, it is not valid to say, "Reading is immediately necessary." When teachers are conscious only of their own values, they will continue their efforts to teach reading, at times even intensifying these endeavors when their original attempts are not successful. Yet, if these individuals knew the culture that characterizes these subpopulations, in many instances they would not even attempt to teach reading to the total group. Instead, new groupings would be determined, based not upon psychological and/or reading tests alone, but upon a knowledge of the subculture.

One teacher in the Los Angeles area, after numerous futile attempts to teach reading, decided upon a compromise based upon the practical dimensions of the social and cultural expectations of the "culturally disadvantaged" groups that comprised the student population of her school. She decided that it was better to teach them only two things: how to read the want ads that were compatible with their potential economic skills, and how to fill out an application form for employment. Beyond that, reading was not important. This proved to be an accurate evaluation by the teacher, for when she instituted her program interest increased significantly, pupils put forth a concerted effort to learn these skills, and the teacher was viewed as one who sincerely understood the problems and the values of these groups to the point where she was willing and able to help them. This evaluation can be contrasted with feelings about other educators in the same school who were looked upon as classical "do-gooders," but who did not truly understand the culture of the children they were trying to teach and hence could not possibly help them. While the teaching of reading selected want ads and employment forms is a restricted achievement, it is a concrete advance for the members of the culturally disadvantaged groups. It is directly related to their ability to attain equal opportunities by helping themselves, rather than by accepting the traditional idea, "We'll help you."

The "do-gooder" concept, which expresses the superordinate–subordinate relationship, is completely contradictory to equal opportunity since it is intimately integrated with an expression of authority: the teacher represents authority and a superordinate position rather than equality and a symmetrical status. Unless the culture of these disadvantaged groups is known, aid that is rendered will usually remain relatively insignificant. Agents who do not know a culture cannot know accurately how to transfer into that subgroup the cultural elements they want internalized.

Recognition of Cultural Variables. This leads us to still another point that is intimately related to the ones previously presented. A complete reversal of the current reading program is not advocated here; this would be ridiculous. We are suggesting that the same differential patterns that exist in the behavior of these culturally disadvantaged groups in their normal daily activities be recognized in the context of the school. We know, and have demonstrated again and again, that all social groups are characterized by divergent behavior that adheres to certain patterns. The very fact that we differentiate among all culturally disadvantaged groups and between these and the hypothetical "middle-class American" culture at least implies this. Yet, conscious recognition of social differentiations stops there. We fail to realize and to utilize the differential behavior and values that characterize any single social group unless they are so apparent that they cannot be ignored, as in the case of a near-genius who may be a member of one of these groups. Only then do we consciously turn our efforts toward understanding that individual and the cultural variations which affected him.

Reading as a means of communication is one of several alternatives. It is characteristic of "middle-class American" culture and is deemed a necessary skill for successful competition in contemporary society. Yet, reading is not always looked upon in the same way among the culturally disadvantaged groups. More frequently, one finds that these individuals communicate more effectively and more familiarly with oral patterns of communication. If this is known for any particular group of individuals, the program of communication should begin with the oral dimension, seizing upon a similarity between the two cultural groups, and utilizing this similarity to introduce whatever concepts of reading are possible. Alternatively, if teachers begin their programs by attempting to teach reading to a group that bases its communication upon oral communication, the probability for success will be very low. Anthropology has recorded many examples of similar situations where representatives of western civilization contacted primitive groups and began attempts to assimilate them. Frequently, reading is one of the first skills offered to a primitive group who are preliterate and who have relied on oral communication. That these attempts have seldom proven successful is not surprising, for the culture and behavioral patterns of a preliterate society obviously do not equate reading with success or happiness, nor do they define it as a necessary skill.

The ideas presented here are simple and general, and apply to all phases of the educational processes as well as to all programs of directed culture change in our society. Conscious recognition of the complete culture must be ascertained specifically and objectively. This information then must be used as an integral part of the educational process or other program of change. Wholesale application of any skill, method, technique, or value to a total social group such as "America" or "California" is based upon an erroneous assumption of homogeneity. This type of application must be foregone in favor of endeavors based upon a recognition of heterogeneity of behavior and of values within and among each subgroup in the society. Such programs are not short-range ones, in spite of the fact that they are constructed in this way and pressure is placed upon directors to demonstrate phenomenal success in a very limited period of time. Rather, all of these programs of directed culture change are long-range programs that may very well require several generations to come to fruition.

Finally, the programs of change in which individuals attempt to transmit "American" cultural elements to subcultures existing in their midst must no longer be construed as static ones; the dynamic variables must be recognized and considered in planning these programs. Precisely, "American culture" is constantly changing, as are the subcultures that characterize the culturally disadvantaged groups. If this dynamic variable is not considered, groups will be expected, erroneously, to accept and internalize cultural elements which we feel will prepare them to achieve equal opportunities, when in fact many elements in the total culture are working in just the opposite way over the long run.

SUMMARY

Early in this chapter it was stated that applied anthropologists do not, as yet, pretend to practice a precise science. The case studies in technical assistance and the discussion of the role of anthropology in urban education should help make clear why this is so.

First, the anthropologist can rarely if ever control all the relevant factors in situations of planned change. Our previous discussion of the obstacles to planned change should illustrate how difficult it is sometimes to control even a few factors where people are concerned. This point, however, has been sufficiently illustrated.

Second, the anthropologist engaged in the application of his knowledge to human situations inevitably becomes involved in questions of ethics or in making value judgments, as the preceding discussion showed. An applied program always makes certain assumptions about what is good or right for the recipient people. But the anthropologist must always ask, "Good or right from whose standpoint?" He is not certain that the values of western civilization (those of technical assistance planners) are applicable to a peasant community in Latin America or Africa. Sometimes he takes the attitude that certain parts of a culture can be and should be changed, because change would mean better health, longer life, or a higher standard of living for the people involved. On the other hand, he may believe that nothing must be done to tamper with a people's religion, beliefs, or value system. Yet, as one who is aware of the functional interrelatedness of all aspects of a culture, the anthropologist knows that the introduction of new agricultural techniques or of new health and medical practices will eventually affect other areas of life, including the value system. Considerations such as these stand in the way of the anthropologist when he attempts to make reasoned judgments about courses of action.

Third, although the anthropologist has more knowledge and insight into culture than any other professional, even the anthropologist's knowledge of the dynamics of the sociocultural system of a recipient group can be only partial. He can, hopefully, predict to some extent what will happen (how people will act) if the technical specialist attempts to introduce new patterns of action, new technical devices, new habits. Such prediction, however, is limited, even under the best of circumstances. Add to this the fact that the anthropologist and the technical or educational specialists themselves are more or less unknown factors in the predictive equation, affecting the course of action because of their own culture-bound value orientations, and the reader can begin to appreciate how complex an actual situation of directed change can become.

In short, try though he may to regard a technical assistance or an educational program as a purely scientific experiment, to be approached objectively and disinterestedly, the anthropologist can never completely succeed. A peasant community in an emergent nation, or an urban classroom, does not present a laboratory situation where all factors can be controlled. The anthropologist applying his knowledge in these circumstances is well aware that his work is at least as much art as it is science. His approach, as Sol Tax has stated, is clinical. As a program of action proceeds, the anthropologist revises his judgments and his recommendations for further action according to the reactions of the recipient group. Many of the anthropologist's judgments are based on his sensitivity to the human, cultural situation. His work is a peculiar blending of art and science, scientific detachment and empathy, human and scientific interest.

Glossary

acculturation—one type of culture change; the continuous first-hand contact between two or more cultures over a significant period of time which results in the transfer of cultural elements from one culture to another.

adaptation—change, either biological or cultural, that results in a more precise and effective adjustment of an organism or society to its environment.

adaptive mechanism—any agent which allows or which is used to achieve a more precise and effective adjustment.

affinal kin—those persons who are related, either directly or indirectly, by some socially recognized marital union.

allele—one of a pair of genes.

anagenesis—an evolutionary process in which a species is transformed into new species through time, but remaining a single species at any given time (*see also* **cladogenesis**).

animism—the belief in spiritual beings; Tylor's minimal definition of religion.

anthropomorphic—in the form of man.

artifacts—man-made objects, part of material culture, e.g., bow and arrow, chair, automobile, etc.

australopithecine—a generic term for the fossils belonging to the earliest recognized stage of human evolution, that preceding the **pithecanthropine.**

avuncular kinship systems—a system of relationships, applied to the first ascendant generation (ego's father's generation).

avunculocal—a type of residence, where a married male takes up residence with his mother's brother.

band—a nomadic community based on territoriality and kinship relations.

barriada—Spanish: city ward or precinct. In Peru, often refers to urban squatters' settlements.

barrio—neighborhood; a territorial and kinship unit in Latin America.

bilateral descent—a system for claiming descent and membership in a social group using both the mother's and the father's lines simultaneously.

bilocal residence—a form of residence whereby individuals in a society reside with about equal frequency with the mother's kinsmen or with the father's kinsmen.

brachiation—a means of locomotion dependent upon the hands and arms for movement in an arboreal environment.

brachydactyly—a condition expressed externally by short-fingeredness in the heterozygous state; lethal or semi-lethal in the homozygous state.

bride-wealth—payment of wealth for a bride by the kinsmen of the groom; one method for the distribution of economic products and wealth in society.

cacique—chief, or "boss"; term used in Mexico to indicate a person who guides and controls the activities of municipal authorities.

caste—a social group traditionally characterized by endogamy, limited occupational alternatives, and distinctive dress and behavior.

caste *panchayat*—an agency of social control in India that deals with violation of caste behavior.

caste system—a system of social organization, frequently associated with India, which is characterized by limited mobility and a rigid structure.

Chalcolithic Age—late Neolithic phase of culture development where copper was an important material; the Copper Age.

Chamar—a low caste in India; leather-workers.

Chinook—an aboriginal group in Oregon and Washington; a *lingua franca* used in the area of Oregon, Washington, and northern California.

chromosomes—the locus of genes; colored or stained bodies.

cladogenesis—process of evolutionary change in which species diversify through time to give rise to several new species (*see also* **anagenesis**).

clan—a social group based on the principle of unilineal descent. The members claim descent from a common ancestor without necessarily being able to demonstrate this relationship genealogically.

class—a ranked social category or social aggregate in which membership is based on criteria such as wealth, education, or power.

comparative method—the method of cross-cultural comparisons in anthropology which stresses the analysis of similarities and differences among cultures in order to derive significant generalizations.

consanguineal kin—those persons society recognizes as being biologically related, either directly or indirectly.

contagious magic—a general category of magic based upon the idea of a continued relationship among two or more items, even though one item is physically removed from the other.

couvade—a custom whereby the father simulates the experience of childbirth at the time his wife is giving birth to a child, such as in tropical South America.

covert culture—non-observable dimensions of culture, e.g., values, beliefs, attitudes, etc. (*see also* **ideal culture**).

Cro-Magnon—a fossil form of man which belongs to the taxonomic category *Homo sapiens*.

cross-cousin—offspring of siblings of opposite sex; category of kinship relations which include a person's mother's brother's children and father's sister's children.

cultural determinism—the concept that human behavior is a result of the culture in which an individual is born, raised, and lives, and that nothing a person does is totally free from cultural influences.

cultural lag—the disproportionate rate of change among the various parts of culture.

culture area—a geographical area characterized by the presence of similar cultures.

culture shock—the trauma which results when a person makes a rapid transition from one culture to another, together with his inability to adapt effectively to the new culture.

dialect—a local variant of any language.

diffusion—the geographical spread of cultural items.

diffusionism—the concept that a culture can be best explained by studying the unique history and spread of culture traits.

directed culture change—change that is consciously introduced and controlled in an attempt to achieve specific results.

distribution—one of the major components of economics; the flow of culturally desired goods and services.

double descent—a system for claiming descent and membership in social groups by using two single lines (the mother's line and the father's line) simultaneously and independently of each other.

dryopithecine—Miocene fossils which are thought to be the common ancestors of man and the great apes.

ecology—that branch of science which studies the relationships between a group (biological or social) and its environment.

economic organization—the social organization of production, distribution, and consumption.

encomienda—Spanish: trusteeship. System instituted by the Spanish following the conquest of the New World. Indians and the land on which they lived were given in trust to a Spaniard, who was then entitled to tribute payments.

enculturation—the process of transmitting traditional culture to new members of a society; training individuals in the ways of the culture.

endogamy—marriage within a specified group or territory.

eolith—a crude stone implement which demonstrates little conscious purpose in its production.

ethnocentrism—the concept that a person's culture is at the center of the universe and which supports the idea that his culture is the "proper and correct" culture.

ethnography—that part of cultural anthropology that emphasizes the description of particular cultures.

ethnology—that part of cultural anthropology that emphasizes explanation, interpretation, and hypothesis formation based upon information derived from many cultures.

exogamy—marriage outside a specified group or territory.

extended family—that form of the family which includes the close relatives of a married couple over three generations.

evolution—a process of change through time in a definite direction; biological and cultural evolution are two dimensions of human evolution.

family of orientation—the family in which a person is born and raised.

family of procreation—the family which an individual creates; the family formed by marriage and the production of offspring.

fertilization—one of the processes of life; the union of the male sperm with the female egg to form a zygote.

fetish—an object which is thought to have unusual powers or characteristics and which, therefore, is held to be sacred and is revered.

fictive kin—those persons who are related on a socially recognized, but fictitious basis, e.g., through adoption.

field research—the collection of information through actual residence among the people being studied.

fossils—the mineralized skeletal remains of earlier life forms.

fraternal polyandry—the marriage of a woman to two or more men who stand in the relationship of brother to each other; a form of multiple marriage.

function—the results of action performed in association with a particular structure.

functionalism—the concept that culture constitutes a unified and integrated system of parts, each part influencing the other parts of the system.

gamete—sex cells produced as a result of meiosis (sperm and egg).

garh—exogamous, non-totemic unit in India, corresponding to a village unit.

gene—the unit of heredity.

genetic drift—a force of biological evolution resulting in the change of gene frequencies.

genetic variation—increase in the variety of genes in a population.

genetics—the study of hereditary units, their results, and their relationships.

genotype—genetic composition; the particular combination of genes in an individual or in a population.

group marriage—the socially recognized union of two or more men to two or more women.

heterozygous—unlike; different; in genetics, two different genes at the same locus, e.g., A and B at the ABO blood locus.

hominidae—the name of the taxonomic family which includes the genus *Homo*.

hominoidea—the name of the taxonomic superfamily which includes men and apes.

Homo—the genus designation for man.

Homo sapiens—the genus and species designation for modern man.

homozygous—like; similar; in genetics, two like genes at a given locus, e.g., A and A at the ABO blood group locus.

human evolution—the combination of biological and cultural evolution as a single interacting process.

hybridization—a force of evolution whereby two genetically distinct populations interbreed to form a third genetically distinct population.

ideal culture—that part of culture which members of a society attempt to achieve, or which is held as a value or goal of a society.

idiosyncratic behavior—individual behavior which varies from the patterned behavior of a particular group; individualistic behavior.

imitative magic—a category of magic based upon the idea that like produces like.

jati—caste or subcaste of India.

kindred—a kinship group (or quasi-kinship group) based on the principle of bilaterality.

kinship—a system of relationships among members in a society.

kinship terminology—the names used to designate certain relations among members in a society.

kula—a system of ceremonial exchange among Trobriand Islanders.

lineage—a social group based upon the principle of unilineal descent, the members of which claim descent from a common ancestor and can trace this descent genealogically.

mal ojo—"evil eye"; a cause, often inadvertent, of illness.

mana—an impersonal supernatural force which can become manifest in persons and things and which is transferable.

manifest culture—the reality of culture. What people actually do. (*See also* **ideal culture.**)

matrilineal descent—descent reckoned along the mother's line of kinsmen.

matrilocal—residence with the bride's mother and her kinsmen.

meiosis—the process of the production of gametes (sperm and egg).

Mesolithic—Middle Stone Age.

mestizo—term used in Latin America to indicate persons of mixed Indian and Spanish ancestry.

microlith—very small stone tools; characteristic of the Mesolithic period.

Miocene—a middle period of the Cenozoic era.

mitosis—a process of growth of the cells of the body.

mizimu—ancestral spirits among the Plateau Tonga of Nigeria.

moiety—a social group resulting from the division of society into half.

molimo—sacred trumpet used by the Pygmies of the Ituri Forest in Africa.

monogamy—singular marriage—unites one male and one female.

morpheme—in linguistics, the minimal sequence of phonemes having meaning.

Mousterian—a Middle Paleolithic cultural complex associated with Neanderthal man.

mutation—change in the structure of a gene.

natural selection—a major force of evolution which acts upon the genetic composition of a population in a given environment.

Neanderthal man—a variety of fossil man during the Middle Paleolithic, associated with Mousterian culture.

negative assortative mating—the mating of persons who are phenotypically different.

Neolithic—the New Stone Age; a period of culture beginning about 8000 B.C.; characterized by the domestication of plants and animals; and ground stone tools.

neolocal residence—new residence; a married couple takes up residence independent of their respective kinsmen.

nuclear family—a basic social unit in society composed of a husband, wife, and their offspring.

overt culture—that part of culture which is openly expressed and therefore is observable (*see also* **manifest culture**).

Paleolithic—Old Stone Age; that period of cultural development characterized by hunting and gathering; embraces most of man's culture history.

paleontology—the study of fossil evidence of previous life on earth.

panchayat—council of five; an agency of social control in India.

parallel cousin—a category of kinship relations which includes a person's mother's sister's children and father's brother's children.

patrilineal descent—descent reckoned along the father's line of kinsmen.

patrilocal—residence with the groom's father and his kinsmen.

phenotype—the overt expression of genetic composition.

phoneme—the smallest significant unit of sound in a language.

phratry—a social group which may be based on unilineal descent; composed of related clans.

pithecanthropine—generic term for the fossils belonging to the second stage of human evolution, following the australopithecine.

Pleiocene—geological epoch preceding the Pleistocene.

Pleistocene—geological epoch commonly called the Ice Age.

polyandry—a form of multiple marriage where one woman is married to two or more men.

polygamy—a general term to indicate multiple marriage of any type.

polygyny—a form of multiple marriage in which one man is married to two or more women.

pongid—the taxonomic category which includes living and extinct varieties of apes. A family within the superfamily Hominoidea.

positive assortative mating—the mating of individuals who are phenotypically similar.

potlatch—ritual among Northwest Coast Indian groups designed to achieve or validate the status of the giver and to distribute economic products.

prescriptions—the rules for preferred and permissible behavior in a society.

primatology—the scientific study of primates.

Proconsul—a Miocene fossil sometimes described as being hominoid; a hominoid genus.

production—one of the necessary components of economics; the organization of raw materials, technology, and human effort to produce goods and services desired by the society.

proscriptions—rules describing behavioral limitations or indicating the taboos of a society.

psychic unity of mankind—the concept that all men share similar mental abilities; a concept characteristic of the classical evolutionary school of thought in the nineteenth century.

rapport—free, sincere, and harmonious interaction between persons, especially those of different cultures.

real action—the actual behavior that occurs in society.

reciprocity—mutual relations of a specified type.

rites de passage—the rituals which attend the life-cycle crises, e.g., birth, puberty, marriage, death.

sanctions—rewards and punishments in a society; means of social control.

selection—a force of evolution crucial to biological adaptation and evolution (*see also* natural selection).

shaman—a type of religious specialist; a curer; a medium.

silent barter—the exchange of economic products without direct contact at the time of exchange, as among the Pygmies and Bantu of the Ituri Forest in Africa.

socialization—the process of adaptation and integration of the members of society.

sodality—a non-residential association which, in tribal society, achieves tribal integration by cross-cutting local groups.

sorcery—behavior by which the practitioner attempts to harm other persons by magical means.

sororal polygyny—the marriage of a man to two or more women who stand in the relationship of sister to each other; a form of multiple marriage.

stimulus diffusion—the spread of ideas resulting in new cultural forms.

structure—a component of organization; the parts and their interrelationships.

taboo—a prohibition; derived from the Polynesian *tapu,* where such prohibitions implied sacredness.

taxonomy—a system of classification, especially of biological organisms.

technology—the tools and related techniques of culture.

totem—an aspect of nature (animal, meteorological phenomena, etc.) which is linked to social groups in a special relationship.

totemism—the relationship between some aspect of nature and human social groups.

tribe—a territorial and/or loosely organized political unit. Segments often united by some form of sodality.

uniformitarianism—the concept that natural principles at work now must be assumed to have been at work in the past.

unilateral—one-sided; along a single line.

Zinjanthropus boisei—fossil type found in the Olduvai Gorge in East Africa.

zygote—the initial cell formed by the union of the sperm and egg at fertilization.

Bibliography

ADAMS, RICHARD N.
    1955   A nutritional research program in Guatemala. In Benjamin D. Paul (ed.), *Health, Culture, and Community*, pp. 435–58.

ALLISON, ANTHONY C.
    1956   Sickle cells and evolution. *Scientific American* 195:87–94.

ARENSBERG, CONRAD M., and ARTHUR H. NIEHOFF
    1964   *Introducing Social Change: A Manual for Americans Overseas.* Chicago, Aldine Publishing Company.

BASCOM, WILLIAM R., and MELVILLE J. HERSKOVITS
    1959   *Continuity and Change in African Cultures.* Chicago, The University of Chicago Press (Phoenix Books).

BEALS, ALAN R.
    1962   *Gopalpur: A South Indian Village. Case Studies in Cultural Anthropology.* New York, Holt, Rinehart and Winston, Inc.

BEALS, RALPH L., and HARRY HOIJER
    1959   *An Introduction to Anthropology*, second edition. New York, The Macmillan Company.

BEARDSLEY, RICHARD D., et al.
    1955   Functional and evolutionary implications of community patterning. In *Seminars in Archeology: 1955.* Memoir No. 11 of the Society for American Archeology.

BEATTIE, JOHN
    1960   *Bunyoro: An African Kingdom. Case Studies in Cultural Anthropology.* New York, Holt, Rinehart and Winston, Inc.

BENEDICT, RUTH
    1946   *Patterns of Culture.* New York, Penguin Books, Inc. (First published 1934, Houghton Mifflin Company).

BERNDT, RONALD M.
    1962   *Excess and Restraint: Social Control Among a New Guinea Mountain People.* Chicago, The University of Chicago Press.

BOAS, FRANZ
    1964   *The Central Eskimo.* Lincoln, University of Nebraska Press.

BOHANNAN, PAUL
    1963   *Social Anthropology.* New York, Holt, Rinehart and Winston, Inc.

BRACE, C. LORING
    1962   Cultural factors in the evolution of the human dentition. In M. F. Ashley Montagu (ed.), *Culture and the Evolution of Man*, pp. 343–54.
    1964   The Problem of the Neanderthals. In Peter B. Hammond (ed.), *Physical Anthropology and Archaeology: Selected Readings*, pp. 107–27.

503

BRACE, C. L., and M. F. ASHLEY MONTAGU
   1965 *Man's Evolution: An Introduction to Physical Anthropology*. New York, The Macmillan Company.

CARRASCO, PEDRO
   1963 The locality referent in residence terms. *American Anthropologist* 65:133–34.

CHANCE, NORMAN A.
   1966 *The Eskimo of North Alaska. Case Studies in Cultural Anthropology*. New York, Holt, Rinehart and Winston, Inc.

CHILDE, V. GORDON
   1936 *Man Makes Himself*. The Thinker's Library, No. 87. London, Watts & Co.

   1960 The New Stone Age. In Harry L. Shapiro (ed.), *Man, Culture and Society*, pp. 94–110.

COHEN, RONALD
   1967 *The Kanuri of Bornu. Case Studies in Cultural Anthropology*. New York, Holt, Rinehart and Winston, Inc.

COLSON, ELIZABETH
   1958 Ancestral spirits and social structure among the Plateau Tonga. In W. A. Lessa and E. Z. Vogt, *Reader in Comparative Religion*, pp. 395–400.

COON, CARLETON S.
   1948 *A Reader in General Anthropology*. New York, Holt, Rinehart and Winston, Inc.

   1962 *The Origin of Races*. New York, Alfred A. Knopf.

DEVORE, IRVEN (ed.)
   1965 *Primate Behavior: Field Studies of Monkeys and Apes*. New York, Holt, Rinehart and Winston, Inc.

DEVORE, IRVEN, and S. L. WASHBURN
   1963 Baboon ecology and human evolution. In F. Clark Howell and F. Bourlíere (eds.), *African Ecology and Human Evolution*, pp. 335–67.

DOBZHANSKY, THEODOSIUS
   1963 Genetic entities in hominid evolution. In Sherwood L. Washburn (ed.), *Classification and Human Evolution*, pp. 347–62.

DUNN, LESLIE C., and STEPHEN P.
   1957 The Jewish Community of Rome. *Scientific American* 196:119–28.

DURKHEIM, EMILE
   1961 *The Elementary Forms of the Religious Life*. New York, Collier Books.

ELWIN, VERRIER
   1939 *The Baiga*. London, J. Murray.

ERASMUS, CHARLES J.
   1954 An anthropologist looks at technical assistance. *The Scientific Monthly* 78:147–58.

EVANS-PRITCHARD, E. E.
   1951 *Social Anthropology*. New York, The Free Press of Glencoe.

EWALD, ROBERT H.
   1957 San Antonio Sacatepequez: Culture change in a Guatemalan community. *Social Forces* 36:160–65.

FIRTH, RAYMOND (ed.)
  1957 *Man and Culture: An Evaluation of the Work of Bronislaw Malinowski.* New York, Harper and Row.
FISCHER, J. L.
  1958 The classification of residence in censuses. *American Anthropologist* 60:508–17.
FORTES, M., and E. E. EVANS-PRITCHARD (eds.)
  1940 *African Political Systems.* London, Oxford University Press.
FORTUNE, REO F.
  1934 *Manus Religion.* Lincoln, University of Nebraska Press.
FOSTER, GEORGE M.
  1962 *Traditional Cultures: and the Impact of Technological Change.* New York, Harper and Row.
FRASER, THOMAS M., JR.
  1966 *Fishermen of South Thailand: The Malay Villagers. Case Studies in Cultural Anthropology.* New York, Holt, Rinehart and Winston, Inc.
FRIED, MORTON H. (ed.)
  1959a *Readings in Anthropology. Vol. I: Physical Anthropology, Linguistics, Archeology.* New York, Thomas Y. Crowell Company.
  1959b *Readings in Anthropology. Vol. II: Readings in Cultural Anthropology.* New York, Thomas Y. Crowell Company.
GLEASON, H. A., JR.
  1961 *An Introduction to Descriptive Linguistics,* revised edition. New York, Holt, Rinehart and Winston, Inc.
HAMMOND, PETER B. (ed.)
  1964 *Physical Anthropology and Archaeology: Selected Readings.* New York, The Macmillan Company.
HARDING, THOMAS G.
  1967 *Voyagers of the Vitiaz Strait: A Study of a New Guinea Trade System.* Seattle, University of Washington Press. (Monograph 44, The American Ethnological Society).
HARLEY, GEORGE
  1948 The Mano of Liberia. In Carleton Coon (ed.), *A Reader in General Anthropology,* pp. 344–74.
HARRISON, G. A., J. S. WEINER, J. M. TANNER, and N. A. BARNICOT
  1964 *Human Biology: An Introduction to Human Evolution, Variation and Growth.* New York, Oxford University Press.
HART, C. W. M., and ARNOLD R. PILLING
  1960 *The Tiwi of North Australia. Case Studies in Cultural Anthropology.* New York, Holt, Rinehart and Winston, Inc.
HOCKETT, CHARLES F., and ROBERT ASCHER
  1964 The human revolution. *Current Anthropology* 5:135–68.
HOEBEL, E. ADAMSON
  1958 *Man in the Primitive World,* second edition. New York, McGraw-Hill Book Company.
  1960 *The Cheyennes: Indians of the Great Plains. Case Studies in Cultural Anthropology.* New York, Holt, Rinehart and Winston, Inc.
HOGBIN, IAN
  1964 *A Guadalcanal Society: The Kaoka Speakers. Case Studies in Cultural Anthropology.* New York, Holt, Rinehart and Winston, Inc.

HOIJER, HARRY
    1959   The Sapir-Whorf hypothesis. In Morton H. Fried (ed.), *Readings in Anthropology. Vol. I: Physical Anthropology, Linguistics, Archeology*, pp. 219–31.

HOLLINGSHEAD, AUGUST B.
    1961   *Elmtown's Youth.* New York, John Wiley & Sons, Inc. (Science Editions.)

HONIGMANN, JOHN J.
    1959   *The World of Man.* New York, Harper and Row.

HOWELL, F. CLARK, and FRANCOIS BOURLIERE
    1963   *African Ecology and Human Evolution. Viking Fund Publications in Anthropology, 36.* New York, Wenner-Gren Foundation for Anthropological Research, Incorporated.

HOWELLS, WILLIAM
    1948   *The Heathens: Primitive Man and His Religions.* Garden City, Doubleday & Company, Inc.

HUXLEY, JULIAN S.
    1956   Evolution, cultural and biological. In William L. Thomas, Jr. (ed.), *Current Anthropology*, pp. 3–25.

JENNINGS, JESSE D., and E. ADAMSON HOEBEL
    1966   *Readings in Anthropology*, second edition. New York, McGraw-Hill Book Company.

KLIMA, GEORGE
    1967   Personal communication.

KLUCKHOHN, CLYDE, and DOROTHEA LEIGHTON
    1962   *The Navaho*, revised edition. Garden City, Doubleday & Company, Inc. (Anchor Book.)

KROEBER, A. L.
    1917   The superorganic. *American Anthropologist* 19:163–213.
    1948   *Anthropology*, new revised edition. New York, Harcourt, Brace and World, Inc.

KROEBER, A. L., and CLYDE KLUCKHOHN
    1952   Culture: a critical review of concepts and definitions. *Papers of the Peabody Museum of American Archaeology and Ethnology, Harvard University*, Vol. XLVII, No. 1.
    1963   *Culture: A Critical Review of Concepts and Definitions.* New York, Random House. (Vintage Book.) (Reprint of 1952 publication.)

KROEBER, A. L., et al.
    1952   *Anthropology Today: An Encyclopedic Inventory.* Chicago, The University of Chicago Press.

KUPER, HILDA
    1963   *The Swazi: a South African Kingdom. Case Studies in Cultural Anthropology.* New York, Holt, Rinehart and Winston, Inc.

LAFARGE, OLIVER
    1947   *Santa Eulalia: The Religion of a Cuchumatan Indian Town.* Chicago, The University of Chicago Press.

LASKER, GABRIEL WARD
    1961   *The Evolution of Man: A Brief Introduction to Physical Anthropology.* New York, Holt, Rinehart and Winston, Inc.

LE GROS CLARK, WILFRID E.
    1959   *The Antecedents of Man.* Chicago, Quadrangle Books.

1967   *Man-Apes or Ape-Men? The Story of Discoveries in Africa.* New York, Holt, Rinehart and Winston, Inc.

LESLIE, CHARLES (ed.)
1960   *Anthropology of Folk Religion.* New York, Random House. (Vintage Book.)

LESSA, WILLIAM A., and EVON Z. VOGT (eds.)
1958   *Reader in Comparative Religion.* New York, Harper and Row.

LEWIS, OSCAR
1955   Medicine and politics in a Mexican village. In Benjamin D. Paul (ed.), *Health, Culture, and Community,* pp. 403–34.

1965   *Village Life in Northern India.* New York, Random House. (Vintage Book.)

1966   The culture of poverty. *Scientific American* 215:19–25.

LIENHARDT, R. GODFREY
1956   Religion. In Harry L. Shapiro (ed.), *Man, Culture and Society,* pp. 310–29.

LINK, EUGENE P., and SUSHILA MEHTA
1966   A new goddess for an old. In Arthur H. Niehoff (ed.), *A Case Book of Social Change,* pp. 219–24.

LINTON, RALPH
1936   *The Study of Man: An Introduction.* New York, Appleton-Century-Crofts.

1966   One hundred per cent American. In Jesse D. Jennings and E. Adamson Hoebel, *Readings in Anthropology,* pp. 253–55.

LIVINGSTON, FRANK
1962   Reconstructing man's Pliocene pongid ancestor. *American Anthropologist* 64:301–5.

LOWIE, ROBERT H.
1948   *Primitive Religion.* New York, Liveright Publishing Corporation.

MADSEN, WILLIAM
1960   Maya paganism and Christianity. In *Nativism and Syncretism,* pp. 1–35. Publication 19, Middle American Research Institute. New Orleans, Tulane University.

MALINOWSKI, BRONISLAW
1961   *Argonauts of the Western Pacific.* New York, E. P. Dutton & Co. Inc.

MAUSS, MARCELL
1954   *The Gift.* New York, The Free Press of Glencoe.

MESSENGER, JOHN C., JR.
1959   Religious acculturation among the Anang Ibibio. In W. R. Bascom and Melville J. Herskovits, *Continuity and Change in African Cultures,* pp. 279–99.

METRAUX, ALFRED
1960   A selection from Voodoo in Haiti. In Charles Leslie (ed.), *Anthropology of Folk Religion,* pp. 391–448.

MIDDLETON, JOHN
1965   *The Lugbara of Uganda. Case Studies in Cultural Anthropology.* New York, Holt, Rinehart and Winston, Inc.

MINER, HORACE
1965   *The Primitive City of Timbuctoo,* revised edition. Garden City, Doubleday & Company, Inc. (Anchor Book.)

MONTAGU, M. F. ASHLEY (ed.)
 1962 *Culture and the Evolution of Man.* New York, Oxford University Press. (Galaxy Book.)
MORGAN, LEWIS H.
 1877 *Ancient Society.* Chicago, Charles H. Kerr & Company.
MURDOCK, GEORGE PETER
 1934 *Our Primitive Contemporaries.* New York, The Macmillan Company.
 1949 *Social Structure.* New York, The Macmillan Company.
NAPIER, JOHN
 1962 The evolution of the hand. *Scientific American* 207:56–62.
NEWMAN, PHILIP L.
 1965 *Knowing the Gururumba. Case Studies in Cultural Anthropology.* New York, Holt, Rinehart and Winston, Inc.
NIEHOFF, ARTHUR H. (ed.)
 1966 *A Casebook of Social Change.* Chicago, Aldine Publishing Company.
OBERG, KALERVO
 1940 The kingdom of Ankole in Uganda. In M. Fortes and E. E. Evans-Pritchard (eds.), *African Political Systems,* pp. 121–62.
OLIVER, DOUGLAS L.
 1955 *A Solomon Island Society.* Cambridge, Harvard University Press.
PAUL, BENJAMIN D.
 1953 Interview techniques and field relationships. In A. L. Kroeber (ed.), *Anthropology Today,* pp. 430–51.
 1958 The role of beliefs and customs in sanitation programs. *American Journal of Public Health* 48:1502–06.
 1961 Problems of introducing public health programs in "underdeveloped" areas. Paper presented at the Tenth Pacific Science Congress of the Pacific Science Association, University of Hawaii, Honolulu, Hawaii, August 21, 1961.
PAUL, BENJAMIN D. (ed.)
 1955 *Health, Culture and Community: Case Studies of Public Reactions to Health Programs.* New York, Russell Sage Foundation.
PEATTIE, LISA R.
 1958 Interventionism and applied science in anthropology. *Human Organization* 17:4–8.
POLANYI, KARL, C. M. ARENSBERG, and H. W. PEARSON (eds.)
 1957 *Trade and Market in the Early Empires.* New York, The Free Press of Glencoe
RADCLIFFE-BROWN, A. R.
 1965 *Structure and Function in Primitive Society.* New York, The Free Press of Glencoe.
RICHARDS, AUDREY I.
 1957 The concept of culture in Malinowski's work. In R. Firth (ed.), *Man and Culture,* pp. 15–31.
ROBINSON, J. T.
 1963 Adaptive radiation in the australopithecines and the origin of man. In F. Clark Howell and Francois Bourliere, *African Ecology and Human Evolution,* pp. 385–416.
RODNICK, DAVID
 1966 *An Introduction to Man and his Development.* New York, Appleton-Century-Crofts.

Roy, Sarat Chandra
1912   *The Mundas and their Country.* Calcutta, Kuntaline Press.
Royal Anthropological Institution of Great Britain and Ireland (RAIG)
1951   *Notes and Queries on Anthropology,* sixth edition. London, Routledge and Kegan Paul Ltd.
Sachchidananda
1957   Crime and punishment in a Munda village. *Man in India* 37:124–32.
Sahlins, Marshall D.
1959   The social life of monkeys, apes and primitive men. In Morton Fried (ed.), *Readings in Anthropology. Vol. II: Readings in Cultural Anthropology,* pp. 186–99.
1960   The Origin of Society. Reprinted from *Scientific American,* September, 1960.
Sahlins, Marshall D., and Elman R. Service (eds.)
1960   *Evolution and Culture.* Ann Arbor, The University of Michigan Press.
Schwartz, Barton M.
n.d.   Participant observation and participant-as-observer in the field situation: a reply. Unpublished manuscript.
1965   Extra-legal activities of the village pandit in Trinidad. *Anthropological Quarterly* 38:62–71.
Service, Elman R.
1958   *A Profile of Primitive Culture.* New York, Harper and Row.
1962   *Primitive Social Organization: An Evolutionary Perspective.* New York, Random House.
1966   *The Hunters.* Foundations of Modern Anthropology Series. Englewood Cliffs, N. J., Prentice-Hall, Inc.
Shapiro, Harry L. (ed.)
1960   *Man, Culture, and Society.* New York, Oxford University Press.
Spicer, Edward H. (ed.)
1952   *Human Problems in Technological Change: A Casebook.* New York, Russell Sage Foundation.
Spindler, George D.
1959   *The Transmission of American Culture.* Cambridge, Harvard University Press.
Spindler, George D. (ed.)
1963   *Education and Culture.* New York, Holt, Rinehart and Winston, Inc.
Stefansson, Vilhjalmur
1962   *My Life With The Eskimo.* New York, Collier Books.
Stein, William W.
1961   *Hualcan: Life in the Highlands of Peru.* Ithaca, Cornell University Press.
Stern, Curt
1960   *Principles of Human Genetics,* second edition. San Francisco, W. H. Freeman and Company.
Steward, Julian H.
1955   *Theory of Culture Change: The Methodology of Multilineal Evolution.* Urbana, Illinois University Press.

STEWARD, JULIAN H., and LOUIS C. FARON
1959 *Native Peoples of South America.* New York, McGraw-Hill Book
Company.
SWANSON, GUY E.
1960 *The Birth of the Gods: The Origin of Primitive Beliefs.* Ann Arbor,
University of Michigan Press.
TAX, SOL
1966 The uses of anthropology. In Jesse D. Jennings and E. Adamson
Hoebel, *Readings in Anthropology,* pp. 417–21.
THOMAS, ELIZABETH MARSHALL
1965 *The Harmless People.* New York, Random House. (Vintage Book.)
THOMAS, WILLIAM L., JR. (ed.)
1956 *Current Anthropology: A Supplement to Anthropology Today.* Chicago, The University of Chicago Press.
TINDALE, NORMAN B.
1965 Stone implement making among the Nakako, Ngadadjara and Pitjandjara of the Great Western Desert. *Records of the South Australian Museum* 15:131–64.
TURNBULL, COLIN M.
1961 *The Forest People.* New York: Simon & Schuster, Inc.
TYLOR, EDWARD BURNETT
1958a *The Origins of Culture.* New York, Harper and Row. (Originally
published as chapters i–x of *Primitive Culture.* London, John Murray
Publishers, 1871.)
1958b *Religion in Primitive Culture.* New York, Harper and Row. (Part
II of *Primitive Culture.* Chapters xi–xix.)
UCHENDU, VICTOR C.
1965 *The Igbo of Southeast Nigeria. Case Studies in Cultural Anthropology.* New York, Holt, Rinehart and Winston, Inc.
VAN GENNEP, ARNOLD
1960 *The Rites of Passage.* Chicago, The University of Chicago Press.
WAGLEY, CHARLES
1963 *An Introduction to Brazil.* New York, Columbia University Press.
WALLACE, ANTHONY F. C.
1956 Revitalization movements. *American Anthropologist* 58:264–81.
WASHBURN, SHERWOOD L.
1960 Tools and human evolution. Reprinted from *Scientific American,*
203(3).
WASHBURN, SHERWOOD L. (ed.)
1963 *Classification and Human Evolution. Viking Fund Publications in
Anthropology,* 37. Wenner-Gren Foundation for Anthropological Research, Incorporated.
WASHBURN, SHERWOOD L., and DAVID A. HAMBURG
1965 The implications of primate research. In Irven DeVore (ed.), *Primate Behavior,* pp. 607–22.
WHETTEN, NATHAN L.
1948 *Rural Mexico.* Chicago, The University of Chicago Press.
WHITE, LESLIE A.
1949 *The Science of Culture: A Study of Man and Civilization.* New York,
Farrar, Straus and Company.
1959 *The Evolution of Culture.* New York, McGraw-Hill Book Company.

WILLIAMS, THOMAS RHYS

1965 *The Dusun: A North Borneo Society. Case Studies in Cultural Anthropology.* New York, Holt, Rinehart and Winston, Inc.

WISER, CHARLOTTE VIALL, and WILLIAM H.

1963 *Behind Mud Walls.* Berkeley, University of California Press.

WITTFOGEL, KARL A.

1959 The theory of oriental society. In Morton Fried (ed.), *Readings in Anthropology. Vol. II: Readings in Cultural Anthropology,* pp. 94–113.

WOLF, ERIC R.

1962 *Sons of the Shaking Earth.* Chicago, The University of Chicago Press. (Phoenix Book.)

1966 *Peasants.* Englewood Cliffs, N. J., Prentice-Hall, Inc.

WYLIE, LAURENCE

1964 *Village in the Vaucluse,* second edition. New York, Harper and Row.

Index

513